BLACKSTONE'S GUIDE TO

The Criminal Justice and Immigra

HMP EDMUNDS HILL

BLACKSTONE'S GUIDE TO

The Criminal Justice and Immigration Act 2008

Edited by
Maya Sikand

With contributions by
Kate Aubrey-Johnson, Adrian Berry,
Brenda Campbell, Anya Lewis, Anna Morris,
and Tom Wainwright

OXFORD
UNIVERSITY PRESS

OXFORD

UNIVERSITY PRESS

Great Clarendon Street, Oxford OX2 6DP

Oxford University Press is a department of the University of Oxford.
It furthers the University's objective of excellence in research, scholarship,
and education by publishing worldwide in

Oxford New York

Auckland Cape Town Dar es Salaam Hong Kong Karachi
Kuala Lumpur Madrid Melbourne Mexico City Nairobi
New Delhi Shanghai Taipei Toronto

With offices in

Argentina Austria Brazil Chile Czech Republic France Greece
Guatemala Hungary Italy Japan Poland Portugal Singapore
South Korea Switzerland Thailand Turkey Ukraine Vietnam

Oxford is a registered trade mark of Oxford University Press
in the UK and in certain other countries

Published in the United States
by Oxford University Press Inc., New York

British Library Cataloguing in Publication Data

Data available

Library of Congress Cataloging-in-Publication Data

Blackstone's guide to the criminal justice and immigration act 2008 / edited by
Maya Sikand; with contributions by Kate Aubrey-Johnson, Adrian Berry,
Brenda Campbell, Anya Lewis, Anna Morris, and Tom Wainwright.
  p. cm.
Includes bibliographical references and index.
ISBN 978-0-19-955382-2 (pbk. : alk. paper) 1. Great Britain. Criminal Justice
and Immigration Act 2008. 2. Criminal justice, Administration of—Great Britain.
I. Sikand, Maya.
KD7876.A3282008.A3 2009
345.41'05—dc22

                                              2008050445

Typeset by Cepha Imaging Private Ltd, Bangalore, India
Printed in Great Britain
on acid-free paper by
CPI Antony Rowe, Chippenham, Wiltshire

ISBN 978-0-19-955382-2

1 3 5 7 9 10 8 6 4 2

Foreword

You will expect a Foreword to fulfil two functions: first, to commend the authors to the reader and second, to make an observation which transcends the learning contained in this book.

In the case of this book the task I have the pleasure to discharge is easy.

First of all, the authors are all practitioners at Garden Court Chambers. They can be depended upon for their familiarity with the detail of the criminal and immigration law onto which this statute has been grafted. Their approach is insightful and helpful to the practitioner, as well as highlighting the civil liberties and human rights implications throughout. They know what you need to know in order to understand and apply the statute recently passed into law. You can depend on the fruits of their labour.

Secondly, the observation I feel bound to make will find a resonance in lawyer and lay citizen alike.

We are driven to reflect upon the role of the Criminal Justice and Immigration Act 2008 and in particular the role it plays in the Rule of Law. It is not long ago that Lord Bingham reminded us[1] of the paramount prerequisite that,

the law must be accessible and so far as possible intelligible, clear and predicable.

Is the CJIA 2008 accessible? Or another product of what Lord Bingham called 'legislative hyperactivity'? Is it intelligible? Or clear? Far from constituting a clear statement of the law it depends so 'heavily on cross-reference and incorporation as on occasion to baffle'. Furthermore there is a reliance upon subsidiary legislation that increases the opacity of what, to a citizen wishing to order his or her life, ought to be transparent. Lord Bingham also says that the law,

must be stated in terms which a judge can without undue difficulty explain to a jury or an unqualified clerk to a bench of lay justices.

Does this statute satisfy that test? I fear not.

Is it predictable? There are sentencing measures within this Act that make it quite impossible for a would-be offender to be sure of the criminal sanction his or her ascertainable transgressions will attract. Sentences passed into law as recently as 2003 and brought into force soon after are abandoned and new initiatives are put out without the resources to put them into effect. There can be no confidence that innovations in this statute will survive the next, inevitable Criminal Justice Act and further tampering.

The media driven aspect of this hopscotch of a statute is perhaps clearest in the new provision dealing with the clarification of the law on self-defence (the 'Tony Martin' section).[2] It is no different from the law as I have always understood it to be.

---

[1] Lecture given to the Centre for Public law (16 November 2006) (<http://www.cpl.law.cam.ac.uk/past_activities/the_rt_hon_lord_bingham_the_rule_of_law.php>).

[2] CJIA 2008, Part 5, s 76, dealt with in Chapter 4.

Tony Martin, the Norfolk farmer who shot dead a teenage burglar, would just as much have been convicted by a jury under this section as under the common law. Yet the Ministry of Justice, in its press release, commended the new section as if it had allowed people to defend their property when before they ran the risk of being sent to prison. Announcing that the reforms are designed to clarify and reinforce the law and 'articulating the state's responsibility to stand by those acting in good faith when using force in self-defence', Jack Straw, the Justice Secretary said,

In the case of a passer-by witnessing a crime in the street for example, or a householder faced with a burglar in his home, we are reassuring them that if they intervene and necessarily use force which is not excessive or disproportionate, the law really is behind them.[3]

For a government committed to eradicating crime and the causes of crime this statute is an indictment of a legislative process that has reached the point of being merely a tool for persuading us that action is being taken. If there is a perceived problem—so goes the thinking—create another criminal offence or a new kind of penal sanction and the problem will go away as the sea recedes upon the command of the monarch.

I suppose we should not complain. As lawyers there will be plenty of work to assist the judiciary in grappling with the layer upon layer of primary and subsidiary legislation, the dates of it coming into force and the meaning of the applicable provisions that can be identified.

We need this book.

Owen Davies QC
Joint Head of Chambers
Garden Court Chambers
Recorder of the Crown Court
September 2008

---

[3] <http://www.justice.gov.uk/news/newsrelease191207a.htm>.

Contents—Summary

Contents—Detailed

Tables of Cases

References are to Paragraph Numbers

European Court of Human Rights

Tables of Primary Legislation

References are to Paragraph Numbers

Tables of Secondary Legislation

References are to Paragraph Numbers

List of Abbreviations

ACAS	Advisory, Conciliation and Arbitration Service
AJA 1999	Access to Justice Act 1999
ASBA 2003	Anti-social Behaviour Act 2003
BA 1976	Bail Act 1976
BBFC	British Board of Film Classification
BTPA	British Transport Police Authority
CAA 1968	Criminal Appeal Act 1968
CCRC	Criminal Case Review Commission
CDA 1998	Crime and Disorder Act 1998
CJA 2003	Criminal Justice Act 2003
CJIA 2008	Criminal Justice and Immigration Act 2008
CJPOA 1994	Criminal Justice and Public Order Act 1994
COE	Council of Europe
CPPNM	Convention on the Physical Protection of Nuclear Material
CPS	Crown Prosecution Service
DCWs	Designated Caseworker
DPP	detention for public protection
DSI investigation	Death or Serious Injury investigation
DWP	Department for Work and Pensions
ERS	Early Removal Scheme
HMIC	Her Majesty's Inspectorate of Constabulary
HMRC	Her Majesty's Revenue and Customs
IAA 1999	Immigration and Asylum Act 1999
IANA 2006	Immigration, Asylum and Nationality Act 2006
IPCC	Independent Police Complaints Commission
IPP	imprisonment for public protection
ISOs	Individual Support Order
IVOO	interim VOO
JCHR	Joint Committee on Human Rights
JIRPA	Joint Industrial Relations Protocol Agreement
MCA 1980	Magistrates' Court Act 1980
MDA 1987	Ministry of Defence Police Act 1987
MDP	Ministry of Defence Police
NIAA 2002	Nationality, Immigration and Asylum Act 2002
NM(O)A 1983	Nuclear Material (Offences) Act 1983
OAPA 1861	Offences Against the Person Act 1861
OPA 1959	Obscene Publications Act 1959
PA 1996	Police Act 1996
PAT	Police Appeal Tribunal
PCC(S)A 2000	Powers of Criminal Courts (Sentencing) Act 2000
PCSOs	Police Community Support Officers

POA	Prisoner Officer's Association
POA 1986	Public Order Act 1986
PRA 2002	Police Reform Act 2002
PRB	Pay Review Body
PSR	Pre-sentence Report
ROA 1974	Rehabilitation of Offenders Act 1974
RPA 1984	Repatriation of Prisoners Act 1984
RTSA 2003	Railways and Transport Safety Act 2003
SCPO	Serious Crime Prevention Order
SFO	Serious Fraud Office
SSHD	Secretary of State for the Home Department
UKBA 2007	UK Borders Act 2007
VOO	Violent Offender Order
YOS	Youth Offending Service
YRO	Youth Rehabilitation Order

1

INTRODUCTION

A. OVERVIEW

According to the Ministry of Justice website, the Criminal Justice and Immigration   1.01
Act (CJIA) 2008, which received Royal Assent on 8 May 2008, 'takes forward the
government's programme of reform of the criminal justice system'. It states that the
reform 'will help to protect the public, promote and improve access to justice, and
increase public confidence in the justice system'. It is difficult to conceive of a piece
of legislation less likely to inspire public confidence than this one, not only because
it lacks any kind of thematic structure and is inconsistent in its aims but because the
drafting of large parts of it are testimony to the last-minute amendments which
characterized the Bill.

The Act sprawls lazily across three hundred odd pages, comprising 12 Parts and   1.02
28 Schedules. Despite its short title, only one Part of the Act deals exclusively with
'immigration' and the other Parts deal with issues that go far beyond the remit of
'criminal justice'. Indeed, so wide is its breadth that an overview is impossible. Each
chapter of this book therefore contains a detailed analysis of the political or other
motivations for reform.

During its passage through Parliament, the Bill was criticized as ill-conceived and   1.03
poorly constructed. At the Committee stage in the Commons, Nick Herbert, the
Shadow Secretary of State for Justice, described it as a typical 'Christmas tree Bill'[1]
suggesting that the government were certain that they wished to legislate about
something but were not sure what.

---

[1] HC Deb 8 October 2007 c71.

1.04   During the Public Bill Committee debates, Edward Garnier MP (Conservative), a Crown Court Recorder and vociferous critic of the Bill, described it as having been 'pulled together without a theme; no central argument seems to push through its core. It is simply a collection of nice ideas, in the government's thinking, which have been pulled together under one title, the Criminal Justice and Immigration Bill.'[2] Although Opposition criticism of proposed legislation is hardly uncommon, Mr Garnier's comments are apposite.

1.05   By the Report Stage in the House of Commons, Mr Garnier was describing the Bill as 'a mis-shapen tree in the first place'. How else, he said, 'can one describe a Bill that deals with youth justice, adult sentencing, the creation of a commissioner for offender management and prisons, a Northern Ireland commissioner for prison complaints, proceedings in magistrates courts, international co-operation in criminal justice matters, violent offender orders, antisocial behaviour and disturbances in hospitals, parenting orders, financial assistance for police authorities, inspection of police authorities, misconduct proceedings against police officers, special immigration status, the disclosure of information about sex offenders, sales of tobacco to those under 18, and amendments to armed forces legislation?'[3]

1.06   His enduring complaint was that despite this vast landscape of proposed changes, there was insufficient time allowed for debate. The number of rapid changes and subsequent timetabling of the debate on them caused great consternation, not just to Mr Garnier, but in Parliament generally. In the House of Lords, Lord Thomas of Gresford observed that the government first overloaded and then accelerated the passage of the Bill.[4] It started off in the House of Commons with 139 clauses, and by the time it reached the House of Lords on Report, it had accumulated over 200 changes, the vast majority of which were never debated by the Commons.

1.07   There is of course a discernible strand of connectivity to past criminal justice initiatives contained in the new initiatives in the Act and these are signposted in each chapter. Other parts of the Act, such as the changes to criminal procedure in Part 3 are a tinkering with existing procedure, including a re-writing of some parts of the Criminal Justice Act (CJA) 2003 which are still not in force. New offences have been introduced which legal academics have daubed unnecessary. More politically controversial is the re-instatement of the statutory ban on the right of prison officers to take industrial action, which was introduced by the Conservatives in 1994 and repealed by Labour in 2005, as well as the new immigration limbo for 'foreign criminals'. By far the most impacting changes for legal practitioners, however, are the sentencing reforms and the expansion of civil orders.

B. SENTENCING AND PRISON OVERCROWDING

1.08 Amongst the most controversial parts of the Act are the new sentencing provisions, detailed in Chapter 2 of this book. They are controversial because they purport to

---

[2] PBC Deb 16 October 2007 c5.
[3] HC Deb 1 January 2008 c311.
[4] HL Deb 27 February 2008 vol 695 cc660–61.

remedy a problem largely seen to be of the government's own making—problems caused by the previous piece of significant sentencing legislation, which came into force only three years ago, ie the Criminal Justice Act 2003. Where the 2003 Act culled judicial discretion, and directly led to an unprecedented level of prison overcrowding, the CJIA 2008 now seeks to alleviate this phenomenon.

The motivation for reform came in part from Lord Carter's Review of Prisons[5] (December 2007), which found a 60 per cent increase in the prison population in England and Wales between 1995 and 2007, identifying this is as the highest prison population per capita in Western Europe, and in part from the Ministry of Justice Penal Policy Paper (May 2007) which noted a 47 per cent increase of recalled prisoners between April 2005 and February 2007.   1.09

The CJIA 2008 removes statutory assumptions and restores judicial discretion in the sentencing of dangerous offenders. The restoration of discretion is not, however, the thread underpinning the new sentencing and release provisions. In a further attempt to reduce overcrowding, the Act creates an automatic early release at the halfway point provision for those serving extended sentences for violent or sexual offences. Previously, the Parole Board's input and approval was required before early release was permitted. The Act also brings forward the early release date for long-term prisoners who were sentenced before 4 April 2005, and who were not convicted under the 2003 Act's dangerous offender provisions.   1.10

This reform and with it the acknowledgement of past errors, as well as other initiatives such as the crediting of time on remand for those subject to stringent bail conditions, is of course welcome, but as the detailed analysis in Chapter 2 highlights, it is more akin to the dressing of a wound than a constructive, long-term change. Unfortunately, the errors of the past are relatively recent ones, and the resultant changes in procedure could well undermine confidence in the Home Office and will almost certainly create greater confusion within the judiciary.   1.11

C. NEW CIVIL ORDERS

Continuing the government's love-affair with ASBO-type civil orders, the CJIA 2008 creates the Violent Offender Order (VOO), close on the heels of the Serious Crime Prevention Order, introduced only last year by the Serious Crime Act 2007. The Act also expands the existing 'crack house' Closure Order regime to include premises on which anti-social behaviour takes place. The effect of such orders can be far-reaching (VOOs, for example, attract automatic notification requirements, mirroring those required of sex offenders) and breaches attract penal sanctions.   1.12

The government's expressed aim in introducing VOOs was to fill a gap to protect the public from violent harm from 'dangerous offenders' convicted pre-4 April 2005, and not therefore subject to the dangerous offender regime under the CJA 2003. Ironically, as indicated above, those provisions have now been re-written in the CJIA 2008, and the scope for such sentences dramatically reduced.   1.13

---

[5] 'Securing the future—Proposals for the efficient and sustainable use of custody in England and Wales'.

1.14   The new premises Closure Orders permit the closure of any premises (including homes or businesses) that are associated with both anti-social behaviour and either significant and persistent disorder or serious nuisance. They can remove people from their homes for three to six months. Significant concerns arise with the potential for enforced homelessness, both for the period of the order and for permanent loss of possession that may occur as a result of an inability to make rent or mortgage payments. Serious concerns also arise in respect of children and other vulnerable occupants caught up in the order.

1.15   Both these new orders raise important human rights issues, dealt with in Chapter 6. Like all the civil orders that have gone before (some of which have been amended by the CJIA 2008 and are also dealt with in Chapter 6), it is likely that breaches of their terms will simply result in increasing the prison population that other parts of this Act are dedicated to decreasing.

D. NEW CRIMES

1.16   These are detailed in Chapter 4. Laudable changes to the criminal law include the assertion of jurisdiction over extra-territorial child sex offenders, the inclusion of sexual orientation under hate crime legislation, and the elimination of blasphemy as an offence. However, there are a number of unnecessary additions to the calendar of criminal offences, such as the offence of simple possession of 'extreme pornography' and the offence of nuisance on NHS premises. The NHS nuisances provisions make it an offence to cause a disturbance on NHS premises, but drafted with so many exceptions that the section is arguably unworkable in practice.

1.17   The new extreme pornography sections make it an offence to possess pornography deemed to be 'extreme'—the most controversial criminalization in the Act. They are grounded in the aftermath of the murder by strangulation of Jane Longhurst,[6] but by changing the wording from the Obscene Publications Act 1959, the provisions have the potential to criminalize individuals who do not actually abuse or promote the abuse of others. The vague definition of the crime means the occurrence of a criminal act can only really be determined after a trial to define the offence. As a result, people have no way of knowing whether or not they are breaking the law at the time of viewing the material in question.

E. FOREIGN CRIMINALS

1.18   Dealt with in Chapter 8 of this book, Part 10 of the Act creates a new class of broadly defined 'foreign criminals', who have no right to reside in Britain but cannot be removed from the country. Inspired by the much publicized Afghan hijack case which left the government's hands tied, the new status precludes designated persons

---

[6] HC Deb 8 October 2007 vol 464 c60. The defendant, Coutts, had hundreds of images of strangulation and necrophilia on his computer.

from applying for discretionary leave to remain in the UK. The Act vastly reduces the support obligations ordinarily available from the Secretary of State.

It also raises questions about its concordance with the Human Rights Act 1998   1.19 and the Refugee Convention, as well as about the imposition of punitive restrictions on both the individual concerned and any dependants. Such restrictions could well legislate for an underclass of non-citizens who have to seek permission for the most basic opportunities of personal advancement.

F. OTHER CHANGES

As already mentioned, the Act's remit is wide and a single introduction cannot do it   1.20 justice. Within the Act, in addition to the changes outlined above, the police misconduct regime has been reformed; the UK's EC obligations have resulted in new enactments in a number of areas, including the international enforcement of fines; a brand new and very complex youth community penalty is born (the Youth Rehabilitation Order); the 'double jeopardy' discount in AG's references has been abolished in relation to all life sentences (including IPP); the mode of trial procedure has been radically overhauled; and there are changes to the rights of appeal to the Court of Appeal.

G. CONCLUSIONS

In introducing the Criminal Justice and Immigration Bill, the government noted that   1.21 while framework legislation was acceptable in other areas of public administration, where it could be supplemented by regulation, the criminal law demanded more detail from the outset. The Secretary of State for Justice and Lord Chancellor, Jack Straw, noted that 'in this area, where we are dealing with critical issues concerning the safety of the public and the liberty of the individual, the detail itself has to be contained in the primary legislation'.

In fact the over-breadth of the CJIA 2008 has meant that the detail has been left   1.22 to secondary legislation. Throughout it are references to the fact that the Secretary of State can or will make further provision or issue regulations 'by order'. As a result only parts of the Act are in force,[7] and practitioners will have to keep a keen eye on the Ministry of Justice website—not just for commencement orders, but also for regulations, without which some sections are inoperable.

---

[7] Each chapter of this book indicates exactly which section is in force and its effect at the time of writing.

2

SENTENCING

A. INTRODUCTION

By the time the Criminal Justice and Immigration Bill was first introduced in June 2007, 2.01 a number of consultations had been undertaken and reports and papers produced which provided a much needed analysis into the criminal justice sentencing system. Among them, 'Making Sentencing Clearer', a consultation and a report of a review by none other than the Home Secretary, the Lord Chancellor, and the Attorney General, provided a detailed analysis of the current system, made concrete proposals and raised challenging questions for the future.

In a similar vein, the Ministry of Justice and NOMS background paper on 'Penal 2.02 Policy' identified a number of areas for improvement. It set out proposals for a way forward to ensure an effective penal policy which actively reduced offending and one in which the public could have confidence. Despite this background of careful consultation, an examination of the sentencing provisions in the CJIA 2008 raises a real doubt over whether anyone in the government actually read or digested these papers in the holistic spirit in which they were delivered. Regrettably, while the CJIA 2008, Parts 1 and 2 make significant amendments to the sentencing regime, many of the changes called for have simply not been delivered.

When the Bill was first introduced, the sentencing provisions (described as forming 2.03 a large part of the Bill[1]) ran to 25 clauses. When it received Royal Assent on 8 May 2008, 41 sections of the Act related to sentencing. In a manner which is becoming uncomfortably familiar, some of the most significant sentencing provisions were inserted into the Bill by the government at the last minute, hastily drafted and too late for debate.

---

[1] Research Paper 07/65, 9 August 2007, summary of main points.

Among these are the new dangerous offender provisions, piggy-backed on to the Bill at the eleventh hour in a transparent attempt to stave off, at least temporarily, the rapidly approaching prison population crisis.

2.04 These provisions represent a major about turn by the government from the much lauded dangerous offender provisions of the CJA 2003. The judiciary's hands, once tied, have now been untied. Only three years have passed since these trumpeted provisions were brought into force and now legislative change has become imperative to save the United Kingdom from its present prison crisis. Whether it will in fact achieve that aim remains to be seen.

2.05 One of the reasons for the late insertion of many provisions aimed at reducing the prison population was the timely publication in December 2007 of Lord Carter's Review of Prisons. Lord Carter had been asked to consider options for improving the balance between the supply of prison places and the demand for them and to make recommendations on how this could be achieved. His Review, 'Securing the future—Proposals for the efficient and sustainable use of custody in England and Wales', set out some worrying statistics. There had been a 60 per cent increase in the prison population in England and Wales between 1995 and 2007, with England and Wales having the highest prison population per capita in Western Europe. On 16 November 2007, the prison population was at 81,547—the highest on record. On current projections the demand for prison places will continue to outstrip the supply of prison places.[2]

2.06 The Carter Review recommended the implementation of five new measures to reduce the projected need for new prison places. Three of those measure were introduced into Part 2 of the Bill on 9 January 2008, at Report Stage in the House of Commons: reform of indeterminate and extended sentences for public protection (CJIA 2008, ss 13–18); credit for period of remand on bail subject to curfew (CJIA 2008, ss 21–23); and the alignment of release mechanisms for prisoners serving sentences under the CJA 1991 with those serving sentences under the CJA 2003 (CJIA 2008, ss 26 and 28).[3] These new measures are estimated to reduce the projected increase by between 3,500 and 4,500 places.[4]

2.07 The CJIA 2008, Part 1 and ss 35–37 and 39 of Part 2 relate to young offenders and were included in the Criminal Justice and Immigration Bill as originally introduced in June 2007. They are considered in Part F below. Described as the most significant development in youth sentencing in the last ten years, the CJIA 2008 seeks to implement reforms to the youth justice system foreshadowed in the government's discussion paper 'Youth Justice—the next steps' which accompanied the 'Every Child Matters' Green Paper published in September 2003. The Act introduces Youth Rehabilitation Orders, Youth Default Orders and youth conditional cautions. It also extends the scope of Referral Orders and clarifies the purpose of sentencing for the youth justice system.

---

[2] See p 2.
[3] The Review supported the proposal already included in the Criminal Justice and Immigration Bill to introduce fixed terms recalls. It further supported the proposal in the original Criminal Justice and Immigration Bill to limit suspended sentences, although this proposal was not finally enacted.
[4] See p 3.

The Youth Justice provisions are apparently designed to improve the range of   2.08
sentencing options and provide a stepped approach which will deter the use of custodial
sentences for children and young people. Regrettably, however, the government did
not adopt proposed amendments to make the *primary consideration* of sentencing
policy the welfare of the child, nor the proposals to ensure that custodial sentences
for children and young people were only used as a last resort.[5]

Despite an increasingly urgent need for wholesale reform of the use of prisons   2.09
and an increasingly vocal body of opinion advocating the long-term rehabilitative
benefit of structured community sentences, the government has tinkered around the
edges of an already complex sentencing system, putting right some of the wrongs
implemented by the CJA 2003, but has failed to enact legislation which will lead to
real, necessary and long-term improvement.

B. CUSTODIAL SENTENCES

1. Imprisonment for public protection (adult offenders)

(a) *Introduction*

Few would dispute that the provisions of the CJA 2003, ss 225–229 relating to   2.10
dangerousness created a flawed system. That prisons were dangerously near to maximum capacity was due, to a significant extent, to the numbers of prisoners serving
indeterminate sentences, often with relatively short minimum tariffs and with no
clear prospect of release. What was arguably needed to address problems within the
system was a thorough and reasoned review with appropriate and timely legislative
response. Instead, far-reaching legislative changes were inserted into the Bill at the
eleventh hour. The amending provisions were announced on 9 January 2008 when
the Bill was due for its Report stage and, as a result, changes to the dangerous offender
provisions of the CJA 2003 were passed in the Commons within a day—with little
or no opportunity for debate.

In his Review of Prisons delivered in December 2007, Lord Carter identified   2.11
indeterminate sentences of imprisonment for public protection (IPP) as one of the
drivers of the overall increase in prison population.[6] In the two and a half years
between the implementation of the relevant provisions of the CJA 2003 in April
2005 and October 2007, 3,400 offenders were sentenced to IPP. At the same time,
projections indicated that in the absence of change, there could be as many as 11,500
IPP prisoners by 2014.[7] These statistics cannot have been welcome news in the
corridors of Whitehall.

At the same time, legal challenges had been launched by IPP prisoners who   2.12
remained in custody well beyond the expiry of their minimum tariff, due to lack of
access to resources whilst in custody and a subsequent, related inability to convince
an increasingly risk averse Parole Board that they no longer presented a significant

---

[5] See for example JCHRR Legislative Scrutiny: Criminal Justice and Immigration Bill, 25 January 2008,
pp 37–8.
[6] See p 6.
[7] Page 7, para 18.

risk of serious harm to the public. It cannot be a coincidence that on the same day that amendments to the Bill were announced in the Commons by the Secretary of State for Justice, the then Lord Chief Justice, handing down judgment in *Secretary of State for Justice v David Walker & Brett James*,[8] observed

This appeal has demonstrated an unhappy state of affairs. There has been a systemic failure on the part of the Secretary of State to put in place the resources necessary to implement the scheme of rehabilitation necessary to enable the relevant provisions of the 2003 Act to function as intended . . . For the reasons that we have given . . . The prevailing situation is likely to result in infringement of Article 5(4) and may ultimately also result in infringement of Article 5(1).

(b) *Amendments to the existing IPP regime*

2.13   Against this background, the CJIA 2008, s 13 and Sch 5, which came into force on 14 July 2008[9] and apply to all cases which fall to be sentenced on or after that date, introduce significant amendments to s 225 of the CJA 2003. One of the most significant changes is the removal of the mandatory requirement to impose an IPP sentence, which had been contained in the CJA 2003, s 225(3), replacing it with room for judicial discretion. Where an offender is to be sentenced for a serious specified offence[10] but a sentence of life imprisonment is not deemed justified, the court retains a power—but no longer has a duty—to impose a sentence of IPP. This discretionary power, however, only arises under the CJIA 2008, s 13(1) if the court is of the opinion (a) that the offender presents a significant risk to members of the public of serious harm occasioned by the commission of further specified offences; and (b) from that threshold, one of two further conditions is met.

2.14   The first condition[11] is that at the time when the offence for which the offender is to be sentenced was committed, the offender had been convicted in any part of the UK of an offence specified in a new Sch 15A to the CJA 2003 (as inserted by the CJIA 2008, Sch 5). Schedule 15A contains a significantly streamlined list of specified offences. Although the list contains some new additions (Sexual Offences Act 2003, s 62 (committing any offence with intent to commit a sexual offence)) and specifically extends to the Armed Forces, many offences which had previously been deemed specified offences under the CJA 2003, Sch 15 have been purposefully omitted. Notable omissions include offences contrary to ss 20 and 47 of the Offences Against the Person Act 1861, possession of a firearm with intent to cause fear of violence contrary to s 16A of the Firearms Act 1968, arson and offences contrary to s 1 of the Criminal Damage Act 1971, and offences contrary to ss 1, 2, and 3 of the Public Order Act 1986 (riot, violent disorder, and affray). Attempts, conspiracy, or incitement to commit any specified offence are included in the list, as are aiding, abetting, counselling, or procuring the commission of a listed offence. Importantly, although robbery remains a specified offence, such an offence only becomes specified if 'at some time

---

[8] [2008] EWCA Civ 30, para 72.

[9] Criminal Justice and Immigration Act 2008 (Commencement No 2 and Transitional and Saving Provisions) Order 2008 (SI 2008/1586). See A-G's Reference (No 55 of 2008) sub nom *R v C & 9 Ors* [2008] EWCA Crim 2790 for a full analysis of these new provisions.

[10] CJA 2003, s 224(2).

[11] See CJA 2003, s 225(3)(3A), as inserted by CJIA 2008, s 13(1).

during the commission of the offence, the offender had in his possession a firearm or an imitation firearm'.[12]

If the first condition does not apply, the second condition[13] falls to be considered 2.15 by the sentencing court. It stipulates that an offender who has not been previously convicted of a specified offence under Sch 15A can only be sentenced to imprisonment for public protection if 'the notional minimum term is at least two years'. The 'notional minimum term' is defined in the CJA 2003, s 225(3C).[14]

(c) *Tariff setting*

The court should follow the now familiar practice for setting minimum tariffs for 2.16 IPP sentences, save that it should not credit time spent in custody on remand in arriving at the minimum term. In practice, an IPP can only be imposed on an offender who does not have a previous conviction for an offence specified under Sch 15A, if the notional determinate sentence is at least 4 years imprisonment.[15]

The importance therefore of rigorously calculating the notional determinate sentence 2.17 for those offenders falling into condition two should not be under-estimated. Practitioners will have to pay particular attention to quantifiable discounts for early guilty pleas and specific mitigation.

Further, it is not clear whether the notional determinate term of 4 years can be 2.18 achieved by a series of lesser terms running consecutively or whether it is envisaged that at least one offence would justify a minimum determinate sentence of 4 years. This potential source of work for the Court of Appeal has been highlighted by David Thomas QC in his article 'IPP Amended'.[16]

Assuming that the threshold of significant risk of serious harm has been reached 2.19 together with one of the two conditions for imposing an IPP sentence, the court must then decide whether to exercise its discretion to impose an IPP.[17] Before exercising the discretion to impose a sentence other than a determinate one, consideration must be given to whether an extended sentence might be sufficient for the protection of the public (see paras **2.21** and **2.25** below).

2. Detention for public protection (young offenders)

(a) *Introduction*

The CJIA 2008, s 14, also in force from 14 July 2008[18] (and applicable to all cases 2.20 which fall to be sentenced on or after that date) amends the CJA 2003, s 226 (detention for life, or detention for public protection in the case of those under 18). The 2003 Act imposed a duty on the sentencing court to impose a sentence of detention for public protection (DPP) unless an extended sentence was considered adequate.

---

[12] CJA 2003, Sch 15A, para 10, as inserted by CJIA 2008, Sch 5.

[13] See CJA 2003, s 225(3B), as inserted by CJIA 2008, s 13(1).

[14] Inserted by CJIA 2008, s 13(1).

[15] See CJA 2003, s 225(3B) and (3C), as inserted by CJIA 2008, s 13(1).

[16] *Archbold News*, Issue 5, June 6, 2008. See also *Langstone* [2001] 2 Cr App R (S) 98 (p 439). See A-G's Reference (No 55 of 2008) sub nom *R v C & 9 Ors* [2008] EWCA Crim 2790 for a full analysis of these new provisions.

[17] See the discretion contained in CJA 2003, s 225(3), as inserted by CJIA 2008, s 13(1).

[18] Criminal Justice and Immigration Act 2008 (Commencement No 2 and Transitional and Saving Provisions) Order 2008, SI 2008/1586.

The effect of the amendment is to substitute that duty with a power to impose DPP. As with adults, that power can only be exercised when the notional minimum term is at least 2 years. Similarly, the process of calculation of the notional minimum term is the same as that for adult offenders. It should be noted, however, that unlike the related adult provisions, a previous conviction in the case of a youth for a specified offence under Sch 15A is not a trigger for either DPP or an extended sentence.

3. Extended sentences

(a) *Adult offenders*

2.21   The CJIA 2008, s 15 makes substantial amendments to the CJA 2003, s 227 and came into force on 14 July 2008.[19] The restriction contained in the CJA 2003, s 227(1)(a) on the use of extended sentences to specified offences 'other than a serious offence' has been revoked, empowering sentencing courts to impose extended sentences for serious violent and sexual offences (ie specified offences which carry a maximum of 10 years or more). It is however, as with IPP sentences, a power and not a duty. In all cases therefore, where the offence is a serious specified offence, the court will have a discretion to impose an IPP, an extended sentence, or indeed a determinate one.

2.22   Again as with IPP sentences, the power of the court to impose an extended sentence can only be invoked when certain qualifying conditions are met. Conditions inserted into the CJA 2003, s 227 by the CJIA 2008, s 15(4), ensure that an extended sentence may only be imposed on an offender who presents a significant risk of serious harm if, at the time the offence was committed the offender had a previous conviction in any part of the UK for a Sch 15A offence or the immediate offence would attract an immediate custodial term of at least 4 years.[20] By extension therefore, an extended sentence cannot be imposed (as they have been in the past) for persistent but relatively low level offending that demonstrates worrying and dangerous tendencies but could not justify a 4 year determinate minimum term (eg relatively low level sexual assaults).

2.23   Other amendments[21] inserted into the CJA 2003, s 227 by the CJIA 2008 include s 15(4)(2C), which reasserts the structure of an extended sentence (an appropriate custodial term followed by a further licence period), and the CJIA 2008, s 15(6) which preserves a power by the Secretary of State to amend the minimum custodial tariff of 4 years (as set out in the new CJA 2003, s 227(2B)) should the power to release on licence at the halfway point be changed. As the purpose of the minimum 4 year determinate tariff is to ensure a minimum of 2 years is spent in custody, any amendment to the proportion of sentence to be served before release on licence could undermine that purpose. The Secretary of State therefore retains a discretion to change the 4 year figure accordingly.[22]

---

[19] Criminal Justice and Immigration Act 2008 (Commencement No 2 and Transitional and Saving Provisions) Order 2008, SI 2008/1586. See A-G's Reference (No 55 of 2008) sub nom *R v C & 9 Ors* [2008] EWCA Crim 2790 for a full analysis of these new provisions.

[20] See CJA 2003, s 227(2A) and (2B), as inserted by CJIA 2008 s 15(4).

[21] Also in force from 14 July 2008 by virtue of Criminal Justice and Immigration Act 2008 (Commencement No 2 and Transitional and Saving Provisions) Order 2008, SI 2008/1586.

[22] See Explanatory Notes to the CJIA 2008, p 36.

(b) *Young offenders*

As with the amendments to the provisions relating to adult offenders, the CJIA 2008, s 16 amends the CJA 2003, s 228. The effect of the amendment, which came into force on 14 July 2008,[23] is to give the court the power rather than a duty to impose an extended sentence. The power can only be exercised where the offence for which the young person is to be sentenced would attract a custodial term of at least 4 years. 2.24

(c) *IPP or extended sentence?*

There seems little therefore to distinguish between the conditions meriting the consideration of the imposition of an IPP and those relating to extended sentences. The fine dividing line is a matter for the discretion of the sentencing court when considering the balance between the least onerous sentence which can be imposed on the offender and which is at the same time adequate for the protection of the public. Only if a commensurate determinate sentence can be excluded, should the court consider imposing an extended sentence. Only if both a determinate sentence and an extended sentence can be excluded, should the court invoke its power to impose imprisonment for detention for public protection. 2.25

4. Assessment of dangerousness

The CJIA 2008, s 17, in force from 14 July 2008[24] and applicable to all case which fall to be sentenced on or after that date, provides for the wholesale review of the assumption of dangerousness, which was enshrined in the CJA 2003, s 229. Gone is the assumption of dangerousness and gone is the distinction between offenders aged under and over 18. Instead, s 229(2) is re-worked to allow the court, in the case of all offenders, to make an assessment of dangerousness taking into consideration all information about the nature and circumstances of the offence for which the individual is to be sentenced, all available information about previous convictions before courts worldwide, any information about relevant patterns of behaviour, and any information about the offender.[25] 2.26

5. Appeals where previous convictions set aside

The CJIA 2008, s 18, in force from 14 July 2008[26] amends the CJA 2003, ss 231, 232 and 234 to reflect the amendments made to ss 225–229. The effect of the amendments is to provide a framework for appeal if the imposition of an IPP or extended sentence was justified on the basis of a previous conviction for an offence under Sch 15A and that conviction is subsequently overturned on appeal. 2.27

---

[23] Criminal Justice and Immigration Act 2008 (Commencement No 2 and Transitional and Saving Provisions) Order 2008, SI 2008/1586.

[24] Ibid.

[25] See CJIA 2008, s 17(2).

[26] Criminal Justice and Immigration Act 2008 (Commencement No 2 and Transitional and Saving Provisions) Order 2008, SI 2008/1586.

2.28   The CJA 2003, s 231 as amended provides that a notice of appeal against the sentence should be lodged within 28 days from the date in which the previous conviction was set aside. Amendments introduced by the CJIA 2008, s 18(2) simply brings the CJA 2003, s 232 (certificates of conviction) up to date with the changes made under ss 225 to 229. Similarly, the CJIA 2008, s 18(3) omits the CJA 2003, s 234 ('Determination of a day when offence committed') in light of the amendments to s 229.

6. Consequential amendments to Armed Forces Act 2006

2.29   The CJIA 2008, s 145 and Sch 25, paras 10–18 introduce consequential amendments to the corresponding dangerous offender provisions of the Armed Forces Act 2006.[27] As would be expected, the amendments are in the spirit of the changes made to the CJA 2003, ss 225–229.

7. Indeterminate sentences: determination of tariffs

2.30   When it comes into force,[28] the CJIA 2008, s 19 will amend s 82A of the Powers of Criminal Courts (Sentencing) Act 2000 to empower the court tasked with determining the minimum period to be served in custody under a discretionary life sentence or an indeterminate sentence for public protection, to reduce the notional determinate term by less than half in certain serious cases. This amendment was prompted by headline grabbing cases such as *R v Sweeney* (Cardiff Crown Court, 12 June 2006) where, for an offence of kidnap and three offences of sexual assault of a child under 13 by penetration, Sweeney was sentenced to life imprisonment with a minimum term of less than 6 years. Although in reality, Sweeney could not have expected to be released until long after the expiry of the minimum term, the sentence was criticized by both the Home Office and members of the public. By July 2006, A Home Office White Paper[29] observed:

> 2.25 In fact, very few offenders on unlimited sentences will be released at the half way point—it is just the earliest point at which their release can be considered by the parole board. But it gives the public the impression that dangerous people might be released after a very short time; and we believe it is wrong to automatically apply this principle to 'halving' the sentence tariffs for dangerous offenders. We will consult on a range of options for ending this convention and will give the courts the discretion to make dangerous offenders serve a higher proportion of their tariff.

2.31   By November 2006, a Home Office Consultation Paper, 'Making Sentencing Clearer', proposed several options for reform of the system. The paper recognized that part of the concern about these sentences related to the way the sentence is expressed. A proposal was therefore made to 'make the headline sentence clearer', possibly by borrowing from the American phraseology and referring to a sentence of,

---

[27] Not yet in force.
[28] The provisions will come into force on such a day as the Secretary of State may by order appoint (CJA 2008, s 53(7)). At the time of writing there is no proposed implementation date.
[29] 'Rebalancing the criminal justice system in favour of the law-abiding majority: cutting crime, reducing re-offending and protecting the public', July 2006.

for example, six years to life. Another option proposed, and favoured by Liberty,[30] was to allow the sentencing judge to make a recommendation to the Parole Board on the minimum period to be served for public protection in addition to the minimum term for punishment.

Ultimately, neither of these options (nor a further two proposed) found favour with the legislators. Instead, a proposal from the more radical end of the scale was adopted: the amendment of the Powers of Criminal Courts (Sentencing) Act (PCC(S)A) 2000, s 82A to remove the requirement to take into account the duty to release determinate prisoners at the halfway point where an exceptionally high seriousness test is met.[31]   2.32

Although the principle behind the clause was generally approved in its passage through Parliament, practitioners will no doubt agree with the criticism from opposition parties, who lamented the lack of clarity of the drafting.[32] In essence, the CJIA 2008, s 19 leaves intact the arrangements under the PCC(S)A 2000, s 82A for setting tariffs but purports to give courts more flexibility when dealing with exceptionally serious cases.[33] The two circumstances in which the discretion to reduce the notional determinate sentence by less than half can be exercised are as follows: 2.33

(i) Case A:[34] applies to offenders aged over 18 when the offence was committed and to offences for which the court is determining the tariff for a discretionary life sentence. If the circumstances of the offence, or of the offence and one or more other offences associated with it, makes the crime exceptionally serious (but not serious enough to attract the imposition of a 'whole-life' tariff) and the court determines that half of the determinate term would be inadequate to reflect the seriousness presented by the offence or offences, the court retains a discretion not to reduce the notional determinate tariff at all, or to reduce it by less than half.

(ii) Case B:[35] arises where, in the case of a youth or adult offender, the court is determining the tariff for a discretionary life sentence or an indeterminate sentence of imprisonment for public protection. Courts may reduce the notional determinate tariff by less that half, but no less than one third where to reduce the tariff by a full half would result in the offender not serving any extra time in custody, ie where the offender is already serving a determinate custodial sentence and would not be eligible for release until after the minimum term for the indeterminate sentence had expired. This provision aims to address the fact that

[30] Liberty's response to the Home Office Consultation, 'Making Sentencing Clearer', January 2007.

[31] 'Making Sentencing Clearer, A consultation and report of a review by the Home Secretary, Lord Chancellor and Attorney General', Home Office, November 2006, para 3.9.

[32] Described as 'gobbledegook' by the Conservatives who put forward a 'plea for simplicity in English' and observed, 'it is not quite impenetrable, but it is getting close': see PBC Deb 20 November 2007 c345. To the Liberal Democrats it represented 'the antithesis of clear drafting': see PBC Deb 20 November 2007 c347.

[33] Although a definition of 'exceptionally serious' has not been provided, It was suggested in the Consultation Paper, to ensure consistency with the determination of the minimum term for mandatory life sentences, that the exceptionally high seriousness test in CJA 2003, para 4 of Sch 21 could be used as a starting point.

[34] PCC(S)A 2000, s 82A(3A), as inserted by CJIA 2008, s19(3).

[35] Ibid.

indeterminate sentences cannot be served consecutively with determinate sentences of imprisonment.

2.34   The CJIA 2008, s 19 has attracted criticism and concern in equal measure. In advancing the proposal, the authors of the Home Office report 'Making Sentencing Clearer', recognized a potential problem—that the section does not allow for the consideration during sentence of any lessening of the risk posed by the offender, where, for example, there has been positive treatment of a mental illness. It will also result in very different periods of imprisonment where the offender receives an indeterminate rather than a determinate sentence for the same offence.

2.35   These concerns, together with others, were echoed in the briefing papers from Liberty, the Law Society,[36] and the Prison Reform Trust.[37] Liberty observed that the creation of a two-tier system will lead to much harsher sentences for those who meet the criteria of 'exceptionally serious'. As noted by the Prison Reform Trust, of the cases that are not deemed to meet the criteria, some are still likely to be viewed by the public and/or victims as exceptionally serious and the rationale for invoking the discretion in some exceptionally serious cases, but not other still extremely serious cases, may be difficult to justify.

2.36   Beyond reference to the facts in *Sweeney* there is no real guidance on the application of this section and significant reason for concern exists as to how exceptionally serious cases are to be identified. Against that background, it seems inevitable that guidance will ultimately be delivered by the appellate courts.

8. Consecutive terms of imprisonment and intermittent custody

2.37   The CJIA 2008, s 20 amends various sections of the CJA 2003, Part 12. While s 20 came into force on 14 July 2008,[38] the relevant sections of the CJA 2003 are not yet in force.

2.38   The CJIA 2008, s 20(2) amends the CJA 2003, s 181 (prison sentences of less than 12 months) by inserting a new subsection (7A). The CJA 2003, s 181(7)(a) states that when, in accordance with this section, a court imposes two or more prison sentences to be served consecutively, the aggregate length of the terms of imprisonment must not be more that 65 weeks. The effect of (7A) is that, when considering whether the consecutive terms are within the 65-week maximum period, all periods in custody should be calculated but only the longest of the licence periods.

2.39   The CJIA 2008, s 20(3) amends the CJA 2003, s 264A(3), 4(b) and (5) (consecutive terms; intermittent custody). In essence, where consecutive sentences of intermittent custody are imposed, the offender will be required to serve all the custodial periods consecutively, followed by all the licence periods.

2.40   The CJIA 2008, s 20(4) amends the CJA 2003, s 265 (restrictions on consecutive sentences for released prisoners). Subsection 4(a) amends s 265(1) to extend its

---

[36] The Law Society, Parliamentary Brief Criminal Justice and Immigration Bill Second Reading, House of Commons, 23 July 2007.

[37] Prison Reform Trust, 'Criminal Justice and Immigration Bill: Initial Briefing Paper', July 2007.

[38] Criminal Justice and Immigration Act 2008 (Commencement No 2 and Transitional and Saving Provisions) Order 2008, SI 2008/1586.

application to offenders released under Criminal Justice Act 1991, Part 2 by inserting subsections (1A) and (1B). Subsection (1A) dictates that, under the amended s 265(1), a subsequent sentence may not be ordered to be served consecutively to a sentence imposed under the CJA 2003, Part 12 or the CJA 1991, Part 2 from which the offender has already been released. Section 20(4)(b) ensures that the amended s 265(1) applies to all terms of imprisonment including;

- sentences imposed for offences committed before 4 April 2005 (ie the coming into force of the CJA 2003 provisions); or
- sentences of less than 12 months imposed for offences committed on or after that date.

The CJIA 2008, s 20(4)(b) inserts into the CJA 2003 a new s 265(1B) to ensure   2.41 that the reference to 'release' in the CJA 2003, s 265(1) does include periods of temporary release on licence, where an intermittent custody order applies, before the custodial days specified in s 183(1)(a) have been served.

Section 20(5) removes any saving which might continue to apply by virtue of   2.42 PCC(S)A 2000, s 84 (despite the repeal of that section by the CJA 2003).

C. NON-CUSTODIAL SENTENCES

1. Introduction

A series of papers and reports, produced or commissioned by the Home Office and   2.43 the Ministry of Justice have, in acknowledgment of the rapidly increasing prison population in England and Wales, re-emphasized the principle that prison must only be used when necessary and for the most serious offenders. There is also widespread recognition that alternatives to custody can be more effective in reducing re-offending.

The Home Office consultation paper 'Making Sentencing Clearer'[39] observed: 2.44

There are often better options than imprisonment for dealing with less serious non-violent offenders. More of these offenders should be dealt with through robust community sentences that ask a lot of them. Community orders are often more challenging than a short period in custody for less serious offenders. The evidence so far is that the courts are not using community orders as fully as they might. The anticipated switch to these new community sentences from short terms of imprisonment that was envisaged has not happened but is a crucial part of the package of sentencing reform we wish to achieve.

In a similar vein, in the Ministry of Justice paper of May 2007, 'Penal Policy—   2.45 a background paper', Lord Falconer, the Lord Chancellor, and the Secretary of State for Justice outlined how 'ensuring that we build on those non-custodial sentences that offer tough, safe and effective alternative punishments, but are more effective in reducing re-offending' would form part of an effective penal policy.

Although these sentiments have not been specifically reproduced in particular   2.46 sections of the CJIA 2008, there is a tangible theme in the sentencing provisions of the re-introduction of judicial discretion and the saving of valuable probation resources for those who need them most.

---

[39] November 2006; at 1.16.

2. Community sentences

2.47   The CJIA 2008, ss 10 and 11, both in force from 14 July 2008,[40] introduce restrictions on the courts' powers to impose community sentences.[41] Section 10 amends the CJA 2003, s 148 to emphasize the discretion available to the sentencing court—both with regard to the imposition of a community sentence *per se* and the imposition of restrictions on any such sentence. In essence, it dictates that nothing in the CJA 2003, s 148 obliges the court to impose a community sentence, even where the offence is serious enough to justify such a sentence. Further, even where a power exists to impose particular restrictions on liberty available under such orders, there is no requirement on the court to impose them (CJA 2003, s 148 (5), as amended).

2.48   The CJIA 2008, s 11 introduces into the CJA 2003 an entirely new s 150A and makes amendments to s 151. As suggested in the title, 'Community order only available for offences punishable with imprisonment or for persistent offenders previously fined', this section ensures that the power to make a community order is exercisable only if:

- the offence is punishable with imprisonment; or
- the offender is aged over 16 on conviction and since he has attained the age of 16, for offences for which he was convicted before UK courts, he has been fined three or more times.

2.49   When it comes into force, however, the CJIA 2008, Sch 4, para 76 will amend the CJA 2003, s 151 to restrict the application of this section to offenders over the age of 18.

2.50   The CJIA 2008, s 38 makes amendments to the powers of both magistrates' and Crown Courts to deal with those in breach of their community orders under the CJA 2003, Sch 8, paras 9 and 10.[42] Where the court proposes to deal with the breach by amending the terms of the order by the imposition of more onerous requirements, the minimum period of unpaid work that may be imposed has been reduced from 40 hours to 20 hours. However, as before, where the community order already contains an unpaid work requirement, there is no minimum amount by which the hours of unpaid work may be increased.

3. Fines

2.51   The CJIA 2008, s 41, when it comes into force, will amend the Courts Act 2003, Sch 5, Part 3 by inserting new paragraphs (9A), (9B), and (9C). The effect of these amendments is to allow for the disclosure by the Secretary of State, on request by a designated officer of a magistrates' court, of information[43] relating to an individual for the purposes of enforcement of fines. The information should be requested to

---

[40] Criminal Justice and Immigration Act 2008 (Commencement No 2 and Transitional and Saving Provisions) Order 2008, SI 2008/1586.

[41] Consequential amendments have also be introduced to the relevant provisions of the Armed Forces Act 2006, see CJIA 2008, s 145 which gives effect to CJIA 2008, Sch 25, Part 2, paras 24–27.

[42] Ibid.

[43] Full name, address(es), date of birth, national insurance number, and benefit status.

facilitate 'the making of a decision by the court as to whether it is practicable or appropriate to make an application for benefit deduction[44] 'in relation to a person who has defaulted on a fine or fines imposed. Once obtained, para (9B) restricts the purposes for which the information can be shared and used and creates an offence for the unauthorized disclosure or use of such material. New para (9C) defines, for the purposes of para (9A) and (9B); the terms 'benefit status', 'information', and 'prescribed' and provides that nothing in these paragraphs authorizes the making of disclosure in contravention of the Data Protection Act 1998.

4. Pre-sentence Reports

The CJIA 2008, s 12, in force from 14 July 2008,[45] amends the CJA 2003, s 158 to   2.52
permit the court, in most circumstances, to accept an oral pre-sentence report. However, where an offender is aged under 18 and the court is considering whether to impose a discretionary custodial sentence, a written report must be obtained.[46]

D. CREDIT FOR PERIODS OF REMAND ON BAIL

1. Introduction

The CJIA 2008, ss 21 to 23 and Sch 6[47] enable a sentencing court to direct that time   2.53
spent on bail under an electronically monitored curfew should be credited against a custodial sentence at a rate of half-a-day per day spent on bail (subject to certain requirements) in a similar way to the manner in which remands in custody are credited. The provisions were added to the proposed Bill only at Report Stage in the House of Commons on 9 January 2008, as a result of Lord Carter's Review of Prisons.

The government defended the measures against criticism that it was arbitrary that   2.54
9 hours on curfew should count toward sentence but not shorter curfew periods or bail hostel conditions on the basis that it was a useful measure which would help with the reduction of the prison population.[48] An opposition attempt to exclude the proposals from the Act was unsuccessful.[49] Interestingly, in a judgment handed down on 17 July 2008, the Court of Appeal refused an appeal, the basis of which was that the sentence should have been reduced to take into account the time spent on bail with extremely stringent conditions, including tagging and virtual house arrest. The court held that the judge was entitled to hold that there was a difference between onerous bail conditions and custody.[50]

---

[44] Courts Act 2003, Sch 5, para (9A)(1), as inserted by CJIA 2008, s 41(2).
[45] Criminal Justice and Immigration Act 2008 (Commencement No 2 and Transitional and Saving Provisions) Order 2008, SI 2008/1586.
[46] See also para **2.210** below.
[47] Which, with the exception of s 21(2), came into force on 3 November 2008 (SI 2008/2712).
[48] HL Deb 26 February 2008 vol 699, cc642–644.
[49] HL Deb 21 April 2008 vol 700, cc1262–1266.
[50] *R v Peter Kevin Glover* (17 April 2008) but see also *R v Abdul Sherif & 5 Ors* [2008] EWCA Crim 2653.

2. Crediting periods of remand on bail

2.55   The CJA 2003, s 240 sets out, from 4 April 2005, the provision by which a court sentencing an offender to imprisonment can credit periods of remand in custody. The previous regime was set out in the CJA 1967, s 67. The principle behind both regimes is that time spent in custody on remand should count towards the serving of the sentence ultimately imposed. The CJIA 2008, s 21 amends the CJA 2003 by inserting s 240A entitled 'Crediting period on remand on bail: terms of imprisonment and detention'.

(a) *When do the new provisions apply?*

2.56   The provisions of the CJA 2003, s 240A apply whenever a court sentences an offender to imprisonment in respect of an offence committed on or after 4 April 2005 and 'the offender was remanded on bail by a court in the course of or in connection with proceedings for the offence, or any related offence, after the coming into force of section 21'.[51] The CJIA 2008, s 23 and Sch 6 make similar provisions in relation to offenders sentenced to a custodial sentence whose offences were committed before 4 April 2005 and are subject to CJA 1967, s 67. Therefore, the power to credit for periods of remand on bail (subject to certain requirements) applies regardless of when the offence was committed.

2.57   The CJA 2003, s 22 provides that the provisions apply when fixing the tariff in relation to prisoners serving mandatory life sentences (s 22(3)) and discretionary life sentences (s 22(5)). They apply to sentencing after re-trials (s 22(4)) and the making of detention and training orders (s 22(6)).

(b) *Which bail conditions qualify?*

2.58   The CJIA 2008, s 240A applies where an offender's bail was subject to a qualifying curfew condition and an electronic monitoring condition 'the relevant conditions' (s 240A(1)(c)). Section 240A(12) provides that 'electronic monitoring condition' means any electronic monitoring requirements imposed by s 3(6ZAA) of the Bail Act 1976 and 'qualifying curfew condition' means a condition of bail which requires the person granted bail to remain at one or more specified places for a total of not less than 9 hours in any given day.

The provisions do not apply where the offender is on bail subject to an electronically monitored curfew condition and is at the same time subject to an electronically monitored curfew imposed as a consequence of early release from prison or as part of a community order or suspended sentence or is on temporary release from prison, a young offender institution or a secure training centre.[52]

(c) *The court's duty*

2.59   The court must direct that the credit period is to count as time served by the offender unless the CJIA 2008, s 240A(4) applies (s 240A(2)). Section 240A(4) provides that subs (2) does not apply if the following two different circumstances apply. Firstly, s 240A(4)(a) provides that s 240A(2) does not apply if rules made by the Secretary

---

[51] CJA 2003, s 240A(1), as inserted by CJIA 2008, s 21.
[52] See the Remand on Bail (Disqualification of Credit Period) Rules 2008, SI 2008/2793, Rules 3 and 4.

of State so provide.[53] Secondly, s 240A(4)(b) provides that s 240A(2) does not apply if it is in the opinion of the court just in all the circumstances not to give a direction under that subsection. In considering whether it is just, the court must, in particular, take into account whether or not the offender has, at any time whilst on bail subject to the relevant conditions, breached either or both of them. Where the court does not make an order that the whole time remanded on qualifying bail counts it can make an order in relation to a proportion of the time (s 240A(5)).

The time to be credited is the number of days in which the relevant bail conditions   2.60
applied, starting with the first day the conditions applied and excluding the last day, which is then halved (s 240A(3)).

Where the court gives a direction that either the whole time remanded on bail with   2.61
the relevant conditions or part of the time should apply, it shall state in open court the number of days on which the offender was subject to the relevant conditions and the number of days in relation to which the direction is given (s 240A(8)).

Where the court does not allow the whole time to be credited or does not allow   2.62
any time to be credited it must state either that its decision is in accordance with rules under s 240A(4)(a) or that it is of the opinion it is just in all the circumstances not to give a direction in accordance with s 240A(4)(b) and it must state what the circumstances are (s 240A(10)).

Where an offender receives concurrent or consecutive sentences, the time spent on bail subject to an electronically monitored curfew condition should not be credited more than once.[54]

The provisions to a large extent mirror those of the CJA, s 240. In *R v Gordon and*   2.63
Others[55] the Court of Appeal gave general guidance in relation to the CJA 2003, s 240. It made clear that there is a presumption that the direction under s 240 should be given save in cases specifically identified for express reasons.[56] The Court in *Gordon* also considered the difficulties which arose in sentencing courts obtaining accurate information in relation to days spent remanded in custody, a matter that had already been the subject of detailed consideration in the case of *R v Norman*.[57]

The Carter Review, in providing details of its proposed recommendations, suggested   2.64
that the court would receive compliance and curfew data from the tagging contractor. No provisions are made in the new sections for how the Court will be provided with information in relation to compliance with relevant bail conditions or how any disputes will be resolved. The issue is potentially more complicated than in relation to calculating time spent remanded in custody, and the case law demonstrates the many problems which have arisen from the CJA 2003, s 240.

(d) *Consequential amendments*

Consequential amendment is made to the CJA 1991, s 246(4) in relation to Home   2.65
Detention Curfew release (CJIA 2008, s 22(2)). The new provisions do not apply to a service court (s 21(2)) or International Criminal Court sentences (s 22(7)).

---

[53] See further CJA 2003, s 240A(6), as inserted by CJIA 2008, s 21.
[54] See The Remand on Bail (Disqualification of Credit Period) Rules 2008. SI 2008/2793, Rule 2.
[55] [2007] 2 Cr App R (S) 400.
[56] Page 402, at para H10.
[57] 1 Cr App R (S) 509.

E. RELEASE AND RECALL OF PRISONERS

1. Changes to release mechanisms under the CJA 1991

(a) *Introduction*

2.66   Lord Carter suggested that the release mechanisms for prisoners serving sentences under the CJA 1991 should be brought into line with those serving sentences under the CJA 2003, in order to free up Parole Board and prison resources. Under the CJA 2003 the Parole Board now only deals with the release of dangerous offenders. However, a significant number of prisoners were sentenced under the previous legislation and are still subject to discretionary release. Clause 26 (release of certain long-term prisoners) and clause 28 (release of fine defaulters and contemnors) (now sections 26 and 28 respectively) were added to the Bill at Report Stage in the House of Common on 9 January 2008.

(b) *Release of certain long-term prisoners under CJA 1991 (CJIA 2008, s 26)*

2.67   Under the provisions of the Criminal Justice Act 1991, which apply in relation to prisoners sentenced for an offence committed before 4 April 2005, there is a duty to release offenders serving determinate prison sentences of between 12 months and 4 years once they have served half of the sentence. In relation to offenders serving determinate sentences of 4 years or more, the offender may be released between the half and two-thirds point of the sentence subject to a recommendation by the Parole Board. The duty to release the offender does not arise until he has served two-thirds of his sentence. Under the 1991 regime, offenders are released subject to licence until the three-quarter point of their sentence is reached.[58]

2.68   Under the provisions of the CJA 2003 the duty to release offenders serving custodial sentences at the halfway point of their sentence applies in relation to all offenders serving determinate sentences of 12 months and above, other than those serving extended sentences or intermittent custody sentences. All offenders, on being released, are subject to licence in relation to which conditions may be imposed right up to the end of their sentence.[59]

2.69   The CJIA 2008, s 26[60] amends the CJA 1991, s 33 (early release of short-term and long-term prisoners) by imposing on the Secretary of State a duty to release a long-term prisoner on licence as soon as he has served one-half of his sentence.[61] The duty to release at the halfway point does not apply in relation to a long-term prisoner if the offence, or one of the offences, in respect of which he is serving his sentence is specified in Sch 15 to the CJA 2003.[62]

2.70   It is clear, therefore, that the new provision does not completely align the two regimes. An offender serving a determinate sentence for a Schedule 15 specified

---

[58] CJA 1991, ss 32–37.
[59] CJA 2003, ss 244–253.
[60] Which came into force on 9 June 2008 (SI 2008/1466).
[61] Consequential amendments are also made to CJA 1991, s 35.
[62] Schedule 15 includes corresponding armed forces offences (CJA 2003, s 331(1C) and 1(B), as inserted by CJIA 2008, s 26(2)).

offence who falls under the CJA 2003 must be released at the halfway mark whereas such an offender under the CJA 1991 regime only has the right to be released at the two-thirds point. This is so even if he would have been likely to be serving a determinate sentence had he been sentenced under the CJA 2003 regime.

The Commencement Order[63] provides that the coming into force of the CJIA 2008, s 26 will have no effect in relation to prisoners who were already serving their sentence at the time the CJA 1991 came into effect. Further it will have no effect in relation to long-term prisoners who are serving sentences of imprisonment for committing the following offences:[64] (a) ss 11,12, 15 to 18, 54, 56 to 63 of the Terrorism Act 2000; (b) ss 47, 50, and 113 of the Anti-Terrorism, Crime and Security Act 2001; and (c) s 12 of the Sexual Offences Act 1956.   2.71

Section 26 will not apply to long-term prisoners who have already reached the halfway point of their sentence before 9 June 2008[65] or those who are serving a sentence by virtue of having been transferred to the United Kingdom in pursuance of a warrant under s 1 of the Repatriation of Prisoners Act 1984 in certain circumstances.[66]   2.72

The CJIA 2008, s 26(6) inserts a new s37ZA into Part II of the CJA 1991. It brings the licence period and conditions of those released under the newly created CJA 1991, s 33(1A) in line with those of offenders serving determinate sentences of 12 months or more and released under the Criminal Justice Act 2003. Section 37ZA provides that where a long-term prisoner is released on licence under s 33(1A) the licence remains in force for the remainder of the sentence and that the person subject to the licence must comply with conditions specified in the licence. The provisions of the CJA 2003, s 250(1),(4) and (8) (conditions which must and can apply to a licence period) are applicable.   2.73

Those released on licence under Part II of the CJA 1991 were already subject to the recall powers under the CJA 2003, s 254(1).[67] Section 26(4) expressly provides that this section is the applicable recall power.   2.74

Minor and consequential amendments to other legislation as a result of the implementation of s 16 are set out in Sch 16.   2.75

(c) *Release of fine defaulters and contemnors under the CJA 1991 (CJIA 2008, s 28)*

The CJIA 2008, s 28 came into force on 14 July 2008.[68] However, the provisions do not apply to any person released pursuant to the CJA 1991, s 36(1) prior to that date.[69] Section 28 makes a number of amendments to the CJA 1991, s 45, the effect of which is to amend s 36 of that Act so that fine defaulters and contemnors released on compassionate grounds are no longer released on licence. Moreover, the obligation to consult the Parole Board in the case of long-term prisoners is removed, bringing the position into line with the CJA 2003, s 258.   2.76

---

[63] SI 2008/1466.

[64] Including aiding or abetting, conspiring to commit or attempting to commit these offences.

[65] CJIA 2008, Sch 27, para 8.

[66] See CJIA 2008, Sch 27, para 9.

[67] See para 23(1) of Sch 2 to the Criminal Justice Act 2002 (Commencement No 8 and Transitional and Saving Provisions) Order 2005, SI 2006/950.

[68] SI 2008/1586.

[69] CJIA 2008, Sch 27, para 10.

2. Application of the CJA 1991, s 35(1) to prisoners liable to removal from the UK

2.77 The CJIA 2008, s 27[70] was included in the Bill when it was first introduced in the House of Commons in June 2007 in order specifically to address the declaration of incompatibility made in the case of *R (Hindawi and Headley) v Secretary of State for the Home Department*.[71] It has the effect of bringing the parole arrangements for foreign national prisoners sentenced under the CJA 1991 and liable to deportation in line with those applicable to other prisoners under that Act.

2.78　　Prior to the CJA 1991, early release procedures did not distinguish between prisoners liable to be removed form the UK and other prisoners. The distinction between the two procedures was introduced as a result of the Carlisle Committee's 1988 'Report on the Parole System in England and Wales'. The CJA 1991, s 35(1) provides that after a long-term prisoner has served one-half of his sentence, the Secretary of State may, if recommended to do so by the Board, release him on licence. In the case of foreign national prisoners, the necessity for a recommendation by the Board was removed by the CJA 1991, s 46(1). Their Lordships found the provisions incompatible with Article 14 (in conjunction with Article 5) of the ECHR, to the extent that prisoners liable to removal were prevented from having their cases reviewed by the Parole Board in the same manner as other long-term prisoners.

2.79　　The CJIA 2008, s 27(1) provides that the CJA 1991, s 46(1) ceases to have effect. The CJA 1991, s 50(2) is also amended so that the provision which enables the Secretary of State to specify classes of case where the duty to release under s 35(1) is mandatory, applies equally to foreign national prisoners.

2.80　　The CJIA 2008, s 27(1) also makes clear that the Parole Board (Transfer of Functions) Order 1998,[72] which makes it mandatory for the Secretary of State to release prisoners if recommended to do so by the Parole Board if they are serving a sentence of less than 15 years, applies to prisoners liable to removal as it applies to other prisoners.

3. Review and release of determinate sentence prisoners after recall

(a) *Introduction*

2.81 The CJIA 2008, ss 29 and 30, which came into force on 14 July 2008,[73] set out a new regime for the re-release of all fixed-term prisoners,[74] other than those serving extended sentences, recalled after being release on licence under the CJA 2003. They provide for a fixed term, punitive recall to prison for 28 days. These proposals were included in the Bill when it was originally introduced in the House of Commons in June 2007. They arose from a recommendation in the Ministry of Justice Penal Policy Paper published in May of that same year.

---

[70] Which came into force on 14 July 2008 (SI 2008/1586).

[71] [2006] UKHL 54.

[72] SI 1998/3218

[73] Save insofar as s 29(2) inserts subsections (9) and (10) of s 255A into CJA 2003 (SI 2008/1586).

[74] Fixed-term prisoners is defined in CJA 2003 as (a) a person serving a sentence of imprisonment for a determinate term; or (b) a person serving a determinate sentence of detention under s 91 of the Powers of Criminal Courts (Sentencing) Act 2000 or under s 228 of CJA 2003 (extended sentences).

The purpose of the provisions is firstly to address the increase in the prison recall population as a result of the implementation of the early release provisions introduced by the CJA 2003. The Penal Policy Paper noted a 47 per cent increase between April 2005 and February 2007. The government estimates that these provisions will result in a saving of 1000 prison places.[75]   2.82

Secondly the provisions reduce the role of the Parole Board whose Annual Report 2006/07 identified a 58 per cent increase in recall cases being considered by it between 2005/2006 and 2006/2007. This increase was attributed partly to the implementation of the CJA 2003 and partly to the effect of the judgment in *Stafford v UK*[76] and *Smith & West*.[77] The government said the provisions would help to re-focus the heavily burdened Parole Board on looking at the parole needs of serious, dangerous, violent, and sexual offenders.[78]   2.83

During the passage of the Bill concerns were raised in both Houses about the lack of judicial input for those receiving fixed-term release; the application of the provisions to young offenders; and the fact that the 28-day fixed recall period could be amended without a further Act of Parliament. In relation to the latter, it was acknowledged on behalf of the government that it wanted to monitor the provisions and may amend the 28-day fixed recall period if appropriate.[79]   2.84

(b) *CJA 2003, s 254*

Prior to the coming into force of the CJA 2003 recall provisions, it was the Parole Board which both made the decisions as to recall and acted as the body that scrutinized those decisions. The unfairness in that situation was duly recognized and the power to recall given to the Secretary of State (see CJA 2003, s 254(1)). That power, along with the right of prisoners recalled under s 254(1) to make written representations under s 254(2), is retained. However, the CJA 2003, s 254(3) and (4) which set out the obligations of the Secretary of State to refer to the Parole Board and give effect to any recommendation for immediate release cease to have effect and are replaced with three separate procedures contained within the CJA 2003, ss 255A to 255D as inserted by the CJIA 2008, s 29(2).[80]   2.85

(c) *Category One: prisoners eligible and suitable for consideration for automatic release (CJA 2003, s 255B)*

The CJA 2003, s 255B sets out the procedure for prisoners who are *eligible* and *suitable* for automatic release.   2.86

The CJA 2003, 255A(2) provides that a prisoner is eligible to be considered for automatic release *unless* he falls into one of three groups set out below.   2.87

---

[75] Explanatory Notes to Bill 130 page 109.

[76] 35 EHRR 32.

[77] *R (on the application of Smith) v Parole Board: R (on the application of West) v Parole Board* (2005) 1 WLR 350, [2005] UKHL 1.

[78] Hansard, PBC c377 (20 November 2007).

[79] Hansard, HL vol 699, c670 (27 February 2008).

[80] CJA 2003, s 254(5), which deal with the position of intermittent custody prisoners ceases to have effect but its provision are replicated in CJIA 2003, ss 255B(6) and 255C(6), as inserted by CJIA, s 29(2).

2.88　　The first group is extended sentence prisoners[81] or specified offence prisoners. A specified offence prisoner is a prisoner, not being an extended sentence prisoner, who is serving a sentence imposed for a specified offence with the meaning of the CJA 2003, s 224 (ie a violent or sexual offence specified in Sch 15 to the CJA 2003).[82]

2.89　　The second group is prisoners who have been released either on the home detention scheme pursuant to the CJA 2003, s 246 or on compassionate grounds pursuant to the CJA 2003, s 248 and have been recalled before their normal entitlement date (the date on which they would have been entitled to be released under the CJA 2003, s 244).[83]

2.90　　The third group is prisoners who have during the same term of imprisonment previously been recalled and released under the CJA 2003, s 255B(1)(b) or (2) (automatic release or release by Secretary of State) or the CJA 2003, s 255(C)(2) (release by the Secretary of State).

2.91　　If a prisoner is *eligible* for early release (ie does not fall within any of the three groups set out above) then the Secretary of State must, on recalling him, consider whether he is *suitable* for automatic release. This means that he must be satisfied that the prisoner will not present a risk of serious harm to members of the public if he is released at the end of the fixed 28-day period.[84]

2.92　　A prisoner who is both eligible *and* suitable for automatic release must be dealt with in accordance with the CJA 2003, s 255B[85] which provides that at the end of the period of 28 days he must be released on licence. The period of 28 days begins with the date on which the prisoner is returned to prison.[86] The Secretary of State may release him on licence again at any time under s 255B(2) but must not release him under this subsection unless he is satisfied that it is not necessary for the protection of the public that he remain in prison until the end of the 28-day period. The period of 28 days may be amended.[87]

2.93　　A prisoner who is suitable for automatic release must on his return to prison be informed that he will be so released. Such a prisoner retains the right to make representations in writing with respect to his recall under the CJA 2003, s 254(2) before he is automatically released as well as the right to have the Secretary of State refer his case to the Parole Board.[88]

2.94　　Where the Parole Board recommends a prisoner's immediate release on licence the Secretary of State must give effect to the recommendation[89] in the same way as he had to under the old regime.

---

[81] As defined by CJA 2003, s 255A(7).

[82] CJA 2003, s 255A(8), (9) and (1), which are not yet in force, sets out that 'specified offence' includes the relevant armed services offences. See also CJIA 2008, Sch 26, para 11 for the inclusion of certain prisoners transferred to the United Kingdom in pursuance of a warrant under Repatriation of Prisoners Act 1984, s 1 with the meaning of 'specified offence prisoner'.

[83] CJA 2003, s 255A(11), as inserted by CJIA 2008, s 29(2).

[84] CJA 2003, s 255A(3) and (5).

[85] CJA 2003, s 255A(6)(a).

[86] CJA 2003, s 255A(4).

[87] CJA 2003, s 255B(1)(b).

[88] CJA 2003, s 255B(4).

[89] CJA 2003, s 255B(5).

(d) *Category Two: specified offences prisoners and those eligible but not suitable for early release (CJA 2003, s 255C)*

Those who were eligible to be considered for automatic release but who were not 2.95
then considered suitable, as well as those who were ineligible (other than those on
extended sentences[90]), must be dealt with in accordance with the CJA 2003, s 255C.

Under the CJA 2003, s 255C the Secretary of State may re-release a person on 2.96
licence at any time but he must not do so unless he is satisfied that it is not necessary
for the protection of the public that he should remain in prison.[91] If a person makes
representations against his recall under s 254(2) before the end of the period of
28 days, beginning with the date on which he is returned to prison, or if he has not
been released by 28 days, his case must be referred to the Parole Board.[92] Where the
Parole Board recommends a prisoner's immediate release the Secretary of State must
give effect to the recommendation.[93]

(e) *Category Three: extended sentence prisoners (CJA 2003, s 255D)*

Those serving extended sentences must be dealt with pursuant to the CJA 2003, 2.97
s 255D.[94] In relation to this category of prisoners the regime is unchanged from its
original form under the CJA 2003, s 254(3) and (4). The Secretary of State must
refer such prisoners to the Parole Board and must give effect to any recommendation
by the Parole Board for immediate release.

(f) *Further review*

The CJIA 2008, s 30(1) to (5) amends CJA 2003, s 256 (further release after recall). 2.98
Section 256 now provides that where a case is referred to it, and it does not recommend early release on licence, the Parole Board must either fix a date for release
within the next 12 months or make no recommendation. Where a date is fixed it is
the duty of the Secretary of State to release a prisoner on licence on that date. The
section is now entitled 'Review by the Board'.

A further section '256A Further Review' is inserted into the CJA 2003 by the 2.99
CJIA 2008, s 30(6), which requires that the Secretary of State refers recalled prisoners to the Parole Board at least every 12 months after the prisoner's last review. The
Secretary of State may refer a person's case to the Parole Board earlier and the Parole
Board may recommend to the Secretary of State that a person's case be so referred by
him.[95] On each subsequent review the Parole Board's powers remain the same—
it may either recommend immediate release on licence, fix a date for release on licence
or make no recommendation as to release. The Secretary of State must give effect to
any recommendation as to release.[96]

---

[90] CJA 2003, s 255A(6)(b) and (c).
[91] CJA 2003, s 255C(2) and (3).
[92] CJA 2003, s 255C(4).
[93] CJA 2003, s 255C(5).
[94] CJA 2003, s 255A(6)(d).
[95] CJA 2003, s 256A(2) and (3), as inserted by CJIA 2008, s 30(6).
[96] CJA 2003, s 256A (4) and (5), as inserted by CJIA 2008, s 30(6).

4. Recall of life prisoners

2.100   The CJIA 2008, s 31 removes the rule that the Secretary of State may only revoke
the licence of a life-sentencer on the recommendation of the Parole Board (unless it
is expedient in the public interest to recall that person before such a recommendation is practicable). According to the government Research Paper on the Criminal
Justice and Immigration Bill[97] the impetus for the change came from the HM
Inspectorate of Probation Report 'An Independent Review of a Serious Further
Offence case: Anthony Rice' which was published in May 2006, and was set up to
investigate the circumstances in which Anthony Rice murdered Naomi Bryan on
17 August 2005 when he was being supervised on a life licence. However, this
Report made no reference to, or findings in relation to, the Home Secretary's power
to order recall and was focused on the decision to release and, to a lesser extent,
supervision whilst on release. The Report noted that 'over the last 15 years there has
been a series of test cases and judgments that have eroded the Home Secretary's
powers to determine release decisions for lifers by executive action'.[98]

2.101   Concern was expressed during the passage of the Bill in both Houses about the lack
of judicial oversight or involvement in the proposed new provision. The proposal was
justified in the House of Lords on the basis it enabled the Secretary of State to take
swift and preventative action when removing potentially very dangerous offenders
from the community.[99]

2.102   The CJIA 2008, s 31 came into force on 14 July 2008[100] and amends the Crime
(Sentences) Act 1997, s 32. Section 32 gave the Secretary of State the power to
revoke a life prisoner's licence and recall him to prison if it was recommended to do
so by the Parole Board and to recall a life prisoner's licence without a recommendation by the Parole Board where it appeared to him to be expedient in the public
interest to do so before a recommendation by the Parole Board is practicable. Those
two provisions are substituted with a single provision giving the Secretary of State
the discretion to revoke the licence of a life prisoner and recall him to prison.

2.103   Consequential further amendments are also made to the section but the right of
the life prisoner to make representations in relation to his recall and to have his case
referred to the Parole Board are retained.[101] In *R (Hirst) v Home Secretary and Parole
Board*[102] the High Court rejected a claim that the Secretary of State's powers to recall
an offender and then refer the matter to the Board for a hearing pursuant to the CJA
2003, s 31(2) breached Article 5(1)(c) of the ECHR. In view of this it is unlikely
that the new provision will be amenable to challenge.

---

[97] Research Paper 07/65, 9 August 2007.
[98] HM Inspectorate of Probation 'An Independent Review of a Serious Further Offence case: Anthony
Rice', para 11.27 referred to in Research Paper 07/65, 9 August 2007 at p 31.
[99] Hansard, HL vol 699, c670 (27 February 2008).
[100] SI 2008/1586.
[101] C(S)A 1997, s 32(3) and (4).
[102] [2005] EWHC 1480 (Admin).

5. Extension of the Early Removal Scheme

(a) *Introduction*

The CJIA 2008, ss 33 and 34 extend the Early Removal Scheme (ERS) by adding a   2.104
new category of prisoner to those eligible for the ERS and removing some existing
provisions which exclude certain categories of prisoner from the Scheme.[103] The impetus behind the change appears to be the increasing proportion of foreign national
prisoners in the prison population over the last decade. Foreign national prisoners
apparently accounted for almost 8 per cent of the total prison population in the
early and mid-1990s, increasing to approximately 14 per cent by April 2007.[104]

(b) *Amendment of the ERS under the CJA 2003*

The CJA 2003, ss 259–261 introduced the ERS, which enables the Secretary of   2.105
State to remove from prison certain prisoners whose offences had been committed
on or after 4 April 2005 and are liable to removal from the UK up to 270 days[105]
before what would otherwise have been the earliest date of their release in a scheme
which broadly mirrors the Home Detention Curfew scheme.

The CJIA 2008, s 34(2) broadens the ERS under the CJA 2003, ss 259–261 so that   2.106
as well as prisoners liable to removal from the UK, it now includes persons
'eligible for removal from the UK' by inserting s 259A into the CJA 2003.

A person eligible for removal from the UK is defined in the CJA 2003, s 259A as   2.107
a person who shows to the satisfaction of the Secretary of State that he has a settled
intention of residing permanently outside the UK if he is removed from prison
under the ERS and he is not a person who is liable to removal from the UK.

The scheme under the CJA 2003 is further broadened by the CJIA 2008, s 34(5)   2.108
which amends the CJA 2003, s 260(2) so that it now applies to all relevant prisoners
who have served at least one-half of the requisite custodial period. (The original
s 260(2) provided that in order for the Scheme to apply, the length of the requisite
period of any sentence had to be at least 6 weeks, that a prisoner had served at least
4 weeks of his sentence and at least half of the requisite period.)

The ERS scheme under the CJA 2003 applied to fixed-term prisoners[106] except   2.109
those specifically excluded by s 260(3) and (3A). The CJIA 2008, s 34(6) provides
that those subsections cease to have effect with the result that now the Scheme
applies to all relevant fixed-term prisoners.

A number of consequential amendments are made to the CJA 2003 set out in s 34(7)   2.110
to (10). In particular s 34(9) provides that the requisite custodial period in relation to
prisoners serving extended sentences is one-half of the appropriate custodial sentence.

---

[103] Section 33(1), (3), (5) and (6) and s 34 (1), (3), (4)(a), (5), (6), (8) and (9), save insofar as subs (6) provides that s 260(3A) of the CJA 2003 ceases to have effect, came into force on 3 November 2008 (SI
2008/2712). These are the sections which remove some of the existing provisions that exclude certain categories of prisoner from the ERS. The extension of the ERS to a new category of prisoner, i.e. those with a 'settled
intention of residing permanently outside the UK' will come into force on such a day as the Secretary of State
may by order appoint (CJA 2008, s 53(7)).
[104] The Criminal Justice and Immigration Bill Research Paper 07/65.
[105] Originally 135 days amended as from 7 April 2008 by SI 2008/978. (In relation to CJA 1991 discussed
below, see SI 2008/977 amending CJA 1991, s 46A(5).)
[106] Those serving a determinate sentence of imprisonment or detention under C(S)A 1991, s 92, or CJA
2003, s 228 (see CJA 2003, s 237).

(c) *Amendment to the ERS under the CJA 1991*

2.111 Similar provisions to the CJA 2003, ss 259 to 261 were inserted into the Part 2 of the CJA 1991 in relation to those whose offences were committed before 4 April 2005 by the CJA 2003, s 262 and Sch 20. Those provisions are extended by the CJIA, s 33 in a broadly similar way to the way in which the CJA 2003 provisions are extended by the CJIA 2008, s 34.

6. Other miscellaneous provisions

(a) *Minimum conditions for early release under the CJA 2003, s 246(1)*

2.112 The CJIA 2008, s 24 makes technical amendments to the CJA 2003, s 246(1) in relation to conditions for early release.[107]

(b) *Release on licence under CJA 2003 of prisoners serving extended sentences*

2.113 CJIA 2008, s 25,[108] amends the CJA 2003, s 247, the section which governs the release on licence of prisoners serving extended sentences, by omitting subsections 2(b), (3), (4), (5), and (6). Those prisoners will become automatically entitled to release at the halfway point of their sentence and the Parole Board's role in their release will be removed.

(c) *Release of prisoners recalled following release under the CJA 1991*

2.114 The CJIA 2008, s 32 was added to the Bill when it was introduced to the House of Lords in January 2008. It inserts s 50A into the CJA 1991, clarifying that prisoners released on licence under that Act are now covered by the further release provision of the CJA 2003. Section 32 came into force on 14 July 2008[109] and the provisions of the new CJA 1991, s 50A apply to any person who is recalled under s 254(1) of the 2003 Act[110] on or after that date.[111]

F. YOUTH SENTENCING

1. Pre-court interventions

(a) *Introduction*

2.115 The changes to youth sentencing introduced by the CJIA 2008 (other than amendments to the dangerous offender provisions dealt with at paras **2.20** and **2.24** above and crediting periods of remand on bail dealt with at paras **2.53–2.65**), are not yet in force. The Youth Justice Board's target date for implementation is April 2009.[112] Of the changes to be introduced, a key development is conditional cautions for

---

[107] In force from 14 July 2008 (SI 2008/1586).

[108] The provisions will come into force on such a day as the Secretary of State may by order appoint (CJA 2008, s 53(7)). At the time of writing there is no proposed implementation date.

[109] SI 2008/1586.

[110] CJA 2003, s 245 is the relevant recall provision in relation to all determinate sentence prisoners irrespective of the date of the relevant offence.

[111] CJA 2008, Sch 27, para 12.

[112] Youth Justice Board (2008) 'Update on the Youth Justice: The Scaled Approach consultation' [*sic*], Press Release, 18 March 2008.

children and young people. Concerns were raised during the consultation stage that some of the punitive conditions proposed would draw young people into the criminal justice system rather than deter them.[113] The introduction of conditional cautions is to be cautiously welcomed as an additional pre-court intervention for more serious offending (complementing reprimands and final warnings) but much will depend on how they are used in primands. The CJIA 2008 also amends the Rehabilitation of Offenders Act 1974 so as to incorporate reprimands, warnings and conditional cautions.[114]

The changes to youth ASBOs and other related civil orders are dealt with in Chapter 6.   2.116

(b) Conditional cautions

The CJIA 2008, s 48 and Sch 9[115] extend the adult conditional caution scheme[116] to   2.117
children and young people aged between 10 and 17 years (although the government will initially pilot the scheme for 16 and 17 year olds only, from April 2009[117]). Section 65 of the Crime and Disorder Act (CDA) 1998, as amended, sets out the revised framework for reprimands and warnings[118] and CDA 1998, s 66A to H creates the framework for youth conditional cautions. The Act provides that the Secretary of State must prepare a Code of Practice on youth conditional cautions.[119]

The preconditions for imposing a youth conditional caution are that the offender   2.118
admits that he committed the offence and the relevant prosecutor considers that there is sufficient evidence to charge him.[120] The evidential test has a lower threshold than the current test (that there is 'a realistic prospect of his being convicted') and is being amended for reprimands and warnings as well as youth conditional cautions.[121] In the case of youth conditional cautions, an authorized person (a constable, investigating officer or person authorized by a relevant prosecutor[122]) may give a youth conditional caution provided the offender has not previously been convicted of an offence and the five requirements of the CDA 1998, s 66B have been met, namely that:[123]

(1) there is evidence the offender has committed an offence,
(2) there is sufficient evidence to charge and a youth conditional caution should be given;

---

[113] See for example, paras 27–30 of Liberty's Briefing on the Criminal Justice and Immigration Bill, June 2007.

[114] CJIA 2008, s 49 and Sch 10.

[115] CJIA 2008, s 48 and Sch 9, amending CDA 1998, s 65 and inserting ss 66A to H.

[116] As implemented by CJA 2003, ss 22–27. For an overview of how the adult scheme has been introduced, see 'HO Circular 30 / 2005: Cautioning of Adult Offenders' and 'CPS Code of Conduct on Conditional Cautioning'.

[117] Youth Justice Board website <http://www.yjb.gov.uk/en-gb/practitioners/CourtsAndOrders/Criminal JusticeandImmigrationAct/#youthcc>.

[118] It should be noted that under the existing scheme, having received a warning, an offender would be referred to the youth offending team and arrangements made for them to participate in a rehabilitation programme (CDA 1998, s 66(2)). There is no punitive sanction for any failure to participate in the rehabilitation programme, although it may be cited in a person's antecedent history (CDA 1998, s 66(5)(c)).

[119] CDA 1998, s 66G, as inserted by CJIA 2008, Sch 9, para 3.

[120] CDA 1998, s 65(1)(b) and s 66B(2)(a), as amended by CJIA 2008, Sch 9, para 2(2)(b) and para 3.

[121] CDA 1998, s 65(1)(b), as inserted by CJIA 2008, Sch 9, para 2(2)(b).

[122] CDA 1998, s 66A(7), as inserted by CJIA 2008, Sch 9, para 3.

[123] CDA 1998, s 66A(1), as inserted by CJIA 2008, Sch 9, para 3.

(3) the offender admits the offence;

(4) the authorized person explains the effect of the youth conditional caution and warns of failure to comply (if 16 or under the explanation and warning must be given in presence of an appropriate adult) and

(5) the offender signs a document containing the details of the offence, admission that he committed the offence, consent to be given youth conditional caution and the conditions.[124]

2.119   Conditions should have one or more of the following objects: rehabilitation, reparation or punishing the offender.[125] Conditions which may be attached include a financial penalty,[126] and a condition to attend at a specified place at a specified time[127] up to a maximum of 20 hours.[128] Any financial penalty must specify the amount (up to a maximum of £100 in respect of any offence[129]) and the person to whom the financial penalty is to be paid and how.[130] The conditions may only be varied with the consent of the offender.[131]

2.120   If an offender fails to comply with any of the conditions, criminal proceedings may be instituted against the offender for the offence in question,[132] and pursuant to s 24A and B of the CJA 2003 the offender may be arrested.[133] In these circumstances, the conditional caution will cease to have effect.[134] This may be where the conditional caution scheme has the greatest potential to cause injustice; one proposed condition under the adult scheme is 'not to commit further offences' which would leave many young offenders liable to prosecution.[135] A person who is given a youth conditional caution cannot be conditionally discharged within two years of receiving the caution.[136]

2.121   The CJIA 2008, s 48 and Sch 10 extend the scope of the Rehabilitation of Offenders Act (ROA) 1974 to include cautions (i.e. youth conditional cautions,[137] reprimands and warnings[138]). Reprimands and warnings become spent at the time they are given,[139] youth conditional cautions become spent after three months.[140]

---

[124] CDA 1998, s 66B, as inserted by CJIA 2008, Sch 9, para 3.
[125] CDA 1998, s 66A(3), as inserted by CJIA 2008, Sch 9, para 3.
[126] CDA 1998, s 66A(4)(a), as inserted by CJIA 2008, Sch 9, para 3.
[127] CDA 1998, s 66A(4)(b), as inserted by CJIA 2008, Sch 9, para 3.
[128] CDA 1998, s 66A(5), as inserted by CJIA 2008, Sch 9, para 3.
[129] CDA 1998, s 66C(3), as inserted by CJIA 2008, Sch 9, para 3.
[130] CDA 1998, s 66C(5), as inserted by CJIA 2008, Sch 9, para 3.
[131] CDA 1998, s 66D, as inserted by CJIA 2008, Sch 9, para 3.
[132] CDA 1998, s 66E(1), as inserted by CJIA 2008, Sch 9, para 3.
[133] CDA 1998, s 66E(4) and (5), as inserted by CJIA 2008, Sch 9, para 3.
[134] CDA 1998, s 66E(3), as inserted by CJIA 2008, Sch 9, para 3.
[135] See 'CPS Code of Conduct on Conditional Cautioning', para 5: Types of Condition. However, if prosecuted the likely maximum disposal would be a referral order
[136] CDA 1998, s 66F, as inserted by CJIA 2008, Sch 9, para 3.
[137] CJIA 2008, Sch 10, para 2(a).
[138] CJIA 2008, Sch 10, para 2(c).
[139] ROA 1974, Sch 2, para 1(1)(b), as inserted by CJIA 2008, Sch 10, para 6.
[140] ROA 1974, Sch 2, para 1(1)(a), (2), as inserted by CJIA 2008, Sch 10, para 6.

Although this amendment affords children and young people the protection of the ROA 1974, it does not preclude the disclosure of youth conditional cautions for a period of three months, which may impact upon the job opportunities of young offenders. That said, if implemented properly, youth conditional cautions will be reserved for the more serious offences and be used sparingly. For offenders who previously would have been charged, this amendment is similar to the position for Referral Orders (which the young offender might otherwise have received) in that they are spent on completion.[141]   2.122

2. General sentencing principles

(a) *Purposes of sentencing*

Section 9[142] of the CJIA 2008 inserts s 142A into the CJA 2003: 'Purposes etc of sentencing: offenders under 18'. Section 142 currently sets out the purposes of sentencing offenders aged 18 or over. At present the principles for dealing with young offenders and the purpose underpinning the youth justice system are set out in s 44 of the Children and Young Persons Act 1933 and s 37 of the CDA 1998.   2.123

Under the amended s 142A(2)[143] of the CJA 2003, when dealing with an offender aged under 18, the court must have regard to: 2.124

(a) the principal aim of the youth justice system (to prevent offending and re-offending),

(b) the welfare of the offender, and

(c) the purposes of sentencing (punishment, reform and rehabilitation, protection of the public and the making of reparation[144]).

These reflect the purposes of sentencing of adults, with the omission of 'the reduction of crime (including its reduction by deterrence)'.[145]

Another significant change introduced by the CJIA 2008, s 9 is that young offenders who reach 18 at the time of sentence will not benefit from the new statutory purpose of sentencing young offenders. This is because the CJIA 2008, s 9(2) amends the CJA 2003, s 142 (2), and makes the adult purposes of sentencing apply to all offenders aged 18 or over, deleting the words 'at the date of conviction'. It follows therefore that if a young offender crosses the age threshold by the time of conviction or sentence, the adult purposes will apply.   2.125

In *R v Ghafoor (Imran Hussain)*[146] (as applied in *R v Britton (Stephen Kade)*[147]), which dealt with the position of offenders who reached the age of 18 between the date of the offence and date of conviction, the Court of Appeal held that the sentencing regime at the date of the offence was the applicable one. In *R v Bowker,*[148]   2.126

---

[141] Rehabilitation of Offenders Act 1974, s 5(4B), (4C).
[142] At the time of writing these provisions are not in force: see para **2.115** above.
[143] Amended by CJIA 2008, s 9(1).
[144] CJA 2003, s 142A(3), as amended by CJIA 2008, s 9(1).
[145] CJA 2003, s 142(1)(b).
[146] (2003) 1 Cr App R (S) 84.
[147] (2007) 1 Cr App R (S) 121.
[148] (2008) 1 Cr App R (S) 72.

however, the Court of Appeal, considering *Ghafoor*, and noting that it was decided before the enactment of the CJA 2003, held that it was fair and just to take as the starting point the sentence that the offender would be likely to have received if he had been sentenced at the date of the offence; but there was scope for flexibility in that the sentence which would have been imposed at the time of the offence was not a sole or determining factor, though a powerful one.

2.127   The amendments to the CJA 2003 detailed above put beyond doubt that Parliament intended to stipulate that longer, deterrent sentences are permissible for those who reach 18 post-offending *or* post-conviction, shifting the goalpost further from the statutory position at the time when *Bowker* was decided. It must therefore be in the interest of young offenders to be sentenced at the earliest possible date. However, the sentence that would have been applied at the date of the offence must remain a consideration for the sentencing court—the weight to be accorded to it varying according to all the circumstances, including, for example, any delays which are not the fault of the offender.

3. Referral Orders

(a) *Introduction*

2.128   The CJIA 2008 amends ss 16 and 17[149] of the PCC(S)A 2000 to widen the circumstances in which a court may make a Referral Order. These changes reflect the overall success of Referral Orders which, according to the Regulatory Impact Assessment, have a re-conviction rate of 44.7 per cent, which is lower than the other disposals, including a discharge.[150] The changes have the potential to have a positive impact upon the Youth Justice System by increasing the number of Referral Orders, deterring re-offending, and providing a low level intervention.

2.129   There will now be more young offenders who stand to benefit from the Referral Order scheme, but the pre-requisite that the offender has pleaded guilty to an offence remains unchanged (although for a discretionary Referral Order the young offender may have also pleaded not guilty to linked offences). This is because restorative justice plays a significant role in the work of Youth Offender Panels. There is, of course, always a risk that the availability of Referral Orders places an unhappy influence on a young offender's decision on whether or not to plead guilty. To an extent, the relaxing of the criteria will mitigate this concern.

(b) *Modifications to Referral Orders*

2.130   Referral Orders can only be imposed in the Youth Court, where the sentence for the offence(s) is not fixed by law and the court is not proposing to pass a custodial sentence, make a hospital order or grant an absolute discharge.[151] In these circumstances, a

---

[149] At the time of writing these provisions are not in force— see para **2.115** above.

[150] Ministry of Justice, 'Criminal Justice and Immigration Bill Regulatory Impact Assessments', June 2007, p 41 <http://www.justice.gov.uk/docs/regulatory-impact-assess-1.pdf>.

[151] PCC(S)A 2000, s 16 (1) (a), (b), (c).

Referral Order must be made where the offender pleads guilty to an imprisonable offence having never been convicted before.[152]

The changes under the CJIA 2008 will mean that Referral Orders will become available where a young person has previously received a conditional discharge (as this will no longer be treated as a conviction) and where a young offender has been bound over to keep the peace.[153]   2.131

The circumstances in which a Youth Court has the power to make a discretionary Referral Order will be considerably amended. A discretionary Referral Order was previously only available for an offender who had never been convicted before, where he pleads guilty to an offence(s) and not guilty to other connected offence(s).[154] There will now be three gateways through which a discretionary Referral Order may be available: 2.132

- where the offender has never been convicted before (s 17(2A));[155]
- where the offender has been sentenced on one previous occasion but did not receive a Referral Order (s 17(2B));[156]
- where the offender has been sentenced on one or more previous occasions but has only received a Referral Order on one previous occasion, a second Referral Order may be available on recommendation by an appropriate officer that the offender is suitable for a Referral Order and if the court considers there are exceptional circumstances (s 17(2C)).[157]

The length of the order remains between 3 to 12 months[158] and it is considered spent on completion.[159]   2.133

(c) *Extension and revocation of Referral Orders*

The CJIA 2008 modifies other aspects of Referral Orders. Youth Courts will now have the power to revoke a Referral Order where a young offender is making good progress and the Youth Offender Panel refers the offender back to court, it is in the interests of justice.[160] The Panel may also refer the offender back to court to extend the period of the Referral Order by a period of up to 3 months if the Panel consider it in the interests of justice for the length of the Order to be extended (but the total Order must not exceed 12 months).[161]   2.134

---

[152] PCC(S)A 2000, s 17(1).
[153] PCC(S)A 2000, s 17(1)(c) is omitted by CJIA 2008, s 35(2)(c); PCC(S)A 2000, s 17(3) is omitted by CJIA 2008, s 35(2)(c).
[154] PCC(S)A 2000, s 17(2).
[155] PCC(S)A 2000, s 17(2A), as inserted by CJIA 2008, s 35(3).
[156] PCC(S)A 2000, s 17(2B), as inserted by CJIA 2008, s 35(3).
[157] PCC(S)A 2000, s 17(2C), as inserted by CJIA 2008, s 35(3).
[158] PCC(S)A 2000, s 18(1)(c).
[159] Rehabilitation of Offenders Act 1974, s 5(4B), (4C).
[160] PCC(S)A 2000, s 27A, as inserted by CJIA 2008, s 36.
[161] PCCSA 2000, Sch 1, Part 1ZA, as inserted by CJIA 2008, s 37.

4. Youth Rehabilitation Orders

(a) *Introduction*

2.135 The CJIA 2008 introduces the Youth Rehabilitation Order (YRO), a brand new sentence which aims to simplify the sentencing structure for community-based sentences for those under 18. YROs have been devised to enable the sentencing court to tailor sentences to an individual's risk and needs. However, during the consultation process and in the course of the Bill's passage through Parliament, there was real concern that these provisions would lead to an increase (rather than a decrease) in the number of young people in prison, given the onerous nature of some of the conditions attached to such an order.

2.136 The risk is that the courts will be tempted by the large number of potential requirements to impose onerous and unnecessary sentences.[162] In turn, young offenders will receive a custodial sentence sooner than they might otherwise have done through their non-compliance with an onerous order.[163] This is all the more worrying when re-sentencing following breach action already makes a substantial contribution to custody.[164] Concern that courts will impose YROs with severe requirements is reflected in s 10 of the CJIA 2008 which reminds the court that YROs are not mandatory and that it is a matter for the court's discretion whether to pass such a sentence or impose particular restrictions on a young offender's liberty.[165] Further, the CJIA 2008, s 11 restricts courts imposing community orders or YROs for non-imprisonable offences.

2.137 As with all legislative change, much will depend on how the new provisions are implemented. The Youth Justice Board's proposals are set out in 'Youth Justice: the Scaled Approach'.[166] In essence, the proposed level of intervention will be based upon the young offender's assessed risk of re-offending (as derived from the ASSET assessment tool currently used by Youth Offending Teams[167]). In other words, the punishment will be based upon perceived risk of future criminal conduct and not the actual offence for which the young offender is being sentenced.

2.138 The inequality of this approach is obvious. Further, on the basis of the Youth Justice Board's own study, one in six young people predicted to reoffend using ASSET will not do so.[168] The 'Standing Committee for Youth Justice' believes this approach will offend the principles of proportionality and fairness and discriminate against the most deprived children, calls for the current proposals to be reconsidered.[169]

---

[162] See Liberty and Prison Reform Trust papers on the provisions.

[163] This is acknowledged by the Youth Justice Board, p 7, 'Youth Justice: the scaled approach', Youth Justice Board for England and Wales, November 2007.

[164] Twenty five per cent of breaches result in a custodial sentence: Bateman, T (2006) 'Youth justice news' in Youth Justice 6(1).

[165] CJA 2003, s 148(5), as inserted by CJIA 2008, s 10.

[166] 'Youth Justice: the scaled approach', Youth Justice Board for England and Wales, November 2007.

[167] ASSET is a structured assessment tool, produced by the Youth Justice Board for use by YOTs for all young people coming into the youth justice system. Its purpose is to determine why the young person has offended, what factors contributed to their offending behaviour (such as their family and lifestyle circumstances are, whether they have specific mental health or drug and alcohol-related problems, if they are engaged in learning, their level of educational attainment), and what level of risk they pose to themselves and others.

[168] Baker, K, Jones, S, Roberts, C, and Merrington, S (2005) 'The evaluation of the validity and reliability of the youth justice board's assessment for young offenders: Findings from the first two years of the use of ASSET'.

[169] 'Briefing on the Youth Justice Board's "scaled approach"', Standing Committee for Youth Justice, undated.

The provisions are not in force and there are likely to be further refinements to the proposed implementation of YROs which are anticipated to be introduced in April 2009.[170] In reality the success of these orders will depend on whether the budget has been put in place to make them effective.[171]

(b) *General principles*

The CJIA 2008, s 1 and Sch 1 will put/puts in place the framework for YROs by creating a 2.139 generic sentence with 15 different requirements, forming a menu of options for a court.

The requirements seek to engage young offenders and address their offending 2.140 behaviour through positive interventions such as teaching life skills and providing constructive activities. Most of the requirements are modelled on existing provisions in other community orders, and others, such as the activity requirement, mental health treatment and fostering, are new.

Requirements are overseen by the 'responsible officer', who is the person responsible 2.141 for the offender's supervision under the order. The meaning of the responsible officer and their duties are set out in the CJIA 2008, ss 4 and 5.

There are a number of restrictions placed upon a court which is considering 2.142 making a YRO. Before making a YRO the court must

- obtain and consider the offender's family circumstances and the likely effect of such an order;[172]
- consider whether the proposed requirements are compatible if imposing two or more requirements, or two or more YROs;[173]
- ensure that any requirement, as far as practicable, avoids any conflict with the offender's religious beliefs; attendance at work, school or other educational establishment, and the requirements of any other youth rehabilitation order to which the offender may be subject;[174]
- ensure the offender is not already subject to another YRO or a reparation order, which precludes the making of a YRO unless the court revokes the earlier order.[175]

A YRO commences on the day after the order is made.[176] Except where a young 2.143 offender is the subject of a Detention and Training Order, the court may order the YRO to take effect from the date the period of supervision begins, or, on expiry of the Detention and Training Order.[177] Orders can run concurrently and consecutively.[178]

---

[170] 'Youth Justice: the scaled approach', Youth Justice Board for England and Wales, November 2007, p 6.

[171] Concerns were raised during the passage of the Bill that inadequate resources would be available e.g. the Home Office budget for the drugs intervention programme had been cut 13 per cent in 2007 (*Hansard*, 8 Oct 2007). The Consultation revealed similar concerns: For example, a youth offender team manager stated: 'During the seven years that YOTs have been established, apart from limited finance to establish ISSPs, there has been no additional funding made available to enhance the quality of work with those already in the system. This is despite a 26 per cent. increase nationally in youth court business over the past four years.'

[172] CJIA 2008, Sch 1, para 28.

[173] CJIA 2008, Sch 1, para 29(1).

[174] CJIA 2008, Sch 1, para 29(3).

[175] CJIA 2008, Sch 1, para 30(4).

[176] CJIA 2008, Sch 1, para 30(1).

[177] CJIA 2008, Sch 1, para 30.

[178] CJIA 2008, Sch 1, para 31.

The order must specify the date on which all the requirements must have been complied with.[179] The maximum length of the order can be 3 years, but it can be different lengths for different requirements (and a minimum of 6 months for a YRO with ISSP (see paras **2.206–2.210**)).[180]

2.144   The order must specify the local justice area in which the offender will reside[181] and copies of the order should be provided to the young offender (or parent/guardian if aged under 14).[182] Where a Crown Court makes a YRO it may include a direction that further proceedings (such as breach proceedings, or applications to amend or revoke the order) be in a youth court or other magistrates' court.[183]

(c) *Territorial effect*

2.145   The YRO provisions apply in England and Wales.[184] Section 3 and Sch 3 set out the provisions for an offender who resides (or proposes to reside) in Northern Ireland and s 8 makes provision for the Isles of Scilly.

(d) *Abolition of certain youth orders*

2.146   By virtue of the fact that the majority of the YRO requirements reflect existing youth sentences, a large number of youth orders are abolished by the CJIA 2008. These are curfew orders, exclusion orders, attendance centre orders, supervision orders and action plan orders. Existing community orders available to 16 and 17 year olds will also cease to exist i.e. community rehabilitation orders, community punishment orders, community rehabilitation and punishment orders, and drug treatment and testing orders. These changes will be brought into effect by the CJIA 2008, s 6 and Sch 4.

(e) *YRO requirements*

2.147   (i) *Activity requirement*[185]   This is a new sentencing option, and is a central plank of the new provisions. It is a requirement that the young offender must participate in specified activities, including residential exercises, for a maximum of 90 days.[186] There can also be 'an extended activity requirement' of up to 180 days as part of an Intensive Supervision and Surveillance requirement (see para **2.206**).[187]

2.148   A court may only impose this condition if:

- it has consulted a qualifying officer (a member of a youth offending team, an officer of a local probation board or an officer of a provider of probation services);
- it is satisfied that it is feasible to secure compliance with the requirement; and
- such activities are available in the local justice area.[188]

---

[179] CJIA 2008, Sch 1, para 32(1).
[180] CJIA 2008, Sch 1, para 32.
[181] CJIA 2008, Sch 1, para 33.
[182] CJIA 2008, Sch 1, para 34.
[183] CJIA 2008, Sch 1, para 36.
[184] CJIA 2008, s 152(1).
[185] CJIA 2008, Sch 1, para 6(1)(c)
[186] CJIA 2008, Sch 1, para 6(2).
[187] CJIA 2008, Sch 1, para 3
[188] CJIA 2008, Sch 1, para 8(3)

If compliance with the requirement would involve the co-operation of a person 2.149 (other than the young offender or the responsible officer), then the court cannot include this requirement unless that person's consent is given.[189] The order must specify the number of days and the activities the young offender is required to participate in.[190] The young offender must comply with the requirements as directed by the responsible officer,[191] although a requirement to participate in residential activities may only be given with the consent of a parent or guardian.[192]

(ii) *Supervision requirement*[193]   This is a requirement that the young offender must 2.150 attend appointments as directed by the responsible officer.[194]

(iii) *Unpaid work requirement*[195]   This is a requirement that the young offender must 2.151 perform unpaid work for a specified number of hours between 40 and 240 hours, at times directed by the responsible officer.[196] This requirement is only available to 16 and 17 year olds.[197]

The unpaid work requirement must be performed within a period of 12 months[198] 2.152 (although there is provision in the Act for this to be extended[199]) and the order remains in force until the number of hours of unpaid work are completed.[200]

This requirement may only be imposed if the court is satisfied that: 2.153

- the offender is a suitable person to perform work under such a requirement (if the court thinks necessary an appropriate officer[201] can assess the young offender after the hearing[202]); and
- arrangements are in place in the young offenders' local justice area.[203]

(iv) *Programme requirement*[204]   This is a requirement that the young offender must 2.154 participate in specified activities, which may include residential exercises (which require the young offender to reside at a place specified in the order).[205]

---

[189] CJIA 2008, Sch 1, para 8(4).
[190] CJIA 2008, Sch 1, para 6(1).
[191] Further provisions as to the instructions of the responsible officer or pursuant to an activity requirement: CJIA 2008, Sch 1, paras 7 and 8(1).
[192] CJIA 2008, Sch 1, para 7.
[193] CJIA 2008, s 1(1)(b) and Sch 1, para 9.
[194] CJIA 2008, Sch 1, para 9.
[195] CJIA 2008, s 1(1)(c) and Sch 1, para 10.
[196] CJIA 2008, Sch 1, para 10(1), (2) and (5).
[197] CJIA 2008, s 1(c).
[198] CJIA 2008, Sch 1, para 10(6).
[199] CJIA 2008, Sch 2, para 17.
[200] CJIA 2008, Sch 1, para 10(7).
[201] An appropriate officer means a member of the youth offending team, an officer of a local probation board or an officer of a provider of probation services.
[202] CJIA 2008, Sch 1, para 10(3)(a).
[203] CJIA 2008, Sch 1, para 10(3)(b).
[204] CJIA 2008, s 1(1)(d) and Sch 1, para 11.
[205] CJIA 2008, Sch 1, para 11(2).

2.155   This requirement may only be imposed by the court, if:

- The programme the court proposes to specify has been recommended as being suitable for the offender by a qualifying officer (a member of a youth offending team, an officer of a local probation board or an officer of a provider of probation services);[206] and
- a place is available on the proposed programme.[207]

If compliance with the requirement would involve the co-operation of a person (other than the young offender or the responsible officer), then the court cannot include this requirement unless that person's consent is given.[208]

2.156   (v) *Attendance Centre requirement*[209]   This is a requirement that the young offender must attend at an attendance centre for a specified number of hours. The Act provides the number of hours a court can require a young offender to attend: for ten to thirteen year olds, up to 12 hours; for fourteen and fifteen year olds, between 12 and 24 hours; for sixteen and seventeen year olds, 12 to 36 hours.[210]

2.157   The court can only impose this condition if an attendance centre is available with adequate provision for the young offender, the court must also be satisfied the centre is reasonably accessible for the young offender.[211]

2.158   The times and duration the young offender is required to attend the attendance centre will be set firstly by the responsible officer, and then by the officer in charge of the centre, up to a maximum of 3 hours on any occasion, and not more than once a day.[212]

2.159   (vi) *Prohibited activity requirement*[213]   This is a requirement that the young offender must refrain from participating in activities specified in the order on a day(s) specified, or during a period specified.[214] The Act states that a prohibited activity includes a requirement that the offender does not possess, use, or carry a firearm.[215]

2.160   A court may only impose this condition if it has consulted a qualifying officer (a member of a youth offending team, an officer of a local probation a member of a youth offending team, an officer of a local probation board or an officer of a provider of probation services).[216]

---

[206] CJIA 2008, Sch 1, para 11(3)(a).
[207] CJIA 2008, Sch 1, para 11(3)(b).
[208] CJIA 2008, Sch 1, para 11(4).
[209] CJIA 2008, s 1(1)(d) and Sch 1, para 12.
[210] CJIA 2008, Sch 1, para 12(2).
[211] CJIA 2008, Sch 1, para 12(3).
[212] CJIA 2008, Sch 1, para 12(3)–(6).
[213] CJIA 2008, s 1(1)(f) and Sch 1, para 13.
[214] CJIA 2008, Sch 1, para 13(1).
[215] CJIA 2008, Sch 1, para 13(3).
[216] CJIA 2008, Sch 1, para 13(2).

(vii) *Curfew requirement*[217]   This is a requirement that the young offender must   2.161
remain at a place specified in the order for between 2 and 12 hours (in any day).[218]
The curfew requirement period may only be for a maximum of 6 months.[219]

The court must obtain and consider information about the place proposed to be   2.162
specified in the order (including the attitude of those persons likely to be affected by
the enforced presence of the young offender).[220]

(viii) *Exclusion requirement*[221]   This is a requirement prohibiting the young offender   2.163
from entering a place or area specified in the order for a period of up to 3 months.[222]
The order may specify the exclusion only operates during specific periods and may
specify different places, for different periods or days.[223]

(ix) *Electronic monitoring requirement*[224]   This is not a standalone requirement and   2.164
can only be imposed alongside a curfew, exclusion or attendance centre requirements.
Its purpose is to secure the young offender's compliance with other requirements
imposed by the order.

Electronic monitoring *must* be imposed where a court imposes a curfew or exclusion   2.165
requirement,[225] unless the court considers in the particular circumstances of the case
that it is 'inappropriate' to do so[226] or a person (other than the offender) whose
co-operation is required to ensure monitoring takes place has not given their consent.[227]
This requirement can only be imposed if the order specifies the person responsible
for the monitoring and a court is satisfied that there are adequate arrangements for
electronic monitoring.[228]

(x) *Residence requirements*   These are three new options for the court and are likely   2.166
to be controversial given the potential impact upon the young offender's family life.

A residence requirement[229] is either a requirement that the offender must reside   2.167
with a 'specific individual'[230] who must consent to the order[231] or a requirement
that the offender must reside at a place specified in the order ('place of residence
requirement').[232]

---

[217] CJIA 2008, s 1(1)(g) and Sch 1, para 14.
[218] CJIA 2008, Sch 1, para 14(1) and (2).
[219] CJIA 2008, Sch 1, para 14(3).
[220] CJIA 2008, Sch 1, para 14(4).
[221] CJIA 2008, s 1(1)(h) and Sch 1, para 15.
[222] CJIA 2008, Sch 1, para 15(1) and (2), (4).
[223] CJIA 2008, Sch 1, para 15(3).
[224] CJIA 2008, s1(2) and Sch 1, paras 2 and 26.
[225] CJIA 2008, Sch 1, para 2(2).
[226] CJIA 2008, Sch 1, para 2(2).
[227] CJIA 2008, Sch 1, para 26(3).
[228] CJIA 2008, Sch 1, para 26(4)–(7).
[229] CJIA 2008, s 1(1)(i) and Sch 1, para 16.
[230] CJIA 2008, Sch 1, para 16(1)(a).
[231] CJIA 2008, Sch 1, para 16(2).
[232] CJIA 2008, Sch 1, para 16(1)(b) and para 16(3).

2.168　　A place of residence requirement is only available to an offender who was 16 or over at the time of conviction.[233] Before imposing this requirement, the court must consider the home surroundings of the offender.[234] A court may not specify a hostel or other institution as the place of residence except on the recommendation of a member of a youth offending team, an officer of a local probation board, an officer of a provider of probation services or a social worker of a local authority.[235] The young offender may reside elsewhere with the prior approval of the responsible officer.[236]

2.169　　Finally, there is a Local Authority Residence requirement,[237] a requirement that the offender must reside in accommodation provided by or on behalf of the local authority.[238] The requirement may also specify the offender is not to reside with a person specified in the order.[239] The pre-condition for imposing this requirement is that the offender is legally represented during the sentencing hearing[240] or if unrepresented this was the result of the young offender's own actions.[241]

2.170　　This requirement can only be imposed if the court is satisfied that:

- the behaviour which constituted the offence was due to a significant extent the circumstances in which the offender was living; and
- the imposition of that requirement will assist in the offender's rehabilitation.[242]

The court must consult a parent or guardian (unless it is impracticable) and the local authority which is to receive the offender.[243]

2.171　　The requirement must be no longer than 6 months and cannot include any period after the offender has reached 18.[244] The order must specify the local authority in whose area the offender is to reside.[245]

2.172　　(xi) *Mental health treatment requirement,*　A mental health treatment requirement[246] is a new sentencing provision. It is a requirement that the young offender must submit to treatment during the period of the order by or under the direction of a registered medical practitioner or a chartered psychologist[247] (or both, for different periods) with a view to the improvement of the offender's mental condition.[248]

---

[233] CJIA 2008, Sch 1, para 16(4).
[234] CJIA 2008, Sch 1, para 16(6).
[235] CJIA 2008, Sch 1, para 16(7).
[236] CJIA 2008, Sch 1, para 16(5).
[237] CJIA 2008, s 1(1)(j) and Sch 1, para 17.
[238] CJIA 2008, Sch 1, para 17(1).
[239] CJIA 2008, Sch 1, para 17(2).
[240] CJIA 2008, Sch 1, para 19(1).
[241] The young offender was informed of the right to apply for representation funded by the Legal Services Commission, but refused or failed to apply, or such funding was withdrawn because of the offender's conduct (CJIA 2008, Sch 1, para 19(2)).
[242] CJIA 2008, Sch 1, para 17(3).
[243] CJIA 2008, Sch 1, para 17(4).
[244] CJIA 2008, Sch 1, para 17(6).
[245] CJIA 2008, Sch 1, para 18.
[246] CJIA 2008, s 1(1)(k) and Sch 1, para 20.
[247] A person listed in the British Psychological Society's Register of Chartered Psychologists (CJIA 2008, Sch 1, para 20(6)).
[248] CJIA 2008, Sch 1, para 20(1).

This requirement can only be imposed if the court is satisfied that: 2.173

- the offender's mental condition is susceptible to treatment but is not such to warrant a hospital or guardianship order (on the evidence of a medical practitioner approved for the purposes of s 12 of the Mental Health Act 1983[249]);[250]
- arrangements have been made/can be made for the treatment intended;[251] and
- the young offender has expressed a willingness to comply with the requirement.[252]

The order must specify the kind of treatment and the place the young offender is 2.174 to receive treatment. This may be as a resident patient in a hospital or care home (but not hospital premises where high security psychiatric services are provided), non-resident patient, or treatment by or under the direction of a suitably qualified medical practitioner or psychologist (or both).[253] However, the Act does provide for circumstances in which the arrangements can be varied from those specified in the order, if the treatment can be better or more conveniently given elsewhere. These arrangements can only be made if the young offender has expressed a willingness for the treatment to be given.[254]

Criticism was made during the passage of the Bill to the effect that requirements such 2.175 as mental health or intoxicating substance treatment should not form part of a sentence because the treatment should already be available for the young person to access voluntarily.

(xii) *Drug treatment requirement*[255] This is a requirement that the young offender 2.176 must submit to treatment, under the direction of the treatment provider,[256] with a view to the reduction or elimination of the offender's dependency on, or propensity to misuse, drugs,[257] during the period of the order.[258]

This requirement is only available where the court is satisfied that: 2.177

- the offender is dependent on, or has a propensity to misuse drugs,[259] and
- the offender's dependency/propensity is such as requires and is susceptible to treatment.[260]

---

[249] Mental Health Act 1983, s 54(2) and (3) have effect in relation to proof of an offender's mental condition (CJIA 2008, Sch 1, para 20(5)).

[250] CJIA 2008, Sch 1, para 20(3)(a).

[251] CJIA 2008, Sch 1, para 20(3)(b).

[252] CJIA 2008, Sch 1, para 20(3)(c).

[253] CJIA 2008, Sch 1, para 20(2).

[254] CJIA 2008, Sch 1, para 21.

[255] CJIA 2008, s 1(1)(l) and Sch 1, para 22.

[256] For the purposes of this requirement and the drug testing requirement, 'treatment provider' is a person so specified having the necessary qualifications or experience (CJIA 2008, Sch 1, para 22(1)).

[257] For the purposes of this requirement and the drug testing requirement, 'drug' has the definition of a controlled drug as defined by Misuse of Drugs Act 1971, s 2 (CJIA 2008, Sch 1, para 22(5)).

[258] CJIA 2008, Sch 1, para 22(1).

[259] CJIA 2008, Sch 1, para 22(2)(a).

[260] CJIA 2008, Sch 1, para 22(2)(b).

2.178   This requirement can only be imposed if the court is satisfied that:

- the arrangements for this requirement are in place in the young offender's local justice area;[261]
- arrangements have been/can be made for the treatment intended;[262]
- the requirement has been recommended as suitable for the young offender by a qualifying officer (member of a youth offending team, officer of a local probation board or an officer of a provider of probation services);[263] and
- the young offender has expressed a willingness to comply with the requirement.[264]

2.179   The order must specify the length of the treatment or requirement,[265] the kind of treatment and the place the young offender is to receive treatment, either as a resident or non-resident (and the order may specify how often the young offender is required to attend).[266] The court may also wish to consider a drug testing requirement.

2.180   (xiii) *Drug testing requirement*[267]   This is not a standalone requirement and can only be imposed alongside a drug treatment requirement. It is a requirement that the young offender must provide samples in accordance with instructions by the treatment provider during the treatment period,[268] for the purpose of measuring whether there is any drug in the young offender's body.[269]

2.181   This requirement can only be imposed if the court is satisfied that:

- the arrangements for this requirement are in place in the young offender's local justice area;[270]
- the order also imposes a drug treatment requirement; and[271]
- the young offender has expressed a willingness to comply with the requirement.[272]

2.182   The order must specify the minimum number of occasions on which samples are to be provided (the court may also specify descriptions of samples to be provided and the times and circumstances in which they are to be given).[273] If the tests are not to be carried out by the responsible officer, the order must specify that the results are to be communicated to the responsible officer.[274]

---

[261] CJIA 2008, Sch 1, para 22(4)(a).
[262] CJIA 2008, Sch 1, para 22(4)(b).
[263] CJIA 2008, Sch 1, para 22(4)(c).
[264] CJIA 2008, Sch 1, para 22(4)(d).
[265] CJIA 2008, Sch 1, para 22(1).
[266] CJIA 2008, Sch 1, para 22(3).
[267] CJIA 2008, s 1(1)(m) and Sch 1, para 23.
[268] 'Treatment period' means the duration of the drug treatment requirement (CJIA 2008, Sch 1, para 23(2)).
[269] CJIA 2008, Sch 1, para 23(1).
[270] CJIA 2008, Sch 1, para 23(3)(a).
[271] CJIA 2008, Sch 1, para 23(3)(b).
[272] CJIA 2008, Sch 1, para 23(3)(c).
[273] CJIA 2008, Sch 1, para 23(4).
[274] CJIA 2008, Sch 1, para 23(5).

(xiv) *Intoxicating substance treatment requirement*[275]   This is a new sentencing option, and it is yet to be seen whether there are sufficient resources available to make it a realistic and workable disposal. It is a requirement that the young offender must submit to treatment, as directed, with a view to the reduction or elimination of the offender's dependency on, or propensity to misuse, intoxicating substances such as alcohol,[276] during a period or periods specified in the order.[277] 2.183

This requirement is only available where the court is satisfied that: 2.184

- the offender is dependent on, or has a propensity to misuse intoxicating substances;[278] and
- the offender's dependency or propensity is such as requires and is susceptible to treatment.[279]

This requirement can only be imposed if the court is satisfied that: 2.185

- arrangements have been/can be made for the treatment intended;[280]
- the requirement has been recommended as suitable for the young offender by a qualifying officer (member of a youth offending team, officer of a local probation board or an officer of a provider of probation services);[281] and
- the young offender has expressed a willingness to comply with the requirement.[282]

The order must specify the length of the treatment or requirement,[283] the kinds of treatment, and the place the young offender is to receive treatment, either as a resident in a specified institution or place, or non-resident in such institution or place (and the order may specify how often the young offender is required to attend).[284] 2.186

(xv) *Education requirement*[285]   This is a requirement that the young offender must comply with approved education arrangements during the period(s) specified in the order.[286] Approved education arrangements are those made by the young offender's parent or guardian and approved by their local education authority.[287] 2.187

---

[275] CJIA 2008, s 1(1)(n) and Sch 1, para 24.

[276] For the purposes of this requirement 'intoxicating substance' means alcohol or any other substance or product which is (or the fumes of which) are capable of causing intoxication, excluding controlled drugs (see drug treatment requirement above) (CJIA 2008, Sch 1, para 24(5) and (6)).

[277] CJIA 2008, Sch 1, para 24(1).

[278] CJIA 2008, Sch 1, para 24(2)(a).

[279] CJIA 2008, Sch 1, para 24(2)(b).

[280] CJIA 2008, Sch 1, para 24(4)(a).

[281] CJIA 2008, Sch 1, para 24(4)(b).

[282] CJIA 2008, Sch 1, para 24(4)(c).

[283] CJIA 2008, Sch 1, para 24(1).

[284] CJIA 2008, Sch 1, para 24(3).

[285] CJIA 2008, s 1(1)(o) and Sch 1, para 25.

[286] CJIA 2008, Sch 1, para 25(1).

[287] CJIA 2008, Sch 1, para 25(2) and (3); local education authority and parent have same meanings as in the Education Act 1996 (Sch 1, para 25(6)).

2.188   This requirement may only be included if the court:

- has consulted the local education authority to be specified in the order;[288]
- is satisfied that it is the local education authority's view that arrangements exist for the young offender to receive efficient full-time education suitable to the offender's age, ability, aptitude and special education needs (if any);[289] and
- is satisfied it is necessary for securing the good conduct of the offender or for preventing the commission of further offences.[290]

2.189   The order must specify the period of this requirement,[291] which must not include any period when the offender has ceased to be of compulsory school age.[292]

2.190   (xvi) *YROs with Intensive Supervision and Surveillance and Fostering requirement*   The provisions are available as the most intensive community-based sentencing options and are discussed at paras **2.206–2.211** below.

(f) *Breach and enforcement of YROs*

2.191   (i) *Introduction*   The YRO breach provisions are draconian and inflexible, and provide the court with little or no discretion. The Joint Committee on Human Rights identified that the YRO regime with its breach provisions would provide inadequate safeguards against the acceleration of young offenders into custody.[293] In light of the current proposals of a 'scaled approach' which will lead to the most vulnerable young offenders (who are at highest risk of re-offending) receiving YROs with more strenuous requirements, the fact that young offenders who willfully and persistently breach a YRO can receive a 4-month detention and training order for a non-imprisonable offence must give real cause for concern.

2.192   (ii) *Breach*[294]   A breach is where the responsible officer is of the opinion that a young offender has failed *without reasonable excuse* to comply with a YRO.[295] When a breach occurs, the young offender is given a warning ('the first warning'). If there is a further breach during the 'warned period', which is 12 months starting on the day the (first) warning was given,[296] another warning is given. If the young offender fails a third time to comply with the order, the matter will be brought back to court.[297]

---

[288] CJIA 2008, Sch 1, para 25(4)(a).
[289] CJIA 2008, Sch 1, para 25(4)(b)(i).
[290] CJIA 2008, Sch 1, para 25(4)(b)(ii).
[291] CJIA 2008, Sch 1, para 25(1).
[292] CJIA 2008, Sch 1, para 25(5).
[293] Page 9, para 1.21 of the Joint Committee on Human Rights Report, 'Legislative Scrutiny: Criminal Justice and Immigration Bill', 25 January 2008.
[294] CJIA 2008, s 2 and Sch 2.
[295] CJIA 2008, Sch 2, para 3(1).
[296] CJIA 2008, Sch 2, para 3(4).
[297] The responsible officer causes an information to be laid before a justice of the peace (CJIA 2008, Sch 2, para 4(1)).

When a breach occurs the following warning must be given: 2.193

(a) describing the circumstances of the failure;
(b) stating that the failure is unacceptable; and,
(c) stating the young offender will be liable to be brought before a court if the order is breached on more than one occasion within the 'warned period' (or, where the first warning has been given, the young offender will be liable to be brought before a court if the order is breached on one further occasion within the warned period).[298]

The responsible officer must make a record of the warning as soon as practicable after the warning has been given.[299] Surprisingly, there is no requirement for this warning to be in writing, or, for it to be given in the presence of a parent or guardian.

(iii) *Enforcement*   If the responsible officer is of the opinion that there are exceptional 2.194 circumstances which justify not taking the young offender to court, the procedure for commencing court proceedings where two previous warnings have been given need not be followed.[300]

The CJIA 2008 also provides that the responsible officer need not give a warning 2.195 before commencing court proceedings.[301] However, there is no guidance as to the circumstances in which the duty to give a warning may be disregarded. The Explanatory Notes give the example of a particularly serious breach. Given the potentially grave consequences for the young offender, this is an area which would benefit from much greater clarity.

Once an information is laid, the court may issue a summons or (where the infor- 2.196 mation is in writing and on oath) issue a warrant for the offender's arrest.[302] Failure to answer the summons can lead to the court issuing a summons for the offender's arrest.[303] The enforcement proceedings may be heard before the Youth Court, magistrates' court or Crown Court.[304] In relation to mental health, drug and intoxicating substance treatment requirements, the young offender should not be deemed to have failed to comply with the requirement if they have refused to undergo surgery, electrical or other treatment if the court is of the opinion the refusal was reasonable having regard to all the circumstances.[305]

When a young offender appears before the court and it is proved to the court that 2.197 the offender has failed without reasonable excuse to comply with YRO,[306] the court may deal with an offender in one of the following ways:

• by ordering the young offender to pay a fine of an amount up to £1000 (or £250 if the offender is aged under 14);[307]

---

[298] CJIA 2008, Sch 2, para 3(2).
[299] CJIA 2008, Sch 2, para 3(3).
[300] CJIA 2008, Sch 2, para 4(2).
[301] CJIA 2008, Sch 2, para 4(3).
[302] CJIA 2008, Sch 2, para (5)(1).
[303] CJIA 2008, Sch 2, para (5)(6).
[304] The provisions in relation to the powers of the Crown Court to deal with a breach mirror those for magistrates and youth court (CJIA 2008, Sch 2, para 8).
[305] CJIA 2008, Sch 2, para 9.
[306] CJIA 2008, Sch 2, para 6(1).
[307] CJIA 2008, Sch 2, para 6(2)(a).

- by amending the terms of the order in addition to, or, substitution for, the existing requirement(s)[308]—any amendment must be capable of being completed before the end of the order[309] (the maximum length is 3 years[310]);
- by revoking the YRO[311] and re-sentencing the young offender for the original offence in any way in which the original sentencing court could have dealt with the offender for that offence(s).[312]

In dealing with the offender the court must take into account the extent to which the young offender has complied with the order.[313]

2.198   Where the court deals with the young offender by amending the terms of the original order (see above),[314] the following provisions apply:

- If the original YRO did not contain an unpaid work requirement, the minimum number of hours the court can impose is 20 (rather than 40);[315]
- The court may not impose an extended activity requirement or fostering requirement unless the original order already has such a requirement;[316]
- If the original order contained a fostering requirement and the court proposes to substitute a new fostering requirement, the maximum length of the requirement is 18 months (rather than 12 months) starting from the date of the original order;[317]
- The court may also amend the order where the young offender has a change of residence pursuant to the CJIA 2008, Sch 2, para 13.[318]

2.199   Where the original order was imposed by the Crown Court (and the court did not direct that further proceedings take place before the youth court or magistrates' court[319]), the provisions allow for breach proceedings to be heard before the Crown Court and similar powers to those set out above apply.[320]

2.200   (iv) *Wilful and persistent non-compliance*   The CJIA 2008, Sch 2, para 6(13) to (15) apply where the court is revoking the original order and re-sentencing the offender for the original offence[321] and the young offender has *willfully* and *persistently* failed to comply with a youth rehabilitation order.[322] The court may

- impose a YRO with ISSP (notwithstanding the requirements of CJIA 2008, s 1(4)(a) or (b)[323]);

---

308 CJIA 2008, Sch 2, para 6(2)(b).
309 CJIA 2008, Sch 2, para 6(6).
310 CJIA 2008, Sch 1, para 32(1).
311 CJIA 2008, Sch 2, para 11.
312 CJIA 2008, Sch 2, para 6(2)(c).
313 CJIA 2008, Sch 2, para 6(4).
314 CJIA 2008, Sch 2, para 6(2)(b).
315 CJIA 2008, Sch 2, para 6(7), amending Sch 1, para 10(2).
316 CJIA 2008, Sch 2, para 6(8).
317 CJIA 2008, Sch 2, para 6(9), amending Sch 1, para 18(2).
318 CJIA 2008, Sch 2, para 6(10).
319 CJIA 2008, Sch 1, para 36.
320 CJIA 2008, Sch 2, para 7 and 8.
321 Pursuant to CJIA 2008, Sch 2, para 6(2)(c).
322 CJIA 2008, Sch 2, para 6(12).
323 CJIA 2008, Sch 2, para 6(13).

- if the original order being revoked is a YRO with ISSP and the original offence was punishable with imprisonment, then the court may impose a custodial sentence;[324]
- if the original order being revoked is a YRO with ISSP and the original offence was not punishable with imprisonment (ie the young offender has previously breached a YRO and an ISSP requirement was imposed for a non-imprisonable offence), the court has the power to impose a detention and training order not exceeding 4 months.[325]

(v) *Powers to amend and revoke the YRO*   A YRO can be amended if the offender   2.201
or responsible officer applies to the appropriate court and certain conditions apply.[326]
The same powers apply to the Crown Court.[327]

A YRO can be revoked (or revoked and the young offender re-sentenced) where   2.202
the responsible officer applies to the appropriate court, if it appears to the court that
it is in the interests of justice having regard to all the circumstances.[328] These provisions apply where the offender is, for example, making good progress or responding
satisfactorily.[329] The same powers apply to the Crown Court.[330]

Where a young offender is convicted of a further offence, whilst a YRO is in   2.203
force, the court may revoke the order,[331] or, revoke the order and deal with the
offender for the original offence.[332] The court must consider whether it is in the
interest of justice to do so[333] and take into account the young offender's compliance
with the order.[334] The same powers apply to the Crown Court.[335]

5. Youth Default Orders

Youth Default Orders[336] will enable courts to punish young offenders for non-   2.204
payment of a fine. At present magistrates' courts are restricted by the provisions of
the PCC(S)A 2000, s 89.[337] These orders will provide the court with the power to
impose an unpaid work requirement of up to 100 hours; attendance centre requirements of up to 24 hours and a curfew requirement for up to 100 days.[338] The length
of a requirement will depend on the age of an offender and the size of the unpaid
fine. The details can be found in the CJIA 2008, Sch 7. The court also has the power
to impose an electronic monitoring requirement.[339]

---

[324] Notwithstanding the general restrictions on imposing discretionary custodial sentences in s 152(2) of the CJA 2003 (CJIA 2008, Sch 2, para 6(14)).
[325] CJIA 2008, Sch 2, para 6(15).
[326] CJIA 2008, Sch 2, paras 13,15,16.
[327] CJIA 2008, Sch 2, paras 14, 15, 16.
[328] CJIA 2008, Sch 2, para 11(1) and (2).
[329] CJIA 2008, Sch 2, para 11(3).
[330] CJIA 2008, Sch 2, para 12.
[331] CJIA 2008, Sch 2, para 18(3).
[332] CJIA 2008, Sch 2, para 18(4).
[333] CJIA 2008, Sch 2, para 18(5).
[334] CJIA 2008, Sch 2, para 18(6).
[335] CJIA 2008, Sch 2, para 19.
[336] CJIA 2008, s 39. At the time of writing these provisions are not in force—see para **2.115** above.
[337] CJIA 2008, s 39(1).
[338] CJIA 2008, s 39(2).
[339] CJIA 2008, s 39(4).

2.205   The court may postpone making an order, if it thinks it expedient to do so, until such time and on such conditions as it thinks just.[340] Where a Youth Default Order is made and the whole sum is repaid, the order ceases to have effect.[341] If part of the sum is repaid, the number of hours or days will be reduced proportionately.[342] The breach procedures broadly follow those for Youth Rehabilitation Orders.[343]

6. More intensive community sentences and custodial sentences

(a) *Intensive community sentences*

2.206   The CJIA 2008 seeks to strengthen the non-custodial sentencing options for a court considering whether to impose a custodial sentence. The sentencing landscape for children and young people is comprehensively overhauled through the introduction of YROs and these changes provide two intensive community-based disposals: a YRO with Intensive Supervision and Surveillance (modelled on the existing Intensive Supervision and Surveillance Programme (ISSP)); and a YRO with fostering.

2.207   The CJIA 2008, s 1(3) provides that a YRO may be made with either Intensive Supervision and Surveillance or with a fostering requirement (as set out in the CJIA 2008, Sch 18). A court may only impose such an order if:

- the offence is punishable with imprisonment (CJIA 2008, s 1(4)(a));
- the court is of the opinion the offence(s) is/are so serious that a custodial sentence would be appropriate but for the YRO with ISSP and YRO with fostering provisions (or if the young offender is under 12 at the time of conviction, would be appropriate if the offender had been 12)((CJIA 2008, s 1(4)(b)); and
- if the offender is aged under 15 at the time of conviction, the court is of the opinion that the offender is a persistent offender[344] (CJIA 2008, s 1(4)(c)).

2.208   Further provisions in relation to YROs with ISSP are set out in the CJIA 2008, Sch 1, para 3 which provides that:

- if an activity requirement is imposed the court may specify a number of days in relation to that requirement which is more than 90 but not more than 180;
- such an activity requirement is referred to as 'an extended activity requirement'; and
- a YRO which imposes an extended activity requirement must also impose a supervision requirement and a curfew requirement.

2.209   Further provisions in relation to YROs with fostering are set out in the CJIA 2008, Sch 1, para 4 which provides that:

- in order to make a YRO with a fostering requirement the court must be satisfied that the behaviour which constituted the offence was due to a significant extent to the

---

[340] CJIA 2008, s 39(5).
[341] CJIA 2008, s 39(7)(a).
[342] CJIA 2008, s 39(7)(b).
[343] CJIA 2008, s 39(6)(c) and Sch 7, para 5.
[344] See *R v D* [2001] 1 Cr App R (S) 59, CA; *R v B* [2001] 1 Cr App R (S) 18, CA and *R v S(A)* [2001] 1 Cr App R (S) 18, CA as to the meaning of the term 'persistent offender' used within PCC(S)A 2000.

circumstances in which the offender was living and that the imposition of a fostering requirement would assist in the offender's rehabilitation;
• the court may not impose a fostering requirement unless it has consulted the offender's parents or guardians, unless impracticable so to do, and the local authority which is to place the offender with a foster parent; and
• a supervision requirement must also be imposed.

The CJIA 2008, Sch 1, para 19 provides that a court may not include a fostering requirement unless the offender was legally represented at the relevant time in court unless his right to representation funded by the Legal Services Commission was withdrawn because of his conduct or he had been informed of the right to apply for such representation and had the opportunity to do so but had refused or failed to apply. 2.210

(b) *Custodial sentences*
The court, if passing a custodial sentence, must state that a YRO with ISSP or fostering is not appropriate and give reasons why.[345] This is in addition to meeting the existing criteria, ie the court forming the opinion that the offence is so serious that a community sentence cannot be justified. 2.211

7. Pre-sentence Reports

The CJIA 2008, s 12 requires a court to obtain a written Pre-sentence Report (PSR) if it is considering imposing a custodial sentence for an offender aged under 18. This section came into force on 14 July 2008.[346] 2.212

This section, first proposed when the Bill was in its Third Reading before the House of Lords, was tabled in response to concerns that under existing legislation, young people could, in certain circumstances, receive a custodial sentence without the court having a written report before it. It ensures that where a custodial sentence is a possibility for a young offender, the court must obtain a full, written pre-sentence report.[347] 2.213

The requirement to obtain and consider a PSR is also mandatory when imposing a YRO with Intensive Supervision and Surveillance or with fostering.[348] 2.214

---

[345] CJIA 2008, Sch 2, para 48
[346] Criminal Justice and Immigration Act 2008 (Commencement No 2 and Transitional and Saving Provisions) Order 2008, SI 2008/1586.
[347] HL Deb 30 Apr 2008 c245.
[348] CJA 2003, s 156(3)(b), amended by CJIA 2008, s 6(2) and Sch 4, paras 71 and 77.

3
CRIMINAL PROCEDURE AND APPEALS

A. CRIMINAL PROCEDURE

1. Introduction

Part 4 of the CJIA 2008 contains a number of disparate provisions, covering a wide   3.01
range of topics under the general heading 'criminal procedure'. This includes amendments to criminal Legal Aid, bail in summary proceedings and the investigative
powers of the Serious Fraud Office.

For magistrates' court practitioners, there are important changes to bail and trial   3.02
in the absence of the accused. CPS 'Designated Caseworkers' can also now conduct
some summary proceedings.

Part 4 also introduces changes to the procedure for mode of trial and the sending   3.03
of cases from the magistrates' court to the Crown Court. These sections are awaiting
enactment on a date to be appointed and will represent a radical change.

The CJIA 2008, Part 4 needs to be read in conjunction with Schs 11, 12, and   3.04
13 to the Act. Schedule 27, para 18 and Sch 28 list the amendments and repeals
respectively made by Part 4.

2. Bail

(a) *Bail in offences to be tried summarily*

Section 52 of the CJIA 2008 enacts Sch 12 with effect from 14 July 2008.[1] Sch 12   3.05
amends various provisions of the Bail Act (BA) 1976 in relation to bail for summary
only offences and to criminal damage to be tried summarily.

Paragraph 3 of Sch 12 inserts s 9A into the BA 1976 and requires magistrates,   3.06
when considering bail for a defendant under the age of 18 charged with criminal
damage, to determine the value of the damage before they consider whether or not

---

[1] Criminal Justice and Immigration Act 2008 (Commencement No 2 and Transitional and Saving Provisions) Order 2008, SI 2008/1586.

to grant him bail. If the value is under £5000, the matter will be treated as a summary offence.[2]

3.07   For all summary only offences, there are now only a number of specific grounds on which a magistrates' court can refuse bail. These are:

(1) where the defendant has previously been granted bail and has failed to surrender, and the court believes that in view of that failure he will fail to surrender for this offence;[3]

(2) where the defendant was on bail at the time of the commission of the alleged offence and the court is satisfied that he would commit further offences if released on bail;[4]

(3) where the defendant was *not* on bail at the time of the alleged offence, the court can only refuse bail if it is satisfied that he will cause physical or mental injury to another person or cause another person to fear such injury;[5]

(4) if the court is satisfied that the defendant should be held in custody for his own protection, or in the case of a child or young person, for his own welfare;[6]

(5) if the defendant is in custody serving a sentence by a court or a sentence by a military court;[7]

(6) if the defendant has already breached his bail and there are substantial grounds to believe that he would fail to surrender again;[8]

(7) if it has not been practicable to obtain sufficient information for the purpose of taking a decision in relation to bail due to a lack of time since the start of the proceedings against the defendant.[9]

3.08   The provisions of Part 1 of Sch 1 to the BA 1976, setting out the court's powers to refuse bail in the case of confirmed drug users still apply to summary only offences.[10]

3.09   Part 1A of Sch 1 does not specify whether it applies to both adults and young people. However, it is assumed that it does apply to both, given the inclusion of the words 'young person' in para 5 of Part 1A.

3.10   The above changes mean that it will be much harder for magistrates to refuse bail in summary only matters. In order to be satisfied that the defendant will fail to surrender, he must have a proven history of doing so and, in order to be satisfied that he will commit offences on bail, there must be a proven history of doing so, or a real risk of actual injury or fear of actual injury occurring to another person. This liberalization is to be welcomed. Magistrates' court practitioners will know that a large number of bail applications are refused on the wide grounds that a defendant will fail to surrender or commit further offences.

3.11   This liberalization is no doubt a direct response to the findings of Lord Carter's Review Of Prisons, 'Securing the future—Proposals for the efficient and sustainable

---

[2] Sch 2 and s 22, BA 1976.
[3] Para 2 of Part 1A of Sch 1 to the BA 1976.
[4] Para 3 of Part 1A of Sch 1 to the BA 1976.
[5] Para 4 of Part 1A of Sch 1 to the BA 1976.
[6] Para 5 of Part 1A of Sch 1 to the BA 1976.
[7] Para 6 of Part 1A of Sch 1 to the BA 1976.
[8] Para 7 of Part 1A of Sch 1 to the BA 1976.
[9] Para 8 of Part 1A of Sch 1 to the BA 1976.
[10] Para 9 of Part 1A of Sch 1 to the BA 1976.

use of custody in England and Wales'.[11] In the Carter Report, a number of measures are proposed to manage the use of custody in the criminal justice system including 'the continued need to focus prison resources on the most dangerous and serious offenders' given the critical pressure of prison spaces. The Report specifically recommended reform of Bail Act legislation to ensure that custody is reserved for serious and dangerous offenders.[12]

The government has clearly started this review by limiting the numbers of people remanded into custody for less serious, summary matters and will be hoping to reduce the pressure on prison resources.   3.12

(b) *Electronic monitoring of persons released on conditional bail*

Section 51 of the CJIA 2008 brought into force Sch 11 on the 3 November 2008.[13] Schedule 11 makes amendments to s 3 of the BA 1976. They are mostly typographical amendments, with one exception: s 3AC is inserted into the BA 1976, which requires that where the court imposes electronic monitoring as a condition of bail, it must also make a specified person responsible for the monitoring. This person must be of a description specified in an order made by the Secretary of State. The section then gives the Secretary of State power to make further orders or rules under this section by statutory instrument to flesh out these provisions. It is anticipated that the specified person will be likely to be either a member of an approved security organization, a member of the Youth Offending Team, or a police officer.   3.13

3. Mode of trial and transfer of cases to the Crown Court

(a) *Introduction*

Section 53 of the CJIA 2008 brings into force Sch 13 to that Act, which amends Sch 3 to the CJA 2003. Although s 53 and Sch 13 came into force when the Act received Royal Assent on 8 May 2008,[14] Sch 3 to the CJA 2003 is still not yet in force and will require a further commencement order. Effectively, Sch 13 of the 2008 Act amends a Schedule to the CJA 2003 before it has even been brought into force.   3.14

(b) *Determination of mode of trial*

Schedule 3 to the CJA 2003 (as amended by the CJIA 2008, s 53 and Sch 13) will alter the procedure set out in the Magistrates' Court Act (MCA) 1980 for determining mode of trial for either way offences and for sending matters for trial to the Crown Court. The phrase 'mode of trial' will itself be replaced by 'decisions as to allocation'.[15]   3.15

Section 17A of the MCA 1980 (as amended[16]) sets down the procedure for ascertaining a defendant's intention as to plea before the allocation procedure begins.   3.16

---

[11] December 2007 (available at <http://www.justice.gov.uk/publications/securing-the-future.htm>).

[12] Page 28 of the Carter Report.

[13] Criminal Justice and Immigration Act 2008 (Commencement No 3 and Transitional Provisions) Order 2008, SI 2008/2712.

[14] CJIA 2008, s 153.

[15] MCA 1980, s 19 as amended as amended by s 53 of, and Sch 13 to, the CJIA 2008.

[16] By para 2 of Sch 3 to the CJA 2003 (as amended).

It requires the court to explain to the defendant that he must indicate a plea, and that if he pleads guilty he may still be committed for sentence under s 3 of the PCC(S)A 2000. This is effectively the same as the current regime.

3.17   Section 17B of the MCA 1980 will allow the indication of plea to be taken in the absence of the defendant if the defendant is legally represented and is behaving in a disorderly way.

3.18   If the defendant does not indicate a plea, the court is to assume that his plea is not guilty for the purposes of determining allocation. This is the same as the current regime.

3.19   Section 17D of the MCA 1980 (as amended[17]) sets a maximum penalty for an offence of criminal damage with a damage value of under £5000 at 3 months or a level 4 fine and the offence cannot be committed for sentence to the Crown Court. This is the same as the current regime.

3.20   Section 17E of the MCA 1980 (as amended[18]) allows a justice sitting alone to determine allocation under ss 17A to D.

3.21   Section 19 of the MCA 1980 (as amended[19]) deals with the procedure for the determination of allocation for adult defendants by magistrates. The main change will be that for the first time the prosecution will be allowed to inform the bench details of the defendant's previous convictions. This is in order for the magistrates to consider amongst other factors whether, on conviction, their sentencing powers would be adequate.

3.22   This brings the procedure for adults in line with that for young persons under s 24 of the MCA 1980. The High Court ruled in *R (Tullet) v Medway Magistrates' Court*[20] that in making a determination under the MCA 1980, s 24 a Youth Court is entitled to consider the young person's previous convictions (if any) in order to determine whether their sentencing powers are sufficient.

3.23   If the magistrates determine that summary trial is more suitable for the adult defendant, s 20 of the MCA 1980 (as amended[21]) requires them to explain this to the defendant in plain language, to remind him of his right to elect trial at the Crown Court, and to remind him of their powers of committal for sentence following summary trial. This is the same as the current regime.

3.24   Section 20(3) of the MCA 1980 (as amended[22]) will allow the defendant to then ask for an indication of whether a custodial sentence would be likely to be imposed if he were to consent to summary trial and plead guilty. The court is not obliged to give such an indication. This change adopts within the statutory framework a modified version of the practice of '*Goodyear*'[23] indications on sentence given in the Crown Court.

3.25   If an indication is given, the defendant should then be asked if he wishes to reconsider his indication and plead guilty. Where an indication is given, no court can then

---

[17] By para 3 of Sch 3 to the CJA 2003 (as amended).
[18] By para 5 of Sch 3 to the CJA 2003 (as amended).
[19] Ibid.
[20] [2003] EWHC 2279 Admin.
[21] By para 6 of Sch 3 to the CJA 2003 (as amended).
[22] Ibid.
[23] *R v Goodyear* [2005] 1 WLR 2532.

impose a custodial sentence where one was not indicated. With that exception, an indication given is not binding and the passing of a sentence that is inconsistent with an indication cannot be a ground of appeal.

The introduction of *Goodyear* indications in the magistrates' court at the decision as to allocation stage is no doubt part of the government's plans for 'simple, speedy, summary justice', encouraging cases wherever possible to be dealt with in the magistrates' court.   3.26

Section 24 of the MCA 1980 (as amended[24]) creates a presumption that a person under the age of 18 charged with an indictable offence will be tried in the Youth Court unless it is a case which must be sent to the Crown Court by way of CDA 1998, s 51 (adult jointly accused of indictable only offence) or CDA 1998, s 51A (grave crimes as defined by PCC(S)A 2000, s 91).   3.27

Sections 24A and B MCA 1980 replicates the decision as to allocation procedure for those under 18 in accordance with that for adults contained within s 19 as discussed at para **3.21** above.   3.28

(c) *Sending cases to the Crown Court from the magistrates' court*

If the magistrates determine that the case is not suitable for summary trial and is only suitable for trial on indictment, they will be required to follow the procedure in s 21 of the MCA 1980 (as amended[25]). The court must tell the defendant its allocation decision and then proceed in accordance with s 51(1) of the CDA 1998 (as amended[26]) and send the case directly to the Crown Court for trial.   3.29

The magistrates will no longer be required to sit as examining justices and conduct committal proceedings under s 6(1) or (2) of the MCA 1980 before they transfer cases to the Crown Court. Once the magistrates' court has decided that the case should be allocated to the Crown Court, the matter is sent without further ado. Therefore, the appropriate forum for defence submissions that there is no *prima facie* case will be at the Crown Court, before arraignment, in the same way as an application to dismiss is made on an indictable only offence.   3.30

(d) *Sending related offences to the Crown Court on indictment*

Section 51(1) of the CDA 1998 will also be amended by the 2003 Act.[27] Section 51(3) will allow the magistrates' court to send an offence on indictment to the Crown Court and send with it any related either way offence,[28] and/or any summary offence that is related either to the indictable-only offence, or to the either-way offence,[29] but only if it is punishable by imprisonment or involves obligatory of discretionary disqualification from driving.[30] These amendments will remove the need for s 40 (power to join count of common assault on indictment) and s 41 (power to join summary only offence punishable with imprisonment or disqualification) of the CJA 1988.   3.31

---

[24] By para 9 of Sch 3 to the CJA 2003 (as amended).
[25] By para 7 of Sch 3 to the CJA 2003 (as amended).
[26] By para 18 of Sch 3 to the CJA 2003 (as amended).
[27] Ibid.
[28] CDA 1998, s 51(3)(a) (as amended).
[29] CDA 1998, s 51(3)(b) (as amended).
[30] CDA 1998, s 51(11) (as amended).

3.32   If a defendant is sent for trial on indictment, any other defendant jointly charged with a related either-way offence may also be sent for trial for the either-way offence (CDA 1998, s 51(5)[31]).

3.33   Section 51(7) will allow defendants under the age of 18 to be sent for trial with adults if they are either jointly charged with an indictable offence for which the adult has been sent for trial or with an indictable offence which appears to be related to that offence. The court will only be able to send the young person for trial at the Crown Court in this way if it is satisfied that it is in the interests of justice to do so. This is subject to the provisions of s 24A and s 24B of the MCA 1980, which provide for certain cases involving young people to be tried in the Youth Court.[32]

3.34   Section 51A makes provisions for young people to be sent for trial at the Crown Court from the Youth Court for murder and firearms offences that attract a minimum sentence of 5 years imprisonment pursuant to s 5 of the Firearms Act 1968. The procedure under s 51A also applies to cases where the court considers that there is the possibility of a sentence of detention under s 91 of the PCC(S)A 2000 being passed upon conviction. As the maximum period for which a magistrates' court may impose a detention and training order is 24 months (see sections 100 and 101 of the PCC(S)A 2000), detention under s 91 is primarily applicable to cases of such gravity that the court is or may be considering a sentence of at least two years. Further, the procedure under s 51A also applies to young people charged with offences that are specified under s 224 of the CJA 2003 where it appears to the court that the young person, if convicted, would meet the criteria for a sentence of detention for public protection or extended detention in accordance with s 226 or s 228 of the CJA 2003. Finally, it repeats the provisions of s 51 (as amended) that signal which either-way and summary offences can be also be sent with the offence (see para 3.27).[33]

3.35   Section 51B will allow either-way offences of fraud to be sent straight to the Crown Court on the application of the DPP, the Director of the Serious Fraud Office, the Director of Revenue and Customs or the Secretary of State if the case reveals a fraud of such complexity that it is appropriate that the management of the case be taken over by the Crown Court.

3.36   In certain cases where a child is likely to be called as a witness, s 51C will enable the DPP in the case to notify the magistrates' court that the case should be dealt with by the Crown Court in order to avoid any detriment to the welfare of the child.

(e) *Committal to the Crown Court for sentence*
3.37   Schedule 3 of the CJA 2003 as drafted proposed to remove the general power under s 3 of the PCC(S)A 2000 to commit an adult defendant for sentence after conviction

---

[31] As amended by para 18, Sch 3 to the CJA 2003.

[32] Section 51(9) as amended by para 18, Sch 3 to the CJA 2003.

[33] See *R (D) v Manchester City Youth Court* [2002] 1 Cr App R (S) 573, *R (W) v Thetford Youth Justices* [2002] EWHC 1252, [2003] 1 Cr App Rep (S), *R (W) v Southampton Youth Court* [2003] 1 Cr App Rep (S). See also *R (C,D,N) v Sheffield Youth Court* [2003] EWHC Admin 35, 167 JP, *R (C) v Balham Youth Court* [2003] EWHC 1322 Admin, [2004] 1 Cr App Rep (S) 143, *R (H) v Balham Youth Court* [2003] EWHC 3267 Admin, 168 JP 177, *R (CPS) v Redbridge Youth Court* [2005] EWHC 1390 (Admin), 169 JP 393; *R (H,A,O) v Southampton Youth Court* ('Southampton No. 2') [2004] EWHC 2912 (Admin), 169 JP 37, *R(W) v Brent Youth Court* [2006] EWHC 95, (Admin) [2006] All ER (D) 34 (Jan).

for summary trial except where the defendant had been convicted of an offence specified under Sch 15 of the CJA 2003 (specified offences for the purpose of ss 225 and 227 of the CJA 2003—extended sentences and imprisonment for public protection).[34]

Paragraph 22 of the CJA 2003 has not been brought into force and has now been removed from Sch 3 of the CJA 2003 by virtue of Sch 13, para 7 of the CJIA 2008. The general power under s 3 of the PCC(S)A 2000 to commit for sentence where the court is of the opinion that its sentencing powers are insufficient, is therefore preserved.   3.38

Paragraph 23 of Sch 3 of the CJA 2003 will insert s 3A into the PCC(S)A 2000. This new section will require magistrates dealing with an adult convicted after a summary trial of a 'scheduled offence' for the purposes of ss 225 and 227 of the CJA 2003.   3.39

Paragraph 23 of Sch 3 of the CJA 2003 also inserts s 3B into the PCC(S)A 2000 which preserves the Youth Court's power to commit a young offender for sentence following a guilty plea to one of the offences set out in s 91(1) of the PCC(S)A 2000 (certain sexual and firearms offences) if it is of the opinion that the Crown Court should have the power to deal with him under s 91(3) of the PCC(S)A 2000 (passing a sentence for a period of detention above that permitted by a Detention and Training Order).   3.40

Section 3C of the PCC(S)A 2000 will make provision identical to s 3A for those under 18 convicted of a 'scheduled offence'.   3.41

It should be noted that the CJIA 2008 also amends the provisions of the CJA 2003 that deal with extended sentences and imprisonment for public protection and the list of offences under the CJA 2003, Sch 15 (dealt with in Chapter 2). Section 4 of the PCC(S)A 2000 (as amended[35]) will make provision for both adults and young people to be committed for sentence to the Crown Court after they indicate a guilty plea in the magistrates' court or Youth Court. This reflects the existing law.   3.42

Nothing in the amended provisions alters the Youth Court's powers to commit a young person for sentence under s 91 of the PCC(S)A 2000.   3.43

As for the Crown Court's powers once a case has been committed for sentence, s 5 of the PCC(S)A 2000 (as amended[36]) will permit the Crown Court to deal with any offender that is committed for sentence as if they had been convicted on indictment.   3.44

4. Trial in absence of the accused in the magistrates' court

Section 54 of the CJIA 2008 amends s 11 of the MCA 1980 to introduce a presumption in favour of trial in the absence of the accused in the magistrates' court unless it appears to the Court that it would be contrary to the interests of justice to do so. These amendments came into force on 14 July 2008.[37]   3.45

The only caveat to the new presumption is that the Court shall not proceed in absence if it appears that there is an acceptable reason for his failure to appear. However, there is no requirement for the Court even to enquire as to why an accused is not present.   3.46

---

[34] Para 22 of Sch 3 to the CJA 2003 as drafted.
[35] By para 24 of Sch 3 to the CJA 2003 (as amended).
[36] By para 27 of Sch 3 to the CJA 2003 (as amended).
[37] Criminal Justice and Immigration Act 2008 (Commencement No 2 and Transitional and Saving Provisions) Order 2008, SI 2008/1586.

3.47   This statutory provision goes much further than the decision in *R v Jones*.[38] In *Jones*, the House of Lords made it clear that the court had a discretion as to whether to proceed in the defendant's absence having regard to:

(1) the reasons why the defendant was absent;
(2) the extent of the instructions held by the defendant's representatives;
(3) the extent of the disadvantage of not being able to present his defence;
(4) the risk of a jury reaching improper conclusions about the defendant's absence;
(5) general public interest; and
(6) the effect of delay on the memory of witnesses.

3.48   The court still only 'may' proceed in absence in the case of those under the age of 18.

3.49   In all cases where the court proceeds in absence, it must give its reasons for doing so and those reasons must be recorded on the court record.

3.50   Where the court is faced with sentencing the accused in his absence, the new amendments appear contradictory. Section 11(3) of the MCA 1980 is preserved by the CJIA 2008. It states that the court cannot sentence someone to imprisonment or detention or activate a suspended sentence in his absence.

3.51   However, s 54 of the CJIA 2008 inserts s 11(3A), which states that where a sentence of imprisonment or detention or activation of suspended sentence *is* imposed in absence, the offender must be brought to court before being brought to prison to begin serving his sentence. Where this contradiction leaves magistrates deciding whether or not to sentence the accused in his absence is not clear from the statute. However, the Explanatory Notes to the CJIA 2008 state that there should be a presumption that a defendant can be tried in his absence and sentenced if convicted.[39]

3.52   Section 13(5) of the MCA 1980 is also repealed. This section prevented the magistrates when adjourning a trial, or any hearing after the defendant had pleaded guilty, from issuing a bench warrant where a defendant failed to attend unless they felt it was undesirable to continue the case without the presence of the accused.

5. Extension of powers of CPS designated caseworkers in the magistrates' court

3.53   Section 55 of the CJIA 2008 makes controversial changes to the powers of Crown Prosecution Service (CPS) Designated Caseworkers (DCWs) in the magistrates' court. DCWs are non-legally qualified caseworkers who up until now have only been able to perform a limited number of hearings in the magistrates' court.

3.54   Section 55 amends s 7A of the Prosecution of Offences Act 1985 to allow DCWs to conduct summary only trials in cases that do not carry a sentence of imprisonment. A classic example of a trial that a DCW could conduct under the new regime would be for an offence pursuant to s 5 of the Public Order Act 1986.

3.55   DCWs will also be able to conduct hearings of applications for certain civil preventative orders, which includes:

• Restraining orders under s 5 or 5A of the Protection from Harassment Act 1997.

---

[38] *R v Jones (Anthony)* [2003] 1 AC 1, HL.
[39] Explanatory Notes to the CJIA 2008, Part 4 at para 36.

- Parenting orders under s 8 of the CDA 1998.
- Post-conviction ASBOs and variation of the same under s 1C of the CDA 1998.
- Football Banning Orders on complaint under s 14B of the Football Spectator's Act 1989.
- Football Banning Orders on conviction under s 14A of the FSA 1989.

Section 55 of the CJIA 2008 came into force on 14 July 2008.[40]   3.56

However, there is a further extension of DCWs' powers envisaged. Section 7A(10)   3.57
of the Prosecution of Offences Act 1985 (as amended), allows the Attorney General
to modify the application of the section by order and specifically gives the Attorney
General the power to remove the caveat that the only summary trials that DCWs
can conduct are those not punishable by imprisonment. Any such order must be
laid before and approved by both houses of Parliament.[41]

It is little wonder that such a safeguard was put into place given the opposition to   3.58
the proposals when they formed part of the Criminal Justice and Immigration Bill.
At the Bill stage, it was proposed that DCWs would be able to conduct trials of all
summary only matters in the magistrates' court. Both the Law Society and the Bar
Council made it clear that it was their view that having non-lawyers conduct trials
was manifestly against the public interest. Of particular concern was the fact that
DCWs are not bound by any code of practice or conduct nor do they have duties to
the court equivalent to their solicitor and barrister counterparts.

Section 55 of the CJIA 2008 represents a compromise, for now. However, it is   3.59
concerning to say the very least that non-legally qualified caseworkers should be able
to conduct trials of fact and hearings of important civil orders, both of which have
a significant impact on people's private lives.

6. Criminal Legal Aid

(a) *Provisional grants of Criminal Legal Aid*

Section 56 of the CJIA 2008 amends the Access to Justice Act (AJA) 1999 to create   3.60
a framework for the provisional grant of a Representation Order to an individual
before his case even comes to court.

The idea of granting funding in the investigation stage of criminal cases is directly   3.61
linked to the government's strategy in relation to complex fraud cases, although it
applies to criminal investigations generally.

In her consultation paper 'The introduction of a Plea Negotiation Framework for   3.62
Fraud Cases in England and Wales',[42] the Attorney General set out proposals to
enable defence representatives to negotiate on plea even before charge. The stated
aim of allowing such early negotiation was to save the cost of investigation and court
time in these complex cases where apparently 10 per cent of defendants plead guilty
on the first day of trial.

These proposals are still the subject of consultation but make interesting reading.   3.63
For example, there is no proposal to enhance pre-charge disclosure, relying instead on

---

[40] Criminal Justice and Immigration Act 2008 (Commencement No 2 and Transitional and Saving Provisions) Order 2008, SI 2008/1586.
[41] Prosecution of Offences Act 1995, s 7A(12) (as amended).
[42] 3 April 2008.

'Market forces and self-interest'.[43] Few solicitors, whether they have a Representation Order or not, will advise their clients to enter into a plea negotiation without full disclosure, which is unlikely to ever be available pre-charge.

3.64   The particular nature of complex fraud cases means that they invariably involve more than one defendant, often in more than one jurisdiction, resulting in ongoing disclosure right up until the day of trial (and beyond). This creeping disclosure has been the subject of criticism in a number of Court of Appeal rulings (see for example, *R v Early & Others*[44]) and is often the real reason why defendants plead guilty at the door of court.

3.65   Section 56 of the CJIA 2008 is itself really an enabling provision, amending the relevant parts of Sch 3 of the AJA 1999 to allow Parliament to make further regulations to set out the circumstances in which the Legal Services Commission can make a provisional grant of a Representation Order during the investigation of a criminal offence. Those regulations have not yet been drafted and it is anticipated that they will be dependant on the response to the Attorney General's consultation discussed above.

3.66   The legal aid provisions passed unscathed through both Houses and came into force on 14 July 2008.[45]

(b) *Disclosure of information to assess eligibility for Legal Aid*

3.67   Section 57 of the CJIA 2008 further amends Sch 3 to the AJA 1999 by inserting paras 6 and 7. Paragraph 6 of Sch 3 to the AJA 1999 now permits a relevant authority (including a court) to request information from either the Secretary of State (realistically in the form of the Department for Work and Pensions (DWP)) or the Legal Services Commission in order to be able to make a decision regarding a grant of Legal Aid.

3.68   In practical terms this will enable a court to request information from the DWP in order to ascertain whether a defendant is in receipt of certain benefits that 'passport' eligibility for Legal Aid, such as income support. The aim of this amendment is to make decisions on the grant of Legal Aid quicker and more accurate.

3.69   The information that can be disclosed may include personal details such as the person's national insurance number and benefit status, whether he is employed, and by whom.

3.70   Paragraph 7 of Sch 3 to the AJA 1999 (as amended) contains a new offence to criminalize misuse of information requested under para 6. A person who requests information but then uses it for a purpose other than determining an application for Legal Aid will be guilty of an offence. There is a statutory defence within para 7(3) if the disclosure is lawful by any other Act of Parliament or order of a court.

3.71   The new offence is triable either way. If convicted on indictment, the maximum sentence is 2 years, a fine or both.[46] On summary conviction, the maximum sentence is one of 12 months, a fine or both.[47]

---

[43] Page 15.

[44] (2003) 1 Cr App R 19.

[45] Criminal Justice and Immigration Act 2008 (Commencement No 2 and Transitional and Saving Provisions) Order 2008, SI 2008/1586.

[46] Para 5(5)(a) of Sch 3 to the AJA 1999, as amended by CJIA 2008, s 53(3).

[47] Para 5(5)(b) of Sch 3 to the AJA 1999, as amended by CJIA 2008, s 53(3).

Section 57 came into force on 14 July 2008,[48] but like s 56 will require further 3.72
consultation and further regulations to be made before it is put into use. There are
currently Regulations under consultation and these are available from the Ministry
of Justice website.[49]

(c) *Legal Aid Pilot Schemes*

Section 58 of the CJIA 2008 amends s 18 of the AJA 1999. Section 18 of the AJA 1999 3.73
(as amended) allows the Lord Chancellor to initiate pilot schemes for the provision
of Legal Aid services for up to 18 months and can be extended for further periods as
necessary.

Vera Baird, the then Minister for Legal Aid, said in June 2007[50] that pilot schemes 3.74
are a way to give the government flexibility in experimenting with the new powers relating to the grant of Legal Aid as discussed above. Pilot Schemes can cover geographical
areas, types of court or types of offences.

Section 58 of the CJIA 2008 came into force on 14 July 2008.[51] 3.75

7. Defence statements

Section 60 of the CJIA 2008 makes further amendments to the defendant's duty of 3.76
disclosure by way of defence statement under s 6 of the Criminal Procedure and Investigations Act (CPIA) 1996. Section 60 came into force on the 3 November 2008.[52]

Section 6A of the CPIA 1996 (as amended by the CJA 2003[53]) currently requires 3.77
the defendant to:

(1) set out the nature of his defence, including any particular defences (s 6A(a));
(2) indicate the matters of fact with which he takes issue with the prosecution
    (s 6A(b));
(3) set out in each case why he takes issue with the prosecution (s 6A(c)).

Section 60 of the CJA 2008 adds an additional requirement that the defendant 3.78
now has to set out the particulars of the matters of fact on which he intends to rely
for the purposes of his defence (CPIA 1996, s 6A(ca)).

The additional requirement only applies to a case that is tried after the 3 November 3.79
2008 where the criminal investigations began after the 4 April 2005 in England and
Wales or after the 15 July 2005 in Northern Ireland.[54]

---

[48] Criminal Justice and Immigration Act 2008 (Commencement No 2 and Transitional and Saving Provisions) Order 2008, SI 2008/1586.
[49] Available from the Ministry of Justice website <http://www.justice.gov.uk/publications/section-57-criminal-justice-act.htm>.
[50] Letter to Stakeholders, June 2007, as cited in HO Research Paper 07/65 House of Commons Library.
[51] Criminal Justice and Immigration Act 2008 (Commencement No 2 and Transitional and Saving Provisions) Order 2008, SI 2008/1586.
[52] Criminal Justice and Immigration Act 2008 (Commencement No 3 and Transitional Provisions) Order 2008, SI 2008/2712.
[53] CJA 2003, s 33.
[54] Ibid., para 3(a).

8. Serious Fraud Office pre-Investigation powers in cases involving bribery and corruption

3.80   Section 59 of the CJIA 2008 amends s 2 of the CJA 1987 and represents a significant expansion of the Serious Fraud Office's (SFO) powers of investigation into bribery and corruption offences involving foreign officials.

3.81   Pre-CJIA 2008, s 2 of the CJA 1987 allowed the Director of the SFO to direct any individual or corporation under investigation, or any other person with relevant information to answer questions, provide information or produce documents to the investigation.

3.82   The amended CJA 1987, s 2A extends the Director's powers to request information and documents relating to individuals or corporations *before* any investigation has begun in order to determine whether to launch any such investigation in the first place.

3.83   These pre-investigation powers came in response to a Home Office consultation in December 2005, 'Bribery: Reform of the Prevention of Corruption Acts and SFO Powers in Cases of Bribery of Foreign Officials'.[55] This was a broad-ranging consultation into substantive reform of the law of bribery, which is governed by the Prevention of Corruption Acts 1889–1916. This Act is fragmented, out of date and unable to deal with the increasing international nature of bribery investigations.[56]

3.84   As part of the consultation, parties were specifically asked whether the SFO's powers should extend to the vetting stage of an investigation. The response was mixed and only marginally in favour of extension. The Law Society and the Confederation of Business Industry were against it, whilst Transparency International, the All Party group on Africa and the SFO were in favour.[57]

3.85   After the Home Office consultation closed in March 2007, the government asked the Law Commission to undertake its own consultation as to the best way forward. The Law Commission's response was due in late 2008.

3.86   In lieu of substantive reform of the law of bribery, the amendments to s 2A of the CJA 1987 are the only proposals to find their way onto the statute books so far. However, they were not part of the original Criminal Justice and Immigration Bill put before the House of Commons. They were put forward at the Committee stage in October 2007 and only inserted into the Bill when it was introduced to the House of Lords in January 2008 (shortly before the High Court's ruling that the halting of the SFO's investigation into corruption between Saudi Arabian officials and BAE was illegal).[58] They came into force on 14 July 2008.[59]

---

[55] Available from the Home Office website <http://www.homeoffice.gov.uk/documents/450272/2005-consbribery?version=1>.

[56] Executive Summary, 'Bribery: Reform of the Prevention of Corruption Acts and SFO Powers in Cases of Bribery of Foreign Officials'.

[57] See 'Bribery: Reform of the Prevention of Corruption Acts and SFO Powers in Cases of Bribery of Foreign Officials—Summary of Responses' (March 2007).

[58] *R (on the application of Corner House Research) v Director of Serious Fraud Office* [2008] EWHC 714 (Admin), *The Times*, 16 April 2008. This ruling has now been overturned by the House of Lords (*R (on the application of Corner House Research) v Director of Serious Fraud Office* [2008] UKHL 60, *The Times*, 31 July 2008).

[59] Criminal Justice and Immigration Act 2008 (Commencement No 2 and Transitional and Saving Provisions) Order 2008, SI 2008/1586.

Section 2A(3) of the CJA 1987 provides that the new powers also extend to   3.87
Scotland and Northern Ireland.[60]

B. CRIMINAL APPEALS

1. Introduction

Part 3 of the CJIA 2008 introduces substantive changes to the powers of the Court of   3.88
Appeal (Criminal Division) in determining appeals from the Crown Court in the following three situations: on referral from the Criminal Case Review Commission (CCRC),
on appeal against a ruling of the trial judge by the prosecution and upon reference
by the Attorney General of what he considers to be an unduly lenient sentence. The Act
also makes a welcome extension to the 'slip-rule'.

These changes have not been without controversy. However, they do represent   3.89
a greatly watered-down version of the government's initial proposals. In the review
paper 'Rebalancing the Criminal Justice System in favour of the Law-abiding majority',[61] the (then) Home Secretary set out his intention to 'restrict the ability of the
plainly guilty to have their convictions quashed because of procedural irregularity'.

The aim was to address the situation that arose in the case of *R v Mullen*[62] where   3.90
the Court of Appeal, despite strong evidence of the appellant's guilt, quashed his
conviction because he had been brought to the United Kingdom by the Zimbabwean
Authorities in breach of international law instead of being extradited through the
proper channels.

Clause 26 of the Criminal Justice and Immigration Bill suggested an amendment   3.91
to s 2(1) of the Criminal Appeal Act (CAA) 1968 to allow the Court of Appeal not
to consider a conviction to be 'unsafe' if it was satisfied of the appellant's guilt.

This proposal was the subject of a wide-ranging consultation with senior Judges,   3.92
practitioners and human rights organizations.[63] It met significant opposition from
(amongst others) Liberty,[64] the Law Society,[65] and the Criminal Case Review
Commission.[66] By the second reading in the House of Commons, the new Home
Secretary conceded that Clause 26 needed re-consideration.[67] The Clause never
made it into the Act.

However, the spectre of Clause 26 remains and the government's commitment to   3.93
preventing decisions of the court being overturned on a 'technicality' can be seen in
the discussion of s 44 of the CJIA 2008 at para **3.107** below.

The consultation process also highlighted a separate issue, namely how the Court   3.94
of Appeal should approach historic appeals involving miscarriages of justice referred

---

[60] As amended by CJIA 2008, s 59(3).
[61] Home Office, July 2006, 5.
[62] [2000] QB 520, CA.
[63] Home Office, 'Quashing Convictions—A Report of a Review by the Home Secretary, Lord Chancellor
and Attorney General', September 2006.
[64] Liberty, Liberty's Briefing on the Criminal Justice and Immigration Bill, June 2007.
[65] The Law Society, Parliamentary Brief: Criminal Justice and Immigration Bill Second Reading, 23 July 2007.
[66] '"Quashing Convictions" Response of the Criminal Cases Review Commission', 11 December 2006
[67] HC Deb 8 October 2007 vol 464, cc65–66.

to it by the CCRC and whether it should allow appeals on the basis of a change in the law since the time of the conviction.

3.95　On more procedural matters, Sch 8 to the CJIA 2008 introduces a number of minor amendments to the operation of the CAA 1968. Schedule 8 came into force in its entirety on 14 July 2008.[68]

3.96　Also included within this section are the changes to the assessment of compensation for miscarriages of justice. These provisions are found in Part 4 of the CJIA 2008 but are included here for thematic completeness.

2. Appeals following references from the Criminal Case Review Commission (CCRC)

3.97　Section 42 of the CJIA 2008 inserts s 16C into the CAA 1968, which allows the Court of Appeal to dismiss an appeal referred by the CCRC if the only ground for allowing the appeal is a development in the law since the time of the conviction or verdict *and* the Court decides that (if not for the CCRC reference) it would *not* have allowed an application by the appellant for an extension of time within which to seek leave to appeal on the basis of the development in the law.

3.98　Section 43 of the CJIA 2008 inserts an identical provision 13B into the Criminal Appeals (Northern Ireland) Act 1980. Both sections came into force on 14 July 2008.[69] Schedule 27 of the CJIA 2008 states that the new regime under s 16C will only apply to cases in England, Wales, and Northern Ireland that are referred after s 42 came into force on 14 July 2008.[70]

3.99　The Court of Appeal in *R v R*[71] made it clear that its practice is only to grant an extension of time within which to seek leave to appeal where there had been a development in the law post-conviction if a 'substantial injustice' would otherwise occur.

3.100　The introduction of CJIA 2008, s 42 follows the decision of the Court of Appeal in *R v Cottrell; R v Fletcher*.[72] In this case, the Court recognized the growing tension between the Court of Appeal and the CCRC in such 'change of law' cases. The Court was concerned that cases were being referred by the CCRC without consideration being given to applying for an extension of time for leave to appeal, thereby bypassing the Court's own policy and procedure. It held that just as the Court will not normally extend time, a conviction should not normally be referred just on the basis of a change of law.

3.101　In order to make a referral the CCRC only has to be satisfied that there is a 'real possibility' that the conviction would not have been upheld on account of some evidence or argument which led to it and therefore must have been an appeal or application for leave to appeal which has been refused.[73]

---

[68] Criminal Justice and Immigration Act 2008 (Commencement No 2 and Transitional and Saving Provisions) Order 2008, SI 2008/1586.
[69] Ibid.
[70] CJIA 2008, Sch 27, para 14.
[71] [2006] All ER (D) 318 (Jul) CA.
[72] [2007] 1 WLR 3190 CA.
[73] Criminal Appeals Act 1995, s 13.

The effect of the statutory changes are that on referral, the Court of Appeal must consider not only that there is a 'real possibility' that the conviction would not be upheld because of the change in the law, but it must also be satisfied that the change has resulted in a 'substantial injustice' to the appellant.

3.102

Section 16C represents the first statutory limitation on the Court of Appeal's ability to determine cases on referral to the CCRC.

3.103

Paragraph 2 of Sch 25 to the CJIA 2008 will make changes identical to those found in s 42 of the CJIA 2008 to the Courts-Martial (Appeals) Act 1968 by inserting s 25B into that Act. This amendment brings the rules governing referrals from the CCRC to the military Appeal Court arising from convictions by a Courts-Martial into line with the procedure for civilian referrals. Schedule 25 to the CJIA 2008 is not yet in force.

3.104

3. Appeals by the prosecution against terminating rulings by trial judge

Section 44 of the CJIA 2008 amends s 61 of the CJA 2003, which governs the powers of the Court of Appeal when considering an appeal by the prosecution against a terminating ruling by a judge in relation to a trial on indictment. Terminating rulings include a successful submission of no case to answer or where a case is stayed as an abuse of process.

3.105

If the Court of Appeal upholds the trial judge's ruling, it must still order that the defendant be acquitted. The effect of s 61 of the CJA 2003 is that where the Court of Appeal reverses or varies the ruling it may not acquit the defendant unless it considers that he could not have a fair trial by either ordering the trial to resume[74] or by ordering a re-trial.[75] Previously, the Court of Appeal could only order a retrial or a resumption of the trial if it was in the interests of justice to do so. In all other circumstances, it had to acquit the defendant.

3.106

The introduction of this rebuttable presumption in favour of a re-trial is another example of the government's aim to 'restrict the ability of those the courts agree are guilty to have their convictions quashed on a technicality'.[76]

3.107

Section 45 of the CJIA 2008 makes an identical amendment applicable in Northern Ireland.[77]

3.108

Both these paragraphs came into force on 14 July 2008[78] and apply to cases where the prosecution was granted leave to appeal on or after that date.[79]

3.109

4. Attorney General's References

Section 36 of the CJA 1988 provides the statutory framework for the Attorney General to refer a case to the Court of Appeal if it appears to the Attorney General that the sentence was unduly lenient. Prior to the CJA 2003, if the Court of Appeal

3.110

---

[74] CJIA 2008, s 61(4)(b).

[75] CJIA 2008, s 61(4)(c).

[76] 'Quashing Convictions—A Report of a Review by the Home Secretary, Lord Chancellor and Attorney General', Home Office, September 2006, para 2.15.

[77] Section 45 Amends art 20 of the Criminal Justice (Northern Ireland) Order 2004, SI 1500/2004 (NI).

[78] Criminal Justice and Immigration Act 2008 (Commencement No 2 and Transitional and Saving Provisions) Order 2008, SI 2008/1586.

[79] CJIA 2008, Sch 27, para 16.

quashed an unduly lenient sentence and passed in its place one that was more severe, it was the Court's practice to include within the new sentence a discount to reflect the fact that the appellant had been sentenced twice. This was often referred to as the 'double-jeopardy' discount.

3.111 Section 36 of the CJA 1988 was amended by s 272 of the CJA 2003, which introduced a prohibition on the award by the Court of a 'double-jeopardy' discount on appeals concerning minimum terms of mandatory life sentences for murder.[80]

3.112 'Rebalancing the Criminal Justice System in favour of the law-abiding majority' aimed to broaden the scope of the prohibition and 'stop offenders who are re-sentenced after an appeal against a lenient sentence being given a sentence discount simply for the distress of being sentenced again'.[81]

3.113 The government's proposals were no doubt influenced by the media outcry following a number of high-profile cases including that of Tanya French and Alan Webster in June 2006.[82] French and Webster were convicted of serious sex offences involving a baby. Webster was given a life sentence with a minimum term of 6 years. The Attorney General appealed on the basis that the sentence was too lenient and had caused 'public outrage'.

3.114 Before a five-member panel of the Court of Appeal, chaired by the Lord Chief Justice, the Attorney General also argued that 'double-jeopardy' discounts should not apply to discretionary life sentences and should not apply, or should only have limited effect on other significant sentences of imprisonment.[83]

3.115 The Court rejected the Attorney General's submissions and ruled that to expand the prohibition beyond mandatory life sentences would 'constitute an unwarranted interference with the discretion of the court when determining a sentence'.[84] The Court recognized that where a significant sentence was passed at first instance, which was substituted only for a more significant sentence then the distress to the appellant would be minimal and the discount therefore negligible. In these circumstances it could be reasonable to withhold the discount. It further ruled that each case must be decided on its facts. On the facts of Webster's case the Court decided it was not appropriate to award a discount.

3.116 Parliament has now intervened by way of s 46 of the CJIA 2008, which will come into force at a time to be specified.

3.117 Section 46 of the CJIA 2008 inserts a new s 36(3)(A) and s 36(3)(B) into the CJA 1988 and prohibits the award of 'double-jeopardy' discounts in AG's References against:

(1) the minimum term in a mandatory life sentence;[85]
(2) the minimum term in a discretionary life sentence;[86]
(3) the minimum term in a life sentence of imprisonment for public protection;[87]
(4) the minimum term in a life sentence of detention for public protection.[88]

---

[80] CJA 1988, s 36(3)A (as amended).
[81] Home Office (fn 57 above), p 5.
[82] *Attorney General's Reference (No 14 & 15 of 2006) (Tanya French and Alan Webster)* [2007] 1 All ER 718, CA.
[83] Ibid.
[84] Para 62 of the Judgment.
[85] Under CJA 2003, s 269(2).
[86] Under PCC(S)A 2000, s 82A.
[87] Under CJA 2003, s 225.
[88] Under CJA 2003, s 226.

In respect of Northern Ireland, s 47 of the CJIA 2008 prohibits the application of a 'double jeopardy' discount to AG's References against the minimum term in all life sentences.[89]   3.118

Given that the expansion only includes those who received life sentences at first instance, it is submitted that it is a pragmatic one. The impact upon those individuals of an increase in the minimum term on an AG's Reference is likely to be negligible. The real impact is in receiving the life sentence.   3.119

The new provisions do not prohibit the Court of Appeal giving a discount to someone who receives a Community Punishment Order or suspended sentence at first instance and is then sentenced to a period of imprisonment after an AG's Reference. It is clear that these individuals could be said to be caused 'distress' worthy of a discount.   3.120

Paragraph 28 of Sch 25 to the CJIA 2008 amends s 273 of the Armed Forces Act 2006 to remove 'double jeopardy' discounts in references to the Courts Martial Appeal Court by the Attorney General of unduly lenient sentences passed by a Courts Martial. Schedule 25 to the CJIA 2008 is not in force, neither is s 273 of the Armed Forces Act 2006. Both these pieces of legislation will require further commencement orders before these changes can take effect.   3.121

5. Variation of sentences by the Crown Court (the 'slip-rule')

Paragraph 28 of Sch 8 to the CJIA 2008 amends s 155 of the PCC(S)A 2000, otherwise known as the 'slip-rule'. The Crown Court is now able to vary or rescind any sentence imposed or other order made within 56 days of passing sentence or making the order. This doubles the previous time limit of 28 days.   3.122

This will be welcome news to both practitioners and to the Court of Appeal in that it allows uncomplicated sentencing errors to be corrected without the time and expense of seeking leave to appeal if the error is not detected within days of the hearing.   3.123

Paragraph 27 of Sch 8 to the CJIA 2008 makes an identical time limit applicable in Northern Ireland.   3.124

Both these paragraphs came into force on 14 July 2008.[90]   3.125

6. Time limit on grant of certificates of fitness to appeal

Section 1(2)(b) of the CAA 1968 empowers the trial judge sitting in the Crown Court to grant a defendant convicted on indictment a certificate of fitness to appeal to the Court of Appeal. If such a certificate is granted, there is no need for the defendant to seek leave to appeal from the Court of Appeal and his appeal will be heard, without more by the full court.   3.126

A certificate can also be granted to give leave to a defendant's appeal against sentence[91] an appeal against a finding of not guilty by way of insanity[92] and an   3.127

---

[89] CJIA 2008, s 47 amends s 5(1) of the Life Sentences (Northern Ireland) Order 2001, SI 2001/2564 (NI 2).

[90] Criminal Justice and Immigration Act 2008 (Commencement No 2 and Transitional and Saving Provisions) Order 2008, SI 2008/1586.

[91] CAA 1968, s 11.

[92] CAA 1968, s 12.

appeal against a finding that the defendant did an act or omission following a ruling that he is unfit to plead.[93]

3.128　Paragraphs 2–5 of Sch 8 to the CJIA 2008 amend the provisions of the CAA 1968[94] so that certificates of fitness for appeal can only be granted within 28 days from the date of the conviction.

3.129　Paragraphs 15–17 of Sch 8 make amendments with identical effect to ss 1, 12, and 13A of the Criminal Appeal (Northern Ireland) Act 1980.

3.130　The above paragraphs came into force on 14 July 2008.[95]

7. Powers of single judge

3.131　Section 31 of the CAA 1968 sets out the powers of the single judge sitting in the Court of Appeal. Paragraph 11 of Sch 8 amends s 31 of the CAA 1968 and inserts a number of additional powers for the single judge to grant leave of appeal against a judge's ruling at a preparatory hearing on:

- any question as to admissibility of evidence;[96]
- any other question of law relating to the case;[97]
- any question regarding severance or joinder;[98]
- any order that certain fraud trials should take place without a jury;[99]
- any order that the trial should be conducted without a jury where there is a danger of jury tampering.[100]

3.132　In the above cases, as with all powers under s 31, the single judge may exercise his powers in the same way as may be exercised by the full court.

3.133　Paragraph 9 of Sch 8 to the CJIA 2008 also gives the single judge the power to renew an interim hospital order.[101] See further below (at para **3.149**) regarding the Court of Appeal's powers in respect of interim hospital orders.

3.134　Paragraph 25 of Sch 8 makes amendments with identical effect to s 45 of the Criminal Appeals (Northern Ireland) Act 1980. The above paragraphs came into force on 14 July 2008.[102]

---

[93] CAA 1968, s 15.

[94] Paragraphs 2–5 of Sch 8 amend CAA 1968, ss 1, 11, 12, and 15 respectively.

[95] Criminal Justice and Immigration Act 2008 (Commencement No 2 and Transitional and Saving Provisions) Order 2008, SI 2008/1586.

[96] CJA 1987, s 9(3)(b).

[97] CJA 1987, s 9(3)(c).

[98] CJA 1987, s 9(3)(d).

[99] CJA 2003, s 43 (not yet in force).

[100] CJA 2003, s 44 (in force 24 July 2006).

[101] Para 9 amends s 31(2) of the CAA 1968.

[102] Criminal Justice and Immigration Act 2008 (Commencement No 2 and Transitional and Saving Provisions) Order 2008, SI 2008/1586.

8. Appeals against procedural directions

Both the single judge and the Registrar of the Court of Appeal have the power to make procedural directions for the effective preparation of appeals and applications for leave to appeal.[103]

3.135

Paragraph 12 of Sch 8 amends s 31B of the CAA 1968 and removes the power of the Court of Appeal to confirm, vary or set aside directions made by the single judge on appeal. The power of the single judge to confirm, vary or set aside directions of the Registrar on appeal is preserved.

3.136

The above paragraphs came into force on 14 July 2008.[104] The amendments apply to any procedural direction given on or after that date.[105]

3.137

Paragraph 8 of Sch 25 to the CJIA 2008[106] makes identical changes to s 36(C) of the Courts-Martial (Appeal) Act 1968. Schedule 25 to the CJIA 2008 will be brought into force on a date to be appointed.

3.138

9. Evidence on appeal

Section 23 of the CAA 1968 permits the Court of Appeal to call witnesses and order the production of documents whether or not it formed part of the evidence at the original trial.

3.139

Paragraph 10 of Sch 8 amends s 23 of the CAA 1968 to extend this power to receive evidence to applications for leave to appeal.[107] It also specifies that any document, exhibit or thing that is ordered to be produced can be ordered to be produced to any party to the proceedings, as well as the court.

3.140

Paragraph 22 of Sch 8 makes amendments with identical effect to s 25 of the Criminal Appeals (Northern Ireland) Act 1980.

3.141

The above paragraphs came into force on 14 July 2008.[108]

3.142

Paragraph 7 of Sch 25 to the CJIA 2008[109] makes amendments with identical effect to s 28 of the Courts-Martial (Appeals) Act 1968. The effect of these amendments means that a military Appeal Court can call witnesses and order the production of documents in an identical fashion to the civilian Court of Appeal. Schedule 25 to the CJIA 2008 will be brought into force on a date to be appointed.

3.143

---

[103] CAA 1968, s 31B.

[104] Criminal Justice and Immigration Act 2008 (Commencement No 2 and Transitional and Saving Provisions) Order 2008, SI 2008/1586.

[105] Para 6, Sch 2, Transitional and Saving Provisions (Criminal Justice and Immigration Act 2008 (Commencement No 2 and Transitional and Saving Provisions) Order 2008, SI 2008/1586.

[106] As introduced by CJIA 2008, s 145 (not yet in force).

[107] Para 10 inserts s 1(1A) and s (6) into CAA 1968, s 23.

[108] Criminal Justice and Immigration Act 2008 (Commencement No 2 and Transitional and Saving Provisions) Order 2008, SI 2008/1586.

[109] Introduced by CJIA 2008, s 145 (not yet in force).

10. Variation of sentence on appeal

3.144 Section 4 of the CAA 1968 sets out the Court of Appeal's powers when it is dealing with an appeal against conviction for more than one offence and allows the appeal in respect of one (or more) and not the other(s).

3.145 Before the CJIA 2008, the Court had the power to substitute the sentence on any count on which the appellant remained convicted on the same indictment for any sentence that it thought proper, that was authorized by law and that was not more than the total sentence that the lower court passed for the two (or more) offences combined.

3.146 Paragraph 6 of Sch 8 to the CJIA 2008 broadens this power by amending s 4 of the CAA 1968, which now allows the Court to substitute a sentence on any 'related offence' on which the appellant remains convicted, even if the offences are not on the same indictment.

3.147 'Related Offences' (defined by s 4(4) of the CCA 1968 as amended) are sentences that are:

(i) passed on the same day;
(ii) passed on different days but where the Court states that it is treating them as essentially one sentence;
(iii) passed on different days but are different counts on the same indictment.

3.148 Paragraph 18 makes amendments with identical effect to s 4 of the Criminal Appeals (Northern Ireland) Act 1980. The above paragraphs came into force on 14 July 2008[110] and apply to appeal proceedings that began on or after that date.[111]

11. Interim hospital orders

3.149 Paragraphs 7–8 of Sch 8 to the CJIA 2008 are essentially consolidating provisions, clarifying the Court of Appeal's position when it makes or renews an interim hospital order. Section 30A of the CAA 1968 (as amended)[112] now states that when the Court of Appeal has made or renewed an interim hospital order, an offender who absconds during the term of that Order shall be brought back before the Court as soon as practicable for the Court to deal with him under s 38(7) of the Mental Health Act 1983.

3.150 The power of the Crown Court to deal with an offender who is subject to an interim hospital order made by the Court of Appeal has been removed (para 7, Sch 8 to the CJIA 2008).

3.151 Paragraphs 19–21 of Sch 8 make amendments with identical effect to s 10 and s 29 of the Criminal Appeals (Northern Ireland) Act 1980. The above paragraphs came

---

[110] Criminal Justice and Immigration Act 2008 (Commencement No 2 and Transitional and Saving Provisions) Order 2008, SI 2008/1586.

[111] Para 8, Sch 2, Transitional and Saving Provisions (Criminal Justice and Immigration Act 2008 (Commencement No 2 and Transitional and Saving Provisions) Order 2008, SI 2008/1586).

[112] Para 8 inserts s 30A into the CAA 1968.

into force on 14 July 2008[113] and apply in relation to interim hospital orders made on or after that date.[114]

Paragraphs 3–6 of Sch 25 to the CJIA 2008[115] will make amendments identical   3.152
to paras 7–8 of Sch 8 to the Courts-Martial (Appeals) Act 1968 by inserting s 35A into that Act. This amendment means that the effect of an interim hospital order made by a military Appeal Court will be identical to one made in the civilian Court of Appeal. Schedule 25 of the CJIA 2008 will be brought into force on a date to be appointed.

12. Detention on appeal to the House of Lords

Where the prosecutor seeks, or is granted leave to appeal against the decision of the   3.153
Court of Appeal to the House of Lords (soon to be the Supreme Court)[116] the Court of Appeal must consider whether to detain the appellant.

Section 37 of the CAA 1968 as amended by CJIA 2008, Sch 8, para 13 requires   3.154
the Court of Appeal to make an order either to detain the appellant, release him on bail or release without bail. Previously, the Court of Appeal could not make an order to release without bail.

If the appellant is released without bail by the Court of Appeal, the CAA 1968,   3.155
s 37(5) provides that he cannot be liable to be detained again as a result of the decision of the House of Lords.

Paragraph 24 makes amendments with identical effect to s 36 of the Criminal Appeal   3.156
(Northern Ireland) Act 1980. The above paragraphs came into force on 14 July 2008[117] and apply to any case where an appeal lies to the House of Lords if the date of the Court of Appeal decision is on or after that date.[118]

Paragraph 9 of Sch 25[119] makes amendments with identical effect to s 43 of the   3.157
Courts-Martial (Appeals) Act 1968.[120] Schedule 25 to the CJIA 2008 will be brought into force on a date to be appointed.

13. Compensation for miscarriages of justice

Section 61 in Pt 4 of the CJIA 2008 make radical changes to the system of compen-   3.158
sation that can be awarded where a person has been the subject of a miscarriage of justice. Section 61 amends s 133 of the CJA 1988[120a] with the following effect.

---

[113] Criminal Justice and Immigration Act 2008 (Commencement No 2 and Transitional and Saving Provisions) Order 2008, SI 2008/1586.

[114] Para 5, Sch 2, Transitional and Saving Provisions (Criminal Justice and Immigration Act 2008 (Commencement No 2 and Transitional and Saving Provisions) Order 2008, SI 2008/1586).

[115] Introduced by CJIA 2008, s 145 (not yet in force).

[116] From a date to be appointed.

[117] Criminal Justice and Immigration Act 2008 (Commencement No 2 and Transitional and Saving Provisions) Order 2008, SI 2008/1586.

[118] Para 10, Sch 2, Transitional and Saving Provisions (Criminal Justice and Immigration Act 2008 (Commencement No 2 and Transitional and Saving Provisions) Order 2008, SI 2008/1586).

[119] As introduced by CJIA 2008, s 145 (not yet in force).

[120] As amended by the Armed Forces Act 2006 (not yet in force).

[120a] Date in force 1 December 2008, Criminal Justice and Immigration Act 2008 (Commencement No 4 and Saving Provision) Order 2008, SI 2008/2993.

3.159   First, s 61 introduces a time limit of 2 years from a reversal of conviction or pardon within which an application for compensation must be made. The 2-year period can be extended by the Secretary of State in exceptional circumstances. A reversal is defined as an acquittal or where a retrial is not pursued.

3.160   Secondly, an assessor of the amount of compensation due is entitled to make a deduction in the award having regard to the conduct of the person that has either directly or indirectly contributed to the conviction and any other convictions of the person and any other punishment suffered as a result of those convictions. After considering these factors, the assessor is entitled to reduce the compensation payable, and in some circumstances, to a nominal amount.

3.161   This amendment effectively imports the doctrine of contributory negligence into a determination of compensation for a miscarriage of justice.

3.162   Thirdly, the total compensation payable in respect of a person detained for 10 years or under will be capped at £500,000. This is equivalent to the amount available to the victims of crime under the Criminal Injuries Compensation Scheme. In the case of those detained for over 10 years, the amount is capped at £1 million.

3.163   The fourth change is to limit the amount of compensation payable under s133 for a person's loss of earnings capacity in respect of any one year to an amount equal to between one and a half times the median annual gross earnings at the time of the assessment.

3.164   These amendments apply to England, Wales, and Northern Ireland and came into force on 1 December 2008[120b] and will apply to any application for compensation made after this date.[120c]

3.165   The changes were first proposed in 2006 by the then Home Secretary, Charles Clarke, and met with significant opposition from both the Law Society[121] and Liberty.[122] The main concern of both organizations was the attempt to balance compensation awards of those wrongly convicted and those who had been the victims of crime as part of the government's 'rebalancing' agenda.

3.166   Liberty commented:

The position of the state, and its proper responsibility to pay compensation is entirely different in respect of a miscarriage of justice as compared to a victim of crime. The state has, at best, limited control over the criminal actions of individuals on the street. For this reason, it is right that the criminal should themselves bear the main burden, for, as far as possible, restoring the victim to the position they were in before the wrong-doing. By contrast, in the case of a miscarriage of justice the wrongdoing is committed by the state—no-one else can be held to account for this. Where the state makes a mistake and wrongly convicts someone of a crime, there is no justification for the state escaping its responsibility for compensating the victim of the mistake so that as far as possible they are put in the same position as if the mistake never happened. As cases like those of Angela Cannings and Sally Clarke demonstrate so clearly, full financial compensation is not in itself enough to enable people to rebuild their lives after being wrongfully convicted.[123]

[120b] Criminal Justice and Immigration Act 2008 (Commencement No 4 and Saving Provision) Order 2008, SI 2008/2993.
[120c] Section 22, Sch 27, CJIA 2008.
[121] The Law Society, Parliamentary Brief: Criminal Justice and Immigration Bill Second Reading, 23 July 2007.
[122] Liberty, 'Liberty's Briefing on the Criminal Justice and Immigration Bill', June 2007.
[123] Paras 31–33.

In addition, it is submitted that the importation of principles of contributory   3.167
fault by the provisions is an echo of the government's (albeit failed) aim to prevent
those the government considers 'plainly guilty' escaping liability altogether.

Allowing the assessor to reduce awards because of things that an individual may   3.168
have done, is first of all putting that assessor in place of the tribunal of fact, who have
acquitted and secondly, suggests that the individual should be penalized for offences
they are 'plainly guilty' of, or have been convicted of in the past, despite the fact that
they have been the victim of a miscarriage of justice.

The sea-change that these amendments bring about is a controversial one and will   3.169
no doubt be the subject of judicial and academic scrutiny.

Paragraph 29 of Sch 25 to the CJIA 2008[124] amends s 276 of the Armed Forces   3.170
Act 2006 with identical effect to s 61 and s 62 of the CJIA 2008. However, Sch 25
to the CJIA 2008 is not yet in force; neither is s 276 of the Armed Forces Act 2006.
Both these pieces of legislation will require further commencement orders before
these changes can take effect.

Part 3 of Sch 25 to the CJIA 2008 contains transitional provisions regarding the   3.171
implementation of the amendments to s 276 of the Armed Forces Act 2006. Part 3
states that any application for compensation that has been made but not determined
by the time of the commencement of the amendments to s 276 will be caught by its
provisions. If a conviction is quashed or reversed before the commencement date
but an application for compensation has not been made, the time period of 2 years
starts to run from the commencement date, unless the Secretary of State determines
that there are exceptional circumstances in which to extend the time limit.

---

[124] Introduced by CJIA 2008, s 145 (not yet in force).

4

NEW CRIMINAL OFFENCES

A. OVERVIEW

The CJIA 2008 introduces new criminal offences, amends some existing offences and 4.01 extends the jurisdiction of others. These changes are the result of several different government Consultation Papers, with no discernible connection between each new offence. A number of the offences were brought in to the Bill at a late stage with little time for debate and there is no coherent structure to their appearance in the Act.

Most of the offences are contained within CJIA 2008, Part 5 but the new offence 4.02 of causing a nuisance or disturbance on NHS premises is found in the CJIA 2008, Part 8 under the general heading 'Anti-social Behaviour' whilst 'Miscellaneous' Part 11 introduces new powers in relation to those who persistently sell tobacco to under 18 year olds. This section also deals with the clarification of the law on self-defence which appears in Part 5.

Once the offences are located within the Act, close scrutiny reveals that the majority 4.03 are very poorly drafted. The Act introduces a number of new words and phrases to the criminal law lexicon, which are likely to be the subject of future legal argument. The provisions on extreme pornography, for example, will require a court to decide what is 'explicit', 'disgusting', or an 'integral part of the narrative'. Phrases which have been used in previous legislation and case law and which have established legal meaning are replaced without explanation with synonyms. For example 'serious injury' is used in the CJIA 2008, s 63(7)(b) when the intention is to cover 'grievous bodily harm'.

Section 63(5) begins, 'So, for example . . .' introducing what looks like an Explanatory Note into the Act itself. The grammar is similarly tortuous—s 66, for example, contains a triple negative. However, the wording of the Act is in fact the least controversial part of it.

4.04   It is submitted that the majority of the changes introduced are simply unnecessary. The clarification of the law on self-defence, for example, does not change the position at common law. Further, the mischief intended to be dealt with by the new offences of inciting hatred on the grounds of sexual orientation and causing a nuisance on NHS premises is largely covered by existing legislation but the offences were supported in part on the basis that they 'sent out a message'.[1] It remains to be seen, as has happened with a proportion of the 3,000 offences created in the preceding 10 years, how many of these sections actually come into force and, of those that already have, how often they are used.

B. EXTREME PORNOGRAPHY

1. Introduction

4.05   The CJIA 2008, Part 5, s 63 introduces the new offence of possession of extreme pornography. As is often the case with unnecessary legislation, it was introduced as a result of one high profile case. During the trial of Graham Coutts for the murder of Jane Longhurst in March 2003, during what Coutts described as consensual sex, evidence was adduced of Coutt's alleged addiction to violent pornography. A subsequent campaign by the deceased's family led to a Consultation Paper in August 2005.[2]

4.06   The response to the consultation was polarized. Among the critics was the campaign group 'Backlash', a coalition formed from a number of organizations, including the Spanner Trust that was set up in response to the case of *R v Brown*[3] which defined the legal limits of consensual 'violent' behaviour between adults engaged in sado-masochism. There was concern that the proposal would further criminalize sado-masochistic behaviour simply on the grounds that some people found it distasteful.

4.07   One argument consistently put forward by the government in response was that it was simply criminalizing the possession of that which it was already illegal to publish under the Obscene Publications Act (OPA) 1959[4] and it did not intend to change the law in relation to what was obscene or pornographic.[5] This assurance may be of assistance in defining the scope of the new offence as, *prima facie*, this would not appear to be the case. For example, under the OPA 1959 an item is 'obscene' if its effect is '. . . such as to tend to deprave and corrupt persons who are likely, having regard to all relevant circumstances, to read, see or hear the matter contained or embodied in it'.[6] This is a matter to be decided by the tribunal of fact.

---

[1] See PBC Deb 16 October 2007 c62 and Criminal Justice and Immigration Bill 2008, House of Lords Explanatory Notes, para 1168.

[2] 'On the possession of extreme pornographic material' Home Office and Scottish Executive, Aug 2005.

[3] *R v Brown (A)* [1994] 1 AC 212, HL.

[4] HC Deb 8 October 2007 vol 464, c112.

[5] PBC Deb 22 November 2007 c524.

[6] OPA 1959, s 1(1).

Under the CJIA 2008 images of sado-masochism may depict an act where serious injury is likely to be caused and may be found by a jury to be 'disgusting' and therefore 'extreme pornography'. An image can be 'disgusting' without having any tendency to corrupt or deprave. Furthermore, whether publication of a particular article would fall foul of the OPA 1959 may depend upon who is likely to see it.[7] In a case of simple possession, the only person likely to see the image may be the defendant, but there is no scope for considering the effect on him. The corruption or depravity is effectively presumed by the mere nature of the images. It seems therefore that the concerns raised by 'Backlash' may well be valid.   4.08

During the Committee stage, a number of MPs raised concerns as to whether there was any evidence showing a causal link between extreme pornographic images and actual offences of violence. The Government pointed to an assessment carried out by the Ministry of Justice[8] which it relied on to demonstrate that there was 'cause to have concern in certain circumstances for what is, no doubt, a smallish number of the population who might be susceptible to their behaviour being affected by viewing extreme pornography'.[9]   4.09

The evidence of causation may be important as the offence interferes with an individual's right to a private life and their right freely to impart and receive information, including offensive or unpalatable information,[10] under Articles 8 and 10 respectively, of the European Convention on Human Rights (ECHR). The offence therefore has to be justified as a necessary and proportionate response. In addition, in order to comply with Article 7 of the ECHR, the offence has to be sufficiently clear and foreseeable so as to enable individuals to regulate their conduct.[11] The human rights impact is unclear as the UK may be the first western jurisdiction to introduce a ban on simple possession of extreme material.   4.10

The provisions of the CJIA 2008 relating to extreme pornography extend to England, Wales, and Northern Ireland[12] and will come into force on 26 January 2009.[12a]   4.11

2. Elements of the offence

Section 63 creates a new triable either-way offence of being in 'possession' of an 'extreme' 'pornographic' 'image' unless it is an excluded image under s 64 or the defendant can avail themselves of one of the defences under ss 65 or 66. Proceedings for an offence under s 63 may not be instituted except by, or with the consent of, the Director of Public Prosecutions.   4.12

---

[7] *R v Barker* [1962] 1 WLR 349, CA.

[8] 'The evidence of harm to adults relating to exposure to extreme pornographic material: a rapid evidence assessment' Ministry of Justice Research Studies 11/07, September 2007.

[9] PBC Deb 16 October 2007 c31.

[10] *Mueller v Switzerland* Series A No 133, (1991) 13 EHRR 212, para 33.

[11] See *Handyside v UK* (1974) Series A No 24, 1 EHRR 737 for the application of Art 7 to the definition of 'obscene' in the OPA 1959.

[12] CJIA 2008, s 152(3).

[12a] CJIA 2008 (Commencement No 4 and Saving Provision) Order 2008, SI 2008/2993.

(a) *'Possession'*

4.13 Possession was intended to be construed in the same way as in relation to possession of indecent images of children.[13]

(b) *'Pornographic'*

4.14 By the CJIA 2008, s 63(3) an image is pornographic 'if it is of such a nature that it must reasonably be assumed to have been produced solely or principally for the purpose of sexual arousal'. It is not clear how wide a definition is to be given to 'produced'. In relation to a film for example, a narrow definition would require the court simply to look at whether the filming took place for that purpose. A wider definition, would allow the court to consider a film which may not have been filmed for the purpose of sexual arousal but appears to have been subsequently edited for that purpose. The reference to judging the image as it is found in the defendant's possession in s 63(4) (as to which see para **4.16**) would seem to suggest that the wider definition is intended. This will be an issue for the judge to consider before directing the jury on the question of purpose.

4.15 Whether an image must reasonably be assumed to have been produced for the purpose of sexual arousal is an objective test to be decided by the tribunal of fact. 'Sexual arousal' is unlikely to need further definition and is likely to mean the same thing as 'sexual gratification' in the Sexual Offences Act 2003. There does not appear to have been any reason why the same term could not have been used.

4.16 By the CJIA 2008, s 63(4) if the image (as it is found in the person's possession) forms part of a series of images, the question of whether the image is 'pornographic' is to be determined by reference to the context in which it appears. The example is given in s 63(5) of an image which forms an integral part of a narrative whereby, having regard to the images as a whole, the image must not reasonably be assumed to have been produced for the purposes of sexual arousal, even though it might have been found to be pornographic taken by itself. For example, in the case of a film containing a sex scene, the court must consider whether that scene was integral to the plot. If it is deemed gratuitous, the sex scene could be deemed 'pornographic'.

4.17 Clearly, it is farcical that criminal liability could depend upon an artistic judgment as to whether a particular scene sufficiently progressed the protagonist's journey. As outlined at para **4.42** below expert evidence may be admissible on the question of whether a defendant had a legitimate reason for possessing the material and it may be that it would also be admissible on this question.

4.18 Other than the example given in the CJIA 2008, s 63(5) there may be comparatively few examples in which the context can be taken into account. This could prove to be problematic—for example, in relation to an image in an art exhibition. Section 63(4) would seem to exclude consideration of any extraneous material, such as where the image was found. The artist's motive would be irrelevant under an objective test. The possessor of the image would then have the burden of proving that he had a defence of lawful reason under the CJIA 2008, s 65.

---

[13] 'On the possession of extreme pornographic material' Home Office and Scottish Executive, Aug 2005, para 50.

(c) 'Extreme'

Section 63(6) defines an image as extreme if it portrays one of the acts in s 63(7)[14]   4.19
in an explicit and realistic way and a reasonable person looking at the image would
think that any such person or animal was real.

For practical reasons the Act requires that the image 'portrays' a particular act   4.20
rather than requiring that it actually shows such an act. To legislate in the latter way
would have required the prosecution to prove that the act actually took place which
may require finding the 'actors' involved. Despite the defences available, the offence
may therefore make unlawful possession of an image of an act which may not itself
have been illegal. For example, an image which portrays what looks like serious
harm being caused to a person's genitals, when in fact none was caused, will be illegal
for anyone but the participants to possess.

Whether an act is 'explicit' is likely to be left to the tribunal of fact. The original   4.21
Consultation Paper provides a little more guidance, stating that it intended the
offence only to cover activity 'which can be clearly seen and is not hidden, disguised
or implied'.[15]

The condition that the portrayal be 'realistic' would exclude, for example, mock   4.22
depictions involving fake blood and badly made up 'corpses'. The requirement that
a reasonable person would think that any person or animal involved was real would,
most obviously, not include animation or puppets.[16] Although it may be that animated
or unrealistic material has the same effect, given that the research carried out on the
effects of violent pornography only considered realistic depictions, there is as yet no
evidence to support this possibility.

The four acts in the CJIA 2008, s 63(7) are as follows: 4.23

(a) an act which threatens a person's life;
(b) an act which results, or is likely to result, in serious injury to a person's anus,
      breasts or genitals;
(c) an act which involves sexual interference with a human corpse; or
(d) a person performing an act of intercourse or oral sex with an animal (whether
      dead or alive).

In relation to s 63(7)(a), examples of acts which threaten a person's life are given   4.24
in the Explanatory Notes.[17] These include depictions of hanging, suffocation or
sexual assault involving a threat with a weapon.

'Serious' injury for the purposes of s 63(7)(b) would seem at first glance to set   4.25
a lower injury threshold than that required for grievous bodily harm under ss 18 or
20 of the Offences Against the Persons Act 1861 as the ordinary meaning of 'grievous
bodily harm' is 'really serious' bodily harm.[18] However, the Court of Appeal has held
that a summing up which omitted the word 'really' would not necessarily affect the
safety of a conviction.[19] The intention expressed in the Consultation Paper was that

---

[14] See para **4.23** below.
[15] 'On the possession of extreme pornographic material', Home Office 2005, para 38.
[16] Explanatory Notes, para 459.
[17] Explanatory Notes, para 457.
[18] *DPP v Smith* [1961] AC 290, HL.
[19] *R v Janjua* (1999) 1 Cr App R 91, CA.

violence in respect of which a prosecution for grievous bodily harm could be brought would be covered.[20]

4.26   The injury has to be caused to the person's anus, breasts or genitals. By virtue of s 63(9) references to a part of the body include references to a part surgically constructed (in particular through gender reassignment surgery).

4.27   In *R v Bassett*[21] the word 'breasts' was held not to extend to the male chest for the purposes of the offence of voyeurism under s 67 of the Sexual Offences Act 2003. It may be that for the sake of consistency and certainty the same definition will be applied to s 63(7)(b). However, the ruling in *Bassett* was on two bases. Firstly, that the ordinary and normal meaning of the word 'breasts' related to female breasts. Secondly, that the offence of voyeurism was designed to prevent covert viewing of certain acts and parts of the body that people would feel embarrassed about other people viewing without their consent. Although the first justification would apply equally to this case, the second would not. One of the purposes of the offence is to prevent the degradation of women, in which case, injury to the female breast is symbolically offensive in a way injury to other parts of the body or the male breast is not. Another purpose of the offence is that violent sexual imagery encourages some to go on to commit violent sexual offences, in which case it is arguable that injury to any body part is equally corrupting.

4.28   Section 63(7)(c) refers to sexual interference with a human corpse, which is not necessarily an offence in itself. Section 70 of the Sexual Offences Act 2003 creates the offence of sexual penetration of a corpse, but clearly a corpse can be interfered with without it being penetrated. The Consultation Paper uses the term necrophilia to refer to both the image and the act and it may be arguable that 'interference' should be limited to 'penetration'.

4.29   Similarly in relation to s 63(7)(d), performing an act of intercourse or oral sex with an animal (whether dead or alive) is not necessarily illegal. Intercourse with an animal is an offence under s 69 of the Sexual Offences Act 2003, but this does not extend to oral sex—by either party—nor does it cover dead animals.

(d) *'Image'*

4.30   An 'image' is defined in s 63(8) as a moving or still image (produced by any means) (s 63(8)(a)) or data (stored by any means) which is capable of conversion into an image within paragraph (a) (s 63 (8) (b)).

3. Excluded images

4.31   Section 64 of the CJIA 2008 provides that an image may be excluded from the operation of s 63 if it is an image which 'forms part of a series of images contained in a recording of the whole or part of a classified work'. A classified work is a recording of a film for which the British Board of Film Classification has issued a certificate. The BBFC guidance for 18 rated films states that any content in breach of the criminal law is not acceptable. It will now have to bear s 63 in mind when issuing certificates.

[20] 'On the possession of extreme pornographic material' Home Office 2005, para 41.
[21] [2008] EWCA Crim 1174; *The Times* (18 June 2008); (2009) 1 Cr App R 7.

It would only seem necessary to invoke this exemption in relation to films certified before the implementation of this section.

However, due mainly to its poor drafting, the exclusion is not quite as simple as it appears. The simplest example to illustrate the different scenarios is the video recording of a mainstream film from television. The same principles will apply to DVDs, digital recordings and downloading over the Internet as 'recording' means any disc, tape or other device capable of storing data electronically and from which images may be produced by any means (s 64(7)). 4.32

Section 22(3) of the Video Recordings Act 1984 applies for the purposes of s 64. The Video Recordings Act 1984 applies to any series of visual images produced electronically by the use of information contained on any disc, magnetic tape or any other device capable of storing data electronically, and shown as a moving picture.[22] 4.33

Section 22(3) states that any alteration to the classified recording will invalidate the certificate. Therefore, if the video recording is subsequently edited and scenes moved around, it would no longer be a classified film, and would therefore no longer be an 'excluded image'. Otherwise, if a recording contains the whole of the classified work, it is an 'excluded image'. If the recording as it is found does not contain the entirety of the original certified film but only part, then in certain circumstances it may still be caught by s 63. 4.34

First of all it must be determined under s 64(5) whether, for the purposes of the CJIA 2008, the recording is of the whole or part of the film. Any alteration due to technical reasons is to be disregarded for the purposes of this determination (s 64(5)(a)). If the reason that only part of the film has been recorded because of a loss of television signal, it can still be regarded as a recording of the whole of a classified film. By analogy, the downloading of a film over the Internet may be unsuccessful due to technical reasons and therefore fall within the ambit of s 64(5). 4.35

An alteration due to inadvertence on the part of any person is also to be disregarded (s 64(5)(a)). Therefore, if the timer were set incorrectly on the video recorder so that only part of the classified film was recorded, it would still be an 'excluded image'. 4.36

'Alteration' under the Video Recordings Act 1984[23] includes additions to the recording. However, by the CJIA 2008, s 64(5)(b), if the addition is 'extraneous material', the addition is to be disregarded. Advertisements are specifically mentioned in this subsection as an example of 'extraneous material'. It would also cover the situation where a video recorder or DVD player continues recording after a film has finished and records part of the following programme. 4.37

If, having considered these issues, the recording is found to be part of the classified film, the court must go on to consider the part of the classified film in question. If the part in question is of such a nature that it must reasonably be assumed to have been extracted (whether with or without other images) solely or principally for the purpose of sexual arousal it is not an excluded image (s 64(3)(b)). For example, if a classified film contained a scene of sexual violence within the narrative, the recording of that scene alone may take it out of the s 64 exemption. 4.38

---

[22] Video Recordings Act 1984, s 1(2).
[23] See para **4.34** above.

4.39   If non-sexual scenes either side are also recorded this will not necessarily mean that it is an 'excluded image'. The court will have to consider whether the scenes either side provide a context for the scene in question. The same questions that must be asked in relation to s 63(5)[24] also apply here and therefore the court will need to decide whether all the scenes which have been recorded provide a narrative.

4.40   Although badly drafted, the purpose of s 64 is clear. Possession of a BBFC certified film which happens to contain a violent sexual scene is not covered by the CJIA 2008. This will ordinarily be a preliminary issue of law decided by the judge or magistrate. If a violent, sexual scene is the only or predominant part of a BBFC certified film that has been recorded, it will be a matter for the jury to decide 'Why has only that part been recorded?' If it is for the purposes of sexual arousal it may be found to be 'extreme pornography'.

4. Defences

4.41   There are two types of defences to a charge under the CJIA 2008, s 63, both of which place the legal burden on the defendant[25] to be proven to the civil standard. The first type is general defences which mirror those for the possession of child pornography.[26] The second is that the defendant participated in the acts and any harm was consensual.

(a) General defences

4.42   Firstly, it is a defence to prove that the person had a legitimate reason for being in possession of the image concerned (s 65(2)(a)). In relation to Internet Service Providers which may come into possession of such material, special rules are provided by virtue of the CJIA 2008, s 68 and Sch 14. As far as other legitimate reasons are concerned, each case is to be judged on its own facts. In relation to the offence of publishing obscene articles under s 2 of the OPA 1959, it is a defence to prove that the publication is justified in the interests of art or literature, and therefore 'legitimate reason' should also cover possessing meritorious artwork. The OPA 1959 specifically provides that experts may be called to give evidence as to the merits of an article. Whilst there is no corresponding provision for experts in the CJIA 2008 it is likely that such evidence would be admissible.

4.43   Secondly, it is a defence to prove that the person had not seen the image concerned and did not know, nor had any cause to suspect it to be an extreme pornographic image (s 65(2)(b)).

4.44   Thirdly, it is a defence to prove that the person was sent the image concerned without any prior request having been made by or on behalf of the person, and did not keep it for an unreasonable time (s 65(2)(c)).

---

[24] See para 4.16 above.
[25] As with indecent images of children. See *Collier* [2005] WLR 843, CA.
[26] Criminal Justice Act 1988, s 160(2).

(b) *Participation in consensual acts*

Firstly, the defendant must prove to the civil standard that he 'directly participated'   4.45
in the act or any of the acts portrayed (s 66 (2)(a)). Clearly the defendant will have to
be confident that he is able to prove the remainder of this defence before admitting
that he was involved. It is not clear what 'direct participation' involves. If a person
carrying out the act in question is able to avail themselves of a defence under this
section, namely that the act depicted was not illegal and he was entitled to be in
possession of such images, it would be unfair if the cameraman or director were
unable to avail themselves of the same defence.

Secondly, the defendant must prove that the act or acts did not involve the infliction   4.46
of any non-consensual harm on any person (s 66(2)(b)). Non-consensual harm
includes both harm to which a person does not consent and harm to which a person
cannot consent in law (s 66(3)).

Therefore, if the image appears to show grievous bodily harm being inflicted, it   4.47
will not be a defence simply to prove that in fact only actual bodily harm was caused as
a person cannot consent to either type of harm unless it is within one of the exceptions
recognized in the case law.

The recognized exceptions will provide a defence in the case of pornographic   4.48
images of a defendant taking part in 'properly conducted lawful games and sports,
lawful chastisement, reasonable surgical interference, dangerous exhibitions etc.',[27]
'rough and undisciplined horseplay' if there was no intent to injure,[28] and amateur
tattooing.[29] The infliction of harm for the purpose of satisfying sado-masochistic
desires does not constitute a good reason for inflicting harm.[30]

In relation to an image depicting sexual interference with a human corpse, it is   4.49
a defence to prove that what is portrayed as a human corpse was not in fact a corpse
(s 66(2)(c)). Again, if the harm caused by such images is the effect on the offender's
imagination, it is not clear why realistic depictions should not be covered simply
because a corpse was not in fact involved. The defence does not apply to images
of bestiality, even if it is shown that what appeared to be an animal was in fact not
(s 66(1)(b)).

5. Penalties

For offences under the CJIA 2008, s 63(7)(a) or (b) the maximum penalty is 3 years   4.50
imprisonment (s 67(2)). Anyone aged 18 or over at the time of the offence, who
receives a sentence of over two years imprisonment will be subject to the notification
requirements under Part 2 of the Sexual Offences Act 2003.[31]

For images depicting necrophilia or bestiality the maximum penalty is 2 years   4.51
imprisonment (s 67(3)). This is on the basis that the corresponding offences under
ss 69 and 70 of the Sexual Offences Act 2003 only carry a maximum of 2 years
imprisonment. For the sake of proportionality the CJIA 2008, s 71 increases the

---

[27] Attorney-General's Reference (No 6 of 1980) [1981] QB 715, 719 CA.
[28] *R v Jones (T)* (1986) 83 Cr App R 375, CA; *R v Aitken* [1992] 1 WLR 1006, Ct MAC.
[29] *R v Wilson (A)* [1997] QB 47, CA.
[30] *R v Brown (A)* [1994] 1 AC 212, HL.
[31] Sexual Offences Act 2003, Sch 3, paras 35A and 92A, inserted by CJIA 2008, Sch 26, para 58.

maximum penalty for publication of an obscene article under the OPA 1959, s 2 to five years, for offences taking place after 26 January 2009.[32]

C. INDECENT IMAGES OF CHILDREN

1. Introduction

4.52 The CJIA 2008, Part 5, s 69 extends the definition of a 'photograph' when dealing with offences involving indecent images of children. The amendment follows a separate Home Office consultation.[33] This was as a result of reports by police and children's welfare groups that interest in images of child abuse contained in computer generated images, drawings and animation was increasing. However, although there was particular concern about indecent drawings or animations of children on the basis that cartoons and fantasy images could be used in 'grooming' children for sexual abuse, these images are not covered by the extended offence.

4.53　The amendments relating to child pornography extend to England, Wales, and Northern Ireland and came into force on 8 July 2008.[34] They do not apply to anything done before that date.[35]

4.54　Section 69(2) extends to members of the Secret Intelligence Service, the immunity from prosecution if it was necessary to make an indecent photograph or pseudo-photograph of a child in the exercise of the Service's functions.

2. Definition of 'photograph'

4.55 The CJIA 2008, s 69 amends the Protection of Children Act 1978 to extend the definition of photograph by inserting a new s 7(4A) into that Act so as to include:

(a) a tracing or other image, whether made by electronic or other means (of whatever nature) which is not itself a photograph or pseudo-photograph, but which is derived from the whole or part of a photograph or pseudo-photograph (or a combination of either or both); and

(b) data stored on a computer disc or by other electronic means which is capable of conversion into an image within paragraph (a).

Section 70 makes equivalent provisions in relation to Northern Ireland.

4.56　This will mean that the offences under the Protection of Children Act 1978, s 1 and the Criminal Justice Act 1988, s 160 will include pencil-traced images and computer-traced images of photographs taken on mobile phones.

4.57　The CJIA 2008, s 69(4) amends a drafting error in the Protection of Children Act 1978 so that s 7(9) of that Act now provides that references to an indecent

---

[32] CJIA 2008, Sch 27, para 25. CJIA 2008 (Commencement No 4 and Saving Provision) Order 2008, SI 2008/2993.

[33] 'Consultation on possession of non-photographic visual depictions of child sex abuse', Home Office, April 2007.

[34] CJIA 2008, s 153.

[35] CJIA 2008 s 153 and Sch 27, para 24.

pseudo-photograph include data which is capable of conversion into an indecent pseudo-photograph. Whether this had ever caused any difficulty in practice is not clear.

D. CHILD SEX OFFENCES

1. Introduction

The CJIA 2008, Part 5, ss 72–73 and Sch 15 were introduced to the Bill as government amendments at the Committee Stage. Section 72 was introduced in order to fulfil the UK's obligations under the Council of Europe Convention on the Protection of Children against Sexual Exploitation and Sexual Abuse.   4.58

The provisions relating to child sex offences committed outside the UK and grooming came into force on 14 July 2008.[36] The provisions relating to sexual offences involving adopted children came into force on 8 July 2008.[37]   4.59

2. Sexual offences committed overseas

The extended jurisdiction will vary depending upon the status of the offender. The main change introduced by s 72 is to amend s 72 of the Sexual Offences Act 2003 so that, in relation to UK nationals committing sexual offences against children outside the UK, there is no longer a requirement that the act in question must also be criminal in the country in which it is committed before it can be prosecuted in the UK.   4.60

(a) *Conditions*
The three conditions which may apply, depending on the status of the offender in question, are that: 4.61

  (i) a person does an act in a country (which also includes territory) outside the United Kingdom;
 (ii) the act constitutes an offence under the law in force in that country;
(iii) the act if done in England and Wales or Northern Ireland, would constitute a sexual offence to which Sch 2 to the Sexual Offences Act 2003 applies.

In relation to the second condition, an offence under the law in force in a particular country applies to an act punishable under the law in force in that country, however it is described in that law. If the proposed defendant believes that this condition is not met he must serve on the prosecution a notice informing them of his opinion, the grounds for that opinion and informing them that they are required to prove that it is met.   4.62

Rules of court may provide for a time limit for such a notice and the court may waive the requirement if it thinks fit. In the Crown Court the question whether the condition is met is to be decided by the judge alone (Sexual Offences Act 2003, s 72(6)–(8), as amended by the CJIA 2008, s 72(1)).   4.63

---

[36] CJIA (Commencement No 2 and Transitional and Saving Provisions) Order 2008, SI 2008/1586.
[37] CJIA 2008, s 153.

4.64   In relation to the third condition, the scope of the Sexual Offences Act 2003, Sch 2 is extended so that in relation to England and Wales it now applies to the following offences under the Sexual Offences Act 2003:

  (i) ss 1–4 (rape, assault by penetration, sexual assault and causing a person to engage in sexual activity without consent) if the victim was under 18 at the time;
  (ii) ss 5–8 (sexual offences against children under 13);
  (iii) ss 9–15 (child sex offences);
  (iv) ss 16–19 (abuse of a position of trust);
  (v) ss 25–26 (familial child sex offences);
  (vi) ss 30–33 (offences against persons with a mental disorder impeding choice) if the victim was under 18 at the time;
  (vii) ss 34–37 (inducements etc. to persons with a mental disorder) if the victim was under 18 at the time;
  (viii) ss 38–41 (offences by care workers for persons with a mental disorder) if the victim was under 18 at the time;
  (ix) ss 47–50 (abuse of children through prostitution and pornography);
  (x) ss 61–63 (preparatory offences) where the victim of the offence or the intended offence was under 18 at the time.

4.65   Schedule 2 to the Sexual Offences Act 2003 (as amended) also includes offences under the Protection of Children Act 1978, s 1 and the Criminal Justice Act 1988, s 160 (indecent images) where the image relates to a person under the age of 18[38] and includes attempts and conspiracies, inciting, aiding, abetting, counselling or procuring such offences. The schedule of offences as it applies to Northern Ireland is also amended.

(b) *Offences*

4.66   The new s 72(1) applies to UK nationals. This means a British citizen, a British overseas territories citizen, a British National (Overseas) or a British Overseas citizen or a person who is a British subject or a British protected person under the British Nationality Act 1981.[39] If such a person fulfils conditions (i) and (iii) (see para **4.61** above) that person is thereby guilty in the relevant part of the United Kingdom of that sexual offence.

4.67   The new s 72(2) applies to UK residents, which simply means someone who is resident in the United Kingdom. If that person fulfils conditions (i), (ii), and (iii), he is thereby guilty in the relevant part of the United Kingdom of that sexual offence.

4.68   The new s 72(3) applies to a person who was not a UK national or UK resident at the time condition (i) was fulfilled but is a UK national or resident when proceedings are brought. If such a person also satisfies conditions (ii) and (iii) then proceedings

---

[38] The words 'in relation to a photograph or pseudo-photograph showing a child under 16' are removed by CJIA 2008, Sch 28 and therefore the sections within the Acts which define a child as a person under the age of 18 apply.
[39] Sexual Offences Act 2003, s 72(9), as amended by the CJIA 2008, s 72(1)).

may be brought against that person in the relevant part of the United Kingdom for that sexual offence as if the person had done the act there.

3. Grooming

Section 73 introduces the CJIA 2008, Sch 15. Schedule 15, para 1 amends the   4.69
Sexual Offences Act 2003, s 15 which deals with meeting a child following sexual grooming. Under the original section it is an offence if:

(a) the offender (over the age of 18) has met or communicated on at least two earlier occasions with a child (under the age of 16);
(b) the offender intentionally meets or travels with the intention of meeting the child; and
(c) at the time the offender intends to commit a relevant offence in respect of the child during or after the meeting.

The amendments mean that it will also be an offence if, with (a) and (c) fulfilled,   4.70
the offender simply arranges to meet the child or if the child travels with the intention of meeting the offender.

4. Sexual offences involving adopted children

The Adoption and Children Act 2002, s 67 provides that when a child is adopted   4.71
he becomes legally the child of his adopted parents. The Sexual Offences Act 2003, s 27 states that for the purposes of familial sex offences a relationship is prohibited if it is one of those listed (parent and child, brother and sister etc) or it would be one of those listed if it were not for s 67. Therefore a relationship between the natural parent and their child is still prohibited even if the child has been adopted and is therefore otherwise treated in law as someone else's child. The Sexual Offences Act 2003, s 29 provides that if a lawful sexual relationship exists between a person adopted under the Adoption and Children Act 2002 and a member of their adopted family, no offence is committed if the sexual relationship predates the adoption.

The Adoption and Children Act 2002 only applies to adoptions which took place   4.72
after 30 December 2005. The CJIA 2008, Sch 15, paras 2–4 amend ss 27 and 29 so that they also apply to adoptions which took place prior to 30 December 2005 under the Adoption Act 1976.

Schedule 15, paras 5 and 6 amend the provisions of the Sexual Offences Act 2003   4.73
which deal with sex with an adult relative. The prohibited sexual relationships are amended to include adoptive parent and child. Whereas a person will ordinarily only be committing an offence by penetrating, or consenting to be penetrated by, a member of their family if they are aged 16 or over, an adopted child will only commit an offence by penetrating, or consenting to be penetrated by, their adopted parent if they are aged 18 or over.

Further provisions ensure that the sections of the Adoption Act 1976 and the   4.74
Adoption and Children Act 2002, which ordinarily provide that for the purposes of offences of familial sex and sex with an adult relative, an adopted child is not to be treated in law as the child of its adopted parents, do not prevent the application of the above sections.

E. HATRED ON THE GROUNDS OF SEXUAL ORIENTATION

1. Introduction

4.75 The CJIA 2008, Part 5, s 74 and Sch 16 extend the public order provisions relating to inciting religious hatred to include inciting hatred on the grounds of sexual orientation. These provisions were introduced by a new clause at the Committee stage, having been announced at the Second Reading of the Bill.[40]

4.76 The impetus for reform came in part from the organization Stonewall, which works for 'equality and justice for lesbians, gay men and bisexuals'[41] and in particular their campaign against certain reggae artists whose lyrics were said to be calling for violence against homosexuals. The Chief Executive of Stonewall gave evidence to the Committee[42] reporting a 167 per cent increase in convictions for offences involving a homophobic element, although this was disputed by other organizations. Views were invited as to whether the provisions should be extended to include hatred of transgender or disabled persons[43] but due to a lack of evidence of any organizations deliberately stirring up hatred towards these groups, no such proposals are included in the CJIA 2008.

4.77 Broadly the principle behind the proposal was welcomed, although some groups felt that the offending behaviour in question could already be covered by existing legislation, in particular the use of threatening words and behaviour under the Public Order Act 1986, s 5 or the offence of harassment under the Protection from Harassment Act 1997.

4.78 Much of the behaviour intended to be dealt with by the new offences will be covered by the offences of assisting or encouraging offences in the Serious Crime Act 2007 when the relevant sections come into force. Section 146 of the Criminal Justice Act 2003 provides that the court is obliged to treat any hostility on the grounds of sexual orientation as an aggravating factor in sentencing.

4.79 Concerns were raised about whether some religious discourse would fall foul of any such legislation and whether people could 'unintentionally stumble' into committing an offence by telling a joke, hence the limitation to threatening behaviour intended to stir up hatred and the introduction of a provision specifically outlining the right to freedom of expression.

4.80 Similar legislation has been in force in Northern Ireland since 2004[44] although during the Committee stage the government was not aware of any prosecutions having been brought under this legislation.[45]

4.81 The provisions of the Act creating the offence of hatred on the grounds of sexual orientation extend to England and Wales and are not in force at the time of writing.

---

[40] HC Deb 8 October 2007 vol 464 c66.
[41] <http://www.stonewall.org.uk>.
[42] PBC Deb 16 October 2007 c74.
[43] HC Deb 8 October 2007 vol 464 c68.
[44] Criminal Justice (No 2) (Northern Ireland) Order 2004.
[45] PBC Deb 29 November 2007 c666.

However, the provisions protecting freedom of expression in relation to sexual orientation came into force on 8 May 2008.[46]

2. Incitement to hatred on the grounds of sexual orientation

The amendments are contained wholly within the CJIA 2008, Sch 16 which amends the Public Order Act (POA) 1986, Part 3A, ss 29A to N.   4.82

Part 3A of the POA 1986[47] previously only dealt with acts intended to stir up religious hatred. The acts covered are the use of words or behaviour, the display of written material, publishing or distributing written material, public performance of a play, distributing, showing or playing a recording, broadcasting, including a programme in a programme service, and possession of inflammatory material. Schedule 16 makes it an offence if these acts are done to stir up hatred on the grounds of sexual orientation.   4.83

As with the offences relating to religious hatred, and in contrast to the similar offences of racial hatred in the POA 1986, the offences can only be committed with the intention to stir up hatred on the grounds of sexual orientation and not simply because they are likely to stir up such hatred. Similarly, although abusive or insulting words and behaviour are sufficient for racial hatred, they are not sufficient under the amended POA 1986, s 29B. The words and behaviour must be threatening.   4.84

Hatred on the grounds of sexual orientation is defined as meaning hatred against a group of persons who are defined by reference to sexual orientation (whether towards persons of the same sex, the opposite sex or both).[48] The Act will therefore cover offences against people on the basis that they are homosexual, heterosexual or bisexual. In the debate relating to extreme pornography, the pressure group 'Backlash' described sado-masochism as an 'orientation' and it may be argued that other sexual preferences could be covered. However, the words in parentheses appear to be exhaustive rather than explanatory and therefore the Act would seem to be limited only to those orientations set out.   4.85

3. Freedom of expression

The Public Order Act 1986, s 29JA[49] specifically provides that 'for the avoidance of doubt' freedom of expression is protected. It states that the discussion or criticism of sexual conduct or practices or the urging of persons to refrain from or modify such conduct or practices shall not be taken, of itself, to be threatening or intended to stir up hatred. It is not intended to change the threshold of conduct required for the offences to be made out.[50]   4.86

By comparison, the corresponding provision relating to incitement of religious hatred protects freedom of expression not only in relation to discussion or criticism of particular religions but also expressions of antipathy, dislike, ridicule, insult or   4.87

---

[46] CJIA 2008, s 153.
[47] Inserted by the Schedule to the Racial and Religious Hatred Act 2006.
[48] CJIA 2008, Sch 16, para 4.
[49] Inserted by CJIA 2008, Sch 16, para 14.
[50] Explanatory Notes, para 501.

abuse of religion.[51] It would seem that this clause adds little but confusion for the courts and is a sop to religious groups who campaigned against the new provisions.

4. Exceptions, procedure, and penalties

4.88   The amended POA 1986, Part 3A does not apply to fair and accurate reports of anything done in the United Kingdom Parliament, Scottish Parliament and National Assembly for Wales or fair, accurate and contemporaneous reports of judicial proceedings.[52] Proceedings may only be instigated with the consent of the Attorney General.[53]

4.89   The maximum punishment is 7 years imprisonment on indictment. Any person committing an offence under the amended s 3A whilst at or travelling to a football match may be made subject to a banning order under the Football Spectators Act 1989.[54]

F. OFFENCES RELATING TO NUCLEAR MATERIALS AND FACILITIES

1. Introduction

4.90   The CJIA 2008, Part 5, s 75 introduces new offences relating to nuclear material and facilities to enable the UK to ratify a number of changes to the Convention on the Physical Protection of Nuclear Material (CPPNM). The original Convention was signed by the UK in 1980 and ratified in 1991. In July 2005, the International Atomic Energy Agency Diplomatic Conference in Vienna approved amendments to the Convention. In part the amendment was borne out of concerns relating to the protection of nuclear materials and the amended Preamble suggests that the States involved were concerned by, amongst other things, the worldwide escalation of acts of terrorism, the threat posed by organized crime and the dangers posed by illicit trafficking of nuclear material.

4.91   Section 75 gives effect to Sch 17 which sets out a number of amendments to be made to the Nuclear Material (Offences) Act (NM(O)A) 1983.

4.92   In the same way that the original Act only applied to nuclear material used for peaceful purposes, nuclear facilities are defined as only those used for peaceful purposes. Nothing in the NM(O)A 1983 applies to the proper activities of the armed forces.

4.93   The provisions of the CJIA 2008 dealing with offences relating to nuclear material extend to England, Wales, Scotland and Northern Ireland and are not in force at the time of writing. The sections provide universal jurisdiction, regardless of where the offences are committed or who they are committed by or against. The Government has indicated that, in relation to acts committed overseas, it would wait to see

---

[51] POA 1986, s 29J.
[52] POA 1986, s 29K.
[53] POA 1986, s 29L(1).
[54] Part II and Sch 1 as amended by the CJIA 2008, Sch 26, para 26.

whether there was a prosecution in the jurisdiction where the offence took place, before commencing one here.[55]

2. Attacks and thefts relating to nuclear material

The Nuclear Material (Offences) Act 1983 (as amended) distinguishes between two   4.94
types of offences. Firstly there are what may be termed 'physical offences': murder, manslaughter, culpable homicide, assault to injury, malicious mischief or causing injury, or endangering the life of the lieges, by reckless conduct and offences contrary to ss 18 or 20 of the Offences Against the Person Act 1861, s 1 of the Criminal Damage Act 1971, Article 3 of the Criminal Damage (Northern Ireland) Order 1977, and s 52 of the Criminal Law (Consolidation) Scotland Act 1995.[56]

Secondly, there are what may be termed 'dishonesty offences': theft, embezzlement,   4.95
robbery, assault with intent to rob, burglary, aggravated burglary, fraud, extortion, and offences pursuant to ss 15 or 21 of the Theft Act 1968 and ss 15 or 20 of the Theft Act (Northern Ireland) 1969.[57]

(a) *Offences*
Section 1(1) of the Nuclear Material (Offences) Act (NM(O)A) 1983 provides that   4.96
if a person of any nationality does an act outside the United Kingdom which is:

(i) an act 'in relation to or by means of nuclear material'; and
(ii) had he done that act in the UK, it would make him guilty of one of the physical offences or one of the dishonesty offences,

then he will be guilty of such an offence in the United Kingdom.

The new NM(O)A) 1983, s 1(1A)[58] provides that if such a person of any nationality   4.97
does an act outside the United Kingdom which is:

(i) directed at a nuclear facility or which interferes with the operation of a nuclear facility; and
(ii) the act causes death, injury or damage resulting from the emission of ionizing radiation or the release of radioactive material; and
(iii) had he done that act in the United Kingdom it would make him guilty of one of the physical offences,

then he will be guilty of such an offence in the United Kingdom.

The new section broadens the scope of the Act so as to include not simply direct   4.98
attacks on nuclear material but also attacks on the facilities in which they are housed which may have the same effect. For example, interfering with the computer systems of a nuclear power plant may not be an act 'in relation to' nuclear material but will be an act directed at a nuclear facility or which interferes with the operation of a nuclear facility.

---

[55] PBC Deb 27 November 2007 c577.
[56] NM(O)A 1983, s 1(1)(a)(b) as amended by CJIA 2008, Sch 17, s 2(1)(2).
[57] NM(O)A 1983, s 1(1)(c)(d).
[58] Inserted by CJIA 2008, Sch 17, para 2(3).

4.99   'Act' is no longer defined so as to include omission.[59] Therefore, should a company negligently fail to repair or properly maintain a nuclear power station thereby causing injury, it may evade criminal liability.

(b) *Penalty*

4.100   The new NM(O)A) 1983, s 1A[60] provides that if someone is convicted of one of the physical or dishonesty offences which was 'done in relation to or by means of nuclear material' or if they are convicted of one of the physical offences whereby they 'caused death, injury or damage resulting from the emission of ionizing radiation or the release of radioactive material' and the act took place in England, Wales or Northern Ireland the maximum penalty is life imprisonment.

4.101   Although the maximum penalty for most of the offences relevant to this section is already life imprisonment, it is not for all and this amendment was made to implement the CPPNM requirement that relevant offences should be punishable by penalties severe enough to reflect the grave nature of the offences. The offences under Scottish law which are likely to be used to prosecute such acts already carry a maximum punishment of life imprisonment and so no amendment is necessary.

4.102   For offences committed outside England, Wales or Northern Ireland which are dealt with in those jurisdictions under NM(O)A 1983, ss 1(1) or 1(1A) the maximum penalty is life imprisonment.

3. Damage to environment caused by nuclear material

4.103   The new NM(O)A 1983 s 1B[61] applies to offences committed by anyone, both in the United Kingdom and elsewhere in the world. 'The environment' includes land, air and water and living organisms supported by any of those media.[62]

(a) *Offences*

4.104   A person commits an offence if, without lawful authority, he receives, holds or deals with nuclear material, and does so either:

(i) intending to cause, or for the purpose of enabling another to cause, damage to the environment by means of that material; or

(ii) being reckless as to whether, as a result of his so receiving, holding or dealing with that material, damage would be caused to the environment by means of that material.[63]

4.105   A person commits an offence if, without lawful authority, he does an act directed at a nuclear facility, or which interferes with the operation of such a facility, and does so either:

(i) intending to cause, or for the purpose of enabling another to cause, damage to the environment by means of the emission of ionizing radiation or the release of radioactive material, or

---

[59] CJIA 2008, Sch 17, Sch 28, para 2(4).
[60] Inserted by CJIA 2008, Sch 17, para 3.
[61] Ibid.
[62] NM(O)A 1983, s 6(6), as inserted by CJIA 2008, Sch 17, para 6(6).
[63] NM(O)A 1983, s 1B(2), as inserted by CJIA 2008, Sch 17, para 3.

(ii) being reckless as to whether, as a result of his act, damage would be caused to the environment by means of such an emission or release.[64]

As well as extending the scope of the NM(O)A 1983 in order to deal with offences against nuclear facilities under s 1B(3), both offences in this section extend the heads of damage to cover offences affecting the environment. Damage to the environment caused by ionizing radiation is likely to lead to injury to people in the long term, however it may be difficult to prove the necessary causation as the effects may not be noticed for several years. These sections therefore circumvent this difficulty. The offence goes further than required by the CPPNM as the latter requires that the intended or foreseen damage to the environment is 'serious'. 4.106

(b) *Penalty*
The offences are indictable only and the maximum penalty for either is imprisonment for life.[65] 4.107

4. Importing or exporting nuclear material

The new NM(O)A 1983, s 1C[66] applies to offences committed by anyone, which take place outside the United Kingdom. 4.108

(a) *Offences*
A person commits an offence if he is knowingly concerned in the unlawful export, import or shipment as stores of nuclear material from one country (including a territory) to another. The export, import or shipment will be unlawful if it is contrary to any prohibition or restriction having effect under or by virtue of the law of that country.[67] The unlawfulness can be evidenced by a statement in a certificate to that effect, issued by or on behalf of the government of the relevant country outside the United Kingdom to the effect.[68] 4.109

The new CJIA 2008, s 1D extends the powers of Her Majesty's Revenue and Customs under the Customs and Excise Management Act 1979 relating to investigation, arrest and procedure to offences under s 1C. 4.110

(b) *Penalty*
The maximum penalty is 14 years imprisonment. Part 2 of Sch 17 amends the Customs and Excise Management Act 1979 so that the same penalty applies to offences of importation, exportation and fraudulent evasion of duty under that Act when done in relation to nuclear material.[69] Whilst severe in itself, it is questionable whether this satisfies the Convention obligation that the offences be punishable by 4.111

---

[64] NM(O)A 1983, s 1B(3), as inserted by CJIA 2008, Sch 17, para 3.
[65] NM(O)A 1983, s 1B(4), as inserted by CJIA 2008, Sch 17 para 3.
[66] Inserted by CJIA 2008, Sch 17, para 3.
[67] NM(O)A 1983, s 1C(3) inserted by CJIA 2008, Sch 17, para 3.
[68] NM(O)A 1983, s 1C(4) inserted by CJIA 2008, Sch 17, para 3.
[69] Customs and Excise Management Act 1979, s 50(4) and (5C), s 68(3) and (4B), 170(3), and (4C), as amended by CJIA 2008, Sch 17, para 8.

penalties that are severe enough to reflect the grave nature of the offences[70] given that all other offences are punishable with life imprisonment and 14 years is the same maximum penalty as is available for importing a Class B drug and is less serious than the penalty for importing a Class A drug, which is life imprisonment.

5. Preparatory acts and threats

4.112 The substituted NM(O)A 1983, s 2[71] applies to a person, whatever his nationality, in the UK or elsewhere but does not apply to anything done before Sch 17 comes into force.[72]

(a) *Offences*

4.113 A person commits an offence if, without lawful authority, he receives, holds or deals with nuclear material or does an act directed at, or which interferes with the operation of a nuclear facility. The act must be done intending, being reckless or with the purpose of enabling another, to cause the type of injury or damage which would be sufficient for one of the physical offences. Where the act is directed at a nuclear facility or interferes with the operation of such a facility the injury or damage must be caused by the emission of ionizing radiation or the release of radioactive material.[73]

4.114 A person also commits an offence[74] if he threatens:

(i) either to cause damage to the environment or to cause the type of injury or damage which would be sufficient for one of the physical offences;
(ii) by means of nuclear material, or by means of the emission of ionizing radiation or the release of radioactive material resulting from an act which is directed at a nuclear facility, or which interferes with the operation of such a facility; and
(iii) he intends that the person to whom the threat is made shall fear that it will be carried out.

4.115 A person commits an offence if he attempts to blackmail a State, international organization or person by threatening to steal nuclear material.[75]

(b) *Penalty*

4.116 The maximum penalty for any of these offences is imprisonment for life.[76]

6. Jurisdiction and inchoate and secondary offences

4.117 The new NM(O)A 1983, s 2A[77] extends to anyone outside the UK the jurisdiction for attempting, conspiring, inciting, aiding, abetting, counselling or procuring the

---

[70] Explanatory Notes, para 514.
[71] Inserted by CJIA 2008, Sch 17, para 4.
[72] CJIA 2008, Sch 27, para 26.
[73] NM(O)A 1983, s 2(2) and (3), as substituted by CJIA 2008, Sch 17, para 4.
[74] NM(O)A 1983, s 2(4)–(6), as substituted by CJIA 2008, Sch 17, para 4.
[75] NM(O)A 1983, s 2(7), as substituted by CJIA 2008, Sch 17, para 4.
[76] NM(O)A 1983, s 2(8), as substituted by CJIA 2008, Sch 17, para 4.
[77] Inserted by CJIA 2008, Sch 17, para 4.

above offences, other than attempting to threaten or blackmail. Incitement refers to the common law offence of incitement in Scotland and, until Part 2 of the Serious Crime Act 2007 comes into force, the common law offence in England, Wales or Northern Ireland.

G. DATA PROTECTION OFFENCES

1. Introduction

The power to increase the penalty for unlawfully obtaining or disclosing personal data was introduced by the CJIA 2008, Part 5, s 77 following a report by the Information Commissioner's Office calling for such an increase.[78] The Department for Constitutional Affairs subsequently published a Consultation Paper[79] on the proposals. After concerns were raised about the prospect of journalists having to show that a *prima facie* breach was justified in the public interest in order to avoid custody, the CJIA 2008, s 78 was introduced to allay such fears. The 'reasonable belief' defence in this section mirrors the defence in the Data Protection Act 1998, s 32 relating to civil proceedings.   4.118

The CJIA 2008, ss 77, 78, and 144 apply to England, Wales, Scotland and Northern Ireland. Section 77 which gives the Secretary of State the power to increase the penalty for data protection offences came into force on the 8 May 2008.[80] The power has not yet been exercised. Section 78 which provides a defence for journalists, is not in force at the time of writing and the defence will not apply to offences committed before the commencement of s 78.[81] Section 144 is not in force at the time of writing.   4.119

2. Unlawfully obtaining etc personal data

Unlawfully obtaining personal data is an offence under the Data Protection Act 1998, s 55(1), which provides that: 4.120

A person must not knowingly or recklessly, without the consent of the data controller—

(a) obtain or disclose personal data or the information contained in personal data, or

(b) procure the disclosure to another person of the information contained in personal data.

There are then created separate offences of contravening s 55(1), and selling or offering to sell personal data obtained in contravention of s 55(1). The original penalty was an unlimited fine.

Section 77 of the CJIA 2008 confers on the Secretary of State the power to alter the penalty for unlawfully obtaining etc personal data up to a maximum of 2 years   4.121

---

[78] 'What price privacy? The unlawful trade in confidential personal information', Information Commissioner's Office, May 2006.

[79] 'Increasing penalties for deliberate and wilful misuse of personal data', Department for Constitutional Affairs, July 2006.

[80] CJIA 2008, s 153.

[81] CJIA 2008, Sch 27, para 28.

imprisonment on indictment. Before doing so he must consult the Information Commissioner and such media organizations and other persons as he considers appropriate (s 77 (4)).

3. Defence for the purposes of journalism, etc

4.122   The previous defences in the Data Protection Act 1998[82] were that it was for the defendant to show that:

(a) the obtaining, disclosing or procuring was either necessary for the purpose of preventing or detecting crime, or was required or authorized by or under any enactment, by any rule of law or by the order of a court; or

(b) that he acted in the reasonable belief that he had in law the right to obtain or disclose the data or information or, as the case may be, to procure the disclosure of the information to the other person; or

(c) that he acted in the reasonable belief that he would have had the consent of the data controller if the data controller had known of the obtaining, disclosing or procuring and the circumstances of it; or

(d) that in the particular circumstances the obtaining, disclosing or procuring was justified as being in the public interest.

4.123   Section 78 of the CJIA 2008 creates a new defence. The defendant must prove that:

(i)   he acted for the 'special purposes' (these are defined in the Data Protection Act 1998, s 3 as the purposes of journalism, artistic purposes, and literary purposes), and

(ii) he acted with a view to the publication by any person of any journalistic, literary or artistic material, and

(iii) in the reasonable belief that in the particular circumstances the obtaining, disclosing or procuring was justified as being in the public interest.

4. Power to require data controllers to pay monetary penalty

4.124   The CJIA 2008, s144 inserts new ss 55A to E into the Data Protection Act 1998.

4.125   The new s 55A provides that the Information Commissioner may serve a data controller (other than the Crown Estate Commissioners or those controlling data for the Royal household, the Duchy of Lancaster or the Duchy of Cornwall) with a monetary penalty notice if he is satisfied that:

(a) there has been a serious contravention of their duty to comply with data protection principles in relation to personal data;

(b) the contravention was of a kind likely to cause substantial damage or substantial distress;

(c) the contravention was either deliberate or the data controller knew (or ought to have known) that there was a risk that the contravention would occur, and that such a contravention would be of a kind likely to cause substantial damage

---

[82] CJIA 2008, s 55(2).

or substantial distress, but failed to take reasonable steps to prevent the contravention.

The data protection principles are set out in the Data Protection Act 1998, Chapter 1, 4.126 Part I. Guidance on their application is provided in Sch 1, Part II and Sch 2 to 4 but, as they are principles and not rules, a great deal is left to the judgment of the data controller. It is hoped therefore that the guidance which may be issued by the Information Commissioner under the new s 55C will provide that monetary penalty notices will only be issued where it is clear there has been a breach.

Before serving a monetary penalty notice, the Commissioner must serve the data 4.127 controller with a notice of intent, informing him that the Information Commissioner proposes to serve a monetary penalty notice and informing the data controller that he may make written representations within a specified period.[83] Once the specified period has expired the Information Commissioner may serve a monetary penalty notice.

A monetary penalty notice is a notice requiring the data controller to pay to the 4.128 Information Commissioner a monetary penalty of a specified amount, determined by the Commissioner, not exceeding an amount to be prescribed, within a specified period.[84] The person on whom the monetary penalty notice is served may appeal to the Data Protection Tribunal against the issue of the notice or the amount of the specified penalty.[85] The penalty may be recovered in England, Wales, and Northern Ireland as payable under an order of the County or High Court and in Scotland as an extract registered decree arbitral bearing a warrant for execution issued by the sheriff court of any sheriffdom in Scotland.[86]

H. NUISANCE OR DISTURBANCE ON NHS PREMISES

1. Introduction

The CJIA 2008, Part 8, s 119 introduces a new offence of nuisance or disturbance 4.129 on NHS premises. The problem of violence on NHS premises was raised in a Consultation Paper published by the Department of Health in June 2006.[87] The paper stated that 20 per cent of staff felt that the NHS did not provide them with a safe working environment and that violence against staff cost the NHS between £10m and 270m per annum. It argued that measures were needed to pre-empt violence occurring on NHS premises and to allow offenders to be removed if they were causing a disturbance.

In response, concerns were raised by mental health charities as to the potential 4.130 impact on those suffering from mental health problems or otherwise with behavioural difficulties. Others highlighted the need to address the reasons for such behaviour rather than to criminalize individuals. Another issue highlighted was whether the

---

[83] Data Protection Act 1998, s 55B(1)–(3), as inserted by CJIA 2008, s 144.
[84] Data Protection Act 1998, s 55A(4), as inserted by CJIA 2008, s 144.
[85] Data Protection Act 1998, s 55B(4), as inserted by CJIA 2008, s 144.
[86] Data Protection Act 1998, s 55D(2)–(4), as inserted by CJIA 2008, s 144.
[87] 'Tackling nuisance or disturbance behaviour on NHS healthcare premises: A paper for consultation', June 2006.

offence should only apply to hospitals or should be more widely defined. The proposals were not extended to GP's surgeries and other places where NHS staff were employed due to a concern about lack of suitable staff.

4.131　　The new offence is modelled on the Education Act 1996, s 547, which creates an offence of causing or permitting a nuisance whilst on school premises. There is little data on how effective this offence has been.

4.132　　The provisions relating to the offence of creating a nuisance on NHS premises will come into force on a day appointed by the Secretary of State in relation to England, the Welsh Ministers in relation to Wales.[88] The corresponding provisions relating to Northern Ireland in s 122 and Sch 21 will come into force on a day appointed by the Department of Health, Social Services and Public Order.[89] None are in force at the time of writing.

2. Causing a nuisance or disturbance on NHS premises

4.133　　The CJIA 2008, s 119 creates the new offence of causing a nuisance or disturbance on NHS premises in England or Wales.

4.134　　The offence only relates to relevant NHS bodies which are defined as:

- a National Health Service trust, all or most of whose hospitals, establishments and facilities are situated in either England or Wales; or
- in England, a Primary Care Trust or an NHS foundation trust;
- in Wales, a Local Health Board.

(a) *Elements of the offence*

4.135　　The elements of the offence are conjunctive and set out at s 119(1). They are that:

- a person, without reasonable excuse, causes a nuisance or disturbance (s 119(1)(a));
- to an NHS staff member who is working there or is otherwise there in connection with work (s 119(1)(a));
- the person is on NHS premises (s 119(1)(a));
- the person refuses, without reasonable excuse, to leave the NHS premises when asked to do so by a constable or an NHS staff member (s 119(1)(b)); and
- the person is not on the premises for the purpose of obtaining medical advice, treatment or care for himself (s 119(c)).

4.136　　(i) *A person, without reasonable excuse, causes a nuisance or disturbance*　　Nuisance is not defined within the CJIA 2008 but in the course of the Commons debate it was said that it was assumed to be an ordinary word of the English language, and would be left to the courts to decide if an offence had been committed.[90] The Explanatory Notes to the Act state that a nuisance or disturbance can include any form of non-physical behaviour which breaches the peace such as verbal aggression or intimidating gestures.[91] The reference to 'breach of the peace' is concerning, as is the fact that the provisions

---

[88] CJIA 2008, s 153(5).
[89] CJIA 2008, s 153(6).
[90] HC Deb 20 February 2007 vol 472 c676.
[91] Explanatory Notes, para 674.

are to be found in Part 8 of the CJIA 2008 under the title 'Anti-Social Behaviour'. Both these phrases have been applied widely in the past to include any behaviour which others may find distasteful or annoying.

Respondents to the Consultation Paper identified specific behaviour which they 4.137 wished to be covered which included habitual attendees who visit the Emergency Department who do not require treatment; the obstruction of thoroughfares and the drinking of alcohol on hospital premises. It is doubtful whether some of this behaviour could properly be classified as a nuisance nor is it usually directed at a particular staff member. Even if it were, it is to be hoped that the person would be given the opportunity to desist before being asked to leave.

The nuisance has to be committed without reasonable excuse for an offence to 4.138 have been committed. An example of a reasonable excuse given in the Explanatory Notes to the Act is behaviour consequential to the receipt of upsetting news or bereavement.[92] The Explanatory Notes to the Bill as introduced also suggest communication problems due to a language barrier.

(ii) *to an NHS staff member who is working there or is otherwise there in connection with* 4.139 *work* An 'NHS staff member' is a person employed by a relevant NHS body or otherwise working for such a body (whether as or on behalf of a contractor, as a volunteer or otherwise).[93] This would include therefore agency workers and students. Being on NHS premises otherwise 'in connection with work' would include staff members travelling to work, walking between buildings or taking a break.

The causation required is not clear. Shouting abuse at patients would not, for 4.140 example, be behaviour directed at an NHS staff member. However, a staff member may feel the need to intervene to keep the peace or the person abused may complain, causing a staff member to take time out from their other work. Either of these scenarios may well be a nuisance to the staff member. It remains to be seen whether this would be sufficient for the nuisance to have been 'caused' by the person shouting abuse or whether the other party's actions would break the chain of causation.

(iii) *the person is on NHS premises* NHS premises are defined in s 119(4) as: 4.141

- any hospital vested in, or managed by, a relevant NHS body,
- any building or other structure, or vehicle (including air ambulance), associated with the hospital and situated on hospital grounds (whether or not vested in, or managed by, a relevant NHS body), and
- the hospital grounds (land in the vicinity of a hospital and associated with it).

(iv) *the person refuses, without reasonable excuse, to leave the NHS premises when asked to* 4.142 *do so by a constable or an NHS staff member(s 119(b))* The Explanatory Notes to the Act[94] suggest that a person may be asked to leave *once* the elements of s 119(1)(a) (namely the elements identified (i), (ii), and (iii) above) are satisfied. This would suggest that a constable or NHS staff member is required to form an objective view

---

[92] Para 674.
[93] CJIA 2008, s 119(4)(c).
[94] Para 675.

of whether the nuisance was caused without reasonable excuse, before moving on to the next stage of asking someone to leave.

4.143   Further, once the behaviour has been deemed to be unreasonable, and a person is asked to leave and refuses to, a further judgement call has to be made before a person exercises his power to remove a person (as to which see para **4.147** below).

4.144   A potential example of a reasonable excuse for refusing to leave, given in the Explanatory Notes, is where a dependent is on the premises and the person concerned has a responsibility to remain on the premises with that person.

4.145   It remains to be seen how this section will operate in practice, and whether ultimately, the courts will have to decide whether the behaviour that led to being asked to leave was without reasonable excuse and if so, whether any subsequent refusal to leave was without reasonable excuse. As with all 'reasonable excuse' defences, the evidential burden will be on the defendant to the civil standard.

4.146   (v) *the person is not on the premises for the purpose of obtaining medical advice, treatment or care for himself (s 119(c))*   By the CJIA 2008, s 119(3) a person ceases to be on NHS premises for the purpose of obtaining medical advice, treatment or care for himself once the person has received the advice, treatment or care, or if the person has been refused the advice, treatment or care during the last 8 hours.

3. Power to remove

4.147   The CJIA 2008, s 120 provides for the power to remove any person causing nuisance or disturbance. The power can be exercised by either a police constable or an authorized officer. An authorized officer is any NHS staff member authorized by the relevant NHS body to exercise these powers (s 120(5)).

4.148   The threshold criterion is that the constable or authorized officer reasonably suspects that a person is committing or has committed an offence under the CJIA 2008, s 119. He may then remove the person from the NHS premises, using reasonable force if necessary (s 120(3)). An authorized officer may also choose to authorize an 'appropriate NHS staff member' to remove the person (s 120(2)). An 'appropriate NHS staff member' means the same as 'NHS staff member' in s 119 (s 120(5)). The word 'appropriate' therefore seems to add nothing but a potential challenge if the person authorized was not suitable in the ordinary meaning of the word.

4.149   One fetter on the power of an authorized officer under this section is that he cannot remove a person or authorize another person to do so if he has reason to believe the person to be removed requires medical advice, treatment or care for himself or herself, or the removal would endanger the person's physical or mental health (s 120(4)). Worryingly, a police constable does not have to make any such checks.

4.150   The CJIA 2008, s 121 provides that the Secretary of State or Welsh Minister may from time to time prepare and publish guidance to relevant NHS bodies and authorized officers about the power to remove. This may relate to, in particular, the authorization and training requirements of staff members and matters to be considered when deciding whether an offence has been committed under s 119 and whether removal would endanger the person's physical or mental health. It may also provide guidance on the procedure to be followed before using the power of removal and the degree of force that may be appropriate. An authorized officer must have regard to any such guidance when exercising the power of removal (s 121(4)).

4. Penalty

The maximum penalty on conviction is a fine not exceeding level 3 (s 119(2)).   4.151

I. PERSISTENT SALES OF TOBACCO TO PERSONS UNDER 18

1. Introduction

The CJIA 2008, Part 11, s 143 introduces new powers to deal with the persistent   4.152
selling of tobacco to persons under the age of 18. The intention to enact legislation
to ban retailers from selling tobacco if they repeatedly flouted the law was announced
in a Ministry of Health White Paper.[95] Following consultation, the 'negative licensing
scheme' in relation to tobacco was introduced at the Committee stage of the Bill's
passage through Parliament in order to encourage retailers to comply with the increase
in the minimum legal age for buying tobacco from 16 to 18, which took effect in
October 2007.

By way of comparison, in relation to alcohol sales a premises licence may be   4.153
suspended for up to 3 months if alcohol is sold to under 18-year-olds on three occasions in a period of three consecutive months.[96] A similar time period for tobacco
offences was rejected on the basis of the potentially serious consequences on the sale
of alcohol and the infrequency of test purchases in relation to tobacco.

The provisions relating to persistent sales of tobacco are not in force at the time   4.154
of writing and do not apply where the relevant offences were committed before the
commencement of that section.[97]

2. Restricted premises orders and restricted sales orders

The CJIA 2008, s 143, provides for two new civil orders, with a penal sanction upon   4.155
breach, to prevent retailers repeatedly selling tobacco to under 18-year-olds. A magistrates' court may impose either a restricted premises order or a restricted sales
order upon application following a conviction for a 'tobacco offence'. The choice of
order is one for the person bringing the complaint and is likely to depend on the
position of the person committing the offence. The manager of a shop is likely to be
more affected by a restricted sales order which takes effect against him and remains
in force even if he moves to a different premises. Where the offence is committed by
a cashier and the view is taken that there is a problem with the management or
supervision of a particular premises, a restricted premises order is likely to be more
effective.

---

[95] 'Choosing Health: Making Healthy Choices Easier', Cm 6374.
[96] Violent Crime Reduction Act 2006, s 23.
[97] CJIA 2008, Sch 27, para 37.

4.156   Any person selling tobacco in breach of a restricted premises order or failing to comply with a restricted sales order commits a criminal offence. The amendment is created by inserting new ss 12A–D into the Children and Young Persons Act 1933.

4.157   A restricted premises order takes effect against the premises and creates an outright ban on the sale of tobacco or cigarette papers from those premises, whether by the defendant or by any other person or by machine (s 12A(3)). Such an order takes effect as a local land charge and is therefore registered against the premises (s 12C(5)).

4.158   A restricted sales order takes effect solely against the defendant just convicted and prevents him from selling tobacco or cigarette papers; keeping or permitting to be kept on any premises a cigarette machine and from having any management functions in respect of the sale of tobacco or cigarette papers or the keeping of a cigarette machine in relation to any premises (s 12B(3)).

4.159   Both orders may have effect for up to one year (s 12A(5) and 12B(4)) unless varied or discharged. (See para **4.165** below.) Any person aggrieved by the making of either order may appeal to the Crown Court.[98]

3. Necessary conditions

4.160   In accordance with s 12D, a 'tobacco offence' is an offence under the Children and Young Persons Act 1933, s 7[99] which provides that '[a]ny person who sells to a person under the age of eighteen years any tobacco or cigarette papers, whether for his own use or not, shall be liable, on summary conviction to a fine not exceeding level 4 on the standard scale'. A due diligence defence is provided by the CYPA 1933, s 1A.

4.161   Following such a conviction, 'the person who brought the proceedings', may apply by complaint to the magistrates' court for either a restricted premises order or a restricted sales order (s 12A(2) and s12B(2)).

4.162   The court may only make either order if it is satisfied that 'on at least 2 occasions within the period of 2 years ending with the date on which the relevant offence was committed' the defendant has committed other tobacco offences in relation to the relevant premises (ss 12A(7) and s 12B(5)). The two occasions do not include the offence for which the defendant has just been convicted.

4.163   It should be possible to argue that although the legislation does not refer to two 'separate' occasions, that there must be some distance in time or else it would simply be one occasion. Otherwise the sale of two items of tobacco to the same person would fulfil this requirement. Controversially, the Explanatory Notes state that the court may be so satisfied even if the defendant has not been convicted of any such offences.[100] No standard of proof is provided for and it is likely that a similar procedure will be followed as for the making of Anti-social Behaviour Orders and other civil orders, and that hearsay evidence will be admissible.[101]

---

[98] CYPA 1933, s 102(1)(f), as inserted by CJIA 2008, s 143(3).
[99] As amended by the Children and Young Persons (Protection from Tobacco) Act 1991 and the Children and Young Persons (Sale of Tobacco etc) Order 2007, SI 2007/767.
[100] Explanatory Notes paras 823 and 826.
[101] See Chapter 6 on other civil orders and associated procedure.

The commencement provisions of the CJIA 2008[102] provide that the new powers   4.164
created by s 143 do not apply where '*any* of the offences mentioned in those new
sections' were committed before the commencement of s 143. This would therefore
seem to include the two occasions necessary for the making of an order.

4. Procedure

Before applying for a restricted premises order the person bringing the complaint   4.165
must make reasonable enquiries and give notice of the application in writing to the
occupier of the premises and any person with an interest in the premises (s 12A(6)
and (11)). Any such person is entitled to make representations on whether the order
should be made (s 12A(8)). Before making such an order, the court must satisfy itself
that reasonable enquiries have been made and the appropriate notice been given
(s 12A(7)). If it later transpires that a relevant person did not receive such a notice, he
is entitled to apply on complaint to vary or discharge the order (s 12A(9)).

5. Breaches of orders

Selling tobacco or cigarette papers in contravention of a restricted premises order is   4.166
an offence if the seller knew, or ought reasonably to have known, that the sale was
in contravention of the order (s 12C(1)). Failing to comply with a restricted sale
order is an offence, although it is a defence for the defendant to prove that he took
all reasonable precautions and exercised all due diligence to avoid the commission of
the offence (s 12C(2) and (3)).

Either offence is punishable by a maximum penalty of a fine not exceeding   4.167
£20,000 (s 12C(4)).

J. CLARIFICATION OF THE LAW OF SELF-DEFENCE

1. Introduction

A review of the law of self-defence was announced by the Justice Secretary at the end   4.168
of the Labour Party conference in 2007 to ensure 'that those who seek to protect
themselves, their loved ones and their homes, as well as other citizens, have confidence that the law is on their side'. He went on to say that 'the law on self defence
works much better than most people think; but not as well as it could or should'. It
is submitted that the so-called clarification does nothing to improve the working of
the law. Indeed, it arguably makes it less clear. The intention to take another look at
the law on self-defence was repeated at the Second Reading of the Criminal Justice
and Immigration Bill and the new clause was introduced in December 2007. The
Conservative Party proposed that the test should be amended so that force is allowed
so long as it was not 'grossly disproportionate' but this was dismissed as potentially
incompatible with the European Convention on Human Rights.

---

[102] CJIA 2008, Sch 27, para 37.

4.169   The main question was whether the section was necessary and there was an unsuccessful attempt to throw it out in the House of Lords. It was agreed that the real
problems were firstly, the prolonged investigation of cases involving the use of
self-defence by people protecting their property and secondly, a lack of public under-
standing of the law. Guidance had previously been issued in relation to the former
and a leaflet was published by the Crown Prosecution Service and the Association of
Chief Police Officers to assist with the latter. It remains to be seen whether this new
legislation will have any effect on either of these problems.

4.170   The 'new' law applies to England, Wales, and Northern Ireland and applies
whether the offence took place before or after 14 July 2008 when the CJIA 2008,
s 76 came into force.[103] However, it will not apply where, in relation to trial on
indictment, arraignment took place before that date and, in relation to summary
trial, the hearing began before that date.[104]

2. The 'new' law

4.171   The CJIA 2008, s76 is intended to clarify the operation of the existing defences of
self-defence (including defence of another) under the common law, the Criminal
Law Act 1967, s 3(1) and the Criminal Law Act (Northern Ireland) 1967, s 3(1).
The previous law is not abolished and the new section does not cover all elements of
self-defence.

4.172   The new definition applies whenever an issue arises as to whether a defendant is
entitled to rely on either of the above defences. Section 76(3) states that the question
of whether the degree of force used by a defendant was reasonable in the circumstances is to be decided by reference to the circumstances as the defendant believed
them to be. The applicable criteria for deciding that question are dealt with below.

(a) Honest belief as to circumstances

4.173   Section 76(4)(a) provides that if a defendant claims to have held a particular belief
as regards the existence of any circumstances 'the reasonableness or otherwise of that
belief is relevant to the question of whether [he] genuinely held it'. In other words,
'the reasonableness or unreasonableness of the defendant's belief is material to the
question of whether the belief was held by the defendant at all'.[105]

4.174   Section 76(4)(b) goes on to provide that 'if it is determined that [the defendant]
did genuinely hold that belief, he is entitled to rely on it whether or not it was
mistaken, or (if it was mistaken) the mistake was a reasonable one to have made'.
Put another way, '[i]f the belief was in fact held, its unreasonableness, so far as
guilt or innocence is concerned, is neither here nor there. It is irrelevant.'[106]
This section could be open to challenge, as allowing a defence on the basis of an
honest but unreasonable belief that force was necessary may provide insufficient

---

[103] CJIA (Commencement No 2 and Transitional and Saving Provisions) Order 2008, SI 2008/1586.
[104] CJIA 2008, Sch 27, para 27.
[105] *R v Williams (Gladstone)* (1987) 3 All ER 411.
[106] *R v Williams (Gladstone)* (1987) 3 All ER 411.

protection for the victim's right to life under Article 2 of the European Convention on Human Rights.

(b) *Voluntary intoxication*

The CJIA 2008, s 76(5) provides that a defendant is not entitled 'to rely on any   4.175
mistaken belief attributable to intoxication that was voluntarily induced'. This means that, 'where the jury are satisfied that the defendant was mistaken in his belief that any force or the force which he in fact used was necessary to defend himself and are further satisfied that the mistake was caused by voluntarily induced intoxication, the defence must fail'.[107]

(c) *Proportionality of response*

Section 76(6) provides that 'The degree of force, by which is meant the type and   4.176
amount of force, used by a defendant is not to be regarded as having been reasonable, in the circumstances as the defendant believed them to be, if it was disproportionate in those circumstances.' For example, '[i]f there is some relatively minor attack, it would not be common sense to permit some act of retaliation which was wholly out of proportion to the necessities of the situation.'[108]

(d) *Other considerations*

Section 76(7) provides that whenever it is relevant the following considerations   4.177
must also be taken into account.

Firstly, that a person acting in self-defence may not be able to weigh to a nicety the   4.178
exact measure of any necessary action. That is to say that, 'If there has been an attack so that defence is reasonably necessary, it will be recognized that a person defending himself cannot weigh to a nicety the exact measure of his necessary defensive action.'[109]

Secondly, it must be taken into account that evidence of a person 'having only   4.179
done what the person honestly and instinctively thought was necessary for a legitimate purpose constitutes strong evidence that only reasonable action was taken by that person for that purpose'. Therefore, '[i]f a jury thought that in a moment of unexpected anguish a person attacked had only done what he honestly and instinctively thought was necessary, that would be most potent evidence that only reasonable defensive action had been taken'.[110] It does not seem that this section is intended to introduce any evidential rule to this effect,[111] but simply puts the common law pronouncement above on a statutory footing in order to provide guidance for police, prosecutors and jury directions.

Section 76(8) provides that other matters may be taken into account where they   4.180
are relevant. This is likely to include the *obiter* observations of Lord Hoffman in *R v Jones*[112] that what is reasonable in the circumstances includes an objective element,

---

[107] *R v O'Grady* 1987 QB 995 at 999.
[108] *Palmer v R* [1971] AC 814 at 831.
[109] *Palmer v R* [1971] AC 814 at 832.
[110] Ibid.
[111] See criticism in Editorial [2008] Crim LR 507.
[112] [2007] 1 AC 136 at 178.

so that in relation to trials of direct action protestors, their actions must be considered in the context of a functioning state in which disputes about what should be law or government policy can be submitted to the democratic process.

K. MINOR AND CONSEQUENTIAL AMENDMENTS

4.181   The CJIA 2008, s 79 and Sch 28 abolish the common law offences of blasphemy and blasphemous libel in relation to England and Wales. The move was made following a Liberal Democrat amendment to the Bill and was largely unopposed. Although attempts to abolish the offences have been discussed before, on the basis that the law was rarely used and potentially in breach of Articles 10 and 14 of the ECHR (as it threatened the right to free speech and only applied to criticism of Christianity), the final impetus finally came from the failed attempt to bring a private prosecution against the producers of the play 'Jerry Springer: the Opera'.

4.182   The power of a constable under the Public Order Act 1984 to arrest without warrant a person he suspects of using words or behaviour intending to stir up religious hatred is removed with effect from 8 May 2008.[113] The power of arrest without warrant for this offence can only be exercised by a constable if the general arrest criteria in the Police and Criminal Evidence Act 1984, s 24[114] are fulfilled.

---

[113] CJIA 2008, s 74, Sch 16, para 6(3).
[114] As amended by Serious Organised Crime and Police Act 2005.

5

INTERNATIONAL CO-OPERATION

A. INTRODUCTION

The provisions in Part 6 of the CJIA 2008 relate to three different areas of international   5.01
co-operation in criminal justice matters. Sections 80–92 and Schedules 18 and 19 give
effect to the European Council Framework Decision on the application of the principle
of mutual recognition to financial penalties.[1]

Sections 93–96 amend the Repatriation of Prisoners Act 1984 to enable the   5.02
United Kingdom to ratify the Additional Protocol to the Council of Europe Convention
on the Transfer of Sentenced Persons.

Section 97 amends the Crime (International Co-operation) Act 2003 so that the   5.03
Treasury may, by order, provide for functions conferred on the Secretary of State, in
relation to requests for mutual legal assistance from overseas authorities, to be exercisable by HMRC in relation to direct tax matters (as is already the position in relation
to indirect tax matters).

Sections 80–92 come into force on such day as the Lord Chancellor may by order   5.04
appoint.[2] Sections 93–97 came into force on 14 July 2008.[3]

B. RECOGNITION OF FINANCIAL PENALTIES

1. Background

A detailed analysis of the background to the European Council Framework Decision   5.05
on the application of the principle of mutual recognition to financial penalties is

---

[1] 2005/214/JHA; 24 February 2005.
[2] CJIA 2008, s 153(4).
[3] Criminal Justice and Immigration Act 2008 (Commencement No 2 and Transitional and Saving Provisions)
Order 2008, SI 2008/1586.

outside the scope of this book. Systematic co-operation at a European level in the field of justice and home affairs was introduced by the Maastricht Treaty of 1992 and developed through the provisions of the Treaty of Amsterdam, signed in 1997 and incorporating the Schengen Convention in relation to which the UK has partial participation, and the Treaty of Nice, signed in 2001.

5.06   Policing and judicial co-operation in criminal matters remain areas within the 'third pillar' of the European Union which means that legislation requires unanimity of Member States in the Council of Ministers. Because of this, progress in this area can be slow with third pillar procedures leading to stalled measures and poor quality compromises which Member States often fail to implement properly.[4]

5.07   At the European Council summit in Tampere in 1999 the first comprehensive agenda for Justice and Home Affairs at EU level was set with the goal of constructing an 'Area of Freedom, Security and Justice' across the EU. The principle of 'mutual recognition', as opposed to 'harmonisation' or 'practical co-operation', was endorsed thereby becoming the cornerstone of judicial co-operation in both civil and criminal matters within the European Union.

5.08   The five-year agenda from Tampere was followed in 2004 by the 'Hague Programme', a new programme for the years 2005–2010. The Hague Programme anticipated the coming into force of the Constitutional Treaty in 2006 and the failure of the Treaty has posed some difficulties for the Programme's implementation. There has been continuing debate about the correct principle on which to base justice and home affairs co-operation.

5.09   The government's research paper notes that the Centre for European Policy Studies has suggested that it was the UK which 'very strongly pushed' mutual recognition (as opposed to harmonization) as a founding principle of the Hague Programme, arguing that 'it has been very much a UK project'.[5]

5.10   To date a number of proposals based on mutual recognition have been agreed: the 2002 Framework Decision introduced the European Arrest Warrant (implemented in the UK by Extradition Act 2003); the 2003 Framework Decision on the execution of orders freezing property or evidence (implemented in the UK by Crime (International Co-operation) Act 2003); the 2005 Framework Decision applying mutual recognition to financial penalties and the 2006 Framework Decision on the mutual recognition of confiscation orders.

5.11   In July 2001, a European Council Framework Decision on the application of the principle of mutual recognition of financial penalties was proposed, as a joint initiative by France, Sweden and the UK. The Decision was agreed on 24 February 2005. It was promoted on behalf of the government in the UK during Standing Committee as an instrument which would fill a significant gap in EU judicial co-operation by providing a mechanism for enforcing financial penalties imposed in other member states, whilst also providing important safeguards to ensure that individuals have had an adequate opportunity to defend themselves in proceedings abroad.[6]

---

[4] House of Commons Home Affairs Committee Justice and Home Affairs Issues at European Union Level Third Report of Session 2006–2007, paras 304–10.

[5] Research Paper 07/65, p 67.

[6] Bob Ainsworth, Parliamentary Under Secretary of State for the Home Department, European Standing Committee B Debates, Wednesday 29 January 2003.

The European Scrutiny Committee finally cleared the Decision on 4 February 5.12
2004 despite maintaining a number of doubts about the adequacy of the certificate
referred to in Article 4 of the Framework Decision. In particular the Committee was
concerned that the certificate does not require an indication of the defendant's
wishes (in relation to contesting the case) to be given in writing. Further they raised
concerns about the lack of judicial certification in the issuing state that a defendant's
rights under Article 6 ECHR have been respected. They identified a clear risk of
orders being presented for enforcement under the Framework Decision against
defendants who have not in fact been informed in the detail required by Article 6
ECHR or at all of the accusations made against them.[7]

It is against this background that the CJIA 2008, ss 80–92 purport to give effect 5.13
to the Framework Decision.

2. Requests to other member states

The CJIA 2008, ss 80 and 81 set out the procedure for requests to be made to other 5.14
member states for enforcement of financial penalties imposed in England and Wales.
The Courts Act 2003, Sch 5, para 38 sets out the range of 'further steps'[8] available in
order to enforce a fine against a person over the age of 18. Section 80(1) of the CJIA 2008
adds the issuing of a certificate requesting enforcement under the Framework
Decision on financial penalties to that list of further steps.[9] A certificate requesting
enforcement under the Framework Decision may only be issued where the sum due
is a financial penalty within the meaning of the CJIA 2008, s 80.[10]

Financial penalty is defined by the CJIA 2008, s 80(5) to mean: 5.15

- a fine imposed by a court in England and Wales on a person's conviction for an
  offence;
- any sum payable under a compensation order within the meaning of PCC(S)A 2006,
  s 130(1);
- a surcharge under CJA 2003, s 161A;
- orders for payment of costs as mentioned in Administration of Justice Act 1970, Sch 9,
  paras 1 to 9;
- orders requiring parents to pay fines etc under PCC(S)A 2000, s 137(1) or (1A);
- any fine or other sum mentioned in CJIA 2008, s 82(4)(b)(i) to (iv) in relation to
  Northern Ireland, or any fine imposed by a court in Scotland, which is enforceable in
  a local justice area in England and Wales by virtue of Magistrates' Courts Act 1980,
  s 91(c. 43); and
- any other financial penalty, within the meaning of the Framework Decision on
  financial penalties, specified in an order made by the Lord Chancellor. Further, it
  may only be issued where it appears to the fines officer or the court that the person

---

[7] Select Committee on European Scrutiny 9th Report Session 2003–2004, 4 February 2004.
[8] See Courts Act 2003, Sch 5 which sets out the powers of the courts and fines officers to enforce fines,
costs and compensation.
[9] CJIA 2008, s 80(1)(a), inserting Courts Act 2003, Sch 5, para 38(1)(e).
[10] CJIA 2008, s80(1)(b), inserting Courts Act 2003, Sch 5, para 38(4)(a).

is normally resident, or has property or income, in a member state other than the United Kingdom.[11]

5.16   The CJIA 2008, s 80(2)–(4) sets out the power and procedure for the issuing of a certificate requesting enforcement of a financial penalty under the Framework Decision in circumstances not covered by the Courts Act 2003, Sch 5, that is to say in relation to an offender under 18 or a legal person. A certificate may be issued in such circumstance where the person is required to pay a financial penalty;[12] that penalty is not paid in full within the time allowed; there is no appeal outstanding[13] and it appears to the designated officer that the person is normally resident in, or has property or income in, a member state other than the United Kingdom (or in the case of a body corporate has its registered office in a member state other than the UK[14]).

5.17   The CJIA 2008, s 81 provides that where a certificate requesting enforcement under the Framework Decision has been issued (either under the Courts Act 2003, Sch 5 or CJIA 2008, s 80(2)) the fines officer or the designated officer for the magistrates' court must give the Lord Chancellor the certificate together with a certified copy of the decision requiring payment of the financial penalty.[15] The Lord Chancellor must then give those documents to the central authority or competent authority of the member state in which the person required to pay the penalty appears to be normally resident or has property or income in[16] or, in the case of a body corporate, in which the person appears to have its registered office.[17] No further steps to enforce the decision may then be taken in England or Wales except in accordance with provision made by order by the Lord Chancellor.[18]

5.18   Sections 82 and 83 correspond to ss 80 and 81 in relation to requests to other Member States for the enforcement of financial penalties imposed in Northern Ireland where the Courts Act 2003, Sch 5 does not apply.

3. Requests from other member states

5.19   The CJIA 2008, ss 84–86 and 91 set out the procedure to be followed when a request is received from another member state for the enforcement in England and Wales of a financial penalty. The procedure is envoked if two conditions are met.[19] Firstly, the Lord Chancellor must be given by the competent authority[20] of a member state (i) a certificate requesting enforcement of a financial penalty under

---

[11] CJIA 2008, s 80(1)(b), inserting Courts Act 2003, Sch 5 para 38(4)(b).

[12] As defined by CJIA 2008, s 80(5).

[13] CJIA 2008, s 80(3) provides that there is no appeal outstanding if no appeal has been brought within the time allowed or such an appeal has been brought but the proceedings have been concluded.

[14] CJIA 2008, s 80(4).

[15] CJIA 2008, s 81(2).

[16] CJIA 2008, s 81(3).

[17] CJIA 2008, s 81(5).

[18] CJIA 2008, s 81(4), see also Explanatory Notes to the Act at para 550.

[19] CJIA 2008, s 84(1).

[20] CJIA 2008, s 84(6) extends the application of the section to requests from other member states received by the central authority for Scotland for the enforcement of financial penalties, which are then forwarded to the Lord Chancellor.

the Framework Decision ('the certificate'), and (ii) the decision or a certified copy of the decision ('the decision') requiring payment of the penalty. Secondly, the financial penalty must be suitable for enforcement in England and Wales.

The CJIA 2008, s 91(1) provides that Sch 18 specifies when a financial penalty is   5.20
suitable for enforcement in England and Wales (and Northern Ireland[21]) against persons:

- residing in England and Wales;
- residing in Northern Ireland;
- having property etc in England and Wales;
- having property etc in Northern Ireland;
- having property etc in England and Wales and Northern Ireland;
- having property etc in England and Wales and Scotland;
- having property etc in Northern Ireland and Scotland;
- having property etc in England and Wales, Scotland and Northern Ireland.

If the relevant information has been received by the Lord Chancellor and the pen-   5.21
alty is suitable for enforcement in England and Wales, he must give the certificate and the decision to the designated officer for the local justice area in which it appears that the person required to pay the financial penalty is normally resident[22] or where the body corporate has its registered office.[23] Where the person is not normally resident but has property or income in England and Wales the Lord Chancellor must give the certificate and decision to the designated officer for such local justice area as appears appropriate.[24]

In addition, however, the CJIA 2008, s 84(4) requires that as well as providing a   5.22
copy of the certificate and decision, the Lord Chancellor must also give the designated officer a notice stating whether he thinks that any of the grounds for refusal to enforce the penalty might apply, together with reasons for that opinion. In this regard, the CJIA 2008, s 91(2) and Sch 19 specify the grounds on which a request may be refused. Amongst them are the following considerations:[25]

- the principle of double jeopardy;
- the absence of dual criminality,[26] save where the penalty was imposed in respect of conduct that is specified in Sch 19, Part 2;[27]
- the principle of territoriality, if the conduct took place outside the territory of the state issuing the certificate;
- the age of criminal responsibility;
- the manner and fairness of the proceedings giving rise to the penalty;
- the value of the financial penalty.

---

[21] See para **5.26** below.
[22] CJIA 2008, s 84(2).
[23] CJIA 2008, s 84(5).
[24] CJIA 2008, s 84(3).
[25] As set out in the CJIA 2008, Sch 19, Part 1.
[26] Where the conduct is unlawful under the laws of both the surrendering and requesting state.
[27] A list of offences, mirroring Art 5(1) of the Framework Decision where it has been agreed that co-operation should not be subject to a dual criminality requirement.

5.23   The CJIA 2008, s 85 governs the procedure to be adopted on receipt, by a designated officer for a local justice area, of a certificate requesting the enforcement of financial penalties sent by the Lord Chancellor. Section 85(2)–(4) dictates that:

- the designated officer must refer the matter to the magistrates' court acting for that area;
- the magistrates' court must determine whether it is satisfied whether any of the grounds for refusal apply; and
- the designated officer must inform the Lord Chancellor of the decision taken in the magistrates' court.

5.24   Unless a ground for refusal is deemed to exist, the court must treat any outstanding balance of the penalty as if it were a sum payable on summary conviction in that jurisdiction, from the date of the magistrates' court decision. The relevant provisions of Part 3 of the Magistrates' Court Act 1980, Schs 5 and 6 to the Courts Act 2003, and any subordinate legislation will therefore govern the enforcement and collection of the penalty.[28]

5.25   The power contained in the Magistrates' Courts Act 1980, s 90(1) to transfer a fine to another jurisdiction within the UK is amended and extended by the CJIA 2008, s 86 to allow for the transfer of a penalty to Northern Ireland where it appears that the individual is residing, or has property or a source of income there.

5.26   Further, ss 87 and 88 correspond to ss 84 and 85 in relation to requests to other Member States for enforcement of financial penalties imposed in Northern Ireland. The CJIA 2008, s 89 makes subsequent necessary modifications to the Magistrates' Courts (Northern Ireland) Order 1981.

C. REPATRIATION OF PRISONERS

1. Background

5.27   The provisions which now appear at ss 93 to 96 of the CJIA 2008 were inserted into the Bill when it was due for its Report Stage on 9 January 2008.[29] As a result, the opportunity for debate was extremely limited. The government justified the proposals as a means of amending the Repatriation of Prisoners Act 1984 to enable the United Kingdom to ratify the Additional Protocol to the Council of Europe Convention on the Transfer of Sentenced Persons and to support the government's belief that, when possible, foreign national prisoners should serve their sentences in their home countries.[30]

5.28   The Additional Protocol provides at Article 2(1) that:

Where a national of a Party who is the subject of a sentence imposed in the territory of another Party as a part of a final judgment, seeks to avoid the execution or further execution of the sentence in the sentencing State by fleeing to the territory of the former Party before having served the sentence, the sentencing State may request the other Party to take over the execution of the sentence.

---

[28] CJIA 2008, s 85(5)–(8).
[29] Some would say 'plonked': see HC Deb 9 Jan 2008 col 426.
[30] HC Deb 9 Jan 2008 col 430.

Article 3(1) provides: 5.29

Upon being requested by the sentencing State, the administering State may, subject to the provisions of this Article, agree to the transfer of a sentenced person without the consent of that person, where the sentence passed on the latter, or an administrative decision consequential to that sentence, includes an expulsion or deportation order or any other measure as the result of which that person will no longer be allowed to remain in the territory of the sentencing State once he or she is released from prison.

Although the UK has had ample legislation to address the transfer of prisoners 5.30 subject to deportation for some time, the essence of the CJIA 2008, ss 94 and 95 is to create a framework for the transfer of responsibility for the execution and enforcement of a sentence on an individual who has fled from the jurisdiction of one State that is party to the Additional Protocol to another.

The CJIA 2008, ss 93–95[31] introduce amendments to the Repatriation of Prisoners 5.31 Act (RPA) 1984. Section 96 introduces amendments specifically relating to Scotland. These sections mirror to a significant extent the language and provisions relating to the transfer of a sentenced person already in place in the 1984 Act.

Section 93 amends s 2(1) of the 1984 Act which relates to the delivery of a pris- 5.32 oner to a place abroad for the purposes of executing a transfer out of the United Kingdom. Section 2(1) of the 1984 Act had previously restricted the effect of a warrant providing for the transfer of the prisoner to delivering the prisoner *at a point of departure* in the UK to the custody of an authorized person representing the country or territory to which the prisoner is being transferred. This power is now extended to enable the transfer of the prisoner into the custody of an appropriate person *at the place of arrival* in the receiving state.

2. Warrants transferring responsibility

CJIA 2008, s 94 inserts new ss 4A, 4B, and 4C after s 4 of the 1984 Act. 5.33

The new s 4A relates to the issuing of a warrant transferring, to or from the UK, 5.34 the responsibility for the detention and release of an offender who has escaped or absconded from lawful custody[32] and fled to another country. It provides in s 4A(5) that where:

(a) the UK is party to international agreements to transfer between the UK and another country or territory responsibility for the detention and release of persons who are:
    (i) subject to a lawful order imposed in the UK and have fled to another country or territory; or
    (ii) subject to a lawful order imposed in another country or territory and have fled to the UK,

---

[31] In force since 14 July 2008, see para **5.02** above.
[32] Having been detained in a prison, hospital or other institution (s 1(7) of the RPA 1984). But see also s 4B(6), as inserted by CJIA 2008, s 94.

(b) the relevant Minister[33] and the appropriate authority of the other country or territory agree to a transfer of responsibility; and

(c) if necessary, the relevant person's consent has been given,[34]

the Minister shall issue a warrant authorizing the transfer of responsibility for the detention and release either from that Minister or to that Minister as appropriate.

5.35   Sections 4A(6)–(8) introduce a number of caveats to the issuing of a warrant by a relevant Minister in the UK. Of note is that a warrant should not be issued providing for the transfer of responsibility to the UK for the detention and release of an individual *unless* that person is a British Citizen or the transfer appears to the Minister to be appropriate having regard to any close ties that person has with the UK. The interpretation of the phrase 'close ties' attracted debate during the passage of the Bill in the House of Commons.[35] It was advanced by the government as mirroring existing provisions in the RPA 1984 and including, for example, 'the right of residence in the United Kingdom, or having close family here'.[36]

5.36   An additional caveat requires that the relevant Minister should not issue a warrant unless satisfied that all reasonable steps have been taken to communicate to the relevant person the substance of the international arrangements and the effect of the warrant and transfer of responsibility.[37]

(a) *Transfer of responsibility from the UK*

5.37   Section 4B focuses in greater detail on the transfer of responsibility by virtue of s 4A from the UK to another country or territory in relation to a person who has fled from lawful custody in the UK. The UK retains a power under the warrant to deal with the individual if, at any time when under the order in relation to which the warrant was issued, he returns to the UK.[38] Similarly, at any time after the transfer of responsibility, the relevant Minister[39] retains a power, if it appears to him to be appropriate, to vary the order or to provide that the order should cease to have effect.[40]

(b) *Transfer of responsibility to the UK*

5.38   Section 4C focuses in greater detail on the transfer of responsibility by virtue of s 4A to the UK from another country or territory. This section authorizes the taking into custody and detention in a prison, hospital or other institution in the UK of the relevant individual in accordance with the provisions of the warrant. In the limited debate which took place in the House of Commons in relation to these provisions, some concern was raised about the expressed lack of a right of appeal by virtue of s 4C(6),[41]

---

[33] See RPA 1984, s 4A(10), as inserted by CJIA 2008, s 94.
[34] See also RPA 1984, s 4A(9), as inserted by CJIA 2008, s 94.
[35] As to the parliamentary debate on the interpretation of 'close ties' see HC Deb 9 Jan 2008 cols 426–30.
[36] See HC Deb 9 Jan 2008 c 430.
[37] RPA 1984, s 4A(8), as inserted by CJIA 2008, s 94.
[38] RPA 1984, s 4B(2), as inserted by CJIA 2008, s 94.
[39] See RPA 1984, s 4B(4), as inserted by CJIA 2008, s 94.
[40] See RPA 1984, s 4B(3) and (5), as inserted by CJIA 2008, s 94.
[41] See HC Deb 9 Jan 2008 cc428–430.

although it seems clear that the provisions of any warrant issued in a UK court could be subject to challenge by way of judicial review.

3. Powers of arrest and detention

Sections 4D, 4E and 4F have been inserted into the RPA 1984 by virtue of the CJIA 2008, s 95 and are aimed at ensuring that a person can be arrested and detained in custody while the relevant Minister 'determines whether or not to issue a warrant transferring responsibility for the continued enforcement of the prisoner's sentence from the country in which it was imposed to the United Kingdom'.[42]

5.39

(a) *Arrest of persons suspected of falling within s 4A(3)*

Under the new s 4D, the Secretary of State[43] (ie the relevant Minister) may issue a certificate indicating firstly that there are reasonable grounds for believing that an individual in the UK falls within s 4A(3)[44] and secondly that further written confirmation from the territory or country concerned is being sought.

5.40

If an appropriate judge[45] is satisfied that reasonable grounds for believing that the person falls within s 4A(3) exist, this certificate may be acted upon to issue a warrant for the arrest of the person concerned. A person arrested under such a warrant must be given a copy of the warrant for his arrest as soon as is practicable and be brought before the appropriate judge.[46] The judge can make an order for the individual's detention for a period of no more than 7 days while appropriate enquiries are being made.[47]

5.41

(b) *Arrest of persons believed to fall within s 4A(3)*

The new s 4E applies where the relevant Minister has issued a certificate indicating that the issuing authority considers[48] that a person in the UK is a person falling within s 4A(3) and has received written confirmation from a representative of the country or territory concerned of the details of that person's case. It is immaterial for the purposes of this section whether the person concerned has previously been arrested or detained under s 4D.

5.42

On the basis of such a certificate, the appropriate judge[49] may, if satisfied that there are reasonable grounds for believing that the person falls within s 4A(3), issue an arrest warrant. A person arrested under such a warrant must, as soon as is practicable, be given a copy of the warrant for his arrest and be brought before the appropriate judge.[50] The judge can, on the application by the appropriate minister, make an

5.43

---

[42] Explanatory Notes to the CJIA 2008, para 576.

[43] Or, in the case of Scotland, the Scottish Ministers.

[44] That is, a person present in the UK and unlawfully at large from an order imposed in another country or territory.

[45] See RPA 1984, s 4F(3) as inserted by CJIA 2008, s 95. In England and Wales the appropriate judge is a designated District Judge.

[46] RPA 1984, s 4D(5), as inserted by CJIA 2008, s 95.

[47] RPA 1984, s 4D(6) and (7), as inserted by CJIA 2008, s 95.

[48] As distinct from having a 'reasonable belief' as is necessary for RPA 1984, s 4D(1).

[49] See RPA 1984, s 4F(3), as inserted by CJIA 2008, s 95.

[50] RPA 1984, s 4F(5), as inserted by CJIA 2008, s 95.

order for the individual's detention for a period of no more than 14 days while it is determined whether to issue a warrant under s 4A and, if appropriate, such a warrant is issued.[51]

(c) *Further powers of arrest and detention*

5.44 It is apparent that a person arrested under ss 4D and 4E above can be detained for a period up to 21 days. It is suggested in the Explanatory Notes to CJIA 2008 that:

> it is intended that a person detained under [these procedures] would not be detained for more than 21 days while the relevant Minister consults the sentencing State and determines whether or not to issue a warrant to transfer responsibility for the continued enforcement of the prisoner's sentence.[52]

5.45 It is to be noted however, that ss 4D(10) and 4E(10) specifically permit further arrests and detention under s 4D or 4E (although arguments could be raised before the appropriate judge as to the continued existence of reasonable grounds for believing that a person falls within s 4A(3)). According to the Explanatory Notes all time spent in custody under ss 4D or 4E will be credited as 'time served' and deducted from the remaining balance of the sentence if a warrant transferring responsibility under s 4A is issued.[53]

D. MUTUAL LEGAL ASSISTANCE IN REVENUE MATTERS

5.46 The CJIA 2008, s 97 amends s 27(1) of the Crime (International Co-operation) Act 2003 and repeals para 14 of Sch 2 to the Commissioners for Revenue and Customs Act 2005. The effect of the amendment is to enable the Treasury, by order, to provide for functions conferred on the Secretary of State, in relation to requests for mutual legal assistance from overseas authorities, to be exercisable by HMRC in relation to direct tax matters (as is already the position in relation to indirect tax matters).

---

[51] RPA 1984, 4F(6) and (7), as inserted by CJIA 2008, s 95.
[52] Paragraph 585.
[53] Paragraph 586.

6

CIVIL ORDERS IN THE CRIMINAL COURTS

A. VIOLENT OFFENDER ORDERS

1. Introduction

The CJIA 2008, Part 7, introduces a brand new kind of civil order: the violent 6.01 offender order (VOO).[1] Such orders will prevent or restrict certain 'qualifying' violent offenders (whether or not their qualifying offence was committed before or after the coming into force of the CJIA 2008) from going to specified places and events and associating with certain individuals after the expiry of their licences. The VOO will also impose automatic notification requirements on them, akin to those required of sex offenders. The purpose of a VOO is to protect the public from the risk of 'serious violent harm' caused by the offender.

Many will be wondering why we need yet another civil order, the ink barely dry 6.02 on the pages of the Serious Crime Act 2007 which heralded the latest in the line of such orders, the Serious Crime Prevention Order (SCPO), colloquially known as the 'Super ASBO'.[2] The purpose of an SCPO is 'to protect the public by preventing, restricting or disrupting involvement by the person in serious crime in England and Wales'.[3] A breach of an SCPO, like an ASBO, can attract a sentence of up to 5 years imprisonment.[4]

Barely, had the SCPO been in force a month, when the CJIA 2008 received 6.03 Royal Assent,[5] introducing the new civil 'behaviour' order, this time to protect the public from the risk of 'serious violent harm' (as opposed to 'serious crime'),

---

[1] Part 7 is not yet in force, with no implementation date at the time of publication.
[2] In force as of 6 April 2008.
[3] SCA 2007, s 1.
[4] SCA 2007, s 25.
[5] 8 May 2008.

with breaches attracting up to 5 years imprisonment. And this despite the fact that our prisons are full to breaking point.[6] So what is the rationale?

6.04   On 28 February 2006, Charles Clarke, the then Home Secretary, made a written statement to the House of Commons following the publication of the report by the Chief Inspector of Probation on the murder of the Chelsea banker, John Monckton by Damien Hanson and Elliot White, both of whom were under the supervision of the London Probation Area at the time.[7] He reported that 'The Chief Inspector describes a sustained and repeated failure on the part of the London Probation Area, over 2003 and 2004, to assess and manage these two offenders to a professional standard.' He went on to say that he would be examining whether there are any means by which the approach in the dangerous offender provisions of the CJA 2003 (indeterminate sentences) could be applied to those convicted before 4 April 2005 (those provisions only being applicable to those convicted of certain offences after that date).

6.05   Mr Clarke followed this with an oral statement on 20 April 2006 in which he set out further measures that the government intended to take to protect the public from dangerous offenders. In the course of his statement he expressed the view that there are some offenders who do not cease to be a risk to the public just because their licence has come to an end and that there was therefore a strong case for introducing a violent offender order along the same lines that have proved effective in the case of sex offenders.[8]

6.06   The proposal to introduce violent offender orders (VOOs) was also set out in the July 2006 Home Office Report 'Rebalancing the criminal justice system in favour of the law-abiding majority':

We will do more, by legislating to:

. . . introduce Violent Offender Orders, which will enable the court to impose requirements on those convicted of violent offences—for example, placing restrictions on where the offender can live, or preventing them associating with certain organisations or individuals. We will be able to apply them to people convicted before our new unlimited sentences were introduced, and will target the most dangerous offenders. Breach will be a criminal offence punishable by a maximum of five years' imprisonment.[9]

6.07   The reference to 'our new unlimited sentences' is to the dangerous offender provisions brought in by the CJA 2003, which ironically, Part 2 of the CJIA 2008 signals a hasty retreat from, apparently as a result of Lord Carter's Review of Prisons in December 2007.[10] Indeed the assumption of dangerousness for certain qualifying offenders has now been abolished.[11] This may well result in the greater use of VOOs, as opposed to confining them to a smaller class of pre-April 2005 violent offenders.

---

[6] See Lord Carter's Review of Prisons, December 2007.

[7] HC Deb 28 February 2006 vol 457 c13WS.

[8] HC Deb 20 Apr 2006 vol 445 cc244–5, quoted in Research Paper 07-065, 71–72.

[9] 'Rebalancing the criminal justice system in favour of the law-abiding majority: Cutting crime, reducing reoffending and protecting the public', Home Office July 2006, para 3.40 <http://www.homeoffice.gov.uk/documents/CJS-review.pdf/CJS-review-english.pdf?view=Binary>.

[10] See Chapter 2 for the changes to these provisions, which are already in force.

[11] See Chapter 2, at para 2.26.

During Committee stage, the Minister set out the principal aim of VOOs: 6.08

. . . to protect the public from the most dangerous violent offenders who still present a risk of serious, violent harm at the end of their sentences, when there is no other risk management mechanism in place.[12]

These orders would seem therefore to reflect the government's lack of faith in our   6.09
current penal system. The Monckton murder was committed by those who were in fact subject to a 'risk management mechanism'. If sentencing policy, the prison system and the probation services were working properly, surely there would be very few, if any, offenders who still presented 'a risk of serious violent harm at the end of their sentences'? Instead of resources being directed at building a viable and effective probation service so the kind of serious mistakes that were made in relation to Hanson and White are not repeated, the government has sought to bandage an ailing system with an extremely costly 'quick fix' to compensate for the implied failure of its other agencies and of penal policy generally.

At the time of writing, the VOO scheme is not yet in force, with no published   6.10
implementation date.

(a) ECHR considerations

VOO legislation is intended to parallel, as much as possible, the ASBO and sexual   6.11
offences prevention order (SOPO) procedures:

Part 8 of the Criminal Justice and Immigration Bill is intended to provide for the introduction of VOOs. The provisions concerning VOOs are intended to mirror as far as possible the arrangements for other types of civil order, such as Anti-Social Behaviour Orders and Sexual Offences Prevention Orders, breach of both of which results in a criminal conviction.[13]

The criteria for obtaining a VOO differ in one major respect from an ASBO (but   6.12
not a SOPO), namely that a prerequisite for obtaining a VOO is demonstrating that the individual has been convicted of a specified offence.[14] The Joint Committee on Human Rights (JCHR) raised a number of concerns about VOOs, in particular whether such orders should properly be classified as criminal not civil in order to attract the full protection of Article 6 of the ECHR and whether in fact such orders constituted a retrospective penalty within the meaning of Article 7(1).

The government in its response to the first of the two concerns listed above, relying   6.13
upon the decision in McCann,[15] said it did not think it appropriate for the criminal fairness guarantees to apply to VOOs.[16] The JCHR remained of the view that VOOs are distinguishable from ASBOs in this context.[17]

---

[12] PBC Deb 27 November 2007 c596.

[13] The Criminal Justice and Immigration Bill, Bill 130 of 2006–07: Research Paper 07/65, 9 August 2007. House of Commons Library, at 73.

[14] CJIA 2008, s 98.

[15] [2002] UKHL 39, [2003] 1 AC 787.

[16] Letter dated 6 December 2007 from David Hanson MP, Appendix 3, Fifth Report of the Joint Committee on Human Rights (Session 2007–8), Legislative Scrutiny: Criminal Justice and Immigration Bill, HL Paper 37/HC 269.

[17] Fifth Report of the Joint Committee on Human Rights (Session 2007–8), Legislative Scrutiny: Criminal Justice and Immigration Bill, HL Paper 37/HC 269, para 1.89.

6.14   No doubt there will be litigation on this point when the regime comes into force. However, given the House of Lords decision in *Secretary of State for the Home Department v MB*[18] in relation to the classification of control orders (i.e. that such proceedings do not amount to the determination of a criminal charge for the purposes of Article 6 of the ECHR), it is an argument that is probably unlikely to succeed. That said, as their Lordships have said in both *MB* and *McCann*, procedural protections must be commensurate with the gravity of the consequences for the individual subject to such orders, and it may be that future litigation will determine the standard of proof to be applied as well as the nature of the hearing which decides whether or not a VOO is to be imposed.

6.15   On the question of retrospectivity, the government's response was as follows:

Violent Offender Orders are not imposed as an additional punishment for an offence. They are a preventative measure aimed to protect the public from the most dangerous violent offenders who still present a risk of serious violent harm after their licence has expired and who are not subject to any other measures (e.g. public protection sentences, community sentences, other civil orders) to manage that risk. *A Violent Offender order will always be made on the basis of an up to date assessment of risk and only when the court considers an Order necessary to protect the public from serious violent harm. Further, the terms of the Order must be directly linked to the risk of future harm . . .* Breach would be a new criminal offence and therefore not constitute retrospective punishment. We therefore do not need to introduce any additional safeguards to ensure that an individual is not retrospectively punished for an offence committed before the coming into force of the Act.[19] (emphasis added)

6.16   The JCHR remained unconvinced on this point.[20] Article 7(1) prohibits a retroactive increase in the penalty applicable to an offence. The term 'penalty' has an autonomous meaning, defined by reference to criteria analogous to those which apply to the term 'criminal charge' in Article 6 of the ECHR. In *Welch v UK*,[21] a confiscation order made under the Drug Trafficking Offences Act 1986 in respect of an offence committed before the Act entered into force was held to be in breach of Article 7. In *Ibbotson v UK*,[22] by contrast, the Commission held that the registration requirements of the Sex Offenders Act 1997 (now superseded by the Sexual Offences Act 2003) were preventative rather than punitive in character and did not therefore constitute a 'penalty' for the purposes of Article 7. The notification requirements in VOOs are broadly similar to those under the Sexual Offences Act 2003, but of course notification is just one aspect of a VOO.

6.17   A VOO has the potential to be an extremely severe measure and a person who becomes subject to one, having been convicted of a qualifying offence prior to the coming into force of the CJIA 2008, may well have a compelling Article 7 challenge.

---

[18] [2007] UKHL 46.
[19] Letter dated 6 December 2007 from David Hanson MP (note 16 above).
[20] Fifth Report of the Joint Committee on Human Rights (Session 2007–8), Legislative Scrutiny: Criminal Justice and Immigration Bill, HL Paper 37/HC 269, para 1.102.
[21] 20 EHRR 247.
[22] [1999] Crim LR 153.

(b) *Rules, regulations and guidance*

Before this scheme comes into force, it is essential that Home Office guidance on the scheme, as well as specific rules of court and regulations in relation to notification requirements are published. These being civil orders, applied for in the magistrates' court, the Magistrates' Court (Hearsay Evidence in Civil Proceedings) Rules 1999[23] will undoubtedly apply (see para **6.32** below). **6.18**

2. Defining Violent Offender Orders (s 98)

A VOO will be available in relation to a person aged 18 or over who has been convicted of an offence specified in the CJIA 2008, s 98(2) and who satisfies the terms of s 99 ('a qualifying offender'—as to which see para **6.24** below). The government had initially wanted VOOs to apply to all offenders, including juveniles, and the original Bill did not contain an age limit, but following extensive debates in Committee, it would seem that it was eventually persuaded to reserve the order for adult offenders.[24] **6.19**

The specified offences are limited to manslaughter, soliciting murder, wounding with intent to cause GBH (Offences Against the Person Act (OAPA) 1861, s 18), malicious wounding (OAPA 1861, s 20), attempted murder, conspiracy to murder and relevant 'service offences' (s 98(3)(a) to (f)). Service offences are defined at CJIA 2008, s 98(4) which essentially refers to the corresponding civil offences as defined by s 70 of the Army Act 1955, s 70 of the Air Force Act 1955 and s 42 of the Naval Discipline Act 1957,[25] as well as those defined by s 42 of the Armed Forces Act 2006,[26] which would also amount to specified offences within the meaning of the CJIA 2008, s 98(3)(a) to (e) above. Offences under s 42 include attempts, conspiracy etc as defined by s 48 of the Armed Forces Act 2006[27] (s 98(5)). **6.20**

A VOO is defined as an order that contains such prohibitions, restrictions or conditions authorized by the CJIA 2008, s 102 (for which see para **6.39** below), 'as the court making the order considers necessary for the purpose of protecting the public from the risk of serious violent harm caused by the offender' (s 98(1)(a)). VOOs can be made for a period of not less than 2 years and not more than 5 years, *unless* renewed or discharged (s 98(1)(b)). **6.21**

(a) *Risk to the public*

'The public' includes the public in the United Kingdom or any particular members of the public in the United Kingdom (s 98(2)(a) and (b)). 'Risk of serious violent harm caused by a person' is a *'current* risk of serious physical or psychological harm caused by that person committing one or more specified offences' (s 98(2)).[28] **6.22**

At the time of writing, there is no government guidance on the operation of this scheme and in particular the kind of evidence that can be expected to satisfy a court that such a risk exists. In Committee, when asked what evidence would be admissible, **6.23**

---

[23] SI 1999/681.
[24] PBC Deb 27 November 2007 c606.
[25] These sections will be repealed by the Armed Forces Act 2006.
[26] Not yet in force.
[27] Ibid.
[28] See also para **6.13** above.

the Minister confirmed that, as with ASBOs, hearsay evidence would be admissible,[29] that written rather than oral evidence would be the norm,[30] and that guidance would be issued which would relate, amongst other things, to issues of evidence and how applications are to be made.[31] Given that the terms of a VOO are very likely to engage Article 8 of the ECHR, and that the consequences of a breach could be grave, it is submitted that there ought to be a full adversarial hearing in accordance with Article 6(1).

3. Qualifying offenders (s 99)

6.24   A VOO can only be made if the court is satisfied that the person is a 'qualifying offender' and that he has since the relevant conviction acted in such a way as to make it necessary to make a VOO for the purpose of protecting the public from the risk of serious violent harm caused by him (CJIA 2008, s 101(3)) (explained further at para **6.32** below). A 'qualifying offender' means a person who is aged 18 or over who comes within the CJIA 2008, s 99(2) *or* (4).

(a) *Convicted of a specified offence (s 99(2))*

6.25   A person comes within s 99(2) if he has been convicted of a specified offence (see para **6.20** above), regardless of whether the conviction occurred before or after the commencement of Part 8.[32] In order to qualify, a person must also have either received a custodial sentence[33] of at least 12 months upon being convicted of a specified offence or having received a hospital order[34] (with or without a restriction order[35]) (s 99(2)(a)); or been found not guilty of a specified offence by reason of insanity *and* have received a hospital order (with or without a restriction order) or a supervision order[36] (s 99(2)(b) and (3)); or been found to have been under a disability and have done the act charged[37] in relation to a specified offence *and* have received a hospital order (with or without a restriction order) or a supervision order (s 99(2)(c) and (3)).

(b) *Convictions outside England and Wales (s 99(4))*

6.26   A person could still qualify for a VOO if the conviction for the equivalent of a specified offence was obtained outside England and Wales i.e. the offence would have to have constituted an offence in the country in question as well as have constituted a specified offence if it had been committed in England and Wales (a 'relevant offence') (s 99(5)). An offence is an act punishable under the law of the particular country, however it is described in that law (s 99(6)). Additionally, just as with

---

[29] PBC Debate, 27 November 2007, col 613.
[30] Ibid., col 612.
[31] Ibid.
[32] For a discussion on Art 7 of the ECHR and potential retrospectivity challenges, see paras **6.13** and **6.14**.
[33] As defined by CJIA 2008, s 117(1)(a) and (b) and (2).
[34] Ibid.
[35] Ibid.
[36] Ibid.
[37] In accordance with CJIA 2008, s 117(1), these expressions have the same meaning as they do under Part 2 of the Sexual Offences Act 2003, s 135.

convictions in England and Wales, the offender would either have to have received a sentence of imprisonment[38] of at least 12 months or the equivalent of a hospital order (s 99(4)(a)) or the court would have had to have made the equivalent findings and disposals in relation to insanity and fitness to plead (s 99(4)(b) and (c)).

The court can assume that the relevant offence would have constituted a specified   6.27 offence in England and Wales, unless the person to whom the application relates ('P'), serves a notice in accordance with rules of court[39] denying that the facts as alleged constitute a specified offence and giving reasons why that is the case, and requiring the applicant to prove that it would have constituted a specified offence (s 99(7)). The court has the power to permit P to require the condition to be proved even if a notice has not been served (s 99(8)).

It remains to be seen what kind of time limits will be imposed for the service of a   6.28 notice in any future rules of court. It is hoped that they will reflect the fact that enquiring into foreign convictions can sometimes be a lengthy process.

4. Applications for VOOs (s 100)

Like ASBOs and some other civil orders, applications are made by complaint to   6.29 a magistrates' court. Currently only the chief officer of police may make such a complaint, although the CJIA 2008, s 100(4) gives the Secretary of State a very broad discretion to confer powers on other persons or bodies by way of secondary legislation (s 100(4)). The person to whom an application relates must be given notice of any such application and the details of the hearing a reasonable time before the hearing (see s 105).

A chief officer of police can make an application for a VOO in relation to a resident   6.30 of his police area or in relation to a person he believes is in or intending to come to that area (s 100(1)), if it appears to him that person is a qualifying offender and that the person has, since becoming a qualifying offender ('the appropriate date') (s 100(5)), 'acted in such a way as to give reasonable cause to believe that it is necessary for a VOO to be made' (s 100(2)). At this stage therefore, the chief officer of police does not have to satisfy the court the conditions for a making a VOO are met. It would seem that he simply has to form the view that the person may be a qualifying offender and that there may be reasonable cause to believe he has acted in a particular way.

The application can either be made to any magistrates' court that covers the   6.31 applicant's police area or covers the area where the behaviour that led to the belief that a VOO was necessary took place (s 100(3)).

5. Making of VOOs: the statutory test (s 101)

Once an application for a VOO is made to the court, the court will hear from the   6.32 police and P, if P wishes to be heard. The statute is silent on procedure, but like all

---

[38] In accordance with CJIA 2008, s 117 (1), this expression has the same meaning as it does under Part 2 of the Sexual Offences Act 2003, s 131.

[39] No such rules have yet been published.

other such civil behaviour orders applied for in the criminal courts, it is submitted that there will have to be a full adversarial hearing in order to be compliant with Article 6(1) of the ECHR. Further, if there is to be reliance on hearsay evidence, then the Magistrates' Court (Hearsay Evidence in Civil Proceedings) Rules 1999 will have to be complied with. If police intelligence records are to be relied on it may be that s 9 of the Civil Evidence Act 1995 (which deals with records of public authorities) will have to be complied with.[40]

6.33   The court has to be satisfied of two things before a VOO can be made: that P is a qualifying offender[41] and 'that P has, since the appropriate date,[42] acted in such a way as to make it necessary to make a violent offender order for the purpose of protecting the public from the risk of serious violent harm caused by P' (s 101(3)). As laid out at s 98(2) of the CJIA 2008, the risk to the public (whether it is the public in general or specified members of it) has to be a current risk of serious physical or psychological harm caused by that person committing one or more specified offences.[43]

6.34   Even if a court is satisfied that P is a qualifying offender and that he has acted in such a way that causes the court to have the relevant concerns about P's future conduct, the court still has to consider whether a VOO is necessary. To that end, in deciding whether an order is necessary, the court is specifically required by the CJIA 2008, s 101(4) to have regard to whether P would be subject to any other measure which operated to protect the public.

6.35   Although an application for a VOO can be made whilst a person is subject to a custodial term or on licence or subject to a hospital order or supervision order imposed for an offence, the statute prohibits it from coming into force at any time during the currency of those sentences or orders (s 102(5) and (6)). This is in line with the government's desire to protect the public from certain violent offenders who are not subject to any form of risk management. However, s 101(6) contemplates the application being made whilst there is such management in place, so that a person could in theory be subject to a VOO the moment his licence expires.

(a)   *The standard of proof*

6.36   The burden will be on the applicant to satisfy the court to the requisite standard. However, the statute is silent on what that standard is. In *R (on the application of McCann & Ors) v Crown Court at Manchester; Clingham v K & C Royal Borough Council*,[44] the House of Lords held that the criminal standard of proof should apply to ASBOs, despite the fact that they were civil orders, due to 'the seriousness of matters involved'.[45] Following the Court of Appeal decisions in relation to sex offender orders[46] and football banning orders,[47] the House of Lords was accepting

---

[40] See *Wadmore and Foreman v R* (2007) 1 WLR 339 110 at [36]–[38] in the ASBO context.
[41] See para **6.24** above.
[42] See para **6.20** above.
[43] See para **6.30** above.
[44] [2002] UKHL 39, [2003] 1 AC 787.
[45] Lord Steyn at [37], *McCann*, op. cit.
[46] *B v Chief Constable of Avon & Somerset Constabulary* [2001] 1 WLR 340.
[47] *Gough v Chief Constable of the Derbyshire Constabulary* [2002] 3 WLR 289.

that there should be procedural safeguards in place when Convention rights are engaged and when the consequences of breach are potentially very serious.

During the Committee stage, there was considerable debate as to whether or not the standard of proof beyond reasonable doubt should be on the face of the Bill.[48] The Minister, relying upon *McCann*, stated:

> . . . there is a sliding scale . . . and a standard of proof virtually indistinguishable from the criminal standard should be the standard of proof that is used.[49]

In fact, the House of Lords recently confirmed in *In re B (Children)*[50] that there is no intermediate standard of proof, there is just one civil standard of proof, and that in *McCann* their Lordships had adopted the criminal standard because of the nature of the consequences of ASBOs.[51] Although, unlike ASBOs, VOOs are aimed at a relatively small, defined and adult group of persons, it is submitted that the reasoning in *McCann* applies equally and the criminal standard of proof should be applied when deciding whether a person is a 'qualifying offender' and whether he has 'acted in such a way as to make it necessary to make a violent offender order for the purpose of protecting the public from the risk of serious violent harm caused by P'. As was said in *McCann*, deciding upon 'necessity' does not involve applying a standard of proof as it is an exercise of judgment or evaluation.[52]

6. Provisions that a VOO may contain (s 102)

Section 98 of the CJIA 2008 states that a VOO may contain such prohibitions, restrictions or conditions authorized by s 102. Section 102(1) currently authorizes prohibitions, etc that prevent the offender from going to a particular place or premises (the person can be prevented altogether or have specified access); from attending a specified event (presumably that could be anything from a wedding to a football match); from having any contact or a specified description of contact with an individual (a person could therefore, for example, have no face to face contact but have telephone contact). Section 102(3) gives the Secretary of State power to amend s 102(1) by way of secondary legislation, thereby leaving open the possibility of a host of further provisions.

Any of the provisions, etc in a VOO may also relate to conduct in Scotland or Northern Ireland (s 102(2)). Presumably a court would have to find it necessary for a prohibition, etc to so extend and so specify.

7. Variation, renewal or discharge (s 103)

Section 98(1)(b) of the CJIA 2008 defines a VOO as having effect for a minimum period of 2 years and a maximum period of 5 years, unless renewed or discharged

6.37

6.38

6.39

6.40

6.41

---

[48] PBC Deb 27 November 2007 cc607–614.
[49] PBC Deb 27 November 2007 c613.
[50] [2008] UKHL 35. See also *In Re D* [2008] UKHL 33.
[51] Lord Hoffmann at [13]; Baroness Hale at [69].
[52] *McCann*, op cit, at [37].

under s 103. By s 103(1) and (2), the offender and various chief officers of police can apply for variation, renewal or discharge of a VOO (although the likelihood of an offender seeking a renewal must be slim).

(a) *Renewal and variation*

6.42 An order can be renewed for a period of up to 5 years (s 103(1)(b)). Reading the CJIA 2008, s 98(1)(b) together with s 103(1)(b) suggests that a 'renewal order' can be made for a maximum period of 5 years. However, before a court can renew or vary so as to impose *additional* prohibitions, etc, it must be satisfied of the necessity in accordance with s 103(5). Each prohibition, etc must be necessary for the purpose specified and can only be a prohibition, etc authorized by s 102 (see para **6.39** above).

(b) *Discharge*

6.43 The minimum term of a VOO is 2 years,[53] unless discharged. Discharge of a VOO upon application by the offender before that period is ended is only possible with the consent of the chief officer of police *for the area in which he resides* (s 103(7)(b)). If the application for discharge is made by a chief officer of police, then that officer's consent is required (s 103(7)(a)). The offender's consent is required in both scenarios (although it is unlikely that any offender would withhold his consent).

(c) *Procedure*

6.44 An application for variation, discharge or renewal is made by complaint to the appropriate magistrates' court, depending on who is seeking the order (s 103(1) and (3)). The person to whom such an application relates must be given notice of any such application and the details of the hearing a reasonable time before the hearing (see s 105). It is hoped that any future rules of court will include the details of the procedural processes.

8. Interim VOOs (s 104)

6.45 VOOs are available on an interim basis before the main application under s 100 has been determined (CJIA 2008, s 104(1)). There is no limit on the duration of an interim VOO (IVOO) but it will have effect 'only for such period as specified in the order' (s 104(6)(a)). Certainly at the stage that the Bill was considered by the Joint Committee on Human Rights (before the Second Reading in the House of Lords), there was a maximum period of 4 weeks, although subject to unlimited renewal.[54] It will cease to have effect once the main application has either been withdrawn or refused or if granted, when the VOO actually comes into force (s 104(7)).

6.46 Section 104(8) makes the variation and discharge powers in s 103 applicable to IVOOs (with the exception of s 103(7) which deals with the requirement for consent when VOOs are discharged before the expiration of 2 years). Notably, s 104(8) does not make the renewal powers applicable to IVOOs. An appeal against

---

[53] Beginning on the date the VOO came into force (as opposed to when it was made) (s 103(7)).
[54] Clause 153(5) and (6).

an IVOO lies to the Crown Court, in the same way as it does for a full VOO (see para **6.50** below).

An application for an IVOO can be made by the same complaint as the main **6.47** application or later by further complaint (s 104(2)). It is hoped that any future rules of court will include the procedure to be adopted when applying for an IVOO, and make explicit the evidence that ought to be included in the complaint. An IVOO is subject to the same notice requirement as a full VOO (s 105(1)(b)).

(a) *When can a court make an IVOO?*

Such an order can be made if it 'appears' to the court that 'P' is a qualifying offender **6.48** and that it would be likely to make a VOO if it was determining the full application and that it is 'desirable' to act before the full application is heard 'with a view to securing the immediate protection of the public from the risk of serious violent harm caused by P' (s 103(3)). It is submitted that in order for the court to make any such decisions, in particular since the court is required to evaluate whether it would be likely to make a full VOO, there would have to be compelling evidence of risk to the public of the kind of harm the statute seeks to prevent, as well as evidence that the risk is an immediate one.

An IVOO attracts the same notification requirements as a full VOO (as to which **6.49** see para **6.54** below) and a breach of an IVOO and/or a failure to comply with notification requirements and/or the provision of false information in relation to those requirements are all criminal offences (see para **6.63** below).

9. Appeals (s 106)

A person subject to a VOO or an IVOO can appeal to the Crown Court 'as of right'. **6.50** Such an appeal, like other appeals from the magistrates' court to the Crown Court, is conducted by way of a re-hearing.[55] Such a person can also appeal to the Crown Court against the making or refusal to make an order under s 103 (namely, the variation, renewal or discharge of a VOO) (s 106(2)).

As s 103 applies in relation to the variation or discharge of an IVOO (s 104(8)), **6.51** an appeal will also lie to the Crown Court against the variation or discharge, or refusal to vary or discharge an IVOO.

Under the ASBO regime, there is no appeal to the Crown Court available against **6.52** variation or discharge, only against 'the making' of an ASBO.[56] The decision to include such a right of appeal in the VOO legislation is undoubtedly a pragmatic one as the alternative would be a flood of public law challenges.

The Crown Court has wide powers on appeal. It can make such orders as necessary **6.53** to give effect to its determination (s 106(3)) as well as such incidental or consequential orders as appear to it to be just (s 106(3)(b)). Any order made by the Crown Court on appeal from the magistrates' court is treated, for the purposes of any application to vary, renew or discharge, as an order of the magistrates' court from which the appeal was brought (s 106(4)).

---

[55] Pursuant to 79(3) of the Supreme Court Act 1981.

[56] CDA 1998, s 4. See also *R(Langley) v Preston Crown Court (defendant) and West Lancashire District Council and The secretary of state (interest parties)* [2008] EWHC 2623 (Admin).

10. Notification requirements (ss 107–112)

6.54 Notification requirements are automatic once a VOO or IVOO is in force (CJIA 2008, s 107(1)). Those subject to IVOOs are not subject to the periodic notification requirements in s 110 (for which see para **6.59** below). The notification requirements are broadly similar to the requirements which apply to offenders convicted of sex offences under Part 2 of the Sexual Offences Act 2003 (also known as the 'sex offenders' register').

(a) *Required information*

6.55 Section 108(1) requires an offender to provide 'required information' within 3 days of a VOO or IVOO coming into force ('the relevant date'). 'Required information' consists of the following:

(a) date of birth;
(b) national insurance number;
(c) name or names of the offender on the relevant date;
(d) home address on the relevant date;[57]
(e) name or names on the date of notification;
(f) home address on the date of notification;
(g) any other address in the UK at which on the date of notification the offender regularly resides or stays;
(h) any information prescribed by the regulations made by the Secretary of State.[58]

6.56 By s 108(4) of the CJIA 2008, the 3 days mentioned in s 108(1) exclude any time when the offender is in custody pursuant to a court order or kept in service custody[59] or serving a sentence of imprisonment[60] or a term of service detention[61] or is detained in hospital[62] or is outside the UK.

(b) *Change of circumstances*

6.57 Section 109 sets out a complex list of requirements in the event of relevant changes occurring in an offender's circumstances. Relevant changes are those that qualify as a 'notifiable event', which are set out at s 109(2), and include a change of name or address and the residing at an address which has not been previously notified for

---

[57] Further defined at CJIA 2008, s 108(5) to include offenders who are homeless or of no fixed abode. In those circumstances, a park bench or a friend's house may suffice (see Explanatory Notes at para 628).

[58] CJIA 2008, s 108(3).

[59] 'Kept in service custody' means kept in service custody by virtue of an order under s 105(2) of the Armed Forces Act 2006 (not yet in force) (CJIA 2008, s 117(1)), but see also Sch 27, Part 7, para 32(1) (Transitory, transitional and saving provisions) for the definition prior to the commencement of the Armed Forces Act 2006.

[60] 'Sentence of imprisonment' has the same meaning as it does in Part 2 of the Sexual Offences Act 2003, ss 133 and 135 (CJIA 2008, s 117(1)).

[61] 'Service detention' has the meaning given by s 374 of the Armed Forces Act 2006 (not yet in force) (CJIA 2008, s 117(1)) but see also Sch 27, Part 7, para 32(1) (Transitory, transitional and saving provisions) for the definition prior to the commencement of the Armed Forces Act 2006.

[62] This has the same meaning as it does in Part 2 of the Sexual Offences Act 2003, ss 133 and 135 (CJIA 2008, s 117).

a period of 7 days (which is not necessarily 7 consecutive days and can mean two or more periods that amount to 7 days in a 12 month period[63]).

Once there has been a notifiable event, there is a requirement to provide the 'required new information' (as set out at s 109(3)) within 3 days[64] of the date on which the event occurred (s 109(1)). There is room for an offender to notify in advance of a notifiable event, but that is subject to various provisos and does not necessarily displace the requirement to notify within 3 days of the event (see s 109(4), (5), and (6)). 6.58

(c) *Periodic notification*

Those subject to IVOOs are exempt from the periodic notification requirements (s 110(7)). Basically, an offender is required to repeat the notification requirements in s 108 within one year (s 110(5)(b)), or in certain defined circumstances, within such period as the Secretary of State prescribes (s 110(5)(a) and (6)), unless he has already notified changes under s 109(1) within that period. The period is extended if the requirement to notify arises at a time when an offender is in custody, etc (s 110(3) and (4)). 6.59

(d) *Travel outside UK*

Section 111 gives the Secretary of State power to make regulations requiring offenders who leave the United Kingdom to disclose to the police the date on which they leave, the country to be visited, information about their return, and any other information prescribed by the regulations.[65] 6.60

(e) *Method of notification*

Notification under CJIA 2008, ss 108(1), 109(1), and 110(1), is given by attending a police station in the offender's local police area[66] and by giving the notification orally to a police officer or authorized person (s 112(a) and (b)). If the notification involves a change of address the notification can take place at the police station local to that address (s 112(2)). Any such notification has to be acknowledged in writing and in a form directed by the Secretary of State (s 112(3)[67]). 6.61

If requested to by the police or other authorized person, the offender *must* allow that person to take his fingerprints, photograph him or any part of him or both in order to verify his identity (s 112(3)). The failure to comply without reasonable excuse is a criminal offence (see para **6.63** below). This requirement mirrors the requirement in the Sexual Offences Act 2003. 6.62

---

[63] CJIA 2008, s 109(9).

[64] Subject to CJIA 2008, s 108(4), as explained at para **6.56** above.

[65] For parallel regulations under the Sexual Offences Act 2003, see Sexual Offences Act 2003 (Travel Notification Requirements) Regulations 2004, SI 2004/1220.

[66] Defined at CJIA 2008, s 112(5).

[67] For parallel regulations, see the Sexual Offences Act 2003 (Prescribed Police Stations) Regulations 2005, SI 2005/210.

11. Criminal offences (s 113)

(a) *Extent*

6.63 Offences under this section apply throughout the UK even though VOOs can be imposed only by courts in England and Wales.[68]

(b) *The penalty*

6.64 There are three types of offences provided for by the CJIA 2008, s 113, all of which attract the same penalty: on summary conviction a term not exceeding 12[69] months in England, Wales, and Scotland and 6 months in Northern Ireland or a fine or both; on indictment a term not exceeding 5 years or a fine or both (s 113(6) and (7)).

(c) *Non-compliance with a term of an order*

6.65 The first offence is the failure, without reasonable excuse, to comply with any prohibition, restriction or condition contained in a VOO or IVOO (s 113(1)).

(d) *Non-compliance with notification requirements*

6.66 The second is the failure, without reasonable excuse, to comply with initial notification requirements under the CJIA 2008, s 108(1) or notification of changes under s 109(1) or (6)(b) or periodic notification requirements under s 110(1) or the fingerprint and photograph requirements in s 112(4) or any regulations imposed by the travel notification requirements under s 111(1) (s 113(2)).

6.67 In relation to non-compliance with the CJIA 2008, ss 108(1), 109(1), 110(1) or any regulations made under s 111(1), this is a continuing offence. A person commits an offence on the first day on which the person fails, without reasonable excuse, to comply with any of these provisions, and continues to commit it throughout any period during which the failure continues (s 113(4)). However, a person cannot be prosecuted more than once in respect of the same failure (s 113(5)).

6.68 In *R v Clark (James)*[70] and *R v Bowman (Maximus John)*,[71] sentencing cases under the almost identical notification provisions in the Sexual Offences Act 2003, the court acknowledged the complexities that could arise where an offender, who was subject to notification requirements, was not of fixed abode and at times had been homeless.

(e) *Providing false information*

6.69 The third is knowingly providing false information in relation to purported compliance with the notification requirements in the CJIA 2008, ss 108(1), 109(1), 110(1) or any regulations made under s 111(1).

---

[68] CJIA 2008, s 152(2).

[69] In England and Wales, the reference to 12 months is to be read as a reference to 6 months in relation to an offence committed prior to the commencement of the CJA 2003, s 154(1) (CJIA 2008, Sch 27, Part 7, para 31).

[70] [2003] 1 Cr App R (S) 2.

[71] [2006] 2 Cr App R (S) 40.

(f) *The defence of 'reasonable excuse'*

As with other criminal offences which include a statutory defence of 'reasonable   6.70
excuse', the standard of proof (on the defendant) is the balance of probabilities.[72]

Whether the defence is made out will depend on the facts of each case. In a jury   6.71
trial whether a defence amounts to a reasonable excuse is for the jury to decide and
judges should be slow to withdraw any such defence from them.[73] If the defendant
raises the issue that he believed that the conduct about which the complaint is made
was permitted by the order, the prosecution will have to prove that the defendant
did not have reasonable excuse for the prohibited conduct. Acting under a reasonable misapprehension as to the scope and meaning of the order is capable of being a
reasonable excuse for acting in a manner which is prohibited by the order.[74]

12. The supply of information (ss 114–116)

(a) *Supply of information to Secretary of State, etc*

Section 114 of the CJIA 2008 provides that a chief officer of police has the power to   6.72
check the accuracy of information notified to the police under ss 108(1), 109(1) and
110(1) for the purposes of the prevention, detection, investigation or prosecution of
offences under the CJIA 2008, Part 7. He can do so by supplying it to the Secretary
of State (or a person providing services to the Secretary of State in connection with
a 'relevant function'[75]) who can in turn compare it with information held in relation
to that function.

The Secretary of State, etc can then compile a report of that comparison (s 114(3)(b)) and   6.73
supply it to the chief officer of police (s 115(1)). The chief of police is authorized to retain the
information, whether or not it is used for the prevention, etc of offences under Part 7 and to
use it for the prevention, etc of offences generally, but for no other purpose (s 115(3)).

Such supply of information under the CJIA 2008, ss 114 and 115 will not breach   6.74
any restrictions on disclosure of information as long as it does not contravene the
Data Protection Act 1998, nor does it affect any power to supply information that
exists apart from ss 114 and 115 (see ss 114(4)–(6) and 115(4)).

(b) *Information about release or transfer*

Section 116 gives the Secretary of State power to make provision by regulations that   6.75
require certain persons who will be responsible for an offender[76] subject to notification
requirements who is serving a sentence of imprisonment[77] or service detention[78]

---

[72] See for example *R v Brown*, 55 Cr App R 478.

[73] See *R v Heather Shirley Nicholson* [2006] 2 Cr App R 30.

[74] *R v Dorothy Evans* [2005] 1 Cr App R 549 at [21].

[75] Defined at CJIA 2008, s 114(7) as social security, child support, employment, training or passport functions
or a function under Part 3 of the Road Traffic Act 1988 (the licensing of drivers of vehicles).

[76] CJIA 2008, s 116(4) states that the regulations may make provisions for determining who is to be taken
to be the person responsible.

[77] 'Sentence of imprisonment' has the same meaning as it does in Part 2 of the Sexual Offences Act 2003,
ss 133 and 135 (see CJIA 2008, s 117(1)).

[78] 'Service detention' has the meaning given by s 374 of the Armed Forces Act 2006 (not yet in force) (CJIA
2008, s 117(1)) but see also Sch 27, Part 7, para 32(1) (Transitory, transitional and saving provisions) for the
definition prior to the commencement of the Armed Forces Act 2006.

or is detained in a hospital[79] to give notice to persons (who will be specified in the regulations) that they have become responsible for the offender and to inform them if the offender is released or if somebody else has become responsible for them.

B. PREMISES CLOSURE ORDERS

1. Introduction

6.76 Part 8, s 118 inserts Sch 20 into the CJIA 2008,[80] which in turn inserts a new Part 1A (which contains ss 11A–K) into the Anti-social Behaviour Act (ASBA) 2003.[81] Part 1A makes provision about the issue of closure notices and the making of closure orders in respect of premises associated with persistent disorder or nuisance. It mirrors the ASBA 2003, Part 1 (the scheme currently in force for 'crack house' closure orders). Part 1 has eleven sections; hence the first section inserted by the CJIA 2008 is 11A.

6.77 The 'crack house' closure order scheme introduced in January 2004[82] has been a controversial one. It is designed to close down certain residential premises (be they privately owned or owned by a local authority) within 48 hours of occupiers of such premises being notified of such an intention, and has required judicial intervention to ensure procedural fairness. The power was apparently used over 700 times between January 2004 and September 2006[83] to close down crack houses.

6.78 In *R (Cleary) v Highbury Corner Magistrates' Court*,[84] May LJ recognized that 'applications for closure orders threaten to trample on defendants' Article 8 rights and defendants may be vulnerable and unrepresented'.[85] The High Court identified a number of difficulties with the legislation: it did nothing to spell out the means whereby the magistrates' court are to be satisfied, nor, importantly, the steps which must be taken to ensure that Article 6 of the ECHR is complied with, so that defendants, who may be at risk of losing their home, have a fair hearing. Further, particular problems arose because the statutory time limits were very short; there was routine reliance on hearsay evidence and the Magistrates' Court (Hearsay Evidence in Civil Proceedings) Rules 1999 are in direct conflict with the time limits for hearing a closure order application.

6.79 Despite the defects in the regime identified by the Court in *Cleary*, the Home Office, in a bid to extend the scheme, described it as delivering 'visible, accountable and speedy summary justice. . . .with all the necessary court and judicial safeguards . . . an example of a new balance between rights and due process'.[86] Not only was the existing scheme not amended to safeguard rights, new Part 1A closure orders, which

---

[79] This has the same meaning as it does in Part 2 of the Sexual Offences Act 2003, ss 133 and 135 (CJIA 2008, s 117(1)).

[80] In force as of 1 December 2008, CJIA 2008 (Commencement No 4 and Saving Provision) Order 2008, SI 2008/2993.

[81] ASBA 2003, Part 1 does not extend to Scotland: see ASBA 2003, s 96(1).

[82] SI 2003/3300.

[83] 'Tools and Powers to Tackle Anti-Social Behaviour', January 2007.

[84] [2007] 1 All ER 270.

[85] At para 34.

[86] 'Strengthening Powers to Tackle Anti-Social Behaviour: Consultation Paper', Home Office, November 2006.

will undoubtedly affect a much larger class of people, have made their way on to the statute book.

Questions remain about the impact of such closure orders on the vulnerable, particularly children. It is conceivable that the behaviour of one person in the household (be it an adult or a child or a young person) could have severe consequences for the entire family. Given the drastic ramifications of eviction, the government has insisted it will issue 'robust guidelines' and that 'clear and sensitive distinctions will need to be made in relation to those who are being targeted as part of the order'.[87]   6.80

Indeed, Part 1A has a new section entitled 'Guidance' (s 11K) which is not included in Part 1, which gives the Secretary of State power to issue guidance and imposes an obligation on those discharging functions under Part 1A to have regard to the guidance.[88] The guidance was published in November 2008, just before part 1A came into force.[88a]   6.81

The making of a closure order in relation to private dwellings undoubtedly engages Article 8 of the ECHR (the right to private life) and in many cases will also engage Article 1 of Protocol No 1 (the right to peaceful enjoyment of possessions).[89] Part 1 orders were limited to premises upon which Class A drugs were used, produced or supplied. By contrast, Part 1A orders do not necessarily require criminal behaviour to be demonstrated. The courts will be required to carry out an extremely careful balancing exercise when deciding whether the activity complained of is serious enough to interfere with family life, otherwise they will fall foul of the Human Rights Act 1998.   6.82

Although this new scheme is closely modelled on the Anti-social Behaviour etc (Scotland) Act 2004,[90] in that Act the sheriff has a statutory obligation to consider both an occupant's ability to find other accommodation as well as the vulnerability of any occupant who has not engaged in anti-social behaviour, before making any such order.   6.83

2. Part 1A closure notices (s 11A)

Section 11A (as inserted by the CJIA 2008, s 118 and Sch 20 into the ASBA 2003) gives a police officer not below the rank of superintendent[91] or the local authority[92] the power to authorize the issue of a closure notice if either has reasonable grounds for believing 'that at any time during the relevant period a person has engaged in anti-social behaviour on the premises'[93] *and* 'that the use of the premises is associated   6.84

---

[87] The *Criminal Justice and Immigration Bill*, Bill 130 of 2006–07: Research Paper 07/65, 9 August 2007. House of Commons Library, at 87–88.

[88] In relation to Part 1 orders it has been said that the guidance does not have a particular legal status but it is capable of being persuasive authority: see *Chief Constable of Cumbria Constabulary v Mark Wright & Fiona Wood* [2006] EWHC 3574 (Admin).

[88a] It is available at <http://www.respect.gov.uk/uploadedFiles/Members_site/Documents_and_images/Enforcement_tools_and_powers/PremisesClosureNov08_0156.pdf>.

[89] *Chief Constable of Merseyside v Harrison* [2007] QB 79 at [21].

[90] Section 30(3).

[91] In the parallel ASBA 2003, Part 1 regime, the police officer can be a designated person not below grade 2.

[92] This is the local authority for the area in which the premises are located (s 11L(7)). 'Local authority' is defined at ss 11L(5) and (6).

[93] For the definition of 'anti-social behaviour', see para **6.92** below.

with significant and persistent disorder or persistent serious nuisance to members of the public' (s 11A(1)). 'Premises' includes 'any land or other place whether enclosed or not' and 'any outbuildings which are or are used as part of premises' (s 11L(13). The 'relevant period' is the three months preceding the date upon which the relevant officer comes to make the authorization decision (s 11A(11)).

6.85   Before such authorization can be given, the relevant officer (or the local authority) must be satisfied that there has been consultation with the local authority (or the police) and that reasonable steps have been taken to establish the identity of any person who lives on the premises or who has control of or responsibility for or an interest in the premises (s 11A(2) and (3)). The authorization can be given orally, but must be confirmed in writing as soon as practicable (s 11A(4)).

6.86   Consultation between the police and local authorities should include discussion about less intrusive interventions, any statutory duties to the occupants[94] as well as their housing obligations and needs. There may or may not be a duty on the local authority to provide housing assistance for those affected by a closure order, depending on whether their homelessness is classified as 'intentionally homeless'.

6.87   In a Public Bill Committee debate, the Secretary of State promised guidance which would emphasis the 'last resort' nature of these applications:

> Premises closure orders are an attempt to plug a difficult gap and they had huge public support. The question is, how do we make them work proportionately and in a way that we can all feel comfortable with? . . . There will be robust guidance on how the orders operate and how the process is put into practice. I will ensure that we include housing considerations as part of the guidance . . . However, as part of the guidance we would also expect the police, the local authority and all of the other statutory agencies to show that consideration has been given to every other possible intervention prior to a premises closure order being applied for. *In other words, the guidance will say that this process is only appropriate if it is an absolute last resort and nothing else seems to be appropriate.*[95] (emphasis added)

6.88   Although the statute does not require it, good practice dictates that a closure notice should contain confirmation of the statutory consultation requirement. The notice must contain various other details, including the date, time and place of the hearing in the magistrates' court, and most importantly, the fact that access to the premises by any person other than a person who habitually resides in the premises or the owner of the premises is prohibited and that the failure to comply with the notice is an offence (s 11A(5)). The notice should also give information about 'relevant legal advice providers' (s 11A(5)(f)).[96]

6.89   That said, in the parallel 'crack house' closure order regime (Part 1 orders), the High Court has ruled that the making of a closure order is not contingent on the original closure notice being valid, although defects in the notice may affect subsequent criminal proceedings insofar as they depended upon the validity of the notice.[97]

---

[94] For example under the NHS and Community Care Act 1990 or the Children Act 1989.

[95] PBC 27 November 2007 c621.

[96] Details of those who provide advice on legal and housing matters (s 11A(11)).

[97] *R (Errington) v Metropolitan Police Authority* (2006) EWHC 1155 (Admin); 171 JP 89; at [23].

Details of how service of the notice is effected, by whom, and upon whom, are contained in s 11A(6)–(9).

3. Making a Part 1A closure order (s 11B)

Once a closure notice has been issued, a constable or the local authority[98] (depending   6.90
on which body authorized it), must apply to a magistrates' court for such a closure
order (s 11B(1) and (2)). The application must be heard no later than 48 hours after
the notice was served (s 11B(3)). A Part 1A closure order is an order that the premises
in respect of which the order is made are closed to all persons for such period (not
exceeding three months) as the court decides (s 11B(5)). It may be made in respect of
all or any part of the premises in respect of which the notice was issued (s 11B(9)).

The statutory test for a Part 1A closure order requires the magistrates' court to be   6.91
satisfied of each of the following three conditions pursuant to s 11B(4):

(a) a person has engaged in anti-social behaviour on the premises in respect of which
the Part 1A closure notice was served; *and*
(b) the use of the premises is associated with significant *and* persistent disorder *or*
persistent serious nuisance to members of the public; *and*
(c) the making of the order is necessary to prevent the occurrence of such disorder
or nuisance for the period specified in the order. [emphasis added]

The justices would have to be satisfied of each of the three matters specified in (a),   6.92
(b), and (c), although there is a 'choice' in (b) of either 'significant *and* persistent
disorder' or 'persistent serious nuisance'.[99] As to (a), borrowing from the ASBO
regime, 'anti-social behaviour' is defined as 'behaviour by a person which causes or
is likely to cause harassment, alarm or distress to one or more other persons not of
the same household as the person' (s 11L).[100] In *R (on the application of Gosport LBC)
v Fareham Magistrates Court*[101] it was said that this criterion could not be satisfied
where there was no potential victim present at the time of the past events relied on.
The word 'likely' in this context means 'more probable than not'.[102] The use of the
words 'not of the same household' deliberately excludes from this regime anti-social
behaviour displayed towards a co-habitee.[103]

As to (b), neither phrase is defined in the Act, and it is difficult to understand   6.93
the seemingly deliberate omission of the word 'and' in the second phrase ('persistent
serious'), or to consider that its exclusion makes any material difference to the
interpretation of either term.

---

[98] This is the local authority for the area in which the premises are located (s 11L(7)). 'Local authority' is defined at ss 11L(5) and (6).

[99] See *Chief Constable of Cumbria Constabulary v Mark Wright & Fiona Wood* [2006] EWHC 3574 (Admin) for a discussion of the inter-relationship between the sub-sections in ASBA 2003, Part 1 cases.

[100] The test in CDA 1998, s 1(1)(a) is that the defendant 'Has acted in an anti-social manner, that is to say, in a manner that caused or was likely to cause harassment, alarm or distress to one or more persons not of the same household as himself.'

[101] [2007] 1 WLR 634, QBD.

[102] *Chief Constable of Lancashire v Potter* [2003] EWHC 2272 (Admin).

[103] See *R v Gowan (Jason)*[2007] Crim LR 812, CA on the meaning of the same phrase in the ASBO context.

6.94   In the law of tort, nuisance is defined as 'an act or omission which is an interference with, disturbance of or annoyance to, a person in the exercise or enjoyment of (a) right belonging to him as a member of the public, when it is a public nuisance, or (b) his ownership or occupation of land or of some easement, profit, or other right used or enjoyed in connection with land, when it is a private nuisance'.[104] Public nuisance is also a common law criminal offence.[105]

6.95   'Significant', 'persistent', and 'serious' are obviously ordinary English words and we will have to see how the courts interpret them in this context. The guidance provides examples at para 3.1.2 of conduct that the Home Office considers should act as a guideline on the level of nuisance in and around the premises to be considered serious.

6.96   As to (c), since a closure order may dispossess a person from his home, Article 8 of the ECHR is of central importance, and the court will have to be satisfied that it is both necessary and proportionate to make such an order.[106] As to the procedure for obtaining a closure order and the relationship with the hearsay rules,[107] see *R (Cleary) v Highbury Corner Magistrates' Court*.[108]

6.97   Even if a closure order is made, it may include such provision as the court thinks appropriate relating to access to any other part of the building or structure of which the premises form part (s 11B(6)).

4. The standard of proof

6.98   The statute is silent on this issue, however the High Court has had to consider it in relation to Part 1 orders. The burden of proof is of course on the police[109] and the standard of proof is the normal civil standard.[110] However, in *R (Cleary) v Highbury Corner Magistrates' Court*,[111] the court emphasized that the civil standard of proof is plainly coloured by the fact that Article 8 is engaged.

5. Adjournment of the application

6.99   Section 11B(7) gives the magistrates' court a statutory power to adjourn the hearing of an application for 14 days to allow the occupier of the premises, or the person who has control or responsibility for the premises, or any other person with an interest to show why a closure order should not be made. A magistrates' court may order the closure notice to continue in effect until the end of the adjournment (s 11B(7)).

6.100   Given that an application has to be heard within 48 hours of the notice being served, it is hardly surprising that those who stand to be deprived of their homes often need time to prepare for the hearing properly. In *Commissioner of the*

---

[104] *Clerk & Lindsell on Torts* at 20-01.
[105] See *R v Rimmington* [2006] 1 AC 459 for a discussion of the elements of this offence.
[106] *R (Cleary) v Highbury Corner Magistrates' Court* [2007] 1 All ER 270.
[107] The Magistrates' Court (Hearsay Evidence in Civil Proceedings) Rules 1999 provide for 21 days notice of reliance on hearsay which is at odds with the 48-hour timetable.
[108] [2007] 1 All ER 270.
[109] Ibid.
[110] *Chief Constable of the Merseyside Police v Harrison* [2007] QB 79.
[111] [2007] 1 All ER 270.

Metropolitan Police v Hooper[112] (a decision relating to Part 1 closure orders) it was held that a further adjournment, beyond 14 days, was possible under s 54 of the MCA 1980, but the power should be exercised in exceptional circumstances since the notice will lapse if any adjournment beyond the 14-day period is allowed.[113]

6. Duration and extension of orders

Section 11B(5) stipulates that a Part 1A closure order can initially be made for any period not exceeding three months. Any application to extend or further extend must be made by the police or the local authority (depending on who the original applicant was) at any time before a closure order's designated period ends (s 11(E)(1)). The court has the power to extend the order for a period of up to three months (s 11E(5)) but the overall length of the order must not exceed six months (s 11E(6)).   6.101

An application to extend is made by complaint (s 11E(1)) and must be authorized by a police officer not below the rank of superintendent or the local authority, as appropriate, and such a person must have reasonable grounds for believing that it is necessary to extend the order for the purpose of preventing the occurrence of significant and persistent disorder or persistent serious nuisance (s 11E(2) and (3)). Additionally, the relevant person must be satisfied that the local authority has consulted the appropriate chief officer[114] or vice versa (s 11E(2) and (3)).   6.102

Once a complaint is made, the magistrates' court can issue a summons requiring the person or persons upon whom the closure notice was served (usually the excluded occupier) or any other person who appears to have an interest in the premises to attend court to answer the complaint, but it is not obliged to (s 11E(4)). The High Court in *R (Derek Smith) v Snaresbrook Crown Court*[115] endorsed the proposition that fair procedure requires that where possible proper notice should be given to the excluded occupier.[116] Section 11E(10) deals with details of what the summons, if issued, should contain.   6.103

Before a court can make such an extension it must be satisfied 'that the order is necessary to prevent the occurrence of significant and persistent disorder or persistent serious nuisance to members of the public for a further period' (s 11E(5)). The Home Office guidance states at para 11.1.1 that it does not expect extensions after 3 months to be routine.[117] For guidance on how the court should approach the test for extension in the Part 1 regime, see *R (Derek Smith) v Snaresbrook Crown Court.*[118]   6.104

---

[112] [2005] 4 All ER 1095.

[113] See also *R (Turner) v Highbury Corner Magistrates' Court* [2005] EWHC 2568.

[114] Defined by s 11L(3) as the chief officer of police of the area in which the premises are situated.

[115] [2008] EWHC 1282 (Admin).

[116] At paragraph 7(3).

[117] Available on the Home Office website <http://www.respect.gov.uk/uploadedFiles/Members_site/Documents_and_images/Enforcement_tools_and_powers/PremisesClosureNov08_0156.pdf>.

[118] [2008] EWHC 1282 (Admin) at para 19.

7. Discharge

6.105   A constable, the local authority, a person on whom the closure notice was served or a person who has an interest in the closed premises but upon whom a notice was not served can make an application by way of complaint to the magistrates' court for the discharge of a Part 1A closure order (s 11E(7)). The court must not make an order discharging a closure order unless it is satisfied that the closure order is no longer necessary to prevent the occurrence of significant and persistent disorder or persistent serious nuisance to members of the public (s 11E(9)). Sections 11E(8) and (10) deal with who the court may summons in relation to such a complaint and the details that the summons should contain.

8. Appeals (s 11F)

6.106   Section 11F confers a right of appeal against a decision to make an order or to extend an order (s 11F(1)(a)). Such an appeal is also available against a decision not to make either of those orders (s 11F(1)(b)). An appeal must be brought before the Crown Court within 21 days beginning on the day of decision (s 11(2)). In *R (Errington) v Metropolitan Police Authority*,[119] Collin J said that Crown Courts should give such appeals priority and hear them in a matter of days.[120]

6.107   An appeal against the making of an order or the extension of an order may be brought either by someone who was served with the notice, or someone who has an interest in the premises but was not served with the notice (s 11F(3)). Conversely, either a local authority or a constable (depending on who the original applicant was) may appeal against the decision of a court not to make or extend an order (s 11F(4)). Such appeals are 'as of right' and by way of full rehearing, do not require permission and, as such, do not require the appellant to specify the grounds upon which he appeals. On appeal the Crown Court may make such order as it thinks appropriate (s 11F(5)).

9. Access to other premises (s 11G)

6.108   Sections 11G(1) and (2) give anyone who either lives in or owns any part of a building or structure in which closed premises are situated and in respect of which the closure order does not have effect the right to apply to the magistrates' court (or the Crown Court where an order was made on appeal) to obtain access. Section 11G(3) requires notice of such an application to be given to various parties. The court may make such order as it thinks appropriate in relation to access (s 11G(4)). It is immaterial whether any provision has been made pursuant to s 11B(6) (see para **6.97** above).

---

[119] (2006) EWHC 1155 (Admin).
[120] At para 12.

10. Powers of entry (s 11C)

A constable (or a person authorized by the chief constable) or a person authorized   6.109
by the local authority ('a relevant person')[121] has a power under s 11C(2) to enter
the premises in respect of which a closure order has been made and to do anything
reasonably necessary to secure the premises against entry by any person.

Section 11C(3) authorizes that person to use reasonable force to enter or to secure   6.110
the premises in accordance with s 11C(2)(b). However, such a person must, if
required to do so by or on behalf of the owner, occupier or other person in charge of
the premises, produce evidence of his identity and authority before entering the
premises (s 11C(5)).

A relevant person may also enter closed premises to carry out essential maintenance   6.111
or repairs (s 11C(5)). A similar power exists in relation to premises in respect of
which a closure notice has been authorized but is limited to entry for the sole purpose
of effecting service of a notice (s 11A(9)).

11. Criminal offences (s 11D)

Section 11D(1) provides that a person commits an offence if he remains on or enters   6.112
premises in contravention of either a closure notice (s 11D(1)) or a closure order
(s 11D (2)(b) and (c)). It is also an offence under s 11D(2) to obstruct a constable
or a local authority employee seeking to effect the service of a closure notice under
s 11A(7) or a relevant person[122] seeking to enter and secure the closure of premises
in accordance with s 11C(2).

(a) *The penalty*
A person guilty of an offence under s 11D is liable on summary conviction to   6.113
imprisonment for a period of up to 51 weeks in relation to offences committed after
the commencement of the CJA 2003, 281(5)[123]and up to six months for those
committed before that date or a fine not exceeding level 5 (s 11D(3) and (5)).
A constable may arrest a person he reasonably suspects of committing or having
committed an offence under s 4.

(b) *Defences*
There is a statutory defence of reasonable excuse available for entering or remaining   6.114
on a closed premises or in contravention of a closure notice (s 11D(4)).[124]

In *R (Errington) v Metropolitan Police Authority*[125] Collins J expressed the view   6.115
(at [23]) that an invalid notice may afford a defence to a criminal charge (see para
6.89 above).

---

[121] See s 11C(6) for the definition of 'a relevant person'.
[122] Ibid.
[123] Not yet in force.
[124] See also para **6.70** above.
[125] (2007) 171 JP 89.

12. Reimbursement of expenditure (s 11H)

6.116 Either the police or a local authority which incurs expenditure for the purpose of clearing, securing or maintaining the closed premises may apply for an order to be made for those costs (s 11H(1)). The court may make such order for reimbursement as it considers appropriate against the owner[126] of the premises. The limitation period for such applications is 3 months, starting with the day on which the closure order ceases to have effect (s 11H(2)). The application has to be served on the relevant police authority if made by the local authority (and vice-versa) and the owner (s 11H(4)).

13. Exemption from liability (s 11I)

6.117 Section 11I seeks to protect the police and the local authority when carrying out their functions under Part 1A against claims for damages in judicial review proceedings or in negligence claims or in claims for misfeasance in public office (s 11I(6)). However, it provides only a partial exemption in that the exemption does not cover acts or omissions made in bad faith or damages that a person may be entitled to by virtue of s 6(1) of the Human Rights Act 1998 (s 11I(4)).[127]

14. Compensation (s 11J)

6.118 Anyone who suffers financial loss as a result of either a closure notice or a closure order may apply to the court where it was made or extended for compensation from central funds (s 11J(1)).

6.119 Such an application has to made to the magistrates' court who considered the application for an order or the Crown Court that made or extended an order on appeal (s 11J(2)). The limitation period is 3 months starting with the day the court decided not to make a closure order, or the day the Crown Court dismissed an appeal, or the day an order ceases to have effect (whichever is latest) (s 11J(3)).

6.120 In order for compensation to be granted, the court must be satisfied that the person had no association with the significant and persistent disorder or the persistent serious nuisance[128] or, if that person is the owner[129] or occupier of the premises, that he took reasonable steps to prevent such use of the premises, and that he has incurred financial loss and it is appropriate to grant it (s 11J(4)).

---

[126] 'The owner' is defined at s 11L(9) and includes certain leaseholders.
[127] Human Rights Act 1998, s 6(1) makes it unlawful for a public authority to act in a way which is incompatible with a Convention right.
[128] As described in s 11A(1)(b).
[129] 'The owner' is defined at s 11L(9) and includes certain leaseholders.

C. YOUTH ASBOS AND RELATED ORDERS

1. Introduction

On 21 December 2005, Home Office Minister Hazel Blears announced that all 6.121
youth ASBOs would be reviewed after a period of one year (despite the statutory
minimum term of 2 years, subject to discharge). The Home Office guide to ASBOs
published in 2006[130] advised that all orders issued to young people should be
reviewed every year. The guide also indicated that 'this should become a statutory
requirement in the near future'.[131]

The CJIA 2008, Part 8, s 123(1) inserts two new sections, 1J and 1K, into Part 1 6.122
of the Crime and Disorder Act (CDA) 1998. Section 1J creates the obligation to
carry out a one year review of ASBOs issued to under 17 year olds and 1K sets out
which agencies are responsible for carrying out the reviews. Despite the fact that this
legislation has been promised for some years now, this section is still not in force.

This section also deals with the changes to other related youth orders, namely 6.123
individual support orders (ISOs), parenting contracts and parenting orders.

2. The review of the youth ASBO (s 1J)

All ASBOs imposed on those who were aged under 17 at the time the order was 6.124
made, regardless of whether they were made on a 'stand-alone' basis or on conviction
or in the county court, are subject to review (s 1J(1)). However, the review will only
be carried out if the person is still aged under 18 at the end of a 'review period' (for
which see para **6.125** below) (s 1J(1)(a)). If they are, then a review must be carried
out before the end of each review period. If an order is discharged before the end of
a review period, then a review is not carried out (s 1J(5)).

(a) *Types of review*
There are two types of review period specified. The first is 12 months beginning on 6.125
the day the order was made or if there was either a further order varying the original
ASBO or an ISO made in that period ('a supplemental order'), the clock will begin
to run from that date instead (s 1J(3)(a)). According to the Explanatory Notes to
the CJIA 2008, this is apparently to avoid a review having to be carried out when
a similar process will have been gone through for the purposes of variation or to
obtain an ISO.

The second and subsequent reviews are to be carried out on a 12 month cycle, 6.126
beginning on the day after the previous review, unless, as in the first review, a supplemental order was made (s 1J(3)(b)).

For transitional provisions which affect whether an ASBO is subject to review, see 6.127
para **6.134** below.

---

[130] A Guide to Anti-social Behaviour Orders (Home Office, 2006).
[131] Page 45.

(b) *Purpose of the review*

6.128 Section 1J(6) sets out a non-exhaustive of issues to be considered at any such review (extent of compliance, adequacy of available support and any other matters relevant to discharge or variation) but the statute lacks teeth insofar as it does not specify actions that should flow from such reviews, in particular when an ASBO should be discharged. Instead it leaves details of how reviews should be conducted and what action should follow to 'any guidance issued by the Secretary of State' (s 1J(7)).[132]

3. Responsibility for, and participation in, reviews (s 1K)

(a) *Which agency should conduct the review?*

6.129 Reviews of 'stand-alone'[133] and county court[134] ASBOs are to be carried out by the 'relevant authority' that applied for the order. 'Relevant authority' is defined in CDA 1998, s 1(1A) and that meaning is extended to s 1K by the CJIA 2008, s 123(2).

6.130 A post-conviction ASBO[135] is applied for by the CPS or imposed by a court of its own motion. A review will be carried out by the police unless another relevant authority is stipulated at the time of the ASBO is made or varied (s 1K(2)). The power to stipulate is introduced by amending the CDA 1998, s 1C to add a new s 1C(9ZA).[136]

(b) *Participation in the review*

6.131 A local authority carrying out a review has a duty to act in co-operation with 'the appropriate chief officer of police'[137] and the chief officer of police carrying out a review must act in co-operation with 'the appropriate local authority'[138] (s 1K(3) and (4)). The Act makes it a statutory duty to so co-operate.

6.132 If it is another relevant authority carrying out the review, than it has to co-operate with both the appropriate local authority and the appropriate chief officer of police, who in turn have an obligation to so co-operate (s 1K(5)).

6.133 Importantly, an authority carrying out a review, can invite the participation of a person or a body who is not required by statute to co-operate. Given that these reviews relate to youth ASBOs, it would seem eminently sensible to invite the participation of the Youth Offending Service (YOS)[139] or Social Services where a young person is 'looked after' or 'in need' within the meaning of the Children Act 1989 (s 1K(6)).

---

[132] No such guidance has been issued to date.
[133] CDA 1998, s 1.
[134] CDA 1998, s 1B.
[135] CDA 1998, s 1C.
[136] CDA 1998, s 1K(3), as inserted by CJIA 2008, s 123(3).
[137] Defined at CDA 1998, 1K(7), as inserted by CJIA 2008, s 123(1).
[138] Ibid.
[139] Formerly the Youth Offending Team (YOT).

(c) *Transitional, etc provisions*

The CJIA 2008, Sch 27, para 33 states that in order to qualify for a review, an ASBO   6.134
must be less than 9 months old when these provisions come into force, or have been
varied 9 months (or less) before the provisions come into force.

4. Individual support orders (ISOs)

ISOs were introduced by the CJA 2003 which inserted s 1AA into the CDA 1998.   6.135
They have been in force since 1 May 2004. The court is required to consider the
making of such an order when a stand-alone ASBO is made against a child or
young person (10 to 17 year olds) pursuant to the CDA 1998, s 1. ISOs last for up
to 6 months and impose specified activities designed to tackle the underlying causes
of the young person's anti-social behaviour. Under the current regime, the court has
to be satisfied of various pre-conditions before it can make such an order, in particular
that an individual support order would be desirable in the interests of preventing
any repetition of the kind of behaviour which led to the making of the anti-social
behaviour order (CDA 1998, s 1AA(3)).

Section 124 of the CJIA 2008 amends the existing regime by amending parts of   6.136
the CDA 1998, ss 1AA, 1AB, 1B, and 1C. At the time of writing, these provisions
are not yet in force.

Section 124(1) inserts new sections into the CDA 1998, s 1AA which now allow   6.137
ISOs to be made more than once and to be made *subsequent* to the making of the
ASBO, provided that at the time an application for an ISO is made, the ASBO is
still in force and the defendant is still a child or young person (in other words, still
under 18) and the application is made by the same relevant authority[140] that applied
for the ASBO. Further, by s 124(5) of the CJIA 2008,[141] the ISO cannot be made
to last beyond the lifetime of the original ASBO.

Section 124(2) amends the CDA 1998, s 1AA(3) to give the court the power to   6.138
impose an ISO to prevent not just the repetition of the kind of behaviour which led
to the making of the ASBO but also behaviour which led to a variation of that
ASBO (where the variation is made as a result of further anti-social behaviour by the
defendant). There is a corresponding amendment to the CDA 1998, s 1AA(5) by
virtue of s 142(3) of the CJIA 2008.

Section 142(6) allows for the making of ISOs in relation to county court ASBOs[142]   6.139
and s 142(7) does the same in relation to post-conviction ASBOs.[143] ISOs can also
be applied for by the relevant authority carrying out a review of the post-conviction
ASBO pursuant to s 1K of the CDA 1998 (as inserted by the CJIA 2008).[144]

The transitional provisions (CJIA 2008, Sch 27, para 34) provide that the amend-   6.140
ments made by the CJIA 2008, s 124 do not apply in relation to any ASBOs if they

---

[140] The definition of 'relevant authority' in CDA 1998, s 1(1A) is applied to the ISO regime by virtue of
CJIA 2008, s 142(4).
[141] Amending CDA 1998, s 1AB.
[142] Amending CDA 1998, s 1B.
[143] Amending CDA 1998, s 1C.
[144] See para **6.129** above.

were made more than 9 months before the date the section comes into force, unless the ASBO had been varied no more than 9 months before that date.

5. Parenting contracts and parenting orders

6.141   Parenting contracts were introduced by the ASBA 2003[145] and were subsequently amended by the Police and Justice Act 2006 and the Education and Inspections Act 2006. Like acceptable behaviour contracts, such a contract is a voluntary agreement between a parent and a local authority or the governing body of a school or a social landlord which is not legally enforceable and does not attract a criminal penalty on breach. The purpose is to prevent the child or young person from engaging in anti-social behaviour or further anti-social behaviour or behaviour that warrants school exclusion.

6.142   Parenting orders were initially introduced by s 8 of the CDA 1998 and have been available since 30 September 1998.[146] Various statutes since have amended the section, including the ASBA 2003, the Education and Inspections Act 2006, and the Police and Justice Act 2006. They are available in a number of circumstances including when an ASBO is made in respect of a child or young person. The purpose is to impose requirements on parents to prevent, for example, the repetition of the kind of behaviour which led to the making of the ASBO or exclusion from school. They can be applied for by local authorities, schools and registered social landlords.

6.143   The CJIA 2008, s 125(1) amends the definition of a local authority in the interpretation provisions of the ASBA 2003 (s 29(1)), so as to include 'district councils' as well as county councils within the list of councils which may enter into a parenting contract or apply for a parenting order.

6.144   Section 125(3) inserts a new subsection (8A) into the ASBA 2003, s 26B, which obliges a registered social landlord to consult with both a county council and a district council, before applying for a parenting order in relation to a child living in a district council.

6.145   Section 125 (4) amends s 27 of the ASBA 2003 to re-define which local authority can bring breach proceedings in relation to parenting orders. The amendments mean that breach proceedings are no longer to be brought by the local authority where the child (or young person) or parent (or guardian) resides, but rather the local authority who originally applied for the order, unless the child, etc or parent, etc is living in the area of another local authority. Where there is both a district council and a county council, either council can bring breach proceedings.

---

[145] ASBA 2003, ss 19 and 25.
[146] SI 1998/2327.

D. SEXUAL OFFENCES: ORDERS AND NOTIFICATION REQUIREMENTS

1. Sexual offences prevention orders (SOPOs)

SOPOs were introduced by the Sexual Offences Act 2003 and have been in force   6.146
since 1 May 2004. The purpose of these orders is to protect the public or any particular members of the public from serious sexual harm from the defendant.

The CJIA 2008, s 141, in force from 14 July 2008,[147] amends s 106 of the SOA   6.147
2003. The amendment removes the necessity under the Sexual Offences Act 2003,
ss 104 and 106 to meet certain conditions listed in Sch 3 to the 2003 Act when considering whether to make a SOPO. The conditions no longer applicable are those
that relate to the age of the victim, the age of the offender or the length of sentence
imposed. This means that SOPOs will now be available in relation to a larger group
of qualifying offenders.

Such an amendment will mean that young offenders convicted of offences listed   6.148
in Sch 3, who were previously excluded because of an age limitation, will become
eligible for a SOPO.

2. The sex offenders' register: notification requirements

The CJIA 2008, s 142, also in force from 14 July 2008,[148] introduces amendments   6.149
to the Sexual Offences Act 2003, ss 83 to 85 and s 138(2). The effect of the amendments is to allow the Secretary of State to amend, through secondary legislation, the
notification requirements of those on the sex offenders' register or those cautioned
or convicted of relevant sexual offences.

In addition to the comprehensive list of information required to be notified as   6.150
outlined in the Sexual Offences Act 2003, s 83(5), the amendment introduced by
virtue of the CJIA 2008, s 142(1), allows for the notification of 'any prescribed
information', prescribed by regulations made by the Secretary of State. Should the
Secretary of State add to the list of prescribed information, the CJIA 2008, ss 142(2)
to 142(5) apply the 3-day timescale in which the offender must notify the relevant
authorities of a change in any such prescribed circumstance.

Sections 142(6) to 142(9) amend the Sexual Offences Act 2003, s 85 to differen-   6.151
tiate between the periodic notification of those who have a sole or main residence in
the UK and those who do not. For those who benefit from a stable home address,
the periodic notification requirement remains annual. For those who do not, the
periodic notification may be prescribed in regulations made by the Secretary of State
and will no doubt, once prescribed, be more frequent.

---

[147] Criminal Justice and Immigration Act 2008 (Commencement No 2 and Transitional and Saving Provisions) Order 2008, SI 2008/1586.
[148] Ibid.

7

POLICE MISCONDUCT AND
INDUSTRIAL ACTION BY
PRISON OFFICERS

A. POLICE MISCONDUCT

1. Introduction

Part 9 of the CJIA 2008 makes changes to both the procedure governing disciplinary   7.01
proceedings for misconduct by police officers (s 126) and to the investigation of
complaints of police officer's misconduct by members of the public (s 127).

Police officers' conduct is currently governed by the Code of Conduct contained   7.02
in the Police (Conduct) Regulations 2004, made pursuant to ss 50 and 51 of the
Police Act (PA) 1996.[1] For there to be misconduct, there must be a failure to meet
the standard set out in the Code.

To date, guidance has been issued by way of Regulations on how to manage miscon-   7.03
duct proceedings. This guidance is found in 'Unsatisfactory Performance, Complaints
and Misconduct Procedures'[2] issued by the Home Office pursuant to ss 83 and 87 of
the PA 1996.

Where police inefficiency and unsatisfactory performance falls short of misconduct,   7.04
the procedure for resolution is set down in the Police (Efficiency) Regulations 1999[3]
made pursuant to ss 50 and 84 of the PA 1996. The existing procedures cover both
police officers and special constables.

Schedule 22, para 9 of the CJIA 2008 permits the Secretary of State to publish   7.05
new Regulations and Guidance in relation to disciplinary proceedings that concern
not only police officers and special constables but also extends the procedures to

---

[1] SI 2004/645, Sch 1.
[2] Home Office Circular 055/2002.
[3] SI 1999/732.

cover police staff, such as Police Community Support Officers (PCSOs) and police escort staff.

7.06   These new Regulations under the CJIA 2008 currently exist only as draft Statutory Instruments (SIs) referred to as the Draft Police (Conduct) Regulations 2008,[4] the Draft Police (Performance) Regulations 2008,[5] and the Draft Police Appeal Tribunal Rules 2008.[6] These Regulations have been laid before Parliament and are currently expected to come into force on 1 December 2008. A detailed discussion of these Regulations is outside the scope of this text but the relevant sections are highlighted below.

7.07   Each set of Regulations that have been made will require the approval of each House of Parliament[7] before they enter into force (referred to as the 'affirmative resolution procedure'[8]). Any subsequent Regulations may be annulled by a resolution of either House of Parliament[9] (referred to as the 'negative resolution procedure').

7.08   The procedure for the investigation of complaints of police misconduct by members of the public is governed by the Police Reform Act (PRA) 2002. Schedule 23 to the CJIA 2008 amends the provisions of the PRA 2002.

2. Background to the changes

7.09   The way in which both public complaints about police officers' conduct and internal disciplinary affairs are handled has been an area of intense scrutiny in recent years.

7.10   The PRA 2002 and specifically, its creation of the Independent Police Complaints Commission (IPCC) was itself a response to the need for radical reform of the police misconduct complaints system voiced within the *Macpherson Report* into the death of Stephen Lawrence in 1999.[10]

7.11   In 2004, an inquiry was ordered into the way in which internal complaints about ethnic minorities officers were being handled by the Metropolitan Police Service. This inquiry was chaired by Sir William Morris and the report that followed reflected the overwhelming criticism the inquiry received of the current regime.[11] The inquiry followed a number of high-profile cases including that of Superintendent Ali Dizaei, who was acquitted of criminal charges of dishonesty in 2003. He later complained that the police investigation against him had been nothing short of a 'witch hunt'.

---

[4] Tabled on 22 July 2008 (available at <http://www.opsi.gov.uk/si/si2008/draft/ukdsi_9780110835174_en_2#pt1-l1g1>).

[5] Ibid., (<available at http://www.opsi.gov.uk/si/si2008/draft/ukdsi_9780110835181_en_2>).

[6] Ibid.,(<available at http://www.opsi.gov.uk/si/si2008/draft/ukdsi_9780110835150_en_1>).

[7] PA 1996, s 84(8), as amended by CJIA 2008, Sch 22, para 7.

[8] Explanatory Notes to the CJIA 2008 at para 727.

[9] PA 1996, s 84(7), as amended by CJIA 2008, Sch 22, para 7.

[10] Cm 4262-I (1999).

[11] Full Report of the Morris Inquiry (available at <http://www.mpa.gov.uk/morrisinquiry/default.htm>).

Informed by the findings of the Morris Inquiry, a 'Fundamental Review of Police Disciplinary Arrangements' was conducted in 2004–2005, chaired by William Taylor CBE. The *Taylor Report* was published in January 2005.[12] 7.12

The reports of both the Morris Inquiry and the Taylor Review recommended that there should be a new single Code for police officers, incorporating both ethics and conduct. It was proposed that this Code should be modelled on the Council of Europe (COE) Code of Ethics.[13] 7.13

As a result, the Home Office and the Police Advisory Board published a new Code for Professional Standards for the Police, based on the COE Model. This code was put out for consultation in May 2006. There is currently a draft code of 'Standards for Professional Behaviour' attached as Sch 1 to the Draft Police (Conduct) Regulations 2008, which follows the COE Model.[14] 7.14

The *Taylor Report* further recommended that disciplinary arrangements should be established on the basis of thirteen key areas; 7.15

- (i) Disciplinary arrangements of police officers are most appropriately determined by Parliament (and not by an Employment Tribunal);
- (ii) The regulatory framework should avoid an overly legalistic or adversarial environment;
- (iii) Sanctions should play a part, but improvement must be an integral part of any outcome;
- (iv) Language and environment for handling police discipline should be open and transparent, less quasi-judicial and less adversarial;
- (v) Initial reports should be formally assessed with the full range of options available for responding;
- (vi) Conduct issues should be separated into two groups, 'misconduct' and 'gross misconduct';
- (vii) Conduct matters should be dealt with at the lowest possible line management level;
- (viii) Investigation hearings should be less formal where possible;
- (ix) There should be a single appeal mechanism for the policing environment;
- (x) The police service must handle complaints dynamically and promote the acceptance of responsibility;
- (xi) IPCC, Police Authorities and HMIC all have roles to play in protecting the public interest;
- (xii) All parts of the process must have a designated time limit with consequences for failure to do so;
- (xiii) Further guidance is required to make sure that issues of capability and performance are not dealt with as 'misconduct'.

Clause 111 of, and Sch 19 to, the Criminal Justice and Immigration Bill (as first introduced) set out the proposed changes to the primary legislation to accommodate 7.16

---

[12] 'Fundamental Review of Police Disciplinary Arrangements Report' January 2005 (available at <http://press.homeoffice.gov.uk/documents/police-disciplinary-arrangements/>).

[13] Set out at Appendix H of the *Taylor Report*, above.

[14] Tabled on 22 July 2008 (see **n 4** above).

new Regulations which in turn implemented the recommendations of the *Taylor Report*. The majority of the detail of the new framework will be set out through secondary legislation as discussed below.

3. Police misconduct and performance procedures

7.17 Section 126 of the CJIA 2008 introduces the provisions contained in Sch 22 to the Act. Section 126 was brought into force on 14 July 2008.[15] Paragraph 6 of Sch 22 came into force on 14 July 2008. Paragraphs 1 and 2 of Part 1 of Sch 22 came into force on 3 November 2008. Parts 3, 4 and 7 came into force on the same date but only for the purposes of making Regulations. Paragraph 8 also came into force on 3 November 2008 but only for the purpose of making Rules.[16] The rest of Sch 22 will be brought into force by way of a further commencement order on a date to be appointed.[16]

7.18 Section 126 of, and Sch 22 to, the CJIA 2008, as well as any Regulations issued by way of Statutory Instrument will only extend to England and Wales. The Draft Police (Conduct) Regulations 2008, when in force, will only apply to cases where the behaviour complained of came to the attention of the relevant authority on or after the date they came into force.[17] The Draft Police (Performance) Regulations 2008 will apply to unsatisfactory performance or attendance that came to the attention of a manager on or after the date that the Regulations came into force.[18]

7.19 Schedule 22 comprises of three Parts. Part 1 of Sch 22 amends the PA 1996 to make provisions for, or in connection with, disciplinary and other proceedings in respect of the conduct and performance of members of the police force and special constables. It also makes other minor amendments to the PA 1996.

7.20 Part 2 of Sch 22 makes equivalent amendments to the Ministry of Defence Police Act 1987 for the purposes of Ministry of Defence Police.

7.21 Part 3 of Sch 22 makes equivalent amendments to the Railways and Transport Safety Act 2003 for the purposes of the British Transport Police.

(a) *Sch 22, Part 1: the police and special constables*

7.22 Part 1, para 2 amends s 36(2)(d) of the PA 1996 to include within the Secretary of State's general duties to exercise his powers in a way that is best calculated to maximize the efficiency and effectiveness of the police, the remit of representation of officers at disciplinary hearings.[19] Part 1, para 2 came into force on 3 November 2008.[20]

7.23 Paragraphs 3 and 4 of Part 1 of Sch 22 amend ss 50 (regulations for police forces) and 51 (regulations for special constables) of the PA 1986. The effect of these amendments is that the Secretary of State can establish Regulations to govern procedures for disciplinary proceedings relating to the conduct, efficiency and effectiveness of members

---

[15] Criminal Justice and Immigration Act 2008 (Commencement No 2 and Transitional and Saving Provisions) Order 2008, SI 2008/1586.

[16] Criminal Justice and Immigration Act 2008 (Commencement No 3 and Transitional Provisions) Order 2008, SI 2008/2712.

[17] Regulation 2 of the Draft Police (Conduct) Regulations 2008.

[18] Regulation 2 of the Draft Police (Performance) Regulations 2008.

[19] Under s 84 of the PA 1996.

[20] Criminal Justice and Immigration Act 2008 (Commencement No 3 and Transitional and Provisions) Order 2008, SI 2008/2712.

of police forces and special constables including procedures in dismissal cases. The draft Regulations that have been tabled under s 50 of the PA 1996 (as amended) are the Draft Police (Performance) Regulations 2008.[21] Part 1, paras 3 and 4 came into force in full on 1 December 2008.[22]

The amendments only require the Regulations to set down procedure for cases 7.24 where dismissal is a sanction. They do not mention procedures resulting in any other sanction. It is clear from the explanatory notes to the CJIA 2008 that the new disciplinary proceedings system will not have the sanction of 'required to resign' as an outcome.[23]

In fact, under the Draft Police Draft (Conduct) Regulations 2008[24] the only 7.25 sanctions that a person or persons conducting misconduct proceedings can impose upon a finding of misconduct or gross misconduct are management advice, written warning, final written warning, dismissal with notice and dismissal without notice.[25]

Paragraphs 5 and 6 of Part 1 of Sch 22 make minor amendments to the wording 7.26 of ss 59(3) and 63(3) of the PA 1996 regarding representation by a police officer at disciplinary proceedings. There are no substantive changes made by these paragraphs. Part 1, para 5 came into force on 1 December 2008.[25a] Paragraph 6 of Sch 22 came into force on 14 July 2008.[26]

Paragraph 7 of Part 1 amends s 84 of the PA 1996 to allow the Secretary of State 7.27 to make Regulations by Statutory Instrument to govern the provision of:

- legal representation of police officers or special constables during disciplinary proceedings,[27]
- legal representation for the police force to which the officer or special constable belongs (or the IPCC) during disciplinary proceedings;[28]
- legal advice to the panel conducting disciplinary proceedings.[29]

Draft Regulations have been issued under s 84 of the PA 1996 (as amended). 7.28 They are the Draft Police (Performance) Regulations 2008.[30]

Section 84 previously allowed any officer below the rank of Superintendent to 7.29 elect legal representation in proceedings where he may be dismissed, required to resign or reduced in rank. If he elected, he could be represented by counsel or a solicitor. If he did not so elect, he could only be represented by a member of the police force. Part 1, para 7 came into force in full on 1 December 2008.[31]

---

[21] Tabled on 22 July 2008 (see **n 5** above).
[22] Criminal Justice and Immigration Act 2008 (Commencement No 4 and Saving Provision) Order 2008, SI 2008/2993.
[23] Explanatory Note to the CJIA 2008, para 732 (<http://www.opsi.gov.uk/acts/acts2008/en/08en04-j.htm>).
[24] Tabled on 22 July 2008 (see **n 4** above).
[25] Regulation 35 of the Draft Police Draft (Conduct) Regulations 2008.
[25a] Criminal Justice and Immigration Act 2008 (Commencement No 4 and Saving Provision) Order 2008, SI 2008/2993.
[26] Criminal Justice and Immigration Act 2008 (Commencement No 2 and Transitional and Saving Provisions) Order 2008. SI 2008/1586.
[27] PA 1996, s 84(1)(a), as amended by CJIA 2008, Sch 22, para 7.
[28] PA 1996, s 84(1)(a), as amended by CJIA 2008, Sch 22, para 7.
[29] PA 1996, s 84(1)(b), as amended by CJIA 2008, Sch 22, para 7.
[30] Tabled on 22 July 2008 (see **n 5** above).
[31] Criminal Justice and Immigration Act 2008 (Commencement No 4 and Saving Provision) Order 2008, SI 2008/2993.

7.30   Part 2 of the Draft (Conduct) Regulations 2008 deals with legal representation and allows an officer to nominate a 'police friend' who can advise that officer and represent him if he does not elect to be represented by a lawyer.[32] If the officer faces misconduct proceedings or a special case hearing, he is entitled to be represented by a lawyer of his choice.[33]

7.31   Section 84(3)(c) of the PA 1996 (as amended) states that any Regulations made under s 84 shall ensure that any proceedings at which the officer may be dismissed *and* is entitled to legal representation under the Regulations are not to take place until that officer has been notified of his right to legal representation. Previously, if an officer failed without reasonable cause to notify his intention to elect legal representation, he could be dismissed without being legally represented.[34]

7.32   Regulation 7 of the Draft (Conduct) Regulations 2008 echoes this section and states that if the officer concerned chooses not to be legally represented at a misconduct hearing he may be dismissed or receive any other outcome without his being so represented.

7.33   The *Taylor Report* recommended that the use of lawyers should generally be kept to a minimum and whilst they may have a part to play in hearings regarding gross misconduct, their role should be carefully prescribed.[35]

7.34   Under s 85 PA 1996 an officer has an automatic right of appeal against dismissal to the Police Appeal Tribunal (PAT). Section 85(1) (as amended) removes this automatic right and directs that the circumstances in which an officer *may* appeal will be prescribed by Regulations issued under this section. Part 1, para 8 came into force in full on 1 December 2008.[36]

7.35   These Regulations are the Draft Police Appeal Tribunals Rules 2008,[37] which will replace the Police Appeals Tribunal Rules 1999.[38] These Rules will come into force on 1 December 2008.[39] When in force, they will apply to England and Wales[40] and to appeals that are made against decisions under the Draft Police (Performance) Regulations 2008 and the Draft Police (Conduct) Regulations 2008 only.[41]

7.36   The Draft Police Appeal Tribunals Rules 2008 will set out the procedure on appeal to the PAT. In particular they make provision for:

• The PAT to determine a case without a hearing if the appellant so consents;[42]
• The appellant and respondent to be entitled to legal representation (further to s 84 of the PA 1996);[43]
• To enable the PAT to require any person to attend a hearing and give evidence or produce documents.[44]

---

[32] Regulations 6 of the Draft (Conduct) Regulations 2008.
[33] Regulation 7 of the Draft (Conduct) Regulations 2008.
[34] PA 1996, s 84(5).
[35] *Taylor Report*, para 4.3.2 at p 28.
[36] Criminal Justice and Immigration Act 2008 (Commencement No 4 and Saving Provision) Order 2008, SI 2008/2993.
[37] Tabled on 22 July 2008 (see **n 6** above).
[38] SI 1999/818 (enabling provision, PA 1996, s 85). In force 1 April 1999.
[39] Draft Police Appeal Tribunals Rules 2008, reg 1.
[40] Draft Police Appeal Tribunals Rules 2008, reg 1.
[41] Draft Police Appeal Tribunals Rules 2008, reg 2.
[42] Draft Police Appeal Tribunals Rules 2008, reg 12(2).
[43] Draft Police Appeal Tribunals Rules 2008, reg 15.
[44] Draft Police Appeal Tribunals Rules 2008, reg 13.

The constitution of the PAT is currently governed by Sch 6 of the PA 1996, which   7.37
will be amended by para 11 of Sch 22 of the CJIA 2008 when it comes into force.

For Senior Officers, the PAT will consist of three members appointed by the   7.38
Secretary of State, one of whom must be the Chief Inspector of Constabulary (or one
Inspector nominated by the Chief Inspector) and one permanent secretary to the
Secretary of State (or a Home Office director nominated by the permanent secretary).

For appeals by other members of the police force (including special constables),   7.39
the PAT will consist of four members. One of these 4 members must be a person
chosen from the Lord Chancellor's list of those who satisfy the judicial appointment
eligibility on a 5 year basis;[45] one must be a senior officer;[46] one must be a member
of the police force of which the appellant is a member[47] and one must be a retired
member of either the Police Superintendents' Association England or the Police
Federation of England and Wales.[48]

Schedule 22, para 9 of the CJIA 2008 will amend s 87 of the PA 1996 to allow   7.40
the Secretary of State to issue guidance concerning disciplinary proceedings for
police authorities; chief officers of police; other members of police forces; special
constables and persons employed by a police authority. This therefore includes
PCSOs (technically police staff) and any other members of police staff. Paragraph 9
came into force on 1 December 2008.[48a]

The current guidance issued pursuant to s 87 of the PA 1996, 'Unsatisfactory   7.41
Performance, Complaints and Misconduct Procedures'[49] does not extend to special
constables or police staff. It was a key recommendation of the *Taylor Report* that the
disciplinary process should apply to all members of a police force.[50]

The Draft Police (Performance) Regulations 2008[51] issued under s 87 of the   7.42
PA 1996, will apply to a much broader category of people. The inclusion of police
staff is no doubt a pragmatic recognition that the modern police force depends
increasingly on those outside the officer class such as PCSOs.

Sch 22, Part 1, para 10 of the CJIA 2008 amends s 97 of the PA 1996 to remove   7.43
references to the sanction of 'required to resign' for officers who are subject to
disciplinary proceedings whilst they are engaged in service outside their force. This
is because the sanction of 'required to resign' is not intended to play a part in
the new disciplinary procedures that will be brought in by way of further legislation
(see para **7.24**).[52]

(b) *Sch 22, Part 2: Ministry of Defence Police*
Part 2 of Sch 22 makes amendments to the Ministry of Defence Police Act (MDA)   7.44
1987 and therefore affects the disciplinary procedure for Ministry of Defence Police
(MDP).

---

[45] PA 1996, Sch 6, para 1(1)(a).
[46] PA 1996, Sch 6, para 2(1)(b).
[47] PA 1996, Sch 6, para 2(1)(c).
[48] PA 1996, Sch 6, para 10(c).
[48a] Criminal Justice and Immigration Act 2008 (Commencement No 4 and Saving Provision) Order 2008,
SI 2008/2993.
[49] Home Office Circular 055/2002.
[50] *Taylor Report,* para 4.3.1 at page 28.
[51] Tabled on 22 July 2008 (see **n 6** above).
[52] Explanatory Note to the CJIA 2008, para 732 (<http://www.opsi.gov.uk/acts/acts2008/en/08en04-j.htm>).

7.45   Paragraph 13 of Sch 22 will amend s 3(4) of the MDA 1987 so that a member of the MDP will be represented at police disciplinary proceedings by another member of the MDP unless the member is entitled to legal representation under s 4 of the MDA 1987.

7.46   Section 4 of the MDA 1987 will be amended by para 15 of Sch 22 to the CJIA 2008 to mirror the changes to s 84 of the PA 1996, thereby permitting the Secretary of State to make further Regulations regarding the legal representation of parties before disciplinary proceedings and the ability of the disciplinary panel to receive legal advice (see discussion of s 84 of the PA 1996 at paras **7.26–7.30** above).

7.47   Paragraph 16 of Sch 22 will amend s 4A of the MDA 1987 to allow the Secretary of State for the Home Department to make Regulations setting out a framework for members of the MDP to appeal to the Police Appeals Tribunal which will be equivalent to the provisions for other police officers under Sch 6 of the PA 1996. Any Regulations passed under s 4A of the MDA 1987 will have to follow the same legislative procedure outlined at para **7.07** above.

(c) *Sch 22, Part 3: British Transport Police*

7.48   Part 3 of Sch 22 of the CJIA 2008 amends the Railways and Transport Safety Act (RTSA) 2003 and therefore affects the disciplinary procedure for the British Transport Police (BTP).

7.49   Paragraph 18 will amend s 36 of the RTSA 2003 to allow the British Transport Police Authority (BTPA) to make Regulations similar to those under ss 84 (legal representation before disciplinary proceedings) and 85 (appeals against dismissal) and Sch 6 (appeals to PAT) of the PA 1996. Paragraph 19 gives the BTPA the power to make similar Regulations for its special constables.

7.50   It is anticipated that in light of the *Taylor Report*'s recommendations about the unification of police disciplinary procedure across the police force,[53] that the Secretary of State for the Home Department will make Regulations further to the amendments to the BTPA and the Ministry of Defence Police Authority that apply to all types of officer. Paragraphs 17 to 21 of Schedule 22 came into force on 1 December 2008.[53a]

4. Investigation of complaints of police misconduct

7.51   Section 127 of the CJIA 2008 inserts Sch 23 into the Act. Section 127 is only in force insofar as it relates to paragraphs 1–3, 5, 12(1), 12(4) and 19 of Sch 23 which were also brought into force on 3 November 2008.[54] Schedule 23 amends the Police Reform Act (PRA) 2002.

7.52   Section 127 and Sch 23 of the CJIA 2008 and any Regulations passed by way of Statutory Instrument will only extend to England and Wales.

7.53   Although there are a number of statutory changes made by Sch 23, they are difficult to decipher without the secondary legislation that is envisaged to complement them. The secondary legislation (as discussed at para **7.06** above) is the Draft Police

---

[53] *Taylor Report*, para 4.3.1 at page 28.

[53a] Criminal Justice and Immigration Act 2008 (Commencement No 4 and Saving Provision) Order 2008, SI 2008/2993.

[54] Criminal Justice and Immigration Act 2008 (Commencement No 3 and Transitional Provisions) Order 2008, SI 2008/2712.

(Conduct) Regulations 2008,[55] Draft Police (Performance) Regulations 2008,[56] and the Draft Police Appeal Tribunals Rules 2008.[57] These Regulations are due to come into force on 1 December 2008.[58]

Schedule 23 therefore merely creates the statutory framework within which the   7.54
new Regulations will operate. This chapter will set out the statutory amendments to the PRA 2002 made by Sch 23 and will signpost the main provisions of the relevant Draft Regulations. However, a full discussion of the Draft Regulations is outside the scope of this text.

In summary, the new framework introduces the following: 7.55

- Introduces the concepts of 'misconduct' and 'gross misconduct';
- Encourages the use of an accelerated procedure in all cases that do not involve 'gross misconduct';
- Increases the scope for legal representation and advice during disciplinary proceedings and appeals;
- Removes the sanction of 'requirement to resign';
- Limits the category of cases that must be referred to the DPP.

Paragraph 2 of Sch 23 amends s 23(2) of the Police Reform Act 2002 to gives the   7.56
Secretary of State the power to specify by way of Regulations who, apart from a legal representative, can make representations to the IPCC on behalf of someone whose conduct is under investigation. The Secretary of State can already make Regulations in a number of areas under s 23 of the PRA 2002 and this amendment is essentially an insertion of an additional power(see reg 7 of the Draft Police (Conduct) Regulations 2008). Paragraph 2 of Sch 23 came into force on 3 November 2008.[59]

Paragraph 4 of Sch 23 amends para 6(4) of Sch 3 to the PRA 2002 which deals   7.57
with the handling of complaints by an appropriate authority. It removes from para 6(4) any reference to the sanction of a 'requirement to resign', 'reduction in rank or other demotion' or the 'imposition of a fine' and replaces it with 'the giving of a final written warning'. This is because the sanction of 'required to resign' will not play a part in the new disciplinary and complaint procedures[60] (see the discussion at para 7.25 above). Paragraph 4 of Schedule 23 came into force on 1 December 2008.[60a]

Paragraph 5 of Sch 23 inserts paras 19A–E into Sch 3 to the PRA 2002. These   7.58
new paragraphs set out a special procedure to be adopted on the investigation of a complaint or recordable conduct matter of either a police officer or special constable. Paragraph 5 of Sch 23 came into force in full on 1 December 2008.[60b] It came into force for this purpose alone on 3 November 2008.[61] The remaining amendments

---

[55] Tabled on 22 July 2008 (see **n 4** above).
[56] Ibid., (see **n 5** above).
[57] Tabled on 22 July 2008 (see **n 6** above).
[58] Draft Rules, s 1.
[59] Criminal Justice and Immigration Act 2008 (Commencement No 3 and Transitional Provisions) Order 2008, SI 2008/2712.
[60] Explanatory Note to the CJIA 2008 para 732 (http://www.opsi.gov.uk/acts/acts2008/en/08en04-j.htm).
[60a] Criminal Justice and Immigration Act 2008 (Commencement No 4 and Saving Provision) Order 2008, SI 2008/2993.
[60b] Ibid.
[61] Criminal Justice and Immigration Act 2008 (Commencement No 3 and Transitional Provisions) Order 2008, SI 2008/2712.

made by para 5 will have to be brought into force by a further commencement order on a date to be appointed. However, the full amendments made by para 5 are discussed here for completeness.

7.59   This special procedure that is introduced by paras 19A–E of Sch 3 to the PRA 2002 (as amended) is as follows: if during the course of an investigation of a complaint it appears to the person investigating that there is an indication that the subject of the investigation may have either committed a criminal offence or behaved in a way that could justify the bringing of disciplinary proceedings, they must certify the investigation as being subject to the special procedure under Sch 3, para 19A.[62]

7.60   Once the investigation is certified as being subject to the special procedure, the investigator must carry out a 'severity assessment' as soon as reasonably practicable.[63] A severity assessment involves determining whether the conduct, if proved could amount to either 'misconduct' or 'gross misconduct' and if the conduct were to become the subject of disciplinary proceedings, the form that the proceedings would be likely to take (see reg 12 of the Draft Police (Conduct) Regulations 2008).

7.61   The assessment must be made after consultation with the 'appropriate authority.' In the case of a senior officer this is the Police Authority for the area of police force he serves under. In the case of any other officer, it is the Chief Officer with direct control of that officer.[64]

7.62   'Misconduct' and 'gross misconduct' are both defined by para 29 of Sch 3 to the PRA 2002.[65] Misconduct means a breach of the 'Standards of Professional Behaviour'. Gross misconduct means a breach of the "Standards of Professional Behaviour' that is so serious as to warrant dismissal.

7.63   The 'Standards of Professional Behaviour' is a reference to the new code for Standards of Professional Behaviour that forms Sch 1 to the Draft Police (Conduct) Regulations 2008[66] (see discussion at paras 7.02 and 7.14 above).

7.64   The determination of whether a complaint could amount to either 'misconduct' or 'gross misconduct' was a key recommendation of the *Taylor Report*. The Report placed great emphasis on an initial assessment of police complaints taking place to ensure that the complaint is dealt with correctly and at the right level.[67]

7.65   Once the severity assessment has taken place, the investigator must notify the person concerned[68] giving them information about the results of the assessment[69] and the effect of the assessment[70] as long as giving him this information would not prejudice the current investigation or any other investigation[71] (see reg 15 of the Draft Police (Conduct) Regulations 2008).

---

[62] PRA 2002, Sch 3, para 19B (as amended).
[63] What is as soon as reasonably practicable will depend on whether it is an investigation into a complaint or a recordable conduct matter, see para 19B(2) and (3) of Sch 3, PRA 2002 (as amended).
[64] PA 1996, s 84(4) (as amended by CJIA 2008, Sch 22, para 7).
[65] Inserted by CJIA 2008, Sch 23, para 19.
[66] Tabled on 22 July 2008 (see **n 4** above).
[67] Para 5.1 of the *Taylor Report* (2005).
[68] PRA 2002, Sch 3, para 19B(6).
[69] PRA 2002, Sch 3, para 19B(7)(a).
[70] PRA 2002, Sch 3, para 19B(7)(b).
[71] PRA 2002, Sch 3, para 19B(8).

The notification must also set out the time limits for providing the investigation with relevant statements and documents.[72] If the person concerned provides the investigation with a statement or document before the expiration of a set time limit, the person investigating must consider the document[73] (see reg 16 of the Draft Police (Conduct) Regulations 2008). 7.66

Once a severity assessment has taken place, it can later be revised by the same investigator.[74] If a revision takes place, the person concerned must be notified of any outcome.[75] 7.67

Paragraph 19D of Sch 3 to the PRA 2002 as amended gives the Secretary of State the power to make Regulations regarding the procedure to be followed in interviewing a person whose conduct is under investigation. These Regulations may in particular determine what information is to be provided to the interviewee[76] and regulate who may accompany the interviewee during the interview.[77] Regulation 17 of the Draft Police (Conduct) Regulations 2008 deals with interviews during an investigation. 7.68

Paragraph 19E places a duty on the person investigating to provide the appropriate authority (see para 7.61 above) with any information that they reasonably request in order to determine whether the person under investigation should be suspended or remain under suspension. 7.69

Paragraph 20A of Sch 3 to the PRA 2002, which sets out a special accelerated investigation procedure, is amended by para 6 of Sch 23 to the CJIA 2008. This accelerated procedure currently applies in cases where the evidence suggests that an imprisonable offence has occurred and that the person's conduct is of a serious nature. Following the CJIA 2008 amendments, the accelerated procedure will now only apply where there is sufficient evidence of 'gross misconduct'. This effectively lowers the threshold for the use of the accelerated procedure as what constitutes gross misconduct may not equate to an imprisonable offence. This may result in a wider use of this procedure. 7.70

Part 5 of the Draft Police (Conduct) Regulations 2008 sets out the Fast Track procedure for 'Special Cases'. A case is 'special' if the 'special conditions' are satisfied. These conditions are satisfied if: 7.71

(a) there is sufficient evidence, in the form of written statements or other documents, without the need for further evidence, whether written or oral, to establish on the balance of probabilities that the conduct of the officer concerned constitutes gross misconduct; and

(b) it is in the public interest for the officer concerned to cease to be a police officer without delay.[78]

---

[72] PRA 2002, Sch 3, para 19B(7)(c).
[73] PRA 2002, Sch 3, para 19C.
[74] PRA 2002, Sch 3, para 19B(9).
[75] PRA 2002, Sch 3, para 19B(10).
[76] PRA 2002, Sch 3, para 19D(2)(b).
[77] PRA 2002, Sch 3, para 19D(2)(c).
[78] Draft Police (Conduct) Regulations 2008, reg 3.

7.72   If the case is certified as a special case, a hearing will take place 10 to 15 days after notice has been served on the officer under investigation. The procedure for these hearings is set out at regs 42–54. At the end of a special case hearing, if the panel finds on the balance of probabilities that gross misconduct took place, they can either issue a final warning or dismiss without notice.[79]

7.73   Paragraphs 7 and 9 of Sch 23 of the CJIA 2008 amend paras 20B(5) and 20E(5) of Sch 3 to the PRA 2002 which deal with the accelerated procedure in investigations being managed or supervised by the IPCC. Where the appropriate authority certifies that the accelerated disciplinary procedures apply to this sort of investigation, there will no longer be an automatic requirement to send a copy of the file to the DPP.

7.74   Paragraph 10 of Sch 23 of the CJIA 2008 repeals para 20G of Sch 3 to the PRA 2002 (which gives the DPP the power to ask the appropriate authority not to take disciplinary action without prior agreement if it is felt that they may prejudice future criminal proceedings).

7.75   Paragraph 11 of Sch 23 to the CJIA 2008 amends para 21A of Sch 3 to the PRA 2002 which governs the procedure where an investigation into a Death or Serious Injury (a DSI investigation) reveals that a serving police officer may have committed a criminal offence or behaved in a manner that would justify the bringing of disciplinary proceedings. If the investigation is re-classified as a conduct matter (because of a breach of the Standards of Professional Behaviour), the original investigator for the DSI investigation will be able to continue as the investigator in the conduct matter.[80] This is no doubt aimed at improving continuity of investigations and thereby preventing the repetition of work by an investigator. Paragraphs 6 to 11 of Sch 23 came into force on 1 December 2008.[80a]

7.76   Paragraph 16 of Sch 23 makes identical amendments to para 24B of Sch 23 to the PRA 2002.[80b] The amendments clarify that following a DSI investigation being completed and recorded as a conduct matter, the person who conducted the DSI investigation may continue as the investigator of the conduct matter.[81]

7.77   Paragraph 12 of Sch 23 to the CJIA 2008 inserts sub paragraphs (7) and (10) into para 22 of Sch 3 to the PRA 2002. Paragraph 22(7) empowers the Secretary of State to make regulations to require a final report to be produced on an investigation where conduct has been identified that may lead to disciplinary proceedings under para 19B(1)(a) or (b) of Sch 3 to the PRA 2002. Regulation 18 of the Draft Police (Conduct) Regulations 2008[82] deals with final reports of an investigation.

7.78   Paragraph 12 of Sch 23 also inserts sub paragraphs (8) and (9) into para 22 of Sch 3 to the PRA 2002, which place a duty on the person who submits the investigation

---

[79] Ibid, reg 55.

[80] PRA 2002, Sch 3, para 21A(6)(a) (as amended) and subject to the IPPC determining under PRA 2002, Sch 3, para 15(5) that the investigation should take a different form.

[80a] Criminal Justice and Immigration Act 2008 (Commencement No 4 and Saving Provision) Order 2008, SI 2008/2993.

[80b] Para 16, Sch 23, CJIA 2008 in force 1 December 2008. CJIA 2008 (Commencement No 4 and Saving Provision) Order 2008, SI 2008/2993.

[81] Subject to the IPPC determining under PRA 2002, Sch 3, para 15(5) that the investigation should take a different form.

[82] Tabled on 22 July 2008 (see **n 4** above).

report to supply the appropriate authority with copies of the report and any such items to ensure that the authority can comply with its obligations under the misconduct procedures in place or to ensure that the officer under investigation receives a fair hearing. This provision will really only be used where the investigation report fails to attach the documents that the appropriate authority considers relevant for these purposes. Paragraph 12(1) of Sch 23 came into force on 3 November 2008. The rest of para 12 came into force on 1 December 2008.[82a] Paragraph 12(4) of Sch 23 came into force on the same date but only for the purpose of making Regulations.[83] The remaining amendments made by para 12 will have to be brought into force by a further commencement order on a date to be appointed.

Paragraphs 13(2) and (3) of Sch 23 amend para 23 of Sch 3 to the PRA 2002.[83a] **7.79**
Paragraph 23 deals with the situations in which the IPCC has a duty to refer to the DPP any report on an investigation it has managed[84] or undertaken itself.[85] Currently the IPCC is required to refer a case to the DPP whenever an investigation report reveals that a criminal offence may have been committed. Under the amended para 23, it will only be required to refer if the report indicates to the IPCC that a criminal offence may have been committed *and* either the IPCC considers the case should be referred *or* the case falls within any prescribed category of cases. The prescribed category of cases will be set out by Regulations.[86]

It was a clear recommendation of the *Taylor Report* that criminal sanctions should **7.80**
only be considered in the most serious of cases and that the majority of conduct matters should be dealt with by disciplinary proceedings. The Report recommended that 'low-level' matters should not automatically be referred to the prosecuting authorities but should be dealt with as conduct matters.[87] This would explain the removal of the automatic referral to the DPP and the increased prescription of cases that should be referred.

Paragraph 13(5) of Sch 23 substitutes new sub-paragraphs (6) and (7) into para 23 **7.81**
of Sch 3 to the PRA 2002. They provide that on receipt of an investigation report, the IPCC must require the appropriate authority to determine whether any person to whose conduct the investigation relates has a case to answer in respect of misconduct or gross misconduct and decide what action it will (or must) take.[88] The authority must then submit a memorandum to the IPCC setting out its decision.[89]

The Draft Police (Conduct) Regulations 2008 set out at reg 19 the disciplinary **7.82**
action the appropriate authority must or may take as a result of its decision of whether there is a case to answer for misconduct or gross misconduct.

[82a] Criminal Justice and Immigration Act 2008 (Commencement No 4 and Saving Provision) Order 2008, SI 2008/2993.

[83] Criminal Justice and Immigration Act 2008 (Commencement No 3 and Transitional Provisions) Order 2008, SI 2008/2712.

[83a] Para 13, Sch 23, CJIA 2008 in force 1 December 2008. CJIA 2008 (Commencement No 4 and Saving Provision) Order 2008, SI 2008/2993.

[84] Under para 18 of PRA 2002, Sch 3.

[85] Under para 19 of PRA 2002, Sch 3.

[86] CJIA 2008, Sch 23, para 19.

[87] Para 4.3.7 of the *Taylor Report* (2005).

[88] PRA 2002, para 23(6) (as amended).

[89] PRA 2002, para 23(7) (as amended).

7.83   Paragraph 14 of Sch 23 amends para 24 of Sch 3 to the PRA 2002[89a] to put an identical duty on appropriate authorities conducting their own investigations or conducting an investigation that is supervised by the IPCC as is placed on the IPCC itself under para 23 of Sch 3 (see para **7.68** above).

7.84   In cases where the IPCC has supervised an investigation by an appropriate authority into a recordable conduct matter, the authority will be responsible for notifying the IPCC whether it determines that the matter should be referred to the DPP.[90] Where it determines that the conditions are not satisfied, then the IPCC will still be able to make its own decision and may still direct the appropriate authority to refer.[91]

7.85   Paragraph 14(6) of Sch 23 inserts a new para 24(6) into Sch 3 to the PRA 2002, which requires that the appropriate authority on receipt of an investigator's report in an investigation conducted by the authority itself[92] or an investigation that is supervised by the IPCC[93] must determine whether the person whose conduct is the subject of the investigation has a case to answer in relation to either misconduct or gross misconduct and what action it will (or must) take. This includes both disciplinary action and other action.

7.86   Paragraph 17(2) of Sch 23 to the CJIA 2008 amends para 25 of Sch 3 to the PRA 2002[93a] to give complainants concerned with investigations by appropriate authorities in their own right, or those supervised by the IPCC, new rights of appeal to the IPCC against the decisions that the authority is required to make in respect of (a)whether there is a case to answer for misconduct or gross misconduct; (b) whether to take (or not take) action in respect of matters in an investigation report and (c) any decision not to send a copy of the investigation report to the DPP.

7.87   This amendment merely adds rights of appeal to the IPCC in respect of the additional decisions that an appropriate authority is required to make as a consequence of paras 19–24 of Sch 3 to the PRA 2002 (as amended) (discussed at paras **7.62–7.78** above).

7.88   Paragraph 17(3) of Sch 23 to the CJIA 2008 amends para 25(3) of Sch 3 to the PRA 2002 to extend the matters that the IPCC can require the appropriate authority to cover in its formal memorandum to the IPCC where there is an appeal. The memorandum can now include (a) the determination on a case to answer, (b) the action that it decided to take, and (c) whether the case has not been referred to the DPP, the reasons for that decision. This is a pragmatic amendment that will allow the IPCC to know the full procedural history of a matter that it is considering on appeal.

7.89   Paragraph 17(6) of Sch 23 to the CJIA 2008 inserts a new para 25(9A) into Sch 3 to the PRA 2002, which requires that where the appropriate authority has determined that the conditions for referring a case to the DPP are not met and the complainant in the matter has appealed to the IPCC, the IPCC will be required to determine itself whether it feels the conditions for referral are satisfied. Where it feels

---

[89a] Amendment in force 1 December 2008. CJIA 2008 (Commencement No 4 and Saving Provision) Order 2008, SI 2008/2993.

[90] PRA 2002, Sch 3, para 24(5A) (as amended).

[91] PRA 2002, Sch 3, para 24(5B) (as amended).

[92] Under PRA 2002, Sch 3, para 16.

[93] Under PRA 2002, Sch 3, para 17.

[93a] Para 17, Sch 23, CJIA 2008 in force 1 December 2008. CJIA 2008 (Commencement No 4 and Saving Provision) Order 2008, SI 2008/2993.

that they are satisfied, the IPCC must direct the authority to refer the case to the DPP. This will give complainants an extra safeguard in cases where there may be concern that a police authority investigating a complaint against its own officers is not willing to refer the matter for prosecution.

Paragraph 18 of Sch 23 amends para 27 of Sch 3[93b] which sets out the circum-   7.90 stances in which an appropriate authority must give notification to the IPCC of its determination of whether there is a case to answer of misconduct or gross miscon- duct and/or any action it proposes to take. Under the amended para 27, once the IPCC has received the notification, it may make recommendations to the appropri- ate authority in respect of whether there is a case to answer and if so, what proceed- ings should be brought and what form they should take.

Under the current provisions, the authority must then indicate whether it accepts   7.91 the recommendations. If it does not, the IPCC can direct that the recommended steps be taken. It is the duty of the authority to comply with that direction.

B. INDUSTRIAL ACTION BY PRISON OFFICERS

1. The statutory prohibition on industrial action by prison officers

Part 11, s 138 of the CJIA 2008 amends s 127 of the Criminal Justice and Public   7.92 Order Act (CJPOA) 1994, and re-introduces a statutory prohibition on industrial action by prison officers. Section 138 came into force on the 8 May 2008 when the CJIA received Royal Assent, [94] apart from s 138(5) (which relates to Scotland). The provision came into force on Royal Assent for England, Wales, and Northern Ireland, but the enactment in relation to Scotland will come into force by way of a commencement order.

'Industrial action' is now defined as 'the withholding of services as a prison   7.93 officer',[95] and 'any action that would be likely to put at risk the safety of any person (whether a prisoner, a person working at or visiting a prison, a person working with prisoners or a member of the public)'.[96]

Section 139 of the CJIA 2008 inserts s 127A into the CJPOA 1994 and gives the   7.94 SSHD the power to suspend or later revive the statutory prohibition in s 138 by way of an order by way of a Statutory Instrument. Both Houses of Parliament, ie the 'affirmative resolution procedure', must approve any order. Section 139 also came into force on Royal Assent.[97]

2. The history of s 127 of the CJPOA 1994

A prohibition on industrial action by prison officers was first introduced by the   7.95 original s 127 of the CJPOA 1994. This legislation was part of the Conservative

---

[93b] Para 18, Sch 23, CJIA 2008 in force 1 December 2008. CJIA 2008 (Commencement No 4 and Saving Provision) Order 2008, SI 2008/2993.
[94] CJIA 2008, s 153.
[95] CJPOA 1994, s 127(1A)(a) (as amended).
[96] CJPOA 1994, s 127(1A)(b) (as amended).
[97] CJIA 2008, s 153.

government's 'strike-breaking' measures to undermine the influence of the Trade Unions on industrial relations in the public sector. The Labour party in opposition (with the then shadow Home Secretary, one Tony Blair), attacked s 127 calling it a 'wholly unwarranted attack on the rights of prison officers'.[98] Both Tony Blair and John Prescott gave written undertakings in correspondence that their government would 'put the situation right again'.[99]

7.96   After litigation brought in 2004 by the Prisoner Officer's Association (POA) to the International Labour Organisation regarding the right of its members to strike, an agreement was formed in 2005 between the POA and the Prison Service known as the Joint Industrial Relations Protocol Agreement (JIRPA).

7.97   Under the JIRPA, the Labour government agreed to adhere to the recommendations of an independent Pay Review Body[100] (PRB) in order to address the POA's concerns about its members receiving below inflation pay increases. The only limitation to the government's acceptance of the PRB recommendations could be in 'exceptional circumstances' including affordability. In return, the POA agreed not to stage industrial action.

7.98   In response to the POA's 'no strike' agreement, the government repealed s 127 of the CJPOA 1994 on March 22 2005.[101] The government claims to have made it clear that if the POA walked away from JIRPA without alternative arrangement being put in place, it would seek Parliament's permission to re-instate s 127 of the CJPOA 1994.[102] The JIRPA itself required the POA to give 12 months notice if it wished to terminate the agreement.

7.99   However, in August 2006, the POA voiced strong concerns that the PRB was not truly independent and was not delivering appropriate pay reviews to its members. In March 2007, the PRB recommended a pay increase of 2.5 per cent to take effect in April 2007. The government stated that this was 'unaffordable' and claimed that under the JIRPA, exceptional circumstances meant that they did not have to give effect to the PRB recommendations. Instead it suggested a two-stage increase of 1.5 per cent, followed by 1 per cent the following year.

7.100   In April 2007, the National Chairman of the POA, Colin Moses asked his members to consider withdrawing from the JIRPA and return to collective bargaining in light of the government's position in respect of the pay increase.[103] After a series of litigation by both the POA and the prison service, at the POA annual conference on 7 May 2007, members voted to instigate a work to rule policy[104] and gave the government their notice of termination of the JIRPA on 8 May 2007. The effect of this notice was that the JIRPA would terminate on the 8 May 2008.

---

[98] Letter from Tony Blair to the Prison Officers Association, 6 July 1994—cited in *Hansard*, HC col 326 (9 Jan 2008).

[99] Ibid.

[100] Set up by the Prison Service (Pay Review Body) Regulations 2001, SI 2001/1161, reg 8.

[101] Regulatory Reform (Prison Officers) (Industrial Action) Order 2005, SI 2005/908 made under the Regulatory Reform Act 2001.

[102] Prisons Minister Gerry Sutcliffe, *Hansard*, Vol 449 HC col 1897 (4 Sept 2006).

[103] Colin Moses (April 2007) <http://www.poauk.org.uk/the-national-chairman-0407.asp>.

[104] 'Prison Officers Launch Industrial Action Over Pay', *The Guardian*, 7 May 2008 (available at http://www.guardian.co.uk/society/2008/may/07/prison.officers.industrial.action).

In August 2007, members of the POA voted for strike action by ballot and at 07:00 hours on 29 August 2007 began a 24-hour strike, which led to a number of prison riots. Particularly serious was the disorder at Lancaster Farm's Buttermere Wing, which houses violent young offenders, where the riots resulted in criminal damage and arson.[105] At 13.20 hours on the 29 August 2007, the Secretary of State obtained a High Court injunction to prevent prison officers from continuing with their industrial action.[106] The judgment of Ramsey J indicated that the POA was in breach of the JIRPA by inducing strike action. This injunction was extended by the consent of the parties on 19 October 2007.[107]

As a result of the strike action, the Chairman of the Advisory, Conciliation and Arbitration Service (ACAS), Ed Sweeney was asked to produce a report setting out a framework as to how negotiations between the POA and the Prison Service could move forward. His report was published on 7 January 2008 but did not recommend against a statutory prohibition on industrial action.

3. The legislative history of s 137 of the CJIA 2008

On 9 January 2008, only 48 hours after the publication of the *Sweeney Report*, the Home Secretary tabled clause 37 of the Criminal Justice and Immigration Bill 2008 which proposed a re-introduction of s 127 of the CJPOA 1994. It was not envisaged at that time that the prohibition would come into force with Royal Assent on 8 May 2008—the powers, it was said, would only be used as 'reserve powers'.[108]

The main criticism of the Clause during the Commons debate was that it was 'designed to hold a gun to their [the POA's] head in negotiations' that had not yet begun.[109] The government was clearly hoping that before the 8 May 2008 (the date that the JIRPA would be terminated), negotiations would have been concluded in its favour as the POA would buckle under the threat of the re-introduction of s 127 of the CJPOA 1994 and there would therefore be no need to re-instate it.

On 18 February 2008, the High Court was once again asked to consider whether the injunction obtained on 29 August 2007 against 'strike action' could extend until the expiration of the JIRPA on the 8 May 2008.[110] The Court held that the injunction could be extended and that the government had not acted unlawfully by refusing to comply with the PRB's recommendations. The High Court further ruled that the prohibition on strike action did not conflict with prison officers' rights under Article 11 of the ECHR as there was a 'strong public interest' in preventing the POA from breaching the agreement.[111]

The effect of the High Court judgment was that the government could prevent strike action up to and until 8 May 2008 but not beyond. It is clear that the

7.101

7.102

7.103

7.104

7.105

7.106

---

[105] Home Secretary HC Deb 9 January 2008 c329.
[106] Ramsey J, *Ministry of Justice v POA (formerly Prison Officers' Association)* (29 August 2007).
[107] By Saunders J, *Ministry of Justice v POA (formerly Prison Officers' Association)* (19 October 2007).
[108] Home Secretary HC Deb 9 January 2008 c331.
[109] Neil Gerrard (Labour MP, Walthamstow), HC Deb 9 January 2008 c336.
[110] *Ministry of Justice v POA (formerly Prison Officers' Association)* [2008] EWHC 239 (QB), [2008] ICR 702 (18 Feb 2008).
[111] Para 63 of Judgment of Wynn Willams J, ibid.

relationship between the Prison Service and the POA was deteriorating and the government was not confident that the prohibition on strike action would be able to be renewed by way of voluntary agreement after 8 May.

7.107   What followed was a steady shift from the introduction of 'reserve powers' to the clear statutory prohibition that is found in s 127 of the CJPOA 1994 (as amended). The Bill that was presented to the House of Lords largely contained the wording that now forms ss 137 and 138 of the CJIA 2008,[112] although they were still at this stage being presented as 'reserve powers'.[113]

7.108   The Lords were concerned with the need for the prohibition and the lack of time that had been spent debating the topic. They were also concerned with the inclusion within the definition of 'industrial action' of 'any action likely to affect the normal working of a prison'. The effect of this inclusion is to prohibit by statute any action that could otherwise be properly considered a 'disciplinary matter'. The original s 127 of the CJPOA 1994 did include a prohibition on inducing a prison officer to 'commit any breach of discipline'.[114] However, 'any action' is a much broader prohibition.

7.109   A broad interpretation of 'any action likely to affect the normal working of a prison' could, for example, include a single officer refusing to undertake a specific task within a prison without it being part of a collective act. The fact that 'any action' is not specifically defined also concerned the Lords. The Lords felt that including what were effectively disciplinary matters within the prohibition was using a 'sledgehammer to crack a nut when it comes to industrial relations within the Prison Service by proposing legislation even more draconian than proposed by a previous Conservative Government'.[115]

7.110   Despite the reservations of the House of Lords, an amendment was tabled on 30 April 2008 to broaden the prohibition further and it is this broader definition, which formed the wording of the amendments to s 138 of the CJIA 2008.[116] 'Industrial action' is now defined as 'the withholding of services as a prison officer',[117] and 'any action that would be likely to put at risk the safety of any person (whether a prisoner, a person working at or visiting a prison, a person working with prisoners or a member of the public)'.[118]

7.111   Although these prohibitions were sold to both Houses of Parliament as 'reserve powers' the prohibition under s 127 was brought into force on the very day the Act received Royal Assent on 8 May 2008. On 7 May 2008, Lord Dear noted that the government had 'lost the trust of the prison service officers' and said, 'I do not think that they will regain it for a very long time.'[119]

---

[112] As clauses 189 and 190 of the Criminal Justice and Immigration Bill 2008, HL Bill 16.
[113] Parliamentary Under Secretary of State Lord Hunt, HL Deb 22 January 2008 c130.
[114] CJPOA 1994, s 127(1)(b) (as enacted).
[115] Lord Graham of Edmonton, HL Deb 10 March 2008 c1357.
[116] Lord Hunt of Kings Heath, HL Deb 30 April 2008 c1546.
[117] CJPOA 1994, s 127(1A)(a) (as amended).
[118] CJPOA 1994, s 127(1A)(b) (as amended).
[119] Lord Dear, HL Deb 7 May 2008 c593.

4. Conclusion

The effect of the amended ss 127 and 127A of the CJPOA 1994 is to put industrial   7.112
relations between the government and prison officers back to exactly where it was
under a Thatcherite Conservative government. The government has reneged on its
promise to give prison officers the same employment rights as other public sector
workers and has delivered a punishing blow to any future negotiations. It is difficult
to see how this will be resolved with this statutory stronghold in place.

The Joint Committee on Human Rights has also questioned whether the legisla-   7.113
tive steps taken were a proportionate interference with prison officers' rights under
Article 11 of the ECHR (freedom of association, including within trade unions) and
whether they were necessary as a point of last resort or whether in fact other measures
could have been taken.[120]

There is a real concern that this government or future governments could use s 127   7.114
as a blue print for introducing prohibitions on industrial action in other areas of the
public sector. The only possible reprieve is the power to remove the prohibition
by way of delegated legislation under s 127A. It is impossible to understand why
a Labour government failed to heed the calls from both Houses of Parliament to
introduce the prohibition by way of secondary legislation, *if necessary*, rather than
to introduce such draconian and regressive measures onto the statute book.

---

[120] Joint Committee on Human Rights, 5th Report <http://www.publications.parliament.uk/pa/jt200708/
jtselect/jtrights/37/3704.htm#a9>.

8

FOREIGN CRIMINALS

A. INTRODUCTION

The immigration provisions of the Criminal Justice and Immigration Act 2008   8.01
provide for two matters. Firstly, Part 10 (ss 130–137) creates and regulates a status
known as 'special immigration status'. Secondly, s 146 creates an additional exception
to the automatic deportation provisions in the UK Borders Act 2007.

In respect of the first matter, the Secretary of State for Justice, Jack Straw MP stated: 8.02

The new special immigration status will ensure that foreign criminals and terrorists who cannot
be deported cannot expect a settled status in this country.[1]

In respect of the second matter, the government has declared an intention to   8.03
ratify the Council of Europe Convention Against Trafficking in Human Beings
(European Trafficking Convention).[2] The United Kingdom signed the Convention
on 23 March 2007.

The objective of ratification forms part of the government's UK Action Plan on   8.04
Human Trafficking.[3] It also provides the motivation for including s 146 of the CJIA
2008. As the Explanatory Notes to the Act state:

. . . Section 146 ensures that the UK can comply with the Convention once it has been ratified.[4]

In a letter of 27 March 2008, Lord Hunt, Parliamentary Under Secretary of State,   8.05
Ministry of Justice, wrote to Lord Kingsland QC, re-iterating the government's

---

[1] HC Deb 8 October 2007 vol 464 c69.
[2] Warsaw, 16 May 2005; CETS 197 (2008).
[3] See also JCHR 21st Report Human Trafficking: Update (2006–07) HL Paper 179 HC. 1056; JCHR
Government Response to the Committee's Twenty-First Report of Session 2006–07: Human Trafficking:
Update (2007–08) HL Paper 31 HC 220.
[4] Para 99.

commitment, first announced by the Home Secretary on 14 January 2008, to ratify the European Trafficking Convention before the end of 2008.

B. BACKGROUND

1. Special immigration status: the purpose behind the legislation

8.06   The motivation for introducing special immigration status was the judgment in *S and Others v Secretary of State for the Home Department*[5] (better known as the Afghan Hijackers' case). The Explanatory Notes to the Act state:

> Part 10 gives effect to the Home Secretary's commitment to legislate to deny leave to enter or remain to certain foreign nationals who can not be removed from the UK compatibly with the United Kingdom's obligations under the European Convention on Human Rights (ECHR). The commitment was made following the judgment of the Court of Appeal in *S and others vs Secretary of State for the Home Department* in August 2006.[6]

8.07   The introduction of the new status was criticized by Keith Vaz MP (Labour), Chairman of the Home Affairs Select Committee, at the Second Reading of the Bill in the House of Commons, on the grounds that the criteria for designating persons were remarkably broad and that persons posing no threat to the United Kingdom would be encompassed within the legislation.[7]

8.08   During consideration of the Bill in Committee, David Heath MP (Liberal Democrat) found it impossible to reconcile the Home Secretary's stated objective of simplifying immigration law with the introduction of a new status.[8]

8.09   The new status was justified in the Regulatory Impact Assessment for the Bill[9] by Liam Byrne MP, Minister of State, Home Office:

> This is addressing the risk that individuals who have committed serious crimes will become settled in the United Kingdom. Currently those who would be affected by this provision are granted short periods of leave (Discretionary Leave (DL)), generally for 6 months at a time, after which they have to apply for further leave. DL allows them to access employment and mainstream benefits, increasing their links with the UK and making their eventual removal more problematic. Legislation is required to take the power to deny them leave. Local management information suggests that the policy will affect fewer than 50 people at first, although it is possible that the number will rise over time depending on the difficulty of overcoming the legal barriers to their removal.[10]

---

[5] At first instance [2006] EWHC 1111 (Admin), and on appeal; [2006] EWCA Civ 1157 (Court of Appeal); [2006] Immigration and Nationality Law Reports 575.
[6] Para 93.
[7] HC Deb 8 October 2007 vol 464 cc84–85.
[8] PBC Deb 14th Sitting 27 November 2007 c640.
[9] June 2007.
[10] Page 156.

2. The context: immigration law on leave to enter or remain and the Afghan Hijackers' case

To understand the role of special immigration status within immigration law following   8.10
the judgments in the Afghan Hijackers' case, it is necessary to consider the pre-existing
statutory structure. The latter can be pared down to its key elements necessary for this
purpose.

Persons with the right of abode in the United Kingdom (British citizens and a few   8.11
others) are broadly free to live in, and to come and go from, the United Kingdom.[11]

Persons without the right of abode, may live, work and settle in the United Kingdom   8.12
by permission and subject to such regulation and control on their entry into, stay in
and departure from the United Kingdom as may be imposed.[12] Such persons *require
leave to enter or remain* and may be said to be *subject to immigration control.*

Persons who are entitled to enter or remain by virtue of an enforceable Community   8.13
right or under a provision made under the European Communities Act 1972, s 2(2),
do not require leave to enter or remain.[13] However, absent the exercise of those
rights, leave is required.

Persons arriving at a port may be examined by an immigration officer to determine   8.14
whether they are British citizens, whether they may enter without leave, whether
they may have extant leave, or whether where required they should be given or refused
leave.[14] Such persons may be detained by an immigration officer pending examination
or pending a decision to give or refuse leave to enter.[15]

Persons who are detained or liable to detention under the Immigration Act 1971,   8.15
Sch 2, para 16, may be temporarily admitted to the United Kingdom under the
written authority of an immigration officer.[16]

In the Afghan Hijackers' case, *S and Others v Secretary of State for the Home Department*   8.16
(referred to at para **8.06** above), the Home Secretary sought to rely on the Immigration
Act 1971, Sch 2, para 16(1), to confer temporary admission on, and deny Discretionary
Leave to those whom immigration adjudicators had found to be at risk on return to
Afghanistan.

The claimants had hijacked an aircraft to escape from Afghanistan, arrived in the   8.17
United Kingdom, and claimed asylum. They were convicted of offences relating to
the hijacking. On appeal, the Court of Appeal quashed the convictions. No retrial
was ordered.

An immigration appeal against refusal of leave to enter was dismissed on asylum   8.18
grounds as the claimants were held to be excluded from the Convention Relating to
the Status of Refugees (the Refugee Convention).[17] However the appeal was allowed

---

[11] Immigration Act 1971, ss 1–2.
[12] Immigration Act 1971, ss 1 and 3–4.
[13] Immigration Act 1988, s 7.
[14] Immigration Act 1971, Sch 2, para 2(1).
[15] Immigration Act 1971, Sch 2, para 16(1).
[16] Immigration Act 1971, Sch 2, para 21(1).
[17] Geneva, 28 July 1951; UNTS 2545 (1954) and Protocol Relating to the Status of Refugees of 31 January
1967 (UNTS 8791 (1967)) by application of Article 1F(b).

on the basis there would be a risk on return to Afghanistan contrary to Article 3 of the ECHR (the prohibition on torture).

8.19 Under the then policy for granting leave to remain those at risk on this basis could have been excluded from Humanitarian Protection, where there were serious reasons for considering they had committed a serious crime in the United Kingdom or overseas. They could normally expect to be granted Discretionary Leave.

8.20 However, the Home Secretary issued a revised policy whereby, in circumstances where Ministers decided it was 'inappropriate' to grant any leave in all the circumstances of the case, a person could be placed on 'temporary admission'. Thereafter, the Home Secretary refused the claimants' Discretionary Leave and decided they should remain on temporary admission. By withholding such leave and placing them on temporary admission, the Home Secretary was aiming to exclude the claimants from access to ordinary social security benefits and access to social housing and to prohibit their employment.

8.21 The claimants asserted that the decision and the new policy were unlawful as being inconsistent with the scheme under the Immigration Act 1971. The High Court held that there was an improper use of the powers contained in the Immigration Act 1971, Sch 2, paras 16(1) and 21. The power to grant temporary admission under para 21 was parasitic upon the power to detain. The conditions for the exercise of the power to detain under para 16(1) were not fulfilled.

8.22 On appeal, the Home Secretary unsuccessfully challenged the conclusion that the revised policy was unlawful. In giving judgment Brook LJ, Vice-President of the Court of Appeal (Civil Division), foreshadowed the introduction of special immigration status by observing that it would be open to Parliament to introduce a new statutory category to accommodate those disentitled by conduct to discretionary leave.[18]

C. SPECIAL IMMIGRATION STATUS

1. Introduction

8.23 Part 10 of the CJIA 2008 (ss 130 to 137) creates and regulates special immigration status. By s 137(9), it forms part of the body of immigration statute law known as 'the Immigration Acts'.[19]

8.24 CJIA 2008, s 152(2)(d) provides that Part 10 applies to England and Wales, Scotland and Northern Ireland.

8.25 At the time of writing, Part 10 is not in force and no date has been set for its commencement.

2. The designation of persons

8.26 The CJIA 2008, s 130 confers a power on the Secretary of State to designate a person who satisfies one of two conditions. The power is subject to two provisions restricting its exercise.

---

[18] *S and Others v Secretary of State for the Home Department* [2006] EWCA Civ 1157 (Court of Appeal), [2006] Immigration and Nationality Law Reports 575, at para 47.
[19] Defined in the UK Borders Act 2007, s 61.

(a) *The first condition: foreign criminals who are liable to deportation but who cannot be removed*

Condition 1 is set out in s 130(2) and contains two elements. Firstly, a person must   8.27
be a foreign criminal within the meaning of s 131 (see paras **8.37–8.46** below).
Secondly, a person must be liable to deportation but someone who cannot be removed
from the United Kingdom on account of the obligation on public authorities not to
act contrary to the ECHR, pursuant to the Human Rights Act 1998, s 6.

(b) *The second condition: the family members of foreign criminals*

Condition 2 is set out in the CJIA 2008, s 130(3). A person must be the family   8.28
member of a person who satisfies Condition 1.

Section 137(3) provides that 'family' is to be construed in accordance with the   8.29
Immigration Act 1971, s 5(4). The latter provides:

(4) For purposes of deportation the following shall be those who are regarded as belonging to
another person's family—

    (a)   where that other person is a man, his wife [or civil partner,][20] and his or her children
under the age of eighteen; and

    [(b) where that other person is a woman, her husband [or civil partner,][21] and her or his children under the age of eighteen;][22]

and for purposes of this subsection an adopted child, whether legally adopted or not, may be
treated as the child of the adopter and, if legally adopted, shall be regarded as the child only of
the adopter; an illegitimate child (subject to the foregoing rule as to adoptions) shall be
regarded as the child of the mother; and 'wife' includes each of two or more wives.

At the Committee Stage of the Bill, Harry Cohen MP (Labour) voiced concern   8.30
that special immigration status would disadvantage children on account of their parents'
actions contrary to the Convention on the Rights of the Child.[23] He considered that
children would be left in limbo, potentially unable to work or to have access to
education or childcare.[24]

For the government, Vernon Coaker MP, Parliamentary Under Secretary of State   8.31
for the Home Department, stated:

. . . As a matter of policy, the Border and Immigration Agency does not grant dependants with leave
in line—a form of leave that is more favourable than that given to the principal applicant . . .

. . . a family member who has been designated will be able to apply for leave in their own right
and, if they qualify, be granted it. . . There are two aims behind the conditions that can be
imposed: first, to prevent a foreign criminal from establishing links with this country that might
constitute an additional obstacle to his eventual deportation; and, secondly, to maintain contact
with a foreign criminal and his immediate family until such time as his removal becomes possible.

---

[20] Inserted by the Civil Partnership Act 2004, s 261(1), Sch 27, para 37.
[21] Ibid.
[22] Substituted by the Asylum and Immigration Act 1996, s 12(1), Sch 2, para 2.
[23] New York, 20 November 1989; UNTS 27531(1990), art 2.2
[24] PBC Deb 14th Sitting 27 November 2007 c637.

The purpose of the conditions is not punishment, but merely to allow a situation to be managed.[25]

(c) *Restrictions on designation*

8.32   The first restriction is contained in the CJIA 2008, s 130(4). A person with the right of abode may not be designated. By s 137(4), 'right of abode in the United Kingdom' has the meaning given by the Immigration Act 1971, s 2.

8.33   The second restriction is contained in the CJIA 2008, s 130(5). Where the Secretary of State thinks that an effect of designation would breach the United Kingdom's obligations under the Refugee Convention or a person's rights under the Community Treaties[26] he may not designate a person.

8.34   The Joint Committee on Human Rights commented:[27]

. . . We were concerned by the subjective language used in this provision and therefore wrote to the Government. We welcome the Government's clarification that the Secretary of State's designation of a person under clause 181 of the Bill would be unlawful if, in the opinion of a court, the effect of designation would breach the UK's obligations under the Refugee Convention.

8.35   It would also be unlawful for the Secretary of State to designate a person, if to do so would be incompatible with a right under the ECHR and thus contrary to the Human Rights Act 1998, s 6.

8.36   There is no right of appeal against designation. A challenge may only be brought by a claim for judicial review or by proceedings under the Human Rights Act 1998, s 7 in a claim that a public authority has acted incompatibly with the ECHR.

3. Foreign criminals

(a) *The definition of 'foreign criminal'*

8.37   The CJIA 2008, s 131 provides the definition 'foreign criminal' for the purposes of designation under s 130. By s 131(1) a 'foreign criminal' is a person who is not a British citizen and who satisfies any one of three conditions.

8.38   Condition 1 in s 131(2) draws on provisions of the Nationality, Immigration and Asylum Act (NIAA) 2002, ss 72(2)(a) and (b) or s 72(3)(a) to (c), for its requirements. Within the NIAA 2002, s 72 applies for the purpose of the construction and application of Article 33(2) of the Refugee Convention (exclusion from protection). Concerns about the width of this broad statutory definition of Article 33(2) have been expressed by the United Nations High Commission for Refugees (UNHCR) and the Joint Committee on Human Rights.[28]

---

[25] PBC Deb 14th Sitting 27 November 2007 cc638–9.

[26] The Community Treaties are defined in the European Communities Act 1972, s 1.

[27] JCHR Legislative Scrutiny: Criminal Justice and Immigration Bill 5th Report, (2007–08) HL Paper 37 HC 269 pp 33–34.

[28] UNHCR Comments on the Nationality, Immigration and Asylum Act 2002 (Specification of Particularly Serious Crimes) Order 2004, November 2004; JCHR 22nd Report (2003–04) HL Paper 190 HC 1212.

Condition 1 is satisfied in one of two ways. Firstly, under the NIAA 2002, s 72(2)(a) **8.39** and (b), which provides:

(2) A person shall be presumed to have been convicted by a final judgment of a particularly serious crime and to constitute a danger to the community of the United Kingdom if he is—
   (a) convicted in the United Kingdom of an offence, and
   (b) sentenced to a period of imprisonment of at least two years.

Secondly, under the NIAA 2002, s 72(3)(a) to (c), which provides: **8.40**

(3) A person shall be presumed to have been convicted by a final judgment of a particularly serious crime and to constitute a danger to the community of the United Kingdom if—
   (a) he is convicted outside the United Kingdom of an offence,
   (b) he is sentenced to a period of imprisonment of at least two years, and
   (c) he could have been sentenced to a period of imprisonment of at least two years had his conviction been a conviction in the United Kingdom of a similar offence.

Section 137(6) of the CJIA 2008 provides that a 'period of imprisonment' is to be con- **8.41** strued in accordance with the NIAA 2002, s 72(11)(b)(i) and (ii). The latter provides:

(b) a reference to a person who is sentenced to a period of imprisonment of at least two years—
   (i) does not include a reference to a person who receives a suspended sentence [(unless a court subsequently orders that the sentence or any part of it is to take effect)][29],
   . . .
   (ii) includes a reference to a person who is sentenced to detention, or ordered or directed to be detained, in an institution other than a prison (including, in particular, a hospital or an institution for young offenders), and
   . . .

Condition 2 is found in the CJIA 2008, s 131(3). It draws on provisions of the **8.42** NIAA 2002, s 72(4)(a) or (b), for its requirements and is satisfied in one or two ways. Section 72(4) provides:

(4) A person shall be presumed to have been convicted by a final judgment of a particularly serious crime and to constitute a danger to the community of the United Kingdom if—
   (a) he is convicted of an offence specified by order of the Secretary of State, or
   (b) he is convicted outside the United Kingdom of an offence and the Secretary of State certifies that in his opinion the offence is similar to an offence specified by order under paragraph (a).

The order specifying the offences under the NIAA 2002, s 72(4)(a) is the Nationality, **8.43** Immigration and Asylum Act 2002 (Specification of Particularly Serious Crimes) Order 2004.[30] It contains a list of criminal offences including theft and criminal damage. A person satisfies Condition 2 where s 72(4)(a) or (b) applies and he has been sentenced to a term of imprisonment of any length.

---

[29] Substituted by the UK Borders Act 2007, s 39, in force 1 August 2008 by the UK Borders Act 2007 (Commencement No 3 and Transitional Provisions) Order 2008, SI 2008/1818, art 2.
[30] SI 2004/1910.

8.44   Sub-sections (2), (3) and (4) of s 72 of the NIAA 2002 each contain a provision that a person who falls within it shall be presumed to have been convicted by a final judgment of a particularly serious crime and to constitute a danger to the United Kingdom. Section 72(6) of the NIAA 2002 makes that presumption rebuttable. However, by s 131(5) of the CJIA 2008, s 72(6) of the NIAA 2002 has no effect in relation to Condition 1 or 2. For CJIA 2008 purposes the presumption is not relevant and accordingly is made of no effect.

8.45   Similarly, the NIAA 2002, s 72(7), states that the presumption contained in s 72(2), (3) and (4) of the same Act does not apply while an appeal against conviction or sentence is pending or could be brought. However, by the CJIA 2008, s 131(6), the NIAA 2002, s 72(7), has no effect in relation to Condition 1 or 2. Again the presumption is not relevant for CJIA 2008 purposes and so the provision that applies to it is made of no effect.

8.46   Condition 3 is found in s 131(4). It applies if Article 1F of the Refugee Convention applies to the person.

(b) *Issues arising under Article 1F of the Refugee Convention*

8.47   There are serious concerns about the number of persons who may satisfy Condition 3 of the definition of foreign criminal, without having committed a criminal offence, because of the width of the statutory definition of Article 1F (c) of the Refugee Convention in the Immigration, Asylum and Nationality Act 2006, s 54.[31] The latter provides as material:

> 54. Refugee Convention: construction
>> (1) In the construction and application of Article 1(F)(c) of the Refugee Convention the reference to acts contrary to the purposes and principles of the United Nations shall be taken as including, in particular—
>>> (a) acts of committing, preparing or instigating terrorism (whether or not the acts amount to an actual or inchoate offence), and
>>> (b) acts of encouraging or inducing others to commit, prepare or instigate terrorism (whether or not the acts amount to an actual or inchoate offence).
>> (2) In this section—
>>> . . .
>> 'terrorism' has the meaning given by section 1 of the Terrorism Act 2000 (c 11).

8.48   Concerns about Condition 3 in the CJIA 2008, s 131, and Article 1F(c) of the Refugee Convention were set out at the Committee Stage of the Bill by Harry Cohen MP (Labour).[32] He noted that the narrow construction of Article 1F(c) contended for by the United Nations High Commissioner for Refugees (UNHCR) had not been adopted by Parliament and that the broad statutory definition in the IANA 2006, s 54, is capable of catching political refugees who have opposed repressive regimes in their home countries. The concerns that UNHCR had about IANA 2006, s 54, were set out by David Heath MP (Liberal Democrat).[33]

---

[31] In relation to criminal offences covering similar or overlapping actions, see Terrorism Act 2006, ss 1–4 and 20.
[32] PBC Deb 14th Sitting 27 November 2007 c643.
[33] Ibid., cc643–4.

In reply, Vernon Coaker, MP, Parliamentary Under Secretary of State for the   8.49
Home Department, stated:

My hon. Friend says that designation should be limited to cases where we are certain that a criminal offence has been committed, as evidenced by the fact of the conviction. However, we are not talking about cases in which there is a vague suspicion of wrongdoing on the part of an individual, but about cases where there are serious grounds for considering that an individual is guilty of actions so serious that even if he has a well-founded fear of persecution in his country of nationality, he is to be denied the protection normally afforded to a refugee by the international community. The requirement to have serious grounds before making any consideration means that there will need to be clear and credible evidence on which to base a decision to exclude. Often, people will not have been prosecuted, still less convicted. Indeed, sometimes, the reason why such people cannot be prosecuted is that they are in the United Kingdom. We are unable to bring them to trial here, and we are unable to remove them for human rights reasons.

Sometimes, people cannot be tried here for procedural reasons: in other words, the events happened abroad and the evidence was gathered there, and witnesses would have to be brought here. In other instances, our courts do not have jurisdiction, even for serious offences. For example, our courts have no jurisdiction to try a foreign national for a murder committed overseas. Ideally, we would prefer to deport rather than designate such individuals, but if our international human rights obligations mean that we cannot deport a person, we want to be in a position to designate, so we are not forced into a position whereby we are forced to grant leave for the person to remain here.[34]

The Joint Committee on Human Rights commented: 8.50

In our view, however, the clause still gives rise to a significant human rights issue, because of its reliance on the so-called statutory construction of Article 1F of the Refugee Convention by s. 54 of the Immigration, Asylum and Nationality Act 2006. The Government confirmed in its response to our inquiry that this statutory construction of Article 1F of the Refugee Convention would apply in any court proceedings when deciding whether the effect of designation would breach the UK's obligations under the Convention. In a previous report we have reported that this statutory construction undermines the protection afforded by the Refugee Convention because it expands the scope of the exclusions from refugee protection well beyond the narrow scope given to those exclusions in the Convention itself. These concerns continue to be shared by the UNHCR. **We are therefore concerned that this Part of the Bill gives rise to a further risk of breaches of the Refugee Convention by the UK and we recommend that the statutory construction of Article 1F of that Convention be repealed.**[35]

(c) *The separate definition of 'foreign criminal' for deportation purposes under s 32 of the UK Borders Act 2007*
The definition of 'foreign criminal' in the UK Borders Act (UKBA) 2007, s 32(1)–(3),   8.51
for deportation purposes is narrower than that in the CJIA 2008, s 131. Care must

---

[34] Ibid., cc 645–6.
[35] JCHR Legislative Scrutiny: Criminal Justice and Immigration Bill 5th Report, (2007–08) HL Paper 37 HC 269 pp 33–4.

be taken to ascertain which definition is being used by the UK Borders Agency in relation to a particular person. Section 32(1)–(3) of the UKBA 2007 provides:[36]

32 Automatic deportation

    (1) In this section 'foreign criminal' means a person—

        (a) who is not a British citizen,

        (b) who is convicted in the United Kingdom of an offence, and

        (c) to whom Condition 1 or 2 applies.

    (2) Condition 1 is that the person is sentenced to a period of imprisonment of at least 12 months.

    (3) Condition 2 is that—

        (a) the offence is specified by order of the Secretary of State under section 72(4)(a) of the Nationality, Immigration and Asylum Act 2002 (c 41) (serious criminal), and

        (b) the person is sentenced to a period of imprisonment.

4. The effect of designation

8.52   Designation isolates a person from forms of status or benefit conferred by other provisions of immigration and nationality law. Special immigration status is indefinite until brought to an end under the CJIA 2008, s 136. It may apply to someone who poses no risk to the United Kingdom, who has been convicted of a minor offence, who has no convictions, or who has been denied Refugee Status by operation of the overbroad definition of Article 1F(c) of the Refugee Convention in the IANA 2006, s 54.

8.53   Family members entirely free from blame may be designated and their ability, to work, study and access benefits and healthcare restricted.

8.54   Designation and any conditions imposed following designation may violate rights enjoyed under the ECHR. Full consideration of this issue can be found in the Joint Council for the Welfare of Immigrants Bill submissions to the Joint Committee on Human Rights.

(a) *The effect on immigration status*

8.55   The CJIA 2008, s 132(1) provides that a designated person does not have leave to enter or remain in the United Kingdom. This prevents the person from making applications under immigration and nationality law that would otherwise apply to persons subject to immigration control.

8.56   Section 132(2) and (4) describes how the status of a person designated under s 130 fits into immigration and nationality law. Section 132(2) provides that for the purposes of a provision of the Immigration Acts and other enactments which concern or refer to immigration or nationality, a designated person has three characteristics, notwithstanding that he does not have leave to enter or remain. He is:

(a) a person subject to immigration control,

(b) not to be treated as an asylum-seeker or a former asylum-seeker, and

(c) not in the United Kingdom in breach of immigration laws.

---

[36] By the UK Borders Act 2007 (Commencement No 3 and Transitional Provisions) Order 2008, SI 2008/1818, art 2, automatic deportation for those satisfying Condition 1 came into force on 1 August 2008. The provisions are not yet in force for those satisfying Condition 2.

Section 132(4)(a) provides that a designated person shall not be deemed to have been given leave to enter in accordance with the Immigration Act 1971, Sch 2, para 6.   8.57

Section 132(4)(b) provides that a designated person may not be granted temporary admission to the United Kingdom under the Immigration Act 1971, Sch 2, para 21.   8.58

A designated person does not have the right of abode. Consequently he requires leave to enter or remain under the Immigration Act 1971, ss 1–3. Section 132 of the CJIA 2008 provides that he does not have leave to enter or remain yet he is, nonetheless, a person subject to immigration control. For such a person there is no obvious route to settlement in the United Kingdom under the Immigration Rules.[37] Even the requirements for indefinite leave to remain on the ground of long residence (14 years), paras 276A–D of the Immigration Rules, could not be satisfied by the inclusion of any time spent following service of a notice of liability to removal, a decision to remove by way of directions, or an intention to deport (see para 276B(i)(b) of the Immigration Rules).   8.59

(b) The effect of access to welfare benefits and tax credits

A designated person is excluded from welfare benefits by the Immigration and Asylum Act (IAA) 1999, s 115, as he is a person who requires leave to enter or remain (not having the right of abode)[38] who does not have such leave. Section 115 of the IAA 1999 excludes income-based jobseeker's allowance, pension credit, income-related allowance, attendance allowance, severe disablement allowance, carer's allowance, disability living allowance, income support, a social fund payment, child benefit, housing benefit, and council tax benefit.   8.60

There is an equivalent restriction on access to Tax Credits under the Tax Credits Act 2002, s 42, and the Tax Credits (Immigration) Regulations 2003, SI 2003/653.   8.61

(c) The effect for the purposes of nationality law

CJIA 2008, s 132(3) prevents the use of designated status for the purposes of satisfying relevant criteria in nationality law. Notwithstanding the fact that a designated person is not in the United Kingdom in breach of immigration law, by s 132(2)(c) time spent in the United Kingdom as a designated person may not be relied upon for the purposes of an enactment about nationality.   8.62

It follows that NIAA 2002, s 11, still applies, so that a designated person will be in the United Kingdom in breach of immigration law for nationality law purposes. Such a person will therefore fail to satisfy a requirement of nationality law, where imposed, not to be in the United Kingdom in breach of immigration law (for example the provisions for naturalization in the British Nationality Act 1981, Sch 1, paras 1 and 2). Furthermore, time spent as a designated person will not count for satisfying the residence and presence requirements of nationality law.   8.63

5. Conditions

(a) The power to impose conditions

The CJIA 2008, s 133(1) confers a power on the Secretary of State or an immigration officer to impose a condition on a designated person by notice in writing.   8.64

---

[37] HC 395 of 1993–1994 as amended.
[38] Immigration Act 1971, ss 1–3.

8.65   At Committee Stage of the Bill, Vernon Coaker MP, Parliamentary Under Secretary of State for the Home Department, stated:

> The new status is not an additional punishment, and the purpose of the conditions that might be imposed is not to punish. The condition relating to employment is designed to prevent the designated person establishing firm roots within the UK, as I have already said. The conditions relating to residence and reporting are designed to enable the BIA to maintain contact until such time as the ECHR barrier to removal has passed, so that the removal can be effected.
>
> . . . the purpose of any conditions that may be imposed is not to prevent the commission of further offences. Again, discussion on that has revealed a misunderstanding of the purpose of creating the new status. As it is has been stated, the aim of imposing conditions is not crime prevention or reduction, and that holds good whether or not the clause is amended to state that explicitly. The purpose of conditions is to manage the situation.[39]

(b) *The conditions that may be imposed*

8.66   Section 133(2) provides that a condition 'may relate to':

(a) residence,
(b) employment or occupation, or
(c) reporting to the police, the Secretary of State or an immigration officer.

8.67   The words 'may relate to' mean that, potentially, the power to impose conditions is very wide.[40]

8.68   A designated person may be subjected to electronic monitoring. Section 133(3) applies the Asylum and Immigration (Treatment of Claimants, etc) Act 2004, s 36, in relation to conditions imposed on a designated person, as the latter applies to restrictions imposed on those granted temporary admission under the Immigration Act 1971, Sch 2, para 21.

8.69   It may be that the long term denial of the ability to work or otherwise earn money, may become unlawful (see the opinion of Baroness Hale in *R (Khadir) v Secretary of State for the Home Department*).[41]

8.70   A designated person may receive travel expenses in relation to complying with reporting restrictions. Section 133(4) applies the NIAA 2002, s 69, to designated persons who have a reporting condition imposed, as the latter applies to those granted temporary admission subject to restrictions imposed under the Immigration Act 1971, Sch 2, para 21.

8.71   The Home Office policy made under s 69 of the NIAA 2002 is 'Travelling expenses policy: Contact management policy, processes, and implementation'.[42] Where a person has to make a journey of three miles or more to a reporting centre, or where there are exceptional needs, expenses will be paid.

(c) *Criminal sanctions for failure to comply with conditions*

8.72   Section 133(5) of the CJIA 2008 provides that a person who without reasonable excuse fails to comply with a condition imposed under s 133 commits an offence.

---

[39] PBC Deb 14th Sitting 27 November 2007 c648.
[40] Cf the power to impose obligations under a control order in the Prevention of Terrorism Act 2005, s 1(4).
[41] [2006] 1 AC 207 at para 4.
[42] Version 5, June 2006.

Section 133(6) provides that a person guilty of the offence is liable on summary conviction to a fine not exceeding level 5 on the standard scale, imprisonment for a period not exceeding 51 weeks, or both.

Paragraph 36 of Sch 27 of the CJIA 2008 provides that in the application of s 133   8.73
to England and Wales in relation to an offence committed before the commencement of the Criminal Justice Act 2003, s 281(5), the reference in s 133(6)(b) to 51 weeks is to be read as a reference to 6 months. At the time of writing the CJA 2003, s 281(5) is not in force.

Section 133(7) of the CJIA 2008 provides that in Scotland and Northern Ireland   8.74
the reference to 51 weeks is to be treated as a reference to 6 months.

(d) *Powers of arrest, search, entry and seizure in connection with the offence*
Section 133(7) of the CJIA 2008 provides that the provisions of the Immigration   8.75
Act 1971 that apply in relation to an offence under the Immigration Act 1971, s 24(1), also apply in relation to the offence under s 133(5) of the CJIA 2008. Under the Immigration Act 1971 there are powers of arrest, search, entry and seizure in relation to an offence under s 24(1). These powers can be found in the Immigration Act 1971, ss 28A–K. They may be applied in relation to an offence under the CJIA 2008, s 133(5).

(e) *A comparison with the power to impose conditions on those with other forms of status*
The permissible conditions that may be imposed on those with other forms of status   8.76
may be found in the following places:

(a) temporary admission: Immigration Act 1971, para 21 of Sch 2,
(b) subject to deportation proceedings: Immigration Act, 1971, Sch 3,
(c) on immigration bail: Immigration Act 1971, para 22 of Sch 2,
(d) limited leave to enter or remain: Immigration Act 1971, s 3(1)(c),
(e) subject to a control order: Prevention of Terrorism Act 2005, s 1(4).

Given the power to impose conditions as to employment or occupation, reporting   8.77
and residence, on those with limited leave to enter or remain and on those subject to a control order, it is hard to see the true rationale for introducing special immigration status with its attendant conditions.

6. Accommodation and support

Section 134(1) of the CJIA 2008 provides that the provision made for the support   8.78
of asylum-seekers under the Immigration and Asylum Act 1999, Part VI, applies in relation to designated persons and their dependants, as it applies in relation to asylum-seekers and their dependants.

Asylum support is set at 70 per cent of income support rates for adults and   8.79
100 per cent for children.[43]

Temporary support may be provided under the IAA 1999, s 98. Thereafter, sup-   8.80
port may be provided under the IAA 1999, s 95, where designated persons or their

---

[43] House of Commons Library Research Paper 07/65 The Criminal Justice and Immigration Bill, Bill 130 of 2006–07, p 110.

dependants appear to the Secretary of State to be destitute or likely to become so within a prescribed period.

(a) *The application of a modified asylum support regime*

8.81   Section 134(2) modifies the general application of the IAA 1999, Part VI. Section 96 of the IAA 1999 ('Ways in which support may be provided') does not apply to designated persons and their dependants. Instead, s 134(3) provides, that support may be provided under the IAA 1999, s 95, by providing accommodation that appears to the Secretary of State to be adequate for a person's needs, by providing what appears to the Secretary of State to be essential living needs, or in other ways the Secretary of States thinks necessary to reflect the exceptional circumstances of a particular case.

8.82   As s 96 of the IAA 1999 does not apply to designated persons and their dependants and s 134(3) of the CJIA 2008 governs the ways in which support may be provided, supplemental provision is made in s 135(1) to reflect this modification to the statutory regime of support. Further, a reference to asylum-seekers is to be treated as including a reference to designated persons.

8.83   Section 134(2) of the CJIA 2008 relieves the Secretary of State, when exercising the power to provide accommodation under the IAA 1999, s 95, to designated persons and dependants, of the requirement under the IAA 1999, s 97(1)(b), to have regard to the desirability in general of providing accommodation in areas in which there is a ready supply of accommodation.

8.84   Local Authorities are relieved of the duty to co-operate in providing accommodation under the IAA 1999, s 100, in respect of designated persons and their dependants, by the CJIA 2008, s 134(2).

8.85   Section 134(2) of the CJIA 2008 provides that s 108 ('Failure of sponsor to maintain'), s 111 ('Grants to voluntary organisations') and s 113 ('Recovery of expenditure from sponsor') of the IAA 1999 are not to apply to designated person and their dependants.

8.86   Section 135(2) of the CJIA 2008 provides that a provision of the IAA 1999, Part VI, that requires or permits the Secretary of State to have regard to the *temporary nature of support*, is to be treated as requiring him to have regard to the nature and circumstances of support provided by virtue of s 134 of the CJIA 2008. Section 97(5) of the IAA 1999 provides an example of where the *temporary nature of support* is required to be taken into account.

8.87   Section 135(4) permits a statutory instrument to make the same or different provision for designated persons and their dependants, as is made for asylum-seekers and their dependants.

8.88   A designated person may appeal against the refusal of support. Under the IAA 1999, s 103, a person may appeal to an Asylum Support Adjudicator of the Asylum Support Tribunal, against the decision that he does not qualify for support under the IAA 1999, s 95, or against the decision to stop providing such support before it would otherwise have come to an end. Section 135(3) of the CJIA 2008 provides that rules made under the IAA 1999, s 104, in respect of appeals by asylum-seekers and failed asylum-seekers, have effect for the purposes of Part VI of that Act as it applies by virtue of the CJIA 2008, s 134, so that designated persons may appeal against the refusal of support.

There are also specific provisions in the IAA 1999, Sch 8, para 9 governing the making of regulations in respect of a Notice to Quit where a person has a tenancy or licence to occupy accommodation by virtue of support provided under s 95 of that Act. Section 135(5) of the CJIA 2008 modifies the IAA 1999, Sch 8, para 9(2)(b), so that a reference to the determination of a claim for asylum is to be treated as a reference to ceasing to be a designated person. The provisions governing Notices to Quit are found in the Asylum Support Regulations 2000, SI 2000/704, reg 22.   **8.89**

Other than were expressly excluded or modified, the provisions of the IA 1999, Part VI, apply to designated persons and their dependants.   **8.90**

For example, there is no definition of a dependant in the CJIA 2008, Part 10. The definition of a dependant of a designated person is the same as for the dependant of an asylum seeker. It is found in the IAA 1999, s 94 and the Asylum Support Regulations 2000, (SI 2000/704).   **8.91**

Section 134(5) of the CJIA 2008 provides that s 4 of the IAA 1999, known as 'hard cases' accommodation, does not apply in relation to designated persons. The latter section is found in Part I of the IAA 1999. It gives the Secretary of State power to provide accommodation to persons who are temporarily admitted to the United Kingdom under the Immigration Act 1971, Sch 2, para 21; those released from immigration detention; those released on immigration bail; or failed asylum-seekers.   **8.92**

(b) *The limited role of cash in the provision of support*

Section 134(4) of the CJIA 2008 provides that the support may not be provided wholly or mainly by way of cash unless the Secretary of State thinks it appropriate because of exceptional circumstances. Section 137(7) provides that a voucher is not cash.   **8.93**

At the Committee Stage in the House of Commons, there were concerns about the use of vouchers. Harry Cohen MP (Labour) noted that the Refugee Council had pointed out there was no allowance for clothing or shoe repairs and that there would be progressive poverty under the proposals. The Refugee Council had noted that vouchers for asylum-seekers had previously been withdrawn due to their stigmatizing role and impoverishing impact.[44]   **8.94**

By s 135(6), the Secretary of State may by order repeal, modify or disapply to any extent s 134(4). By virtue of s 147(5)(g) a statutory instrument containing an order under s 135(6) is to be made under the affirmative resolution procedure.   **8.95**

In response to a request for information by the Delegated Powers and Regulatory Reform Committee of the House of Lords, Lord Hunt of Kings Heath, Minister of State, Ministry of Justice, providing the following further information about the clause containing the power to make the order: **8.96**

. . . our experience of running the asylum seeker support arrangements has shown that it is not always possible to predict developments. For example, if a chain of stores in a region were to decide that it would no longer accept vouchers, this might make it necessary to review the way in which support was provided in that area.

---

[44] PBC Deb 14th Sitting 27 November 2007 c649.

Bearing in mind that support will only be provided to people who are, or who are likely to become, destitute, The Government needs to be able to respond quickly to developments which affect the ability to provide support. The Government does not believe that primary legislation could be enacted sufficiently quickly to allow the provision of support to continue; nor would it be flexible enough to accommodate temporary suspensions of the restriction—which might be limited to a particular area—while new arrangements were made . . .[45]

(c) *Modifications to statutory regimes for the provision of housing and homelessness assistance*

8.97   Section 134(6) of the CJIA 2008 modifies provisions relating to homelessness found in other statutes. A designated person is not to be treated as a person subject to immigration control for the purposes of the IAA 1999, s 119(1)(b) in Scotland and Northern Ireland. Further, a designated person is not to be treated as a person from abroad who is not eligible for housing assistance for the purposes of the Housing Act 1996, s 185(4) in England and Wales. These provisions prevent a designated person from being disregarded in determining whether another person is homeless or threatened with homelessness or whether she has a priority need for accommodation.

8.98   By s 135(7) an order under the Human Rights Act 1998, s 10, amending a provision mentioned in s 134(6) may amend or repeal s 134(6). An order under the Human Rights Act 1998, s 10, may make amendments to legislation that has been declared to be incompatible with rights under the ECHR.

8.99   A Memorandum by the Ministry of Justice, provided during the passage of the Bill, considering the clause conferring the power to make the order stated:

> . . . In the case of *R (Morris) v Westminster City Council and another* the Court of Appeal made a declaration of incompatibility in relation to section 185(4) of the Housing Act.
>
> Action has not yet been taken to remove the incompatibility and so clause 186(6) is necessary. However, if a remedial order under section 10 of the Human Rights Act 1998 is used to remove the incompatibility, clause 186(7) provides that clauses 185(6) may be amended or repealed . . .[46]

8.100   However, there will be no remedial order. Instead, the Housing and Regeneration Act 2008, Sch 15, makes various amendments to the Housing Act 1996, the Housing (Scotland) Act 1987, the Housing (Northern Ireland) Order 1988, and the IAA 1999, in an attempt to address the declaration of incompatibility made in *R (Morris) City Council and another v Westminster*.[47] The amendments have not yet come into force. As a result of the amendments, the Housing and Regeneration 2008, Sch 15, paras 23 and 24, repeals CJIA 2008, ss 134(6) and 135(7). No date has been set for the commencement of these consequential amendments.

---

[45] HL Delegated Powers and Regulatory Reform Committee 6th Report (2007–08) HL Paper 76 pp 103–104.

[46] HL Delegated Powers and Regulatory Reform Committee 4th Report (2007–08) HL Paper 49 p 64.

[47] (CA) [2006] 1 WLR 505.

7. The end of designation

(a) *The ways in which designation may end*

Section 136 of the CJIA 2008 provides that designation lapses if the person is granted leave to enter or remain in the United Kingdom, is notified by the Secretary of State or an immigration officer of a right of residence in the United Kingdom by virtue of the Community treaties,[48] leaves the United Kingdom, or is made the subject of a deportation order under the Immigration Act 1971, s 5. **8.101**

(b) *The consequences for the provision of support*

Section 135(2) provides that after designation lapses support may not be provided by virtue of s 134 unless one of two exceptions applies. **8.102**

Exception 1 applies where designation lapses as the person is granted leave to enter or remain in the United Kingdom or is notified by the Secretary of State or an immigration officer of a right of residence in the United Kingdom by virtue of the Community treaties. Support may be provided for a period beginning when designation lapses and ending on a date determined in accordance with an order of the Secretary of State (s 136(3)). **8.103**

Exception 2 is where designation lapses as the person is made the subject of a deportation order under the Immigration Act 1971, s 5. Support may be provided for any period during which an appeal against the deportation order may be brought; for any period during which an appeal against the deportation order is pending; and after the appeal ceases to be pending, such period as the Secretary of State may specify by order (s 136(4)). **8.104**

By s 137(8) of the CJIA 2008 a reference to a pending appeal has the meaning given by the NIAA 2002, s 104(1). **8.105**

D. A NEW EXCEPTION TO AUTOMATIC DEPORTATION

1. Introduction

Section 146 of the CJIA 2008 inserts s 33(6A) into the UK Borders Act 2007, creating a further exception to automatic deportation where the Secretary of State thinks that the application of the UKBA 2007, s 32(4) and (5), would contravene the United Kingdom's obligations under the European Trafficking Convention (see paras **8.03–8.05** above). **8.106**

Section 33(6A) of the UKBA 2007 applies to England and Wales, Scotland and Northern Ireland. **8.107**

At the time of writing, s 146 is not in force and no date has been set for commencement. **8.108**

---

[48] The Community Treaties are defined in the European Communities Act 1972, s 1.

2. The automatic deportation measures in the UK Borders Act 2007

8.109 The UKBA 2007, ss 32–39 makes provision for the automatic deportation of foreign criminals. 'Foreign criminal' is defined in s 32 of that Act for those purposes (see para **8.51** above).

8.110 Section 32(4) and (5) of the UKBA 2007 provides:

> (4) For the purpose of section 3(5)(a) of the Immigration Act 1971 (c 77), the deportation of a foreign criminal is conducive to the public good.
>
> (5) The Secretary of State must make a deportation order in respect of a foreign criminal (subject to section 33).

8.111 However, s 33(1)(a) of the UKBA 2007 provides:

> 33 Exceptions
>
> (1) Section 32(4) and (5)—
>
>   (a) do not apply where an exception in this section applies (subject to subsection (7) below), and
>
>   . . .

3. The new exception to automatic deportation

8.112 Section 33(6A) of the UKBA 2007, as inserted by the CJIA 2008, s 146, creates a further exception, Exception 6, to the exceptions to the automatic deportation provisions already contained in the UKBA 2007, s 33.

8.113 Thus the UKBA 2007, s 32(4), which provides by statute rather than by individual administrative decision, that the deportation of a foreign criminal is conducive to the public good and s 32(5), which requires the Secretary of State to make a deportation order, will not apply where the Secretary of State thinks their application would contravene the European Trafficking Convention.

8.114 If the Secretary of State considers that the UKBA 2007, s 32(5) applies, the person concerned may bring an appeal under the NIAA 2002, s 82(3A), that Exception 6 applies and there ought to be no automatic deportation order.

8.115 While Exception 6, contained in the UKBA 2007, s 33(6A) may disapply the automatic provisions of the UKBA 2007, s 32(4) and (5), it does not prevent an individual administrative decision that deportation is conducive to the public good, nor the making of a deportation order at discretion (UKBA 2007, s 33(7)). Where a decision to deport at discretion is made, the person may be able to rely on the European Trafficking Convention on appeal to the Asylum and Immigration Tribunal under the NIAA 2002, s 82(2)(j).

APPENDIX 1

Criminal Justice and Immigration Act 2008

CHAPTER 4

CONTENTS

PART 1
YOUTH REHABILITATION ORDERS

Youth rehabilitation orders

Supplementary

PART 2
SENTENCING

General sentencing provisions

Custodial sentences

PART 3
APPEALS

PART 5
CRIMINAL LAW

PART 6
INTERNATIONAL CO-OPERATION IN RELATION
TO CRIMINAL JUSTICE MATTERS

PART 7
VIOLENT OFFENDER ORDERS

Violent offender orders

CRIMINAL JUSTICE AND IMMIGRATION ACT 2008

2008 CHAPTER 4

An Act to make further provision about criminal justice (including provision about the police) and dealing with offenders and defaulters; to make further provision about the management of offenders; to amend the criminal law; to make further provision for combatting crime and disorder; to make provision about the mutual recognition of financial penalties; to amend the Repatriation of Prisoners Act 1984; to make provision for a new immigration status in certain cases involving criminality; to make provision about the automatic deportation of criminals under the UK Borders Act 2007; to amend section 127 of the Criminal Justice and Public Order Act 1994 and to confer power to suspend the operation of that section; and for connected purposes.

[8th May 2008]

BE IT ENACTED by the Queen's most Excellent Majesty, by and with the advice and consent of the Lords Spiritual and Temporal, and Commons, in this present Parliament assembled, and by the authority of the same, as follows:—

PART 1
YOUTH REHABILITATION ORDERS

Youth rehabilitation orders

1 Youth rehabilitation orders

(1) Where a person aged under 18 is convicted of an offence, the court by or before which the person is convicted may in accordance with Schedule 1 make an order (in this Part referred to as a "youth rehabilitation order") imposing on the person any one or more of the following requirements—

(a) an activity requirement (see paragraphs 6 to 8 of Schedule 1),

(b) a supervision requirement (see paragraph 9 of that Schedule),

(c) in a case where the offender is aged 16 or 17 at the time of the conviction, an unpaid work requirement (see paragraph 10 of that Schedule),

(d) a programme requirement (see paragraph 11 of that Schedule),

(e) an attendance centre requirement (see paragraph 12 of that Schedule),

(f) a prohibited activity requirement (see paragraph 13 of that Schedule),

(g) a curfew requirement (see paragraph 14 of that Schedule),

(h) an exclusion requirement (see paragraph 15 of that Schedule),

(i) a residence requirement (see paragraph 16 of that Schedule),

(j) a local authority residence requirement (see paragraph 17 of that Schedule),

(k) a mental health treatment requirement (see paragraph 20 of that Schedule),

(l) a drug treatment requirement (see paragraph 22 of that Schedule),

(m) a drug testing requirement (see paragraph 23 of that Schedule),

(n) an intoxicating substance treatment requirement (see paragraph 24 of that Schedule), and

(o) an education requirement (see paragraph 25 of that Schedule).

(2) A youth rehabilitation order—

    (a) may also impose an electronic monitoring requirement (see paragraph 26 of Schedule 1), and

    (b) must do so if paragraph 2 of that Schedule so requires.

(3) A youth rehabilitation order may be—

    (a) a youth rehabilitation order with intensive supervision and surveillance (see paragraph 3 of Schedule 1), or

    (b) a youth rehabilitation order with fostering (see paragraph 4 of that Schedule).

(4) But a court may only make an order mentioned in subsection (3)(a) or (b) if—

    (a) the court is dealing with the offender for an offence which is punishable with imprisonment,

    (b) the court is of the opinion that the offence, or the combination of the offence and one or more offences associated with it, was so serious that, but for paragraph 3 or 4 of Schedule 1, a custodial sentence would be appropriate (or, if the offender was aged under 12 at the time of conviction, would be appropriate if the offender had been aged 12), and

    (c) if the offender was aged under 15 at the time of conviction, the court is of the opinion that the offender is a persistent offender.

(5) Schedule 1 makes further provision about youth rehabilitation orders.

(6) This section is subject to—

    (a) sections 148 and 150 of the Criminal Justice Act 2003 (c. 44) (restrictions on community sentences etc.), and

    (b) the provisions of Parts 1 and 3 of Schedule 1.

2 Breach, revocation or amendment of youth rehabilitation orders

Schedule 2 makes provision about failures to comply with the requirements of youth rehabilitation orders and about the revocation or amendment of such orders.

3 Transfer of youth rehabilitation orders to Northern Ireland

Schedule 3 makes provision about the transfer of youth rehabilitation orders to Northern Ireland.

4 Meaning of "the responsible officer"

(1) For the purposes of this Part, "the responsible officer", in relation to an offender to whom a youth rehabilitation order relates, means—

    (a) in a case where the order—

        (i) imposes a curfew requirement or an exclusion requirement but no other requirement mentioned in section 1(1), and

        (ii) imposes an electronic monitoring requirement, the person who under paragraph 26(4) of Schedule 1 is responsible for the electronic monitoring required by the order;

    (b) in a case where the only requirement imposed by the order is an attendance centre requirement, the officer in charge of the attendance centre in question;

    (c) in any other case, the qualifying officer who, as respects the offender, is for the time being responsible for discharging the functions conferred by this Part on the responsible officer.

(2) In this section "qualifying officer", in relation to a youth rehabilitation order, means—

    (a) a member of a youth offending team established by a local authority for the time being specified in the order for the purposes of this section, or

    (b) an officer of a local probation board appointed for or assigned to the local justice area for the time being so specified or (as the case may be) an officer of a provider of probation services acting in the local justice area for the time being so specified.

(3) The Secretary of State may by order—
    (a) amend subsections (1) and (2), and
    (b) make any other amendments of—
        (i) this Part, or
        (ii) Chapter 1 of Part 12 of the Criminal Justice Act 2003 (c. 44) (general provisions about sentencing),
        that appear to be necessary or expedient in consequence of any amendment made by virtue of paragraph (a).

(4) An order under subsection (3) may, in particular, provide for the court to determine which of two or more descriptions of responsible officer is to apply in relation to any youth rehabilitation order.

5 Responsible officer and offender: duties in relation to the other

(1) Where a youth rehabilitation order has effect, it is the duty of the responsible officer—
    (a) to make any arrangements that are necessary in connection with the requirements imposed by the order,
    (b) to promote the offender's compliance with those requirements, and
    (c) where appropriate, to take steps to enforce those requirements.

(2) In subsection (1) "responsible officer" does not include a person falling within section 4(1)(a).

(3) In giving instructions in pursuance of a youth rehabilitation order relating to an offender, the responsible officer must ensure, as far as practicable, that any instruction is such as to avoid—
    (a) any conflict with the offender's religious beliefs,
    (b) any interference with the times, if any, at which the offender normally works or attends school or any other educational establishment, and
    (c) any conflict with the requirements of any other youth rehabilitation order to which the offender may be subject.

(4) The Secretary of State may by order provide that subsection (3) is to have effect with such additional restrictions as may be specified in the order.

(5) An offender in respect of whom a youth rehabilitation order is in force—
    (a) must keep in touch with the responsible officer in accordance with such instructions as the offender may from time to time be given by that officer, and
    (b) must notify the responsible officer of any change of address.

(6) The obligation imposed by subsection (5) is enforceable as if it were a requirement imposed by the order.

Supplementary

6 Abolition of certain youth orders and related amendments

(1) Chapters 1, 2, 4 and 5 of Part 4 of (and Schedules 3 and 5 to 7 to) the Powers of Criminal Courts (Sentencing) Act 2000 (c. 6) (curfew orders, exclusion orders, attendance centre orders, supervision orders and action plan orders) cease to have effect.

(2) Part 1 of Schedule 4 makes amendments consequential on provisions of this Part.

(3) Part 2 of Schedule 4 makes minor amendments regarding other community orders which are related to the consequential amendments in Part 1 of that Schedule.

7 Youth rehabilitation orders: interpretation

(1) In this Part, except where the contrary intention appears—
    "accommodation provided by or on behalf of a local authority" has the same meaning as it has in the Children Act 1989 (c. 41) by virtue of section 105 of that Act;

"activity requirement", in relation to a youth rehabilitation order, has the meaning given by paragraph 6 of Schedule 1;

"associated", in relation to offences, is to be read in accordance with section 161(1) of the Powers of Criminal Courts (Sentencing) Act 2000 (c. 6);

"attendance centre" has the meaning given by section 221(2) of the Criminal Justice Act 2003 (c. 44);

"attendance centre requirement", in relation to a youth rehabilitation order, has the meaning given by paragraph 12 of Schedule 1;

"curfew requirement", in relation to a youth rehabilitation order, has the meaning given by paragraph 14 of Schedule 1;

"custodial sentence" has the meaning given by section 76 of the Powers of Criminal Courts (Sentencing) Act 2000;

"detention and training order" has the same meaning as it has in that Act by virtue of section 163 of that Act;

"drug treatment requirement", in relation to a youth rehabilitation order, has the meaning given by paragraph 22 of Schedule 1;

"drug testing requirement", in relation to a youth rehabilitation order, has the meaning given by paragraph 23 of Schedule 1;

"education requirement", in relation to a youth rehabilitation order, has the meaning given by paragraph 25 of Schedule 1;

"electronic monitoring requirement", in relation to a youth rehabilitation order, has the meaning given by paragraph 26 of Schedule 1;

"exclusion requirement", in relation to a youth rehabilitation order, has the meaning given by paragraph 15 of Schedule 1;

"extended activity requirement", in relation to a youth rehabilitation order, has the meaning given by paragraph 3 of Schedule 1;

"fostering requirement", in relation to a youth rehabilitation order with fostering, has the meaning given by paragraph 18 of Schedule 1;

"guardian" has the same meaning as in the Children and Young Persons Act 1933 (c. 12);

"intoxicating substance treatment requirement", in relation to a youth rehabilitation order, has the meaning given by paragraph 24 of Schedule 1;

"local authority" means—
  (a) in relation to England—
    (i) a county council,
    (ii) a district council whose district does not form part of an area that has a county council,
    (iii) a London borough council, or
    (iv) the Common Council of the City of London in its capacity as a local authority, and
  (b) in relation to Wales—
    (i) a county council, or
    (ii) a county borough council;

"local authority residence requirement", in relation to a youth rehabilitation order, has the meaning given by paragraph 17 of Schedule 1;

"local probation board" means a local probation board established under section 4 of the Criminal Justice and Court Services Act 2000 (c. 43);

"mental health treatment requirement", in relation to a youth rehabilitation order, has the meaning given by paragraph 20 of Schedule 1;

"programme requirement", in relation to a youth rehabilitation order, has the meaning given by paragraph 11 of Schedule 1;

"prohibited activity requirement", in relation to a youth rehabilitation order, has the meaning given by paragraph 13 of Schedule 1;

"residence requirement", in relation to a youth rehabilitation order, has the meaning given by paragraph 16 of Schedule 1;

"the responsible officer", in relation to an offender to whom a youth rehabilitation order relates, has the meaning given by section 4;

"supervision requirement", in relation to a youth rehabilitation order, has the meaning given by paragraph 9 of Schedule 1;

"unpaid work requirement", in relation to a youth rehabilitation order, has the meaning given by paragraph 10 of Schedule 1;

"youth offending team" means a team established under section 39 of the Crime and Disorder Act 1998 (c. 37);

"youth rehabilitation order" has the meaning given by section 1;

"youth rehabilitation order with fostering" has the meaning given by paragraph 4 of Schedule 1;

"youth rehabilitation order with intensive supervision and surveillance" has the meaning given by paragraph 3 of Schedule 1.

(2) For the purposes of any provision of this Part which requires the determination of the age of a person by the court, the Secretary of State or a local authority, the person's age is to be taken to be that which it appears to the court or (as the case may be) the Secretary of State or a local authority to be after considering any available evidence.

(3) Any reference in this Part to an offence punishable with imprisonment is to be read without regard to any prohibition or restriction imposed by or under any Act on the imprisonment of young offenders.

(4) If a local authority has parental responsibility for an offender who is in its care or provided with accommodation by it in the exercise of any social services functions, any reference in this Part (except in paragraphs 4 and 25 of Schedule 1) to the offender's parent or guardian is to be read as a reference to that authority.

(5) In subsection (4)—

"parental responsibility" has the same meaning as it has in the Children Act 1989 (c. 41) by virtue of section 3 of that Act, and

"social services functions" has the same meaning as it has in the Local Authority Social Services Act 1970 (c. 42) by virtue of section 1A of that Act.

8 Isles of Scilly

This Part has effect in relation to the Isles of Scilly with such exceptions, adaptations and modifications as the Secretary of State may by order specify.

PART 2
SENTENCING

General sentencing provisions

9 Purposes etc. of sentencing: offenders under 18

(1) After section 142 of the Criminal Justice Act 2003 (c. 44) insert—

"142A Purposes etc. of sentencing: offenders under 18

(1) This section applies where a court is dealing with an offender aged under 18 in respect of an offence.

(2) The court must have regard to—

    (a) the principal aim of the youth justice system (which is to prevent offending (or re-offending) by persons aged under 18: see section 37(1) of the Crime and Disorder Act 1998),

    (b) in accordance with section 44 of the Children and Young Persons Act 1933, the welfare of the offender, and

    (c) the purposes of sentencing mentioned in subsection (3) (so far as it is not required to do so by paragraph (a)).

(3) Those purposes of sentencing are—

    (a) the punishment of offenders,

    (b) the reform and rehabilitation of offenders,

    (c) the protection of the public, and

    (d) the making of reparation by offenders to persons affected by their offences.

(4) This section does not apply—

    (a) to an offence the sentence for which is fixed by law,

    (b) to an offence the sentence for which falls to be imposed under—

        (i) section 51A(2) of the Firearms Act 1968 (minimum sentence for certain firearms offences),

        (ii) section 29(6) of the Violent Crime Reduction Act 2006 (minimum sentences in certain cases of using someone to mind a weapon), or

        (iii) section 226(2) of this Act (detention for life for certain dangerous offenders), or

    (c) in relation to the making under Part 3 of the Mental Health Act 1983 of a hospital order (with or without a restriction order), an interim hospital order, a hospital direction or a limitation direction."

(2) In section 142 of the Criminal Justice Act 2003 (purposes of sentencing in relation to offenders aged 18 or over at the time of conviction)—

(a) in the heading, at the end insert ": offenders aged 18 or over", and

(b) in subsection (2)(a) omit "at the time of conviction".

(3) In section 44 of the Children and Young Persons Act 1933 (c. 12) (general considerations) after subsection (1) insert—

"(1A) Subsection (1) is to be read with paragraphs (a) and (c) of section 142A(2) of the Criminal Justice Act 2003 (which require a court dealing with an offender aged under 18 also to have regard to the principal aim of the youth justice system and the specified purposes of sentencing).

 (1B) Accordingly, in determining in the case of an offender whether it should take steps as mentioned in subsection (1), the court shall also have regard to the matters mentioned in those paragraphs."

(4) In section 42(1) of the Crime and Disorder Act 1998 (c. 37) (interpretation of Part 3 of Act), after the definition of "local authority" insert—

""offending" includes re-offending;".

10 Effect of restriction on imposing community sentences

In section 148 of the Criminal Justice Act 2003 (c. 44) (restrictions on imposing community sentences), after subsection (4) insert—

"(5) The fact that by virtue of any provision of this section—

    (a) a community sentence may be passed in relation to an offence; or

    (b) particular restrictions on liberty may be imposed by a community order or youth rehabilitation order,

does not require a court to pass such a sentence or to impose those restrictions."

11 Restriction on power to make a community order

(1) After section 150 of the Criminal Justice Act 2003 (community sentence not available where sentence fixed by law etc.) insert—

"**150A Community order available only for offences punishable with imprisonment or for persistent offenders previously fined**

   (1) The power to make a community order is only exercisable in respect of an offence if—
       (a) the offence is punishable with imprisonment; or
       (b) in any other case, section 151(2) confers power to make such an order.
   (2) For the purposes of this section and section 151 an offence triable either way that was tried summarily is to be regarded as punishable with imprisonment only if it is so punishable by the sentencing court (and for this purpose section 148(1) is to be disregarded)."

(2) Section 151 of that Act (community order for persistent offender previously fined) is amended as follows.

(3) Before subsection (1) insert—
   "(A1) Subsection (2) provides for the making of a community order by the court in respect of an offence ("the current offence") committed by a person to whom subsection (1) or (1A) applies."

(4) In subsection (1)—
   (a) for "Subsection (2) applies where" substitute "This subsection applies to the offender if—
       (za) the current offence is punishable with imprisonment;";
   (b) for paragraph (a) substitute—
       "(a) the offender was aged 16 or over when he was convicted;";
   (c) in paragraph (b) for "he" substitute "the offender".

(5) After subsection (1) insert—
   "(1A) This subsection applies to the offender if—
       (a) the current offence is not punishable with imprisonment;
       (b) the offender was aged 16 or over when he was convicted; and
       (c) on three or more previous occasions the offender has, on conviction by a court in the United Kingdom of any offence committed by him after attaining the age of 16, had passed on him a sentence consisting only of a fine."

(6) In subsection (3)(a) after "(1)(b)" insert "or (1A)(b) (as the case may be)".

(7) In subsections (4), (5) and (6), for "subsection (1)(b)" insert "subsections (1)(b) and (1A)(b)".

(8) In section 166 of that Act (savings for powers to mitigate etc.), in subsection (1)(a), after "148" insert "or 151(2)".

12 Pre-sentence reports

In section 158 of the Criminal Justice Act 2003 (c. 44) (meaning of "pre-sentence report"), after subsection (1) insert—
   "(1A) Subject to any rules made under subsection (1)(b) and to subsection (1B), the court may accept a pre-sentence report given orally in open court.
   (1B) But a pre-sentence report that—
       (a) relates to an offender aged under 18, and
       (b) is required to be obtained and considered before the court forms an opinion mentioned in section 156(3)(a),
       must be in writing."

Custodial sentences

13 Sentences of imprisonment for public protection

(1) In section 225 of the Criminal Justice Act 2003 (life sentence or imprisonment for public protection), for subsection (3) substitute—
   "(3) In a case not falling within subsection (2), the court may impose a sentence of imprisonment for public protection if the condition in subsection (3A) or the condition in subsection (3B) is met.
   (3A) The condition in this subsection is that, at the time the offence was committed, the offender had been convicted of an offence specified in Schedule 15A.
   (3B) The condition in this subsection is that the notional minimum term is at least two years.
   (3C) The notional minimum term is the part of the sentence that the court would specify under section 82A(2) of the Sentencing Act (determination of tariff) if it imposed a sentence of imprisonment for public protection but was required to disregard the matter mentioned in section 82A(3)(b) of that Act (crediting periods of remand)."
(2) After Schedule 15 to that Act, insert the Schedule set out in Schedule 5 to this Act.

14 Sentences of detention for public protection

In section 226 of the Criminal Justice Act 2003 (c. 44) (detention for life or detention for public protection), for subsection (3) substitute—
   "(3) In a case not falling within subsection (2), the court may impose a sentence of detention for public protection if the notional minimum term is at least two years.
   (3A) The notional minimum term is the part of the sentence that the court would specify under section 82A(2) of the Sentencing Act (determination of tariff) if it imposed a sentence of detention for public protection but was required to disregard the matter mentioned in section 82A(3)(b) of that Act (crediting periods of remand)."

15 Extended sentences for certain violent or sexual offences: persons 18 or over

(1) Section 227 of the Criminal Justice Act 2003 (extended sentence for certain violent or sexual offences: persons 18 or over) is amended as follows.
(2) In subsection (1)—
   (a) in paragraph (a) the words ", other than a serious offence," are omitted, and
   (b) after paragraph (b) insert ", but
      (c) the court is not required by section 225(2) to impose a sentence of imprisonment for life."
(3) In subsection (2) —
   (a) for "The court must" substitute "The court may", and
   (b) for the words from "that is to say" to the end substitute "if the condition in subsection (2A) or the condition in subsection (2B) is met."
(4) After subsection (2) insert—
   "(2A) The condition in this subsection is that, at the time the offence was committed, the offender had been convicted of an offence specified in Schedule 15A.
   (2B) The condition in this subsection is that, if the court were to impose an extended sentence of imprisonment, the term that it would specify as the appropriate custodial term would be at least 4 years.
   (2C) An extended sentence of imprisonment is a sentence of imprisonment the term of which is equal to the aggregate of—
      (a) the appropriate custodial term, and
      (b) a further period ("the extension period") for which the offender is to be subject to a licence and which is of such length as the court considers necessary for the purpose of protecting members of the public from serious harm occasioned by the commission by him of further specified offences."

(5) In subsection (3) for "subsection (2)" substitute "subsections (2B) and (2C)".

(6) After subsection (5) insert—

   "(6) The Secretary of State may by order amend subsection (2B) so as to substitute a different period for the period for the time being specified in that subsection."

16 Extended sentences for certain violent or sexual offences: persons under 18

(1) Section 228 of the Criminal Justice Act 2003 (c. 44) (extended sentence for certain violent or sexual offences: persons under 18) is amended as follows.

(2) In subsection (1)(b)(ii) the words from "or by section 226(3)" to the end are omitted.

(3) In subsection (2) —

   (a) for "The court must" substitute "The court may", and

   (b) for the words from ", that is to say" to the end substitute "if the condition in subsection (2A) is met."

(4) After subsection (2) insert—

   "(2A) The condition in this subsection is that, if the court were to impose an extended sentence of detention, the term that it would specify as the appropriate custodial term would be at least 4 years.

   (2B) An extended sentence of detention is a sentence of detention the term of which is equal to the aggregate of—

      (a) the appropriate custodial term, and

      (b) a further period ("the extension period") for which the offender is to be subject to a licence and which is of such length as the court considers necessary for the purpose of protecting members of the public from serious harm occasioned by the commission by him of further specified offences."

(5) In subsection (3)—

   (a) for "subsection (2)" substitute "subsections (2A) and (2B)", and

   (b) paragraph (a) is omitted.

(6) After subsection (6) insert—

   "(7) The Secretary of State may by order amend subsection (2A) so as to substitute a different period for the period for the time being specified in that subsection."

17 The assessment of dangerousness

(1) Section 229 of the Criminal Justice Act 2003 (the assessment of dangerousness) is amended as follows.

(2) In subsection (2)—

   (a) the words from the beginning to "18" are omitted,

   (b) after paragraph (a) insert—

      "(aa) may take into account all such information as is available to it about the nature and circumstances of any other offences of which the offender has been convicted by a court anywhere in the world,", and

   (c) in paragraph (b) for "the offence" substitute "any of the offences mentioned in paragraph (a) or (aa)".

(3) After subsection (2) insert—

   "(2A) The reference in subsection (2)(aa) to a conviction by a court includes a reference to—

      (a) a finding of guilt in service disciplinary proceedings, and

      (b) a conviction of a service offence within the meaning of the Armed Forces Act 2006 ("conviction" here including anything that under section 376(1) and (2) of that Act is to be treated as a conviction)."

(4) Subsections (3) and (4) are omitted.

(5) Schedules 16 and 17 to that Act are omitted.

18 Further amendments relating to sentences for public protection

(1) In section 231 of the Criminal Justice Act 2003 (c. 44) (appeals where previous convictions set aside), for subsection (1) substitute—

"(1) This section applies where—

(a) a sentence has been imposed on any person under section 225(3) or 227(2),

(b) the condition in section 225(3A) or (as the case may be) 227(2A) was met but the condition in section 225(3B) or (as the case may be) 227(2B) was not, and

(c) any previous conviction of his without which the condition in section 225(3A) or (as the case may be) 227(2A) would not have been met has been subsequently set aside on appeal."

(2) In section 232 of that Act (certificates for purposes of section 229)—

(a) in the heading for "section 229" substitute "sections 225 and 227",

(b) in paragraph (a)—

(i) for "the commencement of this section" substitute "the commencement of Schedule 15A", and

(ii) for "a relevant offence" substitute "an offence specified in that Schedule", and

(c) for "section 229" substitute "sections 225(3A) and 227(2A)".

(3) Section 234 of that Act (determination of day when offence committed) is omitted.

19 Indeterminate sentences: determination of tariffs

(1) Section 82A of the Powers of Criminal Courts (Sentencing) Act 2000 (c. 6) (determination of tariffs in cases where the sentence is not fixed by law) is amended as follows.

(2) In subsection (3) (determination of the appropriate part of the sentence) at the end insert—

"In Case A or Case B below, this subsection has effect subject to, and in accordance with, subsection (3C) below."

(3) After subsection (3) insert—

"(3A) Case A is where the offender was aged 18 or over when he committed the offence and the court is of the opinion that the seriousness of the offence, or of the combination of the offence and one or more other offences associated with it,—

(a) is exceptional (but not such that the court proposes to make an order under subsection (4) below), and

(b) would not be adequately reflected by the period which the court would otherwise specify under subsection (2) above.

(3B) Case B is where the court is of the opinion that the period which it would otherwise specify under subsection (2) above would have little or no effect on time spent in custody, taking into account all the circumstances of the particular offender.

(3C) In Case A or Case B above, in deciding the effect which the comparison required by subsection (3)(c) above is to have on reducing the period which the court determines for the purposes of subsection (3)(a) (and before giving effect to subsection (3)(b) above), the court may, instead of reducing that period by one-half,—

(a) in Case A above, reduce it by such lesser amount (including nil) as the court may consider appropriate according to the seriousness of the offence, or

(b) in Case B above, reduce it by such lesser amount (but not by less than one-third) as the court may consider appropriate in the circumstances."

(4) In subsection (4A) (no order to be made under subsection (4) in the case of certain sentences) after "No order under subsection (4) above may be made" insert ", and Case A above does not apply,".

20 Consecutive terms of imprisonment

(1) Part 12 of the Criminal Justice Act 2003 (c. 44) (sentencing) is amended as follows.

(2) In section 181 (consecutive terms of imprisonment complying with section 181) after subsection (7) insert—

"(7A) For the purposes of subsection (7)(a) the aggregate length of the terms of imprisonment is not to be regarded as being more than 65 weeks if the aggregate of all the custodial periods and the longest of the licence periods in relation to those terms is not more than 65 weeks."

(3) In section 264A (consecutive terms: intermittent custody)—

(a) in subsection (3), omit the words from "and none" to the end;

(b) in subsection (4)(b), for "the longest of the total" substitute "all the"; and

(c) in subsection (5), for the definition of "total licence period" substitute—

""licence period" has the same meaning as in section 183(3);".

(4) In section 265 (restriction on consecutive sentences for released prisoners)—

(a) in subsection (1), for "early under this Chapter" substitute "—

(a) under this Chapter; or

(b) under Part 2 of the Criminal Justice Act 1991."; and

(b) after that subsection insert—

"(1A) Subsection (1) applies to a court sentencing a person to—

(a) a term of imprisonment for an offence committed before 4 April 2005, or

(b) a term of imprisonment of less than 12 months for an offence committed on or after that date,

as it applies to the imposition of any other term of imprisonment.

(1B) Where an intermittent custody order applies to the other sentence, the reference in subsection (1) to release under this Chapter does not include release by virtue of section 183(1)(b)(i) (periods of temporary release on licence before the custodial days specified under section 183(1)(a) have been served)."

(5) Any saving by virtue of which section 84 of the Powers of Criminal Courts (Sentencing) Act 2000 (c. 6) (restrictions on consecutive sentences for released prisoners) continues to apply in certain cases (despite the repeal of that section by the Criminal Justice Act 2003) shall cease to have effect.

Release and recall of prisoners

21 Credit for period of remand on bail: terms of imprisonment and detention

(1) The Criminal Justice Act 2003 (c. 44) is amended as follows.

(2) In section 237 (meaning of "fixed term prisoner"), in subsection (1B), after "Armed Forces Act 2006)" insert "or section 240A".

(3) In the italic heading before section 240, after "*custody*" insert "*or on bail subject to certain types of condition*".

(4) After section 240 insert—

"240A Crediting periods of remand on bail: terms of imprisonment and detention

(1) This section applies where—

(a) a court sentences an offender to imprisonment for a term in respect of an offence committed on or after 4th April 2005,

(b) the offender was remanded on bail by a court in course of or in connection with proceedings for the offence, or any related offence, after the coming into force of section 21 of the Criminal Justice and Immigration Act 2008, and

(c) the offender's bail was subject to a qualifying curfew condition and an electronic monitoring condition ("the relevant conditions").

(2) Subject to subsection (4), the court must direct that the credit period is to count as time served by the offender as part of the sentence.

(3) The "credit period" is the number of days represented by half of the sum of—

    (a) the day on which the offender's bail was first subject to conditions that, had they applied throughout the day in question, would have been relevant conditions, and

    (b) the number of other days on which the offender's bail was subject to those conditions (excluding the last day on which it was so subject), rounded up to the nearest whole number.

(4) Subsection (2) does not apply if and to the extent that—

    (a) rules made by the Secretary of State so provide, or

    (b) it is in the opinion of the court just in all the circumstances not to give a direction under that subsection.

(5) Where as a result of paragraph (a) or (b) of subsection (4) the court does not give a direction under subsection (2), it may give a direction in accordance with either of those paragraphs to the effect that a period of days which is less than the credit period is to count as time served by the offender as part of the sentence.

(6) Rules made under subsection (4)(a) may, in particular, make provision in relation to—

    (a) sentences of imprisonment for consecutive terms;

    (b) sentences of imprisonment for terms which are wholly or partly concurrent;

    (c) periods during which a person granted bail subject to the relevant conditions is also subject to electronic monitoring required by an order made by a court or the Secretary of State.

(7) In considering whether it is of the opinion mentioned in subsection (4)(b) the court must, in particular, take into account whether or not the offender has, at any time whilst on bail subject to the relevant conditions, broken either or both of them.

(8) Where the court gives a direction under subsection (2) or (5) it shall state in open court—

    (a) the number of days on which the offender was subject to the relevant conditions, and

    (b) the number of days in relation to which the direction is given.

(9) Subsection (10) applies where the court—

    (a) does not give a direction under subsection (2) but gives a direction under subsection (5), or

    (b) decides not to give a direction under this section.

(10) The court shall state in open court—

    (a) that its decision is in accordance with rules made under paragraph (a) of subsection (4), or

    (b) that it is of the opinion mentioned in paragraph (b) of that subsection and what the circumstances are.

(11) Subsections (7) to (10) of section 240 apply for the purposes of this section as they apply for the purposes of that section but as if—

    (a) in subsection (7)—

        (i) the reference to a suspended sentence is to be read as including a reference to a sentence to which an order under section 118(1) of the Sentencing Act relates;

        (ii) in paragraph (a) after "Schedule 12" there were inserted "or section 119(1)(a) or (b) of the Sentencing Act"; and

    (b) in subsection (8) the reference to subsection (3) of section 240 is to be read as a reference to subsection (2) of this section and, in paragraph (b), after "Chapter" there were inserted "or Part 2 of the Criminal Justice Act 1991".

(12) In this section—

"electronic monitoring condition" means any electronic monitoring requirements imposed under section 3(6ZAA) of the Bail Act 1976 for the purpose of securing the electronic monitoring of a person's compliance with a qualifying curfew condition;

"qualifying curfew condition" means a condition of bail which requires the person granted bail to remain at one or more specified places for a total of not less than 9 hours in any given day; and

"related offence" means an offence, other than the offence for which the sentence is imposed ("offence A"), with which the offender was charged and the charge for which was founded on the same facts or evidence as offence A."

(5) In section 241 (effect of direction under section 240 of that Act) after the words "section 240", in each place where they occur (including in the title), insert "or 240A".

(6) In section 242 (interpretation of sections 240 and 241), in the title and in subsection (1), after "sections 240" insert ", 240A".

(7) In section 330 (Parliamentary procedure for subordinate legislation made under that Act), in subsection (5)(d), after "section 240(4)(a)" insert "or 240A(4)(a)".

22 Credit for period of remand on bail: other cases

(1) The Criminal Justice Act 2003 (c. 44) is amended in accordance with subsections (2) and (3).

(2) In section 246(4) (exceptions to power to release prisoner on licence before required to do so), in paragraph (i), after "section 240" insert "or 240A".

(3) In section 269(3) (part of mandatory life prisoner's sentence to be specified for purposes of early release provisions), in paragraph (b), before "if" insert "or under section 240A (crediting periods of remand on bail spent subject to certain types of condition)".

(4) In paragraph 2 of Schedule 2 to the Criminal Appeal Act 1968 (c. 19) (sentence on conviction at retrial), in sub-paragraph (4), for the words from the beginning to "custody:" substitute "Sections 240 and 240A of the Criminal Justice Act 2003 (crediting of periods of remand in custody or on bail subject to certain types of condition:".

(5) In section 82A(3) of the Powers of Criminal Courts (Sentencing) Act 2000 (c. 6) (part of discretionary life prisoner's sentence to be specified for purposes of early release provisions), in paragraph (b), before "if" insert "or under section 240A of that Act of 2003 (crediting periods of remand on bail subject to certain types of condition)".

(6) In section 101 of that Act (detention and training orders: taking account of remand etc.)—

    (a) in subsection (8) for "in custody" substitute "—

        (a) in custody, or

        (b) on bail subject to a qualifying curfew condition and an electronic monitoring condition (within the meaning of section 240A of the Criminal Justice Act 2003),"; and

    (b) in subsection (9) for "in custody" substitute "as mentioned in that subsection".

(7) In paragraph 2(1) of Schedule 7 to the International Criminal Court Act 2001 (c. 17) (provisions of law of England and Wales affecting length of sentence which are not applicable to ICC prisoners), for paragraph (d) substitute—

"(d) sections 240 and 240A of the Criminal Justice Act 2003 (crediting of periods spent on remand in custody or on bail subject to certain types of condition: terms of imprisonment and detention)."

23 Credit for period of remand on bail: transitional provisions

Schedule 6 (which, for the purposes of certain repealed provisions which continue to have effect in relation to persons convicted of certain offences, makes provision similar to that made by sections 21 and 22) has effect.

24 Minimum conditions for early release under section 246(1) of Criminal Justice Act 2003

In section 246(2) of the Criminal Justice Act 2003 (c. 44) (minimum conditions for early release of fixed-term prisoner other than intermittent custody prisoner) for paragraph (b) substitute "and

    (b) he has served—

        (i) at least 4 weeks of that period, and

        (ii) at least one-half of that period."

25 Release on licence under Criminal Justice Act 2003 of prisoners serving extended sentences

(1) Section 247 of the Criminal Justice Act 2003 (release on licence of prisoner serving extended sentence) is amended as follows.

(2) In subsection (2)—

    (a) the word "and" at the end of paragraph (a) is omitted, and

    (b) paragraph (b) is omitted.

(3) Subsections (3), (4), (5) and (6) are omitted.

26 Release of certain long-term prisoners under Criminal Justice Act 1991

(1) Part 2 of the Criminal Justice Act 1991 (c. 53) (early release of prisoners: offences committed before 4th April 2005 etc.) is amended as follows.

(2) In section 33 (duty to release short-term and long-term prisoners), after subsection (1) insert—

    "(1A) As soon as a long-term prisoner has served one-half of his sentence, it shall be the duty of the Secretary of State to release him on licence.

    (1B) Subsection (1A) does not apply to a long-term prisoner if the offence or one of the offences in respect of which he is serving the sentence is specified in Schedule 15 to the Criminal Justice Act 2003 (specified violent offences and specified sexual offences).

    (1C) The reference in subsection (1B) to an offence specified in Schedule 15 to the Criminal Justice Act 2003 includes a reference to—

        (a) an offence under section 70 of the Army Act 1955, section 70 of the Air Force Act 1955 or section 42 of the Naval Discipline Act 1957 as respects which the corresponding civil offence (within the meaning of the Act in question) is an offence specified in that Schedule, and

        (b) an offence under section 42 of the Armed Forces Act 2006 as respects which the corresponding offence under the law of England and Wales (within the meaning given by that section) is an offence specified in that Schedule.

    (1D) Section 48 of the Armed Forces Act 2006 (attempts, conspiracy etc.) applies for the purposes of subsection (1C)(b) as if the reference in subsection (3)(b) of that section to any of the following provisions of that Act were a reference to subsection (1C)(b)."

(3) In that section, in subsection (2) after "a long-term prisoner" insert "to whom subsection (1A) does not apply".

(4) In section 35 (power to release long-term prisoners etc.) after subsection (1) insert—

    "(1A) Subsection (1) does not apply to a long-term prisoner to whom section 33(1A) applies."

(5) In section 37 (duration and conditions of licences)—

    (a) in subsection (1), for "(1B) and (2)" substitute "(1B), (2) and (8)", and

    (b) after subsection (7) insert—

        "(8) This section does not apply in relation to a long-term prisoner to whom section 33(1A) applies (provision as to the duration and conditions of licences for such prisoners being made by section 37ZA)."

(6) After section 37 insert—

> **"37ZA Duration and conditions of licences under section 33(1A) etc.**
>
> (1) Where a long-term prisoner is released on licence under section 33(1A), the licence shall (subject to any revocation under section 254 of the 2003 Act) remain in force for the remainder of the sentence.
>
> (2) Section 250(1), (4) and (8) of the 2003 Act apply in relation to a licence under section 33(1A) of this Act as they apply in relation to a licence under Chapter 6 of Part 12 of the 2003 Act in respect of a prisoner serving a sentence of imprisonment for a term of twelve months or more.
>
> (3) A person subject to a licence under section 33(1A) must comply with such conditions as may for the time being be specified in the licence.
>
> (4) The reference in section 254(1) of the 2003 Act to a person who has been released on licence under Chapter 6 of Part 12 of that Act includes a reference to a person released on licence under section 33(1A).
>
> (5) In this section, "the 2003 Act" means the Criminal Justice Act 2003."

27 Application of section 35(1) of Criminal Justice Act 1991 to prisoners liable to removal from the UK

(1) The following provisions of Part 2 of the Criminal Justice Act 1991 (c. 53) (which apply to persons sentenced for offences committed before 4th April 2005 etc.) cease to have effect—

    (a) section 46(1) (which makes the early release power under section 35(1) exercisable in relation to long term prisoners liable to removal without a Parole Board recommendation), and

    (b) in section 50(2), the words from "but nothing" to the end (which exclude prisoners liable to removal from the cases in which prisoners must be released if recommended for release by the Parole Board);

and, accordingly, the Parole Board (Transfer of Functions) Order 1998 (S.I. 1998/3218) applies to prisoners liable to removal as it applies to other prisoners.

(2) In this section "prisoners liable to removal" means prisoners liable to removal from the United Kingdom (within the meaning of section 46(3) of the Criminal Justice Act 1991).

28 Release of fine defaulters and contemnors under Criminal Justice Act 1991

(1) Section 45 of the Criminal Justice Act 1991 (fine defaulters and contemnors: persons committed to prison before 4th April 2005) is amended as follows.

(2) In subsection (2) after "(3)" insert ", (3A)".

(3) In subsection (3)—

    (a) for "the following subsections" substitute "the following subsection", and

    (b) in the substituted text, subsection (2) is omitted.

(4) After subsection (3) insert—

> "(3A) In section 36 above—
>
>   (a) in subsection (1) for "on licence" there shall be substituted "unconditionally", and
>
>   (b) subsection (2) shall be omitted."

(5) Subsection (4) is omitted.

29 Release of prisoners after recall

(1) In section 254 of the Criminal Justice Act 2003 (c. 44) (recall of prisoners while on licence)—

    (a) subsections (3) to (5) cease to have effect;

    (b) in subsection (7) for "subsections (2) to (6)" substitute "this section".

(2) After section 255 of that Act (recall of prisoners released early under section 246) insert—

"255A Further release after recall: introductory

(1) This section applies for the purpose of identifying which of sections 255B to 255D governs the further release of a person who has been recalled under section 254 ("the prisoner").

(2) The prisoner is eligible to be considered for automatic release unless—

    (a) he is an extended sentence prisoner or a specified offence prisoner;

    (b) in a case where paragraph (a) does not apply, he was recalled under section 254 before the normal entitlement date (having been released before that date under section 246 or 248); or

    (c) in a case where neither of the preceding paragraphs applies, he has, during the same term of imprisonment, already been released under section 255B(1)(b) or (2) or section 255C(2).

(3) If the prisoner is eligible to be considered for automatic release the Secretary of State must, on recalling him, consider whether he is suitable for automatic release.

(4) For this purpose "automatic release" means release at the end of the period of 28 days beginning with the date on which the prisoner is returned to prison.

(5) The person is suitable for automatic release only if the Secretary of State is satisfied that he will not present a risk of serious harm to members of the public if he is released at the end of that period.

(6) The prisoner must be dealt with—

    (a) in accordance with section 255B if he is eligible to be considered for automatic release and is suitable for automatic release;

    (b) in accordance with section 255C if he is eligible to be considered for automatic release but was not considered to be suitable for it;

    (c) in accordance with section 255C if he is a specified offence prisoner or if he is not eligible to be considered for automatic release by virtue of subsection (2)(b) or (c);

    (d) in accordance with section 255D if he is an extended sentence prisoner.

(7) The prisoner is an "extended sentence prisoner" if he is serving an extended sentence imposed under section 227 or 228 of this Act, section 58 of the Crime and Disorder Act 1998 or section 85 of the Powers of Criminal Courts (Sentencing) Act 2000.

(8) The prisoner is a "specified offence prisoner" if (not being an extended sentence prisoner) he is serving a sentence imposed for a specified offence within the meaning of section 224.

(9) The reference in subsection (8) to a specified offence (within the meaning of section 224) includes a reference to—

    (a) an offence under section 70 of the Army Act 1955, section 70 of the Air Force Act 1955 or section 42 of the Naval Discipline Act 1957 as respects which the corresponding civil offence (within the meaning of the Act in question) is a specified offence, and

    (b) an offence under section 42 of the Armed Forces Act 2006 as respects which the corresponding offence under the law of England and Wales (within the meaning given by that section) is a specified offence.

(10) Section 48 of the Armed Forces Act 2006 (attempts, conspiracy etc.) applies for the purposes of subsection (9)(b) as if the reference in subsection (3)(b) of that section to any of the following provisions of that Act were a reference to subsection (9)(b).

(11) In subsection (2)(b) the "normal entitlement date" means the date on which the prisoner would (but for his earlier release) have been entitled to be released under section 244.

(12) For the purposes of subsection (2)(c) terms of imprisonment which are consecutive and terms which are wholly or partly concurrent are to be treated as a single term if—
   (a) the sentences were passed on the same occasion, or
   (b) where they were passed on different occasions, the prisoner has not been released under this Chapter at any time during the period beginning with the first and ending with the last of those occasions.

(13) In subsection (5) "serious harm" means death or serious personal injury, whether physical or psychological.

(14) In this section, "term of imprisonment" includes a determinate sentence of detention under section 91 of the Sentencing Act or under section 228 of this Act.

255B Automatic release

(1) A prisoner who is suitable for automatic release must—
   (a) on his return to prison, be informed that he will be released under this subsection, and
   (b) at the end of the 28 day period mentioned in section 255A(4) (or such other period as is specified for the purposes of that subsection), be released by the Secretary of State on licence under this Chapter (unless he has already been released under subsection (2)).

(2) The Secretary of State may, at any time after a prisoner who is suitable for automatic release is returned to prison, release him again on licence under this Chapter.

(3) The Secretary of State must not release a person under subsection (2) unless the Secretary of State is satisfied that it is not necessary for the protection of the public that he should remain in prison until the end of the period mentioned in subsection (1)(b).

(4) If a prisoner who is suitable for automatic release makes representations under section 254(2) before the end of that period, the Secretary of State must refer his case to the Board on the making of those representations.

(5) Where on a reference under subsection (4) relating to any person the Board recommends his immediate release on licence under this Chapter, the Secretary of State must give effect to the recommendation.

(6) In the case of an intermittent custody prisoner who has not yet served in prison the number of custodial days specified in the intermittent custody order, any recommendation by the Board as to immediate release on licence is to be a recommendation as to his release on licence until the end of one of the licence periods specified by virtue of section 183(1)(b) in the intermittent custody order.

255C Specified offence prisoners and those not suitable for automatic release

(1) This section applies to a prisoner who—
   (a) is a specified offence prisoner,
   (b) is not eligible to be considered for automatic release by virtue of section 255A(2)(b) or (c), or
   (c) was eligible to be considered for automatic release but was not considered to be suitable for it.

(2) The Secretary of State may, at any time after the person is returned to prison, release him again on licence under this Chapter.

(3) The Secretary of State must not release a person under subsection (2) unless the Secretary of State is satisfied that it is not necessary for the protection of the public that he should remain in prison.

(4) The Secretary of State must refer to the Board the case of any person to whom this section applies—
   (a) if the person makes representations under section 254(2) before the end of the period of 28 days beginning with the date on which he is returned to prison, on the making of those representations, or

(b) if, at the end of that period, the person has not been released under subsection (2) and has not made such representations, at that time.

(5) Where on a reference under subsection (4) relating to any person the Board recommends his immediate release on licence under this Chapter, the Secretary of State must give effect to the recommendation.

(6) In the case of an intermittent custody prisoner who has not yet served in prison the number of custodial days specified in the intermittent custody order, any recommendation by the Board as to immediate release on licence is to be a recommendation as to his release on licence until the end of one of the licence periods specified by virtue of section 183(1)(b) in the intermittent custody order.

255D Extended sentence prisoners

(1) The Secretary of State must refer to the Board the case of any extended sentence prisoner.

(2) Where on a reference under subsection (1) relating to any person the Board recommends his immediate release on licence under this Chapter, the Secretary of State must give effect to the recommendation."

(3) In section 256 of that Act (further release after recall) in subsection (1) (powers of Board on a reference) for "section 254(3)" substitute "section 255B(4), 255C(4) or 255D(1)".

30 Further review and release of prisoners after recall

(1) Section 256 of the Criminal Justice Act 2003 (c. 44) (further release after recall) is amended as follows.

(2) In subsection (1) for paragraph (b) substitute—
"(b) determine the reference by making no recommendation as to his release."

(3) In subsection (2) omit "or (b)".

(4) Subsections (3) and (5) cease to have effect.

(5) In consequence of the amendments made by section 29 and this section, the heading to section 256 becomes "Review by the Board".

(6) After section 256 insert—

"256A Further review

(1) The Secretary of State must, not later than the first anniversary of a determination by the Board under section 256(1) or subsection (4) below, refer the person's case to the Board.

(2) The Secretary of State may, at any time before that anniversary, refer the person's case to the Board.

(3) The Board may at any time recommend to the Secretary of State that a person's case be referred under subsection (2).

(4) On a reference under subsection (1) or (2), the Board must determine the reference by—
(a) recommending the person's immediate release on licence under this Chapter,
(b) fixing a date for his release on licence, or
(c) making no recommendation as to his release.

(5) The Secretary of State—
(a) where the Board makes a recommendation under subsection (4)(a) for the person's immediate release on licence, must give effect to the recommendation; and
(b) where the Board fixes a release date under subsection (4)(b), must release the person on licence on that date."

31 Recall of life prisoners: abolition of requirement for recommendation by Parole Board

(1) Section 32 of the Crime (Sentences) Act 1997 (c. 43) (recall of life prisoners while on licence) is amended as follows.

(2) For subsections (1) and (2) (power of Secretary of State to revoke licence) substitute—

"(1) The Secretary of State may, in the case of any life prisoner who has been released on licence under this Chapter, revoke his licence and recall him to prison."

(3) In subsection (3) (representations by prisoner) for "subsection (1) or (2) above" substitute "this section".

(4) In subsection (4) (reference to Parole Board by Secretary of State) for paragraphs (a) and (b) substitute "the case of a life prisoner recalled under this section".

32 Release of prisoners recalled following release under Criminal Justice Act 1991

(1) Before section 51 of the Criminal Justice Act 1991 (c. 53) insert—

"50A Prisoners recalled under section 254 of Criminal Justice Act 2003

(1) This section applies to a person who is—
  (a) released on licence under any provision of this Part, and
  (b) recalled to prison under section 254(1) of the 2003 Act (recall of prisoners while on licence).

(2) Nothing in the following provisions of this Part (which authorise or require the Secretary of State to release prisoners) applies in relation to the person—
  (a) section 33;
  (b) section 33A;
  (c) section 34A;
  (d) section 35;
  (e) section 43(4).

(3) Sections 254(2) and (6) and 255A to 256A of the 2003 Act (which authorise release on licence etc) apply in relation to a person to whom this section applies with the modifications specified in subsection (4).

(4) Section 255A applies as if—
  (a) the reference in subsection (2)(b) to section 246 or 248 of the 2003 Act were a reference to section 34A or 36 of this Act,
  (b) the reference in subsection (11) to section 244 of the 2003 Act were a reference to section 33(1), (1A) or (2) of this Act,
  (c) subsection (12) were omitted (provision to the same effect being made by section 51(2) of this Act, as it applies by virtue of subsection (9) below), and
  (d) subsection (14) provided that "term of imprisonment" included any sentence of detention mentioned in section 43(1) of this Act.

(5) The provisions of Chapter 6 of Part 12 of the 2003 Act specified in subsection (6) apply in relation to—
  (a) a licence under that Chapter granted to a person to whom this section applies, and
  (b) a licence under section 36 of this Act granted to such a person.

(6) The provisions of the 2003 Act specified in this subsection are—
  (a) section 249 (duration of licence), as modified by subsection (7) below;
  (b) section 250(1), (4) and (8) (licence conditions), as modified by subsection (8) below;
  (c) section 252 (duty to comply with licence conditions).

(7) Section 249 of the 2003 Act applies—
  (a) as if the reference in subsection (1) to a fixed-term prisoner were a reference to a person to whom this section applies, and
  (b) as if for subsection (3) there were substituted—
    "(3) Subsection (1) has effect subject to section 51(2) to (2D) of the Criminal Justice Act 1991 (treatment of consecutive and concurrent terms etc.)."

(8) Section 250(4) of the 2003 Act applies as if the reference to a prisoner serving a sentence mentioned in that subsection were a reference to a person to whom this section applies.

(9) In relation to a person to whom this section applies, subsections (2) to (2D) of section 51 of this Act (treatment of consecutive and concurrent terms etc.) apply as if any reference in those subsections to this Part of this Act included the provisions of the 2003 Act mentioned in subsections (3) and (6).

(10) Except as provided by subsections (7)(b) and (9), nothing in this Part applies in relation to the duration and conditions of—

    (a) a licence under Chapter 6 of Part 12 of the 2003 Act granted to a person to whom this section applies, or

    (b) a licence under section 36 of this Act granted to such a person.

(11) In this section, "the 2003 Act" means the Criminal Justice Act 2003."

(2) The savings made by paragraph 19 of Schedule 2 to the Criminal Justice Act 2003 (Commencement No.8 and Transitional and Saving Provisions) Order 2005 (S.I. 2005/950) in respect of sections 249 and 250 of the Criminal Justice Act 2003 (c. 44) do not apply in relation to a licence granted under Chapter 6 of Part 12 of that Act, or under section 36 of the Criminal Justice Act 1991 (c. 53), to a person to whom section 50A of the Criminal Justice Act 1991 applies.

Early removal of prisoners from the United Kingdom

33 Removal under Criminal Justice Act 1991

(1) Part 2 of the Criminal Justice Act 1991 (early release of prisoners: offences before 4th April 2005 etc.) is amended as follows.

(2) After section 46 insert—

"46ZA Persons eligible for removal from the United Kingdom

(1) For the purposes of section 46A below, to be "eligible for removal from the United Kingdom" a person must show, to the satisfaction of the Secretary of State, that the condition in subsection (2) is met.

(2) The condition is that the person has the settled intention of residing permanently outside the United Kingdom if removed from prison under section 46A below.

(3) The person must not be one who is liable to removal from the United Kingdom."

(3) Section 46A (early removal of persons liable to removal from the United Kingdom) is amended as follows.

(4) In subsection (1) (the power of removal) after "is liable to" insert ", or eligible for,".

(5) Also in subsection (1), for "at any time after he has served the requisite period" substitute "at any time in the period—

    (a) beginning when the person has served the requisite period (see subsection (5)), and

    (b) ending when the person has served one-half of the term."

(6) Subsection (2) (cases where subsection (1) does not apply) ceases to have effect.

(7) In subsection (3) (purpose of removal from prison etc.)—

    (a) at the beginning of paragraph (a) insert "if liable to removal from the United Kingdom,";

    (b) for "and" at the end of that paragraph substitute—

       "(aa) if eligible for removal from the United Kingdom, is so removed only for the purpose of enabling the prisoner to leave the United Kingdom in order to reside permanently outside the United Kingdom, and";

    (c) at the beginning of paragraph (b) insert "in either case,".

(8) In consequence of the amendments made by this section, the heading to section 46A becomes "Early removal of persons liable to, or eligible for, removal from United Kingdom".

34 Removal under Criminal Justice Act 2003

(1) In Part 12 of the Criminal Justice Act 2003 (c. 44) (sentencing) Chapter 6 (release on licence) is amended as follows.

(2) After section 259 (persons liable to removal from the United Kingdom) insert—

"259A Persons eligible for removal from the United Kingdom

(1) For the purposes of this Chapter, to be "eligible for removal from the United Kingdom" a person must show, to the satisfaction of the Secretary of State, that the condition in subsection (2) is met.

(2) The condition is that the person has the settled intention of residing permanently outside the United Kingdom if removed from prison under section 260.

(3) The person must not be one who is liable to removal from the United Kingdom."

(3) Section 260 (early removal of prisoners liable to removal from United Kingdom) is amended as follows.

(4) In subsection (1) (the power of removal)—

(a) for "subsections (2) and (3)" substitute "subsection (2)", and

(b) after "is liable to" insert ", or eligible for,".

(5) For subsection (2) (conditions relating to time) substitute—

"(2) Subsection (1) does not apply in relation to a prisoner unless he has served at least one-half of the requisite custodial period."

(6) Subsections (3) and (3A) (cases where subsection (1) does not apply) cease to have effect.

(7) In subsection (4) (purpose of removal from prison etc.)—

(a) at the beginning of paragraph (a) insert "if liable to removal from the United Kingdom,";

(b) for "and" at the end of that paragraph substitute—

"(aa) if eligible for removal from the United Kingdom, is so removed only for the purpose of enabling the prisoner to leave the United Kingdom in order to reside permanently outside the United Kingdom, and";

(c) at the beginning of paragraph (b) insert "in either case,".

(8) In subsection (6) (order-making powers)—

(a) in paragraph (a) omit "or (3)(e)",

(b) omit paragraph (b), and

(c) in paragraph (c) for "subsection (2)(b)(ii)" substitute "subsection (2)".

(9) For subsection (7) (meaning of "requisite custodial period") substitute—

"(7) In this section "requisite custodial period"—

(a) in relation to a prisoner serving an extended sentence imposed under section 227 or 228, means one-half of the appropriate custodial term (determined by the court under that section);

(b) in any other case, has the meaning given by paragraph (a), (b) or (d) of section 244(3)."

(10) In consequence of the amendments made by this section—

(a) the italic heading preceding section 259 becomes "Persons liable to, or eligible for, removal from the United Kingdom", and

(b) the heading to section 260 becomes "Early removal of persons liable to, or eligible for, removal from the United Kingdom".

Referral orders

35 Referral conditions

(1) Section 17 of the Powers of Criminal Courts (Sentencing) Act 2000 (c. 6) (the referral conditions) is amended as follows.

(2) In subsection (1)—
    (a) after "section 16(2) above" insert "and subsection (2) below",
    (b) insert "and" at the end of paragraph (a), and
    (c) omit paragraph (c).
(3) For subsections (1A) and (2) substitute—
    "(2) For the purposes of section 16(3) above, the discretionary referral conditions are satisfied in relation to an offence if—
        (a) the compulsory referral conditions are not satisfied in relation to the offence;
        (b) the offender pleaded guilty—
            (i) to the offence; or
            (ii) if the offender is being dealt with by the court for the offence and any connected offence, to at least one of those offences; and
        (c) subsection (2A), (2B) or (2C) below is satisfied in relation to the offender.
    (2A) This subsection is satisfied in relation to the offender if the offender has never been convicted by or before a court in the United Kingdom ("a UK court") of any offence other than the offence and any connected offence.
    (2B) This subsection is satisfied in relation to the offender if the offender has been dealt with by a UK court for any offence other than the offence and any connected offence on only one previous occasion, but was not referred to a youth offender panel under section 16 above on that occasion.
    (2C) This subsection is satisfied in relation to the offender if—
        (a) the offender has been dealt with by a UK court for any offence other than the offence and any connected offence on one or more previous occasions, but has been referred to a youth offender panel under section 16 above on only one previous occasion;
        (b) an appropriate officer recommends to the court as suitable for the offender a referral to a youth offender panel under that section in respect of the offence; and
        (c) the court considers that there are exceptional circumstances which justify ordering the offender to be so referred.
    (2D) In subsection (2C)(b) above "appropriate officer" means—
        (a) a member of a youth offending team;
        (b) an officer of a local probation board; or
        (c) an officer of a provider of probation services."
(4) Omit subsection (5).

36 Power to revoke a referral order

(1) Part 3 of the Powers of Criminal Courts (Sentencing) Act 2000 (c. 6) (mandatory and discretionary referral of young offenders) is amended as follows.
(2) After section 27 insert—

"Referrals back to court in the interests of justice

27A Revocation of referral order where offender making good progress etc.

    (1) This section applies where, having regard to circumstances which have arisen since a youth offender contract took effect under section 23 above, it appears to the youth offender panel to be in the interests of justice for the referral order (or each of the referral orders) to be revoked.
    (2) The panel may refer the offender back to the appropriate court requesting it—
        (a) to exercise only the power conferred by sub-paragraph (2) of paragraph 5 of Schedule 1 to this Act to revoke the order (or each of the orders); or

    (b) to exercise both—
        (i) the power conferred by that sub-paragraph to revoke the order (or each of the orders); and
        (ii) the power conferred by sub-paragraph (4) of that paragraph to deal with the offender for the offence in respect of which the revoked order was made.

(3) The circumstances in which the panel may make a referral under subsection (2) above include the offender's making good progress under the contract.

(4) Where—
    (a) the panel makes a referral under subsection (2) above in relation to any offender and any youth offender contract, and
    (b) the appropriate court decides not to exercise the power conferred by paragraph 5(2) of Schedule 1 to this Act in consequence of that referral,
    the panel may not make a further referral under that subsection in relation to that offender and contract during the relevant period except with the consent of the appropriate court.

(5) In subsection (4) above "the relevant period" means the period of 3 months beginning with the date on which the appropriate court made the decision mentioned in paragraph (b) of that subsection."

(3) In paragraph 1(1) of Schedule 1 (youth offender panels: further court proceedings), for "or 27(4)" substitute ", 27(4) or 27A(2)".

37   Extension of period for which young offender contract has effect

(1) Part 3 of the Powers of Criminal Courts (Sentencing) Act 2000 (c. 6) (mandatory and discretionary referral of young offenders) is amended as follows.

(2) After section 27A (as inserted by section 36 above) insert—

"27B Extension of period for which young offender contract has effect

(1) This section applies where at any time—
    (a) a youth offender contract has taken effect under section 23 above for a period which is less than twelve months;
    (b) that period has not ended; and
    (c) having regard to circumstances which have arisen since the contract took effect, it appears to the youth offender panel to be in the interests of justice for the length of that period to be extended.

(2) The panel may refer the offender back to the appropriate court requesting it to extend the length of that period.

(3) The requested period of extension must not exceed three months."

(3) In Schedule 1 (youth offender panels: further court proceedings), after Part 1 insert—

"PART 1ZA
REFERRAL BACK TO APPROPRIATE COURT: EXTENSION OF PERIOD FOR WHICH CONTRACT HAS EFFECT

Introductory

9ZB (1) This Part of this Schedule applies where a youth offender panel refers an offender back to the appropriate court under section 27B of this Act with a view to the court extending the period for which the offender's youth offender contract has effect.

    (2) For the purposes of this Part of this Schedule and that section the appropriate court is—
       (a) in the case of an offender aged under 18 at the time when (in pursuance of the referral back) the offender first appears before the court, a youth court acting in

the local justice area in which it appears to the youth offender panel that the offender resides or will reside; and

(b) otherwise, a magistrates' court (other than a youth court) acting in that area.

Mode of referral back to court

9ZC The panel shall make the referral by sending a report to the appropriate court explaining why the offender is being referred back to it.

Power of court

9ZD (1) If it appears to the appropriate court that it would be in the interests of justice to do so having regard to circumstances which have arisen since the contract took effect, the court may make an order extending the length of the period for which the contract has effect.

(2) An order under sub-paragraph (1) above—

(a) must not extend that period by more than three months; and

(b) must not so extend that period as to cause it to exceed twelve months.

(3) In deciding whether to make an order under sub-paragraph (1) above, the court shall have regard to the extent of the offender's compliance with the terms of the contract.

(4) The court may not make an order under sub-paragraph (1) above unless—

(a) the offender is present before it; and

(b) the contract has effect at the time of the order.

Supplementary

9ZE The following paragraphs of Part 1 of this Schedule apply for the purposes of this Part of this Schedule as they apply for the purposes of that Part—

(a) paragraph 3 (bringing the offender before the court);

(b) paragraph 4 (detention and remand of arrested offender); and

(c) paragraph 9ZA (power to adjourn hearing and remand offender)."

Enforcement of sentences

38 Imposition of unpaid work requirement for breach of community order

(1) Part 2 of Schedule 8 to the Criminal Justice Act 2003 (c. 44) (breach of community order) is amended as follows.

(2) In paragraph 9 (powers of magistrates' court) after sub-paragraph (3) insert—

"(3A) Where—

(a) the court is dealing with the offender under sub-paragraph (1)(a), and

(b) the community order does not contain an unpaid work requirement, section 199(2)(a) applies in relation to the inclusion of such a requirement as if for "40" there were substituted "20"."

(3) In paragraph 10 (powers of Crown Court) after sub-paragraph (3) insert—

"(3A) Where—

(a) the court is dealing with the offender under sub-paragraph (1)(a), and

(b) the community order does not contain an unpaid work requirement, section 199(2)(a) applies in relation to the inclusion of such a requirement as if for "40" there were substituted "20"."

39   Youth default orders

(1) Subsection (2) applies in any case where, in respect of a person aged under 18, a magistrates' court would, but for section 89 of the Powers of Criminal Courts (Sentencing) Act 2000 (c. 6) (restrictions on custodial sentences), have power to issue a warrant of commitment for default in paying a sum adjudged to be paid by a conviction (other than a sum ordered to be paid under section 6 of the Proceeds of Crime Act 2002 (c. 29)).

(2) The magistrates' court may, instead of proceeding under section 81 of the Magistrates' Courts Act 1980 (enforcement of fines imposed on young offender), order the person in default to comply with—

   (a) in the case of a person aged 16 or 17, an unpaid work requirement (see paragraph 10 of Schedule 1),

   (b) an attendance centre requirement (see paragraph 12 of that Schedule), or

   (c) a curfew requirement (see paragraph 14 of that Schedule).

(3) In this section (and Schedule 7) "youth default order" means an order under subsection (2).

(4) Section 1(2) and paragraph 2 of Schedule 1 (power or requirement to impose electronic monitoring requirement) have effect in relation to a youth default order as they have effect in relation to a youth rehabilitation order.

(5) Where a magistrates' court has power to make a youth default order, it may, if it thinks it expedient to do so, postpone the making of the order until such time and on such conditions (if any) as it thinks just.

(6) The following provisions have effect in relation to youth default orders as they have effect in relation to youth rehabilitation orders, but subject to the modifications contained in Schedule 7—

   (a) sections 4, 5 and 7,

   (b) paragraphs 1, 10, 12, 14, 26, 27, 29, 33 and 34 of Schedule 1 (youth rehabilitation orders: further provisions),

   (c) Schedule 2 (breach, revocation or amendment of youth rehabilitation orders), and

   (d) Schedule 3 (transfer of youth rehabilitation orders to Northern Ireland).

(7) Where a youth default order has been made for default in paying any sum—

   (a) on payment of the whole sum to any person authorised to receive it, the order ceases to have effect, and

   (b) on payment of a part of the sum to any such person, the total number of hours or days to which the order relates is to be taken to be reduced by a proportion corresponding to that which the part paid bears to the whole sum.

(8) In calculating any reduction required by subsection (7)(b), any fraction of a day or hour is to be disregarded.

40   Power to impose attendance centre requirement on fine defaulter

(1) Section 300 of the Criminal Justice Act 2003 (c. 44) (power to impose unpaid work requirement or curfew requirement on fine defaulter) is amended as follows.

(2) In the heading for "or curfew requirement" substitute "curfew requirement or attendance centre requirement".

(3) In subsection (2), at the end of paragraph (b) insert ", or

   (c) in a case where the person is aged under 25, an attendance centre requirement (as defined by section 214)".

41   Disclosure of information for enforcing fines

(1) Part 3 of Schedule 5 to the Courts Act 2003 (c. 39) (attachment of earnings orders and applications for benefit deductions) is amended as follows.

(2) After paragraph 9 insert—

"Disclosure of information in connection with application for benefit deductions

9A (1) The designated officer for a magistrates' court may make an information request to the Secretary of State for the purpose of facilitating the making of a decision by the court as to whether it is practicable or appropriate to make an application for benefit deductions in respect of P.

(2) An information request is a request for the disclosure of some or all of the following information—

(a) P's full name;

(b) P's address (or any of P's addresses);

(c) P's date of birth;

(d) P's national insurance number;

(e) P's benefit status.

(3) On receiving an information request, the Secretary of State may disclose the information requested to—

(a) the officer who made the request, or

(b) a justices' clerk specified in the request.

Restrictions on disclosure

9B (1) A person to whom information is disclosed under paragraph 9A(3), or this sub-paragraph, may disclose the information to any person to whom its disclosure is necessary or expedient in connection with facilitating the making of a decision by the court as to whether it is practicable or appropriate to make an application for benefit deductions in respect of P.

(2) A person to whom such information is disclosed commits an offence if the person—

(a) discloses or uses the information, and

(b) the disclosure is not authorised by sub-paragraph (1) or (as the case may be) the use is not for the purpose of facilitating the making of such a decision as is mentioned in that subparagraph.

(3) But it is not an offence under sub-paragraph (2)—

(a) to disclose any information in accordance with any enactment or order of a court or for the purposes of any proceedings before a court; or

(b) to disclose any information which has previously been lawfully disclosed to the public.

(4) It is a defence for a person charged with an offence under subparagraph (2) to prove that the person reasonably believed that the disclosure or use was lawful.

(5) A person guilty of an offence under sub-paragraph (2) is liable on summary conviction to a fine not exceeding level 4 on the standard scale.

Paragraphs 9A and 9B: supplementary

9C (1) This paragraph applies for the purposes of paragraphs 9A and 9B.

(2) "Benefit status", in relation to P, means whether or not P is in receipt of any prescribed benefit or benefits and, if so (in the case of each benefit)—

(a) which benefit it is,

(b) where it is already subject to deductions under any enactment, the nature of the deductions concerned, and

(c) the amount received by P by way of the benefit, after allowing for any such deductions.

(3) "Information" means information held in any form.

(4) "Prescribed" means prescribed by regulations made by the Lord Chancellor.

(5) Nothing in paragraph 9A or 9B authorises the making of a disclosure which contravenes the Data Protection Act 1998."

PART 3

APPEALS

Appeals by defendant

42   Power to dismiss certain appeals following references by the CCRC: England and Wales

After section 16B of the Criminal Appeal Act 1968 (c. 19) insert—

"Appeals following references by the CCRC

16C Power to dismiss certain appeals following references by the CCRC

(1) This section applies where there is an appeal under this Part following a reference by the Criminal Cases Review Commission under section 9(1)(a), (5) or (6) of the Criminal Appeal Act 1995 or section 1(1) of the Criminal Cases Review (Insanity) Act 1999.

(2) Notwithstanding anything in section 2, 13 or 16 of this Act, the Court of Appeal may dismiss the appeal if—

    (a) the only ground for allowing it would be that there has been a development in the law since the date of the conviction, verdict or finding that is the subject of the appeal, and

    (b) the condition in subsection (3) is met.

(3) The condition in this subsection is that if—

    (a) the reference had not been made, but

    (b) the appellant had made (and had been entitled to make) an application for an extension of time within which to seek leave to appeal on the ground of the development in the law,

the Court would not think it appropriate to grant the application by exercising the power conferred by section 18(3)."

43   Power to dismiss certain appeals following references by the CCRC: Northern Ireland

After section 13A of the Criminal Appeal (Northern Ireland) Act 1980 (c. 47) insert—

"Appeals following references by the CCRC

13B Power to dismiss certain appeals following references by the CCRC

(1) This section applies where there is an appeal under this Part following a reference by the Criminal Cases Review Commission under section 10(1)(a), (6) or (7) of the Criminal Appeal Act 1995 or section 1(1) of the Criminal Cases Review (Insanity) Act 1999.

(2) Notwithstanding anything in section 2, 12 or 13A of this Act, the Court of Appeal may dismiss the appeal if—

    (a) the only ground for allowing it would be that there has been a development in the law since the date of the conviction, verdict or finding that is the subject of the appeal, and

    (b) the condition in subsection (3) is met.

(3) The condition in this subsection is that if—

    (a) the reference had not been made, but

    (b) the appellant had made (and had been entitled to make) an application for an extension of time within which to seek leave to appeal on the ground of the development in the law,

the Court would not think it appropriate to grant the application by exercising the power conferred by section 16(2)."

Appeals by prosecution

44 Determination of prosecution appeals: England and Wales

In section 61 of the Criminal Justice Act 2003 (c. 44) (determination of prosecution appeal by Court of Appeal) for subsection (5) substitute—

"(5) But the Court of Appeal may not make an order under subsection (4)(c) in respect of an offence unless it considers that the defendant could not receive a fair trial if an order were made under subsection (4)(a) or (b)."

45 Determination of prosecution appeals: Northern Ireland

In Article 20 of the Criminal Justice (Northern Ireland) Order 2004 (S.I. 2004/1500 (N.I.9)) (determination of prosecution appeal by Court of Appeal) for paragraph (5) substitute—

"(5) But the Court of Appeal may not make an order under paragraph (4)(c) in respect of an offence unless it considers that the defendant could not receive a fair trial if an order were made under paragraph (4)(a) or (b)."

Miscellaneous

46 Review of sentence on reference by Attorney General

(1) Section 36 of the Criminal Justice Act 1988 (c. 33) (reviews of sentencing) is amended as follows.

(2) For subsection (3A) substitute—

"(3A) Where a reference under this section relates to a case in which the judge made an order specified in subsection (3B), the Court of Appeal shall not, in deciding what sentence is appropriate for the case, make any allowance for the fact that the person to whom it relates is being sentenced for a second time.

(3B) The orders specified in this subsection are—

(a) an order under section 269(2) of the Criminal Justice Act 2003 (determination of minimum term in relation to mandatory life sentence);

(b) an order under section 82A(2) of the Powers of Criminal Courts (Sentencing) Act 2000 (determination of minimum term in relation to discretionary life sentences and certain other sentences)."

(3) In subsection (9) after paragraph (b) insert ", and

(c) the reference in subsection (3A) to an order specified in subsection (3B) shall be construed as a reference to an order under Article 5(1) of the Life Sentences (Northern Ireland) Order 2001."

47 Further amendments relating to appeals in criminal cases

Schedule 8 amends the Criminal Appeal Act 1968 (c. 19), the Criminal Appeal (Northern Ireland) Act 1980 (c. 47) and other Acts relating to appeals in criminal cases.

PART 4
OTHER CRIMINAL JUSTICE PROVISIONS

Alternatives to prosecution

48 Alternatives to prosecution for offenders under 18

(1) Schedule 9 amends the Crime and Disorder Act 1998 (c. 37)—

(a) to make provision for the giving of youth conditional cautions to children and young persons, and

    (b) to make minor amendments relating to reprimands and warnings under section 65 of that Act.

(2) The Secretary of State may by order amend the Crime and Disorder Act 1998 (c. 37), as amended by Schedule 9, so as to vary the provision made by it for the giving of youth conditional cautions to children and young persons under the age of 16 (including doing so by adding or omitting any provision).

49   Protection for spent cautions under Rehabilitation of Offenders Act 1974

(1) Schedule 10 amends the Rehabilitation of Offenders Act 1974 (c. 53) so as to provide for the protection of spent cautions.

(2) The provisions of Schedule 10 (and this section) extend only to England and Wales.

50   Criminal conviction certificates and criminal record certificates

(1) Part 5 of the Police Act 1997 (c. 50) (certificates of criminal records) is amended as follows.

(2) In section 112 (criminal conviction certificates)—

    (a) in the definition of "central records", after "convictions" insert "and conditional cautions";

    (b) after that definition insert—

""conditional caution" means a caution given under section 22 of the Criminal Justice Act 2003 (c. 44) or section 66A of the Crime and Disorder Act 1998, other than one that is spent for the purposes of Schedule 2 to the Rehabilitation of Offenders Act 1974."

(3) In section 113A(6) (criminal record certificates)—

    (a) in the definition of "exempted question", after "a question" insert "which—

        "(a) so far as it applies to convictions, is a question";

    (b) in that definition, at the end insert "; and—

        "(b) so far as it applies to cautions, is a question to which paragraph 3(3) or (4) of Schedule 2 to that Act has been excluded by an order of the Secretary of State under paragraph 4 of that Schedule;";

    (c) in the definition of "relevant matter", after "caution" insert ", including a caution that is spent for the purposes of Schedule 2 to that Act".

(4) This section extends to England and Wales only.

Bail

51   Bail conditions: electronic monitoring

Schedule 11 makes provision in connection with the electronic monitoring of persons released on bail subject to conditions.

52   Bail for summary offences and certain other offences to be tried summarily

Schedule 12—

    (a) imposes a duty on a magistrates' court considering whether to withhold or grant bail in relation to a person under 18 accused of an offence mentioned in Schedule 2 to the Magistrates' Courts Act 1980 (c. 43) (offences for which the value involved is relevant to the mode of trial) to consider the value involved in the offence; and

    (b) amends Schedule 1 to the Bail Act 1976 (persons entitled to bail: supplementary provisions).

Proceedings in magistrates' courts

53 Allocation of offences triable either way etc.

Schedule 13 amends Schedule 3 to the Criminal Justice Act 2003 (c. 44) (which makes provision in relation to the allocation and other treatment of offences triable either way, and the sending of cases to the Crown Court).

54 Trial or sentencing in absence of accused in magistrates' courts

(1) Section 11 of the Magistrates' Courts Act 1980 (non-appearance of accused) is amended as follows.

(2) In subsection (1), for "the court may proceed in his absence" substitute "—
   (a) if the accused is under 18 years of age, the court may proceed in his absence; and
   (b) if the accused has attained the age of 18 years, the court shall proceed in his absence unless it appears to the court to be contrary to the interests of justice to do so.
   This is subject to subsections (2), (2A), (3) and (4)."

(3) After subsection (2) insert—
   "(2A) The court shall not proceed in the absence of the accused if it considers that there is an acceptable reason for his failure to appear."

(4) In each of subsections (3) and (4), for "A magistrates' court" substitute "In proceedings to which this subsection applies, the court."

(5) After subsection (3) insert—
   "(3A) But where a sentence or order of a kind mentioned in subsection (3) is imposed or given in the absence of the offender, the offender must be brought before the court before being taken to a prison or other institution to begin serving his sentence (and the sentence or order is not to be regarded as taking effect until he is brought before the court)."

(6) After subsection (4) insert—
   "(5) Subsections (3) and (4) apply to—
      (a) proceedings instituted by an information, where a summons has been issued; and
      (b) proceedings instituted by a written charge.
   (6) Nothing in this section requires the court to enquire into the reasons for the accused's failure to appear before deciding whether to proceed in his absence.
   (7) The court shall state in open court its reasons for not proceeding under this section in the absence of an accused who has attained the age of 18 years; and the court shall cause those reasons to be entered in its register of proceedings."

(7) Section 13(5) of that Act (non-appearance of accused: issue of warrant) ceases to have effect.

55 Extension of powers of non-legal staff

(1) Section 7A of the Prosecution of Offences Act 1985 (c. 23) (powers of non-legal staff) is amended as follows.

(2) In subsection (2) (powers of designated non-legal staff)—
   (a) in paragraph (a)(ii), after "trials" insert "of offences triable either way or offences which are punishable with imprisonment in the case of persons aged 21 or over";
   (b) after paragraph (a)(ii) insert—
      "(iii) the conduct of applications or other proceedings relating to preventative civil orders;
      (iv) the conduct of proceedings (other than criminal proceedings) in, or in connection with, the discharge of functions assigned to the Director under section 3(2)(g) above.";
   (c) for paragraph (b) substitute—
      "(b) any powers of a Crown Prosecutor that do not involve the exercise of such rights of audience as are mentioned in paragraph (a) above but are exercisable in relation to the conduct of—
         (i) criminal proceedings in magistrates' courts, or
         (ii) applications or proceedings falling within paragraph (a)(iii) or (iv)."

(3) For subsection (5) (interpretation) substitute—
    "(5) In this section—
        "bail in criminal proceedings" has the same meaning as in the Bail Act 1976 (see section 1 of that Act);
        "preventative civil orders" means—
            (a) orders within section 3(2)(fa) to (fe) above;
            (b) orders under section 5 or 5A of the Protection from Harassment Act 1997 (restraining orders); or
            (c) orders under section 8 of the Crime and Disorder Act 1998 (parenting orders).
    (5A) For the purposes of this section a trial begins with the opening of the prosecution case after the entry of a plea of not guilty and ends with the conviction or acquittal of the accused."
(4) Omit subsection (6) (powers not applicable to offences triable only on indictment etc.).
(5) After subsection (7) insert—
    "(8) As from 1 May 2011 nothing in this section confers on persons designated under this section—
        (a) any rights of audience, or
        (b) any right to conduct litigation,
        for the purposes of Part 3 of the Legal Services Act 2007 (reserved legal activities).
    (9) As from that date the following provisions of that Act accordingly do not apply to persons designated under this section—
        (a) paragraph 1(3) of Schedule 3 (exemption for persons with statutory rights of audience), and
        (b) paragraph 2(3) of that Schedule (exemption for persons with statutory right to conduct litigation).
    (10) The Attorney General may by order make such modifications in the application of any enactment (including this section) in relation to persons designated under this section as the Attorney General considers appropriate in consequence of, or in connection with, the matters provided for by subsections (8) and (9).
    (11) The Attorney General may also by order amend subsection (2)(a)(ii) so as to omit the words "or offences which are punishable with imprisonment in the case of persons aged 21 or over".
    (12) The power to make an order under subsection (10) or (11) is exercisable by statutory instrument, but a statutory instrument containing such an order may not be made unless a draft of the instrument has been laid before, and approved by a resolution of, each House of Parliament."
(6) In section 15 of that Act (interpretation of Part 1) in subsection (4) (provisions for the purposes of which binding over proceedings are to be taken to be criminal proceedings) for "and 7(1)" substitute ", 7(1) and 7A".

Criminal legal aid

56 Provisional grant of right to representation

(1) Part 1 of the Access to Justice Act 1999 (c. 22) is amended as follows.
(2) In section 14(1) (representation)—
    (a) after "criminal proceedings" insert "and about the provisional grant of a right to representation in prescribed circumstances";
    (b) after "granted" insert ", or provisionally granted,".
(3) In section 15(1) (selection of representative) after "granted" insert ", or provisionally granted,".

(4) In section 25(9) (orders, regulations and directions subject to affirmative resolution procedure) for "paragraph 2A" substitute "paragraph 1A, 2A,".

(5) In section 26 (interpretation) after the definition of "representation" insert—

"and, for the purposes of the definition of "representation", "proceedings" includes, in the context of a provisional grant of a right to representation, proceedings that may result from the investigation concerned."

(6) After paragraph 1 of Schedule 3 (individuals to whom right may be granted) insert—

"Individuals to whom right may be provisionally granted

1A (1) Regulations may provide that, in prescribed circumstances, and subject to any prescribed conditions, a right to representation may be provisionally granted to an individual where—

(a) the individual is involved in an investigation which may result in criminal proceedings, and

(b) the right is so granted for the purposes of criminal proceedings that may result from the investigation.

(2) Regulations under sub-paragraph (1) may, in particular, make provision about—

(a) the stage in an investigation at which a right to representation may be provisionally granted;

(b) the circumstances in which a right which has been so granted—

(i) is to become, or be treated as if it were, a right to representation under paragraph 1, or

(ii) is to be, or may be, withdrawn."

(7) In paragraph 2A of Schedule 3 (grant of right by Commission) at the end of sub-paragraph (1)(b) insert—

"(c) provide that any provisional grant of a right to representation, or any withdrawal of a right so granted, in accordance with regulations under paragraph 1A is to be made by the Commission."

(8) In paragraph 3A(1) of Schedule 3 (form of the grant of a right to representation) after "grant" insert ", or provisional grant,".

(9) In paragraph 3B of Schedule 3 (financial eligibility)—

(a) in sub-paragraph (1)—

(i) after "grant" insert ", or provisionally grant,",

(ii) after "granted" insert ", or provisionally granted,";

(b) in sub-paragraph (2)(a), after "granted" insert ", or provisionally granted,".

(10) In paragraph 4 of Schedule 3 (appeals) at the end insert—

"This paragraph does not apply in relation to any right to representation granted in accordance with paragraph 1A."

(11) In paragraph 5 of Schedule 3 (criteria for grant of right)—

(a) in sub-paragraph (1), after "grant" insert ", or provisionally grant,";

(b) after sub-paragraph (2) insert—

"(2A) For the purposes of sub-paragraph (2), "proceedings" includes, in the context of a provisional grant of a right to representation, proceedings that may result from the investigation in which the individual is involved.";

(c) in sub-paragraph (4), after "grant" insert ", or provisional grant,".

57 Disclosure of information to enable assessment of financial eligibility

(1) The Access to Justice Act 1999 (c. 22) is amended as follows.

(2) In section 25(9) (orders, regulations and directions subject to affirmative resolution procedure), for "or 4" substitute "4 or 6".

(3) In Schedule 3 (criminal defence service: right to representation), after paragraph 5 insert—

"Information requests

6 (1) The relevant authority may make an information request to—
    (a) the Secretary of State, or
    (b) the Commissioners,
    for the purpose of facilitating the making of a decision by the authority about the application of paragraph 3B(1) or (2), or regulations under paragraph 3B(3), in relation to an individual.

    (2) An information request made to the Secretary of State is a request for the disclosure of some or all of the following information—
    (a) the individual's full name;
    (b) the individual's address;
    (c) the individual's date of birth;
    (d) the individual's national insurance number;
    (e) the individual's benefit status;
    (f) information of any description specified in regulations.

    (3) An information request made to the Commissioners is a request for the disclosure of some or all of the following information—
    (a) whether or not the individual is employed;
    (b) the name and address of the employer (if the individual is employed);
    (c) the individual's national insurance number;
    (d) information of any description specified in regulations made with the agreement of the Commissioners.

    (4) The information that may be specified under subsection (3)(d) includes, in particular, information relating to the individual's income (as defined in the regulations) for a period so specified.

    (5) On receiving an information request, the Secretary of State or (as the case may be) the Commissioners may disclose the information requested to the relevant authority.

Restrictions on disclosure

7 (1) A person to whom information is disclosed under paragraph 6(5), or this sub-paragraph, may disclose the information to any person to whom its disclosure is necessary or expedient in connection with facilitating the making of a decision by the relevant authority about the application of paragraph 3B(1) or (2), or regulations under paragraph 3B(3), in relation to an individual.

    (2) A person to whom such information is disclosed commits an offence if the person—
    (a) discloses or uses the information, and
    (b) the disclosure is not authorised by sub-paragraph (1) or (as the case may be) the use is not for the purpose of facilitating the making of such a decision as is mentioned in that subparagraph.

    (3) But it is not an offence under sub-paragraph (2)—
    (a) to disclose any information in accordance with any enactment or order of a court or for the purposes of any proceedings before a court; or
    (b) to disclose any information which has previously been lawfully disclosed to the public.

    (4) It is a defence for a person charged with an offence under subparagraph (2) to prove that the person reasonably believed that the disclosure or use was lawful.

    (5) A person guilty of an offence under sub-paragraph (2) is liable—
    (a) on conviction on indictment, to imprisonment for a term not exceeding 2 years or a fine or both;

(b) on summary conviction, to imprisonment for a term not exceeding 12 months or a fine not exceeding the statutory maximum or both.

(6) In sub-paragraph (5)(b) the reference to 12 months is to be read as a reference to 6 months in relation to an offence committed before the commencement of section 154(1) of the Criminal Justice Act 2003.

(7) Nothing in section 20 applies in relation to the disclosure of information to which sub-paragraph (1) applies.

Paragraphs 6 and 7: supplementary

8 (1) This paragraph applies for the purposes of paragraphs 6 and 7.

(2) "Benefit status", in relation to an individual, means whether or not the individual is in direct or indirect receipt of any prescribed benefit or benefits and, if so (in the case of each benefit)—

(a) which benefit the individual is so receiving, and

(b) (in prescribed cases) the amount the individual is so receiving by way of the benefit.

(3) "The Commissioners" means the Commissioners for Her Majesty's Revenue and Customs.

(4) "Information" means information held in any form.

(5) Nothing in paragraph 6 or 7 authorises the making of a disclosure which contravenes the Data Protection Act 1998."

58 Pilot schemes

(1) The Access to Justice Act 1999 (c. 22) is amended as follows.

(2) In section 17A (contribution orders) omit subsection (5) (piloting of regulations).

(3) After section 18 insert—

"18A Pilot schemes

(1) This section applies to the following instruments—

(a) any order under section 14 or paragraph 5 of Schedule 3,

(b) any regulations under section 12, 13, 15, 17 or 17A or any of paragraphs 1A to 5 of Schedule 3, and

(c) any regulations under section 22(5) having effect in relation to the Criminal Defence Service.

(2) Any instrument to which this section applies may be made so as to have effect for a specified period not exceeding 12 months.

(3) But if the Lord Chancellor thinks that it is necessary or expedient for either of the purposes in subsection (4), the period specified in the instrument—

(a) may in the first instance be a period not exceeding 18 months;

(b) may be varied so as to become a period not exceeding 18 months.

(4) The purposes are—

(a) ensuring the effective operation of the instrument;

(b) co-ordinating the operation of the instrument with the operation of any other provision made under an enactment relating to any aspect of the criminal justice system.

(5) The period for the time being specified in an instrument to which this section applies may also be varied so that the instrument has effect for such further period as the Lord Chancellor thinks necessary for the purpose of securing that it remains in operation until the coming into force of any order or regulations made under the same provision of this Act that will have effect—

(a) generally, or

(b) for purposes wider than those for which the instrument has effect.

(6) In the following provisions of this section "pilot scheme" means any instrument which, in accordance with subsections (2) to (5), is to have effect for a limited period.

(7) A pilot scheme may provide that its provisions are to apply only in relation to—
   (a) one or more specified areas or localities;
   (b) one or more specified descriptions of court;
   (c) one or more specified offences or descriptions of offence;
   (d) one or more specified classes of person;
   (e) persons selected—
      (i) by reference to specified criteria; or
      (ii) on a sampling basis.

(8) A pilot scheme may make consequential or transitional provision with respect to the cessation of the scheme on the expiry of the specified period (or that period as varied under subsection (3)(b) or (5)).

(9) A pilot scheme may be replaced by a further pilot scheme making the same or similar provision."

(4) In section 25 (regulations, orders and directions) after subsection (9A) insert—
   "(9B) No order or regulations which, by virtue of section 18A, is or are to have effect for a limited period shall be made unless a draft of the order or regulations has been laid before, and approved by a resolution of, each House of Parliament."

Miscellaneous

59 SFO's pre-investigation powers in relation to bribery and corruption: foreign officers etc.

(1) The Criminal Justice Act 1987 (c. 38) is amended as follows.

(2) After section 2 insert—

"2A Director's pre-investigation powers in relation to bribery and corruption: foreign officers etc

(1) The powers of the Director under section 2 are also exercisable for the purpose of enabling him to determine whether to start an investigation under section 1 in a case where it appears to him that conduct to which this section applies may have taken place.

(2) But—
   (a) the power under subsection (2) of section 2 is so exercisable only if it appears to the Director that for the purpose of enabling him to make that determination it is expedient to require any person appearing to him to have relevant information to do as mentioned in that subsection, and
   (b) the power under subsection (3) of that section is so exercisable only if it appears to the Director that for that purpose it is expedient to require any person to do as mentioned in that subsection.

(3) Accordingly, where the powers of the Director under section 2 are exercisable in accordance with subsections (1) and (2) above—
   (a) the reference in subsection (2) of that section to the person under investigation or any other person whom the Director has reason to believe has relevant information is to be read as a reference to any such person as is mentioned in subsection (2)(a) above,
   (b) the reference in subsection (3) of that section to the person under investigation or any other person is to be read as a reference to any such person as is mentioned in subsection (2)(b) above, and
   (c) any reference in subsection (2), (3) or (4) of that section to the investigation is to be read as a reference to the making of any such determination as is mentioned in subsection (1) above.

(4) Any reference in section 2(16) to the carrying out of an investigation by the Serious Fraud Office into serious or complex fraud includes a reference to the making of any such determination as is mentioned in subsection (1) above.

(5) This section applies to any conduct which, as a result of section 108 of the Anti-terrorism, Crime and Security Act 2001 (bribery and corruption: foreign officers etc), constitutes a corruption offence (wherever committed).

(6) The following are corruption offences for the purposes of this section—

(a) any common law offence of bribery;

(b) the offences under section 1 of the Public Bodies Corrupt Practices Act 1889 (corruption in office); and

(c) the offences under section 1 of the Prevention of Corruption Act 1906 (corrupt transactions with agents)."

(3) In section 17 (extent)—

(a) in subsection (2) (provisions of Act extending to Scotland), for "section 2" substitute "sections 2 and 2A"; and

(b) in subsection (3) (provisions of Act extending to Northern Ireland), after "sections 2" insert ", 2A".

60 Contents of an accused's defence statement

(1) In section 6A(1) of the Criminal Procedure and Investigations Act 1996 (c. 25) (contents of defence statement), after "prosecution," in paragraph (c) insert—

"(ca) setting out particulars of the matters of fact on which he intends to rely for the purposes of his defence,".

(2) In section 11(2)(f)(ii) of that Act (faults in disclosure by accused), after "matter" insert "(or any particular of any matter of fact)".

61 Compensation for miscarriages of justice

(1) The Criminal Justice Act 1988 (c. 33) has effect subject to the following amendments.

(2) Section 133 (compensation for miscarriages of justice) is amended as follows.

(3) At the end of subsection (2) (compensation only payable if application for compensation is made) insert "before the end of the period of 2 years beginning with the date on which the conviction of the person concerned is reversed or he is pardoned.

(2A) But the Secretary of State may direct that an application for compensation made after the end of that period is to be treated as if it had been made within that period if the Secretary of State considers that there are exceptional circumstances which justify doing so."

(4) For subsection (4A) substitute—

"(4A) Section 133A applies in relation to the assessment of the amount of the compensation."

(5) After subsection (5) (meaning of "reversed" in relation to a conviction) insert—

"(5A) But in a case where—

(a) a person's conviction for an offence is quashed on an appeal out of time, and

(b) the person is to be subject to a retrial,

the conviction is not to be treated for the purposes of this section as "reversed" unless and until the person is acquitted of all offences at the retrial or the prosecution indicates that it has decided not to proceed with the retrial.

(5B) In subsection (5A) above any reference to a retrial includes a reference to proceedings held following the remission of a matter to a magistrates' court by the Crown Court under section 48(2)(b) of the Supreme Court Act 1981."

(6) In subsection (6) (meaning of suffering punishment as a result of conviction) after "this section" insert "and section 133A".

(7) After section 133 insert—

"133A Miscarriages of justice: amount of compensation

(1) This section applies where an assessor is required to assess the amount of compensation payable to or in respect of a person under section 133 for a miscarriage of justice.

(2) In assessing so much of any compensation payable under section 133 as is attributable to suffering, harm to reputation or similar damage, the assessor must have regard in particular to—
   (a) the seriousness of the offence of which the person was convicted and the severity of the punishment suffered as a result of the conviction, and
   (b) the conduct of the investigation and prosecution of the offence.

(3) The assessor may make from the total amount of compensation that the assessor would otherwise have assessed as payable under section 133 any deduction or deductions that the assessor considers appropriate by reason of either or both of the following—
   (a) any conduct of the person appearing to the assessor to have directly or indirectly caused, or contributed to, the conviction concerned; and
   (b) any other convictions of the person and any punishment suffered as a result of them.

(4) If, having had regard to any matters falling within subsection (3)(a) or (b), the assessor considers that there are exceptional circumstances which justify doing so, the assessor may determine that the amount of compensation payable under section 133 is to be a nominal amount only.

(5) The total amount of compensation payable to or in respect of a person under section 133 for a particular miscarriage of justice must not exceed the overall compensation limit. That limit is—
   (a) £1 million in a case to which section 133B applies, and
   (b) £500,000 in any other case.

(6) The total amount of compensation payable under section 133 for a person's loss of earnings or earnings capacity in respect of any one year must not exceed the earnings compensation limit. That limit is an amount equal to 1.5 times the median annual gross earnings according to the latest figures published by the Office of National Statistics at the time of the assessment.

(7) The Secretary of State may by order made by statutory instrument amend subsection (5) or (6) so as to alter any amount for the time being specified as the overall compensation limit or the earnings compensation limit.

(8) No order may be made under subsection (7) unless a draft of the order has been laid before and approved by a resolution of each House of Parliament.

133B Cases where person has been detained for at least 10 years

(1) For the purposes of section 133A(5) this section applies to any case where the person concerned ("P") has been in qualifying detention for a period (or total period) of at least 10 years by the time when—
   (a) the conviction is reversed, or
   (b) the pardon is given,
   as mentioned in section 133(1).

(2) P was "in qualifying detention" at any time when P was detained in a prison, a hospital or at any other place, if P was so detained—
   (a) by virtue of a sentence passed in respect of the relevant offence,
   (b) under mental health legislation by reason of P's conviction of that offence (disregarding any conditions other than the fact of the conviction that had to be fulfilled in order for P to be so detained), or
   (c) as a result of P's having been remanded in custody in connection with the relevant offence or with any other offence the charge for which was founded on the same facts or evidence as that for the relevant offence.

(3) In calculating the period (or total period) during which P has been in qualifying detention as mentioned in subsection (1), no account is to be taken of any period of time during which P was both—
  (a) in qualifying detention, and
  (b) in excluded concurrent detention.

(4) P was "in excluded concurrent detention" at any time when P was detained in a prison, a hospital or at any other place, if P was so detained—
  (a) during the term of a sentence passed in respect of an offence other than the relevant offence,
  (b) under mental health legislation by reason of P's conviction of any such other offence (disregarding any conditions other than the fact of the conviction that had to be fulfilled in order for P to be so detained), or
  (c) as a result of P's having been remanded in custody in connection with an offence for which P was subsequently convicted other than—
    (i) the relevant offence, or
    (ii) any other offence the charge for which was founded on the same facts or evidence as that for the relevant offence.

(5) But P was not "in excluded concurrent detention" at any time by virtue of subsection (4)(a), (b) or (c) if P's conviction of the other offence mentioned in that provision was quashed on appeal, or a pardon was given in respect of it.

(6) In this section—
  "mental health legislation" means—
    (a) Part 3 of the Mental Health Act 1983,
    (b) Part 3 of the Mental Health (Northern Ireland) Order 1986, or
    (c) the provisions of any earlier enactment corresponding to Part 3 of that Act or Part 3 of that Order;
  "the relevant offence" means the offence in respect of which the conviction is quashed or the pardon is given (but see subsection (7));
  "remanded in custody" is to be read in accordance with subsections (8) and (9);
  "reversed" has the same meaning as in section 133 of this Act.

(7) If, as a result of the miscarriage of justice—
  (a) two or more convictions are reversed, or
  (b) a pardon is given in respect of two or more offences,
  "the relevant offence" means any of the offences concerned.

(8) In relation to England and Wales, "remanded in custody" has the meaning given by section 242(2) of the Criminal Justice Act 2003, but that subsection applies for the purposes of this section as if any reference there to a provision of the Mental Health Act 1983 included a reference to any corresponding provision of any earlier enactment.

(9) In relation to Northern Ireland, "remanded in custody" means—
  (a) remanded in or committed to custody by an order of a court, or
  (b) remanded, admitted or removed to hospital under Article 42, 43, 45 or 54 of the Mental Health (Northern Ireland) Order 1986 or under any corresponding provision of any earlier enactment."

(8) In section 172 (extent) in subsection (3) (provisions extending to Northern Ireland as well as England and Wales) for "section 133" substitute "sections 133 to 133B".

(9) This section extends to England and Wales and Northern Ireland.

62 Annual report on Criminal Justice (Terrorism and Conspiracy) Act 1998

(1) Section 8 of the Criminal Justice (Terrorism and Conspiracy) Act 1998 (c. 40) (requirement for annual report on working of the Act) ceases to have effect.

(2) The following provisions, namely—
  (a) subsection (1), and
  (b) the repeal of section 8 of that Act in Part 4 of Schedule 28,
extend to England and Wales and Northern Ireland.

PART 5
CRIMINAL LAW

Pornography etc.

63 Possession of extreme pornographic images

(1) It is an offence for a person to be in possession of an extreme pornographic image.
(2) An "extreme pornographic image" is an image which is both—
  (a) pornographic, and
  (b) an extreme image.
(3) An image is "pornographic" if it is of such a nature that it must reasonably be assumed to have been produced solely or principally for the purpose of sexual arousal.
(4) Where (as found in the person's possession) an image forms part of a series of images, the question whether the image is of such a nature as is mentioned in subsection (3) is to be determined by reference to—
  (a) the image itself, and
  (b) (if the series of images is such as to be capable of providing a context for the image) the context in which it occurs in the series of images.
(5) So, for example, where—
  (a) an image forms an integral part of a narrative constituted by a series of images, and
  (b) having regard to those images as a whole, they are not of such a nature that they must reasonably be assumed to have been produced solely or principally for the purpose of sexual arousal,
the image may, by virtue of being part of that narrative, be found not to be pornographic, even though it might have been found to be pornographic if taken by itself.
(6) An "extreme image" is an image which—
  (a) falls within subsection (7), and
  (b) is grossly offensive, disgusting or otherwise of an obscene character.
(7) An image falls within this subsection if it portrays, in an explicit and realistic way, any of the following—
  (a) an act which threatens a person's life,
  (b) an act which results, or is likely to result, in serious injury to a person's anus, breasts or genitals,
  (c) an act which involves sexual interference with a human corpse, or
  (d) a person performing an act of intercourse or oral sex with an animal (whether dead or alive),
  and a reasonable person looking at the image would think that any such person or animal was real.
(8) In this section "image" means—
  (a) a moving or still image (produced by any means); or
  (b) data (stored by any means) which is capable of conversion into an image within paragraph (a).
(9) In this section references to a part of the body include references to a part surgically constructed (in particular through gender reassignment surgery).
(10) Proceedings for an offence under this section may not be instituted—
  (a) in England and Wales, except by or with the consent of the Director of Public Prosecutions; or

(b) in Northern Ireland, except by or with the consent of the Director of Public Prosecutions for Northern Ireland.

64 Exclusion of classified films etc.

(1) Section 63 does not apply to excluded images.

(2) An "excluded image" is an image which forms part of a series of images contained in a recording of the whole or part of a classified work.

(3) But such an image is not an "excluded image" if—

(a) it is contained in a recording of an extract from a classified work, and

(b) it is of such a nature that it must reasonably be assumed to have been extracted (whether with or without other images) solely or principally for the purpose of sexual arousal.

(4) Where an extracted image is one of a series of images contained in the recording, the question whether the image is of such a nature as is mentioned in subsection (3)(b) is to be determined by reference to—

(a) the image itself, and

(b) (if the series of images is such as to be capable of providing a context for the image) the context in which it occurs in the series of images;

and section 63(5) applies in connection with determining that question as it applies in connection with determining whether an image is pornographic.

(5) In determining for the purposes of this section whether a recording is a recording of the whole or part of a classified work, any alteration attributable to—

(a) a defect caused for technical reasons or by inadvertence on the part of any person, or

(b) the inclusion in the recording of any extraneous material (such as advertisements),

is to be disregarded.

(6) Nothing in this section is to be taken as affecting any duty of a designated authority to have regard to section 63 (along with other enactments creating criminal offences) in determining whether a video work is suitable for a classification certificate to be issued in respect of it.

(7) In this section—

"classified work" means (subject to subsection (8)) a video work in respect of which a classification certificate has been issued by a designated authority (whether before or after the commencement of this section);

"classification certificate" and "video work" have the same meanings as in the Video Recordings Act 1984 (c. 39);

"designated authority" means an authority which has been designated by the Secretary of State under section 4 of that Act;

"extract" includes an extract consisting of a single image;

"image" and "pornographic" have the same meanings as in section 63;

"recording" means any disc, tape or other device capable of storing data electronically and from which images may be produced (by any means).

(8) Section 22(3) of the Video Recordings Act 1984 (effect of alterations) applies for the purposes of this section as it applies for the purposes of that Act.

65 Defences: general

(1) Where a person is charged with an offence under section 63, it is a defence for the person to prove any of the matters mentioned in subsection (2).

(2) The matters are—

(a) that the person had a legitimate reason for being in possession of the image concerned;

(b) that the person had not seen the image concerned and did not know, nor had any cause to suspect, it to be an extreme pornographic image;

    (c) that the person—
        (i) was sent the image concerned without any prior request having been made by or on behalf of the person, and
        (ii) did not keep it for an unreasonable time.
(3) In this section "extreme pornographic image" and "image" have the same meanings as in section 63.

66   Defence: participation in consensual acts

(1) This section applies where—
    (a) a person ("D") is charged with an offence under section 63, and
    (b) the offence relates to an image that portrays an act or acts within paragraphs (a) to (c) (but none within paragraph (d)) of subsection (7) of that section.
(2) It is a defence for D to prove—
    (a) that D directly participated in the act or any of the acts portrayed, and
    (b) that the act or acts did not involve the infliction of any non-consensual harm on any person, and
    (c) if the image portrays an act within section 63(7)(c), that what is portrayed as a human corpse was not in fact a corpse.
(3) For the purposes of this section harm inflicted on a person is "non-consensual" harm if—
    (a) the harm is of such a nature that the person cannot, in law, consent to it being inflicted on himself or herself; or
    (b) where the person can, in law, consent to it being so inflicted, the person does not in fact consent to it being so inflicted.

67   Penalties etc. for possession of extreme pornographic images

(1) This section has effect where a person is guilty of an offence under section 63.
(2) Except where subsection (3) applies to the offence, the offender is liable—
    (a) on summary conviction, to imprisonment for a term not exceeding the relevant period or a fine not exceeding the statutory maximum or both;
    (b) on conviction on indictment, to imprisonment for a term not exceeding 3 years or a fine or both.
(3) If the offence relates to an image that does not portray any act within section 63(7)(a) or (b), the offender is liable—
    (a) on summary conviction, to imprisonment for a term not exceeding the relevant period or a fine not exceeding the statutory maximum or both;
    (b) on conviction on indictment, to imprisonment for a term not exceeding 2 years or a fine or both.
(4) In subsection (2)(a) or (3)(a) "the relevant period" means—
    (a) in relation to England and Wales, 12 months;
    (b) in relation to Northern Ireland, 6 months.

68   Special rules relating to providers of information society services

Schedule 14 makes special provision in connection with the operation of section 63 in relation to persons providing information society services within the meaning of that Schedule.

69   Indecent photographs of children: England and Wales

(1) The Protection of Children Act 1978 (c. 37) is amended as follows.
(2) In section 1B(1)(b) (exception for members of the Security Service)—
    (a) after "Security Service" insert "or the Secret Intelligence Service";
    (b) for "the Service" substitute "that Service".

(3) After section 7(4) (meaning of photograph), insert—

"(4A) References to a photograph also include—

(a) a tracing or other image, whether made by electronic or other means (of whatever nature)—

(i) which is not itself a photograph or pseudo-photograph, but

(ii) which is derived from the whole or part of a photograph or pseudo-photograph (or a combination of either or both); and

(b) data stored on a computer disc or by other electronic means which is capable of conversion into an image within paragraph (a);

and subsection (8) applies in relation to such an image as it applies in relation to a pseudo-photograph."

(4) In section 7(9)(b) (meaning of indecent pseudo-photograph), for "a pseudophotograph" substitute "an indecent pseudo-photograph".

70 Indecent photographs of children: Northern Ireland

(1) The Protection of Children (Northern Ireland) Order 1978 (S.I. 1978/1047 (N.I. 17)) is amended as follows.

(2) In Article 2(2) (interpretation) in paragraph (b) of the definition of "indecent pseudo-photograph", for "a pseudo-photograph" substitute "an indecent pseudo-photograph".

(3) After Article 2(2) insert—

"(2A) In this Order, references to a photograph also include—

(a) a tracing or other image, whether made by electronic or other means (of whatever nature)—

(i) which is not itself a photograph or pseudo-photograph, but

(ii) which is derived from the whole or part of a photograph or pseudo-photograph (or a combination of either or both); and

(b) data stored on a computer disc or by other electronic means which is capable of conversion into an image within paragraph (a);

and paragraph (3)(c) applies in relation to such an image as it applies in relation to a pseudo-photograph."

(4) In article 3A(1)(b) (exception for members of the Security Service)—

(a) after "Security Service" insert "or the Secret Intelligence Service";

(b) for "the Service" substitute "that Service".

71 Maximum penalty for publication etc. of obscene articles

In section 2(1)(b) of the Obscene Publications Act 1959 (c. 66) (maximum penalty on indictment for publication etc. of obscene articles) for "three years" substitute "five years".

Sexual offences

72 Offences committed outside the United Kingdom

(1) For section 72 of the Sexual Offences Act 2003 (c. 42) substitute—

"72 Offences outside the United Kingdom

(1) If—

(a) a United Kingdom national does an act in a country outside the United Kingdom, and

(b) the act, if done in England and Wales or Northern Ireland, would constitute a sexual offence to which this section applies,

the United Kingdom national is guilty in that part of the United Kingdom of that sexual offence.

(2) If—
    (a) a United Kingdom resident does an act in a country outside the United Kingdom,
    (b) the act constitutes an offence under the law in force in that country, and
    (c) the act, if done in England and Wales or Northern Ireland, would constitute a sexual offence to which this section applies,
the United Kingdom resident is guilty in that part of the United Kingdom of that sexual offence.

(3) If—
    (a) a person does an act in a country outside the United Kingdom at a time when the person was not a United Kingdom national or a United Kingdom resident,
    (b) the act constituted an offence under the law in force in that country,
    (c) the act, if done in England and Wales or Northern Ireland, would have constituted a sexual offence to which this section applies, and
    (d) the person meets the residence or nationality condition at the relevant time,
proceedings may be brought against the person in that part of the United Kingdom for that sexual offence as if the person had done the act there.

(4) The person meets the residence or nationality condition at the relevant time if the person is a United Kingdom national or a United Kingdom resident at the time when the proceedings are brought.

(5) An act punishable under the law in force in any country constitutes an offence under that law for the purposes of subsections (2) and (3) however it is described in that law.

(6) The condition in subsection (2)(b) or (3)(b) is to be taken to be met unless, not later than rules of court may provide, the defendant serves on the prosecution a notice—
    (a) stating that, on the facts as alleged with respect to the act in question, the condition is not in the defendant's opinion met,
    (b) showing the grounds for that opinion, and
    (c) requiring the prosecution to prove that it is met.

(7) But the court, if it thinks fit, may permit the defendant to require the prosecution to prove that the condition is met without service of a notice under subsection (6).

(8) In the Crown Court the question whether the condition is met is to be decided by the judge alone.

(9) In this section—
"country" includes territory;
"United Kingdom national" means an individual who is—
    (a) a British citizen, a British overseas territories citizen, a British National (Overseas) or a British Overseas citizen;
    (b) a person who under the British Nationality Act 1981 is a British subject; or
    (c) a British protected person within the meaning of that Act;
"United Kingdom resident" means an individual who is resident in the United Kingdom.

(10) Schedule 2 lists the sexual offences to which this section applies."

(2) Schedule 2 to that Act (list of sexual offences to which section 72 applies) is amended as follows.

(3) In paragraph 1 (offences under the law of England and Wales)—
    (a) for paragraphs (a) and (b) substitute—
        "(a) an offence under any of sections 5 to 19, 25 and 26 and 47 to 50;
        (b) an offence under any of sections 1 to 4, 30 to 41 and 61 where the victim of the offence was under 18 at the time of the offence;";
    (b) in paragraph (c), for "16" substitute "18"; and
    (c) in paragraph (d), omit "in relation to a photograph or pseudophotograph showing a child under 16".

(4) In paragraph 2 (offences under the law of Northern Ireland)—
    (a) in sub-paragraph (1)(c)(iv), for "17" substitute "18"; and
    (b) in sub-paragraph (2), for "17" substitute "18".

73 Grooming and adoption

Schedule 15—
    (a) amends section 15 of the Sexual Offences Act 2003 (c. 42) (meeting a child following sexual grooming etc.),
    (b) amends that Act in relation to adoption, and
    (c) amends the Adoption Act 1976 (c. 36) in relation to offences under sections 64 and 65 of the Sexual Offences Act 2003.

Hatred on the grounds of sexual orientation

74 Hatred on the grounds of sexual orientation

Schedule 16—
    (a) amends Part 3A of the Public Order Act 1986 (c. 64) (hatred against persons on religious grounds) to make provision about hatred against a group of persons defined by reference to sexual orientation, and
    (b) makes minor amendments of that Part.

Offences relating to nuclear material and nuclear facilities

75 Offences relating to the physical protection of nuclear material and nuclear facilities

(1) Part 1 of Schedule 17 amends the Nuclear Material (Offences) Act 1983 (c. 18) to create—
    (a) further offences relating to the physical protection of nuclear material, and
    (b) offences relating to the physical protection of nuclear facilities,
and makes other amendments to that Act.
(2) Part 2 of that Schedule makes related amendments to the Customs and Excise Management Act 1979 (c. 2).

Self-defence etc.

76 Reasonable force for purposes of self-defence etc.

(1) This section applies where in proceedings for an offence—
    (a) an issue arises as to whether a person charged with the offence ("D") is entitled to rely on a defence within subsection (2), and
    (b) the question arises whether the degree of force used by D against a person ("V") was reasonable in the circumstances.
(2) The defences are—
    (a) the common law defence of self-defence; and
    (b) the defences provided by section 3(1) of the Criminal Law Act 1967 (c. 58) or section 3(1) of the Criminal Law Act (Northern Ireland) 1967 (c. 18 (N.I.)) (use of force in prevention of crime or making arrest).
(3) The question whether the degree of force used by D was reasonable in the circumstances is to be decided by reference to the circumstances as D believed them to be, and subsections (4) to (8) also apply in connection with deciding that question.
(4) If D claims to have held a particular belief as regards the existence of any circumstances—

    (a) the reasonableness or otherwise of that belief is relevant to the question whether D genuinely held it; but

    (b) if it is determined that D did genuinely hold it, D is entitled to rely on it for the purposes of subsection (3), whether or not—

        (i) it was mistaken, or

        (ii) (if it was mistaken) the mistake was a reasonable one to have made.

(5) But subsection (4)(b) does not enable D to rely on any mistaken belief attributable to intoxication that was voluntarily induced.

(6) The degree of force used by D is not to be regarded as having been reasonable in the circumstances as D believed them to be if it was disproportionate in those circumstances.

(7) In deciding the question mentioned in subsection (3) the following considerations are to be taken into account (so far as relevant in the circumstances of the case)—

    (a) that a person acting for a legitimate purpose may not be able to weigh to a nicety the exact measure of any necessary action; and

    (b) that evidence of a person's having only done what the person honestly and instinctively thought was necessary for a legitimate purpose constitutes strong evidence that only reasonable action was taken by that person for that purpose.

(8) Subsection (7) is not to be read as preventing other matters from being taken into account where they are relevant to deciding the question mentioned in subsection (3).

(9) This section is intended to clarify the operation of the existing defences mentioned in subsection (2).

(10) In this section—

    (a) "legitimate purpose" means—

        (i) the purpose of self-defence under the common law, or

        (ii) the prevention of crime or effecting or assisting in the lawful arrest of persons mentioned in the provisions referred to in subsection (2)(b);

    (b) references to self-defence include acting in defence of another person; and

    (c) references to the degree of force used are to the type and amount of force used.

Unlawfully obtaining etc. personal data

77 Power to alter penalty for unlawfully obtaining etc. personal data

(1) The Secretary of State may by order provide for a person who is guilty of an offence under section 55 of the Data Protection Act 1998 (c. 29) (unlawful obtaining etc. of personal data) to be liable—

    (a) on summary conviction, to imprisonment for a term not exceeding the specified period or to a fine not exceeding the statutory maximum or to both,

    (b) on conviction on indictment, to imprisonment for a term not exceeding the specified period or to a fine or to both.

(2) In subsection (1)(a) and (b) "specified period" means a period provided for by the order but the period must not exceed—

    (a) in the case of summary conviction, 12 months (or, in Northern Ireland, 6 months), and

    (b) in the case of conviction on indictment, two years.

(3) The Secretary of State must ensure that any specified period for England and Wales which, in the case of summary conviction, exceeds 6 months is to be read as a reference to 6 months so far as it relates to an offence committed before the commencement of section 282(1) of the Criminal Justice Act 2003 (c. 44) (increase in sentencing powers of magistrates' courts from 6 to 12 months for certain offences triable either way).

(4) Before making an order under this section, the Secretary of State must consult—

    (a) the Information Commissioner,

    (b) such media organisations as the Secretary of State considers appropriate, and

(c) such other persons as the Secretary of State considers appropriate.

(5) An order under this section may, in particular, amend the Data Protection Act 1998.

78 New defence for purposes of journalism and other special purposes

In section 55(2) of the Data Protection Act 1998 (c. 29) (defences against offence of unlawfully obtaining etc. personal data) after "it," at the end of paragraph (c) insert—

"(ca) that he acted—

(i) for the special purposes,

(ii) with a view to the publication by any person of any journalistic, literary or artistic material, and

(iii) in the reasonable belief that in the particular circumstances the obtaining, disclosing or procuring was justified as being in the public interest,".

Blasphemy

79 Abolition of common law offences of blasphemy and blasphemous libel

(1) The offences of blasphemy and blasphemous libel under the common law of England and Wales are abolished.

(2) In section 1 of the Criminal Libel Act 1819 (60 Geo. 3 & 1 Geo. 4 c. 8) (orders for seizure of copies of blasphemous or seditious libel) the words "any blasphemous libel, or" are omitted.

(3) In sections 3 and 4 of the Law of Libel Amendment Act 1888 (c. 64) (privileged matters) the words "blasphemous or" are omitted.

(4) Subsections (2) and (3) (and the related repeals in Schedule 28) extend to England and Wales only.

PART 6
INTERNATIONAL CO-OPERATION IN RELATION TO CRIMINAL JUSTICE MATTERS

Recognition of financial penalties: requests to other member States

80 Requests to other member States: England and Wales

(1) In Schedule 5 to the Courts Act 2003 (c. 39) (collection of fines and other sums imposed on conviction) in paragraph 38 (the range of further steps available against defaulters)—

(a) after sub-paragraph (1)(e) insert—

"(f) subject to sub-paragraph (4), issuing a certificate requesting enforcement under the Framework Decision on financial penalties;", and

(b) after sub-paragraph (3) insert—

"(4) A certificate requesting enforcement under the Framework Decision on financial penalties may only be issued where—

(a) the sum due is a financial penalty within the meaning of section 80 of the Criminal Justice and Immigration Act 2008, and

(b) it appears to the fines officer or the court that P is normally resident, or has property or income, in a member State other than the United Kingdom.

(5) In this paragraph, references to a certificate requesting enforcement under the Framework Decision on financial penalties are to be construed in accordance with section 92(3) of the Criminal Justice and Immigration Act 2008."

(2) The designated officer for a magistrates' court may issue a certificate requesting enforcement under the Framework Decision on financial penalties where—

    (a) a person is required to pay a financial penalty,

    (b) the penalty is not paid in full within the time allowed for payment,

    (c) there is no appeal outstanding in relation to the penalty,

    (d) Schedule 5 to the Courts Act 2003 (c. 39) does not apply in relation to the enforcement of the penalty, and

    (e) it appears to the designated officer that the person is normally resident in, or has property or income in, a member State other than the United Kingdom.

(3) For the purposes of subsection (2)(c), there is no appeal outstanding in relation to a financial penalty if—

    (a) no appeal has been brought in relation to the imposition of the financial penalty within the time allowed for making such an appeal, or

    (b) such an appeal has been brought but the proceedings on appeal have been concluded.

(4) Where the person required to pay the financial penalty is a body corporate, subsection (2)(e) applies as if the reference to the person being normally resident in a member State other than the United Kingdom were a reference to the person having its registered office in a member State other than the United Kingdom.

(5) In this section, "financial penalty" means—

    (a) a fine imposed by a court in England and Wales on a person's conviction of an offence;

    (b) any sum payable under a compensation order (within the meaning of section 130(1) of the Powers of Criminal Courts (Sentencing) Act 2000 (c. 6));

    (c) a surcharge under section 161A of the Criminal Justice Act 2003 (c. 44);

    (d) any sum payable under any such order as is mentioned in paragraphs 1 to 9 of Schedule 9 to the Administration of Justice Act 1970 (c. 31) (orders for payment of costs);

    (e) any sum payable by virtue of section 137(1) or (1A) of the Powers of Criminal Courts (Sentencing) Act 2000 (orders requiring parents to pay fines etc.);

    (f) any fine or other sum mentioned in section 82(4)(b)(i) to (iv), or any fine imposed by a court in Scotland, which is enforceable in a local justice area in England and Wales by virtue of section 91 of the Magistrates' Courts Act 1980 (c. 43);

    (g) any other financial penalty, within the meaning of the Framework Decision on financial penalties, specified in an order made by the Lord Chancellor.

81 Procedure on issue of certificate: England and Wales

(1) This section applies where—

    (a) a magistrates' court or a fines officer has, under paragraph 39(3)(b) or 40 of Schedule 5 to the Courts Act 2003 (c. 39), issued a certificate requesting enforcement under the Framework Decision on financial penalties, or

    (b) the designated officer for a magistrates' court has issued such a certificate under section 80(2) of this Act.

(2) The fines officer (in the case of a certificate issued by the officer) or the designated officer for the magistrates' court (in any other case) must give the Lord Chancellor the certificate, together with a certified copy of the decision requiring payment of the financial penalty.

(3) On receipt of the documents mentioned in subsection (2), the Lord Chancellor must give those documents to the central authority or competent authority of the member State in which the person required to pay the penalty appears to be normally resident or (as the case may be) to have property or income.

(4) Where a certified copy of the decision is given to the central authority or competent authority of a member State in accordance with subsection (3), no further steps to enforce the decision may be taken in England and Wales except in accordance with provision made by order by the Lord Chancellor.

(5) Where the person required to pay the financial penalty is a body corporate, subsection (3) applies as if the reference to the member State in which the person appears to be normally

resident were a reference to the member State in which the person appears to have its registered office.

82 Requests to other member States: Northern Ireland

(1) A designated officer of the Northern Ireland Court Service may issue a certificate requesting enforcement under the Framework Decision on financial penalties where—

    (a) a person is required to pay a financial penalty,

    (b) the penalty is not paid in full within the time allowed for payment,

    (c) there is no appeal outstanding in relation to the penalty, and

    (d) it appears to the designated officer that the person is normally resident in, or has property or income in, a member State other than the United Kingdom.

(2) For the purposes of subsection (1)(c), there is no appeal outstanding in relation to a financial penalty if—

    (a) no appeal has been brought in relation to the imposition of the financial penalty within the time allowed for making such an appeal, or

    (b) such an appeal has been brought but the proceedings on appeal have been concluded.

(3) Where the person required to pay the financial penalty is a body corporate, subsection (1)(d) applies as if the reference to the person being normally resident in a member State other than the United Kingdom were a reference to the person having its registered office in a member State other than the United Kingdom.

(4) In this section—

    (a) "designated officer of the Northern Ireland Court Service" means a member of the staff of the Northern Ireland Court Service designated by the Lord Chancellor for the purposes of this section;

    (b) "financial penalty" means—

        (i) a fine imposed by a court in Northern Ireland on a person's conviction of an offence;

        (ii) any sum payable under a compensation order (within the meaning of Article 14 of the Criminal Justice (Northern Ireland) Order 1994 (S.I.1994/2795 (N.I.15));

        (iii) any sum payable under an order made under section 2(1), 4(1) or 5(1) of the Costs in Criminal Cases Act (Northern Ireland) 1968 (N.I. 10) or section 41(1) of the Criminal Appeal (Northern Ireland) Act 1980 (c. 47);

        (iv) any sum payable by virtue of Article 35 of the Criminal Justice (Children) (Northern Ireland) Order 1998 (S.I. 1998/1504 (N.I. 9) (orders requiring parents to pay fines etc.);

        (v) any fine or other sum mentioned in section 80(5)(a) to (e), or any fine imposed by a court in Scotland, which is enforceable in a petty sessions district in Northern Ireland by virtue of Article 96 of the Magistrates' Courts (Northern Ireland) Order 1981 (S.I. 1981/1675 (N.I.26));

        (vi) any other financial penalty, within the meaning of the Framework Decision on financial penalties, specified in an order made by the Lord Chancellor.

83 Procedure on issue of certificate: Northern Ireland

(1) This section applies where a designated officer has issued a certificate under section 82(1).

(2) The designated officer must give the Lord Chancellor the certificate, together with a certified copy of the decision requiring payment of the financial penalty.

(3) On receipt of the documents mentioned in subsection (2), the Lord Chancellor must give those documents to the central authority or competent authority of the member State in which the person required to pay the penalty appears to be normally resident or (as the case may be) to have property or income.

(4) Where a certified copy of the decision is given to the central authority or competent authority of a member State in accordance with subsection (3), no further steps to enforce the decision

may be taken in Northern Ireland except in accordance with provision made by order by the Lord Chancellor.

(5) Where the person required to pay the financial penalty is a body corporate, subsection (3) applies as if the reference to the member State in which the person appears to be normally resident were a reference to the member State in which the person appears to have its registered office.

Recognition of financial penalties: requests from other member States

84 Requests from other member States: England and Wales

(1) This section applies where—
  (a) the competent authority or central authority of a member State other than the United Kingdom gives the Lord Chancellor—
    (i) a certificate requesting enforcement under the Framework Decision on financial penalties, and
    (ii) the decision, or a certified copy of the decision, requiring payment of the financial penalty to which the certificate relates, and
  (b) the financial penalty is suitable for enforcement in England and Wales (see section 91(1)).

(2) If the certificate states that the person required to pay the financial penalty is normally resident in England and Wales, the Lord Chancellor must give the documents mentioned in subsection (1)(a) to the designated officer for the local justice area in which it appears that the person is normally resident.

(3) Otherwise, the Lord Chancellor must give the documents mentioned in subsection (1)(a) to the designated officer for such local justice area as appears appropriate.

(4) Where the Lord Chancellor acts under subsection (2) or (3), the Lord Chancellor must also give the designated officer a notice—
  (a) stating whether the Lord Chancellor thinks that any of the grounds for refusal apply (see section 91(2)), and
  (b) giving reasons for that opinion.

(5) Where the person required to pay the financial penalty is a body corporate, subsection (2) applies as if the reference to the local justice area in which it appears that the person is normally resident were a reference to the local justice area in which it appears that the person has its registered office.

(6) Where—
  (a) the competent authority or central authority of a member State other than the United Kingdom gives the central authority for Scotland the documents mentioned in subsection (1)(a), and
  (b) without taking any action to enforce the financial penalty in Scotland, the central authority for Scotland gives the documents to the Lord Chancellor,
  this section applies as if the competent authority or central authority of the other member State gave the documents to the Lord Chancellor.

85 Procedure on receipt of certificate by designated officer

(1) This section applies where the Lord Chancellor gives the designated officer for a local justice area—
  (a) a certificate requesting enforcement under the Framework Decision on financial penalties,
  (b) the decision, or a certified copy of the decision, requiring payment of the financial penalty to which the certificate relates, and
  (c) a notice under section 84(4).

(2) The designated officer must refer the matter to a magistrates' court acting for that area.

(3) The magistrates' court must decide whether it is satisfied that any of the grounds for refusal apply (see section 91(2)).

(4) The designated officer must inform the Lord Chancellor of the decision of the magistrates' court.

(5) Subsection (6) applies unless the magistrates' court is satisfied that one or more of the grounds for refusal apply.

(6) The enactments specified in subsection (7) apply in relation to the financial penalty as if it were a sum adjudged to be paid by a conviction of the magistrates' court on the date when the court made the decision mentioned in subsection (4).

(7) The enactments specified in this subsection are—

(a) Part 3 of the Magistrates' Courts Act 1980 (c. 43) (satisfaction and enforcement);

(b) Schedules 5 and 6 to the Courts Act 2003 (c. 39) (collection of fines etc. and discharge of fines etc. by unpaid work);

(c) any subordinate legislation (within the meaning of the Interpretation Act 1978 (c. 30)) made under the enactments specified in paragraphs (a) and (b).

(8) If the certificate requesting enforcement under the Framework Decision on financial penalties states that part of the financial penalty has been paid, the reference in subsection (6) to the financial penalty is to be read as a reference to such part of the penalty as remains unpaid.

86 Modification of Magistrates' Courts Act 1980

(1) Section 90 of the Magistrates' Courts Act 1980 is modified as follows in its application to financial penalties by virtue of section 85(6) of this Act.

(2) Subsection (1) applies as if for the words from "he is residing" to the end of that subsection there were substituted "he is residing, or has property or a source of income, in any petty sessions district in Northern Ireland—

(a) the court or the fines officer (as the case may be) may order that payment of the sum shall be enforceable in that petty sessions district, and

(b) if such an order is made, the court or the fines officer must notify the Lord Chancellor."

87 Requests from other member States: Northern Ireland

(1) This section applies where—

(a) the competent authority or central authority of a member State other than the United Kingdom gives the Lord Chancellor—

(i) a certificate requesting enforcement under the Framework Decision on financial penalties, and

(ii) the decision, or a certified copy of the decision, requiring payment of the financial penalty to which the certificate relates, and

(b) the financial penalty is suitable for enforcement in Northern Ireland (see section 91(1)).

(2) If the certificate states that the person required to pay the financial penalty is normally resident in Northern Ireland, the Lord Chancellor must give the documents mentioned in subsection (1)(a) to the clerk of petty sessions for the petty sessions district in which it appears that the person is normally resident.

(3) Otherwise, the Lord Chancellor must give the documents mentioned in subsection (1)(a) to the clerk of petty sessions for such petty sessions district as appears appropriate.

(4) Where the Lord Chancellor acts under subsection (2) or (3), the Lord Chancellor must also give the clerk of petty sessions a notice—

(a) stating whether the Lord Chancellor thinks that any of the grounds for refusal apply (see section 91(2)), and

(b) giving reasons for that opinion.

(5) Where the person required to pay the financial penalty is a body corporate, subsection (2) applies as if the reference to the petty sessions district in which it appears that the person is

normally resident were a reference to the petty sessions district in which it appears that the person has its registered office.

(6) Where—

    (a) the competent authority or central authority of a member State other than the United Kingdom gives the central authority for Scotland the documents mentioned in sub-section (1)(a), and

    (b) without taking any action to enforce the financial penalty in Scotland, the central authority for Scotland gives the documents to the Lord Chancellor,

this section applies as if the competent authority or central authority of the other member State gave the documents to the Lord Chancellor.

88 Procedure on receipt of certificate by clerk of petty sessions

(1) This section applies where the Lord Chancellor gives the clerk of petty sessions for a petty sessions district—

    (a) a certificate requesting enforcement under the Framework Decision on financial penalties,

    (b) the decision, or a certified copy of the decision, requiring payment of the financial penalty to which the certificate relates, and

    (c) a notice under section 87(4).

(2) The clerk must refer the matter to a magistrates' court acting for the petty sessions district.

(3) The magistrates' court must decide whether it is satisfied that any of the grounds for refusal apply (see section 91(2)).

(4) The clerk must inform the Lord Chancellor of the decision of the magistrates' court.

(5) Subsection (6) applies unless the magistrates' court is satisfied that one or more of the grounds for refusal apply.

(6) Part 9 of the Magistrates' Courts (Northern Ireland) Order 1981 (S.I. 1981/1675 (N.I.26)), and any instrument made under that Part, apply in relation to the financial penalty as if it were a sum adjudged to be paid by a conviction of the magistrates' court on the date when the court made the decision mentioned in subsection (4).

(7) If the certificate requesting enforcement under the Framework Decision on financial penalties states that part of the financial penalty has been paid, the reference in subsection (6) to the financial penalty is to be read as a reference to such part of the penalty as remains unpaid.

89 Modification of Magistrates' Courts (Northern Ireland) Order 1981

(1) Part 9 of the Magistrates' Courts (Northern Ireland) Order 1981 is modified as follows in its application to financial penalties by virtue of section 88(6) of this Act.

(2) Article 92 applies in relation to any financial penalty for an amount exceeding £20,000 as if for paragraph (5) there were substituted—

    "(5) The period for which a person may be committed to prison under this Article in default of payment or levy of any sum or part of such sum shall not exceed the maximum period which the Crown Court could have fixed under section 35(1)(c) of the Criminal Justice Act (Northern Ireland) 1945 had the financial penalty been a fine imposed by the Crown Court."

(3) For the purposes of subsection (2), if the amount of a financial penalty is specified in a currency other than sterling, that amount must be converted to sterling by reference to the London closing exchange rate on the relevant date.

(4) In subsection (3), the "relevant date" means the date on which the decision imposing the financial penalty was made.

(5) Article 95 applies as if for the words from "he is residing" in paragraph (1) to the end of that paragraph there were substituted "he is residing, or has property or a source of income, in any local justice area in England and Wales—

    (a) the court may order that payment of the sum shall be enforceable in that local justice area, and

    (b) if such an order is made, the court must notify the Lord Chancellor."

90   Transfer of certificates to central authority for Scotland

(1) This section applies where—

    (a) the competent authority or central authority of a member State other than the United Kingdom gives the Lord Chancellor—

        (i) a certificate requesting enforcement under the Framework Decision on financial penalties, and

        (ii) the decision, or a certified copy of the decision, requiring payment of the financial penalty to which the certificate relates, but

    (b) the Lord Chancellor is not required by section 84 or 87 to give the documents to a designated officer for a local justice area in England and Wales or to a clerk of petty sessions for a petty sessions district in Northern Ireland.

(2) If the certificate states that the person is normally resident or has property or a source of income in Scotland, the Lord Chancellor must give the documents to the central authority for Scotland.

Recognition of financial penalties: miscellaneous

91   Recognition of financial penalties: general

(1) Schedule 18 specifies when a financial penalty is suitable for enforcement in England and Wales for the purposes of section 84(1) and when a financial penalty is suitable for enforcement in Northern Ireland for the purposes of section 87(1).

(2) Schedule 19 specifies the grounds for refusal for the purposes of sections 84(4)(a), 85(3) and (5), 87(4)(a) and 88(3) and (5).

(3) The Lord Chancellor may by order make further provision for or in connection with giving effect to the Framework Decision on financial penalties.

(4) An order under section 81(4), 83(4) or subsection (3) of this section may in particular modify, amend, repeal or revoke any provision of—

    (a) any Act (including this Act and any Act passed in the same Session as this Act);

    (b) subordinate legislation (within the meaning of the Interpretation Act 1978 (c. 30)) made before the passing of this Act;

    (c) Northern Ireland legislation passed, or made, before the passing of this Act;

    (d) any instrument made, before the passing of this Act, under Northern Ireland legislation.

92   Interpretation of sections 80 to 91 etc.

(1) In sections 80 to 91 and Schedules 18 and 19—

"central authority", in relation to a member State other than the United Kingdom, means an authority designated by the State as a central authority for the purposes of the Framework Decision on financial penalties;

"central authority for Scotland" means the person or body which, by virtue of an order under section 56 of the Criminal Proceedings etc. (Reform) (Scotland) Act 2007 (asp 6) (recognition of EU financial penalties), acts as the central authority in relation to Scotland for the purposes of the Framework Decision;

"competent authority", in relation to a member State, means an authority designated by the State as a competent authority for the purposes of that Decision;

"the Framework Decision on financial penalties" means the Framework Decision of the Council of the European Union made on 24 February 2005 on the application of the principle of mutual recognition to financial penalties (2005/214/JHA).

(2) In sections 84 to 91 and Schedules 18 and 19—

"decision" has the meaning given by Article 1 of the Framework Decision on financial penalties (except in sections 85(4) and 88(4));

"financial penalty" has the meaning given by that Article.

(3) References in sections 80 to 91 to a certificate requesting enforcement under the Framework Decision on financial penalties are references to such a certificate as is provided for by Article 4 of that Decision.

Repatriation of prisoners

93 Delivery of prisoner to place abroad for purposes of transfer out of the United Kingdom

In section 2(1) of the Repatriation of Prisoners Act 1984 (c. 47) (transfer out of the UK), for subsection (1) substitute—

"(1) The effect of a warrant under section 1 providing for the transfer of the prisoner out of the United Kingdom shall be to authorise—

(a) the taking of the prisoner to any place in any part of the United Kingdom, his delivery at a place of departure from the United Kingdom into the custody of an appropriate person and his removal by that person from the United Kingdom to a place outside the United Kingdom; or

(b) the taking of the prisoner to any place in any part of the United Kingdom, his removal from the United Kingdom and his delivery, at the place of arrival from the United Kingdom, into the custody of an appropriate person.

(1A) In subsection (1) "appropriate person" means a person representing the appropriate authority of the country or territory to which the prisoner is to be transferred."

94 Issue of warrant transferring responsibility for detention and release of an offender to or from the relevant Minister

After section 4 of the Repatriation of Prisoners Act 1984 (transfer into the United Kingdom) insert—

"Transfer of responsibility for detention and release of offender present outside the country or territory in which he is required to be detained

4A Issue of warrant transferring responsibility for detention and release of offender

(1) This section enables responsibility for the detention and release of a person to whom subsection (2) or (3) applies to be transferred between the relevant Minister in the United Kingdom and the appropriate authority in a country or territory outside the British Islands.

(2) A person falls within this subsection if that person—

(a) is a person to whom section 1(7) applies by virtue of—

(i) an order made in the course of the exercise by a court or tribunal in any part of the United Kingdom of its criminal jurisdiction; or

(ii) any of the provisions of this Act or any similar provisions of the law of any part of the United Kingdom; and

(b) is present in a country or territory outside the British Islands.

(3) A person falls within this subsection if that person—
    (a) is a person to whom section 1(7) applies by virtue of —
        (i) an order made in the course of the exercise by a court or tribunal in a country or territory outside the British Islands of its criminal jurisdiction; or
        (ii) any provisions of the law of such a country or territory which are similar to any of the provisions of this Act; and
    (b) is present in the United Kingdom.

(4) Terms used in subsection (2)(a) and (3)(a) have the same meaning as in section 1(7).

(5) Subject to the following provisions of this section, where—
    (a) the United Kingdom is a party to international arrangements providing for the transfer between the United Kingdom and a country or territory outside the British Islands of responsibility for the detention and release of persons to whom subsection (2) or (3) applies,
    (b) the relevant Minister and the appropriate authority of that country or territory have each agreed to the transfer under those arrangements of responsibility for the detention and release of a particular person to whom subsection (2) or (3) applies (in this Act referred to as "the relevant person"), and
    (c) in a case in which the terms of those arrangements provide for the transfer of responsibility to take place only with the relevant person's consent, that consent has been given,
the relevant Minister shall issue a warrant providing for the transfer of responsibility for the detention and release of the relevant person from that Minister (where subsection (2) applies) or to that Minister (where subsection (3) applies).

(6) The relevant Minister shall not issue a warrant under this section providing for the transfer of responsibility for the detention and release of a person to the relevant Minister unless—
    (a) that person is a British citizen;
    (b) the transfer appears to the relevant Minister to be appropriate having regard to any close ties which that person has with the United Kingdom.

(7) The relevant Minister shall not issue a warrant under this section where, after the duty in subsection (5) has arisen, circumstances arise or are brought to his attention which in his opinion make it inappropriate that the transfer of responsibility should take place.

(8) The relevant Minister shall not issue a warrant under this section (other than one superseding an earlier warrant) unless he is satisfied that all reasonable steps have been taken to inform the relevant person in writing in his own language—
    (a) of the substance, so far as relevant to the case, of the international arrangements in accordance with which it is proposed to transfer responsibility for his detention and release;
    (b) of the effect in relation to the relevant person of the warrant which it is proposed to issue under this section;
    (c) in the case of a person to whom subsection (2) applies, of the effect in relation to his case of so much of the law of the country or territory concerned as has effect with respect to transfers under those arrangements of responsibility for his detention and release;
    (d) in the case of a person to whom subsection (3) applies, of the effect in relation to his case of the law relating to his detention under that warrant and subsequent release (including the effect of any enactment or instrument under which he may be released earlier than provided for by the terms of the warrant); and
    (e) of the powers of the relevant Minister under section 6;
and the relevant Minister shall not issue a warrant superseding an earlier warrant under this section unless the requirements of this subsection were fulfilled in relation to the earlier warrant.

(9) A consent given for the purposes of subsection (5)(c) shall not be capable of being withdrawn after a warrant under this section has been issued in respect of the relevant person; and, accordingly, a purported withdrawal of that consent after that time shall not affect the validity of the warrant, or of any provision which by virtue of section 6 subsequently supersedes provisions of that warrant, or of any direction given in relation to the prisoner under section 4B(3).

(10) In this section "relevant Minister" means—

    (a) the Scottish Ministers in a case where the person who is the subject of the proposed transfer of responsibility is—

        (i) a person to whom subsection (2) applies who is for the time being required to be detained at a place in Scotland; or

        (ii) a person to whom subsection (3) applies, if it is proposed that he will be detained at a place in Scotland;

    (b) the Secretary of State, in any other case.

4B Transfer of responsibility from the United Kingdom

(1) The effect of a warrant under section 4A relating to a person to whom subsection (2) of that section applies shall be to transfer responsibility for the detention and release of that person from the relevant Minister (as defined in section 4A(10)) to the appropriate authority of the country or territory in which he is present.

(2) Subject to subsections (3) to (6), the order by virtue of which the relevant person is required to be detained at the time such a warrant is issued in respect of him shall continue to have effect after the transfer of responsibility so as to apply to him if he comes to be in the United Kingdom at any time when under that order he is to be, or may be, detained.

(3) If, at any time after the transfer of responsibility, it appears to the relevant Minister appropriate to do so in order that effect may be given to the international arrangements in accordance with which the transfer took place, the relevant Minister may give a direction—

    (a) varying the order referred to in subsection (2); or

    (b) providing for the order to cease to have effect.

(4) In subsection (3) "relevant Minister" means—

    (a) the Scottish Ministers, where Scotland is the part of the United Kingdom in which the order referred to in subsection (2) has effect; and

    (b) the Secretary of State in any other case.

(5) The power by direction under subsection (3) to vary the order referred to in subsection (2) includes power by direction—

    (a) to provide for how any period during which the detention and release of the relevant person is, by virtue of a warrant under section 4A, the responsibility of a country or territory outside the United Kingdom is to be treated for the purposes of the order; and

    (b) to provide for the relevant person to be treated as having been released or discharged as mentioned in any paragraph of section 2(4)(b).

(6) Except in relation to any period during which a restriction order is in force in respect of the relevant person, subsection (2) shall not apply in relation to a hospital order; and, accordingly, a hospital order shall cease to have effect in relation to that person—

    (a) at the time of the transfer of responsibility, if no restriction order is in force in respect of him at that time; and

    (b) if at that time a restriction order is in force in respect of him, as soon after the transfer of responsibility as the restriction order ceases to have effect.

(7) In subsection (6) "hospital order" and "restriction order" have the same meaning as in section 2(6).

(8) References in this section to the order by virtue of which a person is required to be detained at the time a warrant under section 4A is issued in respect of him include references to any order by virtue of which he is required to be detained after the order by virtue of which he is required to be detained at that time ceases to have effect.

4C Transfer of responsibility to the United Kingdom

(1) The effect of a warrant under section 4A relating to a person to whom subsection (3) of that section applies shall be to transfer responsibility for the detention and release of that person to the relevant Minister (as defined in section 4A(10)) and to authorise—

    (a) the taking of that person in custody to such place in any part of the United Kingdom as may be specified in the warrant, being a place at which effect may be given to the provisions contained in the warrant by virtue of paragraph (b); and

    (b) the detention of that person in any part of the United Kingdom in accordance with such provisions as may be contained in the warrant, being provisions appearing to the relevant Minister to be appropriate for giving effect to the international arrangements in accordance with which responsibility for that person is transferred.

(2) A provision shall not be contained by virtue of subsection (1)(b) in a warrant under section 4A unless it satisfies the following two conditions, that is to say—

    (a) it is a provision with respect to the detention of a person in a prison, a hospital or any other institution; and

    (b) it is a provision which at the time the warrant is issued may be contained in an order made either—

        (i) in the course of the exercise of its criminal jurisdiction by a court in the part of the United Kingdom in which the person is to be detained; or

        (ii) otherwise than by a court but for the purpose of giving effect to an order made as mentioned in sub-paragraph (i).

(3) Section 3(3) applies for determining for the purposes of paragraph (b) of subsection (1) above what provisions are appropriate for giving effect to the international arrangements mentioned in that paragraph in a relevant person's case as it applies for the purposes of section 3(1)(c) in the case of a prisoner who is to be transferred into the United Kingdom.

(4) Subject to subsection (6) and Part 2 of the Schedule to this Act, a provision contained by virtue of subsection (1)(b) in a warrant under section 4A shall for all purposes have the same effect as the same provision contained in an order made as mentioned in sub-paragraph (i) or, as the case may be, sub-paragraph (ii) of subsection (2)(b).

(5) A provision contained by virtue of subsection (1)(b) in a warrant under section 4A shall take effect with the delivery of the relevant person to the place specified in the warrant for the purposes of subsection (1)(a).

(6) Subsection (4) shall not confer any right of appeal on the relevant person against provisions contained by virtue of subsection (1)(b) in a warrant under this section.

(7) Part 2 of the Schedule to this Act shall have effect with respect to the operation of certain enactments in relation to provisions contained by virtue of subsection (1)(b) in a warrant under section 4A.

(8) For the purposes of determining whether at any particular time any such order as is mentioned in subsection (2)(b) could have been made as so mentioned, there shall be disregarded both—

    (a) any requirement that certain conditions must be satisfied before the order is made; and

    (b) any restriction on the minimum period in respect of which the order may be made."

95 Powers to arrest and detain persons believed to fall within section 4A(3) of Repatriation of Prisoners Act 1984

After section 4C of the Repatriation of Prisoners Act 1984 (c. 47) (as inserted by section 94) insert—

"Persons believed to fall within section 4A(3): powers of arrest and detention

4D Arrest and detention with a view to establishing whether a person falls within section 4A(3) etc.

(1) The Secretary of State or the Scottish Ministers may issue a certificate stating that the issuing authority—

    (a) considers that there are reasonable grounds for believing that a person in the United Kingdom is a person falling within section 4A(3), and

    (b) has requested written confirmation from the country or territory concerned of the details of that person's case.

(2) The issuing authority may send the certificate (with any other documents appearing to the authority to be relevant) to the appropriate judge with a view to obtaining the issue of a warrant under subsection (3).

(3) The appropriate judge may, on receiving the certificate, issue a warrant for the arrest of the person concerned if the judge is satisfied that there are reasonable grounds for believing that the person falls within section 4A(3).

(4) The warrant may be executed anywhere in the United Kingdom by any designated person (and it is immaterial whether or not he is in possession of the warrant or a copy of it).

(5) A person arrested under this section shall, as soon as is practicable—

    (a) be given a copy of the warrant for his arrest; and

    (b) be brought before the appropriate judge.

(6) The appropriate judge may order that a person before him who is the subject of a certificate under this section is to be detained from the time the order is made until the end of the period of seven days beginning with the day after that on which the order is made.

(7) The purpose of an order under subsection (6) is to secure the detention of the person concerned while—

    (a) written confirmation is obtained from a representative of the country or territory concerned of the details of his case;

    (b) it is established whether he is a person falling within section 4A(3); and

    (c) any application for an order under section 4E(6) is made in respect of him.

(8) Subject to subsection (9), a person detained under such an order may be released at any time during the period mentioned in subsection (6) and shall be released at the end of that period (if not released sooner).

(9) Subsection (8) ceases to apply to the detained person if, during that period, an order under section 4E is made in respect of him.

(10) It is immaterial for the purposes of subsection (6) whether or not the person concerned has previously been arrested under this section.

4E Arrest and detention with a view to determining whether to issue a warrant under section 4A

(1) The Secretary of State or the Scottish Ministers may issue a certificate stating that the issuing authority—

    (a) considers that a person in the United Kingdom is a person falling within section 4A(3), and

(b) has received written confirmation from a representative of the country or territory concerned of the details of that person's case;

and it is immaterial for the purposes of this section whether or not the person concerned has been previously arrested or detained under section 4D.

(2) The issuing authority may send the certificate (with a copy of the written confirmation mentioned in subsection (1)(b) and any other documents appearing to that authority to be relevant) to the appropriate judge with a view to obtaining the issue of a warrant under subsection (3).

(3) The appropriate judge may, on receiving the certificate, issue a warrant for the arrest of the person concerned if the judge is satisfied that there are reasonable grounds for believing that the person falls within section 4A(3).

(4) The warrant may be executed anywhere in the United Kingdom by any designated person (and it is immaterial whether or not that person is in possession of the warrant or a copy of it).

(5) A person arrested under this section shall, as soon as is practicable—
    (a) be given a copy of the warrant for his arrest; and
    (b) be brought before the appropriate judge.

(6) The appropriate judge may, on the application of the Secretary of State or the Scottish Ministers, order that a person before the judge who—
    (a) is the subject of a certificate under this section, and
    (b) the judge is satisfied is a person falling within section 4A(3),
    shall be detained from the time the order is made until the end of the period of fourteen days beginning with the day after that on which the order is made.

(7) The purpose of an order under subsection (6) is to secure the detention of the person concerned until—
    (a) it is determined whether to issue a warrant under section 4A; and
    (b) if so determined, such a warrant is issued.

(8) Subject to subsection (9), a person detained under such an order may be released at any time during the period mentioned in subsection (6) and shall be released at the end of that period (if not released sooner).

(9) Subsection (8) ceases to apply to the detained person if, during that period, a warrant under section 4A is issued in respect of him.

(10) It is immaterial for the purposes of subsection (6) whether or not the person concerned has previously been arrested or detained under section 4D or arrested under this section.

4F Sections 4D and 4E: supplementary provisions

(1) This section has effect for the purposes of sections 4D and 4E.

(2) A "designated person" is a person designated by the Secretary of State or the Scottish Ministers.

(3) The appropriate judge is—
    (a) in England and Wales, any District Judge (Magistrates' Courts) who is designated for those purposes by the Lord Chief Justice after consulting the Lord Chancellor;
    (b) in Scotland, the sheriff of Lothian and Borders; and
    (c) in Northern Ireland, any county court judge or resident magistrate who is designated for those purposes by the Lord Chief Justice of Northern Ireland after consulting the Lord Chancellor.

(4) A designation under subsection (2) or (3)(a) or (c) may be made—
    (a) for the purposes of section 4D or 4E (or both); and
    (b) for all cases or only for cases (or cases of a description) specified in the designation.

(5) A designated person shall have all the powers, authority, protection and privileges of a constable in any part of the United Kingdom in which a person who may be arrested under section 4D or 4E is for the time being."

96 Amendments relating to Scotland

(1) The amendments of section 1 of the Repatriation of Prisoners Act 1984 (c. 47) made by section 44(2) and (3) of the Police and Justice Act 2006 (c.48) (which amend the requirement for the prisoner's consent to any transfer to or from the United Kingdom) apply in relation to cases in which the relevant Minister for the purposes of section 1 is the Scottish Ministers as they apply in other cases.

(2) In section 2(6) of the Repatriation of Prisoners Act 1984 (transfer out of the United Kingdom) in the definition of "hospital order", after "1986" insert "or a compulsion order under section 57A of the Criminal Procedure (Scotland) Act 1995".

(3) In section 8(1) (interpretation etc.), before the definition of "international arrangements" insert—

"enactment includes an enactment comprised in, or in an instrument under, an Act of the Scottish Parliament;".

Mutual legal assistance in revenue matters

97 Power to transfer functions under Crime (International Co-operation) Act 2003 in relation to direct taxation

(1) In section 27(1) of the Crime (International Co-operation) Act 2003 (c. 32) (exercise of powers by others)—

(a) in paragraph (a), for "Commissioners of Customs and Excise" substitute "Commissioners for Revenue and Customs"; and

(b) in paragraph (b), for "a customs officer" substitute "an officer of Revenue and Customs".

(2) Paragraph 14 of Schedule 2 to the Commissioners for Revenue and Customs Act 2005 (c. 11) (power under section 27(1) not applicable to former inland revenue matters etc.) ceases to have effect.

PART 7
VIOLENT OFFENDER ORDERS

Violent offender orders

98 Violent offender orders

(1) A violent offender order is an order made in respect of a qualifying offender which—

(a) contains such prohibitions, restrictions or conditions authorised by section 102 as the court making the order considers necessary for the purpose of protecting the public from the risk of serious violent harm caused by the offender, and

(b) has effect for such period of not less than 2, nor more than 5, years as is specified in the order (unless renewed or discharged under section 103).

(2) For the purposes of this Part any reference to protecting the public from the risk of serious violent harm caused by a person is a reference to protecting—

(a) the public in the United Kingdom, or

(b) any particular members of the public in the United Kingdom,

from a current risk of serious physical or psychological harm caused by that person committing one or more specified offences.

(3) In this Part "specified offence" means—
  (a) manslaughter;
  (b) an offence under section 4 of the Offences against the Person Act 1861 (c. 100) (soliciting murder);
  (c) an offence under section 18 of that Act (wounding with intent to cause grievous bodily harm);
  (d) an offence under section 20 of that Act (malicious wounding);
  (e) attempting to commit murder or conspiracy to commit murder; or
  (f) a relevant service offence.
(4) The following are relevant service offences—
  (a) any offence under—
    (i) section 70 of the Army Act 1955 (3 & 4 Eliz. 2 c. 18),
    (ii) section 70 of the Air Force Act 1955 (3 & 4 Eliz. 2 c. 19), or
    (iii) section 42 of the Naval Discipline Act 1957 (c. 53),
  of which the corresponding civil offence (within the meaning of the section in question) is an offence within any of paragraphs (a) to (e) of subsection (3) above; and
  (b) any offence under section 42 of the Armed Forces Act 2006 (c. 52) as respects which the corresponding offence under the law of England and Wales (within the meaning of that section) is an offence within any of those paragraphs.
(5) Section 48 of the Armed Forces Act 2006 (c. 52) (attempts, conspiracy etc.) applies for the purposes of subsection (4)(b) as if the reference in subsection (3)(b) of that section to any of the following provisions of that Act were a reference to subsection (4)(b).

99 Qualifying offenders

(1) In this Part "qualifying offender" means a person aged 18 or over who is within subsection (2) or (4).
(2) A person is within this subsection if (whether before or after the commencement of this Part)—
  (a) the person has been convicted of a specified offence and either—
    (i) a custodial sentence of at least 12 months was imposed for the offence, or
    (ii) a hospital order was made in respect of it (with or without a restriction order),
  (b) the person has been found not guilty of a specified offence by reason of insanity and subsection (3) applies, or
  (c) the person has been found to be under a disability and to have done the act charged in respect of a specified offence and subsection (3) applies.
(3) This subsection applies in the case of a person within (2)(b) or (2)(c) if the court made in respect of the offence—
  (a) a hospital order (with or without a restriction order), or
  (b) a supervision order.
(4) A person is within this subsection if, under the law in force in a country outside England and Wales (and whether before or after the commencement of this Part)—
  (a) the person has been convicted of a relevant offence and either—
    (i) a sentence of imprisonment or other detention for at least 12 months was imposed for the offence, or
    (ii) an order equivalent to that mentioned in subsection (3)(a) was made in respect of it,
  (b) a court exercising jurisdiction under that law has made in respect of a relevant offence a finding equivalent to a finding that the person was not guilty by reason of insanity, and has made in respect of the offence an order equivalent to one mentioned in subsection (3), or
  (c) such a court has, in respect of a relevant offence, made a finding equivalent to a finding that the person was under a disability and did the act charged in respect of the offence, and has made in respect of the offence an order equivalent to one mentioned in subsection (3).

(5) In subsection (4) "relevant offence" means an act which—
   (a) constituted an offence under the law in force in the country concerned, and
   (b) would have constituted a specified offence if it had been done in England and Wales.

(6) An act punishable under the law in force in a country outside England and Wales constitutes an offence under that law for the purposes of subsection (5) however it is described in that law.

(7) Subject to subsection (8), on an application under section 100 the condition in subsection (5)(b) (where relevant) is to be taken as met in relation to the person to whom the application relates ("P") unless, not later than rules of court may provide, P serves on the applicant a notice—
   (a) denying that, on the facts as alleged with respect to the act in question, the condition is met,
   (b) giving the reasons for denying that it is met, and
   (c) requiring the applicant to prove that it is met.

(8) If the court thinks fit, it may permit P to require the applicant to prove that the condition is met even though no notice has been served under subsection (7).

100 Applications for violent offender orders

(1) A chief officer of police may by complaint to a magistrates' court apply for a violent offender order to be made in respect of a person—
   (a) who resides in the chief officer's police area, or
   (b) who the chief officer believes is in, or is intending to come to, that area, if it appears to the chief officer that the conditions in subsection (2) are met.

(2) The conditions are—
   (a) that the person is a qualifying offender, and
   (b) that the person has, since the appropriate date, acted in such a way as to give reasonable cause to believe that it is necessary for a violent offender order to be made in respect of the person.

(3) An application under this section may be made to any magistrates' court whose commission area includes—
   (a) any part of the applicant's police area, or
   (b) any place where it is alleged that the person acted in such a way as is mentioned in subsection (2)(b).

(4) The Secretary of State may by order make provision—
   (a) for applications under this section to be made by such persons or bodies as are specified or described in the order;
   (b) specifying cases or circumstances in which applications may be so made;
   (c) for provisions of this Part to apply, in relation to the making of applications (or cases where applications are made) by any such persons or bodies, with such modifications as are specified in relation to them in the order.

(5) In this Part "the appropriate date" means the date (or, as the case may be, the first date) on which the person became a person within any of paragraphs (a) to (c) of section 99(2) or (4), whether that date fell before or after the commencement of this Part.

101 Making of violent offender orders

(1) This section applies where an application is made to a magistrates' court under section 100 in respect of a person ("P").

(2) After hearing—
   (a) the applicant, and
   (b) P, if P wishes to be heard,
the court may make a violent offender order in respect of P if it is satisfied that the conditions in subsection (3) are met.

(3) The conditions are—
    (a) that P is a qualifying offender, and
    (b) that P has, since the appropriate date, acted in such a way as to make it necessary to make a violent offender order for the purpose of protecting the public from the risk of serious violent harm caused by P.

(4) When deciding whether it is necessary to make such an order for that purpose, the court must have regard to whether P would, at any time when such an order would be in force, be subject under any other enactment to any measures that would operate to protect the public from the risk of such harm.

(5) A violent offender order may not be made so as to come into force at any time when P—
    (a) is subject to a custodial sentence imposed in respect of any offence,
    (b) is on licence for part of the term of such a sentence, or
    (c) is subject to a hospital order or a supervision order made in respect of any offence.

(6) But such an order may be applied for, and made, at such a time.

102 Provisions that orders may contain

(1) A violent offender order may contain prohibitions, restrictions or conditions preventing the offender—
    (a) from going to any specified premises or any other specified place (whether at all, or at or between any specified time or times);
    (b) from attending any specified event;
    (c) from having any, or any specified description of, contact with any specified individual.

(2) Any of the prohibitions, restrictions or conditions contained in a violent offender order may relate to conduct in Scotland or Northern Ireland (as well as to conduct in England or Wales).

(3) The Secretary of State may by order amend subsection (1).

(4) In this section "specified" means specified in the violent offender order concerned.

103 Variation, renewal or discharge of violent offender orders

(1) A person within subsection (2) may by complaint apply to the appropriate magistrates' court—
    (a) for an order varying or discharging a violent offender order;
    (b) for an order (a "renewal order") renewing a violent offender order for such period of not more than 5 years as is specified in the renewal order.

(2) The persons are—
    (a) the offender,
    (b) the chief officer of police who applied for the order,
    (c) (if different) the chief officer of police for the area in which the offender resides, and
    (d) (if different) a chief officer of police who believes that the offender is in, or is intending to come to, his police area.

(3) The "appropriate magistrates' court" means the magistrates' court that made the order or (if different)—
    (a) a magistrates' court for the area in which the offender resides, or
    (b) where the application under this section is made by a chief officer of police, any magistrates' court whose commission area includes any part of the chief officer's police area.

(4) On an application under this section the appropriate magistrates' court may, after hearing—
    (a) the applicant, and
    (b) any other persons mentioned in subsection (2) who wish to be heard,
make such order varying, renewing or discharging the violent offender order as the court considers appropriate.
But this is subject to subsections (5) to (7).

(5) A violent offender order may only be—
  (a) renewed, or
  (b) varied so as to impose additional prohibitions, restrictions or conditions on the offender, if the court considers that it is necessary to do so for the purpose of protecting the public from the risk of serious violent harm caused by the offender (and any renewed or varied order may contain only such prohibitions, restrictions or conditions as the court considers necessary for this purpose).

(6) References in subsection (5) to prohibitions, restrictions or conditions are to prohibitions, restrictions or conditions authorised by section 102.

(7) The court may not discharge the violent offender order before the end of the period of 2 years beginning with the date on which it comes into force under section 101 unless consent to its discharge is given by the offender and—
  (a) where the application under this section is made by a chief officer of police, by that chief officer, or
  (b) where the application is made by the offender, by the chief officer of police for the area in which the offender resides.

104 Interim violent offender orders

(1) This section applies where an application under section 100 ("the main application") has not yet been determined.

(2) An application for an order under this section ("an interim violent offender order") may be made—
  (a) by the complaint by which the main application is made, or
  (b) if the main application has already been made to a court, by means of a further complaint made to that court by the person making the main application.

(3) If it appears to the court—
  (a) that the person to whom the main application relates ("P") is a qualifying offender,
  (b) that, if the court were determining that application, it would be likely to make a violent offender order in respect of P, and
  (c) that it is desirable to act before that application is determined, with a view to securing the immediate protection of the public from the risk of serious violent harm caused by P,
  the court may make an interim violent offender order in respect of P that contains such prohibitions, restrictions or conditions as it considers necessary for the purpose of protecting the public from the risk of such harm.

(4) The reference in subsection (3) to prohibitions, restrictions or conditions is to prohibitions, restrictions or conditions authorised by section 102 in the case of a violent offender order.

(5) But an interim violent offender order may not be made so as to come into force at any time when the person—
  (a) is subject to a custodial sentence for any offence,
  (b) is on licence for part of the term of such a sentence, or
  (c) is subject to a hospital order or a supervision order made in respect of any offence.

(6) An interim violent offender order—
  (a) has effect only for such period as is specified in the order, and
  (b) ceases to have effect (if it has not already done so) at the appropriate time.

(7) "The appropriate time" means—
  (a) if the court grants the main application, the time when a violent offender order made in pursuance of it comes into force;
  (b) if the court decides not to grant the main application or it is withdrawn, the time when the court so decides or the application is withdrawn.

(8) Section 103 applies in relation to the variation or discharge of an interim violent offender order as it applies in relation to the variation or discharge of a violent offender order, but with the omission of subsection (7).

105 Notice of applications

(1) This section applies to—
  (a) any application under section 100 for a violent offender order,
  (b) any application under section 104 for an interim violent offender order, and
  (c) any application under section 103 for the variation, discharge or renewal of a violent offender order, or for the variation or discharge of an interim violent offender order.

(2) A magistrates' court may not begin hearing such an application unless it is satisfied that the relevant person has been given notice of—
  (a) the application, and
  (b) the time and place of the hearing,
  a reasonable time before the hearing.

(3) In this section "the relevant person" means—
  (a) the person to whom the application mentioned in subsection (1)(a) or (b) relates, or
  (b) the person in respect of whom the order mentioned in subsection (1)(c) has been made,
  as the case may be.

106 Appeals

(1) A person in respect of whom—
  (a) a violent offender order, or
  (b) an interim violent offender order,
  has been made may appeal to the Crown Court against the making of the order.

(2) Such a person may also appeal to the Crown Court against—
  (a) the making of an order under section 103, or
  (b) any refusal to make such an order.

(3) On an appeal under this section, the Crown Court—
  (a) may make such orders as may be necessary to give effect to its determination of the appeal; and
  (b) may also make such incidental or consequential orders as appear to it to be just.

(4) For the purposes of section 103(3) an order made by the Crown Court on an appeal made by virtue of subsection (1) or (2) is to be treated as if made by the court from which the appeal was brought.

Notification requirements

107 Offenders subject to notification requirements

(1) References in this Part to an offender subject to notification requirements are references to an offender who is for the time being subject to—
  (a) a violent offender order, or
  (b) an interim violent offender order,
  which is in force under this Part.

(2) Subsection (1) has effect subject to section 110(7) (which excludes from section 110 an offender subject to an interim violent offender order).

108 Notification requirements: initial notification

(1) An offender subject to notification requirements must notify the required information to the police within the period of 3 days beginning with the date on which—
  (a) the violent offender order, or
  (b) the interim violent offender order,
  comes into force in relation to the offender ("the relevant date").

(2) The "required information" is the following information about the offender—
   (a) date of birth;
   (b) national insurance number;
   (c) name on the relevant date or, if the offender used two or more names on that date, each of those names;
   (d) home address on the relevant date;
   (e) name on the date on which the notification is given or, if the offender used two or more names on that date, each of those names;
   (f) home address on the date on which the notification is given;
   (g) the address of any other premises in the United Kingdom at which on that date the offender regularly resides or stays;
   (h) any prescribed information.
(3) In subsection (2)(h) "prescribed" means prescribed by regulations made by the Secretary of State.
(4) When determining the period of 3 days mentioned in subsection (1), there is to be disregarded any time when the offender is—
   (a) remanded in or committed to custody by an order of a court or kept in service custody;
   (b) serving a sentence of imprisonment or a term of service detention;
   (c) detained in a hospital; or
   (d) outside the United Kingdom.
(5) In this Part "home address" means in relation to the offender—
   (a) the address of the offender's sole or main residence in the United Kingdom, or
   (b) if the offender has no such residence, the address or location of a place in the United Kingdom where the offender can regularly be found or, if there is more than one such place, such one of them as the offender selects.

109 Notification requirements: changes

(1) An offender subject to notification requirements must notify to the police—
   (a) the required new information, and
   (b) the information mentioned in section 108(2),
   within the period of 3 days beginning with the date on which any notifiable event occurs.
(2) A "notifiable event" means—
   (a) the use by the offender of a name which has not been notified to the police under section 108 or this section;
   (b) any change of the offender's home address;
   (c) the expiry of any qualifying period during which the offender has resided or stayed at any premises in the United Kingdom the address of which has not been notified to the police under section 108 or this section,
   (d) any prescribed change of circumstances, or
   (e) the release of the offender from custody pursuant to an order of a court or from imprisonment, service detention or detention in a hospital.
(3) The "required new information" is—
   (a) the name referred to in subsection (2)(a),
   (b) the new home address (see subsection (2)(b)),
   (c) the address of the premises referred to in subsection (2)(c),
   (d) the prescribed details, or
   (e) the fact that the offender has been released as mentioned in subsection (2)(e),
   as the case may be.
(4) A notification under subsection (1) may be given before the notifiable event occurs, but in that case the offender must also specify the date when the event is expected to occur.
(5) If a notification is given in accordance with subsection (4) and the event to which it relates occurs more than 2 days before the date specified, the notification does not affect the duty imposed by subsection (1).

(6) If a notification is given in accordance with subsection (4) and the event to which it relates has not occurred by the end of the period of 3 days beginning with the date specified—

    (a) the notification does not affect the duty imposed by subsection (1), and

    (b) the offender must, within the period of 6 days beginning with the date specified, notify to the police the fact that the event did not occur within the period of 3 days beginning with the date specified.

(7) Section 108(4) applies to the determination of—

    (a) any period of 3 days for the purposes of subsection (1), or

    (b) any period of 6 days for the purposes of subsection (6),

as it applies to the determination of the period of 3 days mentioned in section 108(1).

(8) In this section—

    (a) "prescribed change of circumstances" means any change—

        (i) occurring in relation to any matter in respect of which information is required to be notified by virtue of section 108(2)(h), and

        (ii) of a description prescribed by regulations made by the Secretary of State;

    (b) "the prescribed details", in relation to a prescribed change of circumstances, means such details of the change as may be so prescribed.

(9) In this section "qualifying period" means—

    (a) a period of 7 days, or

    (b) two or more periods, in any period of 12 months, which taken together amount to 7 days.

110 Notification requirements: periodic notification

(1) An offender subject to notification requirements must, within the applicable period after each notification date, notify to the police the information mentioned in section 108(2), unless the offender has already given a notification under section 109(1) within that period.

(2) A "notification date" means, in relation to the offender, the date of any notification given by the offender under section 108(1) or 109(1) or subsection (1) above.

(3) Where the applicable period would (apart from this subsection) end while subsection (4) applies, that period is to be treated as continuing until the end of the period of 3 days beginning with the date on which subsection (4) first ceases to apply.

(4) This subsection applies if the offender is—

    (a) remanded in or committed to custody by an order of a court or kept in service custody,

    (b) serving a sentence of imprisonment or a term of service detention,

    (c) detained in a hospital, or

    (d) outside the United Kingdom.

(5) In this section "the applicable period" means—

    (a) in any case where subsection (6) applies, such period as may be prescribed by regulations made by the Secretary of State, and

    (b) in any other case, the period of one year.

(6) This subsection applies if the last home address notified by the offender under section 108(1) or 109(1) or subsection (1) above was the address or location of such a place as is mentioned in section 108(5)(b).

(7) Nothing in this section applies to an offender who is subject to an interim violent offender order.

111 Notification requirements: travel outside United Kingdom

(1) The Secretary of State may by regulations make provision with respect to offenders subject to notification requirements, or any description of such offenders—

    (a) requiring such persons, before they leave the United Kingdom, to give in accordance with the regulations a notification under subsection (2);

    (b) requiring such persons, if they subsequently return to the United Kingdom, to give in accordance with the regulations a notification under subsection (3).

(2) A notification under this subsection must disclose—
   (a) the date on which the offender proposes to leave the United Kingdom;
   (b) the country (or, if there is more than one, the first country) to which the offender proposes to travel and the proposed point of arrival (determined in accordance with the regulations) in that country;
   (c) any other information prescribed by the regulations which the offender holds about the offender's departure from or return to the United Kingdom, or about the offender's movements while outside the United Kingdom.

(3) A notification under this subsection must disclose any information prescribed by the regulations about the offender's return to the United Kingdom.

112 Method of notification and related matters

(1) An offender gives a notification to the police under section 108(1), 109(1) or 110(1) by—
   (a) attending at any police station in the offender's local police area, and
   (b) giving an oral notification to any police officer, or to any person authorised for the purpose by the officer in charge of the station.

(2) An offender giving a notification under section 109(1)—
   (a) in relation to a prospective change of home address, or
   (b) in relation to such premises as are mentioned in section 109(2)(c),
   may also give the notification at a police station that would fall within subsection (1)(a) above if the change of home address had already occurred or (as the case may be) the premises in question were the offender's home address.

(3) Any notification given in accordance with this section must be acknowledged; and the acknowledgement must be—
   (a) in writing, and
   (b) in such form as the Secretary of State may direct.

(4) Where a notification is given under section 108(1), 109(1) or 110(1), the offender must, if requested to do so by the police officer or other person mentioned in subsection (1)(b) above, allow that officer or person to—
   (a) take the offender's fingerprints,
   (b) photograph any part of the offender, or
   (c) do both of those things,
   in order to verify the offender's identity.

(5) In this section—
   "local police area", in relation to the offender, means—
   (a) the police area in England and Wales in which the home address is situated,
   (b) in the absence of a home address in England and Wales, the police area in England and Wales in which the home address last notified is situated, or
   (c) in the absence of such a home address and any such notification, the police area in which the court that made the violent offender order (or, as the case may be, the interim violent offender order) is situated;
   "photograph" includes any process by means of which an image may be produced.

Supplementary

113 Offences

(1) If a person fails, without reasonable excuse, to comply with any prohibition, restriction or condition contained in—
   (a) a violent offender order, or
   (b) an interim violent offender order,
   the person commits an offence.

(2) If a person fails, without reasonable excuse, to comply with—
  (a) section 108(1), 109(1) or (6)(b), 110(1) or 112(4), or
  (b) any requirement imposed by regulations made under section 111(1),
  the person commits an offence.
(3) If a person notifies to the police, in purported compliance with—
  (a) section 108(1), 109(1) or 110(1), or
  (b) any requirement imposed by regulations made under section 111(1),
  any information which the person knows to be false, the person commits an offence.
(4) As regards an offence under subsection (2), so far as it relates to noncompliance with—
  (a) section 108(1), 109(1) or 110(1), or
  (b) any requirement imposed by regulations made under section 111(1),
  a person commits such an offence on the first day on which the person first fails, without reasonable excuse, to comply with the provision mentioned in paragraph (a) or (as the case may be) the requirement mentioned in paragraph (b), and continues to commit it throughout any period during which the failure continues.
(5) But a person must not be prosecuted under subsection (2) more than once in respect of the same failure.
(6) A person guilty of an offence under this section is liable—
  (a) on summary conviction, to imprisonment for a term not exceeding the relevant period or a fine not exceeding the statutory maximum or both;
  (b) on conviction on indictment, to imprisonment for a term not exceeding 5 years or a fine or both.
(7) In subsection (6)(a) "the relevant period" means—
  (a) in relation to England and Wales and Scotland, 12 months;
  (b) in relation to Northern Ireland, 6 months.
(8) Proceedings for an offence under this section may be commenced in any court having jurisdiction in any place where the person charged with the offence resides or is found.

114 Supply of information to Secretary of State etc.

(1) This section applies to information notified to the police under section 108(1), 109(1) or 110(1).
(2) A chief officer of police may, for the purposes of the prevention, detection, investigation or prosecution of offences under this Part, supply information to which this section applies to—
  (a) the Secretary of State, or
  (b) a person providing services to the Secretary of State in connection with a relevant function,
  for use for the purpose of verifying the information.
(3) In relation to information supplied to any person under subsection (2), the reference to verifying the information is a reference to—
  (a) checking its accuracy by comparing it with information held—
    (i) where the person is the Secretary of State, by that person in connection with the exercise of a relevant function, or
    (ii) where the person is within subsection (2)(b), by that person in connection with the provision of services as mentioned there, and
  (b) compiling a report of that comparison.
(4) Subject to subsection (5), the supply of information under this section is to be taken not to breach any restriction on the disclosure of information (however arising).
(5) This section does not authorise the doing of anything that contravenes the Data Protection Act 1998 (c. 29).
(6) This section does not affect any power to supply information that exists apart from this section.

(7) In this section "relevant function" means—
  (a) a function relating to social security, child support, employment or training,
  (b) a function relating to passports, or
  (c) a function under Part 3 of the Road Traffic Act 1988 (c. 52).

115 Supply of information by Secretary of State etc.

(1) A report compiled under section 114 may be supplied to a chief officer of police by—
  (a) the Secretary of State, or
  (b) a person within section 114(2)(b).
(2) Such a report may contain any information held—
  (a) by the Secretary of State in connection with the exercise of a relevant function, or
  (b) by a person within section 114(2)(b) in connection with the provision of services as mentioned there.
(3) Where such a report contains information within subsection (2), the chief officer to whom it is supplied—
  (a) may retain the information, whether or not used for the purposes of the prevention, detection, investigation or prosecution of offences under this Part, and
  (b) may use the information for any purpose related to the prevention, detection, investigation or prosecution of offences (whether or not under this Part), but for no other purpose.
(4) Subsections (4) to (7) of section 114 apply in relation to this section as they apply in relation to section 114.

116 Information about release or transfer

(1) This section applies to an offender subject to notification requirements who is—
  (a) serving a sentence of imprisonment or a term of service detention, or
  (b) detained in a hospital.
(2) The Secretary of State may by regulations make provision requiring the person who is responsible for such an offender to give notice to specified persons—
  (a) of the fact that that person has become responsible for the offender; and
  (b) of any occasion when—
    (i) the offender is released, or
    (ii) a different person is to become responsible for the offender.
(3) In subsection (2) "specified persons" means persons specified, or of a description specified, in the regulations.
(4) The regulations may make provision for determining who is to be taken for the purposes of this section as being responsible for an offender.

117 Interpretation of Part 7

(1) In this Part—
  "the appropriate date" has the meaning given by section 100(5);
  "country" includes territory;
  "custodial sentence" means—
    (a) a sentence of imprisonment, any other sentence or order mentioned in section 76(1) of the Powers of Criminal Courts (Sentencing) Act 2000 (c. 6) (as in force at any time after the passing of this Act) or any corresponding sentence or order imposed or made under any earlier enactment, or
    (b) a relevant service sentence (see subsection (2) below);
  "home address" has the meaning given by section 108(5);
  "hospital order" means—
    (a) an order under section 37 of the Mental Health Act 1983 (c. 20) or section 60 of the Mental Health Act 1959 (c. 72), or

(b) any other order providing for the admission of a person to hospital following a finding of the kind mentioned in section 99(2)(b) or (c) of this Act;

"interim violent offender order" means an order made under section 104;

"kept in service custody" means kept in service custody by virtue of an order under section 105(2) of the Armed Forces Act 2006 (c. 52);

"the offender", in relation to a violent offender order or an interim violent offender order, means the person in respect of whom the order is made;

"qualifying offender" has the meaning given by section 99(1);

"restriction order" means an order under section 41 of the Mental Health Act 1983 or section 65 of the Mental Health Act 1959;

"service detention" has the meaning given by section 374 of the Armed Forces Act 2006;

"specified offence" has the meaning given by section 98(3);

"supervision order" means—

(a) a supervision order within the meaning of Schedule 1A to the Criminal Procedure (Insanity) Act 1964 (c. 84), or

(b) a supervision and treatment order within the meaning of Schedule 2 to that Act;

"violent offender order" has the meaning given by section 98(1).

(2) The following are relevant service sentences—

(a) a sentence of imprisonment passed under the Army Act 1955 (3 & 4 Eliz. 2 c. 18), the Air Force Act 1955 (3 & 4 Eliz. 2 c. 19) or the Naval Discipline Act 1957 (c. 53);

(b) a sentence of custody for life, or detention, under section 71A of either of those Acts of 1955 or section 43A of that Act of 1957;

(c) a sentence under a custodial order within the meaning of—

(i) section 71AA of, or paragraph 10 of Schedule 5A to, either of those Acts of 1955, or

(ii) section 43AA of, or paragraph 10 of Schedule 4A to, that Act of 1957;

(d) a custodial sentence within the meaning of the Armed Forces Act 2006 (c. 52) (see section 374 of that Act).

(3) References in this Part to protecting the public from the risk of serious violent harm caused by a person are to be read in accordance with section 98(2).

(4) References in this Part to a finding of the kind mentioned in section 99(2)(b) or (c) or (4)(b) or (c) include references to a case where a decision on appeal is to the effect that there should have been such a finding in the proceedings concerned.

(5) References in this Part to an offender subject to notification requirements are to be read in accordance with section 107.

(6) The following expressions have the same meanings as in Part 2 of the Sexual Offences Act 2003 (c. 42) (notifications and orders)—

"detained in a hospital" (see sections 133 and 135 of that Act);

"sentence of imprisonment" (see section 131 of that Act);

and references to a person having been found to be under a disability and to have done the act charged are to be read in accordance with section 135 of that Act.

PART 8
ANTI-SOCIAL BEHAVIOUR

Premises closure orders

118 Closure orders: premises associated with persistent disorder or nuisance

Schedule 20 inserts a new Part 1A into the Anti-social Behaviour Act 2003 (c. 38) which makes provision about the issue of closure notices and the making of closure orders in respect of premises associated with persistent disorder or nuisance.

Nuisance or disturbance on hospital premises

119 Offence of causing nuisance or disturbance on NHS premises

(1) A person commits an offence if—

    (a) the person causes, without reasonable excuse and while on NHS premises, a nuisance or disturbance to an NHS staff member who is working there or is otherwise there in connection with work,

    (b) the person refuses, without reasonable excuse, to leave the NHS premises when asked to do so by a constable or an NHS staff member, and

    (c) the person is not on the NHS premises for the purpose of obtaining medical advice, treatment or care for himself or herself.

(2) A person who commits an offence under this section is liable on summary conviction to a fine not exceeding level 3 on the standard scale.

(3) For the purposes of this section—

    (a) a person ceases to be on NHS premises for the purpose of obtaining medical advice, treatment or care for himself or herself once the person has received the advice, treatment or care, and

    (b) a person is not on NHS premises for the purpose of obtaining medical advice, treatment or care for himself or herself if the person has been refused the advice, treatment or care during the last 8 hours.

(4) In this section—

"English NHS premises" means—

    (a) any hospital vested in, or managed by, a relevant English NHS body,

    (b) any building or other structure, or vehicle, associated with the hospital and situated on hospital grounds (whether or not vested in, or managed by, a relevant English NHS body), and

    (c) the hospital grounds,

"hospital grounds" means land in the vicinity of a hospital and associated with it,

"NHS premises" means English NHS premises or Welsh NHS premises,

"NHS staff member" means a person employed by a relevant English NHS body, or a relevant Welsh NHS body, or otherwise working for such a body (whether as or on behalf of a contractor, as a volunteer or otherwise),

"relevant English NHS body" means—

    (a) a National Health Service trust (see section 25 of the National Health Service Act 2006 (c. 41)), all or most of whose hospitals, establishments and facilities are situated in England,

    (b) a Primary Care Trust (see section 18 of that Act), or

    (c) an NHS foundation trust (see section 30 of that Act),

"relevant Welsh NHS body" means—

    (a) a National Health Service trust (see section 18 of the National Health Service (Wales) Act 2006 (c. 42)), all or most of whose hospitals, establishments and facilities are situated in Wales, or

    (b) a Local Health Board (see section 11 of that Act),

"vehicle" includes an air ambulance,

"Welsh NHS premises" means—

    (a) any hospital vested in, or managed by, a relevant Welsh NHS body,

    (b) any building or other structure, or vehicle, associated with the hospital and situated on hospital grounds (whether or not vested in, or managed by, a relevant Welsh NHS body), and

    (c) the hospital grounds.

120 Power to remove person causing nuisance or disturbance

(1) If a constable reasonably suspects that a person is committing or has committed an offence under section 119, the constable may remove the person from the NHS premises concerned.

(2) If an authorised officer reasonably suspects that a person is committing or has committed an offence under section 119, the authorised officer may—

(a) remove the person from the NHS premises concerned, or

(b) authorise an appropriate NHS staff member to do so.

(3) Any person removing another person from NHS premises under this section may use reasonable force (if necessary).

(4) An authorised officer cannot remove a person under this section or authorise another person to do so if the authorised officer has reason to believe that—

(a) the person to be removed requires medical advice, treatment or care for himself or herself, or

(b) the removal of the person would endanger the person's physical or mental health.

(5) In this section—

"appropriate NHS staff member"—

(a) in relation to English NHS premises, means an English NHS staff member, and

(b) in relation to Welsh NHS premises, means a Welsh NHS staff member,

"authorised officer"—

(a) in relation to English NHS premises, means any English NHS staff member authorised by a relevant English NHS body to exercise the powers which are conferred by this section on an authorised officer in respect of English NHS premises, and

(b) in relation to Welsh NHS premises, means any Welsh NHS staff member authorised by a relevant Welsh NHS body to exercise the powers which are conferred by this section on an authorised officer in respect of Welsh NHS premises,

"English NHS staff member" means a person employed by a relevant English NHS body or otherwise working for it (whether as or on behalf of a contractor, as a volunteer or otherwise),

"Welsh NHS staff member" means a person employed by a relevant Welsh NHS body or otherwise working for it (whether as or on behalf of a contractor, as a volunteer or otherwise).

(6) Terms defined in section 119 have the same meaning in this section as in that section.

121 Guidance about the power to remove etc.

(1) The appropriate national authority may from time to time prepare and publish guidance to relevant NHS bodies and authorised officers about the powers in section 120.

(2) Such guidance may, in particular, relate to—

(a) the authorisation by relevant NHS bodies of authorised officers,

(b) the authorisation by authorised officers of appropriate NHS staff members to remove persons under section 120,

(c) training requirements for authorised officers and persons authorised by them to remove persons under section 120,

(d) matters that may be relevant to a consideration by authorised officers for the purposes of section 120 of whether offences are being, or have been, committed under section 119,

(e) matters to be taken into account by authorised officers in deciding whether there is reason to believe that a person requires medical advice, treatment or care for himself or herself or that the removal of a person would endanger the person's physical or mental health,

(f) the procedure to be followed by authorised officers or persons authorised by them before using the power of removal in section 120,

(g) the degree of force that it may be appropriate for authorised officers or persons authorised by them to use in particular circumstances,

(h) arrangements for ensuring that persons on NHS premises are aware of the offence in section 119 and the powers of removal in section 120, or

(i) the keeping of records.

(3) Before publishing guidance under this section, the appropriate national authority must consult such persons as the authority considers appropriate.

(4) A relevant NHS body and an authorised officer must, when exercising functions under, or in connection with, section 120, have regard to any guidance published by the appropriate national authority under this section.

(5) In this section—

"appropriate national authority"—

> (a) in relation to a relevant English NHS body and authorised officers in respect of English NHS premises, means the Secretary of State, and
>
> (b) in relation to a relevant Welsh NHS body and authorised officers in respect of Welsh NHS premises, means the Welsh Ministers,

"appropriate NHS staff member" and "authorised officer" have the same meaning as in section 120,

"relevant NHS body" means a relevant English NHS body or a relevant Welsh NHS body.

(6) Terms defined in section 119 have the same meaning in this section as in that section.

122 Nuisance or disturbance on HSS premises

Schedule 21 makes provision for Northern Ireland corresponding to the provision made for England and Wales by sections 119 to 121.

Anti-social behaviour orders etc. in respect of children and young persons

123 Review of anti-social behaviour orders etc.

(1) In Part 1 of the Crime and Disorder Act 1998 (c. 37) (prevention of crime and disorder) after section 1I insert—

"**1J Review of orders under sections 1, 1B and 1C**

> (1) This section applies where—
>
> > (a) an anti-social behaviour order,
> >
> > (b) an order under section 1B, or
> >
> > (c) an order under section 1C,
>
> has been made in respect of a person under the age of 17.
>
> (2) If—
>
> > (a) the person subject to the order will be under the age of 18 at the end of a period specified in subsection (3) (a "review period"), and
> >
> > (b) the term of the order runs until the end of that period or beyond, then before the end of that period a review of the operation of the order shall be carried out.
>
> (3) The review periods are—
>
> > (a) the period of 12 months beginning with—
> >
> > > (i) the day on which the order was made, or
> > >
> > > (ii) if during that period there is a supplemental order (or more than one), the date of the supplemental order (or the last of them);
> >
> > (b) a period of 12 months beginning with—
> >
> > > (i) the day after the end of the previous review period, or
> > >
> > > (ii) if during that period there is a supplemental order (or more than one), the date of the supplemental order (or the last of them).
>
> (4) In subsection (3) "supplemental order" means—
>
> > (a) a further order varying the order in question;
> >
> > (b) an individual support order made in relation to the order in question on an application under section 1AA(1A).
>
> (5) Subsection (2) does not apply in relation to any review period if the order is discharged before the end of that period.
>
> (6) A review under this section shall include consideration of—
>
> > (a) the extent to which the person subject to the order has complied with it;

(b) the adequacy of any support available to the person to help him comply with it;

(c) any matters relevant to the question whether an application should be made for the order to be varied or discharged.

(7) Those carrying out or participating in a review under this section shall have regard to any guidance issued by the Secretary of State when considering—

(a) how the review should be carried out;

(b) what particular matters should be dealt with by the review;

(c) what action (if any) it would be appropriate to take in consequence of the findings of the review.

1K Responsibility for, and participation in, reviews under section 1J

(1) A review under section 1J of an anti-social behaviour order or an order under section 1B shall be carried out by the relevant authority that applied for the order.

(2) A review under section 1J of an order under section 1C shall be carried out—

(a) (except where paragraph (b) applies) by the appropriate chief officer of police;

(b) where a relevant authority is specified under section 1C(9ZA), by that authority.

(3) A local authority, in carrying out a review under section 1J, shall act in co-operation with the appropriate chief officer of police; and it shall be the duty of that chief officer to co-operate in the carrying out of the review.

(4) The chief officer of police of a police force, in carrying out a review under section 1J, shall act in co-operation with the appropriate local authority; and it shall be the duty of that local authority to co-operate in the carrying out of the review.

(5) A relevant authority other than a local authority or chief officer of police, in carrying out a review under section 1J, shall act in cooperation with—

(a) the appropriate local authority, and

(b) the appropriate chief officer of police;

and it shall be the duty of that local authority and that chief officer to co-operate in the carrying out of the review.

(6) A chief officer of police or other relevant authority carrying out a review under section 1J may invite the participation in the review of a person or body not required by subsection (3), (4) or (5) to co-operate in the carrying out of the review.

(7) In this section—

"the appropriate chief officer of police" means the chief officer of police of the police force maintained for the police area in which the person subject to the order resides or appears to reside;

"the appropriate local authority" means the council for the local government area (within the meaning given in section 1(12)) in which the person subject to the order resides or appears to reside."

(2) In section 1(1A) of that Act (meaning of "relevant authority") for "1CA, 1E and 1F" substitute "1C, 1CA, 1E, IF and 1K".

(3) In section 1C of that Act (orders on conviction in criminal proceedings) after section (9) insert—

"(9ZA) An order under this section made in respect of a person under the age of 17, or an order varying such an order, may specify a relevant authority (other than the chief officer of police mentioned in section 1K(2)(a)) as being responsible for carrying out a review under section 1J of the operation of the order."

124 Individual support orders

(1) In section 1AA of the Crime and Disorder Act 1998 (c. 37) (individual support orders) for subsection (1) and the words in subsection (2) before paragraph (a) substitute—

"(1) This section applies where a court makes an anti-social behaviour order in respect of a defendant who is a child or young person when that order is made.

    (1A) This section also applies where—

        (a) an anti-social behaviour order has previously been made in respect of such a defendant;

        (b) an application is made by complaint to the court which made that order, by the relevant authority which applied for it, for an order under this section; and

        (c) at the time of the hearing of the application—

            (i) the defendant is still a child or young person, and

            (ii) the anti-social behaviour order is still in force.

    (1B) The court must consider whether the individual support conditions are fulfilled and, if satisfied that they are, must make an individual support order.

    (2) An individual support order is an order which—".

(2) In subsection (3)(a) of that section, for the words after "the kind of behaviour which led to" substitute "the making of—

        (i) the anti-social behaviour order, or

        (ii) an order varying that order (in a case where the variation is made as a result of further anti-social behaviour by the defendant);".

(3) In subsection (5) of that section, for "which led to the making of the anti-social behaviour order" substitute "mentioned in subsection (3)(a) above".

(4) In section 1(1A) of that Act (meaning of "relevant authority") after "and sections" insert "1AA,".

(5) In section 1AB of that Act (which makes further provision about individual support orders) after subsection (5) insert—

    "(5A) The period specified as the term of an individual support order made on an application under section 1AA(1A) above must not be longer than the remaining part of the term of the anti-social behaviour order as a result of which it is made."

(6) In section 1B of that Act (orders in county court proceedings) after subsection (7) insert—

    "(8) Sections 1AA and 1AB apply in relation to orders under this section, with any necessary modifications, as they apply in relation to antisocial behaviour orders.

    (9) In their application by virtue of subsection (8), sections 1AA(1A)(b) and 1AB(6) have effect as if the words "by complaint" were omitted."

(7) In section 1C of that Act (orders on conviction in criminal proceedings) after subsection (9A) insert—

    "(9AA) Sections 1AA and 1AB apply in relation to orders under this section, with any necessary modifications, as they apply in relation to antisocial behaviour orders.

    (9AB) In their application by virtue of subsection (9AA), sections 1AA(1A)(b) and 1AB(6) have effect as if the words "by complaint" were omitted.

    (9AC) In its application by virtue of subsection (9AA), section 1AA(1A)(b) has effect as if the reference to the relevant authority which applied for the anti-social behaviour order were a reference to the chief officer of police, or other relevant authority, responsible under section 1K(2)(a) or (b) for carrying out a review of the order under this section."

Parenting contracts and parenting orders

125 Parenting contracts and parenting orders: local authorities

(1) Part 3 of the Anti-social Behaviour Act 2003 (c. 38) (parental responsibilities) is amended as follows.

(2) In section 29(1) (interpretation) in the definition of "local authority" for paragraphs (b) and (c) substitute—

    "(aa) a district council in England;".

(3) In section 26B (parenting orders: registered social landlords)—

    (a) in subsection (8), after "the local authority" insert "(or, if subsection (8A) applies, each local authority)";

(b) after that subsection insert—

"(8A) This subsection applies if the place where the child or young person resides or appears to reside is within the area of a county council and within the area of a district council.";

(c) in subsection (10)(a), after "the local authority" insert "(or authorities)".

(4) In section 27 (parenting orders: supplemental) for subsection (3A) substitute—

"(3A) Proceedings for an offence under section 9(7) of the 1998 Act (parenting orders: breach of requirement etc.) as applied by subsection (3)(b) above may be brought by any of the following local authorities—

(a) the local authority that applied for the order, if the child or young person, or the person alleged to be in breach, resides or appears to reside in that authority's area;

(b) the local authority of the child or young person, if that child or young person does not reside or appear to reside in the area of the local authority that applied for the order;

(c) the local authority of the person alleged to be in breach, if that person does not reside or appear to reside in the area of the local authority that applied for the order.

(3B) For the purposes of subsection (3A)(b) and (c)—

(a) an individual's local authority is the local authority in whose area the individual resides or appears to reside; but

(b) if the place where an individual resides or appears to reside is within the area of a county council and within the area of a district council, a reference to that individual's local authority is to be read as a reference to either of those authorities."

PART 9

POLICING

Misconduct procedures etc.

126 Police misconduct and performance procedures

(1) Part 1 of Schedule 22—

(a) amends the Police Act 1996 (c. 16) to make provision for or in connection with disciplinary and other proceedings in respect of the conduct and performance of members of police forces and special constables, and

(b) makes other minor amendments to that Act.

(2) Part 2 of that Schedule makes equivalent amendments to the Ministry of Defence Police Act 1987 (c. 4) for the purposes of the Ministry of Defence Police.

(3) Part 3 of that Schedule makes equivalent amendments to the Railways and Transport Safety Act 2003 (c. 20) for the purposes of the British Transport Police.

127 Investigation of complaints of police misconduct etc.

Schedule 23 amends the Police Reform Act 2002 (c. 30) to make further provision about the investigation of complaints of police misconduct and other matters.

Financial assistance

128 Financial assistance under section 57 of Police Act 1996

(1) After section 57(1) of the Police Act 1996 (common services: power for Secretary of State to provide and maintain etc. organisations, facilities and services which promote the efficiency or effectiveness of police) insert—

"(1A) The power conferred by subsection (1) includes power to give financial assistance to any person in connection with the provision or maintenance of such organisations, facilities and services as are mentioned in that subsection.

(1B) Financial assistance under subsection (1)—
- (a) may, in particular, be given in the form of a grant, loan or guarantee or investment in a body corporate; and
- (b) may be given subject to terms and conditions determined by the Secretary of State; but any financial assistance under that subsection other than a grant requires the consent of the Treasury.

(1C) Terms and conditions imposed under subsection (1B)(b) may include terms and conditions as to repayment with or without interest.

(1D) Any sums received by the Secretary of State by virtue of terms and conditions imposed under that subsection are to be paid into the Consolidated Fund."

(2) Any loan made by the Secretary of State by virtue of section 57 of the Police Act 1996 (c. 16) and outstanding on the day on which this Act is passed is to be treated as if it were a loan made in accordance with that section as amended by subsection (1) above.

Inspection

129 Inspection of police authorities

In section 54 of the Police Act 1996 (c. 16) (appointment and functions of inspectors of constabulary) for subsection (2A) substitute—

"(2A) The inspectors of constabulary may carry out an inspection of, and report to the Secretary of State on, a police authority's performance of its functions or of any particular function or functions (including in particular its compliance with the requirements of Part 1 of the Local Government Act 1999 (best value))."

PART 10
SPECIAL IMMIGRATION STATUS

130 Designation

(1) The Secretary of State may designate a person who satisfies Condition 1 or 2 (subject to subsections (4) and (5)).

(2) Condition 1 is that the person—
- (a) is a foreign criminal within the meaning of section 131, and
- (b) is liable to deportation, but cannot be removed from the United Kingdom because of section 6 of the Human Rights Act 1998 (c. 42) (public authority not to act contrary to Convention).

(3) Condition 2 is that the person is a member of the family of a person who satisfies Condition 1.

(4) A person who has the right of abode in the United Kingdom may not be designated.

(5) The Secretary of State may not designate a person if the Secretary of State thinks that an effect of designation would breach—
- (a) the United Kingdom's obligations under the Refugee Convention, or
- (b) the person's rights under the Community treaties.

131 "Foreign criminal"

(1) For the purposes of section 130 "foreign criminal" means a person who—
- (a) is not a British citizen, and
- (b) satisfies any of the following Conditions.

(2) Condition 1 is that section 72(2)(a) and (b) or (3)(a) to (c) of the Nationality, Immigration and Asylum Act 2002 (c. 41) applies to the person (Article 33(2) of the Refugee Convention: imprisonment for at least two years).

(3) Condition 2 is that—
  (a) section 72(4)(a) or (b) of that Act applies to the person (person convicted of specified offence), and
  (b) the person has been sentenced to a period of imprisonment.
(4) Condition 3 is that Article 1F of the Refugee Convention applies to the person (exclusions for criminals etc.).
(5) Section 72(6) of that Act (rebuttal of presumption under section 72(2) to (4)) has no effect in relation to Condition 1 or 2.
(6) Section 72(7) of that Act (non-application pending appeal) has no effect in relation to Condition 1 or 2.

132 Effect of designation

(1) A designated person does not have leave to enter or remain in the United Kingdom.
(2) For the purposes of a provision of the Immigration Acts and any other enactment which concerns or refers to immigration or nationality (including any provision which applies or refers to a provision of the Immigration Acts or any other enactment about immigration or nationality) a designated person—
  (a) is a person subject to immigration control,
  (b) is not to be treated as an asylum-seeker or a former asylum-seeker, and
  (c) is not in the United Kingdom in breach of the immigration laws.
(3) Despite subsection (2)(c), time spent in the United Kingdom as a designated person may not be relied on by a person for the purpose of an enactment about nationality.
(4) A designated person—
  (a) shall not be deemed to have been given leave in accordance with paragraph 6 of Schedule 2 to the Immigration Act 1971 (c. 77) (notice of leave or refusal), and
  (b) may not be granted temporary admission to the United Kingdom under paragraph 21 of that Schedule.
(5) Sections 134 and 135 make provision about support for designated persons and their dependants.

133 Conditions

(1) The Secretary of State or an immigration officer may by notice in writing impose a condition on a designated person.
(2) A condition may relate to—
  (a) residence,
  (b) employment or occupation, or
  (c) reporting to the police, the Secretary of State or an immigration officer.
(3) Section 36 of the Asylum and Immigration (Treatment of Claimants, etc.) Act 2004 (c. 19) (electronic monitoring) shall apply in relation to conditions imposed under this section as it applies to restrictions imposed under paragraph 21 of Schedule 2 to the Immigration Act 1971 (with a reference to the Immigration Acts being treated as including a reference to this section).
(4) Section 69 of the Nationality, Immigration and Asylum Act 2002 (c. 41) (reporting restrictions: travel expenses) shall apply in relation to conditions imposed under subsection (2)(c) above as it applies to restrictions imposed under paragraph 21 of Schedule 2 to the Immigration Act 1971.
(5) A person who without reasonable excuse fails to comply with a condition imposed under this section commits an offence.
(6) A person who is guilty of an offence under subsection (5) shall be liable on summary conviction to—
  (a) a fine not exceeding level 5 on the standard scale,
  (b) imprisonment for a period not exceeding 51 weeks, or
  (c) both.

(7) A provision of the Immigration Act 1971 (c. 77) which applies in relation to an offence under any provision of section 24(1) of that Act (illegal entry etc.) shall also apply in relation to the offence under subsection (5) above.

(8) In the application of this section to Scotland or Northern Ireland the reference in subsection (6)(b) to 51 weeks shall be treated as a reference to six months.

134 Support

(1) Part VI of the Immigration and Asylum Act 1999 (c. 33) (support for asylum-seekers) shall apply in relation to designated persons and their dependants as it applies in relation to asylum-seekers and their dependants.

(2) But the following provisions of that Part shall not apply—
   (a) section 96 (kinds of support),
   (b) section 97(1)(b) (desirability of providing accommodation in well-supplied area),
   (c) section 100 (duty to co-operate in providing accommodation),
   (d) section 101 (reception zones),
   (e) section 108 (failure of sponsor to maintain),
   (f) section 111 (grants to voluntary organisations), and
   (g) section 113 (recovery of expenditure from sponsor).

(3) Support may be provided under section 95 of the 1999 Act as applied by this section—
   (a) by providing accommodation appearing to the Secretary of State to be adequate for a person's needs;
   (b) by providing what appear to the Secretary of State to be essential living needs;
   (c) in other ways which the Secretary of State thinks necessary to reflect exceptional circumstances of a particular case.

(4) Support by virtue of subsection (3) may not be provided wholly or mainly by way of cash unless the Secretary of State thinks it appropriate because of exceptional circumstances.

(5) Section 4 of the 1999 Act (accommodation) shall not apply in relation to designated persons.

(6) A designated person shall not be treated—
   (a) as a person subject to immigration control, for the purposes of section 119(1)(b) of the 1999 Act (homelessness: Scotland and Northern Ireland), or
   (b) as a person from abroad who is not eligible for housing assistance, for the purposes of section 185(4) of the Housing Act 1996 (c. 52) (housing assistance).

135 Support: supplemental

(1) A reference in an enactment to Part VI of the 1999 Act or to a provision of that Part includes a reference to that Part or provision as applied by section 134 above; and for that purpose—
   (a) a reference to section 96 shall be treated as including a reference to section 134(3) above,
   (b) a reference to a provision of section 96 shall be treated as including a reference to the corresponding provision of section 134(3), and
   (c) a reference to asylum-seekers shall be treated as including a reference to designated persons.

(2) A provision of Part VI of the 1999 Act which requires or permits the Secretary of State to have regard to the temporary nature of support shall be treated, in the application of Part VI by virtue of section 134 above, as requiring the Secretary of State to have regard to the nature and circumstances of support by virtue of that section.

(3) Rules under section 104 of the 1999 Act (appeals) shall have effect for the purposes of Part VI of that Act as it applies by virtue of section 134 above.

(4) Any other instrument under Part VI of the 1999 Act—

    (a) may make provision in respect of that Part as it applies by virtue of section 134 above, as it applies otherwise than by virtue of that section, or both, and

    (b) may make different provision for that Part as it applies by virtue of section 134 above and as it applies otherwise than by virtue of that section.

(5) In the application of paragraph 9 of Schedule 8 to the 1999 Act (regulations: notice to quit accommodation) the reference in paragraph (2)(b) to the determination of a claim for asylum shall be treated as a reference to ceasing to be a designated person.

(6) The Secretary of State may by order repeal, modify or disapply (to any extent) section 134(4).

(7) An order under section 10 of the Human Rights Act 1998 (c. 42) (power to remedy incompatibility) which amends a provision mentioned in subsection (6) of section 134 above may amend or repeal that subsection.

136 End of designation

(1) Designation lapses if the designated person—

    (a) is granted leave to enter or remain in the United Kingdom,

    (b) is notified by the Secretary of State or an immigration officer of a right of residence in the United Kingdom by virtue of the Community treaties,

    (c) leaves the United Kingdom, or

    (d) is made the subject of a deportation order under section 5 of the Immigration Act 1971 (c. 77).

(2) After designation lapses support may not be provided by virtue of section 134, subject to the following exceptions.

(3) Exception 1 is that, if designation lapses under subsection (1)(a) or (b), support may be provided in respect of a period which—

    (a) begins when the designation lapses, and

    (b) ends on a date determined in accordance with an order of the Secretary of State.

(4) Exception 2 is that, if designation lapses under subsection (1)(d), support may be provided in respect of—

    (a) any period during which an appeal against the deportation order may be brought (ignoring any possibility of an appeal out of time with permission),

    (b) any period during which an appeal against the deportation order is pending, and

    (c) after an appeal ceases to be pending, such period as the Secretary of State may specify by order.

137 Interpretation: general

(1) This section applies to sections 130 to 136.

(2) A reference to a designated person is a reference to a person designated under section 130.

(3) "Family" shall be construed in accordance with section 5(4) of the Immigration Act 1971 (c. 77) (deportation: definition of "family").

(4) "Right of abode in the United Kingdom" has the meaning given by section 2 of that Act.

(5) "The Refugee Convention" means the Convention relating to the Status of Refugees done at Geneva on 28th July 1951 and its Protocol.

(6) "Period of imprisonment" shall be construed in accordance with section 72(11)(b)(i) and (ii) of the Nationality, Immigration and Asylum Act 2002 (c. 41).

(7) A voucher is not cash.

(8) A reference to a pending appeal has the meaning given by section 104(1) of that Act.

(9) A reference in an enactment to the Immigration Acts includes a reference to sections 130 to 136.

PART 11
MISCELLANEOUS

Industrial action by prison officers

138 Amendment of section 127 of Criminal Justice and Public Order Act 1994

(1) Section 127 of the Criminal Justice and Public Order Act 1994 (c. 33) (inducements to prison officers to withhold services or breach discipline) is amended as follows.

(2) In subsection (1), for paragraph (a) substitute—
"(a) to take (or continue to take) any industrial action;".

(3) After subsection (1) insert—
"(1A) In subsection (1) "industrial action" means—
   (a) the withholding of services as a prison officer; or
   (b) any action that would be likely to put at risk the safety of any person (whether a prisoner, a person working at or visiting a prison, a person working with prisoners or a member of the public)."

(4) In subsection (4), after paragraph (a) insert—
"(aa) holds any post, other than as a chaplain or assistant chaplain, to which he has been appointed for the purposes of section 7 of the Prison Act 1952 (appointment of prison staff),".

(5) In subsection (4), after paragraph (aa) (inserted by subsection (4) above) insert—
"(b) holds any post, otherwise than as a medical officer, to which he has been appointed for the purposes of section 3(1A) of the Prisons (Scotland) Act 1989;".

139 Power to suspend the operation of section 127 of Criminal Justice and Public Order Act 1994

After section 127 of the Criminal Justice and Public Order Act 1994 (c. 33) insert—

"127A Power to suspend the operation of section 127

(1) The Secretary of State may make orders suspending, or later reviving, the operation of section 127.

(2) An order under this section may make different provision in relation to different descriptions of prison officer.

(3) The power to make orders under this section is exercisable by statutory instrument.

(4) A statutory instrument containing an order under this section may not be made unless a draft of the instrument has been laid before, and approved by resolution of, each House of Parliament."

Sex offenders

140 Disclosure of information about convictions etc. of child sex offenders to members of the public

(1) After section 327 of the Criminal Justice Act 2003 (c. 44) insert—

"327A Disclosure of information about convictions etc. of child sex offenders to members of the public

(1) The responsible authority for each area must, in the course of discharging its functions under arrangements established by it under section 325, consider whether to disclose information in its possession about the relevant previous convictions of any child sex offender managed by it to any particular member of the public.

(2) In the case mentioned in subsection (3) there is a presumption that the responsible authority should disclose information in its possession about the relevant previous convictions of the offender to the particular member of the public.

(3) The case is where the responsible authority for the area has reasonable cause to believe that—

   (a) a child sex offender managed by it poses a risk in that or any other area of causing serious harm to any particular child or children or to children of any particular description, and

   (b) the disclosure of information about the relevant previous convictions of the offender to the particular member of the public is necessary for the purpose of protecting the particular child or children, or the children of that description, from serious harm caused by the offender.

(4) The presumption under subsection (2) arises whether or not the person to whom the information is disclosed requests the disclosure.

(5) Where the responsible authority makes a disclosure under this section—

   (a) it may disclose such information about the relevant previous convictions of the offender as it considers appropriate to disclose to the member of the public concerned, and

   (b) it may impose conditions for preventing the member of the public concerned from disclosing the information to any other person.

(6) Any disclosure under this section must be made as soon as is reasonably practicable having regard to all the circumstances.

(7) The responsible authority for each area must compile and maintain a record about the decisions it makes in relation to the discharge of its functions under this section.

(8) The record must include the following information—

   (a) the reasons for making a decision to disclose information under this section,

   (b) the reasons for making a decision not to disclose information under this section, and

   (c) the information which is disclosed under this section, any conditions imposed in relation to its further disclosure and the name and address of the person to whom it is disclosed.

(9) Nothing in this section requires or authorises the making of a disclosure which contravenes the Data Protection Act 1998.

(10) This section is not to be taken as affecting any power of any person to disclose any information about a child sex offender.

327B Section 327A: interpretation

(1) This section applies for the purposes of section 327A.

(2) "Child" means a person under 18.

(3) "Child sex offence" means an offence listed in Schedule 34A, whenever committed.

(4) "Child sex offender" means any person who—

   (a) has been convicted of such an offence,

   (b) has been found not guilty of such an offence by reason of insanity,

   (c) has been found to be under a disability and to have done the act charged against the person in respect of such an offence, or

   (d) has been cautioned in respect of such an offence.

(5) In relation to a responsible authority, references to information about the relevant previous convictions of a child sex offender are references to information about—

   (a) convictions, findings and cautions mentioned in subsection (4)(a) to (d) which relate to the offender, and

   (b) anything under the law of any country or territory outside England and Wales which in the opinion of the responsible authority corresponds to any conviction, finding or caution within paragraph (a) (however described).

(6) References to serious harm caused by a child sex offender are references to serious physical or psychological harm caused by the offender committing any offence listed in any paragraph of Schedule 34A other than paragraphs 1 to 6 (offences under provisions repealed by Sexual Offences Act 2003).

(7) A responsible authority for any area manages a child sex offender if the offender is a person who poses risks in that area which fall to be managed by the authority under the arrangements established by it under section 325.

(8) For the purposes of this section the provisions of section 4 of, and paragraph 3 of Schedule 2 to, the Rehabilitation of Offenders Act 1974 (protection for spent convictions and cautions) are to be disregarded.

(9) In this section "cautioned", in relation to any person and any offence, means—
  (a) cautioned after the person has admitted the offence, or
  (b) reprimanded or warned within the meaning given by section 65 of the Crime and Disorder Act 1998.

(10) Section 135(1), (2)(a) and (c) and (3) of the Sexual Offences Act 2003 (mentally disordered offenders) apply for the purposes of this section as they apply for the purposes of Part 2 of that Act."

(2) After Schedule 34 to that Act insert the Schedule 34A set out in Schedule 24 to this Act.

141 Sexual offences prevention orders: relevant sexual offences

(1) In section 106 of the Sexual Offences Act 2003 (c. 42) (supplemental provisions about sexual offences prevention orders), at the end insert—
  "(13) Subsection (14) applies for the purposes of section 104 and this section in their application in relation to England and Wales or Northern Ireland.
  (14) In construing any reference to an offence listed in Schedule 3, any condition subject to which an offence is so listed that relates—
    (a) to the way in which the defendant is dealt with in respect of an offence so listed or a relevant finding (as defined by section 132(9)), or
    (b) to the age of any person,
  is to be disregarded."

(2) This section extends to England and Wales and Northern Ireland only.

142 Notification requirements: prescribed information

(1) In section 83 of the Sexual Offences Act 2003 (c. 42) (notification requirements: initial notification)—
  (a) at the end of subsection (5) insert—
    "(h) any prescribed information."; and
  (b) after that subsection insert—
    "(5A) In subsection (5)(h) "prescribed" means prescribed by regulations made by the Secretary of State."

(2) Section 84 of that Act (notification requirements: changes) is amended as follows.

(3) In subsection (1)—
  (a) after "1997," in paragraph (c) insert—
    "(ca) any prescribed change of circumstances,"; and
  (b) after "the address of those premises" insert ", the prescribed details".

(4) In subsection (2) after "home address" insert "or the prescribed change of circumstances".

(5) After subsection (5) insert—
  "(5A) In this section—
    (a) "prescribed change of circumstances" means any change—
      (i) occurring in relation to any matter in respect of which information is required to be notified by virtue of section 83(5)(h), and

(ii) of a description prescribed by regulations made by the Secretary of State;

    (b) "the prescribed details", in relation to a prescribed change of circumstances, means such details of the change as may be so prescribed."

(6) Section 85 of that Act (notification requirements: periodic notification) is amended as follows.

(7) In subsection (1), for "the period of one year" substitute "the applicable period".

(8) In subsection (3), for "the period referred to in subsection (1)" substitute "the applicable period".

(9) After subsection (4) insert—

    "(5) In this section, "the applicable period" means—

        (a) in any case where subsection (6) applies to the relevant offender, such period as may be prescribed by regulations made by the Secretary of State, and

        (b) in any other case, the period of one year.

    (6) This subsection applies to the relevant offender if the last home address notified by him under section 83(1) or 84(1) or subsection (1) was the address or location of such a place as is mentioned in section 83(7)(b)."

(10) In section 138(2) of that Act (orders and regulations subject to the affirmative resolution procedure), for "86 or 130" substitute "any of sections 83 to 86 or section 130".

(11) This section extends to England and Wales and Northern Ireland only.

Persistent sales of tobacco to persons under 18

143 Persistent sales of tobacco to persons under 18

(1) The Children and Young Persons Act 1933 (c. 12) is amended as follows.

(2) After section 12 insert—

"Persistent sales of tobacco to persons under 18

12A Restricted premises orders

(1) This section applies where a person ("the offender") is convicted of a tobacco offence ("the relevant offence").

(2) The person who brought the proceedings for the relevant offence may by complaint to a magistrates' court apply for a restricted premises order to be made in respect of the premises in relation to which that offence was committed ("the relevant premises").

(3) A restricted premises order is an order prohibiting the sale on the premises to which it relates of any tobacco or cigarette papers to any person.

(4) The prohibition applies to sales whether made—

    (a) by the offender or any other person, or

    (b) by means of any machine kept on the premises or any other means.

(5) The order has effect for the period specified in the order, but that period may not exceed one year.

(6) The applicant must, after making reasonable enquiries, give notice of the application to every person appearing to the applicant to be a person affected by it.

(7) The court may make the order if (and only if) it is satisfied that—

    (a) on at least 2 occasions within the period of 2 years ending with the date on which the relevant offence was committed, the offender has committed other tobacco offences in relation to the relevant premises, and

    (b) the applicant has complied with subsection (6).

(8) Persons affected by the application may make representations to the court as to why the order should not be made.

(9) If—

    (a) a person affected by an application for a restricted premises order was not given notice under subsection (6), and

    (b) consequently the person had no opportunity to make representations to the court as to why the order should not be made, the person may by complaint apply to the court for an order varying or discharging it.

(10) On an application under subsection (9) the court may, after hearing—

    (a) that person, and

    (b) the applicant for the restricted premises order,

make such order varying or discharging the restricted premises order as it considers appropriate.

(11) For the purposes of this section the persons affected by an application for a restricted premises order in respect of any premises are—

    (a) the occupier of the premises, and

    (b) any other person who has an interest in the premises.

12B Restricted sale orders

(1) This section applies where a person ("the offender") is convicted of a tobacco offence ("the relevant offence").

(2) The person who brought the proceedings for the relevant offence may by complaint to a magistrates' court apply for a restricted sale order to be made in respect of the offender.

(3) A restricted sale order is an order prohibiting the person to whom it relates—

    (a) from selling any tobacco or cigarette papers to any person,

    (b) from having any management functions in respect of any premises in so far as those functions relate to the sale on the premises of tobacco or cigarette papers to any person,

    (c) from keeping any cigarette machine on any premises for the purpose of selling tobacco or permitting any cigarette machine to be kept on any premises by any other person for that purpose, and

    (d) from having any management functions in respect of any premises in so far as those functions relate to any cigarette machine kept on the premises for the purpose of selling tobacco.

(4) The order has effect for the period specified in the order, but that period may not exceed one year.

(5) The court may make the order if (and only if) it is satisfied that, on at least 2 occasions within the period of 2 years ending with the date on which the relevant offence was committed, the offender has committed other tobacco offences.

(6) In this section any reference to a cigarette machine is a reference to an automatic machine for the sale of tobacco.

12C Enforcement

(1) If—

    (a) a person sells on any premises any tobacco or cigarette papers in contravention of a restricted premises order, and

    (b) the person knew, or ought reasonably to have known, that the sale was in contravention of the order, the person commits an offence.

(2) If a person fails to comply with a restricted sale order, the person commits an offence.

(3) It is a defence for a person charged with an offence under subsection (2) to prove that the person took all reasonable precautions and exercised all due diligence to avoid the commission of the offence.

(4) A person guilty of an offence under this section is liable, on summary conviction, to a fine not exceeding £20,000.

(5) A restricted premises order is a local land charge and in respect of that charge the applicant for the order is the originating authority for the purposes of the Local Land Charges Act 1975.

12D Interpretation

(1) In sections 12A and 12B a "tobacco offence" means—
 (a) an offence committed under section 7(1) on any premises (which are accordingly "the premises in relation to which the offence is committed"), or
 (b) an offence committed under section 7(2) in respect of an order relating to any machine kept on any premises (which are accordingly "the premises in relation to which the offence is committed").

(2) In sections 12A to 12C the expressions "tobacco" and "cigarette" have the same meaning as in section 7.

(3) In sections 12A and 12B "notice" means notice in writing."

(3) In section 102(1) (appeals to the Crown Court), after paragraph (e) insert—
 "(f) in the case of a restricted premises order under section 12A or a restricted sale order under section 12B, by any person aggrieved."

Penalties for serious contraventions of data protection principles

144 Power to require data controllers to pay monetary penalty

(1) After section 55 of the Data Protection Act 1998 (c. 29) insert—

"Monetary penalties

55A Power of Commissioner to impose monetary penalty

(1) The Commissioner may serve a data controller with a monetary penalty notice if the Commissioner is satisfied that—
 (a) there has been a serious contravention of section 4(4) by the data controller,
 (b) the contravention was of a kind likely to cause substantial damage or substantial distress, and
 (c) subsection (2) or (3) applies.

(2) This subsection applies if the contravention was deliberate.

(3) This subsection applies if the data controller—
 (a) knew or ought to have known —
  (i) that there was a risk that the contravention would occur, and
  (ii) that such a contravention would be of a kind likely to cause substantial damage or substantial distress, but
 (b) failed to take reasonable steps to prevent the contravention.

(4) A monetary penalty notice is a notice requiring the data controller to pay to the Commissioner a monetary penalty of an amount determined by the Commissioner and specified in the notice.

(5) The amount determined by the Commissioner must not exceed the prescribed amount.

(6) The monetary penalty must be paid to the Commissioner within the period specified in the notice.

(7) The notice must contain such information as may be prescribed.

(8) Any sum received by the Commissioner by virtue of this section must be paid into the Consolidated Fund.

(9) In this section—

"data controller" does not include the Crown Estate Commissioners or a person who is a data controller by virtue of section 63(3);

"prescribed" means prescribed by regulations made by the Secretary of State.

55B Monetary penalty notices: procedural rights

(1) Before serving a monetary penalty notice, the Commissioner must serve the data controller with a notice of intent.

(2) A notice of intent is a notice that the Commissioner proposes to serve a monetary penalty notice.

(3) A notice of intent must—

(a) inform the data controller that he may make written representations in relation to the Commissioner's proposal within a period specified in the notice, and

(b) contain such other information as may be prescribed.

(4) The Commissioner may not serve a monetary penalty notice until the time within which the data controller may make representations has expired.

(5) A person on whom a monetary penalty notice is served may appeal to the Tribunal against—

(a) the issue of the monetary penalty notice;

(b) the amount of the penalty specified in the notice.

(6) In this section, "prescribed" means prescribed by regulations made by the Secretary of State.

55C Guidance about monetary penalty notices

(1) The Commissioner must prepare and issue guidance on how he proposes to exercise his functions under sections 55A and 55B.

(2) The guidance must, in particular, deal with—

(a) the circumstances in which he would consider it appropriate to issue a monetary penalty notice, and

(b) how he will determine the amount of the penalty.

(3) The Commissioner may alter or replace the guidance.

(4) If the guidance is altered or replaced, the Commissioner must issue the altered or replacement guidance.

(5) The Commissioner may not issue guidance under this section without the approval of the Secretary of State.

(6) The Commissioner must lay any guidance issued under this section before each House of Parliament.

(7) The Commissioner must arrange for the publication of any guidance issued under this section in such form and manner as he considers appropriate.

(8) In subsections (5) to (7), "guidance" includes altered or replacement guidance.

55D Monetary penalty notices: enforcement

(1) This section applies in relation to any penalty payable to the Commissioner by virtue of section 55A.

(2) In England and Wales, the penalty is recoverable—

(a) if a county court so orders, as if it were payable under an order of that court;

(b) if the High Court so orders, as if it were payable under an order of that court.

(3) In Scotland, the penalty may be enforced in the same manner as an extract registered decree arbitral bearing a warrant for execution issued by the sheriff court of any sheriffdom in Scotland.

(4) In Northern Ireland, the penalty is recoverable—

   (a) if a county court so orders, as if it were payable under an order of that court;

   (b) if the High Court so orders, as if it were payable under an order of that court.

55E Notices under sections 55A and 55B: supplemental

(1) The Secretary of State may by order make further provision in connection with monetary penalty notices and notices of intent.

(2) An order under this section may in particular—

   (a) provide that a monetary penalty notice may not be served on a data controller with respect to the processing of personal data for the special purposes except in circumstances specified in the order;

   (b) make provision for the cancellation or variation of monetary penalty notices;

   (c) confer rights of appeal to the Tribunal against decisions of the Commissioner in relation to the cancellation or variation of such notices;

   (d) make provision for the proceedings of the Tribunal in respect of appeals under section 55B(5) or appeals made by virtue of paragraph (c);

   (e) make provision for the determination of such appeals;

   (f) confer rights of appeal against any decision of the Tribunal in relation to monetary penalty notices or their cancellation or variation.

(3) An order under this section may apply any provision of this Act with such modifications as may be specified in the order.

(4) An order under this section may amend this Act."

(2) In section 67 of that Act (orders, regulations, rules)—

   (a) in subsection (4) insert at the appropriate place—
   "section 55E(1),"; and

   (b) in subsection (5) after paragraph (c) insert—
   "(ca) regulations under section 55A(5) or (7) or 55B(3)(b),".

Armed forces legislation

145 Amendments to armed forces legislation

Schedule 25 contains—

   (a) amendments to armed forces legislation (which make provision for service courts etc. corresponding to other provisions of this Act); and

   (b) transitional provision relating to certain of those amendments.

Automatic deportation of criminals

146 Convention against human trafficking

After section 33(6) of the UK Borders Act 2007 (automatic deportation: exceptions) insert—

   "(6A) Exception 6 is where the Secretary of State thinks that the application of section 32(4) and (5) would contravene the United Kingdom's obligations under the Council of Europe Convention on Action against Trafficking in Human Beings (done at Warsaw on 16th May 2005)."

PART 12
GENERAL

147 Orders, rules and regulations

(1) Orders, rules or regulations made by the Secretary of State or the Lord Chancellor under this Act are to be made by statutory instrument.

(2) Any such orders or regulations—

(a) may make provision generally or only for specified cases or circumstances;

(b) may make different provision for different cases, circumstances or areas;

(c) may make incidental, supplementary, consequential, transitional, transitory or saving provision.

(3) Subject to subsection (4), a statutory instrument containing any order or regulations under this Act is subject to annulment in pursuance of a resolution of either House of Parliament.

(4) Subsection (3) does not apply to—

(a) a statutory instrument containing an order under section 153,

(b) a statutory instrument containing an order under paragraph 26(5) of Schedule 1,

(c) a statutory instrument containing an Order in Council under paragraph 9 of Schedule 17, or

(d) a statutory instrument to which subsection (5) applies.

(5) A statutory instrument containing (whether alone or with other provision)—

(a) an order under section 4(3),

(b) an order under section 48(2),

(c) an order under section 77,

(d) an order under section 81(4), 83(4) or 91(3) which amends or repeals any provision of an Act,

(e) an order under section 102,

(f) regulations under any of sections 108 to 111,

(g) an order under section 135(6),

(h) an order under section 148(3) which amends or repeals any provision of an Act,

(i) an order under paragraph 27 or 35 of Schedule 1,

(j) an order under paragraph 25 of Schedule 2,

(k) rules under paragraph 2(4)(a) of Schedule 6, or

(l) an order under paragraph 6 of Schedule 7,

may not be made unless a draft of the instrument has been laid before, and approved by a resolution of, each House of Parliament.

(6) An order under section 153(5)(b) is to be made by statutory instrument.

(7) An order under section 153(6) is to be made by statutory rule for the purposes of the Statutory Rules (Northern Ireland) Order 1979 (S.I. 1979/1573 (N.I. 12)).

148 Consequential etc. amendments and transitional and saving provision

(1) Schedule 26 contains minor and consequential amendments.

(2) Schedule 27 contains transitory, transitional and saving provisions.

(3) The Secretary of State may by order make—

(a) such supplementary, incidental or consequential provision, or

(b) such transitory, transitional or saving provision,

as the Secretary of State considers appropriate for the general purposes, or any particular purposes, of this Act, or in consequence of, or for giving full effect to, any provision made by this Act.

(4) An order under subsection (3) may, in particular—

(a) provide for any amendment or other provision made by this Act which comes into force before any other provision (whether made by this or any other Act or by any subordinate legislation) has come into force to have effect, until that other provision has come into force, with specified modifications, and

(b) amend, repeal or revoke any provision of—
  (i) any Act (including this Act and any Act passed in the same Session as this Act);
  (ii) subordinate legislation made before the passing of this Act;
  (iii) Northern Ireland legislation passed, or made, before the passing of this Act; and
  (iv) any instrument made, before the passing of this Act, under Northern Ireland legislation.

(5) Nothing in this section limits the power under section 153(8) to include provision for transitory, transitional or saving purposes in an order under that section.

(6) The amendments that may be made by virtue of subsection (4)(b) are in addition to those made by or which may be made under any other provision of this Act.

(7) In this section "subordinate legislation" has the same meaning as in the Interpretation Act 1978 (c. 30).

(8) Her Majesty may by Order in Council extend any provision made by virtue of subsection (4)(b), with such modifications as may appear to Her Majesty to be appropriate, to the Isle of Man or any British overseas territory.

(9) The power under subsection (8) includes power to make supplementary, incidental, consequential, transitory, transitional or saving provision.

(10) Subsection (8) does not apply in relation to amendments of the Armed Forces Act 2006 (c. 52).

149 Repeals and revocations

Schedule 28 contains repeals and revocations, including repeals of spent enactments.

150 Financial provisions

There is to be paid out of money provided by Parliament—
(a) any expenditure incurred by virtue of this Act by a Minister of the Crown; and
(b) any increase attributable to this Act in the sums payable under any other Act out of money so provided.

151 Effect of amendments to criminal justice provisions applied for purposes of service law

(1) In this section "relevant criminal justice provisions" means provisions of, or made under, an Act which—
  (a) relate to criminal justice; and
  (b) have been applied (with or without modifications) for any purposes of service law by any provision of, or made under, any Act.

(2) Unless the contrary intention appears, any amendment by this Act of relevant criminal justice provisions also amends those provisions as so applied.

(3) Subsection (2) does not apply to any amendments made by Part 1.

(4) In this section "service law" means—
  (a) the system of service law established by the Armed Forces Act 2006 (c. 52); or
  (b) any of the systems of service law superseded by that Act (namely, military law, air force law and the Naval Discipline Act 1957 (c. 53)).

152 Extent

(1) Subject as follows and to any other provision of this Act, this Act extends to England and Wales only.

(2) The following provisions of this Act extend to England and Wales, Scotland and Northern Ireland—

(a) section 77;

(b) section 96;

(c) section 113 (together with such of the other provisions of Part 7 as relate to the commission of offences under that section);

(d) Part 10;

(e) this Part (subject to subsection (5)).

(3) The following provisions of this Act extend to England and Wales and Northern Ireland—

(a) section 3 and Schedule 3;

(b) section 39(3) and (6)(d) and paragraph 7 of Schedule 7;

(c) sections 63 to 68 and Schedule 14;

(d) section 76;

(e) section 85(6) and (7) (so far as relating to any provision of Part 3 of the Magistrates' Courts Act 1980 which extends to Northern Ireland);

(f) sections 86 and 90 to 92 and Schedules 18 and 19.

(4) The following provisions of this Act extend to Northern Ireland only—

(a) sections 82 and 83;

(b) sections 87 to 89;

(c) section 122 and Schedule 21.

(5) Except as otherwise provided by this Act, an amendment, repeal or revocation of any enactment by any provision of this Act extends to the part or parts of the United Kingdom to which the enactment extends.

(6) The following amendments and repeals also extend to the Channel Islands and the Isle of Man—

(a) the amendments of sections 26 and 70(1) of the Children and Young Persons Act 1969 (c. 54) (transfers between England or Wales and the Channel Islands or Isle of Man) made by Schedule 4, and

(b) the repeals in Part 1 of Schedule 28 relating to those amendments.

(7) In section 7(2) of the Nuclear Material (Offences) Act 1983 (c. 18) (application to Channel Islands, Isle of Man, etc.) the reference to that Act includes a reference to that Act as amended by Schedule 17.

(8) In section 9(4) of the Repatriation of Prisoners Act 1984 (c. 47) (power to extend provisions of that Act to the Channel Islands etc.) the reference to that Act includes a reference to that Act as amended by any provision of this Act.

(9) In section 384 of the Armed Forces Act 2006 (c. 52) (extent to Channel Islands, Isle of Man, etc.) any reference to that Act includes a reference to—

(a) that Act as amended by or under any provision of this Act,

(b) section 151, and

(c) paragraph 34 of Schedule 25.

(10) Nothing in this section restricts the operation of section 76 and paragraph 27 of Schedule 27 in their application in relation to service offences (within the meaning of that paragraph).

153 Commencement

(1) The following provisions of this Act come into force on the day on which this Act is passed—

(a) section 53, Schedule 13, paragraph 77 of Schedule 26 and the repeals in Part 4 of Schedule 28 relating to—

(i) paragraphs 13 and 22 of Schedule 3 to the Criminal Justice Act 2003 (c. 44), and

(ii) Part 4 of Schedule 37 to that Act;

    (b) section 77;

    (c) section 128;

    (d) sections 138(1) to (4) and 139;

    (e) section 147;

    (f) section 148(3) to (7);

    (g) sections 150 and 152;

    (h) this section;

    (i) section 154;

    (j) paragraphs 6(3) and 12 to 16 of Schedule 16 and the repeals in Part 5 of Schedule 28 relating to Part 3A of the Public Order Act 1986 (c. 64);

    (k) paragraphs 35 to 39 of Schedule 26.

(2) The following provisions of this Act come into force at the end of the period of 2 months beginning with the day on which it is passed—

    (a) section 62 and the related repeal in Part 4 of Schedule 28;

    (b) section 69 and paragraph 24 of Schedule 26;

    (c) section 70 and paragraph 25 of Schedule 26;

    (d) section 79 and the related repeals in Part 5 of Schedule 28;

    (e) paragraphs 2 to 7 of Schedule 15;

    (f) paragraph 24 of Schedule 27.

(3) Where any particular provision or provisions of a Schedule come into force in accordance with subsection (1) or (2), the section introducing the Schedule also comes into force in accordance with that subsection so far as relating to the particular provision or provisions.

(4) The following provisions come into force on such day as the Lord Chancellor may by order appoint—

    (a) section 19;

    (b) section 41;

    (c) sections 56 to 58;

    (d) sections 80 to 92 and Schedules 18 and 19;

    (e) paragraph 29 of Schedule 27.

(5) Sections 119 to 121 come into force—

    (a) in relation to English NHS premises, on such day as the Secretary of State may by order appoint, and

    (b) in relation to Welsh NHS premises, on such day as the Welsh Ministers may by order appoint.

(6) Section 122 and Schedule 21 come into force on such day as the Department of Health, Social Services and Public Safety may by order appoint.

(7) The other provisions of this Act come into force on such day as the Secretary of State may by order appoint.

(8) An order under any of subsections (4) to (7) may—

    (a) appoint different days for different purposes and in relation to different areas;

    (b) make such provision as the person making the order considers necessary or expedient for transitory, transitional or saving purposes in connection with the coming into force of any provision falling within that subsection.

154 Short title

This Act may be cited as the Criminal Justice and Immigration Act 2008.

SCHEDULES

SCHEDULE 1   Section 1
FURTHER PROVISIONS ABOUT YOUTH REHABILITATION ORDERS

PART 1
PROVISIONS TO BE INCLUDED IN YOUTH REHABILITATION ORDERS

Imposition of requirements

1 Subsection (1) of section 1 has effect subject to the following provisions of Part 2 of this
Schedule which relate to particular requirements—
   (a) paragraph 8(3) and (4) (activity requirement),
   (b) paragraph 10(3) (unpaid work requirement),
   (c) paragraph 11(3) and (4) (programme requirement),
   (d) paragraph 12(3) (attendance centre requirement),
   (e) paragraph 13(2) (prohibited activity requirement),
   (f) paragraph 16(2), (4) and (7) (residence requirement),
   (g) paragraphs 17(3) and (4) and 19 (local authority residence requirement),
   (h) paragraph 20(3) (mental health treatment requirement),
   (i) paragraph 22(2) and (4) (drug treatment requirement),
   (j) paragraph 23(3) (drug testing requirement),
   (k) paragraph 24(2) and (4) (intoxicating substance treatment requirement), and
   (l) paragraph 25(4) (education requirement).

Electronic monitoring requirement

2 (1) Sub-paragraph (2) applies to a youth rehabilitation order which—
      (a) imposes a curfew requirement (whether by virtue of paragraph 3(4)(b) or otherwise), or
      (b) imposes an exclusion requirement.
  (2) The order must also impose an electronic monitoring requirement unless—
      (a) in the particular circumstances of the case, the court considers it inappropriate for the
          order to do so, or
      (b) the court is prevented by paragraph 26(3) or (6) from including such a requirement in
          the order.
  (3) Subsection (2)(a) of section 1 has effect subject to paragraph 26(3) and (6).

Youth rehabilitation order with intensive supervision and surveillance

3 (1) This paragraph applies where paragraphs (a) to (c) of section 1(4) are satisfied.
  (2) The court, if it makes a youth rehabilitation order which imposes an activity requirement,
      may specify in relation to that requirement a number of days which is more than 90 but
      not more than 180.
  (3) Such an activity requirement is referred to in this Part of this Act as "an extended activity
      requirement".
  (4) A youth rehabilitation order which imposes an extended activity requirement must also
      impose—
      (a) a supervision requirement, and
      (b) a curfew requirement (and, accordingly, if so required by paragraph 2, an electronic
          monitoring requirement).
  (5) A youth rehabilitation order which imposes an extended activity requirement (and other
      requirements in accordance with sub-paragraph (4)) is referred to in this Part of this Act as

288

"a youth rehabilitation order with intensive supervision and surveillance" (whether or not it also imposes any other requirement mentioned in section 1(1)).

Youth rehabilitation order with fostering

4 (1) This paragraph applies where paragraphs (a) to (c) of section 1(4) are satisfied.

(2) If the court is satisfied—

(a) that the behaviour which constituted the offence was due to a significant extent to the circumstances in which the offender was living, and

(b) that the imposition of a fostering requirement (see paragraph 18) would assist in the offender's rehabilitation,

it may make a youth rehabilitation order in accordance with section 1 which imposes a fostering requirement.

(3) But a court may not impose a fostering requirement unless—

(a) it has consulted the offender's parents or guardians (unless it is impracticable to do so), and

(b) it has consulted the local authority which is to place the offender with a local authority foster parent.

(4) A youth rehabilitation order which imposes a fostering requirement must also impose a supervision requirement.

(5) This paragraph has effect subject to paragraphs 18(7) and 19 (pre-conditions to imposing fostering requirement).

(6) A youth rehabilitation order which imposes a fostering requirement is referred to in this Part of this Act as "a youth rehabilitation order with fostering" (whatever other requirements mentioned in section 1(1) or (2) it imposes).

Intensive supervision and surveillance and fostering: further provisions

5 (1) A youth rehabilitation order with intensive supervision and surveillance may not impose a fostering requirement.

(2) Nothing in—

(a) section 1(4)(b), or

(b) section 148(1) or (2)(b) of the Criminal Justice Act 2003 (c. 44) (restrictions on imposing community sentences),

prevents a court from making a youth rehabilitation order with intensive supervision and surveillance in respect of an offender if the offender fails to comply with an order under section 161(2) of the Criminal Justice Act 2003 (pre-sentence drug testing).

PART 2
REQUIREMENTS

Activity requirement

6 (1) In this Part of this Act "activity requirement", in relation to a youth rehabilitation order, means a requirement that the offender must do any or all of the following—

(a) participate, on such number of days as may be specified in the order, in activities at a place, or places, so specified;

(b) participate in an activity, or activities, specified in the order on such number of days as may be so specified;

(c) participate in one or more residential exercises for a continuous period or periods comprising such number or numbers of days as may be specified in the order;

(d) in accordance with paragraph 7, engage in activities in accordance with instructions of the responsible officer on such number of days as may be specified in the order.

(2) Subject to paragraph 3(2), the number of days specified in the order under sub-paragraph (1) must not, in aggregate, be more than 90.

(3) A requirement such as is mentioned in sub-paragraph (1)(a) or (b) operates to require the offender, in accordance with instructions given by the responsible officer, on the number of days specified in the order in relation to the requirement—

    (a) in the case of a requirement such as is mentioned in sub-paragraph (1)(a), to present himself or herself at a place specified in the order to a person of a description so specified, or

    (b) in the case of a requirement such as is mentioned in sub-paragraph (1)(b), to participate in an activity specified in the order,

and, on each such day, to comply with instructions given by, or under the authority of, the person in charge of the place or the activity (as the case may be).

(4) Where the order requires the offender to participate in a residential exercise, it must specify, in relation to the exercise—

    (a) a place, or

    (b) an activity.

(5) A requirement to participate in a residential exercise operates to require the offender, in accordance with instructions given by the responsible officer—

    (a) if a place is specified under sub-paragraph (4)(a)—

        (i) to present himself or herself at the beginning of the period specified in the order in relation to the exercise, at the place so specified to a person of a description specified in the instructions, and

        (ii) to reside there for that period,

    (b) if an activity is specified under sub-paragraph (4)(b), to participate, for the period specified in the order in relation to the exercise, in the activity so specified,

and, during that period, to comply with instructions given by, or under the authority of, the person in charge of the place or the activity (as the case may be).

Activity requirement: instructions of responsible officer under paragraph 6(1)(d)

7 (1) Subject to sub-paragraph (3), instructions under paragraph 6(1)(d) relating to any day must require the offender to do either of the following—

    (a) present himself or herself to a person or persons of a description specified in the instructions at a place so specified;

    (b) participate in an activity specified in the instructions.

(2) Any such instructions operate to require the offender, on that day or while participating in that activity, to comply with instructions given by, or under the authority of, the person in charge of the place or, as the case may be, the activity.

(3) If the order so provides, instructions under paragraph 6(1)(d) may require the offender to participate in a residential exercise for a period comprising not more than 7 days, and, for that purpose—

    (a) to present himself or herself at the beginning of that period to a person of a description specified in the instructions at a place so specified and to reside there for that period, or

    (b) to participate for that period in an activity specified in the instructions.

(4) Instructions such as are mentioned in sub-paragraph (3)—

    (a) may not be given except with the consent of a parent or guardian of the offender, and

    (b) operate to require the offender, during the period specified under that sub-paragraph, to comply with instructions given by, or under the authority of, the person in charge of the place or activity specified under sub-paragraph (3)(a) or (b) (as the case may be).

Activity requirement: further provisions

8 (1) Instructions given by, or under the authority of, a person in charge of any place under any of the following provisions—

(a) paragraph 6(3),

(b) paragraph 6(5),

(c) paragraph 7(2), or

(d) paragraph 7(4)(b),

may require the offender to engage in activities otherwise than at that place.

(2) An activity specified—

(a) in an order under paragraph 6(1)(b), or

(b) in instructions given under paragraph 6(1)(d),

may consist of or include an activity whose purpose is that of reparation, such as an activity involving contact between an offender and persons affected by the offences in respect of which the order was made.

(3) A court may not include an activity requirement in a youth rehabilitation order unless—

(a) it has consulted a member of a youth offending team, an officer of a local probation board or an officer of a provider of probation services,

(b) it is satisfied that it is feasible to secure compliance with the requirement, and

(c) it is satisfied that provision for the offender to participate in the activities proposed to be specified in the order can be made under the arrangements for persons to participate in such activities which exist in the local justice area in which the offender resides or is to reside.

(4) A court may not include an activity requirement in a youth rehabilitation order if compliance with that requirement would involve the co-operation of a person other than the offender and the responsible officer, unless that other person consents to its inclusion.

Supervision requirement

9 In this Part of this Act "supervision requirement", in relation to a youth rehabilitation order, means a requirement that, during the period for which the order remains in force, the offender must attend appointments with the responsible officer or another person determined by the responsible officer, at such times and places as may be determined by the responsible officer.

Unpaid work requirement

10 (1) In this Part of this Act "unpaid work requirement", in relation to a youth rehabilitation order, means a requirement that the offender must perform unpaid work in accordance with this paragraph.

(2) The number of hours which a person may be required to work under an unpaid work requirement must be specified in the youth rehabilitation order and must be, in aggregate—

(a) not less than 40, and

(b) not more than 240.

(3) A court may not impose an unpaid work requirement in respect of an offender unless—

(a) after hearing (if the court thinks necessary) an appropriate officer, the court is satisfied that the offender is a suitable person to perform work under such a requirement, and

(b) the court is satisfied that provision for the offender to work under such a requirement can be made under the arrangements for persons to perform work under such a requirement which exist in the local justice area in which the offender resides or is to reside.

(4) In sub-paragraph (3)(a) "an appropriate officer" means a member of a youth offending team, an officer of a local probation board or an officer of a provider of probation services.

(5) An offender in respect of whom an unpaid work requirement of a youth rehabilitation order is in force must perform for the number of hours specified in the order such work at such times as the responsible officer may specify in instructions.

(6) Subject to paragraph 17 of Schedule 2, the work required to be performed under an unpaid work requirement of a youth rehabilitation order must be performed during the period of 12 months beginning with the day on which the order takes effect.

(7) Unless revoked, a youth rehabilitation order imposing an unpaid work requirement remains in force until the offender has worked under it for the number of hours specified in it.

Programme requirement

11 (1) In this Part of this Act "programme requirement", in relation to a youth rehabilitation order, means a requirement that the offender must participate in a systematic set of activities ("a programme") specified in the order at a place or places so specified on such number of days as may be so specified.

(2) A programme requirement may require the offender to reside at any place specified in the order under sub-paragraph (1) for any period so specified if it is necessary for the offender to reside there for that period in order to participate in the programme.

(3) A court may not include a programme requirement in a youth rehabilitation order unless—
   (a) the programme which the court proposes to specify in the order has been recommended to the court by—
      (i) a member of a youth offending team,
      (ii) an officer of a local probation board, or
      (iii) an officer of a provider of probation services,
      as being suitable for the offender, and
   (b) the court is satisfied that the programme is available at the place or places proposed to be specified.

(4) A court may not include a programme requirement in a youth rehabilitation order if compliance with that requirement would involve the co-operation of a person other than the offender and the offender's responsible officer, unless that other person consents to its inclusion.

(5) A requirement to participate in a programme operates to require the offender—
   (a) in accordance with instructions given by the responsible officer to participate in the programme at the place or places specified in the order on the number of days so specified, and
   (b) while at any of those places, to comply with instructions given by, or under the authority of, the person in charge of the programme.

Attendance centre requirement

12 (1) In this Part of this Act "attendance centre requirement", in relation to a youth rehabilitation order, means a requirement that the offender must attend at an attendance centre specified in the order for such number of hours as may be so specified.

(2) The aggregate number of hours for which the offender may be required to attend at an attendance centre—
   (a) if the offender is aged 16 or over at the time of conviction, must be—
      (i) not less than 12, and
      (ii) not more than 36;
   (b) if the offender is aged 14 or over but under 16 at the time of conviction, must be—
      (i) not less than 12, and
      (ii) not more than 24;
   (c) if the offender is aged under 14 at the time of conviction, must not be more than 12.

(3) A court may not include an attendance centre requirement in a youth rehabilitation order unless it—
   (a) has been notified by the Secretary of State that—
      (i) an attendance centre is available for persons of the offender's description, and

(ii) provision can be made at the centre for the offender, and

(b) is satisfied that the attendance centre proposed to be specified is reasonably accessible to the offender, having regard to the means of access available to the offender and any other circumstances.

(4) The first time at which the offender is required to attend at the attendance centre is a time notified to the offender by the responsible officer.

(5) The subsequent hours are to be fixed by the officer in charge of the centre—

(a) in accordance with arrangements made by the responsible officer, and

(b) having regard to the offender's circumstances.

(6) An offender may not be required under this paragraph to attend at an attendance centre—

(a) on more than one occasion on any day, or

(b) for more than three hours on any occasion.

(7) A requirement to attend at an attendance centre for any period on any occasion operates as a requirement—

(a) to attend at the centre at the beginning of the period, and

(b) during that period, to engage in occupation, or receive instruction, under the supervision of and in accordance with instructions given by, or under the authority of, the officer in charge of the centre, whether at the centre or elsewhere.

Prohibited activity requirement

13 (1) In this Part of this Act "prohibited activity requirement", in relation to a youth rehabilitation order, means a requirement that the offender must refrain from participating in activities specified in the order—

(a) on a day or days so specified, or

(b) during a period so specified.

(2) A court may not include a prohibited activity requirement in a youth rehabilitation order unless it has consulted—

(a) a member of a youth offending team,

(b) an officer of a local probation board, or

(c) an officer of a provider of probation services.

(3) The requirements that may by virtue of this paragraph be included in a youth rehabilitation order include a requirement that the offender does not possess, use or carry a firearm within the meaning of the Firearms Act 1968 (c. 27).

Curfew requirement

14 (1) In this Part of this Act "curfew requirement", in relation to a youth rehabilitation order, means a requirement that the offender must remain, for periods specified in the order, at a place so specified.

(2) A youth rehabilitation order imposing a curfew requirement may specify different places or different periods for different days, but may not specify periods which amount to less than 2 hours or more than 12 hours in any day.

(3) A youth rehabilitation order imposing a curfew requirement may not specify periods which fall outside the period of 6 months beginning with the day on which the requirement first takes effect.

(4) Before making a youth rehabilitation order imposing a curfew requirement, the court must obtain and consider information about the place proposed to be specified in the order (including information as to the attitude of persons likely to be affected by the enforced presence there of the offender).

Exclusion requirement

15 (1) In this Part of this Act "exclusion requirement", in relation to a youth rehabilitation order, means a provision prohibiting the offender from entering a place specified in the order for a period so specified.

(2) The period specified must not be more than 3 months.

(3) An exclusion requirement—

    (a) may provide for the prohibition to operate only during the periods specified in the order, and

    (b) may specify different places for different periods or days.

(4) In this paragraph "place" includes an area.

Residence requirement

16 (1) In this Part of this Act, "residence requirement", in relation to a youth rehabilitation order, means a requirement that, during the period specified in the order, the offender must reside—

    (a) with an individual specified in the order, or

    (b) at a place specified in the order.

(2) A court may not by virtue of sub-paragraph (1)(a) include in a youth rehabilitation order a requirement that the offender reside with an individual unless that individual has consented to the requirement.

(3) In this paragraph, a residence requirement falling within sub-paragraph (1)(b) is referred to as "a place of residence requirement".

(4) A court may not include a place of residence requirement in a youth rehabilitation order unless the offender was aged 16 or over at the time of conviction.

(5) If the order so provides, a place of residence requirement does not prohibit the offender from residing, with the prior approval of the responsible officer, at a place other than that specified in the order.

(6) Before making a youth rehabilitation order containing a place of residence requirement, the court must consider the home surroundings of the offender.

(7) A court may not specify a hostel or other institution as the place where an offender must reside for the purposes of a place of residence requirement except on the recommendation of—

    (a) a member of a youth offending team,

    (b) an officer of a local probation board,

    (c) an officer of a provider of probation services, or

    (d) a social worker of a local authority.

Local authority residence requirement

17 (1) In this Part of this Act, "local authority residence requirement", in relation to a youth rehabilitation order, means a requirement that, during the period specified in the order, the offender must reside in accommodation provided by or on behalf of a local authority specified in the order for the purposes of the requirement.

(2) A youth rehabilitation order which imposes a local authority residence requirement may also stipulate that the offender is not to reside with a person specified in the order.

(3) A court may not include a local authority residence requirement in a youth rehabilitation order made in respect of an offence unless it is satisfied—

    (a) that the behaviour which constituted the offence was due to a significant extent to the circumstances in which the offender was living, and

    (b) that the imposition of that requirement will assist in the offender's rehabilitation.

(4) A court may not include a local authority residence requirement in a youth rehabilitation order unless it has consulted—

    (a) a parent or guardian of the offender (unless it is impracticable to consult such a person), and

(b) the local authority which is to receive the offender.

(5) A youth rehabilitation order which imposes a local authority residence requirement must specify, as the local authority which is to receive the offender, the local authority in whose area the offender resides or is to reside.

(6) Any period specified in a youth rehabilitation order as a period for which the offender must reside in accommodation provided by or on behalf of a local authority must—

    (a) not be longer than 6 months, and

    (b) not include any period after the offender has reached the age of 18.

Fostering requirement

18 (1) In this Part of this Act "fostering requirement", in relation to a youth rehabilitation order, means a requirement that, for a period specified in the order, the offender must reside with a local authority foster parent.

(2) A period specified in a youth rehabilitation order as a period for which the offender must reside with a local authority foster parent must—

    (a) end no later than the end of the period of 12 months beginning with the date on which the requirement first has effect (but subject to paragraphs 6(9), 8(9) and 16(2) of Schedule 2), and

    (b) not include any period after the offender has reached the age of 18.

(3) A youth rehabilitation order which imposes a fostering requirement must specify the local authority which is to place the offender with a local authority foster parent under section 23(2)(a) of the Children Act 1989 (c. 41).

(4) The authority so specified must be the local authority in whose area the offender resides or is to reside.

(5) If at any time during the period specified under sub-paragraph (1), the responsible officer notifies the offender—

    (a) that no suitable local authority foster parent is available, and

    (b) that the responsible officer has applied or proposes to apply under Part 3 or 4 of Schedule 2 for the revocation or amendment of the order,

the fostering requirement is, until the determination of the application, to be taken to require the offender to reside in accommodation provided by or on behalf of a local authority.

(6) This paragraph does not affect the power of a local authority to place with a local authority foster parent an offender in respect of whom a local authority residence requirement is imposed.

(7) A court may not include a fostering requirement in a youth rehabilitation order unless the court has been notified by the Secretary of State that arrangements for implementing such a requirement are available in the area of the local authority which is to place the offender with a local authority foster parent.

(8) In this paragraph, "local authority foster parent" has the same meaning as it has in the Children Act 1989.

Pre-conditions to imposing local authority residence requirement or fostering requirement

19 (1) A court may not include a local authority residence requirement or a fostering requirement in a youth rehabilitation order in respect of an offender unless—

    (a) the offender was legally represented at the relevant time in court, or

    (b) either of the conditions in sub-paragraph (2) is satisfied.

(2) Those conditions are—

    (a) that the offender was granted a right to representation funded by the Legal Services Commission as part of the Criminal Defence Service for the purposes of the proceedings but the right was withdrawn because of the offender's conduct, or

(b) that the offender has been informed of the right to apply for such representation for the purposes of the proceedings and has had the opportunity to do so, but nevertheless refused or failed to apply.

(3) In this paragraph—
"the proceedings" means—
(a) the whole proceedings, or
(b) the part of the proceedings relating to the imposition of the local authority residence requirement or the fostering requirement;
"the relevant time" means the time when the court is considering whether to impose that requirement.

Mental health treatment requirement

20 (1) In this Part of this Act "mental health treatment requirement", in relation to a youth rehabilitation order, means a requirement that the offender must submit, during a period or periods specified in the order, to treatment by or under the direction of a registered medical practitioner or a chartered psychologist (or both, for different periods) with a view to the improvement of the offender's mental condition.

(2) The treatment required during a period specified under sub-paragraph (1) must be such one of the following kinds of treatment as may be specified in the youth rehabilitation order—
(a) treatment as a resident patient in an independent hospital or care home within the meaning of the Care Standards Act 2000 (c. 14) or a hospital within the meaning of the Mental Health Act 1983 (c. 20), but not in hospital premises where high security psychiatric services within the meaning of that Act are provided;
(b) treatment as a non-resident patient at such institution or place as may be specified in the order;
(c) treatment by or under the direction of such registered medical practitioner or chartered psychologist (or both) as may be so specified;
but the order must not otherwise specify the nature of the treatment.

(3) A court may not include a mental health treatment requirement in a youth rehabilitation order unless—
(a) the court is satisfied, on the evidence of a registered medical practitioner approved for the purposes of section 12 of the Mental Health Act 1983 (c. 20), that the mental condition of the offender—
(i) is such as requires and may be susceptible to treatment, but
(ii) is not such as to warrant the making of a hospital order or guardianship order within the meaning of that Act,
(b) the court is also satisfied that arrangements have been or can be made for the treatment intended to be specified in the order (including, where the offender is to be required to submit to treatment as a resident patient, arrangements for the reception of the offender), and
(c) the offender has expressed willingness to comply with the requirement.

(4) While the offender is under treatment as a resident patient in pursuance of a mental health treatment requirement of a youth rehabilitation order, the responsible officer is to carry out the supervision of the offender to such extent only as may be necessary for the purpose of the revocation or amendment of the order.

(5) Subsections (2) and (3) of section 54 of the Mental Health Act 1983 have effect with respect to proof of an offender's mental condition for the purposes of sub-paragraph (3)(a) as they have effect with respect to proof of an offender's mental condition for the purposes of section 37(2)(a) of that Act.

(6) In this paragraph and paragraph 21, "chartered psychologist" means a person for the time being listed in the British Psychological Society's Register of Chartered Psychologists.

Mental health treatment at place other than that specified in order

21 (1) Where the registered medical practitioner or chartered psychologist by whom or under whose direction an offender is being treated in pursuance of a mental health treatment requirement is of the opinion that part of the treatment can be better or more conveniently given in or at an institution or place which—

(a) is not specified in the youth rehabilitation order, and

(b) is one in or at which the treatment of the offender will be given by or under the direction of a registered medical practitioner or chartered psychologist,

the medical practitioner or psychologist may make arrangements for the offender to be treated accordingly.

(2) Such arrangements as are mentioned in sub-paragraph (1) may only be made if the offender has expressed willingness for the treatment to be given as mentioned in that sub-paragraph.

(3) Such arrangements as are mentioned in sub-paragraph (1) may provide for part of the treatment to be provided to the offender as a resident patient in an institution or place notwithstanding that the institution or place is not one which could have been specified for that purpose in the youth rehabilitation order.

(4) Where any such arrangements as are mentioned in sub-paragraph (1) are made for the treatment of an offender—

(a) the registered medical practitioner or chartered psychologist by whom the arrangements are made must give notice in writing to the offender's responsible officer, specifying the institution or place in or at which the treatment is to be carried out, and

(b) the treatment provided for by the arrangements is deemed to be treatment to which the offender is required to submit in pursuance of the youth rehabilitation order.

Drug treatment requirement

22 (1) In this Part of this Act, "drug treatment requirement", in relation to a youth rehabilitation order, means a requirement that the offender must submit, during a period or periods specified in the order, to treatment, by or under the direction of a person so specified having the necessary qualifications or experience ("the treatment provider"), with a view to the reduction or elimination of the offender's dependency on, or propensity to misuse, drugs.

(2) A court may not include a drug treatment requirement in a youth rehabilitation order unless it is satisfied—

(a) that the offender is dependent on, or has a propensity to misuse, drugs, and

(b) that the offender's dependency or propensity is such as requires and may be susceptible to treatment.

(3) The treatment required during a period specified under sub-paragraph (1) must be such one of the following kinds of treatment as may be specified in the youth rehabilitation order—

(a) treatment as a resident in such institution or place as may be specified in the order, or

(b) treatment as a non-resident at such institution or place, and at such intervals, as may be so specified,

but the order must not otherwise specify the nature of the treatment.

(4) A court may not include a drug treatment requirement in a youth rehabilitation order unless—

(a) the court has been notified by the Secretary of State that arrangements for implementing drug treatment requirements are in force in the local justice area in which the offender resides or is to reside,

(b) the court is satisfied that arrangements have been or can be made for the treatment intended to be specified in the order (including, where the offender is to be required to submit to treatment as a resident, arrangements for the reception of the offender),

    (c) the requirement has been recommended to the court as suitable for the offender by a member of a youth offending team, an officer of a local probation board or an officer of a provider of probation services, and

    (d) the offender has expressed willingness to comply with the requirement.

(5) In this paragraph "drug" means a controlled drug as defined by section 2 of the Misuse of Drugs Act 1971 (c. 38).

Drug testing requirement

23 (1) In this Part of this Act, "drug testing requirement", in relation to a youth rehabilitation order, means a requirement that, for the purpose of ascertaining whether there is any drug in the offender's body during any treatment period, the offender must, during that period, provide samples in accordance with instructions given by the responsible officer or the treatment provider.

(2) In sub-paragraph (1)—

    "drug" has the same meaning as in paragraph 22,

    "treatment period" means a period specified in the youth rehabilitation order as a period during which the offender must submit to treatment as mentioned in sub-paragraph (1) of that paragraph, and

    "the treatment provider" has the meaning given by that sub-paragraph.

(3) A court may not include a drug testing requirement in a youth rehabilitation order unless—

    (a) the court has been notified by the Secretary of State that arrangements for implementing drug testing requirements are in force in the local justice area in which the offender resides or is to reside,

    (b) the order also imposes a drug treatment requirement, and

    (c) the offender has expressed willingness to comply with the requirement.

(4) A youth rehabilitation order which imposes a drug testing requirement—

    (a) must specify for each month the minimum number of occasions on which samples are to be provided, and

    (b) may specify—

        (i) times at which and circumstances in which the responsible officer or treatment provider may require samples to be provided, and

        (ii) descriptions of the samples which may be so required.

(5) A youth rehabilitation order which imposes a drug testing requirement must provide for the results of tests carried out otherwise than by the responsible officer on samples provided by the offender in pursuance of the requirement to be communicated to the responsible officer.

Intoxicating substance treatment requirement

24 (1) In this Part of this Act, "intoxicating substance treatment requirement", in relation to a youth rehabilitation order, means a requirement that the offender must submit, during a period or periods specified in the order, to treatment, by or under the direction of a person so specified having the necessary qualifications or experience, with a view to the reduction or elimination of the offender's dependency on or propensity to misuse intoxicating substances.

(2) A court may not include an intoxicating substance treatment requirement in a youth rehabilitation order unless it is satisfied—

    (a) that the offender is dependent on, or has a propensity to misuse, intoxicating substances, and

    (b) that the offender's dependency or propensity is such as requires and may be susceptible to treatment.

(3) The treatment required during a period specified under sub-paragraph (1) must be such one of the following kinds of treatment as may be specified in the youth rehabilitation order—
  (a) treatment as a resident in such institution or place as may be specified in the order, or
  (b) treatment as a non-resident at such institution or place, and at such intervals, as may be so specified,
but the order must not otherwise specify the nature of the treatment.

(4) A court may not include an intoxicating substance treatment requirement in a youth rehabilitation order unless—
  (a) the court is satisfied that arrangements have been or can be made for the treatment intended to be specified in the order (including, where the offender is to be required to submit to treatment as a resident, arrangements for the reception of the offender),
  (b) the requirement has been recommended to the court as suitable for the offender by a member of a youth offending team, an officer of a local probation board or an officer of a provider of probation services, and
  (c) the offender has expressed willingness to comply with the requirement.

(5) In this paragraph "intoxicating substance" means—
  (a) alcohol, or
  (b) any other substance or product (other than a drug) which is, or the fumes of which are, capable of being inhaled or otherwise used for the purpose of causing intoxication.

(6) In sub-paragraph (5)(b) "drug" means a controlled drug as defined by section 2 of the Misuse of Drugs Act 1971 (c. 38).

Education requirement

25 (1) In this Part of this Act "education requirement", in relation to a youth rehabilitation order, means a requirement that the offender must comply, during a period or periods specified in the order, with approved education arrangements.

(2) For this purpose, "approved education arrangements" means arrangements for the offender's education—
  (a) made for the time being by the offender's parent or guardian, and
  (b) approved by the local education authority specified in the order.

(3) The local education authority so specified must be the local education authority for the area in which the offender resides or is to reside.

(4) A court may not include an education requirement in a youth rehabilitation order unless—
  (a) it has consulted the local education authority proposed to be specified in the order with regard to the proposal to include the requirement, and
  (b) it is satisfied—
    (i) that, in the view of that local education authority, arrangements exist for the offender to receive efficient fulltime education suitable to the offender's age, ability, aptitude and special educational needs (if any), and
    (ii) that, having regard to the circumstances of the case, the inclusion of the education requirement is necessary for securing the good conduct of the offender or for preventing the commission of further offences.

(5) Any period specified in a youth rehabilitation order as a period during which an offender must comply with approved education arrangements must not include any period after the offender has ceased to be of compulsory school age.

(6) In this paragraph, "local education authority" and "parent" have the same meanings as in the Education Act 1996 (c. 56).

Electronic monitoring requirement

26 (1) In this Part of this Act "electronic monitoring requirement", in relation to a youth rehabilitation order, means a requirement for securing the electronic monitoring of the offender's

compliance with other requirements imposed by the order during a period specified in the order or determined by the responsible officer in accordance with the order.

(2) Where an electronic monitoring requirement is required to take effect during a period determined by the responsible officer in accordance with the youth rehabilitation order, the responsible officer must, before the beginning of that period, notify—

(a) the offender,

(b) the person responsible for the monitoring, and

(c) any person falling within sub-paragraph (3)(b),

of the time when the period is to begin.

(3) Where—

(a) it is proposed to include an electronic monitoring requirement in a youth rehabilitation order, but

(b) there is a person (other than the offender) without whose cooperation it will not be practicable to secure that the monitoring takes place,

the requirement may not be included in the order without that person's consent.

(4) A youth rehabilitation order which imposes an electronic monitoring requirement must include provision for making a person responsible for the monitoring.

(5) The person who is made responsible for the monitoring must be of a description specified in an order made by the Secretary of State.

(6) A court may not include an electronic monitoring requirement in a youth rehabilitation order unless the court—

(a) has been notified by the Secretary of State that arrangements for electronic monitoring of offenders are available—

(i) in the local justice area proposed to be specified in the order, and

(ii) for each requirement mentioned in the first column of the Table in sub-paragraph (7) which the court proposes to include in the order, in the area in which the relevant place is situated, and

(b) is satisfied that the necessary provision can be made under the arrangements currently available.

(7) For the purposes of sub-paragraph (6), "relevant place", in relation to a requirement mentioned in the first column of the following Table which the court proposes to include in the order, means the place mentioned in relation to it in the second column of the Table.

Proposed requirement of youth rehabilitation order	Relevant place
Curfew requirement.	The place which the court proposes to specify in the order for the purposes of that requirement.
Exclusion requirement	The place (within the meaning of paragraph 15) which the court proposes to specify in the order.
Attendance centre requirement	The attendance centre which the court proposes to specify in the order.

Power to amend limits

27 (1) The Secretary of State may by order amend—

(a) paragraph 10(2) (unpaid work requirement), or

(b) paragraph 14(2) (curfew requirement),

by substituting, for the maximum number of hours for the time being specified in that provision, such other number of hours as may be specified in the order.

(2) The Secretary of State may by order amend any of the provisions mentioned in sub-paragraph (3) by substituting, for any period for the time being specified in the provision, such other period as may be specified in the order.

(3) Those provisions are—
   (a) paragraph 14(3) (curfew requirement);
   (b) paragraph 15(2) (exclusion requirement);
   (c) paragraph 17(6) (local authority residence requirement);
   (d) paragraph 18(2) (fostering requirement).

(4) An order under this paragraph which amends paragraph 18(2) may also make consequential amendments of paragraphs 6(9), 8(9) and 16(2) of Schedule 2.

PART 3
PROVISIONS APPLYING WHERE COURT PROPOSES TO MAKE YOUTH REHABILITATION ORDER

Family circumstances

28 Before making a youth rehabilitation order, the court must obtain and consider information about the offender's family circumstances and the likely effect of such an order on those circumstances.

Compatibility of requirements, requirement to avoid conflict with religious beliefs, etc.

29 (1) Before making—
   (a) a youth rehabilitation order imposing two or more requirements, or
   (b) two or more youth rehabilitation orders in respect of associated offences,
   the court must consider whether, in the circumstances of the case, the requirements to be imposed by the order or orders are compatible with each other.

(2) Sub-paragraph (1) is subject to paragraphs 2, 3(4) and 4(4).

(3) The court must ensure, as far as practicable, that any requirement imposed by a youth rehabilitation order is such as to avoid—
   (a) any conflict with the offender's religious beliefs,
   (b) any interference with the times, if any, at which the offender normally works or attends school or any other educational establishment, and
   (c) any conflict with the requirements of any other youth rehabilitation order to which the offender may be subject.

(4) The Secretary of State may by order provide that sub-paragraph (3) is to have effect with such additional restrictions as may be specified in the order.

Date of taking effect and other existing orders

30 (1) Subject to sub-paragraph (2), a youth rehabilitation order takes effect on the day after the day on which the order is made.

(2) If a detention and training order is in force in respect of an offender, a court making a youth rehabilitation order in respect of the offender may order that it is to take effect instead—
   (a) when the period of supervision begins in relation to the detention and training order in accordance with section 103(1)(a) of the Powers of Criminal Courts (Sentencing) Act 2000 (c. 6), or
   (b) on the expiry of the term of the detention and training order.

(3) In sub-paragraph (2)—
   (a) the references to a detention and training order include an order made under section 211 of the Armed Forces Act 2006 (c. 52) (detention and training orders made by service courts); and

(b) the reference to section 103(1)(a) of the Powers of Criminal Courts (Sentencing) Act 2000 includes that provision as applied by section 213(1) of the Armed Forces Act 2006.

(4) A court must not make a youth rehabilitation order in respect of an offender at a time when—

(a) another youth rehabilitation order, or

(b) a reparation order made under section 73(1) of the Powers of Criminal Courts (Sentencing) Act 2000 (c. 6),

is in force in respect of the offender, unless when it makes the order it revokes the earlier order.

(5) Where the earlier order is revoked under sub-paragraph (4), paragraph 24 of Schedule 2 (provision of copies of orders) applies to the revocation as it applies to the revocation of a youth rehabilitation order.

Concurrent and consecutive orders

31 (1) This paragraph applies where the court is dealing with an offender who has been convicted of two or more associated offences.

(2) If, in respect of one of the offences, the court makes an order of any of the following kinds—

(a) a youth rehabilitation order with intensive supervision and surveillance,

(b) a youth rehabilitation order with fostering, or

(c) any other youth rehabilitation order,

it may not make an order of any other of those kinds in respect of the other offence, or any of the other offences.

(3) If the court makes two or more youth rehabilitation orders with intensive supervision and surveillance, or with fostering, both or all of the orders must take effect at the same time (in accordance with paragraph 30(1) or (2)).

(4) Where the court includes requirements of the same kind in two or more youth rehabilitation orders, it must direct, in relation to each requirement of that kind, whether—

(a) it is to be concurrent with the other requirement or requirements of that kind, or any of them, or

(b) it and the other requirement or requirements of that kind, or any of them, are to be consecutive.

(5) But the court may not direct that two or more fostering requirements are to be consecutive.

(6) Where the court directs that two or more requirements of the same kind are to be consecutive—

(a) the number of hours, days or months specified in relation to one of them is additional to the number of hours, days, or months specified in relation to the other or others, but

(b) the aggregate number of hours, days or months specified in relation to both or all of them must not exceed the maximum number which may be specified in relation to any one of them.

(7) For the purposes of sub-paragraphs (4) and (6), requirements are of the same kind if they fall within the same paragraph of Part 2 of this Schedule.

PART 4

PROVISIONS APPLYING WHERE COURT MAKES YOUTH REHABILITATION ORDER ETC.

Date for compliance with requirements to be specified in order

32 (1) A youth rehabilitation order must specify a date, not more than 3 years after the date on which the order takes effect, by which all the requirements in it must have been complied with.

(2) A youth rehabilitation order which imposes two or more different requirements falling within Part 2 of this Schedule may also specify an earlier date or dates in relation to compliance with any one or more of them.

(3) In the case of a youth rehabilitation order with intensive supervision and surveillance, the date specified for the purposes of sub-paragraph (1) must not be earlier than 6 months after the date on which the order takes effect.

Local justice area to be specified in order

33 A youth rehabilitation order must specify the local justice area in which the offender resides or will reside.

Provision of copies of orders

34 (1) The court by which any youth rehabilitation order is made must forthwith provide copies of the order—
  (a) to the offender,
  (b) if the offender is aged under 14, to the offender's parent or guardian, and
  (c) to a member of a youth offending team assigned to the court, to an officer of a local probation board assigned to the court or to an officer of a provider of probation services.

  (2) Sub-paragraph (3) applies where a youth rehabilitation order—
  (a) is made by the Crown Court, or
  (b) is made by a magistrates' court which does not act in the local justice area specified in the order.

  (3) The court making the order must—
  (a) provide to the magistrates' court acting in the local justice area specified in the order—
    (i) a copy of the order, and
    (ii) such documents and information relating to the case as it considers likely to be of assistance to a court acting in that area in the exercise of its functions in relation to the order, and
  (b) provide a copy of the order to the local probation board acting for that area or (as the case may be) a provider of probation services operating in that area.

  (4) Where a youth rehabilitation order imposes any requirement specified in the first column of the following Table, the court by which the order is made must also forthwith provide the person specified in relation to that requirement in the second column of that Table with a copy of so much of the order as relates to that requirement.

Requirement	*Person to whom copy of requirement is to be given*
An activity requirement specifying a place under paragraph 6(1)(a).	The person in charge of that place.
An activity requirement specifying an activity under paragraph 6(1)(b).	The person in charge of that activity.
An activity requirement specifying a residential exercise under paragraph 6(1)(c).	The person in charge of the place or activity specified under paragraph 6(4) in relation to that residential exercise.
An attendance centre requirement.	The officer in charge of the attendance centre specified under paragraph 12(1).
An exclusion requirement imposed for the purpose (or partly for the purpose) of protecting a person from being approached by the offender.	The person intended to be protected.
A residence requirement requiring residence with an individual.	The individual specified under paragraph 16(1)(a).

Requirement	Person to whom copy of requirement is to be given
A place of residence requirement (within the meaning of paragraph 16) relating to residence in an institution.	The person in charge of the institution.
A local authority residence requirement.	The local authority specified under paragraph 17(1).
A mental health treatment requirement.	The person in charge of the institution or place specified under sub-paragraph (2)(a) or (b) of paragraph 20, or the person specified under sub-paragraph (2)(c) of that paragraph.
A drug treatment requirement.	The treatment provider specified under paragraph 22(1).
A drug testing requirement.	The treatment provider specified under paragraph 22(1).
An intoxicating substance treatment requirement.	The person specified under paragraph 24(1).
An education requirement.	The local education authority specified under paragraph 25(2).
An electronic monitoring requirement.	Any person who by virtue of paragraph 26(4) will be responsible for the electronic monitoring. Any person without whose consent the requirement could not have been included in the order.

Power to provide for court review of orders

35 (1) The Secretary of State may by order—
   (a) enable or require a court making a youth rehabilitation order to provide for the order to be reviewed periodically by that or another court,
   (b) enable a court to amend a youth rehabilitation order so as to include or remove a provision for review by a court, and
   (c) make provision as to the timing and conduct of reviews and as to the powers of the court on a review.
(2) An order under this paragraph may, in particular, make provision in relation to youth rehabilitation orders corresponding to any provision made by sections 191 and 192 of the Criminal Justice Act 2003 (c. 44) (reviews of suspended sentence orders) in relation to suspended sentence orders.
(3) An order under this paragraph may repeal or amend any provision of—
   (a) this Part of this Act, or
   (b) Chapter 1 of Part 12 of the Criminal Justice Act 2003 (general provisions about sentencing).

Order made by Crown Court: direction in relation to further proceedings

36 (1) Where the Crown Court makes a youth rehabilitation order, it may include in the order a direction that further proceedings relating to the order be in a youth court or other magistrates' court (subject to paragraph 7 of Schedule 2).
(2) In sub-paragraph (1), "further proceedings", in relation to a youth rehabilitation order, means proceedings—
   (a) for any failure to comply with the order within the meaning given by paragraph 1(2)(b) of Schedule 2, or
   (b) on any application for amendment or revocation of the order under Part 3 or 4 of that Schedule.

SCHEDULE 2   Section 2
BREACH, REVOCATION OR AMENDMENT OF YOUTH REHABILITATION
ORDERS

PART 1
PRELIMINARY

Interpretation

1 (1) In this Schedule, "the offender", in relation to a youth rehabilitation order, means the person in respect of whom the order is made.

(2) In this Schedule—

(a) any reference (however expressed) to an offender's compliance with a youth rehabilitation order is a reference to the offender's compliance with—

(i) the requirement or requirements imposed by the order, and

(ii) if the order imposes an attendance centre requirement, rules made under section 222(1)(d) or (e) of the Criminal Justice Act 2003 (c. 44) ("attendance centre rules"), and

(b) any reference (however expressed) to the offender's failure to comply with the order is a reference to any failure of the offender to comply—

(i) with a requirement imposed by the order, or

(ii) if the order imposes an attendance centre requirement, with attendance centre rules.

(3) For the purposes of this Schedule—

(a) a requirement falling within any paragraph of Part 2 of Schedule 1 is of the same kind as any other requirement falling within that paragraph, and

(b) an electronic monitoring requirement is a requirement of the same kind as any requirement falling within Part 2 of Schedule 1 to which it relates.

Orders made on appeal

2 Where a youth rehabilitation order has been made on appeal, for the purposes of this Schedule it is to be treated—

(a) if it was made on an appeal from a magistrates' court, as having been made by a magistrates' court;

(b) if it was made on an appeal brought from the Crown Court or from the criminal division of the Court of Appeal, as having been made by the Crown Court.

PART 2
BREACH OF REQUIREMENT OF ORDER

Duty to give warning

3 (1) If the responsible officer is of the opinion that the offender has failed without reasonable excuse to comply with a youth rehabilitation order, the responsible officer must give the offender a warning under this paragraph unless under paragraph 4(1) or (3) the responsible officer causes an information to be laid before a justice of the peace in respect of the failure.

(2) A warning under this paragraph must—

(a) describe the circumstances of the failure,

(b) state that the failure is unacceptable, and

(c) state that the offender will be liable to be brought before a court—

    (i) in a case where the warning is given during the warned period relating to a previous warning under this paragraph, if during that period the offender again fails to comply with the order, or

    (ii) in any other case, if during the warned period relating to the warning, the offender fails on more than one occasion to comply with the order.

(3) The responsible officer must, as soon as practicable after the warning has been given, record that fact.

(4) In this paragraph, "warned period", in relation to a warning under this paragraph, means the period of 12 months beginning with the date on which the warning was given.

Breach of order

4 (1) If the responsible officer—

    (a) has given a warning ("the first warning") under paragraph 3 to the offender in respect of a youth rehabilitation order,

    (b) during the warned period relating to the first warning, has given another warning under that paragraph to the offender in respect of a failure to comply with the order, and

    (c) is of the opinion that, during the warned period relating to the first warning, the offender has again failed without reasonable excuse to comply with the order,

the responsible officer must cause an information to be laid before a justice of the peace in respect of the failure mentioned in paragraph (c).

(2) But sub-paragraph (1) does not apply if the responsible officer is of the opinion that there are exceptional circumstances which justify not causing an information to be so laid.

(3) If—

    (a) the responsible officer is of the opinion that the offender has failed without reasonable excuse to comply with a youth rehabilitation order, and

    (b) sub-paragraph (1) does not apply (in a case not within subparagraph (2)),

the responsible officer may cause an information to be laid before a justice of the peace in respect of that failure.

(4) In this paragraph, "warned period" has the same meaning as in paragraph 3.

Issue of summons or warrant by justice of the peace

5 (1) If at any time while a youth rehabilitation order is in force it appears on information to a justice of the peace that an offender has failed to comply with a youth rehabilitation order, the justice may—

    (a) issue a summons requiring the offender to appear at the place and time specified in it, or

    (b) if the information is in writing and on oath, issue a warrant for the offender's arrest.

(2) Any summons or warrant issued under this paragraph must direct the offender to appear or be brought—

    (a) if the youth rehabilitation order was made by the Crown Court and does not include a direction under paragraph 36 of Schedule 1, before the Crown Court, and

    (b) in any other case, before the appropriate court.

(3) In sub-paragraph (2), "appropriate court" means—

    (a) if the offender is aged under 18, a youth court acting in the relevant local justice area, and

    (b) if the offender is aged 18 or over, a magistrates' court (other than a youth court) acting in that local justice area.

(4) In sub-paragraph (3), "relevant local justice area" means—

    (a) the local justice area in which the offender resides, or

    (b) if it is not known where the offender resides, the local justice area specified in the youth rehabilitation order.

(5) Sub-paragraphs (6) and (7) apply where the offender does not appear in answer to a summons issued under this paragraph.

(6) If the summons required the offender to appear before the Crown Court, the Crown Court may—

    (a) unless the summons was issued under this sub-paragraph, issue a further summons requiring the offender to appear at the place and time specified in it, or

    (b) in any case, issue a warrant for the arrest of the offender.

(7) If the summons required the offender to appear before a magistrates' court, the magistrates' court may issue a warrant for the arrest of the offender.

Powers of magistrates' court

6 (1) This paragraph applies where—

    (a) an offender appears or is brought before a youth court or other magistrates' court under paragraph 5, and

    (b) it is proved to the satisfaction of the court that the offender has failed without reasonable excuse to comply with the youth rehabilitation order.

(2) The court may deal with the offender in respect of that failure in any one of the following ways—

    (a) by ordering the offender to pay a fine of an amount not exceeding—

        (i) £250, if the offender is aged under 14, or

        (ii) £1,000, in any other case;

    (b) by amending the terms of the youth rehabilitation order so as to impose any requirement which could have been included in the order when it was made—

        (i) in addition to, or

        (ii) in substitution for,

    any requirement or requirements already imposed by the order;

    (c) by dealing with the offender, for the offence in respect of which the order was made, in any way in which the court could have dealt with the offender for that offence (had the offender been before that court to be dealt with for it).

(3) Sub-paragraph (2)(b) is subject to sub-paragraphs (6) to (9).

(4) In dealing with the offender under sub-paragraph (2), the court must take into account the extent to which the offender has complied with the youth rehabilitation order.

(5) A fine imposed under sub-paragraph (2)(a) is to be treated, for the purposes of any enactment, as being a sum adjudged to be paid by a conviction.

(6) Any requirement imposed under sub-paragraph (2)(b) must be capable of being complied with before the date specified under paragraph 32(1) of Schedule 1.

(7) Where—

    (a) the court is dealing with the offender under sub-paragraph (2)(b), and

    (b) the youth rehabilitation order does not contain an unpaid work requirement,

paragraph 10(2) of Schedule 1 applies in relation to the inclusion of such a requirement as if for "40" there were substituted "20".

(8) The court may not under sub-paragraph (2)(b) impose—

    (a) an extended activity requirement, or

    (b) a fostering requirement,

if the order does not already impose such a requirement.

(9) Where—

    (a) the order imposes a fostering requirement (the "original requirement"), and

    (b) under sub-paragraph (2)(b) the court proposes to substitute a new fostering requirement ("the substitute requirement") for the original requirement,

paragraph 18(2) of Schedule 1 applies in relation to the substitute requirement as if the reference to the period of 12 months beginning with the date on which the original requirement first had effect were a reference to the period of 18 months beginning with that date.

(10) Where—
- (a) the court deals with the offender under sub-paragraph (2)(b), and
- (b) it would not otherwise have the power to amend the youth rehabilitation order under paragraph 13 (amendment by reason of change of residence),

that paragraph has effect as if references in it to the appropriate court were references to the court which is dealing with the offender.

(11) Where the court deals with the offender under sub-paragraph (2)(c), it must revoke the youth rehabilitation order if it is still in force.

(12) Sub-paragraphs (13) to (15) apply where—
- (a) the court is dealing with the offender under sub-paragraph (2)(c), and
- (b) the offender has wilfully and persistently failed to comply with a youth rehabilitation order.

(13) The court may impose a youth rehabilitation order with intensive supervision and surveillance notwithstanding anything in section 1(4)(a) or (b).

(14) If—
- (a) the order is a youth rehabilitation order with intensive supervision and surveillance, and
- (b) the offence mentioned in sub-paragraph (2)(c) was punishable with imprisonment,

the court may impose a custodial sentence notwithstanding anything in section 152(2) of the Criminal Justice Act 2003 (c. 44) (general restrictions on imposing discretionary custodial sentences).

(15) If—
- (a) the order is a youth rehabilitation order with intensive supervision and surveillance which was imposed by virtue of sub-paragraph (13) or paragraph 8(12), and
- (b) the offence mentioned in sub-paragraph (2)(c) was not punishable with imprisonment,

for the purposes of dealing with the offender under sub-paragraph (2)(c), the court is to be taken to have had power to deal with the offender for that offence by making a detention and training order for a term not exceeding 4 months.

(16) An offender may appeal to the Crown Court against a sentence imposed under sub-paragraph (2)(c).

Power of magistrates' court to refer offender to Crown Court

7 (1) Sub-paragraph (2) applies if—
- (a) the youth rehabilitation order was made by the Crown Court and contains a direction under paragraph 36 of Schedule 1, and
- (b) a youth court or other magistrates' court would (apart from that subparagraph) be required, or has the power, to deal with the offender in one of the ways mentioned in paragraph 6(2).

(2) The court may instead—
- (a) commit the offender in custody, or
- (b) release the offender on bail,

until the offender can be brought or appear before the Crown Court.

(3) Where a court deals with the offender's case under sub-paragraph (2) it must send to the Crown Court—
- (a) a certificate signed by a justice of the peace certifying that the offender has failed to comply with the youth rehabilitation order in the respect specified in the certificate, and
- (b) such other particulars of the case as may be desirable;

and a certificate purporting to be so signed is admissible as evidence of the failure before the Crown Court.

Powers of Crown Court

8 (1) This paragraph applies where—
- (a) an offender appears or is brought before the Crown Court under paragraph 5 or by virtue of paragraph 7(2), and

   (b) it is proved to the satisfaction of that court that the offender has failed without reasonable excuse to comply with the youth rehabilitation order.

(2) The Crown Court may deal with the offender in respect of that failure in any one of the following ways—

   (a) by ordering the offender to pay a fine of an amount not exceeding—

      (i) £250, if the offender is aged under 14, or

      (ii) £1,000, in any other case;

   (b) by amending the terms of the youth rehabilitation order so as to impose any requirement which could have been included in the order when it was made—

      (i) in addition to, or

      (ii) in substitution for,

     any requirement or requirements already imposed by the order;

   (c) by dealing with the offender, for the offence in respect of which the order was made, in any way in which the Crown Court could have dealt with the offender for that offence.

(3) Sub-paragraph (2)(b) is subject to sub-paragraphs (6) to (9).

(4) In dealing with the offender under sub-paragraph (2), the Crown Court must take into account the extent to which the offender has complied with the youth rehabilitation order.

(5) A fine imposed under sub-paragraph (2)(a) is to be treated, for the purposes of any enactment, as being a sum adjudged to be paid by a conviction.

(6) Any requirement imposed under sub-paragraph (2)(b) must be capable of being complied with before the date specified under paragraph 32(1) of Schedule 1.

(7) Where—

   (a) the court is dealing with the offender under sub-paragraph (2)(b), and

   (b) the youth rehabilitation order does not contain an unpaid work requirement,

   paragraph 10(2) of Schedule 1 applies in relation to the inclusion of such a requirement as if for "40" there were substituted "20".

(8) The court may not under sub-paragraph (2)(b) impose—

   (a) an extended activity requirement, or

   (b) a fostering requirement,

   if the order does not already impose such a requirement.

(9) Where—

   (a) the order imposes a fostering requirement (the "original requirement"), and

   (b) under sub-paragraph (2)(b) the court proposes to substitute a new fostering requirement ("the substitute requirement") for the original requirement,

   paragraph 18(2) of Schedule 1 applies in relation to the substitute requirement as if the reference to the period of 12 months beginning with the date on which the original requirement first had effect were a reference to the period of 18 months beginning with that date.

(10) Where the Crown Court deals with an offender under sub-paragraph (2)(c), it must revoke the youth rehabilitation order if it is still in force.

(11) Sub-paragraphs (12) to (14) apply where—

   (a) an offender has wilfully and persistently failed to comply with a youth rehabilitation order; and

   (b) the Crown Court is dealing with the offender under sub-paragraph (2)(c).

(12) The court may impose a youth rehabilitation order with intensive supervision and surveillance notwithstanding anything in section 1(4)(a) or (b).

(13) If—

   (a) the order is a youth rehabilitation order with intensive supervision and surveillance, and

   (b) the offence mentioned in sub-paragraph (2)(c) was punishable with imprisonment,

   the court may impose a custodial sentence notwithstanding anything in section 152(2) of the Criminal Justice Act 2003 (c. 44) (general restrictions on imposing discretionary custodial sentences).

(14) If—

(a) the order is a youth rehabilitation order with intensive supervision and surveillance which was imposed by virtue of paragraph 6(13) or sub-paragraph (12), and

(b) the offence mentioned in sub-paragraph (2)(c) was not punishable with imprisonment,

for the purposes of dealing with the offender under sub-paragraph (2)(c), the Crown Court is to be taken to have had power to deal with the offender for that offence by making a detention and training order for a term not exceeding 4 months.

(15) In proceedings before the Crown Court under this paragraph any question whether the offender has failed to comply with the youth rehabilitation order is to be determined by the court and not by the verdict of a jury.

Restriction of powers in paragraphs 6 and 8 where treatment required

9 (1) Sub-paragraph (2) applies where a youth rehabilitation order imposes any of the following requirements in respect of an offender—

(a) a mental health treatment requirement;

(b) a drug treatment requirement;

(c) an intoxicating substance treatment requirement.

(2) The offender is not to be treated for the purposes of paragraph 6 or 8 as having failed to comply with the order on the ground only that the offender had refused to undergo any surgical, electrical or other treatment required by that requirement if, in the opinion of the court, the refusal was reasonable having regard to all the circumstances.

Power to amend amounts of fines

10 (1) The Secretary of State may by order amend any sum for the time being specified in paragraph 6(2)(a)(i) or (ii) or 8(2)(a)(i) or (ii).

(2) The power conferred by sub-paragraph (1) may be exercised only if it appears to the Secretary of State that there has been a change in the value of money since the relevant date which justifies the change.

(3) In sub-paragraph (2), "the relevant date" means—

(a) if the sum specified in paragraph 6(2)(a)(i) or (ii) or 8(2)(a)(i) or (ii) (as the case may be) has been substituted by an order under subparagraph (1), the date on which the sum was last so substituted;

(b) otherwise, the date on which this Act was passed.

(4) An order under sub-paragraph (1) (a "fine amendment order") must not have effect in relation to any youth rehabilitation order made in respect of an offence committed before the fine amendment order comes into force.

PART 3

REVOCATION OF ORDER

Revocation of order with or without re-sentencing: powers of appropriate court

11 (1) This paragraph applies where—

(a) a youth rehabilitation order is in force in respect of any offender,

(b) the order—

(i) was made by a youth court or other magistrates' court, or

(ii) was made by the Crown Court and contains a direction under paragraph 36 of Schedule 1, and

(c) the offender or the responsible officer makes an application to the appropriate court under this sub-paragraph.

(2) If it appears to the appropriate court to be in the interests of justice to do so, having regard to circumstances which have arisen since the order was made, the appropriate court may—

    (a) revoke the order, or

    (b) both—

        (i) revoke the order, and

        (ii) deal with the offender, for the offence in respect of which the order was made, in any way in which the appropriate court could have dealt with the offender for that offence (had the offender been before that court to be dealt with for it).

(3) The circumstances in which a youth rehabilitation order may be revoked under sub-paragraph (2) include the offender's making good progress or responding satisfactorily to supervision or treatment (as the case requires).

(4) In dealing with an offender under sub-paragraph (2)(b), the appropriate court must take into account the extent to which the offender has complied with the requirements of the youth rehabilitation order.

(5) A person sentenced under sub-paragraph (2)(b) for an offence may appeal to the Crown Court against the sentence.

(6) No application may be made by the offender under sub-paragraph (1) while an appeal against the youth rehabilitation order is pending.

(7) If an application under sub-paragraph (1) relating to a youth rehabilitation order is dismissed, then during the period of three months beginning with the date on which it was dismissed no further such application may be made in relation to the order by any person except with the consent of the appropriate court.

(8) In this paragraph, "the appropriate court" means—

    (a) if the offender is aged under 18 when the application under subparagraph (1) was made, a youth court acting in the local justice area specified in the youth rehabilitation order, and

    (b) if the offender is aged 18 or over at that time, a magistrates' court (other than a youth court) acting in that local justice area.

Revocation of order with or without re-sentencing: powers of Crown Court

12 (1) This paragraph applies where—

    (a) a youth rehabilitation order is in force in respect of an offender,

    (b) the order—

        (i) was made by the Crown Court, and

        (ii) does not contain a direction under paragraph 36 of Schedule 1, and

    (c) the offender or the responsible officer makes an application to the Crown Court under this sub-paragraph.

(2) If it appears to the Crown Court to be in the interests of justice to do so, having regard to circumstances which have arisen since the youth rehabilitation order was made, the Crown Court may—

    (a) revoke the order, or

    (b) both—

        (i) revoke the order, and

        (ii) deal with the offender, for the offence in respect of which the order was made, in any way in which the Crown Court could have dealt with the offender for that offence.

(3) The circumstances in which a youth rehabilitation order may be revoked under sub-paragraph (2) include the offender's making good progress or responding satisfactorily to supervision or treatment (as the case requires).

(4) In dealing with an offender under sub-paragraph (2)(b), the Crown Court must take into account the extent to which the offender has complied with the youth rehabilitation order.

(5) No application may be made by the offender under sub-paragraph (1) while an appeal against the youth rehabilitation order is pending.

(6) If an application under sub-paragraph (1) relating to a youth rehabilitation order is dismissed, then during the period of three months beginning with the date on which it was dismissed no further such application may be made in relation to the order by any person except with the consent of the Crown Court.

PART 4
AMENDMENT OF ORDER

Amendment by appropriate court

13 (1) This paragraph applies where—
    (a) a youth rehabilitation order is in force in respect of an offender,
    (b) the order—
        (i) was made by a youth court or other magistrates' court, or
        (ii) was made by the Crown Court and contains a direction under paragraph 36 of Schedule 1, and
    (c) an application for the amendment of the order is made to the appropriate court by the offender or the responsible officer.

(2) If the appropriate court is satisfied that the offender proposes to reside, or is residing, in a local justice area ("the new local justice area") other than the local justice area for the time being specified in the order, the court—
    (a) must, if the application under sub-paragraph (1)(c) was made by the responsible officer, or
    (b) may, in any other case,
amend the youth rehabilitation order by substituting the new local justice area for the area specified in the order.

(3) Sub-paragraph (2) is subject to paragraph 15.

(4) The appropriate court may by order amend the youth rehabilitation order—
    (a) by cancelling any of the requirements of the order, or
    (b) by replacing any of those requirements with a requirement of the same kind which could have been included in the order when it was made.

(5) Sub-paragraph (4) is subject to paragraph 16.

(6) In this paragraph, "the appropriate court" means—
    (a) if the offender is aged under 18 when the application under subparagraph (1) was made, a youth court acting in the local justice area specified in the youth rehabilitation order, and
    (b) if the offender is aged 18 or over at that time, a magistrates' court (other than a youth court) acting in that local justice area.

Amendment by Crown Court

14 (1) This paragraph applies where—
    (a) a youth rehabilitation order is in force in respect of an offender,
    (b) the order—
        (i) was made by the Crown Court, and
        (ii) does not contain a direction under paragraph 36 of Schedule 1, and
    (c) an application for the amendment of the order is made to the Crown Court by the offender or the responsible officer.

(2) If the Crown Court is satisfied that the offender proposes to reside, or is residing, in a local justice area ("the new local justice area") other than the local justice area for the time being specified in the order, the court—
    (a) must, if the application under sub-paragraph (1)(c) was made by the responsible officer, or
    (b) may, in any other case,

amend the youth rehabilitation order by substituting the new local justice area for the area specified in the order.

(3) Sub-paragraph (2) is subject to paragraph 15.

(4) The Crown Court may by order amend the youth rehabilitation order—

    (a) by cancelling any of the requirements of the order, or

    (b) by replacing any of those requirements with a requirement of the same kind which could have been included in the order when it was made.

(5) Sub-paragraph (4) is subject to paragraph 16.

Exercise of powers under paragraph 13(2) or 14(2): further provisions

15 (1) In sub-paragraphs (2) and (3), "specific area requirement", in relation to a youth rehabilitation order, means a requirement contained in the order which, in the opinion of the court, cannot be complied with unless the offender continues to reside in the local justice area specified in the youth rehabilitation order.

    (2) A court may not under paragraph 13(2) or 14(2) amend a youth rehabilitation order which contains specific area requirements unless, in accordance with paragraph 13(4) or, as the case may be, 14(4), it either—

        (a) cancels those requirements, or

        (b) substitutes for those requirements other requirements which can be complied with if the offender resides in the new local justice area mentioned in paragraph 13(2) or (as the case may be) 14(2).

    (3) If—

        (a) the application under paragraph 13(1)(c) or 14(1)(c) was made by the responsible officer, and

        (b) the youth rehabilitation order contains specific area requirements,

    the court must, unless it considers it inappropriate to do so, so exercise its powers under paragraph 13(4) or, as the case may be, 14(4) that it is not prevented by sub-paragraph (2) from amending the order under paragraph 13(2) or, as the case may be, 14(2).

    (4) The court may not under paragraph 13(2) or, as the case may be, 14(2) amend a youth rehabilitation order imposing a programme requirement unless the court is satisfied that a programme which—

        (a) corresponds as nearly as practicable to the programme specified in the order for the purposes of that requirement, and

        (b) is suitable for the offender,

    is available in the new local justice area.

Exercise of powers under paragraph 13(4) or 14(4): further provisions

16 (1) Any requirement imposed under paragraph 13(4)(b) or 14(4)(b) must be capable of being complied with before the date specified under paragraph 32(1) of Schedule 1.

    (2) Where—

        (a) a youth rehabilitation order imposes a fostering requirement (the "original requirement"), and

        (b) under paragraph 13(4)(b) or 14(4)(b) a court proposes to substitute a new fostering requirement ("the substitute requirement") for the original requirement,

    paragraph 18(2) of Schedule 1 applies in relation to the substitute requirement as if the reference to the period of 12 months beginning with the date on which the original requirement first had effect were a reference to the period of 18 months beginning with that date.

    (3) The court may not under paragraph 13(4) or 14(4) impose—

        (a) a mental health treatment requirement,

        (b) a drug treatment requirement, or

        (c) a drug testing requirement,

    unless the offender has expressed willingness to comply with the requirement.

(4) If an offender fails to express willingness to comply with a mental health treatment requirement, a drug treatment requirement or a drug testing requirement which the court proposes to impose under paragraph 13(4) or 14(4), the court may—

    (a) revoke the youth rehabilitation order, and

    (b) deal with the offender, for the offence in respect of which the order was made, in any way in which that court could have dealt with the offender for that offence (had the offender been before that court to be dealt with for it).

(5) In dealing with the offender under sub-paragraph (4)(b), the court must take into account the extent to which the offender has complied with the order.

Extension of unpaid work requirement

17 Where—

    (a) a youth rehabilitation order imposing an unpaid work requirement is in force in respect of an offender, and

    (b) on the application of the offender or the responsible officer, it appears to the appropriate court that it would be in the interests of justice to do so having regard to circumstances which have arisen since the order was made,

the court may, in relation to the order, extend the period of 12 months specified in paragraph 10(6) of Schedule 1.

PART 5
POWERS OF COURT IN RELATION TO ORDER FOLLOWING SUBSEQUENT CONVICTION

Powers of magistrates' court following subsequent conviction

18 (1) This paragraph applies where—

    (a) a youth rehabilitation order is in force in respect of an offender, and

    (b) the offender is convicted of an offence (the "further offence") by a youth court or other magistrates' court ("the convicting court").

(2) Sub-paragraphs (3) and (4) apply where—

    (a) the youth rehabilitation order—

        (i) was made by a youth court or other magistrates' court, or

        (ii) was made by the Crown Court and contains a direction under paragraph 36 of Schedule 1, and

    (b) the convicting court is dealing with the offender for the further offence.

(3) The convicting court may revoke the order.

(4) Where the convicting court revokes the order under sub-paragraph (3), it may deal with the offender, for the offence in respect of which the order was made, in any way in which it could have dealt with the offender for that offence (had the offender been before that court to be dealt with for the offence).

(5) The convicting court may not exercise its powers under sub-paragraph (3) or (4) unless it considers that it would be in the interests of justice to do so, having regard to circumstances which have arisen since the youth rehabilitation order was made.

(6) In dealing with an offender under sub-paragraph (4), the sentencing court must take into account the extent to which the offender has complied with the order.

(7) A person sentenced under sub-paragraph (4) for an offence may appeal to the Crown Court against the sentence.

(8) Sub-paragraph (9) applies where—

    (a) the youth rehabilitation order was made by the Crown Court and contains a direction under paragraph 36 of Schedule 1, and

(b) the convicting court would, but for that sub-paragraph, deal with the offender for the further offence.

(9) The convicting court may, instead of proceeding under sub-paragraph (3)—

(a) commit the offender in custody, or

(b) release the offender on bail,

until the offender can be brought before the Crown Court.

(10) Sub-paragraph (11) applies if the youth rehabilitation order was made by the Crown court and does not contain a direction under paragraph 36 of Schedule 1.

(11) The convicting court may—

(a) commit the offender in custody, or

(b) release the offender on bail,

until the offender can be brought or appear before the Crown Court.

(12) Where the convicting court deals with an offender's case under subparagraph (9) or (11), it must send to the Crown Court such particulars of the case as may be desirable.

Powers of Crown Court following subsequent conviction

19 (1) This paragraph applies where—

(a) a youth rehabilitation order is in force in respect of an offender, and

(b) the offender—

(i) is convicted by the Crown Court of an offence, or

(ii) is brought or appears before the Crown Court by virtue of paragraph 18(9) or (11) or having been committed by the magistrates' court to the Crown Court for sentence.

(2) The Crown Court may revoke the order.

(3) Where the Crown Court revokes the order under sub-paragraph (2), the Crown Court may deal with the offender, for the offence in respect of which the order was made, in any way in which the court which made the order could have dealt with the offender for that offence.

(4) The Crown Court must not exercise its powers under sub-paragraph (2) or (3) unless it considers that it would be in the interests of justice to do so, having regard to circumstances which have arisen since the youth rehabilitation order was made.

(5) In dealing with an offender under sub-paragraph (3), the Crown Court must take into account the extent to which the offender has complied with the order.

(6) If the offender is brought or appears before the Crown Court by virtue of paragraph 18(9) or (11), the Crown Court may deal with the offender for the further offence in any way which the convicting court could have dealt with the offender for that offence.

(7) In sub-paragraph (6), "further offence" and "the convicting court" have the same meanings as in paragraph 18.

PART 6

SUPPLEMENTARY

Appearance of offender before court

20 (1) Subject to sub-paragraph (2), where, otherwise than on the application of the offender, a court proposes to exercise its powers under Part 3, 4 or 5 of this Schedule, the court—

(a) must summon the offender to appear before the court, and

(b) if the offender does not appear in answer to the summons, may issue a warrant for the offender's arrest.

(2) Sub-paragraph (1) does not apply where a court proposes to make an order—

(a) revoking a youth rehabilitation order,

(b) cancelling, or reducing the duration of, a requirement of a youth rehabilitation order, or

(c) substituting a new local justice area or place for one specified in a youth rehabilitation order.

Warrants

21 (1) Sub-paragraph (2) applies where an offender is arrested in pursuance of a warrant issued by virtue of this Schedule and cannot be brought immediately before the court before which the warrant directs the offender to be brought ("the relevant court").

(2) The person in whose custody the offender is—

(a) may make arrangements for the offender's detention in a place of safety for a period of not more than 72 hours from the time of the arrest, and

(b) must within that period bring the offender before a magistrates' court.

(3) In the case of a warrant issued by the Crown Court, section 81(5) of the Supreme Court Act 1981 (c. 54) (duty to bring person before magistrates' court) does not apply.

(4) A person who is detained under arrangements made under sub-paragraph (2)(a) is deemed to be in legal custody.

(5) In sub-paragraph (2)(a) "place of safety" has the same meaning as in the Children and Young Persons Act 1933.

(6) Sub-paragraphs (7) to (10) apply where, under sub-paragraph (2), the offender is brought before a court ("the alternative court") which is not the relevant court.

(7) If the relevant court is a magistrates' court—

(a) the alternative court may—

(i) direct that the offender be released forthwith, or

(ii) remand the offender, and

(b) for the purposes of paragraph (a), section 128 of the Magistrates' Courts Act 1980 (c. 43) (remand in custody or on bail) has effect as if the court referred to in subsections (1)(a), (3), (4)(a) and (5) were the relevant court.

(8) If the relevant court is the Crown Court, section 43A of that Act (functions of magistrates' court where a person in custody is brought before it with a view to appearance before the Crown Court) applies as if, in subsection (1)—

(a) the words "issued by the Crown Court" were omitted, and

(b) the reference to section 81(5) of the Supreme Court Act 1981 were a reference to sub-paragraph (2)(b).

(9) Any power to remand the offender in custody which is conferred by section 43A or 128 of the Magistrates' Courts Act 1980 is to be taken to be a power—

(a) if the offender is aged under 18, to remand the offender to accommodation provided by or on behalf of a local authority, and

(b) in any other case, to remand the offender to a prison.

(10) Where the court remands the offender to accommodation provided by or on behalf of a local authority, the court must designate, as the authority which is to receive the offender, the local authority for the area in which it appears to the court that the offender resides.

Adjournment of proceedings

22 (1) This paragraph applies to any hearing relating to an offender held by a youth court or other magistrates' court in any proceedings under this Schedule.

(2) The court may adjourn the hearing, and, where it does so, may—

(a) direct that the offender be released forthwith, or

(b) remand the offender.

(3) Where the court remands the offender under sub-paragraph (2)—

(a) it must fix the time and place at which the hearing is to be resumed, and

(b) that time and place must be the time and place at which the offender is required to appear or be brought before the court by virtue of the remand.

(4) Where the court adjourns the hearing under sub-paragraph (2) but does not remand the offender—

    (a) it may fix the time and place at which the hearing is to be resumed, but

    (b) if it does not do so, must not resume the hearing unless it is satisfied that the offender, the responsible officer and, if the offender is aged under 14, a parent or guardian of the offender have had adequate notice of the time and place of the resumed hearing.

(5) The powers of a magistrates' court under this paragraph may be exercised by a single justice of the peace, notwithstanding anything in the Magistrates' Courts Act 1980 (c. 43).

(6) This paragraph—

    (a) applies to any hearing in any proceedings under this Schedule in place of section 10 of the Magistrates' Courts Act 1980 (adjournment of trial) where that section would otherwise apply, but

    (b) is not to be taken to affect the application of that section to hearings of any other description.

Restrictions on imposition of intensive supervision and surveillance or fostering

23 Subsection (4), and the provisions mentioned in subsection (6), of section 1 apply in relation to a power conferred by paragraph 6(2)(b), 8(2)(b), 13(4)(b) or 14(4)(b) to impose a requirement as they apply in relation to any power conferred by section 1 or Part 1 of Schedule 1 to make a youth rehabilitation order which includes such a requirement.

Provision of copies of orders etc.

24 (1) Where a court makes an order under this Schedule revoking or amending a youth rehabilitation order, the proper officer of the court must forthwith—

    (a) provide copies of the revoking or amending order to the offender and, if the offender is aged under 14, to the offender's parent or guardian,

    (b) provide a copy of the revoking or amending order to the responsible officer,

    (c) in the case of an amending order which substitutes a new local justice area, provide copies of the amending order to—

        (i) the local probation board acting for that area or (as the case may be) a provider of probation services operating in that area, and

        (ii) the magistrates' court acting in that area,

    (d) in the case of an amending order which imposes or cancels a requirement specified in the first column of the Table in paragraph 34(4) of Schedule 1, provide a copy of so much of the amending order as relates to that requirement to the person specified in relation to that requirement in the second column of that Table,

    (e) in the case of an order which revokes a requirement specified in the first column of that Table, provide a copy of the revoking order to the person specified in relation to that requirement in the second column of that Table, and

    (f) if the court is a magistrates' court acting in a local justice area other than the area specified in the youth rehabilitation order, provide a copy of the revoking or amending order to a magistrates' court acting in the local justice area specified in the order.

(2) Where under sub-paragraph (1)(c) the proper officer of the court provides a copy of an amending order to a magistrates' court acting in a different area, the officer must also provide to that court such documents and information relating to the case as appear likely to be of assistance to a court acting in that area in the exercise of its functions in relation to the order.

(3) In this paragraph "proper officer" means—

    (a) in relation to a magistrates' court, the designated officer for the court, and

    (b) in relation to the Crown Court, the appropriate officer.

Power to amend maximum period of fostering requirement

25 The Secretary of State may by order amend paragraph 6(9), 8(9) or 16(2) by substituting, for—
    (a) the period of 18 months specified in the provision, or
    (b) any other period which may be so specified by virtue of a previous order under this paragraph,
such other period as may be specified in the order.

SCHEDULE 3   Section 3

TRANSFER OF YOUTH REHABILITATION ORDERS TO NORTHERN IRELAND

PART 1

MAKING OR AMENDMENT OF A YOUTH REHABILITATION ORDER WHERE OFFENDER RESIDES OR PROPOSES TO RESIDE IN NORTHERN IRELAND

Making of youth rehabilitation order where offender resides or will reside in Northern Ireland

1 (1) This paragraph applies where a court considering the making of a youth rehabilitation order is satisfied that the offender—
    (a) resides in Northern Ireland, or
    (b) will reside there when the order takes effect.
  (2) The court may not make a youth rehabilitation order in respect of the offender unless it appears to the court that—
    (a) in the case of an order imposing a requirement mentioned in subparagraph (6), the conditions in sub-paragraphs (3), (4) and (5) are satisfied, or
    (b) in any other case, that the conditions in sub-paragraphs (3) and (4) are satisfied.
  (3) The condition in this sub-paragraph is satisfied if the number of hours, days or months in respect of which any requirement of the order is imposed is no greater than the number of hours, days or months which may be imposed by a court in Northern Ireland in respect of a similar requirement in the order which the court proposes to specify as the corresponding order under paragraph 3(b).
  (4) The condition in this sub-paragraph is satisfied if suitable arrangements for the offender's supervision can be made by the Probation Board for Northern Ireland or any other body designated by the Secretary of State by order.
  (5) The condition in this sub-paragraph is satisfied in relation to an order imposing a requirement mentioned in sub-paragraph (6) if—
    (a) arrangements exist for persons to comply with such a requirement in the petty sessions district in Northern Ireland in which the offender resides, or will be residing when the order takes effect, and
    (b) provision can be made for the offender to comply with the requirement under those arrangements.
  (6) The requirements referred to in sub-paragraphs (2)(a) and (5) are—
    (a) an activity requirement (including an extended activity requirement);
    (b) an unpaid work requirement;
    (c) a programme requirement;
    (d) an attendance centre requirement;
    (e) a mental health treatment requirement;
    (f) a drug treatment requirement;

    (g) a drug testing requirement;
    (h) an education requirement;
    (i) an electronic monitoring requirement.
  (7) The court may not by virtue of this paragraph require a local authority residence requirement or a fostering requirement to be complied with in Northern Ireland.

Amendment of youth rehabilitation order where offender resides or proposes to reside in Northern Ireland

2 (1) This paragraph applies where the appropriate court for the purposes of paragraph 13(2) of Schedule 2 (amendment by reason of change of residence) or the Crown Court is satisfied that an offender in respect of whom a youth rehabilitation order is in force is residing or proposes to reside in Northern Ireland.

  (2) The power of the court to amend the order under Part 4 of Schedule 2 includes power to amend it by requiring it to be complied with in Northern Ireland if it appears to the court that—
    (a) in the case of an order which once amended will impose a requirement mentioned in sub-paragraph (6), that the conditions in sub-paragraphs (3), (4) and (5) are satisfied, or
    (b) in any other case, that the conditions in sub-paragraphs (3) and (4) are satisfied.

  (3) The condition in this sub-paragraph is satisfied if the number of hours, days or months in respect of which any requirement of the order is imposed is no greater than the number of hours, days or months which may be imposed by a court in Northern Ireland in respect of a similar requirement in the order which the court proposes to specify as the corresponding order under paragraph 3(b).

  (4) The condition in this sub-paragraph is satisfied if suitable arrangements for the offender's supervision can be made by the Probation Board for Northern Ireland or any other body designated by the Secretary of State by order.

  (5) The condition in this sub-paragraph is satisfied in relation to an order that will impose a requirement mentioned in sub-paragraph (6) if—
    (a) arrangements exist for persons to comply with such a requirement in the petty sessions district in Northern Ireland in which the offender resides, or will be residing when the amendment to the order takes effect, and
    (b) provision can be made for the offender to comply with the requirement under those arrangements.

  (6) The requirements referred to in sub-paragraphs (2)(a) and (5) are—
    (a) an activity requirement (including an extended activity requirement);
    (b) an unpaid work requirement;
    (c) a programme requirement;
    (d) an attendance centre requirement;
    (e) a mental health treatment requirement;
    (f) a drug treatment requirement;
    (g) a drug testing requirement;
    (h) an education requirement;
    (i) an electronic monitoring requirement.
  (7) The court may not by virtue of this paragraph require a local authority residence requirement or a fostering requirement to be complied with in Northern Ireland.

Further provisions regarding the making or amending of youth rehabilitation orders under paragraph 1 or 2

3 A youth rehabilitation order made or amended in accordance with paragraph 1 or 2 must—
    (a) specify the petty sessions district in Northern Ireland in which the offender resides or will be residing when the order or amendment takes effect, and

(b) specify as the corresponding order for the purposes of this Schedule an order that may be made by a court in Northern Ireland,

and paragraph 33 of Schedule 1 (local justice area to be specified in order) does not apply in relation to an order so made or amended.

4 (1) Before making or amending a youth rehabilitation order in accordance with paragraph 1 or 2, the court must explain to the offender in ordinary language—

(a) the requirements of the legislation in Northern Ireland relating to the order to be specified under paragraph 3(b),

(b) the powers of the home court under that legislation, as modified by Part 2 of this Schedule, and

(c) its own powers under Part 2 of this Schedule.

(2) The court which makes or amends the order must—

(a) provide the persons mentioned in sub-paragraph (3) with a copy of the order as made or amended, and

(b) provide the home court with such other documents and information relating to the case as it considers likely to be of assistance to that court;

and sub-paragraphs (1) to (3) of paragraph 34 of Schedule 1 (provision of copies of orders) do not apply.

(3) The persons referred to in sub-paragraph (2)(a) are—

(a) the offender,

(b) where the offender is aged under 14—

(i) the offender's parent or guardian, or

(ii) if an authority in Northern Ireland has parental responsibility for, and is looking after, the offender, the authority,

(c) the body which is to make suitable arrangements for the offender's supervision under the order, and

(d) the home court.

(4) In sub-paragraph (3)(b)(ii)—

(a) "authority" has the meaning given by Article 2 of the Children (Northern Ireland) Order 1995 (S.I. 1995/755 (N.I. 2)),

(b) references to an offender who is looked after by an authority are to be construed in accordance with Article 25 of that Order, and

(c) "parental responsibility" has the same meaning as in that Order.

(5) In this paragraph, "home court" has the meaning given by paragraph 8.

Modifications to Part 1

5 (1) Where a court is considering the making or amendment of a youth rehabilitation order by virtue of paragraph 1 or 2, Part 1 of this Act (youth rehabilitation orders) has effect subject to the following modifications.

(2) The following provisions of Schedule 1 are omitted—

(a) in paragraph 8(3)(a) (activity requirement: further provisions), the words "a member of a youth offending team or",

(b) paragraphs 8(3)(c), 10(3)(b) and 12(3)(a) (availability of arrangements in local area: activity requirement, unpaid work requirement and attendance centre requirement),

(c) paragraph 16(7) (residence requirement: restriction on requiring residence at hostel or institution), and

(d) paragraphs 18(7), 22(4)(a), 23(3)(a) and 26(6) and (7) (availability of arrangements in local area: fostering requirement, drug treatment and testing requirements and electronic monitoring requirement).

(3) In paragraph 12 of Schedule 1 (attendance centre requirement) any reference to an attendance centre has effect as a reference to an attendance centre as defined by Article

50(1) of the Criminal Justice (Children) (Northern Ireland) Order 1998 (S.I. 1998/1504 (N.I. 9)).

(4) In paragraph 20 of that Schedule (mental health treatment requirement), for sub-paragraph (2)(a) there is substituted—

"(a) treatment as a resident patient at such hospital as may be specified in the order, being a hospital within the meaning of the Health and Personal Social Services (Northern Ireland) Order 1972 (S.I. 1972/1265 (N.I. 14)), approved by the Department of Health, Social Services and Public Safety for the purposes of paragraph 4(3) of Schedule 1 to the Criminal Justice (Northern Ireland) Order 1996 (S.I. 1996/3160 (N.I. 24));".

(5) In paragraphs 25 (education requirement) and 34(4) (additional persons to whom court must give a copy of the order) of that Schedule, any reference to a local education authority (except in sub-paragraph (6) of paragraph 25) has effect as a reference to an Education and Library Board established under Article 3 of the Education and Libraries (Northern Ireland) Order 1986 (S.I. 1986/594 (N.I. 3)).

(6) In paragraph 26 of that Schedule (electronic monitoring requirements: common provisions) sub-paragraph (5) is omitted.

(7) Paragraph 36 of that Schedule has effect as if it required the Crown Court, where it makes a direction under that paragraph, to specify the youth court or other magistrates' court in England and Wales which is to be the relevant court in England or Wales for the purposes of Part 2 of this Schedule.

(8) Any reference to the responsible officer has effect as a reference to the person who is to be responsible for the offender's supervision under the order.

Meaning of "supervision"

6 In this Part of this Schedule "supervision", in relation to a youth rehabilitation order which a court is considering making or amending in accordance with paragraph 1 or 2, means the performance of supervisory, enforcement and other related functions conferred by the legislation which has effect in Northern Ireland relating to corresponding orders of the kind which the court proposes to specify under paragraph 3(b).

PART 2
PROVISIONS RELATING TO AN ORDER MADE OR
AMENDED UNDER PART 1

Application of this Part

7 This Part of this Schedule applies where a youth rehabilitation order is made or amended in accordance with Part 1 of this Schedule.

Interpretation

8 In this Part of this Schedule, in relation to the youth rehabilitation order—
    "corresponding order" means the order specified under paragraph 3(b);
    "home court" means—
        (a) the court of summary jurisdiction acting for the petty sessions district in Northern Ireland in which the offender resides or proposes to reside, or
        (b) where the youth rehabilitation order was made or amended by the Crown Court and the Crown Court in Northern Ireland has not made a direction under paragraph 11, the Crown Court in Northern Ireland;
    "supervision" means the performance of supervisory, enforcement and other related functions conferred by the legislation which has effect in Northern Ireland relating to the corresponding order;

"the relevant court in England or Wales" means—
- (a) the court in England and Wales which made or which last amended the order, or
- (b) if the order was made by the Crown Court and includes a direction under paragraph 36 of Schedule 1, such youth court or other magistrates' court as may be specified in the order;

"the relevant officer" means the person responsible for the offender's supervision under the order.

Effect of the youth rehabilitation order in Northern Ireland

9 (1) The youth rehabilitation order is to be treated in Northern Ireland as if it were a corresponding order and the legislation which has effect in Northern Ireland in relation to such orders applies accordingly.

(2) Sub-paragraph (1) is subject to paragraphs 12 to 16.

Duty of offender to keep in touch with relevant officer

10 In section 5(5) (duty of offender to keep in touch with responsible officer), references to the responsible officer are to be read as references to the relevant officer.

Direction by Crown Court in Northern Ireland that proceedings in Northern Ireland be before a court of summary jurisdiction

11 Where the youth rehabilitation order was made or amended by the Crown Court, the Crown Court in Northern Ireland may direct that any proceedings in Northern Ireland in relation to the order be before the court of summary jurisdiction acting for the petty sessions district in which the offender resides or proposes to reside.

Powers of the home court in respect of the youth rehabilitation order

12 The home court may exercise in relation to the youth rehabilitation order any power which it could exercise in relation to a corresponding order made by a court in Northern Ireland, by virtue of the legislation relating to such orders which has effect there, except the following—
- (a) any power to discharge or revoke the order (other than a power to revoke the order where the offender has been convicted of a further offence and the court has imposed a custodial sentence),
- (b) any power to deal with the offender for the offence in respect of which the order was made, and
- (c) in the case of a youth rehabilitation order imposing a curfew requirement, any power to vary the order by substituting for the period specified in it any longer period than the court which made the order could have specified.

13 (1) The home court may require the offender to appear before the relevant court in England or Wales if sub-paragraph (2) or (3) applies.

(2) This sub-paragraph applies where it appears to the home court upon a complaint being made to a lay magistrate acting for the petty sessions district for the time being specified in the order that the offender has failed to comply with one or more requirements of the order.

(3) This sub-paragraph applies where it appears to the home court, on the application of the offender or the relevant officer, that it would be in the interests of justice for a power conferred by any of paragraphs 11 to 14 of Schedule 2 to be exercised.

14 Where an offender is required by virtue of paragraph 13 to appear before the relevant court in England or Wales—
- (a) the home court must send to that court a certificate certifying that the offender has failed to comply with such of the requirements of the order as may be specified in the certificate, together with such other particulars of the case as may be desirable, and

(b) a certificate purporting to be signed by the clerk of the home court (or, if the home court is the Crown Court in Northern Ireland, by the chief clerk) is admissible as evidence of the failure before the relevant court in England or Wales.

Powers of court in England or Wales before which the offender is required to appear

15 Where an offender is required by virtue of paragraph 13 to appear before the relevant court in England or Wales, that court may—

(a) issue a warrant for the offender's arrest, and

(b) exercise any power which it could exercise in respect of the youth rehabilitation order if the offender resided in England or Wales,

and any enactment relating to the exercise of such powers has effect accordingly, and with any reference to the responsible officer being read as a reference to the relevant officer.

16 (1) Paragraph 15(b) does not enable the relevant court in England or Wales to amend the youth rehabilitation order unless it appears to the court that the conditions in paragraph 2(2)(a) and (b) are satisfied in relation to any requirement to be imposed.

(2) The preceding paragraphs of this Schedule have effect in relation to the amendment of the youth rehabilitation order by virtue of paragraph 15(b) as they have effect in relation to the amendment of such an order by virtue of paragraph 2(2).

Power to amend provisions of Schedule in consequence of changes to the law in Northern Ireland

17 (1) This paragraph applies where a change is made to the law in Northern Ireland adding further descriptions of orders to the kinds of orders which a court in that jurisdiction may impose in dealing with an offender aged under 18 at the time of conviction.

(2) The Secretary of State may by order make such amendments to any of the preceding provisions of this Schedule as appear expedient in consequence of the change.

SCHEDULE 4   Section 6
YOUTH REHABILITATION ORDERS: CONSEQUENTIAL AND RELATED
AMENDMENTS

PART 1
CONSEQUENTIAL AMENDMENTS

Children and Young Persons Act 1933 (c. 12)

1 The Children and Young Persons Act 1933 has effect subject to the following amendments.

2 (1) Section 34 (attendance at court of parent of child or young person charged with an offence, etc.) is amended as follows.

(2) In subsection (7), omit "section 163 of the Powers of Criminal Courts (Sentencing) Act 2000 or".

(3) After subsection (7A) insert—

"(7B) If it appears that at the time of his arrest a youth rehabilitation order, as defined in Part 1 of the Criminal Justice and Immigration Act 2008, is in force in respect of him, the responsible officer, as defined in section 4 of that Act, shall also be informed as described in subsection (3) above as soon as it is reasonably practicable to do so."

3 (1) Section 49 (restrictions on reports of proceedings in which children or young persons are concerned) is amended as follows.

(2) In subsection (2), for paragraphs (c) and (d) substitute—
> "(c) proceedings in a magistrates' court under Schedule 2 to the Criminal Justice and Immigration Act 2008 (proceedings for breach, revocation or amendment of youth rehabilitation orders);
> (d) proceedings on appeal from a magistrates' court arising out of any proceedings mentioned in paragraph (c) (including proceedings by way of case stated)."

(3) In subsection (4A), omit paragraph (d) (but not the word "or" immediately following it).

(4) In subsection (10), for the words from "Schedule 7" to "supervision orders)" substitute the words "Schedule 2 to the Criminal Justice and Immigration Act 2008 (proceedings for breach, revocation or amendment of youth rehabilitation orders)".

(5) In subsection (13), omit paragraph (c)(i).

Criminal Appeal Act 1968 (c. 19)

4 In section 10(2) of the Criminal Appeal Act 1968 (appeal against sentence in other cases dealt with at assizes or quarter sessions), for paragraph (b) substitute—
> "(b) having been given a suspended sentence or made the subject of—
> > (i) an order for conditional discharge,
> > (ii) a youth rehabilitation order within the meaning of Part 1 of the Criminal Justice and Immigration Act 2008, or
> > (iii) a community order within the meaning of Part 12 of the Criminal Justice Act 2003,
> appears or is brought before the Crown Court to be further dealt with for the offence."

Firearms Act 1968 (c. 27)

5 The Firearms Act 1968 has effect subject to the following amendments.

6 In section 21(3ZA)(a) (possession of firearms by persons previously convicted of crime), after "2003", insert ", or a youth rehabilitation order within the meaning of Part 1 of the Criminal Justice and Immigration Act 2008,".

7 In section 52(1A)(a) (forfeiture and disposal of firearms; cancellation of certificate by convicting court), after "2003", insert ", or a youth rehabilitation order within the meaning of Part 1 of the Criminal Justice and Immigration Act 2008,".

Health Services and Public Health Act 1968 (c. 46)

8 The Health Services and Public Health Act 1968 has effect subject to the following amendments.

9 In section 64(3)(a) (financial assistance by the Secretary of State to certain voluntary organisations)—
> (a) in paragraph (xxi) of the definition of "the relevant enactments", for "sections 63 to 66 and 92 of, and Schedules 6 and 7 to," substitute "section 92 of", and
> (b) after that paragraph, insert—
> > "(xxii) Part 1 of the Criminal Justice and Immigration Act 2008;".

10 In section 65(3)(b) (financial and other assistance by local authorities to certain voluntary organisations), for paragraph (xxii) of the definition of "relevant enactments" substitute—
> "(xxii) Part 1 of the Criminal Justice and Immigration Act 2008;".

Social Work (Scotland) Act 1968 (c. 49)

11 The Social Work (Scotland) Act 1968 has effect subject to the following amendments.

12 In section 86(3) (adjustments between authority providing accommodation etc, and authority of area of residence) after "supervision order" insert ", youth rehabilitation order".

13 In section 94(1) (interpretation)—

    (a) for the definition of "probation order" substitute—

        ""probation order", in relation to an order imposed by a court in Northern Ireland, has the same meaning as in the Criminal Justice (Northern Ireland) Order 1996,",

    (b) in the definition of "supervision order", omit "the Powers of Criminal Courts (Sentencing) Act 2000 or", and

    (c) at the end insert—

        ""youth rehabilitation order" means an order made under section 1 of the Criminal Justice and Immigration Act 2008."

Children and Young Persons Act 1969 (c. 54)

14 The Children and Young Persons Act 1969 has effect subject to the following amendments.

15 Omit section 25 (transfers between England or Wales and Northern Ireland).

16 (1) Section 26 (transfers between England or Wales and the Channel Islands or Isle of Man) is amended as follows.

    (2) In subsection (1)(c), for the words from "supervision order" to "2000" substitute "youth rehabilitation order imposing a local authority residence requirement".

    (3) In subsection (2), for the words from "supervision order" to "2000" substitute "youth rehabilitation order imposing a local authority residence requirement".

17 (1) Section 32 (detention of absentees) is amended as follows.

    (2) In subsection (1A)—

        (a) in paragraph (a), for "paragraph 7(4) of Schedule 7 to the Powers of Criminal Courts (Sentencing) Act 2000" substitute "paragraph 21(2) of Schedule 2 to the Criminal Justice and Immigration Act 2008", and

        (b) for paragraph (b) substitute—

            "(b) from local authority accommodation—

                (i) in which he is required to live by virtue of a youth rehabilitation order imposing a local authority residence requirement (within the meaning of Part 1 of the Criminal Justice and Immigration Act 2008); or

                (ii) to which he has been remanded under paragraph 21 of Schedule 2 to that Act; or

                (iii) to which he has been remanded or committed under section 23(1) of this Act,".

    (3) For subsection (1C) substitute—

        "(1C) In this section "the responsible person" means, as the case may be—

            (a) the person who made the arrangements under paragraph 21(2) of Schedule 2 to the Criminal Justice and Immigration Act 2008;

            (b) the authority specified under paragraph 17(5) of Schedule 1 to that Act;

            (c) the authority designated under paragraph 21(10) of Schedule 2 to that Act; or

            (d) the authority designated under section 23 of this Act."

    (4) After subsection (1C) insert—

        "(1D) If a child or young person—

            (a) is required to reside with a local authority foster parent by virtue of a youth rehabilitation order with fostering, and

            (b) is absent, without the consent of the responsible officer (within the meaning of Part 1 of the Criminal Justice and Immigration Act 2008), from the place in which he is required to reside,

        he may be arrested by a constable anywhere in the United Kingdom without a warrant.

        (1E) A person so arrested shall be conducted to—

            (a) the place where he is required to reside, or

325

(b) such other place as the local authority specified under paragraph 18(3) of Schedule 1 to the Criminal Justice and Immigration Act 2008 may direct,

at that local authority's expense."

(5) In subsection (2), for "or (1A)" substitute ", (1A) or (1D)".

(6) In subsection (2A), for the words from "mentioned in subsection" to "this section is in premises" substitute "mentioned in subsection (1), (1A)(a) or (b)(i) or (ii) or (1D) of this section is in premises".

(7) In subsection (2B)—

(a) after "subsection (1A)" insert "or (1D)", and

(b) at the end insert "or the responsible officer, as the case may be."

(8) In subsection (3), for "or (1A)" substitute ", (1A) or (1D)".

(9) In subsection (4), after "(1A)" insert ", (1D)".

18 In section 70(1) (interpretation)—

(a) omit the definition of "supervision order",

(b) after the definition of "local authority accommodation" insert—

""local authority residence requirement" has the same meaning as in Part 1 of the Criminal Justice and Immigration Act 2008;", and

(c) after the definition of "youth offending team" insert—

""youth rehabilitation order" and "youth rehabilitation order with fostering" have the same meanings as in Part 1 of the Criminal Justice and Immigration Act 2008 (see section 1 of that Act);".

19 In section 73(4)(a) (provisions of section 32 extending to Scotland) for "to (1C)" substitute "to (1E)".

Rehabilitation of Offenders Act 1974 (c. 53)

20 The Rehabilitation of Offenders Act 1974 has effect subject to the following amendments.

21 In section 5(5) (rehabilitation periods for particular sentences) after paragraph (d) insert—

"(da) a youth rehabilitation order under Part 1 of the Criminal Justice and Immigration Act 2008;".

22 In section 7(2) (limitations on rehabilitation under Act, etc.) for paragraph (d) substitute—

"(d) in any proceedings relating to the variation or discharge of a youth rehabilitation order under Part 1 of the Criminal Justice and Immigration Act 2008, or on appeal from any such proceedings;".

Bail Act 1976 (c. 63)

23 In section 4(3) of the Bail Act 1976 (general right to bail of accused persons and others)—

(a) omit the words "to be dealt with", and

(b) for paragraph (a), substitute—

"(a) Schedule 2 to the Criminal Justice and Immigration Act 2008 (breach, revocation or amendment of youth rehabilitation orders), or".

Magistrates' Courts Act 1980 (c. 43)

24 In Schedule 6A to the Magistrates' Courts Act 1980 (fines that may be altered under section 143), omit the entries relating to Schedules 3, 5 and 7 to the Powers of Criminal Courts (Sentencing) Act 2000 (c. 6).

Contempt of Court Act 1981 (c. 49)

25 In section 14 of the Contempt of Court Act 1981 (proceedings in England and Wales), omit the subsection (2A) inserted by the Criminal Justice Act 1982 (c. 48).

Criminal Justice Act 1982

26 Part 3 of Schedule 13 to the Criminal Justice Act 1982 (reciprocal arrangements for transfer of community service orders from Northern Ireland) has effect subject to the following amendments.

27 (1) Paragraph 7 (transfer to England and Wales) is amended as follows.

(2) In sub-paragraph (1), in Article 13(4)(b) inserted by that provision, for "such orders" substitute "an unpaid work requirement of a community order under section 177 of the Criminal Justice Act 2003 or youth rehabilitation order under section 1 of the Criminal Justice and Immigration Act 2008".

(3) In sub-paragraph (2)(b)—

(a) after "a community order" insert "or a youth rehabilitation order", and

(b) omit "(within the meaning of Part 12 of the Criminal Justice Act 2003)".

(4) In sub-paragraph (3)—

(a) for "A community service order" substitute "An adult community service order", and

(b) in paragraph (b)—

(i) omit "within the meaning of Part 12 of the Criminal Justice Act 2003", and

(ii) for "by that Part of that Act" substitute "by Part 12 of the Criminal Justice Act 2003".

(5) After sub-paragraph (3) insert—

"(4) A youth community service order made or amended in accordance with this paragraph shall—

(a) specify the local justice area in England or Wales in which the offender resides or will be residing when the order or the amendment comes into force; and

(b) require—

(i) the local probation board for that area established under section 4 of the Criminal Justice and Court Services Act 2000 or (as the case may be) a provider of probation services operating in that area, or

(ii) a youth offending team established under section 39 of the Crime and Disorder Act 1998 by a local authority for the area in which the offender resides or will be residing when the order or amendment comes into force,

to appoint a person who will discharge in respect of the order the functions in respect of youth rehabilitation orders conferred on responsible officers by Part 1 of the Criminal Justice and Immigration Act 2008.

(5) The person appointed under sub-paragraph (4)(b) must be—

(a) where the appointment is made by a local probation board, an officer of that board;

(b) where the appointment is made by a provider of probation services, an officer of that provider;

(c) where the appointment is made by a youth offending team, a member of that team."

28 (1) Paragraph 9 (general provision) is amended as follows.

(2) In sub-paragraph (3)—

(a) in paragraph (a)—

(i) for "a community service order" substitute "an adult community service order";

(ii) omit "under section 177 of the Criminal Justice Act 2003";

(iii) for "of that Act" substitute "of the Criminal Justice Act 2003", and

(b) before "and" at the end of that paragraph insert—

"(aa) a youth community service order made or amended in the circumstances specified in paragraph 7 above shall be treated as if it were a youth rehabilitation order made in England and Wales and the provisions of Part 1 of the Criminal Justice and Immigration Act 2008 shall apply accordingly;".

(3) In sub-paragraph (4)(a)—

(a) after "community orders" insert "or youth rehabilitation orders", and

(b) omit "(within the meaning of Part 12 of the Criminal Justice Act 2003)".

(4) In sub-paragraph (5)—
    (a) after "community order" insert "or youth rehabilitation order", and
    (b) omit "(within the meaning of Part 12 of the Criminal Justice Act 2003)".
(5) In sub-paragraph (6)—
    (a) after "community orders" insert "or youth rehabilitation orders",
    (b) omit "(within the meaning of Part 12 of the Criminal Justice Act 2003)", and
    (c) in paragraph (b)(i), after "2003" insert "or, as the case may be, Part 1 of the Criminal Justice and Immigration Act 2008".

29 After that paragraph insert—

"Community service orders relating to persons residing in England and Wales: interpretation

10 In paragraphs 7 and 9 above—
    "adult community service order" means a community service order made in respect of an offender who was aged at least 18 when convicted of the offence in respect of which the order is made;
    "community order" means an order made under section 177 of the Criminal Justice Act 2003;
    "youth community service order" means a community service order made in respect of an offender who was aged under 18 when convicted of the offence in respect of which the order is made;
    "youth rehabilitation order" means an order made under section 1 of the Criminal Justice and Immigration Act 2008."

Mental Health Act 1983 (c. 20)

30 In section 37(8) of the Mental Health Act 1983 (powers of courts to order hospital admission or guardianship)—
    (a) in paragraph (a), after "Criminal Justice Act 2003)" insert "or a youth rehabilitation order (within the meaning of Part 1 of the Criminal Justice and Immigration Act 2008)", and
    (b) in paragraph (c), omit the words "a supervision order (within the meaning of that Act) or".

Child Abduction Act 1984 (c. 37)

31 In paragraph 2(1) of the Schedule to the Child Abduction Act 1984 (modifications of section 1 for children in certain cases)—
    (a) in paragraph (a), for "paragraph 7(4) of Schedule 7 to the Powers of Criminal Courts (Sentencing) Act 2000" substitute "paragraph 21(2) of Schedule 2 to the Criminal Justice and Immigration Act 2008", and
    (b) in paragraph (b), after "1969" insert "or paragraph 21 of Schedule 2 to the Criminal Justice and Immigration Act 2008".

Prosecution of Offences Act 1985 (c. 23)

32 (1) Section 19 of the Prosecution of Offences Act 1985 (provision for orders as to costs in other circumstances) is amended as follows.
    (2) In subsection (3B)(b)(i), for the words from "in a community order" to "that Act" substitute "a mental health treatment requirement in a community order or youth rehabilitation order".
    (3) After subsection (3B) insert—
        "(3C) For the purposes of subsection (3B)(b)(i)—
        "community order" has the same meaning as in Part 12 of the Criminal Justice Act 2003;
        "mental health treatment requirement" means—
        (a) in relation to a community order, a mental health treatment requirement under section 207 of the Criminal Justice Act 2003, and

(b) in relation to a youth rehabilitation order, a mental health treatment requirement under paragraph 20 of Schedule 1 to the Criminal Justice and Immigration Act 2008;

"youth rehabilitation order" has the same meaning as in Part 1 of the Criminal Justice and Immigration Act 2008."

Children Act 1989 (c. 41)

33 The Children Act 1989 has effect subject to the following amendments.

34 (1) Section 21 (provision of accommodation for children in police protection or detention or on remand, etc.) is amended as follows.

(2) In subsection (2)(c)—

(a) in sub-paragraph (i), omit "paragraph 7(5) of Schedule 7 to the Powers of Criminal Courts (Sentencing) Act 2000 or" and "or" at the end of that sub-paragraph, and

(b) for sub-paragraph (ii), substitute—

"(ii) remanded to accommodation provided by or on behalf of a local authority by virtue of paragraph 21 of Schedule 2 to the Criminal Justice and Immigration Act 2008 (breach etc. of youth rehabilitation orders); or

(iii) the subject of a youth rehabilitation order imposing a local authority residence requirement or a youth rehabilitation order with fostering,".

(3) After subsection (2) insert—

"(2A) In subsection (2)(c)(iii), the following terms have the same meanings as in Part 1 of the Criminal Justice and Immigration Act 2008 (see section 7 of that Act)—

"local authority residence requirement";

"youth rehabilitation order";

"youth rehabilitation order with fostering"."

35 In section 31(7)(b) (care and supervision orders), for sub-paragraph (ii) substitute—

"(ii) a youth rehabilitation order within the meaning of Part 1 of the Criminal Justice and Immigration Act 2008; or".

36 In section 105(6) (interpretation)—

(a) in paragraph (b), omit from the words "or an" to the end of the paragraph, and

(b) after that paragraph insert—

"(ba) in accordance with the requirements of a youth rehabilitation order under Part 1 of the Criminal Justice and Immigration Act 2008; or".

37 (1) Part 3 of Schedule 3 (education supervision orders) is amended as follows.

(2) In paragraph 13(2), for paragraph (c) substitute—

"(c) a youth rehabilitation order made under Part 1 of the Criminal Justice and Immigration Act 2008 with respect to the child, while the education supervision order is in force, may not include an education requirement (within the meaning of that Part);".

(3) In paragraph 14—

(a) in sub-paragraph (1), for "order under section 63(1) of the Powers of Criminal Courts (Sentencing) Act 2000" substitute "youth rehabilitation order (within the meaning of Part 1 of the Criminal Justice and Immigration Act 2008)", and

(b) in sub-paragraph (2), after "direction" (in the second place it occurs) insert "or instruction".

38 In paragraph 3 of Schedule 8 (privately fostered children) for paragraph (a) substitute—

"(a) a youth rehabilitation order made under section 1 of the Criminal Justice and Immigration Act 2008;".

Criminal Justice Act 1991 (c. 53)

39 Part 3 of Schedule 3 to the Criminal Justice Act 1991 (transfer of probation orders from Northern Ireland to England and Wales) has effect subject to the following amendments.

40 (1) Paragraph 10 is amended as follows.

  (2) In sub-paragraph (2)(b), for the words from "the local probation board" to the end substitute "—

    (i) the local probation board for the area which contains the local justice area in which he resides or will reside or (as the case may be) a provider of probation services operating in the local justice area in which he resides or will reside, or

    (ii) a youth offending team established by a local authority for the area in which he resides or will reside,", and

  (3) In sub-paragraph (3)(a), for the words from "an officer of a local probation board" to the end substitute "—

    (i) an officer of a local probation board assigned to the local justice area in England and Wales in which the offender resides or will be residing when the order or amendment comes into force or (as the case may be) an officer of a provider of probation services acting in the local justice area in which the offender resides or will then be residing, or

    (ii) a member of a youth offending team established by a local authority for the area in England and Wales in which the offender resides or will then be residing;".

41 (1) Paragraph 11 is amended as follows.

  (2) In sub-paragraph (2)—

    (a) for "a probation order" substitute "an adult probation order",

    (b) in paragraph (a), omit "under section 177 of the Criminal Justice Act 2003", and

    (c) in paragraph (b), for "of that Act" substitute "of the Criminal Justice Act 2003".

  (3) After that sub-paragraph insert—

    "(2A) Where a youth probation order is made or amended in any of the circumstances specified in paragraph 10 above then, subject to the following provisions of this paragraph—

    (a) the order shall be treated as if it were a youth rehabilitation order made in England and Wales, and

    (b) the provisions of Part 1 of the Criminal Justice and Immigration Act 2008 shall apply accordingly."

  (4) In sub-paragraph (3)—

    (a) for paragraph (a) substitute—

    "(a) the requirements of the legislation relating to community orders or, as the case may be, youth rehabilitation orders;";

    (b) in paragraph (b), for "Schedule 8 to that Act" substitute "that legislation".

  (5) In sub-paragraph (4)—

    (a) after "a community order" insert "or, as the case may be, a youth rehabilitation order",

    (b) omit "under section 177 of the Criminal Justice Act 2003", and

    (c) for "to that Act" substitute "to the Criminal Justice Act 2003 or by paragraph 6(2)(c) or 11(2) of Schedule 2 to the Criminal Justice and Immigration Act 2008".

  (6) In sub-paragraph (5)—

    (a) after "2003" insert "or, as the case may be, Part 1 of the Criminal Justice and Immigration Act 2008",

    (b) for "(2) above" substitute "(2) or (2A) (as the case may be)", and

    (c) in paragraph (b) for the words from "of the" to "board" substitute "of—

    (i) the offender, or

    (ii) the officer of a local probation board, officer of a provider of probation services or member of a youth offending team (as the case may be),".

  (7) In sub-paragraph (8)—

    (a) after "In this paragraph" insert—

    ""adult probation order" means a probation order made in respect of an offender who was aged at least 18 when convicted of the offence in respect of which the order is made;

    "community order" means an order made under section 177 of the Criminal Justice Act 2003;";

(b) at the end insert—

""youth probation order" means a probation order made in respect of an offender who was aged under 18 when convicted of the offence in respect of which the order is made;

"youth rehabilitation order" means an order made under section 1 of the Criminal Justice and Immigration Act 2008."

Criminal Justice and Public Order Act 1994 (c. 33)

42 In section 136 of the Criminal Justice and Public Order Act 1994 (crossborder enforcement: execution of warrants), in subsection (7A), after "youth offender panel)" insert "or under Schedule 2 to the Criminal Justice and Immigration Act 2008 (youth rehabilitation orders: breach etc.)".

Criminal Procedure (Scotland) Act 1995 (c. 46)

43 The Criminal Procedure (Scotland) Act 1995 has effect subject to the following amendments.

44 (1) Section 234 (probation orders: persons residing in England and Wales) is amended as follows.

(2) In subsection (2), at the end insert "(in any case where the offender has attained the age of 18 years) or under section 1 of the Criminal Justice and Immigration Act 2008 (in any other case)".

(3) In subsection (4)—

(a) in paragraph (a), for "and section 207(2) of the Criminal Justice Act 2003" substitute ", section 207(2) of the Criminal Justice Act 2003 and paragraph 20(2) of Schedule 1 to the Criminal Justice and Immigration Act 2008",

(b) in paragraph (a), for "or, as the case may be, community orders under Part 12 of that Act" substitute ", community orders under Part 12 of the Criminal Justice Act 2003 or, as the case may be, youth rehabilitation orders under Part 1 of the Criminal Justice and Immigration Act 2008",

(c) in paragraph (a), for "and section 207 of the Criminal Justice Act 2003" substitute ", section 207 of the Criminal Justice Act 2003 and paragraph 20 of Schedule 1 to the Criminal Justice and Immigration Act 2008",

(d) in paragraph (b), after "2003" insert "or (as the case may be) paragraphs 20(4) and 21(1) to (3) of Schedule 1 to the Criminal Justice and Immigration Act 2008", and

(e) in paragraph (b), at the end insert "or that paragraph".

(4) In subsection (4A) at the end insert "(in any case where the offender has attained the age of 18 years) or in a youth rehabilitation order made under section 1 of the Criminal Justice and Immigration Act 2008 (in any other case)".

(5) In subsection (5) for the words from "subject to subsection (6)" to the end substitute "subject to subsections (6) and (6A) below—

(a) Schedule 8 to the Criminal Justice Act 2003 shall apply as if it were a community order made by a magistrates' court under section 177 of that Act and imposing the requirements specified under subsection (4A) above (in any case where the offender has attained the age of 18 years); and

(b) Schedule 2 to the Criminal Justice and Immigration Act 2008 shall apply as if it were a youth rehabilitation order made by a magistrates' court under section 1 of that Act and imposing the requirements specified under that subsection (in any other case)."

(6) After subsection (6) insert—

"(6A) In its application to a probation order made or amended under this section, Schedule 2 to the Criminal Justice and Immigration Act 2008 has effect subject to the following modifications—

(a) any reference to the responsible officer has effect as a reference to the person appointed or assigned under subsection (1)(a) above,

    (b) in paragraph 6, sub-paragraph (2)(c) is omitted and, in subparagraph (16), the reference to the Crown Court has effect as a reference to a court in Scotland, and

    (c) Parts 3 and 5 are omitted."

45 (1) Section 242 (community service orders: persons residing in England and Wales) is amended as follows.

  (2) In subsection (1)(a)—

    (a) in sub-paragraph (ii), after "Part 12 of the Criminal Justice Act 2003)" insert ", in any case where the offender has attained the age of 18 years, or an unpaid work requirement imposed by a youth rehabilitation order (within the meaning of Part 1 of the Criminal Justice and Immigration Act 2008), in any other case", and

    (b) in sub-paragraph (iii), after "section 177 of the Criminal Justice Act 2003" insert "or, as the case may be, imposed by youth rehabilitation orders made under section 1 of the Criminal Justice and Immigration Act 2008".

  (3) In subsection (2)(b)—

    (a) after "that court" insert ", in any case where the offender has attained the age of 18 years," and

    (b) after "2003" insert "or it appears to that court, in any other case, that provision can be made for the offender to perform work under the order under the arrangements which exist in that area for persons to perform work under unpaid work requirements imposed by youth rehabilitation orders made under section 1 of the Criminal Justice and Immigration Act 2008".

  (4) In subsection (3)(b)—

    (a) after "the board" insert "or (as the case may be) require a provider of probation services to appoint an officer of the provider,",

    (b) after "the order" insert "—

      (a)", and

    (c) at the end insert "; or

      (b) the functions conferred on responsible officers by Part 1 of the Criminal Justice and Immigration Act 2008 in respect of unpaid work requirements imposed by youth rehabilitation orders (within the meaning of that Part) as the case may be."

46 (1) Section 244 (community service orders: general provisions relating to persons residing in England and Wales or Northern Ireland) is amended as follows.

  (2) In subsection (3)(a)—

    (a) after "2003)" insert "or, as the case may be, a youth rehabilitation order (within the meaning of Part 1 of the Criminal Justice and Immigration Act 2008)", and

    (b) after "such community orders" insert "or youth rehabilitation orders".

  (3) In subsection (4)(a)—

    (a) for "or, as the case may be, community orders" substitute ", community orders", and

    (b) after "2003)" insert "or, as the case may be, youth rehabilitation orders (within the meaning of Part 1 of the Criminal Justice and Immigration Act 2008)".

  (4) In subsection (5)—

    (a) for "or, as the case may be, a community order" substitute ", a community order", and

    (b) after "2003)" insert "or, as the case may be, a youth rehabilitation order (within the meaning of Part 1 of the Criminal Justice and Immigration Act 2008)".

  (5) In subsection (6)—

    (a) for "or, as the case may be, community orders" substitute ", community orders",

    (b) after "within the meaning of Part 12 of the Criminal Justice Act 2003)" insert "or, as the case may be, youth rehabilitation orders (within the meaning of Part 1 of the Criminal Justice and Immigration Act 2008)", and

    (c) after "the responsible officer under Part 12 of the Criminal Justice Act 2003" insert "or, as the case may be, under Part 1 of the Criminal Justice and Immigration Act 2008".

Education Act 1996 (c. 56)

47 In section 562(2)(b) of the Education Act 1996 (Act not to apply to persons detained under order of a court), for "community order under section 177 of the Criminal Justice Act 2003" substitute "youth rehabilitation order under section 1 of the Criminal Justice and Immigration Act 2008".

Crime and Disorder Act 1998 (c. 37)

48 The Crime and Disorder Act 1998 has effect subject to the following amendments.

49 In section 38(4) (local provision of youth justice services)—

(a) in paragraph (f), for ", reparation orders and action plan orders" substitute "and reparation orders",

(b) after paragraph (f) insert—

"(fa) the provision of persons to act as responsible officers in relation to youth rehabilitation orders (within the meaning of Part 1 of the Criminal Justice and Immigration Act 2008);

(fb) the supervision of children and young persons sentenced to a youth rehabilitation order under that Part which includes a supervision requirement (within the meaning of that Part);",

(c) omit paragraph (g), and

(d) in paragraph (h), omit "or a supervision order".

50 In Schedule 8 (minor and consequential amendments), in paragraph 13(2), for "that section" substitute "section 10 of that Act".

Powers of Criminal Courts (Sentencing) Act 2000 (c. 6)

51 The Powers of Criminal Courts (Sentencing) Act 2000 has effect subject to the following amendments.

52 In section 19(4)(a) (making of referral orders: effect on court's other sentencing powers), for "community sentence" substitute "sentence which consists of or includes a youth rehabilitation order".

53 In section 73 (reparation orders)—

(a) for subsection (4)(b) substitute—

"(b) to make in respect of him a youth rehabilitation order or a referral order."

(b) after subsection (4) insert—

"(4A) The court shall not make a reparation order in respect of the offender at a time when a youth rehabilitation order is in force in respect of him unless when it makes the reparation order it revokes the youth rehabilitation order.

(4B) Where a youth rehabilitation order is revoked under subsection (4A), paragraph 24 of Schedule 2 to the Criminal Justice and Immigration Act 2008 (breach, revocation or amendment of youth rehabilitation order) applies to the revocation."

54 In section 74(3)(a) (requirements and provisions of reparation order, and obligations of person subject to it), omit "or with the requirements of any community order or any youth community order to which he may be subject".

55 In section 75 (breach, revocation and amendment of reparation orders) omit "action plan orders and" and "so far as relating to reparation orders".

56 In section 91(3) (offenders under 18 convicted of certain serious offences: power to detain for specified period), for "a community sentence" substitute "a youth rehabilitation order".

57 In section 137(2) (power to order parent or guardian to pay fine, costs, compensation or surcharge)—

(a) after "under—" insert—

"(za) paragraph 6(2)(a) or 8(2)(a) of Schedule 2 to the Criminal Justice and Immigration Act 2008 (breach of youth rehabilitation order),", and

     (b) omit paragraphs (a) to (c), and

     (c) in paragraph (d) omit "action plan order or".

58 In section 150(2) (binding over of parent or guardian), for "a community sentence on the offender" substitute "on the offender a sentence which consists of or includes a youth rehabilitation order".

59 In section 159 (execution of process between England and Wales and Scotland)—

     (a) after "Schedule 1 to this Act," insert "or",

     (b) omit "paragraph 3(1), 10(6) or 18(1) of Schedule 3 to this Act,",

     (c) omit "paragraph 1(1) of Schedule 5 to this Act", and

     (d) omit "paragraph 7(2) of Schedule 7 to this Act, or".

60 (1) Section 160 (rules and orders) is amended as follows.

     (2) Omit subsection (2).

     (3) In subsection (3)(a)—

        (a) omit "40(2)(a)," and

        (b) for "103(2) or paragraph 1(1A) of Schedule 3," substitute "or 103(2)".

     (4) Omit subsection (5).

61 In section 163 (general definitions)—

     (a) omit the definitions of "action plan order", "affected person", "attendance centre", "attendance centre order", "community sentence", "curfew order", "exclusion order", "supervision order", "supervisor" and "youth community order",

     (b) in the definition of "responsible officer", omit paragraphs (a), (aa) and (f), and

     (c) at the end add—

     ""youth rehabilitation order" has the meaning given by section 1(1) of the Criminal Justice and Immigration Act 2008."

62 (1) Schedule 8 (breach, revocation and amendment of action plan orders and reparation orders) is amended as follows.

     (2) In the heading to the Schedule omit "action plan orders and".

     (3) In the cross-heading before paragraph 2, omit "action plan order or".

     (4) In paragraph 2—

        (a) in sub-paragraph (1), for "an action plan order or" substitute "a",

        (b) in sub-paragraph (2)—

          (i) in paragraph (a), omit sub-paragraphs (ii) and (iii), and

          (ii) in each of paragraphs (b) and (c), omit "action plan order or",

        (c) in each of sub-paragraphs (5) and (7), omit "action plan order or", and

        (d) in sub-paragraph (8), omit "or action plan order" in both places where it occurs.

     (5) Omit paragraphs 3 and 4.

     (6) In the cross-heading before paragraph 5, omit "action plan order or".

     (7) In paragraph 5—

        (a) in sub-paragraph (1), for "an action plan order or" substitute "a" and, in paragraph (a), omit "action plan order or", and

        (b) in sub-paragraph (3), for "an action plan order or" substitute "a".

     (8) In paragraph 6(9), in each of paragraphs (a), (b) and (c), omit "action plan order or".

     (9) In paragraph 7(b), for "an action plan order or" substitute "a".

63 In Schedule 10 (transitory modifications), omit paragraphs 4 to 6 and 12 to 15.

64 In Schedule 11 (transitional provisions)—

     (a) in paragraph 4, omit—

        (i) paragraph (a) of sub-paragraph (1),

        (ii) sub-paragraph (2), and

        (iii) sub-paragraph (3), and

     (b) omit paragraph 5.

Child Support, Pensions and Social Security Act 2000 (c. 19)

65 The Child Support, Pensions and Social Security Act 2000 has effect subject to the following amendments.

66 (1) Section 62 (loss of benefit for breach of community order) is amended as follows.

    (2) In the definition of "relevant community order" in subsection (8)—

        (a) after "2003;" in paragraph (a) insert—

            "(aa) a youth rehabilitation order made under section 1 of the Criminal Justice and Immigration Act 2008;", and

        (b) in paragraph (b) for "such an order" substitute "an order specified in paragraph (a) or (aa)".

    (3) In subsection (11)(c)(ii) for "and (b)" substitute "to (b)".

67 (1) Section 64 (information provision) is amended as follows.

    (2) In subsection (6)(a) after "2003)" insert ", youth rehabilitation orders (as defined by section 1 of the Criminal Justice and Immigration Act 2008)".

    (3) In subsection (7) after paragraph (b) insert—

        "(ba) a responsible officer within the meaning of Part 1 of the Criminal Justice and Immigration Act 2008;".

Criminal Justice and Court Services Act 2000 (c. 43)

68 The Criminal Justice and Court Services Act 2000 has effect subject to the following amendments.

69 In section 1(2)(a) (purposes of Chapter), after "2003)" insert ", youth rehabilitation orders (as defined by section 1 of the Criminal Justice and Immigration Act 2008)".

70 In section 70 (interpretation, etc.) omit subsection (5).

Criminal Justice Act 2003 (c. 44)

71 Part 12 of the Criminal Justice Act 2003 (sentencing) has effect subject to the following amendments.

72 (1) Section 147 (meaning of "community sentence" etc.) is amended as follows.

    (2) In subsection (1)—

        (a) omit paragraph (b), and

        (b) after that paragraph insert—

        "(c) a youth rehabilitation order."

    (3) Omit subsection (2).

73 (1) Section 148 (restrictions on imposing community sentences) is amended as follows.

    (2) In subsection (2)—

        (a) omit "which consists of or includes a community order", and

        (b) in paragraph (a), after "community order" insert ", or, as the case may be, youth rehabilitation order, comprised in the sentence".

    (3) After that subsection insert—

        "(2A) Subsection (2) is subject to paragraph 3(4) of Schedule 1 to the Criminal Justice and Immigration Act 2008 (youth rehabilitation order with intensive supervision and surveillance)."

    (4) Omit subsection (3).

74 In section 149(1) (passing of community sentence on offender remanded in custody) for "youth community order" substitute "youth rehabilitation order".

75 In section 150 (community sentence not available where sentence fixed by law etc.) for "youth community order" substitute "youth rehabilitation order".

76 (1) Section 151 (community order for persistent offender previously fined) is amended as follows.

(2) In the title, after "community order" insert "or youth rehabilitation order".

(3) In subsections (1)(a) and (1A)(a), for "16" substitute "18".

(4) After subsection (2) insert—

"(2A) Subsection (2B) applies where—

(a) a person aged 16 or 17 is convicted of an offence ("the current offence");

(b) on three or more previous occasions the offender has, on conviction by a court in the United Kingdom of any offence committed by him after attaining the age of 16, had passed on him a sentence consisting only of a fine; and

(c) despite the effect of section 143(2), the court would not (apart from this section) regard the current offence, or the combination of the current offence and one or more offences associated with it, as being serious enough to warrant a youth rehabilitation order.

(2B) The court may make a youth rehabilitation order in respect of the current offence instead of imposing a fine if it considers that, having regard to all the circumstances including the matters mentioned in subsection (3), it would be in the interests of justice to make such an order."

(5) In subsection (3)—

(a) after "(2)" insert "and (2B)"; and

(b) in paragraph (a) for "or (1A)(b)" substitute "(1A)(b) or (2A)(b)".

(6) In subsections (4), (5) and (6), for "and (1A)(b)" substitute "(1A)(b) and (2A)(b)".

(7) In section 166 (savings for powers to mitigate etc.), in subsection (1)(a) after "151(2)" insert "or (2B)".

77 (1) Section 156 (pre-sentence reports and other requirements) is amended as follows.

(2) In subsection (1)—

(a) for ", (2)(b) or (3)(b)" substitute "or (2)(b),", and

(b) after "153(2)," insert "or in section 1(4)(b) or (c) of the Criminal Justice and Immigration Act 2008 (youth rehabilitation orders with intensive supervision and surveillance or fostering),".

(3) In subsection (2) omit "or (3)(a)".

(4) In subsection (3)(b)—

(a) for ", (2)(b) or (3)(b)" substitute "or (2)(b), or in section 1(4)(b) or (c) of the Criminal Justice and Immigration Act 2008,", and

(b) after "community order" insert "or youth rehabilitation order".

78 In section 161 (pre-sentence drug testing)—

(a) in subsection (1), omit "aged 14 or over", and

(b) omit subsection (7).

79 (1) Section 166 (savings for powers to mitigate sentences and deal appropriately with mentally disordered offenders) is amended as follows.

(2) In subsection (1), after paragraph (d) add—

"(e) paragraph 3 of Schedule 1 to the Criminal Justice and Immigration Act 2008 (youth rehabilitation order with intensive supervision and surveillance), or

(f) paragraph 4 of Schedule 1 to that Act (youth rehabilitation order with fostering),".

(3) In subsections (3) and (5), for "(d)" substitute "(f)".

80 (1) Section 174 (duty to give reasons for, and explain effect of, sentence) is amended as follows.

(2) In subsection (2)—

(a) in paragraph (b), after "that section" insert "or any other statutory provision",

(b) in paragraph (c), after "community sentence" insert ", other than one consisting of or including a youth rehabilitation order with intensive supervision and surveillance or fostering,", and

(c) after paragraph (c) insert—

"(ca) where the sentence consists of or includes a youth rehabilitation order with intensive supervision and surveillance and the case does not fall within paragraph 5(2) of

Schedule 1 to the Criminal Justice and Immigration Act 2008, state that it is of the opinion that section 1(4)(a) to (c) of that Act and section 148(1) of this Act apply and why it is of that opinion,

(cb) where the sentence consists of or includes a youth rehabilitation order with fostering, state that it is of the opinion that section 1(4)(a) to (c) of the Criminal Justice and Immigration Act 2008 and section 148(1) of this Act apply and why it is of that opinion,".

(3) After subsection (4) insert—

"(4A) Subsection (4B) applies where—

(a) a court passes a custodial sentence in respect of an offence on an offender who is aged under 18, and

(b) the circumstances are such that the court must, in complying with subsection (1)(a), make the statement referred to in subsection (2)(b).

(4B) That statement must include—

(a) a statement by the court that it is of the opinion that a sentence consisting of or including a youth rehabilitation order with intensive supervision and surveillance or fostering cannot be justified for the offence, and

(b) a statement by the court why it is of that opinion."

81 In section 176 (interpretation of Chapter 1)—

(a) omit the definition of "youth community order", and

(b) at the end add—

""youth rehabilitation order" has the meaning given by section 1(1) of the Criminal Justice and Immigration Act 2008;

"youth rehabilitation order with fostering" has the meaning given by paragraph 4 of Schedule 1 to that Act;

"youth rehabilitation order with intensive supervision and surveillance" has the meaning given by paragraph 3 of Schedule 1 to that Act."

82 In section 177(1) (community orders) for "16" substitute "18".

83 In section 197(1)(b) (meaning of "the responsible officer"), omit "the offender is aged 18 or over and".

84 In section 199 (unpaid work requirement)—

(a) in subsection (3), for "appropriate officer" substitute "officer of a local probation board or an officer of a provider of probation services", and

(b) omit subsection (4).

85 In section 201 (activity requirement), in subsection (3)(a), for sub-paragraphs (i) and (ii) (but not the "and" immediately following sub-paragraph (ii)) substitute "an officer of a local probation board or an officer of a provider of probation services".

86 In section 202 (programme requirement), in subsection (4)(a), for subparagraphs (i) and (ii) (but not the "and" immediately following subparagraph (ii)) substitute "by an officer of a local probation board or an officer of a provider of probation services".

87 In section 203(2), for paragraphs (a) and (b) substitute "an officer of a local probation board or an officer of a provider of probation services".

88 In section 209(2)(c) (drug rehabilitation requirement), for sub-paragraphs (i) and (ii) substitute "by an officer of a local probation board or an officer of a provider of probation services, and".

89 In section 211 (periodic review of drug rehabilitation requirement), omit subsection (5).

90 In section 214 (attendance centre requirement), after subsection (6) add—

"(7) A requirement to attend at an attendance centre for any period on any occasion operates as a requirement, during that period, to engage in occupation, or receive instruction, under the supervision of and in accordance with instructions given by, or under the authority of, the officer in charge of the centre, whether at the centre or elsewhere."

91 In section 217(1)(b) (requirement to avoid conflict with religious beliefs etc.), for "school or any other" substitute "any".

92 In section 221(2) (provision of attendance centres)—
   (a) omit "or" at the end of paragraph (a),
   (b) after that paragraph insert—
       "(aa) attendance centre requirements of youth rehabilitation orders, within the meaning of Part 1 of the Criminal Justice and Immigration Act 2008,", and
   (c) omit paragraph (b).

93 In section 222(1)(e) (rules), after "attendance centre requirements" insert ", or to attendance centre requirements imposed by youth rehabilitation orders under Part 1 of the Criminal Justice and Immigration Act 2008,".

94 Omit section 279 (drug treatment and testing requirement in action plan order or supervision order).

95 In section 330(5)(a) (orders subject to the affirmative resolution procedure), omit the entry relating to section 161(7).

96 In Schedule 8 (breach, revocation or amendment of community order), omit paragraphs 12, 15 and 17(5) (powers of magistrates' court in case of offender reaching 18).

97 Omit Schedule 24 (drug treatment and testing requirement in action plan order or supervision order).

Violent Crime Reduction Act 2006 (c. 38)

98 In section 47 of the Violent Crime Reduction Act 2006 (power to search persons in attendance centres for weapons), in the definition of "relevant person" in subsection (11), for paragraph (b) substitute—
   "(b) a youth rehabilitation order under Part 1 of the Criminal Justice and Immigration Act 2008;".

Offender Management Act 2007 (c. 21)

99 In section 1(4) of the Offender Management Act 2007 (meaning of "the probation purposes"), in the definition of "community order"—
   (a) after paragraph (a) insert—
       "(aa) a youth rehabilitation order within the meaning of Part 1 of the Criminal Justice and Immigration Act 2008 (see section 1 of that Act);", and
   (b) after paragraph (b) insert—
       "(c) a youth community order within the meaning of that Act (as it applies to offences committed before section 1 of the Criminal Justice and Immigration Act 2008 comes into force)".

PART 2
RELATED AMENDMENTS

Children and Young Persons Act 1933 (c. 12)

100 In section 49 of the Children and Young Persons Act 1933 (restrictions on reports of proceedings in which children or young persons are concerned), in subsection (13)(g)(ii), for "the Powers of Criminal Courts (Sentencing) Act 2000" substitute "Part 1 or 2 of Schedule 15 to the Criminal Justice Act 2003".

Children and Young Persons Act 1969 (c. 54)

101 (1) Section 32 of the Children and Young Persons Act 1969 (detention of absentees) is amended as follows.

(2) In subsection (1A)—

  (a) in paragraph (a), after "under" insert "paragraph 4(1)(a) of Schedule 1 or paragraph 6(4)(a) of Schedule 8 to the Powers of Criminal Courts (Sentencing) Act 2000 or",

  (b) in paragraph (b) (as substituted by paragraph 17(2)(b) of this Schedule), in sub-paragraph (ii), after "under" insert "paragraph 4 of Schedule 1 or paragraph 6 of Schedule 8 to the Powers of Criminal Courts (Sentencing) Act 2000 or".

(3) In subsection (1C) (as substituted by paragraph 17(3) of this Schedule)—

  (a) in paragraph (a), after "under" insert "paragraph 4(1)(a) of Schedule 1 or paragraph 6(4)(a) of Schedule 8 to the Powers of Criminal Courts (Sentencing) Act 2000 or", and

  (b) in paragraph (c), after "under" insert "paragraph 4(6) of Schedule 1 or paragraph 6(8) of Schedule 8 to the Powers of Criminal Courts (Sentencing) Act 2000 or".

Bail Act 1976 (c. 63)

102 In section 4(3) of the Bail Act 1976 (general right to bail of accused persons and others), before paragraph (a) (as substituted by paragraph 23(b) of this Schedule) insert—

"(za) Schedule 1 to the Powers of Criminal Courts (Sentencing) Act 2000 (referral orders: referral back to appropriate court),

(zb) Schedule 8 to that Act (breach of reparation order),".

Magistrates' Courts Act 1980 (c. 43)

103 In Schedule 6A to the Magistrates' Courts Act 1980 (fines that may be altered under section 143), at the end insert—

"In Schedule 8, paragraph 2(2)(a)(i) (failure to comply with reparation order)	£1,000".

Child Abduction Act 1984 (c. 37)

104 In paragraph 2(1) of the Schedule to the Child Abduction Act 1984 (modifications of section 1 for children in certain cases)—

  (a) in paragraph (a), after "under" insert "paragraph 4(1)(a) of Schedule 1 or paragraph 6(4)(a) of Schedule 8 to the Powers of Criminal Courts (Sentencing) Act 2000 or", and

  (b) in paragraph (b), before "or" (as inserted by paragraph 31(b) of this Schedule) insert ", paragraph 4 of Schedule 1 or paragraph 6 of Schedule 8 to the Powers of Criminal Courts (Sentencing) Act 2000".

Children Act 1989 (c. 41)

105 In section 21(2)(c) of the Children Act 1989 (provision of accommodation for children in police protection or detention or on remand, etc.), after subparagraph (i) insert—

  "(ia) remanded to accommodation provided by or on behalf of a local authority by virtue of paragraph 4 of Schedule 1 or paragraph 6 of Schedule 8 to the Powers of Criminal Courts (Sentencing) Act 2000 (breach etc. of referral orders and reparation orders);".

Powers of Criminal Courts (Sentencing) Act 2000 (c. 6)

106 The Powers of Criminal Courts (Sentencing) Act 2000 has effect subject to the following amendments.

107 In Schedule 1 (youth offender panels: further court proceedings), after paragraph 9 insert—

"Power to adjourn hearing and remand offender

9ZA (1) This paragraph applies to any hearing relating to an offender held by a youth court or other magistrates' court in proceedings under this Part of this Schedule.

   (2) The court may adjourn the hearing, and, where it does so, may—

     (a) direct that the offender be released forthwith, or

     (b) remand the offender.

   (3) Where the court remands the offender under sub-paragraph (2)—

     (a) it must fix the time and place at which the hearing is to be resumed, and

     (b) that time and place must be the time and place at which the offender is required to appear or be brought before the court by virtue of the remand.

   (4) Where the court adjourns the hearing under sub-paragraph (2) but does not remand the offender—

     (a) it may fix the time and place at which the hearing is to be resumed, but

     (b) if it does not do so, it must not resume the hearing unless it is satisfied that the persons mentioned in sub-paragraph (5) have had adequate notice of the time and place for the resumed hearing.

   (5) The persons referred to in sub-paragraph (4)(b) are—

     (a) the offender,

     (b) if the offender is aged under 14, a parent or guardian of the offender, and

     (c) a member of the youth offending team specified under section 18(1)(a) as responsible for implementing the order.

   (6) If a local authority has parental responsibility for an offender who is in its care or provided with accommodation by it in the exercise of any social services functions, the reference in sub-paragraph (5)(b) to a parent or guardian of the offender is to be read as a reference to that authority.

   (7) In sub-paragraph (6)—

     "local authority" has the same meaning as it has in Part 1 of the Criminal Justice and Immigration Act 2008 by virtue of section 7 of that Act,

     "parental responsibility" has the same meaning as it has in the Children Act 1989 by virtue of section 3 of that Act, and

     "social services functions" has the same meaning as it has in the Local Authority Social Services Act 1970 by virtue of section 1A of that Act.

   (8) The powers of a magistrates' court under this paragraph may be exercised by a single justice of the peace, notwithstanding anything in the Magistrates' Courts Act 1980.

   (9) This paragraph—

     (a) applies to any hearing in proceedings under this Part of this Schedule in place of section 10 of the Magistrates' Courts Act 1980 (adjournment of trial) where that section would otherwise apply, but

     (b) is not to be taken to affect the application of that section to hearings of any other description."

108 (1) Schedule 8 (breach, revocation and amendment of action plan orders and reparation orders) is amended as follows.

   (2) Omit paragraph 1 and the heading before that paragraph.

   (3) In paragraph 2(1), for "the appropriate court," substitute—

     "(a) a youth court acting in the local justice area in which the offender resides, or

     (b) if it is not known where the offender resides, a youth court acting in the local justice area for the time being named in the order in pursuance of section 74(4) of this Act,".

   (4) In paragraph 5—

     (a) in sub-paragraphs (1) and (3), for "appropriate court" substitute "relevant court", and

     (b) at the end insert—

       "(4) In this paragraph, "the relevant court" means—

         (a) a youth court acting in the local justice area for the time being named in the order in pursuance of section 74(4) of this Act, or

      (b) in the case of an application made both under this paragraph and under paragraph 2(1), the court mentioned in paragraph 2(1)."

(5) In paragraph 6—

    (a) in sub-paragraph (1), for "the appropriate court" substitute "a court",

    (b) in sub-paragraph (4), for "the appropriate court" substitute "the court before which the warrant directs the offender to be brought ("the relevant court")",

    (c) in sub-paragraph (5), for "the appropriate court" substitute "the relevant court", and

    (d) in sub-paragraph (7), for "the appropriate court", in each place it occurs, substitute "the relevant court".

(6) After paragraph 6 insert—

"Power to adjourn hearing and remand offender

6A (1) This paragraph applies to any hearing relating to an offender held by a youth court in any proceedings under this Schedule.

(2) The court may adjourn the hearing, and, where it does so, may—

    (a) direct that the offender be released forthwith, or

    (b) remand the offender.

(3) Where the court remands the offender under sub-paragraph (2)—

    (a) it must fix the time and place at which the hearing is to be resumed, and

    (b) that time and place must be the time and place at which the offender is required to appear or be brought before the court by virtue of the remand.

(4) Where the court adjourns the hearing under sub-paragraph (2) but does not remand the offender—

    (a) it may fix the time and place at which the hearing is to be resumed, but

    (b) if it does not do so, it must not resume the hearing unless it is satisfied that the persons mentioned in sub-paragraph (5) have had adequate notice of the time and place for the resumed hearing.

(5) The persons referred to in sub-paragraph (4)(b) are—

    (a) the offender,

    (b) if the offender is aged under 14, a parent or guardian of the offender, and

    (c) the responsible officer.

(6) If a local authority has parental responsibility for an offender who is in its care or provided with accommodation by it in the exercise of any social services functions, the reference in sub-paragraph (5)(b) to a parent or guardian of the offender is to be read as a reference to that authority.

(7) In sub-paragraph (6)—

"local authority" has the same meaning as it has in Part 1 of the Criminal Justice and Immigration Act 2008 by virtue of section 7 of that Act,

"parental responsibility" has the same meaning as it has in the Children Act 1989 by virtue of section 3 of that Act, and

"social services functions" has the same meaning as it has in the Local Authority Social Services Act 1970 by virtue of section 1A of that Act.

(8) The powers of a youth court under this paragraph may be exercised by a single justice of the peace, notwithstanding anything in the Magistrates' Courts Act 1980.

(9) This paragraph—

    (a) applies to any hearing in any proceedings under this Schedule in place of section 10 of the Magistrates' Courts Act 1980 (adjournment of trial) where that section would otherwise apply, but

    (b) is not to be taken to affect the application of that section to hearings of any other description."

Criminal Justice Act 2003 (c. 44)

109 In Schedule 8 to the Criminal Justice Act 2003 (breach, revocation or amendment of community order), after paragraph 25 insert—

"25A(1) This paragraph applies to any hearing relating to an offender held by a magistrates' court in any proceedings under this Schedule.

(2) The court may adjourn the hearing, and, where it does so, may—

(a) direct that the offender be released forthwith, or

(b) remand the offender.

(3) Where the court remands the offender under sub-paragraph (2)—

(a) it must fix the time and place at which the hearing is to be resumed, and

(b) that time and place must be the time and place at which the offender is required to appear or be brought before the court by virtue of the remand.

(4) Where the court adjourns the hearing under sub-paragraph (2) but does not remand the offender—

(a) it may fix the time and place at which the hearing is to be resumed, but

(b) if it does not do so, it must not resume the hearing unless it is satisfied that the offender and the responsible officer have had adequate notice of the time and place for the resumed hearing.

(5) The powers of a magistrates' court under this paragraph may be exercised by a single justice of the peace, notwithstanding anything in the Magistrates' Courts Act 1980.

(6) This paragraph—

(a) applies to any hearing in any proceedings under this Schedule in place of section 10 of the Magistrates' Courts Act 1980 (adjournment of trial) where that section would otherwise apply, but

(b) is not to be taken to affect the application of that section to hearings of any other description."

SCHEDULE 5   Section 13(2)

OFFENCES SPECIFIED FOR THE PURPOSES OF SECTIONS 225(3A) AND 227(2A) OF CRIMINAL JUSTICE ACT 2003

"SCHEDULE 15A

OFFENCES SPECIFIED FOR THE PURPOSES OF SECTIONS 225(3A) AND 227(2A)

PART 1

OFFENCES UNDER THE LAW OF ENGLAND AND WALES

1 Murder.

2 Manslaughter.

3 An offence under section 4 of the Offences against the Person Act 1861 (c. 100) (soliciting murder).

4 An offence under section 18 of that Act (wounding with intent to cause grievous bodily harm).

5 An offence under section 1 of the Sexual Offences Act 1956 (c. 69) (rape).

6 An offence under section 5 of that Act (intercourse with a girl under 13).

7 An offence under section 16 of the Firearms Act 1968 (c. 27) (possession of firearm with intent to endanger life).

8 An offence under section 17(1) of that Act (use of a firearm to resist arrest).

9 An offence under section 18 of that Act (carrying a firearm with criminal intent).

10 An offence of robbery under section 8 of the Theft Act 1968 (c. 60) where, at some time during the commission of the offence, the offender had in his possession a firearm or an imitation firearm within the meaning of the Firearms Act 1968.

11 An offence under section 1 of the Sexual Offences Act 2003 (c. 42) (rape).

12 An offence under section 2 of that Act (assault by penetration).

13 An offence under section 4 of that Act (causing a person to engage in sexual activity without consent) if the offender was liable on conviction on indictment to imprisonment for life.

14 An offence under section 5 of that Act (rape of a child under 13).

15 An offence under section 6 of that Act (assault of a child under 13 by penetration).

16 An offence under section 8 of that Act (causing or inciting a child under 13 to engage in sexual activity) if the offender was liable on conviction on indictment to imprisonment for life.

17 An offence under section 30 of that Act (sexual activity with a person with a mental disorder impeding choice) if the offender was liable on conviction on indictment to imprisonment for life.

18 An offence under section 31 of that Act (causing or inciting a person with a mental disorder to engage in sexual activity) if the offender was liable on conviction on indictment to imprisonment for life.

19 An offence under section 34 of that Act (inducement, threat or deception to procure sexual activity with a person with a mental disorder) if the offender was liable on conviction on indictment to imprisonment for life.

20 An offence under section 35 of that Act (causing a person with a mental disorder to engage in or agree to engage in sexual activity by inducement etc.) if the offender was liable on conviction on indictment to imprisonment for life.

21 An offence under section 47 of that Act (paying for sexual services of a child) if the offender was liable on conviction on indictment to imprisonment for life.

22 An offence under section 62 of that Act (committing an offence with intent to commit a sexual offence) if the offender was liable on conviction on indictment to imprisonment for life.

23 (1) An attempt to commit an offence specified in the preceding paragraphs of this Part of this Schedule ("a listed offence").

(2) Conspiracy to commit a listed offence.

(3) Incitement to commit a listed offence.

(4) An offence under Part 2 of the Serious Crime Act 2007 in relation to which a listed offence is the offence (or one of the offences) which the person intended or believed would be committed.

(5) Aiding, abetting, counselling or procuring the commission of a listed offence.

PART 2
OFFENCES UNDER THE LAW OF SCOTLAND

24 Murder.

25 Culpable homicide.

26 Rape.

27 Assault where the assault—

(a) is aggravated because it caused severe injury or endangered the victim's life, or

(b) was carried out with intent to rape or ravish the victim.

28 Sodomy where the person against whom the offence was committed did not consent.

29 Lewd, indecent or libidinous behaviour or practices.

30 Robbery, where, at some time during the commission of the offence, the offender had in his possession a firearm or an imitation firearm within the meaning of the Firearms Act 1968 (c. 27).

31 An offence under section 16 of the Firearms Act 1968 (possession of firearm with intent to endanger life).

32 An offence under section 17(1) of that Act (use of a firearm to resist arrest).

33 An offence under section 18 of that Act (carrying a firearm with criminal intent).

34 An offence under section 5(1) of the Criminal Law (Consolidation) (Scotland) Act 1995 (c. 39) (unlawful intercourse with a girl under 13).

35 (1) An attempt to commit an offence specified in the preceding paragraphs of this Part of this Schedule ("a listed offence").

(2) Conspiracy to commit a listed offence.

(3) Incitement to commit a listed offence.

(4) Aiding, abetting, counselling or procuring the commission of a listed offence.

PART 3
OFFENCES UNDER THE LAW OF NORTHERN IRELAND

36 Murder.

37 Manslaughter.

38 Rape.

39 An offence under section 4 of the Offences against the Person Act 1861 (c. 100) (soliciting murder).

40 An offence under section 18 of that Act (wounding with intent to cause grievous bodily harm).

41 An offence under section 4 of the Criminal Law Amendment Act 1885 (c. 69) (intercourse with a girl under 14).

42 An offence of robbery under section 8 of the Theft Act (Northern Ireland) 1969 (c. 16) where, at some time during the commission of the offence, the offender had in his possession a firearm or an imitation firearm within the meaning of the Firearms (Northern Ireland) Order 2004 (S.I. 2004/702 (N.I.3)).

43 An offence under Article 17 of the Firearms (Northern Ireland) Order 1981 (S.I. 1981/155 (N.I.2)) (possession of firearm with intent to endanger life).

44 An offence under Article 18(1) of that Order (use of a firearm to resist arrest).

45 An offence under Article 19 of that Order (carrying a firearm with criminal intent).

46 An offence under Article 58 of the Firearms (Northern Ireland) Order 2004 (possession of firearm with intent to endanger life).

47 An offence under Article 59 of that Order (use of a firearm to resist arrest).

48 An offence under Article 60 of that Order (carrying a firearm with criminal intent).

49 An offence under section 47 of the Sexual Offences Act 2003 (paying for sexual services of a child) if the offender was liable on conviction on indictment to imprisonment for life.

50 (1) An attempt to commit an offence specified in the preceding paragraphs of this Part of this Schedule ("a listed offence").

(2) Conspiracy to commit a listed offence.

(3) Incitement to commit a listed offence.

(4) An offence under Part 2 of the Serious Crime Act 2007 in relation to which a listed offence is the offence (or one of the offences) which the person intended or believed would be committed.

(5) Aiding, abetting, counselling or procuring the commission of a listed offence.

PART 4

OFFENCES UNDER SERVICE LAW

51   An offence under section 70 of the Army Act 1955, section 70 of the Air Force Act 1955 or section 42 of the Naval Discipline Act 1957 as respects which the corresponding civil offence (within the meaning of the Act in question) is an offence specified in Part 1 of this Schedule.

52   (1) An offence under section 42 of the Armed Forces Act 2006 as respects which the corresponding offence under the law of England and Wales (within the meaning given by that section) is an offence specified in Part 1 of this Schedule.

(2) Section 48 of the Armed Forces Act 2006 (attempts, conspiracy etc.) applies for the purposes of this paragraph as if the reference in subsection (3)(b) of that section to any of the following provisions of that Act were a reference to this paragraph.

PART 5

INTERPRETATION

53   In this Schedule, "imprisonment for life" includes custody for life and detention for life."

SCHEDULE 6   Section 23

CREDIT FOR PERIOD OF REMAND ON BAIL: TRANSITIONAL PROVISIONS

1   A period specified under paragraph 2 is to be treated as being a relevant period within the meaning of section 67 of the Criminal Justice Act 1967 (c. 80).

2   (1) This paragraph applies where—

(a) a court sentences an offender to a term of imprisonment for an offence that was committed before 4th April 2005,

(b) the offender was remanded on bail by a court in the course of or in connection with proceedings for the offence, or any related offence, after the coming into force of paragraph 1, and

(c) the offender's bail was subject to a qualifying curfew condition and an electronic monitoring condition ("the relevant conditions").

(2) Subject to sub-paragraph (4), the court must by order specify the credit period.

(3) The "credit period" is the number days represented by half of the sum of—

(a) the day on which the offender's bail was first subject to conditions that, had they applied throughout the day in question, would have been relevant conditions, and

(b) the number of other days on which the offender's bail was subject to those conditions (excluding the last day on which it was so subject),

rounded up to the nearest whole number.

(4) Sub-paragraph (2) does not apply if and to the extent that—

(a) rules made by the Secretary of State so provide, or

(b) it is in the opinion of the court just in all the circumstances not to give a direction under that subsection.

(5) Where as a result of paragraph (a) or (b) of sub-paragraph (4) the court does not specify the credit period under sub-paragraph (2), it may in accordance with either of those paragraphs by order specify a lesser period.

(6) Rules under sub-paragraph (4)(a) may, in particular, make provision in relation to—

(a) sentences of imprisonment for consecutive terms;

(b) sentences of imprisonment for terms which are wholly or partly concurrent;

345

   (c) periods during which a person granted bail subject to the relevant conditions is also subject to electronic monitoring required by an order made by a court or the Secretary of State.

(7) In considering whether it is of the opinion mentioned in sub-paragraph (4)(b) the court must, in particular, take into account whether or not the offender has, at any time whilst on bail subject to the relevant conditions, broken either or both of them.

(8) Where the court specifies a period under sub-paragraph (2) or (5) it shall state in open court—

   (a) the number of days on which the offender was subject to the relevant conditions, and

   (b) the number of days in the period specified.

(9) Sub-paragraph (10) applies where the court—

   (a) does not specify the credit period under sub-paragraph (2) but does specify a lesser period under sub-paragraph (5), or

   (b) does not specify a period under either sub-paragraph (2) or (5).

(10) The court shall state in open court—

   (a) that its decision is in accordance with rules made under paragraph (a) of sub-paragraph (4), or

   (b) that it is of the opinion mentioned in paragraph (b) of that subparagraph and what the circumstances are.

(11) In this paragraph—

"electronic monitoring condition" means any electronic monitoring requirements imposed under section 3(6ZAA) of the Bail Act 1976 (c. 63) for the purpose of securing the electronic monitoring of a person's compliance with a qualifying curfew condition;

"qualifying curfew condition" means a condition of bail which requires the person granted bail to remain at one or more specified places for a total of not less than 9 hours in any given day; and

"related offence" means an offence, other than the offence for which the sentence is imposed ("offence A"), with which the offender was charged and the charge for which was founded on the same facts or evidence as offence A.

SCHEDULE 7   Section 39(6)

YOUTH DEFAULT ORDERS: MODIFICATION OF PROVISIONS APPLYING TO YOUTH REHABILITATION ORDERS

General

1 Any reference to the offender is, in relation to a youth default order, to be read as a reference to the person in default; and any reference to the time when the offender is convicted is to be read as a reference to the time when the order is made.

Unpaid work requirement

2 (1) In its application to a youth default order, paragraph 10 of Schedule 1 (unpaid work requirement) is modified as follows.

(2) Sub-paragraph (2) has effect as if for paragraphs (a) and (b) there were substituted—

"(a) not less than 20, and

   (b) in the case of an amount in default which is specified in the first column of the following Table, not more than the number of hours set out opposite that amount in the second column.

Amount	Number of hours
An amount not exceeding £200	40
An amount exceeding £200 but not exceeding £500	60
An amount exceeding £500	100".

(3) Sub-paragraph (7) has effect as if after "Unless revoked" there were inserted "(or section 39(7)(a) applies)".

Attendance centre requirement

3 (1) In its application to a youth default order, paragraph 12 of Schedule 1 (attendance centre requirement) is modified as follows.
   (2) Sub-paragraph (2) has effect as if—
      (a) in paragraph (a), for the words following "conviction" there were substituted "must be, in the case of an amount in default which is specified in the first column of the following Table, not more than the number of hours set out opposite that amount in the second column.

Amount	Number of hours
An amount not exceeding £250	8
An amount exceeding £250 but not exceeding £500	14
An amount exceeding £500	24".

      (b) in paragraph (b), for the words following "conviction" there were substituted "must be, in the case of an amount in default which is specified in the first column of the following Table, not more than the number of hours set out opposite that amount in the second column.

Amount	Number of hours
An amount not exceeding £250	8
An amount exceeding £250 but not exceeding £500	14
An amount exceeding £500	24".

      (c) in paragraph (c), for "must not be more than 12" there were substituted "must be, in the case of an amount in default which is specified in the first column of the following Table, not more than the number of hours set out opposite that amount in the second column.

Amount	Number of hours
An amount not exceeding £250	8
An amount exceeding £250 but not exceeding £500	14
An amount exceeding £500	12".

Curfew requirement

4 (1) In its application to a youth default order, paragraph 14 of Schedule 1 (curfew requirement) is modified as follows.

(2) That paragraph has effect as if after sub-paragraph (2) there were inserted—

"(2A) In the case of an amount in default which is specified in the first column of the following Table, the number of days on which the person in default is subject to the curfew requirement must not exceed the number of days set out opposite that amount in the second column.

Amount	Number of days
An amount not exceeding £200	20
An amount exceeding £200 but not exceeding £500	30
An amount exceeding £500 but not exceeding £1,000	60
An amount exceeding £1,000 but not exceeding £2,000	90
An amount exceeding £2,000	180".

Enforcement, revocation and amendment of youth default order

5 (1) In its application to a youth default order, Schedule 2 (breach, revocation or amendment of youth rehabilitation orders) is modified as follows.

(2) Any reference to the offence in respect of which the youth rehabilitation order was made is to be read as a reference to the default in respect of which the youth default order was made.

(3) Accordingly, any power of the court to revoke a youth rehabilitation order and deal with the offender for the offence is to be taken to be a power to revoke the youth default order and deal with him in any way in which the court which made the youth default order could deal with him for his default in paying the sum in question.

(4) Paragraph 2 has effect as if for paragraphs (a) and (b) there were substituted "as having been made by a magistrates' court".

(5) The following provisions are omitted—

(a) paragraph 6(2)(a) and (b)(i), (5) and (12) to (16),

(b) paragraph 11(5),

(c) paragraph 18(7), and

(d) paragraph 19(3).

Power to alter amount of money or number of hours or days

6 The Secretary of State may by order amend paragraph 2, 3 or 4 by substituting for any reference to an amount of money or a number of hours or days there specified a reference to such other amount or number as may be specified in the order.

Transfer of youth default order to Northern Ireland

7 (1) In its application to a youth default order, Schedule 3 is modified as follows.

 (2) Paragraph 9 has effect as if, after sub-paragraph (2) there were inserted—

   "(3) Nothing in sub-paragraph (1) affects the application of section 39(7) to a youth default order made or amended in accordance with paragraph 1 or 2."

 (3) Paragraph 12 has effect as if, after paragraph (b) there were inserted—

   "(bb) any power to impose a fine on the offender".

SCHEDULE 8   Section 47
APPEALS IN CRIMINAL CASES

PART 1
AMENDMENTS OF CRIMINAL APPEAL ACT 1968

1 The Criminal Appeal Act 1968 (c. 19) has effect subject to the following amendments.

Time limit on grant of certificates of fitness for appeal

2 In section 1 (appeal against conviction), in subsection (2)(b) after "if" insert ", within 28 days from the date of the conviction,".

3 In section 11 (supplementary provisions as to appeal against sentence), in subsection (1A)—

 (a) after "if" insert ", within 28 days from the date on which the sentence was passed,", and

 (b) for "the sentence" substitute "it".

4 In section 12 (appeal against verdict of not guilty on ground of insanity), in subsection (1)(b) after "if" insert ", within 28 days from the date of the verdict,".

5 In section 15 (appeal against finding of disability), in subsection (2)(b) after "if" insert ", within 28 days from the date of the finding that the accused did the act or made the omission charged,".

Powers of Court to substitute different sentence

6 (1) Section 4 (sentence when appeal allowed on part of indictment) is amended as follows.

 (2) For the heading substitute "Power to re-sentence where appellant remains convicted of related offences".

 (3) For subsection (1) substitute—

   "(1) This section applies where—

     (a) two or more related sentences are passed,

     (b) the Court of Appeal allow an appeal against conviction in respect of one or more of the offences for which the sentences were passed ("the related offences"), but

     (c) the appellant remains convicted of one or more of those offences."

 (4) In subsection (2)—

   (a) for "in respect of any count on which the appellant remains convicted" substitute "in respect of any related offence of which the appellant remains convicted", and

   (b) omit "for the offence of which he remains convicted on that count".

 (5) In subsection (3)—

   (a) for "on the indictment as a whole" substitute "(taken as a whole) for all the related offences of which he remains convicted", and

   (b) for "for all offences of which he was convicted on the indictment" substitute "for all the related offences".

(6) After subsection (3) insert—

"(4) For the purposes of subsection (1)(a), two or more sentences are related if—

(a) they are passed on the same day,

(b) they are passed on different days but the court in passing any one of them states that it is treating that one together with the other or others as substantially one sentence, or

(c) they are passed on different days but in respect of counts on the same indictment.

(5) Where—

(a) two or more sentences are related to each other by virtue of subsection (4)(a) or (b), and

(b) any one or more of those sentences is related to one or more other sentences by virtue of subsection (4)(c),

all the sentences are to be treated as related for the purposes of subsection (1)(a)."

Interim hospital orders

7 The following provisions (which relate to the effect of interim hospital orders made by the Court of Appeal) are omitted—

(a) section 6(5) and the definition of interim hospital order in section 6(7),

(b) section 11(6),

(c) section 14(5) and the definition of interim hospital order in section 14(7), and

(d) section 16B(3).

8 Before section 31 (but after the cross-heading preceding it) insert—

"**30A Effect of interim hospital orders**

(1) This section applies where the Court of Appeal—

(a) make an interim hospital order by virtue of any provision of this Part, or

(b) renew an interim hospital order so made.

(2) The court below shall be treated for the purposes of section 38(7) of the Mental Health Act 1983 (absconding offenders) as the court that made the order."

9 In section 31 (powers of Court which are exercisable by single judge) after subsection (2) insert—

"(2ZA) The power of the Court of Appeal to renew an interim hospital order made by them by virtue of any provision of this Part may be exercised by a single judge in the same manner as it may be exercised by the Court."

Evidence

10 (1) Section 23 (evidence) is amended as follows.

(2) In subsection (1) after "an appeal" insert ", or an application for leave to appeal,".

(3) In that subsection, for paragraph (b) substitute—

"(b) order any witness to attend for examination and be examined before the Court (whether or not he was called in the proceedings from which the appeal lies); and".

(4) After subsection (1) insert—

"(1A) The power conferred by subsection (1)(a) may be exercised so as to require the production of any document, exhibit or other thing mentioned in that subsection to—

(a) the Court;

(b) the appellant;

(c) the respondent."

(5) In subsection (4) after "an appeal" insert ", or an application for leave to appeal,".

(6) After subsection (5) insert—

"(6) In this section, "respondent" includes a person who will be a respondent if leave to appeal is granted."

Powers of single judge

11 (1) Section 31 (powers of Court of Appeal which are exercisable by single judge) is amended as follows.

   (2) In the heading, omit "under Part 1".

   (3) After subsection (2C) insert—

      "(2D) The power of the Court of Appeal to grant leave to appeal under section 9(11) of the Criminal Justice Act 1987 may be exercised by a single judge in the same manner as it may be exercised by the Court.

      (2E) The power of the Court of Appeal to grant leave to appeal under section 35(1) of the Criminal Procedure and Investigations Act 1996 may be exercised by a single judge in the same manner as it may be exercised by the Court."

Appeals against procedural directions

12 In section 31C (appeals against procedural directions), omit subsections (1) and (2).

Detention of defendant pending appeal to Supreme Court

13 (1) Section 37 (detention of defendant on appeal by Crown) is amended as follows.

   (2) In subsection (2) for the words from "may make" to the end substitute "shall make—

      (a) an order providing for his detention, or directing that he shall not be released except on bail (which may be granted by the Court as under section 36 above), so long as the appeal is pending, or

      (b) an order that he be released without bail."

   (3) After subsection (2) insert—

      "(2A) The Court may make an order under subsection (2)(b) only if they think that it is in the interests of justice that the defendant should not be liable to be detained as a result of the decision of the Supreme Court on the appeal."

   (4) In subsection (3) for "this section" substitute "subsection (2)(a)".

   (5) In subsection (4) for "this section" (in each place where it occurs) substitute "subsection (2)(a)".

   (6) In subsection (4A) for "this section" (in the first place where it occurs) substitute "subsection (2)(a)".

   (7) For subsection (5) substitute—

      "(5) The defendant shall not be liable to be detained again as a result of the decision of the Supreme Court on the appeal if—

      (a) the Court of Appeal have made an order under subsection (2)(b), or

      (b) the Court have made an order under subsection (2)(a) but the order has ceased to have effect by virtue of subsection (3) or the defendant has been released or discharged by virtue of subsection (4) or (4A)."

PART 2

AMENDMENTS OF CRIMINAL APPEAL (NORTHERN IRELAND) ACT 1980

14 The Criminal Appeal (Northern Ireland) Act 1980 (c. 47) has effect subject to the following amendments.

Time limit on grant of certificates of fitness for appeal

15 In section 1 (appeal against conviction), in paragraph (b) after "if" insert ", within 28 days from the date of the conviction,".

16 In section 12 (appeal against finding of not guilty on ground of insanity), in subsection (1)(b) after "if" insert ", within 28 days from the date of the finding,".

17 In section 13A (appeal against finding of unfitness to be tried), in subsection (2)(b) after "if" insert ", within 28 days from the date of the finding that the person did the act or made the omission charged,".

Powers of Court to substitute different sentence

18 (1) Section 4 (alteration of sentence on appeal against conviction) is amended as follows.
    (2) For subsection (1) substitute—
        "(1) Subsection (1A) applies where—
            (a) two or more related sentences are passed,
            (b) the Court of Appeal allows an appeal against conviction in respect of one or more of the offences for which the sentences were passed ("the related offences"), but
            (c) the appellant remains convicted of one or more of those offences.
        (1A) The Court may, in respect of any related offence of which the appellant remains convicted, pass such sentence, in substitution for the sentence passed thereon at the trial, as it thinks proper and is authorised by law."
    (3) After subsection (2) insert—
        "(3) For the purposes of subsection (1)(a), two or more sentences are related if—
            (a) they are passed on the same day,
            (b) they are passed on different days but the court in passing any one of them states that it is treating that one together with the other or others as substantially one sentence, or
            (c) they are passed on different days but in respect of counts on the same indictment.
    (4) Where—
            (a) two or more sentences are related to each other by virtue of subsection (3)(a) or (b), and
            (b) any one or more of those sentences is related to one or more other sentences by virtue of subsection (3)(c),
        all the sentences are to be treated as related for the purposes of subsection (1)(a)."

Interim hospital orders

19 Section 10(6) (effect of interim hospital orders made by Court of Appeal) is omitted.

20 (1) For the cross-heading preceding section 30 substitute—

        "Supplementary".

    (2) Before section 30 (but after the cross-heading preceding it) insert—
        "29A Effect of interim hospital orders
        (1) This section applies where the Court of Appeal—
            (a) makes an interim hospital order by virtue of any provision of this Part, or
            (b) renews an interim hospital order so made.
        (2) The Crown Court shall be treated for the purposes of Article 45(6) of the Mental Health Order (absconding offenders) as the court that made the order."

21 In section 45 (powers of Court which are exercisable by single judge) after subsection (3) insert—
        "(3ZA) The power of the Court of Appeal to renew an interim hospital order made by it by virtue of any provision of this Act may be exercised by a single judge in the same manner as it may be exercised by the Court."

Evidence

22 (1) Section 25 (evidence) is amended as follows.

    (2) In subsection (1) after "an appeal" insert ", or an application for leave to appeal,".

    (3) In that subsection, for paragraph (b) substitute—

        "(b) order any witness to attend and be examined before the Court (whether or not he was called at the trial); and".

    (4) After subsection (1) insert—

        "(1A) The power conferred by subsection (1)(a) may be exercised so as to require the production of any document, exhibit or other thing mentioned in that subsection to—

            (a) the Court;

            (b) the appellant;

            (c) the respondent."

    (5) After subsection (3) insert—

        "(4) In this section, "respondent" includes a person who will be a respondent if leave to appeal is granted."

23 In section 26 (additional powers of Court), in subsection (1) after "an appeal" insert ", or an application for leave to appeal,".

Detention of defendant pending appeal to Supreme Court

24 (1) Section 36 (detention of defendant on appeal by Crown) is amended as follows.

    (2) In subsection (1) for the words from "may make" to the end substitute "shall make—

        (a) an order providing for his detention, or directing that he shall not be released except on bail (which may be granted by the Court as under section 35 above), so long as the appeal is pending, or

        (b) an order that he be released without bail."

    (3) After subsection (1) insert—

        "(1A) The Court may make an order under subsection (1)(b) only if it thinks that it is in the interests of justice that the defendant should not be liable to be detained as a result of the decision of the Supreme Court on the appeal."

    (4) In subsection (2) for "subsection (1)" substitute "subsection (1)(a)".

    (5) In subsection (3) for "this section" (in each place where it occurs) substitute "subsection (1)(a)".

    (6) In subsection (3A) for "this section" (in the first place where it occurs) substitute "subsection (1)(a)".

    (7) For subsection (4) substitute—

        "(4) The defendant shall not be liable to be detained again as a result of the decision of the Supreme Court on the appeal if—

        (a) the Court of Appeal has made an order under subsection (1)(b), or

        (b) the Court has made an order under subsection (1)(a) but the order has ceased to have effect by virtue of subsection (2) or the defendant has been released or discharged by virtue of subsection (3) or (3A)."

Powers of single judge

25 (1) Section 45 (powers of Court of Appeal which are exercisable by single judge) is amended as follows.

    (2) After subsection (3C) insert—

        "(3D) The power of the Court of Appeal to grant leave to appeal under Article 8(11) of the Criminal Justice (Serious Fraud) (Northern Ireland) Order 1988 may be exercised by a single judge in the same manner as it may be exercised by the Court."

PART 3
AMENDMENTS OF OTHER ACTS

Detention of defendant pending appeal from High Court to Supreme Court

26 (1) Section 5 of the Administration of Justice Act 1960 (c. 65) (power to order detention or admission to bail of defendant) is amended as follows.

(2) In subsection (1) for the words from "may make" to the end substitute "shall make—

(a) an order providing for the detention of the defendant, or directing that he shall not be released except on bail (which may be granted by the court as under section 4 above), so long as the appeal is pending, or

(b) an order that the defendant be released without bail."

(3) After subsection (1) insert—

"(1A) The court may make an order under subsection (1)(b) only if it thinks that it is in the interests of justice that the defendant should not be liable to be detained as a result of the decision of the Supreme Court on the appeal."

(4) In subsection (3) for "subsection (1)" substitute "subsection (1)(a)".

(5) In subsection (4) for "the said subsection (1)" substitute "the said subsection (1)(a)".

(6) In subsection (4A) for "the said subsection (1)" substitute "the said subsection (1)(a)".

(7) For subsection (5) substitute—

"(5) The defendant shall not be liable to be detained again as a result of the decision of the Supreme Court on the appeal if—

(a) the court has made an order under subsection (1)(b), or

(b) the court has made an order under subsection (1)(a) but the order has ceased to have effect by virtue of subsection (3) or the defendant has been released or discharged by virtue of subsection (4) or (4A)."

Variation of sentences by Crown Court

27 (1) Section 49 of the Judicature (Northern Ireland) Act 1978 (c. 23) (sentences imposed and other decisions made by Crown Court) is amended as follows.

(2) In subsection (2)—

(a) for "28 days" substitute "56 days", and

(b) omit the words from "or, where subsection (3) applies," to the end.

(3) After subsection (2) insert—

"(2A) The power conferred by subsection (1) may not be exercised in relation to any sentence or order if an appeal, or an application for leave to appeal, against that sentence or order has been determined."

(4) Subsection (3) is omitted.

28 (1) Section 155 of the Powers of Criminal Courts (Sentencing) Act 2000 (c. 6) (alteration of Crown Court sentence) is amended as follows.

(2) In subsection (1)—

(a) for "28 days" substitute "56 days", and

(b) omit the words from "or, where subsection (2) below applies," to the end.

(3) After subsection (1) insert—

"(1A) The power conferred by subsection (1) may not be exercised in relation to any sentence or order if an appeal, or an application for leave to appeal, against that sentence or order has been determined."

(4) Subsections (2) and (3) are omitted.

SCHEDULE 9   Section 48
ALTERNATIVES TO PROSECUTION FOR PERSONS UNDER 18

1 The Crime and Disorder Act 1998 (c. 37) has effect subject to the following amendments.

2 (1) Section 65 (reprimands and warnings) is amended as follows.

  (2) In subsection (1)—

    (a) for paragraph (b) substitute—

      "(b) the constable considers that there is sufficient evidence to charge the offender with the offence;",

    (b) in paragraph (d), after "an offence" insert "or given a youth conditional caution in respect of an offence", and

    (c) for paragraph (e) substitute

      "(e) the constable does not consider that the offender should be prosecuted or given a youth conditional caution."

  (3) In subsection (3)(b) after "to be brought" insert "or a youth conditional caution to be given".

  (4) In subsection (6), in paragraph (a)(i) after "to be brought" insert "or a youth conditional caution to be given".

  (5) In subsection (7) for "In this section" substitute "In this Chapter".

  (6) For subsection (8) (cautions not to be given to children or young persons) substitute—

    "(8) No caution, other than a youth conditional caution, shall be given to a child or young person."

3 After section 66 insert—

"Young offenders: youth conditional cautions

66A Youth conditional cautions

(1) An authorised person may give a youth conditional caution to a child or young person ("the offender") if—

  (a) the offender has not previously been convicted of an offence, and

  (b) each of the five requirements in section 66B is satisfied.

(2) In this Chapter, "youth conditional caution" means a caution which is given in respect of an offence committed by the offender and which has conditions attached to it with which the offender must comply.

(3) The conditions which may be attached to such a caution are those which have one or more of the following objects—

  (a) facilitating the rehabilitation of the offender;

  (b) ensuring that the offender makes reparation for the offence;

  (c) punishing the offender.

(4) The conditions that may be attached to a youth conditional caution include—

  (a) (subject to section 66C) a condition that the offender pay a financial penalty;

  (b) a condition that the offender attend at a specified place at specified times.

  "Specified" means specified by a relevant prosecutor.

(5) Conditions attached by virtue of subsection (4)(b) may not require the offender to attend for more than 20 hours in total, not including any attendance required by conditions attached for the purpose of facilitating the offender's rehabilitation.

(6) The Secretary of State may by order amend subsection (5) by substituting a different figure.

(7) In this section, "authorised person" means—

  (a) a constable,

  (b) an investigating officer, or

  (c) a person authorised by a relevant prosecutor for the purposes of this section.

66B The five requirements

(1) The first requirement is that the authorised person has evidence that the offender has committed an offence.

(2) The second requirement is that a relevant prosecutor decides—

    (a) that there is sufficient evidence to charge the offender with the offence, and

    (b) that a youth conditional caution should be given to the offender in respect of the offence.

(3) The third requirement is that the offender admits to the authorised person that he committed the offence.

(4) The fourth requirement is that the authorised person explains the effect of the youth conditional caution to the offender and warns him that failure to comply with any of the conditions attached to the caution may result in his being prosecuted for the offence.

(5) If the offender is aged 16 or under, the explanation and warning mentioned in subsection (4) must be given in the presence of an appropriate adult.

(6) The fifth requirement is that the offender signs a document which contains—

    (a) details of the offence,

    (b) an admission by him that he committed the offence,

    (c) his consent to being given the youth conditional caution, and

    (d) the conditions attached to the caution.

66C Financial penalties

(1) A condition that the offender pay a financial penalty (a "financial penalty condition") may not be attached to a youth conditional caution given in respect of an offence unless the offence is one that is prescribed, or of a description prescribed, in an order made by the Secretary of State.

(2) An order under subsection (1) must prescribe, in respect of each offence or description of offence in the order, the maximum amount of the penalty that may be specified under subsection (5)(a).

(3) The amount that may be prescribed in respect of any offence must not exceed £100.

(4) The Secretary of State may by order amend subsection (3) by substituting a different figure.

(5) Where a financial penalty condition is attached to a youth conditional caution, a relevant prosecutor must also specify—

    (a) the amount of the penalty, and

    (b) the person to whom the financial penalty is to be paid and how it may be paid.

(6) To comply with the condition, the offender must pay the penalty in accordance with the provision specified under subsection (5)(b).

(7) Where a financial penalty is (in accordance with the provision specified under subsection (5)(b)) paid to a person other than a designated officer for a local justice area, the person to whom it is paid must give the payment to such an officer.

66D Variation of conditions

A relevant prosecutor may, with the consent of the offender, vary the conditions attached to a youth conditional caution by—

(a) modifying or omitting any of the conditions;

(b) adding a condition.

66E Failure to comply with conditions

(1) If the offender fails, without reasonable excuse, to comply with any of the conditions attached to the youth conditional caution, criminal proceedings may be instituted against the person for the offence in question.

(2) The document mentioned in section 66B(6) is to be admissible in such proceedings.

(3) Where such proceedings are instituted, the youth conditional caution is to cease to have effect.

(4) Section 24A(1) of the Criminal Justice Act 2003 ("the 2003 Act") applies in relation to the conditions attached to a youth conditional caution as it applies in relation to the conditions attached to a conditional caution (within the meaning of Part 3 of that Act).

(5) Sections 24A(2) to (9) and 24B of the 2003 Act apply in relation to a person who is arrested under section 24A(1) of that Act by virtue of subsection (4) above as they apply in relation to a person who is arrested under that section for failing to comply with any of the conditions attached to a conditional caution (within the meaning of Part 3 of that Act).

66F Restriction on sentencing powers where youth conditional caution given

Where a person who has been given a youth conditional caution is convicted of an offence committed within two years of the giving of the caution, the court by or before which the person is so convicted—

(a) may not make an order under section 12(1)(b) of the Powers of Criminal Courts (Sentencing) Act 2000 (conditional discharge) in respect of the offence unless it is of the opinion that there are exceptional circumstances relating to the offence or the offender which justify its doing so; and

(b) where it does make such an order, must state in open court that it is of that opinion and why it is.

66G Code of practice on youth conditional cautions

(1) The Secretary of State must prepare a code of practice in relation to youth conditional cautions.

(2) The code may, in particular, make provision as to—

(a) the circumstances in which youth conditional cautions may be given,

(b) the procedure to be followed in connection with the giving of such cautions,

(c) the conditions which may be attached to such cautions and the time for which they may have effect,

(d) the category of constable or investigating officer by whom such cautions may be given,

(e) the persons who may be authorised by a relevant prosecutor for the purposes of section 66A,

(f) the form which such cautions are to take and the manner in which they are to be given and recorded,

(g) the places where such cautions may be given,

(h) the provision which may be made by a relevant prosecutor under section 66C(5)(b),

(i) the monitoring of compliance with conditions attached to such cautions,

(j) the exercise of the power of arrest conferred by section 24A(1) of the Criminal Justice Act 2003 (c. 44) as it applies by virtue of section 66E(4),

(k) who is to decide how a person should be dealt with under section 24A(2) of that Act as it applies by virtue of section 66E(5).

(3) After preparing a draft of the code the Secretary of State—

(a) must publish the draft,

(b) must consider any representations made to him about the draft, and

(c) may amend the draft accordingly,

but he may not publish or amend the draft without the consent of the Attorney General.

(4) After the Secretary of State has proceeded under subsection (3) he must lay the code before each House of Parliament.

(5) When he has done so he may bring the code into force by order.

(6) The Secretary of State may from time to time revise a code of practice brought into force under this section.

(7) Subsections (3) to (6) are to apply (with appropriate modifications) to a revised code as they apply to an original code.

Interpretation of Chapter 1

66H Interpretation

In this Chapter—

(a) "appropriate adult" has the meaning given by section 65(7);

(b) "authorised person" has the meaning given by section 66A(7);

(c) "investigating officer" means an officer of Revenue and Customs, appointed in accordance with section 2(1) of the Commissioners for Revenue and Customs Act 2005, or a person designated as an investigating officer under section 38 of the Police Reform Act 2002 (c. 30);

(d) "the offender" has the meaning given by section 66A(1);

(e) "relevant prosecutor" means—

   (i) the Attorney General,

   (ii) the Director of the Serious Fraud Office,

   (iii) the Director of Revenue and Customs Prosecutions,

   (iv) the Director of Public Prosecutions,

   (v) the Secretary of State, or

   (vi) a person who is specified in an order made by the Secretary State as being a relevant prosecutor for the purposes of this Chapter;

(f) "youth conditional caution" has the meaning given by section 66A(2)."

4 (1) Section 114 (orders and regulations) is amended as follows.

(2) In subsection (2) (which specifies orders that are subject to annulment in pursuance of a resolution of either House of Parliament), for "or 10(6)" substitute "10(6), 66C(1) or 66H(e)(vi)".

(3) After subsection (2) insert—

"(2A) Subsection (2) also applies to a statutory instrument containing—

   (a) an order under section 66C(4) unless the order makes provision of the kind mentioned in subsection (3A)(a) below, or

   (b) an order under section 66G(5) other than the first such order."

(4) In subsection (3) (which specifies orders that may not be made unless a draft has been approved by a resolution of each House of Parliament) after "41(6)" insert ", 66A(6)".

(5) After subsection (3) insert—

"(3A) Subsection (3) also applies to—

   (a) an order under section 66C(4) which makes provision increasing the figure in section 66C(3) by more than is necessary to reflect changes in the value of money, and

   (b) the first order under section 66G(5)."

SCHEDULE 10   Section 49

PROTECTION FOR SPENT CAUTIONS UNDER REHABILITATION OF OFFENDERS ACT 1974

1 The Rehabilitation of Offenders Act 1974 (c. 53) is amended as follows.

2 In section 6(6) for "the Schedule" substitute "Schedule 1".

3 After section 8 (defamation actions) there is inserted—

"8A Protection afforded to spent cautions

(1) Schedule 2 to this Act (protection for spent cautions) shall have effect.

(2) In this Act "caution" means—

    (a) a conditional caution, that is to say, a caution given under section 22 of the Criminal Justice Act 2003 (c. 44) (conditional cautions for adults) or under section 66A of the Crime and Disorder Act 1998 (c. 37) (conditional cautions for children and young persons);

    (b) any other caution given to a person in England and Wales in respect of an offence which, at the time the caution is given, that person has admitted;

    (c) a reprimand or warning given under section 65 of the Crime and Disorder Act 1998 (reprimands and warnings for persons aged under 18);

    (d) anything corresponding to a caution, reprimand or warning falling within paragraphs (a) to (c) (however described) which is given to a person in respect of an offence under the law of a country outside England and Wales."

4 After section 9 (unauthorised disclosure of spent convictions) insert—

"9A Unauthorised disclosure of spent cautions

(1) In this section—

    (a) "official record" means a record which—

        (i) contains information about persons given a caution for any offence or offences; and

        (ii) is kept for the purposes of its functions by any court, police force, Government department or other public authority in England and Wales;

    (b) "caution information" means information imputing that a named or otherwise identifiable living person ("the named person") has committed, been charged with or prosecuted or cautioned for any offence which is the subject of a spent caution; and

    (c) "relevant person" means any person who, in the course of his official duties (anywhere in the United Kingdom), has or at any time has had custody of or access to any official record or the information contained in it.

(2) Subject to the terms of any order made under subsection (5), a relevant person shall be guilty of an offence if, knowing or having reasonable cause to suspect that any caution information he has obtained in the course of his official duties is caution information, he discloses it, otherwise than in the course of those duties, to another person.

(3) In any proceedings for an offence under subsection (2) it shall be a defence for the defendant to show that the disclosure was made—

    (a) to the named person or to another person at the express request of the named person;

    (b) to a person whom he reasonably believed to be the named person or to another person at the express request of a person whom he reasonably believed to be the named person.

(4) Any person who obtains any caution information from any official record by means of any fraud, dishonesty or bribe shall be guilty of an offence.

(5) The Secretary of State may by order make such provision as appears to him to be appropriate for excepting the disclosure of caution information derived from an official record from the provisions of subsection (2) in such cases or classes of case as may be specified in the order.

(6) A person guilty of an offence under subsection (2) is liable on summary conviction to a fine not exceeding level 4 on the standard scale.

(7) A person guilty of an offence under subsection (4) is liable on summary conviction to a fine not exceeding level 5 on the standard scale, or to imprisonment for a term not exceeding 51 weeks, or to both.

(8) Proceedings for an offence under subsection (2) shall not be instituted except by or on behalf of the Director of Public Prosecutions."

5 The Schedule (service disciplinary proceedings) is re-numbered as Schedule 1.
6 After that Schedule insert—

"SCHEDULE 2
PROTECTION FOR SPENT CAUTIONS

Preliminary

1 (1) For the purposes of this Schedule a caution shall be regarded as a spent caution—
   (a) in the case of a conditional caution (as defined in section 8A(2)(a)), at the end of the relevant period for the caution;
   (b) in any other case, at the time the caution is given.
   (2) In sub-paragraph (1)(a) "the relevant period for the caution" means (subject to sub-paragraph (3)) the period of three months from the date on which the conditional caution was given.
   (3) If the person concerned is subsequently prosecuted and convicted of the offence in respect of which a conditional caution was given—
   (a) the relevant period for the caution shall end at the same time as the rehabilitation period for the offence; and
   (b) if the conviction occurs after the end of the period mentioned in sub-paragraph (1)(a), the caution shall be treated for the purposes of this Schedule as not having become spent in relation to any period before the end of the rehabilitation period for the offence.

2 (1) In this Schedule "ancillary circumstances", in relation to a caution, means any circumstances of the following—
   (a) the offence which was the subject of the caution or the conduct constituting that offence;
   (b) any process preliminary to the caution (including consideration by any person of how to deal with that offence and the procedure for giving the caution);
   (c) any proceedings for that offence which take place before the caution is given (including anything which happens after that time for the purpose of bringing the proceedings to an end);
   (d) any judicial review proceedings relating to the caution;
   (e) in the case of a warning under section 65 of the Crime and Disorder Act 1998 (c. 37), anything done in pursuance of or undergone in compliance with a requirement to participate in a rehabilitation programme under section 66(2) of that Act;
   (f) in the case of a conditional caution, any conditions attached to the caution or anything done in pursuance of or undergone in compliance with those conditions.
   (2) Where the caution relates to two or more offences, references in sub-paragraph (1) to the offence which was the subject of the caution include a reference to each of the offences concerned.
   (3) In this Schedule "proceedings before a judicial authority" has the same meaning as in section 4.

Protection relating to spent cautions and ancillary circumstances

3 (1) A person who is given a caution for an offence shall, from the time the caution is spent, be treated for all purposes in law as a person who has not committed, been charged with or prosecuted for, or been given a caution for the offence; and notwithstanding the provisions of any other enactment or rule of law to the contrary—
   (a) no evidence shall be admissible in any proceedings before a judicial authority exercising its jurisdiction or functions in England and Wales to prove that any such person has

360

committed, been charged with or prosecuted for, or been given a caution for the offence; and

    (b) a person shall not, in any such proceedings, be asked and, if asked, shall not be required to answer, any question relating to his past which cannot be answered without acknowledging or referring to a spent caution or any ancillary circumstances.

(2) Nothing in sub-paragraph (1) applies in relation to any proceedings for the offence which are not part of the ancillary circumstances relating to the caution.

(3) Where a question seeking information with respect to a person's previous cautions, offences, conduct or circumstances is put to him or to any other person otherwise than in proceedings before a judicial authority—

    (a) the question shall be treated as not relating to spent cautions or to any ancillary circumstances, and the answer may be framed accordingly; and

    (b) the person questioned shall not be subjected to any liability or otherwise prejudiced in law by reason of any failure to acknowledge or disclose a spent caution or any ancillary circumstances in his answer to the question.

(4) Any obligation imposed on any person by any rule of law or by the provisions of any agreement or arrangement to disclose any matters to any other person shall not extend to requiring him to disclose a spent caution or any ancillary circumstances (whether the caution is his own or another's).

(5) A caution which has become spent or any ancillary circumstances, or any failure to disclose such a caution or any such circumstances, shall not be a proper ground for dismissing or excluding a person from any office, profession, occupation or employment, or for prejudicing him in any way in any occupation or employment.

(6) This paragraph has effect subject to paragraphs 4 to 6.

4 The Secretary of State may by order—

    (a) make provision for excluding or modifying the application of either or both of paragraphs (a) or (b) of paragraph 3(2) in relation to questions put in such circumstances as may be specified in the order;

    (b) provide for exceptions from the provisions of subparagraphs (4) and (5) of paragraph 3, in such cases or classes of case, and in relation to cautions of such a description, as may be specified in the order.

5 Nothing in paragraph 3 affects—

    (a) the operation of the caution in question; or

    (b) the operation of any enactment by virtue of which, in consequence of any caution, a person is subject to any disqualification, disability, prohibition or other restriction or effect, the period of which extends beyond the rehabilitation period applicable to the caution.

6 (1) Section 7(2), (3) and (4) apply for the purposes of this Schedule as follows.

(2) Subsection (2) (apart from paragraphs (b) and (d)) applies to the determination of any issue, and the admission or requirement of any evidence, relating to a person's previous cautions or to ancillary circumstances as it applies to matters relating to a person's previous convictions and circumstances ancillary thereto.

(3) Subsection (3) applies to evidence of a person's previous cautions and ancillary circumstances as it applies to evidence of a person's convictions and the circumstances ancillary thereto; and for this purpose subsection (3) shall have effect as if—

    (a) any reference to subsection (2) or (4) of section 7 were a reference to that subsection as applied by this paragraph; and

    (b) the words "or proceedings to which section 8 below applies" were omitted.

(4) Subsection (4) applies for the purpose of excluding the application of paragraph 3(1); and for that purpose subsection (4) shall have effect as if the words "(other than proceedings to which section 8 below applies)" were omitted.

(5) References in the provisions applied by this paragraph to section 4(1) are to be read as references to paragraph 3(1)."

SCHEDULE 11   Section 51
ELECTRONIC MONITORING OF PERSONS RELEASED ON BAIL SUBJECT
TO CONDITIONS

1 The Bail Act 1976 (c. 63) has effect subject to the following amendments.
2 In section 3 (general provisions) for subsection (6ZAA) substitute—
     "(6ZAA) The requirements which may be imposed under subsection (6) include electronic
                monitoring requirements.
                The imposition of electronic monitoring requirements is subject to section 3AA
                (in the case of a child or young person), section 3AB (in the case of other persons)
                and section 3AC (in all cases).
     (6ZAB) In this section and sections 3AA to 3AC "electronic monitoring requirements"
                means requirements imposed for the purpose of securing the electronic monitoring
                of a person's compliance with any other requirement imposed on him as a
                condition of bail."
3 (1) Section 3AA (electronic monitoring of compliance with bail conditions) is amended as
          follows.
   (2) In the heading to the section, for "Electronic monitoring of compliance with bail conditions"
          substitute "Conditions for the imposition of electronic monitoring requirements: children
          and young persons".
   (3) For subsection (1) substitute—
          "(1) A court may not impose electronic monitoring requirements on a child or young
                 person unless each of the following conditions is met."
   (4) For subsection (4) substitute—
          "(4) The third condition is that the court is satisfied that the necessary provision for dealing
                 with the person concerned can be made under arrangements for the electronic
                 monitoring of persons released on bail that are currently available in each local justice
                 area which is a relevant area."'
   (5) In subsection (5), for "such a requirement" substitute "electronic monitoring
          requirements".
   (6) Subsections (6) to (10) and (12) (which are superseded by section 3AC) are omitted.
4 After section 3AA insert—

"3AB Conditions for the imposition of electronic monitoring requirements: other persons

(1) A court may not impose electronic monitoring requirements on a person who has
      attained the age of seventeen unless each of the following conditions is met.
(2) The first condition is that the court is satisfied that without the electronic monitoring
      requirements the person would not be granted bail.
(3) The second condition is that the court is satisfied that the necessary provision for dealing
      with the person concerned can be made under arrangements for the electronic monitoring
      of persons released on bail that are currently available in each local justice area which is a
      relevant area.
(4) If the person is aged seventeen, the third condition is that a youth offending team has
      informed the court that in its opinion the imposition of electronic monitoring requirements
      will be suitable in his case.

3AC Electronic monitoring: general provisions

(1) Where a court imposes electronic monitoring requirements as a condition of bail, the requirements must include provision for making a person responsible for the monitoring.

(2) A person may not be made responsible for the electronic monitoring of a person on bail unless he is of a description specified in an order made by the Secretary of State.

(3) The Secretary of State may make rules for regulating—

 (a) the electronic monitoring of persons on bail;

 (b) without prejudice to the generality of paragraph (a), the functions of persons made responsible for such monitoring.

(4) The rules may make different provision for different cases.

(5) Any power of the Secretary of State to make an order or rules under this section is exercisable by statutory instrument.

(6) A statutory instrument containing rules under this section shall be subject to annulment in pursuance of a resolution of either House of Parliament.

(7) For the purposes of section 3AA or 3AB a local justice area is a relevant area in relation to a proposed electronic monitoring requirement if the court considers that it will not be practicable to secure the electronic monitoring in question unless electronic monitoring arrangements are available in that area.

(8) Nothing in sections 3, 3AA or 3AB is to be taken to require the Secretary of State to ensure that arrangements are made for the electronic monitoring of persons released on bail."

SCHEDULE 12   Section 52

BAIL FOR SUMMARY OFFENCES AND CERTAIN OTHER OFFENCES TO BE TRIED SUMMARILY

1 The Bail Act 1976 (c. 63) is amended as follows.

2 In section 3(6D)(a) (condition to be imposed on person in relation to whom paragraph 6B(1)(a) to (c) of Part 1 of Schedule 1 to that Act apply), after "apply" insert "(including where P is a person to whom the provisions of Part 1A of Schedule 1 apply)".

3 After section 9 (offence of agreeing to indemnify sureties in criminal proceedings) insert—

"9A Bail decisions relating to persons aged under 18 who are accused of offences mentioned in Schedule 2 to the Magistrates' Courts Act 1980

(1) This section applies whenever—

 (a) a magistrates' court is considering whether to withhold or grant bail in relation to a person aged under 18 who is accused of a scheduled offence; and

 (b) the trial of that offence has not begun.

(2) The court shall, before deciding whether to withhold or grant bail, consider whether, having regard to any representations made by the prosecutor or the accused person, the value involved does not exceed the relevant sum for the purposes of section 22.

(3) The duty in subsection (2) does not apply in relation to an offence if—

 (a) a determination under subsection (4) has already been made in relation to that offence; or

 (b) the accused person is, in relation to any other offence of which he is accused which is not a scheduled offence, a person to whom Part 1 of Schedule 1 to this Act applies.

(4) If where the duty in subsection (2) applies it appears to the court clear that, for the offence in question, the amount involved does not exceed the relevant sum, the court shall make a determination to that effect.

363

(5) In this section—

    (a) "relevant sum" has the same meaning as in section 22(1) of the Magistrates' Courts Act 1980 (certain either way offences to be tried summarily if value involved is less than the relevant sum);

    (b) "scheduled offence" means an offence mentioned in Schedule 2 to that Act (offences for which the value involved is relevant to the mode of trial); and

    (c) "the value involved" is to be construed in accordance with section 22(10) to (12) of that Act."

4 Schedule 1 (persons entitled to bail: supplementary provisions) is amended as follows.

5 (1) Paragraph 1 (defendants to whom Part 1 applies) becomes sub-paragraph (1) of that paragraph.

(2) In that sub-paragraph at the beginning insert "Subject to sub-paragraph (2),".

(3) After that sub-paragraph insert—

    "(2) But those provisions do not apply by virtue of sub-paragraph (1)(a) if the offence, or each of the offences punishable with imprisonment, is—

        (a) a summary offence; or

        (b) an offence mentioned in Schedule 2 to the Magistrates' Courts Act 1980 (offences for which the value involved is relevant to the mode of trial) in relation to which—

            (i) a determination has been made under section 22(2) of that Act (certain either way offences to be tried summarily if value involved is less than the relevant sum) that it is clear that the value does not exceed the relevant sum for the purposes of that section; or

            (ii) a determination has been made under section 9A(4) of this Act to the same effect."

6 After Part 1 insert—

"PART 1A
DEFENDANTS ACCUSED OR CONVICTED OF IMPRISONABLE OFFENCES TO WHICH PART 1 DOES NOT APPLY

Defendants to whom Part 1A applies

1 The following provisions of this Part apply to the defendant if—

    (a) the offence or one of the offences of which he is accused or convicted is punishable with imprisonment, but

    (b) Part 1 does not apply to him by virtue of paragraph 1(2) of that Part.

Exceptions to right to bail

2 The defendant need not be granted bail if—

    (a) it appears to the court that, having been previously granted bail in criminal proceedings, he has failed to surrender to custody in accordance with his obligations under the grant of bail; and

    (b) the court believes, in view of that failure, that the defendant, if released on bail (whether subject to conditions or not) would fail to surrender to custody.

3 The defendant need not be granted bail if—

    (a) it appears to the court that the defendant was on bail in criminal proceedings on the date of the offence; and

    (b) the court is satisfied that there are substantial grounds for believing that the defendant, if released on bail (whether subject to conditions or not) would commit an offence while on bail.

4 The defendant need not be granted bail if the court is satisfied that there are substantial grounds for believing that the defendant, if released on bail (whether subject to conditions or not), would commit an offence while on bail by engaging in conduct that would, or would be likely to, cause—
(a) physical or mental injury to any person other than the defendant; or
(b) any person other than the defendant to fear physical or mental injury.
5 The defendant need not be granted bail if the court is satisfied that the defendant should be kept in custody for his own protection or, if he is a child or young person, for his own welfare.
6 The defendant need not be granted bail if he is in custody in pursuance of a sentence of a court or a sentence imposed by an officer under the Armed Forces Act 2006.
7 The defendant need not be granted bail if —
(a) having been released on bail in or in connection with the proceedings for the offence, he has been arrested in pursuance of section 7 of this Act; and
(b) the court is satisfied that there are substantial grounds for believing that the defendant, if released on bail (whether subject to conditions or not) would fail to surrender to custody, commit an offence while on bail or interfere with witnesses or otherwise obstruct the course of justice (whether in relation to himself or any other person).
8 The defendant need not be granted bail where the court is satisfied that it has not been practicable to obtain sufficient information for the purpose of taking the decisions required by this Part of this Schedule for want of time since the institution of the proceedings against him.

Application of paragraphs 6A to 6C of Part 1

9 Paragraphs 6A to 6C of Part 1 (exception applicable to drug users in certain areas and related provisions) apply to a defendant to whom this Part applies as they apply to a defendant to whom that Part applies."

SCHEDULE 13   Section 53
ALLOCATION OF CASES TRIABLE EITHER WAY ETC.

1 Schedule 3 to the Criminal Justice Act 2003 (c. 44) (allocation of cases triable either way, and sending cases to the Crown Court etc.) has effect subject to the following amendments.
2 In paragraph 2, in the paragraph set out in sub-paragraph (2), after "committed" insert "for sentence".
3 In paragraph 6, for subsection (2)(c) of the section set out in that paragraph substitute—
"(c) that if he is tried summarily and is convicted by the court, he may be committed for sentence to the Crown Court under section 3 or (if applicable) section 3A of the Powers of Criminal Courts (Sentencing) Act 2000 if the court is of such opinion as is mentioned in subsection (2) of the applicable section."
4 In paragraph 8, in sub-paragraph (2)(a) for "trial on indictment" substitute "summary trial".
5 (1) Paragraph 9 is amended as follows.
(2) In sub-paragraph (3) after "(1A)" insert ", (1B)".
(3) After sub-paragraph (3) insert—
"(4) In subsection (3) for "the said Act of 2000" substitute "the Powers of Criminal Courts (Sentencing) Act 2000"."
6 Paragraph 13 is omitted.
7 Paragraph 22 is omitted.
8 Before paragraph 23 insert—
"22A (1) Section 3 (committal for sentence on summary trial of offence triable either way) is amended as follows.

365

(2) In subsection (2)—

    (a) in paragraph (a) for the words from "greater punishment" to the end of the paragraph substitute "the Crown Court should, in the court's opinion, have the power to deal with the offender in any way it could deal with him if he had been convicted on indictment", and

    (b) omit paragraph (b) (and the word "or" immediately preceding it).

(3) In subsection (4), after "section" insert "17D or".

(4) In subsection (5), in paragraph (b) omit the words "paragraph (b) and"."

9 In paragraph 23, in subsection (5) of the first of the sections inserted by that paragraph (section 3A), for "a specified offence" substitute "an offender convicted of a specified offence".

10 In paragraph 24 after sub-paragraph (4) insert—

    "(4A) In subsection (2) for "committed" substitute "sent"."

SCHEDULE 14   Section 68

SPECIAL RULES RELATING TO PROVIDERS OF INFORMATION SOCIETY SERVICES

Domestic service providers: extension of liability

1 (1) This paragraph applies where a service provider is established in England and Wales or Northern Ireland (a "domestic service provider").

(2) Section 63(1) applies to a domestic service provider who—

    (a) is in possession of an extreme pornographic image in an EEA state other than the United Kingdom, and

    (b) is in possession of it there in the course of providing information society services,

as well as to persons (of any description) who are in possession of such images in England and Wales or Northern Ireland.

(3) In the case of an offence under section 63, as it applies to a domestic service provider by virtue of sub-paragraph (2)—

    (a) proceedings for the offence may be taken at any place in England and Wales or Northern Ireland, and

    (b) the offence may for all incidental purposes be treated as having been committed at any such place.

(4) Nothing in this paragraph is to be read as affecting the operation of any of paragraphs 3 to 5.

Non-UK service providers: restriction on institution of proceedings

2 (1) This paragraph applies where a service provider is established in an EEA state other than the United Kingdom (a "non-UK service provider").

(2) Proceedings for an offence under section 63 may not be instituted against a non-UK service provider in respect of anything done in the course of the provision of information society services unless the derogation condition is satisfied.

(3) The derogation condition is satisfied where the institution of proceedings—

    (a) is necessary for the purposes of the public interest objective;

    (b) relates to an information society service that prejudices that objective or presents a serious and grave risk of prejudice to that objective; and

    (c) is proportionate to that objective.

(4) "The public interest objective" means the pursuit of public policy.

Exceptions for mere conduits

3 (1) A service provider is not capable of being guilty of an offence under section 63 in respect of anything done in the course of providing so much of an information society service as consists in—
  (a) the provision of access to a communication network, or
  (b) the transmission in a communication network of information provided by a recipient of the service,
  if the condition in sub-paragraph (2) is satisfied.
  (2) The condition is that the service provider does not—
  (a) initiate the transmission,
  (b) select the recipient of the transmission, or
  (c) select or modify the information contained in the transmission.
  (3) For the purposes of sub-paragraph (1)—
  (a) the provision of access to a communication network, and
  (b) the transmission of information in a communication network,
  includes the automatic, intermediate and transient storage of the information transmitted so far as the storage is solely for the purpose of carrying out the transmission in the network.
  (4) Sub-paragraph (3) does not apply if the information is stored for longer than is reasonably necessary for the transmission.

Exception for caching

4 (1) This paragraph applies where an information society service consists in the transmission in a communication network of information provided by a recipient of the service.
  (2) The service provider is not capable of being guilty of an offence under section 63 in respect of the automatic, intermediate and temporary storage of information so provided, if—
  (a) the storage of the information is solely for the purpose of making more efficient the onward transmission of the information to other recipients of the service at their request, and
  (b) the condition in sub-paragraph (3) is satisfied.
  (3) The condition is that the service provider—
  (a) does not modify the information,
  (b) complies with any conditions attached to having access to the information, and
  (c) (where sub-paragraph (4) applies) expeditiously removes the information or disables access to it.
  (4) This sub-paragraph applies if the service provider obtains actual knowledge that—
  (a) the information at the initial source of the transmission has been removed from the network,
  (b) access to it has been disabled, or
  (c) a court or administrative authority has ordered the removal from the network of, or the disablement of access to, the information.

Exception for hosting

5 (1) A service provider is not capable of being guilty of an offence under section 63 in respect of anything done in the course of providing so much of an information society service as consists in the storage of information provided by a recipient of the service, if—
  (a) the service provider had no actual knowledge when the information was provided that it contained offending material, or
  (b) on obtaining actual knowledge that the information contained offending material, the service provider expeditiously removed the information or disabled access to it.
  (2) "Offending material" means material the possession of which constitutes an offence under section 63.

(3) Sub-paragraph (1) does not apply if the recipient of the service is acting under the authority or control of the service provider.

Interpretation

6 (1) This paragraph applies for the purposes of this Schedule.

(2) "Extreme pornographic image" has the same meaning as in section 63.

(3) "Information society services"—

    (a) has the meaning given in Article 2(a) of the E-Commerce Directive (which refers to Article 1(2) of Directive 98/34/EC of the European Parliament and of the Council of 22 June 1998 laying down a procedure for the provision of information in the field of technical standards and regulations), and

    (b) is summarised in recital 17 of the E-Commerce Directive as covering "any service normally provided for remuneration, at a distance, by means of electronic equipment for the processing (including digital compression) and storage of data, and at the individual request of a recipient of a service";

and "the E-Commerce Directive" means Directive 2000/31/EC of the European Parliament and of the Council of 8 June 2000 on certain legal aspects of information society services, in particular electronic commerce, in the Internal Market (Directive on electronic commerce).

(4) "Recipient", in relation to a service, means any person who, for professional ends or otherwise, uses an information society service, in particular for the purposes of seeking information or making it accessible.

(5) "Service provider" means a person providing an information society service.

(6) For the purpose of construing references in this Schedule to a service provider who is established in a part of the United Kingdom or in some other EEA state—

    (a) a service provider is established in a particular part of the United Kingdom, or in a particular EEA state, if the service provider—

        (i) effectively pursues an economic activity using a fixed establishment in that part of the United Kingdom, or that EEA state, for an indefinite period, and

        (ii) is a national of an EEA state or a company or firm mentioned in Article 48 of the EEC Treaty;

    (b) the presence or use in a particular place of equipment or other technical means of providing an information society service does not, of itself, constitute the establishment of a service provider;

    (c) where it cannot be determined from which of a number of establishments a given information society service is provided, that service is to be regarded as provided from the establishment at the centre of the service provider's activities relating to that service.

SCHEDULE 15   Section 73

SEXUAL OFFENCES: GROOMING AND ADOPTION

Meeting a child following sexual grooming

1 In section 15(1) of the Sexual Offences Act 2003 (c. 42) (meeting a child following sexual grooming etc) for paragraphs (a) and (b) substitute—

"(a) A has met or communicated with another person (B) on at least two occasions and subsequently—

    (i) A intentionally meets B,

    (ii) A travels with the intention of meeting B in any part of the world or arranges to meet B in any part of the world, or

    (iii) B travels with the intention of meeting A in any part of the world,

(b) A intends to do anything to or in respect of B, during or after the meeting mentioned in paragraph (a)(i) to (iii) and in any part of the world, which if done will involve the commission by A of a relevant offence,".

Adoption

2 The Sexual Offences Act 2003 (c. 42) has effect subject to the following amendments.

3 In section 27(1)(b) (family relationships) after "but for" insert "section 39 of the Adoption Act 1976 or".

4 In section 29(1)(b) (sections 25 and 26: sexual relationships which pre-date family relationships) after "if" insert "section 39 of the Adoption Act 1976 or".

5 (1) Section 64 (sex with an adult relative: penetration) is amended as follows.

   (2) In subsection (1) after "(A)" insert "(subject to subsection (3A))".

   (3) In subsection (3) after "In subsection (2)—" insert—

   "(za) "parent" includes an adoptive parent;
   (zb) "child" includes an adopted person within the meaning of Chapter 4 of Part 1 of the Adoption and Children Act 2002;".

   (4) After that subsection insert—

   "(3A) Where subsection (1) applies in a case where A is related to B as B's child by virtue of subsection (3)(zb), A does not commit an offence under this section unless A is 18 or over."

   (5) After subsection (5) insert—

   "(6) Nothing in—

   (a) section 47 of the Adoption Act 1976 (which disapplies the status provisions in section 39 of that Act for the purposes of this section in relation to adoptions before 30 December 2005), or
   (b) section 74 of the Adoption and Children Act 2002 (which disapplies the status provisions in section 67 of that Act for those purposes in relation to adoptions on or after that date),

   is to be read as preventing the application of section 39 of the Adoption Act 1976 or section 67 of the Adoption and Children Act 2002 for the purposes of subsection (3)(za) and (zb) above."

6 (1) Section 65 (sex with an adult relative: consenting to penetration) is amended as follows.

   (2) In subsection (1) after "(A)" insert "(subject to subsection (3A))".

   (3) In subsection (3) after "In subsection (2)—" insert—

   "(za) "parent" includes an adoptive parent;
   (zb) "child" includes an adopted person within the meaning of Chapter 4 of Part 1 of the Adoption and Children Act 2002;".

   (4) After that subsection insert—

   "(3A) Where subsection (1) applies in a case where A is related to B as B's child by virtue of subsection (3)(zb), A does not commit an offence under this section unless A is 18 or over."

   (5) After subsection (5) insert—

   "(6) Nothing in—

   (a) section 47 of the Adoption Act 1976 (which disapplies the status provisions in section 39 of that Act for the purposes of this section in relation to adoptions before 30 December 2005), or
   (b) section 74 of the Adoption and Children Act 2002 (which disapplies the status provisions in section 67 of that Act for those purposes in relation to adoptions on or after that date),

   is to be read as preventing the application of section 39 of the Adoption Act 1976 or section 67 of the Adoption and Children Act 2002 for the purposes of subsection (3)(za) and (zb) above."

7 In section 47(1) of the Adoption Act 1976 (c. 36) (disapplication of section 39 (status conferred by adoption) for the purposes of miscellaneous enactments) for "sections 10 and 11 (incest) of the Sexual Offences Act 1956" substitute "or sections 64 and 65 of the Sexual Offences Act 2003 (sex with an adult relative)".

SCHEDULE 16   Section 74
HATRED ON THE GROUNDS OF SEXUAL ORIENTATION

1 Part 3A of the Public Order Act 1986 (c. 64) (hatred against persons on religious grounds) has effect subject to the following amendments.
2 In the heading for Part 3A at the end insert "OR GROUNDS OF SEXUAL ORIENTATION".
3 In the italic cross-heading before section 29A at the end insert "*and "hatred on the grounds of sexual orientation"*".
4 After that section insert—

"29AB Meaning of "hatred on the grounds of sexual orientation""

In this Part "hatred on the grounds of sexual orientation" means hatred against a group of persons defined by reference to sexual orientation (whether towards persons of the same sex, the opposite sex or both)."

5 In the italic cross-heading before section 29B at the end insert "*or hatred on the grounds of sexual orientation*".

6 (1) Section 29B (use of words or behaviour or display of written material) is amended as follows.
  (2) In subsection (1), after "religious hatred" insert "or hatred on the grounds of sexual orientation".
  (3) Omit subsection (3).
7 In section 29C(1) (publishing or distributing written material), after "religious hatred" insert "or hatred on the grounds of sexual orientation".
8 In section 29D(1) (public performance of play), after "religious hatred" insert "or hatred on the grounds of sexual orientation".
9 In section 29E(1) (distributing, showing or playing a recording), after "religious hatred" insert "or hatred on the grounds of sexual orientation".
10 In section 29F(1) (broadcasting or including programme in programme service), after "religious hatred" insert "or hatred on the grounds of sexual orientation".
11 In section 29G(1) (possession of inflammatory material), for "religious hatred to be stirred up thereby" substitute "thereby to stir up religious hatred or hatred on the grounds of sexual orientation".
12 (1) Section 29H (powers of entry and search) is amended as follows.
  (2) In subsection (1), omit "in England and Wales".
  (3) Omit subsection (2).
13 (1) Section 29I (power to order forfeiture) is amended as follows.
  (2) In subsection (2)—
    (a) in paragraph (a), omit "in the case of an order made in proceedings in England and Wales,"; and
    (b) omit paragraph (b).
  (3) Omit subsection (4).

14 After section 29J insert—

"**29JA Protection of freedom of expression (sexual orientation)**

In this Part, for the avoidance of doubt, the discussion or criticism of sexual conduct or practices or the urging of persons to refrain from or modify such conduct or practices shall not be taken of itself to be threatening or intended to stir up hatred."

15 In section 29K(1) (savings for reports of parliamentary or judicial proceedings), for "or in the Scottish Parliament" substitute ", in the Scottish Parliament or in the National Assembly for Wales".

16 (1) Section 29L (procedure and punishment) is amended as follows.

(2) In subsections (1) and (2), omit "in England and Wales".

(3) In subsection (3), in paragraph (b), for "six months" substitute "12 months".

(4) After that subsection insert—

"(4) In subsection (3)(b) the reference to 12 months shall be read as a reference to 6 months in relation to an offence committed before the commencement of section 154(1) of the Criminal Justice Act 2003."

17 In section 29N (interpretation), after the definition of "dwelling" insert—

""hatred on the grounds of sexual orientation" has the meaning given by section 29AB;".

SCHEDULE 17   Section 75

OFFENCES RELATING TO NUCLEAR MATERIAL AND NUCLEAR FACILITIES

PART 1

AMENDMENTS OF NUCLEAR MATERIAL (OFFENCES) ACT 1983

1 The Nuclear Material (Offences) Act 1983 (c. 18) has effect subject to the following amendments.

2 (1) Section 1 (extended scope of certain offences) is amended as follows.

(2) In subsection (1)(b) (offences under certain enactments) for "section 78 of the Criminal Justice (Scotland) Act 1980" substitute "section 52 of the Criminal Law (Consolidation) (Scotland) Act 1995".

(3) After subsection (1) insert—

"(1A) If—

(a) a person, whatever his nationality, does outside the United Kingdom an act directed at a nuclear facility, or which interferes with the operation of such a facility,

(b) the act causes death, injury or damage resulting from the emission of ionising radiation or the release of radioactive material, and

(c) had he done that act in any part of the United Kingdom, it would have made him guilty of an offence mentioned in subsection (1)(a) or (b) above,

the person shall in any part of the United Kingdom be guilty of such of the offences mentioned in subsection (1)(a) and (b) as are offences of which the act would have made him guilty had he done it in that part of the United Kingdom."

(4) Omit subsection (2) (definition of "act").

3 After section 1 insert—

"**1A Increase in penalties for offences committed in relation to nuclear material etc.**

(1) If—

(a) a person is guilty of an offence to which subsection (2), (3) or (4) applies, and

    (b) the penalty provided by this subsection would not otherwise apply,

the person shall be liable, on conviction on indictment, to imprisonment for life.

(2) This subsection applies to an offence mentioned in section 1(1)(a) or (b) where the act making the person guilty of the offence was done in England and Wales or Northern Ireland and either—

    (a) the act was done in relation to or by means of nuclear material, or

    (b) the act—

        (i) was directed at a nuclear facility, or interfered with the operation of such a facility, and

        (ii) caused death, injury or damage resulting from the emission of ionising radiation or the release of radioactive material.

(3) This subsection applies to an offence mentioned in section 1(1)(c) or (d) where the act making the person guilty of the offence—

    (a) was done in England and Wales or Northern Ireland, and

    (b) was done in relation to or by means of nuclear material.

(4) This subsection applies to an offence mentioned in section 1(1)(a) to (d) where the offence is an offence in England and Wales or Northern Ireland by virtue of section 1(1) or (1A).

1B Offences relating to damage to environment

(1) If a person, whatever his nationality, in the United Kingdom or elsewhere contravenes subsection (2) or (3) he is guilty of an offence.

(2) A person contravenes this subsection if without lawful authority—

    (a) he receives, holds or deals with nuclear material, and

    (b) he does so either—

        (i) intending to cause, or for the purpose of enabling another to cause, damage to the environment by means of that material, or

        (ii) being reckless as to whether, as a result of his so receiving, holding or dealing with that material, damage would be caused to the environment by means of that material.

(3) A person contravenes this subsection if without lawful authority—

    (a) he does an act directed at a nuclear facility, or which interferes with the operation of such a facility, and

    (b) he does so either—

        (i) intending to cause, or for the purpose of enabling another to cause, damage to the environment by means of the emission of ionising radiation or the release of radioactive material, or

        (ii) being reckless as to whether, as a result of his act, damage would be caused to the environment by means of such an emission or release.

(4) A person guilty of an offence under this section shall be liable, on conviction on indictment, to imprisonment for life.

1C Offences of importing or exporting etc. nuclear material: extended jurisdiction

(1) If a person, whatever his nationality, outside the United Kingdom contravenes subsection (2) below he shall be guilty of an offence.

(2) A person contravenes this subsection if he is knowingly concerned in—

    (a) the unlawful export or shipment as stores of nuclear material from one country to another, or

    (b) the unlawful import of nuclear material into one country from another.

(3) For the purposes of subsection (2)—

    (a) the export or shipment as stores of nuclear material from a country, or

    (b) the import of nuclear material into a country,

is unlawful if it is contrary to any prohibition or restriction on the export, shipment as stores or import (as the case may be) of nuclear material having effect under or by virtue of the law of that country.

(4) A statement in a certificate issued by or on behalf of the government of a country outside the United Kingdom to the effect that a particular export, shipment as stores or import of nuclear material is contrary to such a prohibition or restriction having effect under or by virtue of the law of that country, shall be evidence (in Scotland, sufficient evidence) that the export, shipment or import was unlawful for the purposes of subsection (2).

(5) In any proceedings a document purporting to be a certificate of the kind mentioned in subsection (4) above shall be taken to be such a certificate unless the contrary is proved.

(6) A person guilty of an offence under this section shall be liable, on conviction on indictment, to imprisonment for a term not exceeding 14 years.

(7) In this section "country" includes territory.

1D Offences under section 1C: investigations and proceedings etc.

(1) Where the Commissioners for Her Majesty's Revenue and Customs investigate, or propose to investigate, any matter with a view to determining—
  (a) whether there are grounds for believing that an offence under section 1C above has been committed, or
  (b) whether a person should be prosecuted for such an offence,
  the matter is to be treated as an assigned matter within the meaning of CEMA 1979 (see section 1(1) of that Act).

(2) Section 138 of CEMA 1979 (provisions as to arrest of persons) applies to a person who has committed, or whom there are reasonable grounds to suspect of having committed, an offence under section 1C above as it applies to a person who has committed, or whom there are reasonable grounds to suspect of having committed, an offence for which he is liable to be arrested under the customs and excise Acts.

(3) Sections 145 to 148 and 150 to 155 of CEMA 1979 (provisions as to legal proceedings) apply in relation to an offence under section 1C above, and to the penalty and proceedings for the offence, as they apply in relation to offences, penalties and proceedings under the customs and excise Acts.

(4) In this section—
  "CEMA 1979" means the Customs and Excise Management Act 1979;
  "the customs and excise Acts", "shipment" and "stores" have the same meanings as in CEMA 1979 (see section 1(1) of that Act)."

4 For section 2 substitute—
"2 Offences involving preparatory acts and threats

(1) If a person, whatever his nationality, in the United Kingdom or elsewhere contravenes subsection (2), (3), (4) or (7) he shall be guilty of an offence.

(2) A person contravenes this subsection if without lawful authority—
  (a) he receives, holds or deals with nuclear material, and
  (b) he does so either—
    (i) intending to cause, or for the purpose of enabling another to cause, relevant injury or damage by means of that material, or
    (ii) being reckless as to whether, as a result of his so receiving, holding or dealing with that material, relevant injury or damage would be caused by means of that material.

(3) A person contravenes this subsection if without lawful authority—
  (a) he does an act directed at a nuclear facility, or which interferes with the operation of such a facility, and

(b) he does so either—

  (i) intending to cause, or for the purpose of enabling another to cause, relevant injury or damage by means of the emission of ionising radiation or the release of radioactive material, or

  (ii) being reckless as to whether, as a result of his act, relevant injury or damage would be caused by means of such an emission or release.

(4) A person contravenes this subsection if he—

  (a) makes a threat of a kind falling within subsection (5), and

  (b) intends that the person to whom the threat is made shall fear that it will be carried out.

(5) A threat falls within this subsection if it is a threat that the person making it or any other person will cause any of the consequences set out in subsection (6) either—

  (a) by means of nuclear material, or

  (b) by means of the emission of ionising radiation or the release of radioactive material resulting from an act which is directed at a nuclear facility, or which interferes with the operation of such a facility.

(6) The consequences mentioned in subsection (5) are—

  (a) relevant injury or damage, or

  (b) damage to the environment.

(7) A person contravenes this subsection if, in order to compel a State, international organisation or person to do, or abstain from doing, any act, he threatens that he or any other person will obtain nuclear material by an act which, whether by virtue of section 1(1) above or otherwise, is an offence mentioned in section 1(1)(c) above.

(8) A person guilty of an offence under this section shall be liable, on conviction on indictment, to imprisonment for life.

(9) In this section references to relevant injury or damage are references to death or to injury or damage of a type which constitutes an element of any offence mentioned in section 1(1)(a) or (b) above.

2A Inchoate and secondary offences: extended jurisdiction

(1) If a person, whatever his nationality—

  (a) does an act outside the United Kingdom, and

  (b) his act, if done in any part of the United Kingdom, would constitute an offence falling within subsection (2),

  he shall be guilty in that part of the United Kingdom of the offence.

(2) The offences are—

  (a) attempting to commit a nuclear offence;

  (b) conspiring to commit a nuclear offence;

  (c) inciting the commission of a nuclear offence;

  (d) aiding, abetting, counselling or procuring the commission of a nuclear offence.

(3) In subsection (2) a "nuclear offence" means any of the following (wherever committed)—

  (a) an offence mentioned in section 1(1)(a) to (d) above (other than a blackmail offence), the commission of which is (or would have been) in relation to or by means of nuclear material;

  (b) an offence mentioned in section 1(1)(a) or (b) above, the commission of which involves (or would have involved) an act—

    (i) directed at a nuclear facility, or which interferes with the operation of such a facility, and

    (ii) which causes death, injury or damage resulting from the emission of ionising radiation or the release of radioactive material;

  (c) an offence under section 1B, 1C or 2(1) and (2) or (3) above;

    (d) an offence under section 50(2) or (3), 68(2) or 170(1) or (2) of the Customs and Excise Management Act 1979 the commission of which is (or would have been) in connection with a prohibition or restriction relating to the exportation, shipment as stores or importation of nuclear material;

    (e) for the purposes of subsection (2)(b) to (d)—

        (i) a blackmail offence, the commission of which is in relation to or by means of nuclear material;

        (ii) an offence under section 2(1) and (4) or (7) above;

        (iii) an offence of attempting to commit an offence mentioned in paragraphs (a) to (d).

(4) In subsection (3) "a blackmail offence" means—

    (a) an offence under section 21 of the Theft Act 1968,

    (b) an offence under section 20 of the Theft Act (Northern Ireland) 1969, or

    (c) an offence of extortion.

(5) In subsection (2)(c) the reference to incitement is—

    (a) a reference to incitement under the law of Scotland, or

    (b) in relation to any time before the coming into force of Part 2 of the Serious Crime Act 2007 (encouraging or assisting crime) in relation to England and Wales or Northern Ireland, a reference to incitement under the common law of England and Wales or (as the case may be) of Northern Ireland."

5 After section 3 (supplemental) insert—

"3A Application to activities of armed forces

(1) Nothing in this Act applies in relation to acts done by the armed forces of a country or territory—

    (a) in the course of an armed conflict, or

    (b) in the discharge of their functions.

(2) If in any proceedings a question arises whether an act done by the armed forces of a country or territory was an act falling within subsection (1), a certificate issued by or under the authority of the Secretary of State and stating that it was, or was not, such an act shall be conclusive of that question.

(3) In any proceedings a document purporting to be such a certificate as is mentioned in subsection (2) shall be taken to be such a certificate unless the contrary is proved."

6 (1) Section 6 (material to which the Act applies) is amended as follows.

(2) Before subsection (1) insert—

    "(A1) This section applies for the purposes of this Act."

(3) In subsection (1), omit "in this Act".

(4) After subsection (1) insert—

    "(1A) "A nuclear facility" means a facility (including associated buildings and equipment) used for peaceful purposes in which nuclear material is produced, processed, used, handled, stored or disposed of.

    (1B) For the purposes of subsections (1) and (1A)—

        (a) nuclear material is not used for peaceful purposes if it is used or retained for military purposes, and

        (b) a facility is not used for peaceful purposes if it contains any nuclear material which is used or retained for military purposes."

(5) In subsection (2) (question whether or not nuclear material used for peaceful purposes to be determined conclusively by certificate of Secretary of State to that effect) after "material" insert "or facility".

(6) For subsection (5) substitute—

    "(5) "Act" includes omission.

(6) "The Convention" means the Convention on the Physical Protection of Nuclear Material and Nuclear Facilities (formerly the Convention on the Physical Protection of Nuclear Material and renamed by virtue of the Amendment adopted at Vienna on 8th July 2005).

(7) "The environment" includes land, air and water and living organisms supported by any of those media.

(8) "Radioactive material" means nuclear material or any other radioactive substance which—

    (a) contains nuclides that undergo spontaneous disintegration in a process accompanied by the emission of one or more types of ionising radiation, such as alpha radiation, beta radiation, neutron particles or gamma rays, and

    (b) is capable, owing to its radiological or fissile properties, of—

        (i) causing bodily injury to a person,

        (ii) causing damage or destruction to property,

        (iii) endangering a person's life, or

        (iv) causing damage to the environment."

(7) For the sidenote, substitute "Interpretation".

7 In section 7 (application to the Channel Islands, Isle of Man etc.) in subsection (2), for "any colony" substitute "any British overseas territory".

PART 2

AMENDMENTS OF CUSTOMS AND EXCISE MANAGEMENT ACT 1979

8 (1) The Customs and Excise Management Act 1979 (c. 2) is amended as follows.

(2) In section 1 (interpretation) in subsection (1) insert at the appropriate place—

    ""nuclear material" has the same meaning as in the Nuclear Material (Offences) Act 1983 (see section 6 of that Act);".

(3) In section 50 (penalty for improper importation of goods)—

    (a) in subsection (4) (penalty for offence) for "or (5B)" substitute ", (5B) or (5C)";

    (b) after subsection (5B) insert—

        "(5C) In the case of an offence under subsection (2) or (3) above in connection with a prohibition or restriction relating to the importation of nuclear material, subsection (4)(b) above shall have effect as if for the words "7 years" there were substituted the words "14 years"."

(4) In section 68 (offences in relation to exportation of prohibited or restricted goods)—

    (a) in subsection (3) (penalty for offence) for "or (4A)" substitute ", (4A) or (4B)";

    (b) after subsection (4A) insert—

        "(4B) In the case of an offence under subsection (2) above in connection with a prohibition or restriction relating to the exportation or shipment as stores of nuclear material, subsection (3)(b) above shall have effect as if for the words "7 years" there were substituted the words "14 years"."

    (5) In section 170 (penalty for fraudulent evasion of duty, etc.)—

    (a) in subsection (3) (penalty for offence) for "or (4B)" substitute ", (4B) or (4C)";

    (b) after subsection (4B) insert—

        "(4C) In the case of an offence under subsection (1) or (2) above in connection with a prohibition or restriction relating to the importation, exportation or shipment as stores of nuclear material, subsection (3)(b) above shall have effect as if for the words "7 years" there were substituted the words "14 years"."

9 (1) Her Majesty may by Order in Council provide for any provisions of section 1, 50, 68 or 170 of the Customs and Excise Management Act 1979 (c. 2) as amended by paragraph 8

to extend, with or without modifications, to any of the Channel Islands or any British overseas territory.

(2) Section 147(2) applies in relation to an Order in Council under subparagraph (1) as it applies in relation to an order made by the Secretary of State.

SCHEDULE 18   Section 91(1)

PENALTIES SUITABLE FOR ENFORCEMENT IN ENGLAND AND WALES OR NORTHERN IRELAND

Person residing in England and Wales

1 The financial penalty is suitable for enforcement in England and Wales if the certificate states that the person required to pay the penalty is normally resident in England and Wales.

Person residing in Northern Ireland

2 The financial penalty is suitable for enforcement in Northern Ireland if the certificate states that the person required to pay the penalty is normally resident in Northern Ireland.

Person having property etc. in England and Wales

3 The financial penalty is suitable for enforcement in England and Wales if—
   (a) the certificate states that the person required to pay the penalty has property or a source of income in England and Wales, and
   (b) the certificate does not state—
      (i) that the person has property or a source of income in Northern Ireland or Scotland, or
      (ii) that the person is normally resident in the United Kingdom.

Person having property etc. in Northern Ireland

4 The financial penalty is suitable for enforcement in Northern Ireland if—
   (a) the certificate states that the person required to pay the penalty has property or a source of income in Northern Ireland, and
   (b) the certificate does not state—
      (i) that the person has property or a source of income in England and Wales or Scotland, or
      (ii) that the person is normally resident in the United Kingdom.

Person having property etc. in England and Wales and Northern Ireland

5 (1) This paragraph applies if—
   (a) the certificate states that the person required to pay the financial penalty has property or a source of income in England and Wales,
   (b) the certificate also states that the person has property or a source of income in Northern Ireland, and
   (c) the certificate does not state—
      (i) that the person has property or a source of income in Scotland, or
      (ii) that the person is normally resident in the United Kingdom.

(2) The financial penalty is suitable for enforcement in England and Wales unless it is suitable for enforcement in Northern Ireland by virtue of subparagraph (3).

(3) The financial penalty is suitable for enforcement in Northern Ireland if the Lord Chancellor thinks that it is more appropriate for the penalty to be enforced in Northern Ireland than in England and Wales.

Person having property etc. in England and Wales and Scotland

6 (1) This paragraph applies if—

    (a) the certificate states that the person required to pay the financial penalty has property or a source of income in England and Wales,

    (b) the certificate also states that the person has property or a source of income in Scotland, and

    (c) the certificate does not state—

        (i) that the person has property or a source of income in Northern Ireland, or

        (ii) that the person is normally resident in the United Kingdom.

  (2) The financial penalty is suitable for enforcement in England and Wales unless sub-paragraph (3) applies.

  (3) This sub-paragraph applies if—

    (a) the Lord Chancellor was given the certificate by the competent authority or central authority of another member State (and not by the central authority for Scotland), and

    (b) the Lord Chancellor thinks that it is more appropriate for the financial penalty to be enforced in Scotland than in England and Wales.

Person having property etc. in Northern Ireland and Scotland

7 (1) This paragraph applies if—

    (a) the certificate states that the person required to pay the financial penalty has property or a source of income in Northern Ireland,

    (b) the certificate also states that the person has property or a source of income in Scotland, and

    (c) the certificate does not state —

        (i) that the person has property or a source of income in England and Wales, or

        (ii) that the person is normally resident in the United Kingdom.

  (2) The financial penalty is suitable for enforcement in Northern Ireland unless sub-paragraph (3) applies.

  (3) This sub-paragraph applies if—

    (a) the Lord Chancellor was given the certificate by the competent authority or central authority of another member State (and not by the central authority for Scotland), and

    (b) the Lord Chancellor thinks that it is more appropriate for the financial penalty to be enforced in Scotland than in Northern Ireland.

Person having property etc. in England and Wales, Scotland and Northern Ireland

8 (1) This paragraph applies if—

    (a) the certificate states that the person required to pay the financial penalty has property or a source of income in Northern Ireland,

    (b) the certificate also states that the person has property or a source of income in England and Wales and in Scotland, and

    (c) the certificate does not state that the person is normally resident in the United Kingdom.

  (2) The financial penalty is suitable for enforcement in England and Wales unless—

    (a) the penalty is suitable for enforcement in Northern Ireland by virtue of sub-paragraph (3) or (4), or

    (b) sub-paragraph (5) applies.

  (3) The financial penalty is suitable for enforcement in Northern Ireland if—

    (a) the Lord Chancellor was given the certificate by the competent authority or central authority of another member State (and not by the central authority for Scotland), and

    (b) the Lord Chancellor thinks that it is more appropriate for the financial penalty to be enforced in Northern Ireland than in England and Wales or Scotland.

(4) The financial penalty is suitable for enforcement in Northern Ireland if—

    (a) the Lord Chancellor was given the certificate by the central authority for Scotland, and

    (b) the Lord Chancellor thinks that it is more appropriate for the financial penalty to be enforced in Northern Ireland than in England and Wales.

(5) This sub-paragraph applies if—

    (a) the Lord Chancellor was given the certificate by the competent authority or central authority of another member State (and not by the central authority for Scotland), and

    (b) the Lord Chancellor thinks that it is more appropriate for the financial penalty to be enforced in Scotland than in England and Wales or Northern Ireland.

Interpretation

9 Where the person required to pay the financial penalty is a body corporate, this Schedule applies as if—

    (a) the reference in paragraph 1 to the person being normally resident in England and Wales were a reference to the person having its registered office in England and Wales,

    (b) the reference in paragraph 2 to the person being normally resident in Northern Ireland were a reference to the person having its registered office in Northern Ireland, and

    (c) any reference to the person being normally resident in the United Kingdom were a reference to the person having its registered office in the United Kingdom.

SCHEDULE 19   Section 91(2)

GROUNDS FOR REFUSAL TO ENFORCE FINANCIAL PENALTIES

PART 1

THE GROUNDS FOR REFUSAL

1 A penalty (of any kind) has been imposed on the liable person in respect of the conduct to which the certificate relates under the law of any part of the United Kingdom (whether or not the penalty has been enforced).

2 A penalty (of any kind) has been imposed on the liable person in respect of that conduct under the law of any member State, other than the United Kingdom and the issuing State, and that penalty has been enforced.

3 (1) The decision was made in respect of conduct—

    (a) that is not specified in Part 2 of this Schedule, and

    (b) would not constitute an offence under the law of the relevant part of the United Kingdom if it occurred in that part.

(2) In sub-paragraph (1), "the relevant part of the United Kingdom" means—

    (a) in the application of this Schedule to England and Wales, England and Wales, and

    (b) in the application of this Schedule to Northern Ireland, Northern Ireland.

4 (1) The decision was made in respect of conduct—

    (a) that occurred outside the territory of the issuing State, and

    (b) would not constitute an offence under the law of the relevant part of the United Kingdom if it occurred outside that part.

(2) In sub-paragraph (1), "the relevant part of the United Kingdom" has the same meaning as in paragraph 3(2).

5 The decision was made in respect of conduct by a person who was under the age of 10 when the conduct took place.

6 The certificate does not confirm that—

(a) if the proceedings in which the decision was made were conducted in writing, the liable person was informed of the right to contest the proceedings and of the time limits that applied to the exercise of that right;

(b) if those proceedings provided for a hearing to take place and the liable person did not attend, the liable person was informed of the proceedings or indicated an intention not to contest them.

7 (1) The financial penalty is for an amount less than 70 euros.

(2) For the purposes of sub-paragraph (1), if the amount of a financial penalty is specified in a currency other than the euro, that amount must be converted to euros by reference to the London closing exchange rate on the date the decision was made.

(3) The Lord Chancellor may by order substitute a different amount for the amount for the time being specified in sub-paragraph (1).

PART 2
EUROPEAN FRAMEWORK LIST (FINANCIAL PENALTIES)

8 Participation in a criminal organisation.

9 Terrorism.

10 Trafficking in human beings.

11 Sexual exploitation of children and child pornography.

12 Illicit trafficking in narcotic drugs and psychotropic substances.

13 Illicit trafficking in weapons, munitions and explosives.

14 Corruption.

15 Fraud, including that affecting the financial interests of the European Communities within the meaning of the Convention of 26 July 1995 on the protection of the European Communities' financial interests.

16 Laundering of the proceeds of crime.

17 Counterfeiting currency, including of the euro.

18 Computer-related crime.

19 Environmental crime, including illicit trafficking in endangered animal species and in endangered plant species and varieties.

20 Facilitation of unauthorised entry and residence.

21 Murder, grievous bodily injury.

22 Illicit trade in human organs and tissue.

23 Kidnapping, illegal restraint and hostage-taking.

24 Racism and xenophobia.

25 Organised or armed robbery.

26 Illicit trafficking in cultural goods, including antiques and works of art.

27 Swindling.

28 Racketeering and extortion.

29 Counterfeiting and piracy of products.

30 Forgery of administrative documents and trafficking therein.

31 Forgery of means of payment.

32 Illicit trafficking in hormonal substances and other growth promoters.

33 Illicit trafficking in nuclear or radioactive materials.

34 Trafficking in stolen vehicles.

35 Rape.

36 Arson.

37 Crimes within the jurisdiction of the International Criminal Court.

38 Unlawful seizure of aircraft or ships.

39 Sabotage.

40 Conduct which infringes road traffic regulations, including breaches of regulations pertaining to driving hours and rest periods and regulations on hazardous goods.

41 Smuggling of goods.

42 Infringement of intellectual property rights.

43 Threats and acts of violence against persons, including violence during sport events.

44 Criminal damage.

45 Theft.

46 Offences created by the issuing State and serving the purpose of implementing obligations arising from instruments adopted under the treaty establishing the European Community or under Title VI of the Treaty on European Union.

PART 3

INTERPRETATION

47 (1) In this Schedule—

    (a) "conduct" includes any act or omission;

    (b) "liable person" means the person required to pay the financial penalty to which the certificate relates.

  (2) If the decision was made in respect of conduct by a person other than the liable person, the references in paragraph 6 to the liable person are to be read as references to that other person.

SCHEDULE 20   Section 118

CLOSURE ORDERS: PREMISES ASSOCIATED WITH PERSISTENT DISORDER OR NUISANCE

After Part 1 of the Anti-social Behaviour Act 2003 (c. 38) (premises where drugs used unlawfully) insert the following Part.

"PART 1A

PREMISES ASSOCIATED WITH PERSISTENT DISORDER OR NUISANCE

11A Part 1A closure notice

(1) This section applies to premises if a police officer not below the rank of superintendent ("the authorising officer") or the local authority has reasonable grounds for believing—

    (a) that at any time during the relevant period a person has engaged in anti-social behaviour on the premises, and

    (b) that the use of the premises is associated with significant and persistent disorder or persistent serious nuisance to members of the public.

(2) The authorising officer may authorise the issue of a Part 1A closure notice in respect of the premises if the officer is satisfied—

    (a) that the local authority has been consulted; and

    (b) that reasonable steps have been taken to establish the identity of any person who lives on the premises or who has control of or responsibility for, or an interest in, the premises.

(3) The local authority may authorise the issue of a Part 1A closure notice in respect of the premises if it is satisfied—

(a) that the appropriate chief officer has been consulted; and

(b) that reasonable steps have been taken to establish the identity of any person who lives on the premises or who has control of or responsibility for, or an interest in, the premises.

(4) An authorisation under subsection (2) or (3) may be given orally or in writing, but if it is given orally the authorising officer or local authority (as the case may be) must confirm it in writing as soon as it is practicable.

(5) A Part 1A closure notice must—

(a) give notice that an application will be made under section 11B for the closure of the premises;

(b) state that access to the premises by any person other than a person who habitually resides in the premises or the owner of the premises is prohibited;

(c) specify the date and time when, and the place at which, the application will be heard;

(d) explain the effects of an order made in pursuance of section 11B;

(e) state that failure to comply with the notice amounts to an offence; and

(f) give information about relevant advice providers.

(6) A Part 1A closure notice must be served by—

(a) a constable if its issue was authorised by the authorising officer, or

(b) an employee of the local authority if its issue was authorised by the authority.

(7) Service is effected by—

(a) fixing a copy of the notice to at least one prominent place on the premises,

(b) fixing a copy of the notice to each normal means of access to the premises,

(c) fixing a copy of the notice to any outbuildings which appear to the server of the notice to be used with or as part of the premises,

(d) giving a copy of the notice to at least one person who appears to the server of the notice to have control of or responsibility for the premises, and

(e) giving a copy of the notice to the persons identified in pursuance of subsection (2)(b) or (3)(b) (as the case may be) and to any other person appearing to the server of the notice to be a person of a description mentioned in that provision.

(8) The Part 1A closure notice must also be served on any person who occupies any other part of the building or other structure in which the premises are situated if the server of the notice reasonably believes, at the time of serving the notice under subsection (7), that the person's access to the other part of the building or structure will be impeded if a Part 1A closure order is made under section 11B.

(9) A person acting under subsection (7) may enter any premises, using reasonable force if necessary, for the purposes of complying with subsection (7)(a).

(10) The Secretary of State may by regulations specify premises or descriptions of premises to which this section does not apply.

(11) In this section—

"information about relevant advice providers" means information about the names of, and means of contacting, persons and organisations in the area that provide advice about housing and legal matters;

"the relevant period" means the period of 3 months ending with the day on which the authorising officer or the local authority (as the case may be) considers whether to authorise the issue of a Part 1A closure notice in respect of the premises.

11B Part 1A closure order

(1) If a Part 1A closure notice has been issued under section 11A an application must be made under this section to a magistrates' court for the making of a Part 1A closure order.

(2) An application under subsection (1) must be made by—
(a) a constable if the issue of the Part 1A closure notice was authorised by the authorising officer, or
(b) the local authority if the issue of the Part 1A closure notice was authorised by the authority.

(3) The application must be heard by the magistrates' court not later than 48 hours after the notice was served in pursuance of section 11A(7)(a).

(4) The magistrates' court may make a Part 1A closure order if and only if it is satisfied that each of the following paragraphs applies—
(a) a person has engaged in anti-social behaviour on the premises in respect of which the Part 1A closure notice was issued;
(b) the use of the premises is associated with significant and persistent disorder or persistent serious nuisance to members of the public;
(c) the making of the order is necessary to prevent the occurrence of such disorder or nuisance for the period specified in the order.

(5) A Part 1A closure order is an order that the premises in respect of which the order is made are closed to all persons for such period (not exceeding 3 months) as is specified in the order.

(6) But the order may include such provision as the court thinks appropriate relating to access to any part of the building or structure of which the premises form part.

(7) The magistrates' court may adjourn the hearing on the application for a period of not more than 14 days to enable—
(a) the occupier of the premises,
(b) the person who has control of or responsibility for the premises, or
(c) any other person with an interest in the premises,
to show why a Part 1A closure order should not be made.

(8) If the magistrates' court adjourns the hearing under subsection (7) it may order that the Part 1A closure notice continues in effect until the end of the period of the adjournment.

(9) A Part 1A closure order may be made in respect of the whole or any part of the premises in respect of which the Part 1A closure notice was issued.

11C Part 1A closure order: enforcement

(1) This section applies if a magistrates' court makes an order under section 11B.

(2) A relevant person may—
(a) enter the premises in respect of which the order is made;
(b) do anything reasonably necessary to secure the premises against entry by any person.

(3) A person acting under subsection (2) may use reasonable force.

(4) But a relevant person seeking to enter the premises for the purposes of subsection (2) must, if required to do so by or on behalf of the owner, occupier or other person in charge of the premises, produce evidence of his identity and authority before entering the premises.

(5) A relevant person may also enter the premises at any time while the order has effect for the purpose of carrying out essential maintenance of or repairs to the premises.

(6) In this section "a relevant person"—
(a) in relation to premises in respect of which a police Part 1A closure order has effect, means a constable or a person authorised by the appropriate chief officer;
(b) in relation to premises in respect of which a local authority Part 1A closure order has effect, means a person authorised by the local authority.

11D Closure of premises associated with persistent disorder or nuisance: offences

(1) A person who remains on or enters premises in contravention of a Part 1A closure notice commits an offence.

(2) A person who—
   (a) obstructs a person acting under section 11A(7) or 11C(2),
   (b) remains on closed premises, or
   (c) enters closed premises,
   commits an offence.

(3) A person guilty of an offence under this section is liable on summary conviction—
   (a) to imprisonment for a period not exceeding 51 weeks, or
   (b) to a fine not exceeding level 5 on the standard scale,
   or to both.

(4) A person who has a reasonable excuse for entering or being on the premises does not commit an offence under subsection (1) or (2)(b) or (c) (as the case may be).

(5) In relation to an offence committed before the commencement of section 281(5) of the Criminal Justice Act 2003, the reference in subsection (3)(a) to 51 weeks is to be read as a reference to 6 months.

11E Part 1A closure order: extension and discharge

(1) At any time before the end of the period for which a Part 1A closure order is made or extended, a complaint may be made by—
   (a) a constable if the order is a police Part 1A closure order, or
   (b) the local authority if the order is a local authority Part 1A closure order,
   to a justice of the peace for an extension or further extension of the period for which the order has effect.

(2) A complaint may not be made under subsection (1) in relation to a police Part 1A closure order unless the complaint is authorised by a police officer not below the rank of superintendent—
   (a) who has reasonable grounds for believing that it is necessary to extend the period for which the order has effect for the purpose of preventing the occurrence of significant and persistent disorder or persistent serious nuisance to members of the public, and
   (b) who is satisfied that the local authority has been consulted about the intention to make the complaint.

(3) A complaint may not be made under subsection (1) in relation to a local authority Part 1A closure order unless the local authority—
   (a) has reasonable grounds for believing that it is necessary to extend the period for which the order has effect for the purpose of preventing the occurrence of significant and persistent disorder or persistent serious nuisance to members of the public, and
   (b) is satisfied that the appropriate chief officer has been consulted about the intention to make the complaint.

(4) If a complaint is made to a justice of the peace under subsection (1), the justice may issue a summons directed to—
   (a) any person on whom the Part 1A closure notice relating to the closed premises was served under subsection (7)(d) or (e) or (8) of section 11A, or
   (b) any other person who appears to the justice to have an interest in the closed premises but on whom the Part 1A closure notice was not served,
   requiring such person to appear before the magistrates' court to answer to the complaint.

(5) If the court is satisfied that the order is necessary to prevent the occurrence of significant and persistent disorder or persistent serious nuisance to members of the public for a further period, it may make an order extending the period for which the Part 1A closure order has effect by a period not exceeding 3 months.

(6) But a Part 1A closure order must not have effect for more than 6 months.

(7) Any of the following persons may make a complaint to a justice of the peace for an order that a Part 1A closure order is discharged—

   (a) a constable if the Part 1A closure order is a police Part 1A closure order;

   (b) the local authority if the Part 1A closure order is a local authority Part 1A closure order;

   (c) a person on whom the Part 1A closure notice relating to the closed premises was served under subsection (7)(d) or (e) or (8) of section 11A;

   (d) a person who has an interest in the closed premises but on whom the Part 1A closure notice was not served.

(8) If a complaint is made under subsection (7)—

   (a) in relation to a police Part 1A closure order, by a person other than a constable, or

   (b) in relation to a local authority Part 1A closure order, by a person other than the local authority,

   the justice may issue a summons directed to such constable as the justice thinks appropriate or to the local authority (as the case may be) requiring the constable or authority to appear before the magistrates' court to answer to the complaint.

(9) The court may not make an order discharging a Part 1A closure order unless it is satisfied that the Part 1A closure order is no longer necessary to prevent the occurrence of significant and persistent disorder or persistent serious nuisance to members of the public.

(10) If a summons is issued in accordance with subsection (4) or (8), a notice stating the date, time and place at which the complaint will be heard must be served on—

   (a) if the summons is issued under subsection (4), the persons to whom it is directed;

   (b) if the summons is issued under subsection (8), the persons mentioned in subsection (7)(c) and (d) (other than the complainant);

   (c) if the complaint relates to a police Part 1A closure order, such constable as the justice thinks appropriate (unless a constable is the complainant);

   (d) if the complaint relates to a local authority Part 1A closure order, the local authority (unless it is the complainant).

11F Part 1A closure order: appeals

(1) This section applies to—

   (a) an order under section 11B or 11E;

   (b) a decision by a court not to make an order under either of those sections.

(2) An appeal against an order or decision to which this section applies must be brought to the Crown Court before the end of the period of 21 days beginning with the day on which the order or decision is made.

(3) An appeal against an order under section 11B or 11E(5) may be brought by—

   (a) a person on whom the Part 1A closure notice relating to the closed premises was served under section 11A(7)(d) or (e), or

   (b) a person who has an interest in the closed premises but on whom the Part 1A closure notice was not served.

(4) An appeal against the decision of a court not to make such an order may be brought by—

   (a) a constable if the Part 1A closure order is (or, if made, would have been) a police Part 1A closure order, or

   (b) the local authority if the Part 1A closure order is (or, if made, would have been) a local authority Part 1A closure order.

(5) On an appeal under this section the Crown Court may make such order as it thinks appropriate.

11G Part 1A closure order: access to other premises

(1) This section applies to any person who occupies or owns any part of a building or structure—

(a) in which closed premises are situated, and

(b) in respect of which the Part 1A closure order does not have effect.

(2) A person to whom this section applies may, at any time while a Part 1A closure order has effect, apply to—

(a) the magistrates' court in respect of an order made under section 11B or 11E, or

(b) the Crown Court in respect of an order made under section 11F.

(3) If an application is made under this section notice of the date, time and place of the hearing to consider the application must be given to—

(a) such constable as the court thinks appropriate;

(b) the local authority;

(c) any person on whom the Part 1A closure notice relating to the closed premises was served under subsection (7)(d) or (e) or (8) of section 11A; and

(d) any person who has an interest in the closed premises but on whom the Part 1A closure notice was not served.

(4) On an application under this section the court may make such order as it thinks appropriate in relation to access to any part of a building or structure in which closed premises are situated.

(5) It is immaterial whether any provision has been made as mentioned in section 11B(6).

11H Part 1A closure order: reimbursement of costs

(1) A police authority or a local authority which incurs expenditure for the purpose of clearing, securing or maintaining the premises in respect of which a Part 1A closure order has effect may apply to the court which made the order for an order under this section.

(2) On an application under this section the court may make such order as it thinks appropriate in the circumstances for the reimbursement (in full or in part) by the owner of the premises of the expenditure mentioned in subsection (1).

(3) But an application for an order under this section must not be entertained unless it is made before the end of the period of 3 months starting with the day the Part 1A closure order ceases to have effect.

(4) An application under this section must be served on—

(a) the police authority for the area in which the premises are situated if the application is made by the local authority;

(b) the local authority if the application is made by a police authority; and

(c) the owner of the premises.

11I Part 1A closure notice or order: exemption from liability

(1) A constable is not liable for relevant damages in respect of anything done or omitted to be done by the constable in the performance or purported performance of functions under this Part.

(2) A chief officer of police who has direction or control of a constable is not liable for relevant damages in respect of anything done or omitted to be done by the constable in the performance or purported performance of functions under this Part.

(3) Neither a local authority nor an employee of a local authority is liable for relevant damages in respect of anything done or omitted to be done by or on behalf of the authority in the performance or purported performance of functions under this Part.

(4) Subsections (1) to (3) do not apply—

    (a) if the act or omission is shown to have been in bad faith;

    (b) so as to prevent an award of damages made in respect of an act or omission on the ground that the act or omission was unlawful by virtue of section 6(1) of the Human Rights Act 1998.

(5) This section does not affect any other exemption from liability for damages (whether at common law or otherwise).

(6) In this section "relevant damages" means damages in proceedings for judicial review or for the tort of negligence or misfeasance in public office.

11J Part 1A closure notices and orders: compensation

(1) This section applies to any person who incurs financial loss in consequence of—

    (a) the issue of a Part 1A closure notice, or

    (b) a Part 1A closure order having effect.

(2) A person to whom this section applies may apply to—

    (a) the magistrates' court which considered the application for a Part 1A closure order;

    (b) the Crown Court if the Part 1A closure order was made or extended by an order made by that Court on an appeal under section 11F.

(3) An application under this section must not be entertained unless it is made not later than the end of the period of 3 months starting with whichever is the later of—

    (a) the day the court decides not to make a Part 1A closure order;

    (b) the day the Crown Court dismisses an appeal against a decision not to make a Part 1A closure order;

    (c) the day the Part 1A closure order ceases to have effect.

(4) On an application under this section the court may order the payment of compensation out of central funds if it is satisfied—

    (a) that the person is not associated with such use of the premises as is mentioned in section 11A(1)(b),

    (b) if the person is the owner or occupier of the premises, that the person took reasonable steps to prevent such use of the premises,

    (c) that the person has incurred financial loss as mentioned in subsection (1), and

    (d) having regard to all the circumstances it is appropriate to order payment of compensation in respect of that loss.

(5) In this section "central funds" has the same meaning as in enactments providing for the payment of costs.

11K Guidance

(1) The Secretary of State may issue guidance relating to the discharge of any functions under or for the purposes of this Part.

(2) A person discharging a function to which guidance under this section relates must have regard to the guidance in discharging the function.

11L Interpretation

(1) This section applies for the purposes of this Part.

(2) "Anti-social behaviour" means behaviour by a person which causes or is likely to cause harassment, alarm or distress to one or more other persons not of the same household as the person.

(3) "The appropriate chief officer", in relation to—

    (a) any premises, or

    (b) a Part 1A closure order relating to any premises,

means the chief officer of police for the area in which the premises are situated.

    (4) "Closed premises" means premises in respect of which a Part 1A closure order has effect.

    (5) "Local authority", in relation to England, means—

        (a) a district council;

        (b) a London borough council;

        (c) a county council for an area for which there is no district council;

        (d) the Common Council of the City of London in its capacity as a local authority;

        (e) the Council of the Isles of Scilly.

    (6) "Local authority", in relation to Wales, means—

        (a) a county council;

        (b) a county borough council.

    (7) References to the local authority in relation to—

        (a) any premises,

        (b) a Part 1A closure notice relating to any premises, or

        (c) a Part 1A closure order relating to any premises,

    are references to the local authority for the area in which the premises are situated

    (8) "A local authority Part 1A closure order" means a Part 1A closure order made or extended on the application of the local authority.

    (9) "The owner", in relation to premises, means—

        (a) a person who is for the time being entitled to dispose of the fee simple in the premises, whether in possession or in reversion (apart from a mortgagee not in possession), or

        (b) a person who holds or is entitled to the rents and profits of the premises under a lease which (when granted) was for a term of not less than 3 years.

  (10) "A Part 1A closure notice" means a notice issued under section 11A.

  (11) "A Part 1A closure order" means—

        (a) an order made under section 11B;

        (b) an order extended under section 11E;

        (c) an order made or extended under section 11F which has the like effect as an order made or extended under section 11B or 11E (as the case may be).

  (12) "A police Part 1A closure order" means a Part 1A closure order made or extended on the application of a constable.

  (13) "Premises" includes—

        (a) any land or other place (whether enclosed or not);

        (b) any outbuildings which are or are used as part of premises."

SCHEDULE 21   Section 122

NUISANCE OR DISTURBANCE ON HSS PREMISES

Offence of causing nuisance or disturbance on HSS premises

1 (1) A person commits an offence if—

        (a) the person causes, without reasonable excuse and while on HSS premises, a nuisance or disturbance to an HSS staff member who is working there or is otherwise there in connection with work,

        (b) the person refuses, without reasonable excuse, to leave the HSS premises when asked to do so by a constable or an HSS staff member, and

        (c) the person is not on the HSS premises for the purpose of obtaining medical advice, treatment or care for himself or herself.

    (2) A person who commits an offence under this paragraph is liable on summary conviction to a fine not exceeding level 3 on the standard scale.

(3) For the purposes of this paragraph—
- (a) a person ceases to be on HSS premises for the purpose of obtaining medical advice, treatment or care for himself or herself once the person has received the advice, treatment or care, and
- (b) a person is not on HSS premises for the purpose of obtaining medical advice, treatment or care for himself or herself if the person has been refused the advice, treatment or care during the last 8 hours.

(4) In this paragraph—
"hospital grounds" means land in the vicinity of a hospital and associated with it,
"HSS premises" means—
- (a) any hospital vested in, or managed by, an HSS trust,
- (b) any building or other structure, or vehicle, associated with the hospital and situated on hospital grounds (whether or not vested in, or managed by, an HSS trust), and
- (c) the hospital grounds,
"HSS staff member" means a person employed by an HSS trust or otherwise working for it (whether as or on behalf of a contractor, as a volunteer or otherwise),
"HSS trust" means a Health and Social Services trust established under Article 10 of the Health and Personal Social Services (Northern Ireland) Order 1991 (S.I. 1991/194 (N.I. 1)), and
"vehicle" includes an air ambulance.

Power to remove person causing nuisance or disturbance

2 (1) If a constable reasonably suspects that a person is committing or has committed an offence under paragraph 1, the constable may remove the person from the HSS premises concerned.

(2) If an authorised officer reasonably suspects that a person is committing or has committed an offence under paragraph 1, the authorised officer may—
- (a) remove the person from the HSS premises concerned, or
- (b) authorise an HSS staff member to do so.

(3) Any person removing another person from HSS premises under this paragraph may use reasonable force (if necessary).

(4) An authorised officer cannot remove a person under this paragraph or authorise another person to do so if the authorised officer has reason to believe that—
- (a) the person to be removed requires medical advice, treatment or care for himself or herself, or
- (b) the removal of the person would endanger the person's physical or mental health.

(5) In this paragraph—
"authorised officer" means any HSS staff member authorised by an HSS trust to exercise the powers conferred on an authorised officer by this paragraph, and
"HSS premises", "HSS staff member" and "HSS trust" have the same meaning as in paragraph 1.

Guidance about the power to remove etc.

3 (1) The Department of Health, Social Services and Public Safety may from time to time prepare and publish guidance to HSS trusts and authorised officers about the powers in paragraph 2.

(2) Such guidance may, in particular, relate to—
- (a) the authorisation by HSS trusts of authorised officers,
- (b) the authorisation by authorised officers of HSS staff members to remove persons under paragraph 2,

(c) training requirements for authorised officers and HSS staff members authorised by them to remove persons under paragraph 2,

(d) matters that may be relevant to a consideration by authorised officers for the purposes of paragraph 2 of whether offences are being, or have been, committed under paragraph 1,

(e) matters to be taken into account by authorised officers in deciding whether there is reason to believe that a person requires medical advice, treatment or care for himself or herself or that the removal of a person would endanger the person's physical or mental health,

(f) the procedure to be followed by authorised officers or persons authorised by them before using the power of removal in paragraph 2,

(g) the degree of force that it may be appropriate for authorised officers or persons authorised by them to use in particular circumstances,

(h) arrangements for ensuring that persons on HSS premises are aware of the offence in paragraph 1 and the powers of removal in paragraph 2, or

(i) the keeping of records.

(3) Before publishing guidance under this paragraph, the Department of Health, Social Services and Public Safety must consult such persons as the Department considers appropriate.

(4) An HSS trust and an authorised officer must have regard to any guidance published under this paragraph when exercising functions under, or in connection with, paragraph 2.

(5) In this paragraph—

"authorised officer" has the same meaning as in paragraph 2, and

"HSS premises", "HSS staff member" and "HSS trust" have the same meaning as in paragraph 1.

SCHEDULE 22   Section 126
POLICE MISCONDUCT AND PERFORMANCE PROCEDURES

PART 1
AMENDMENTS OF POLICE ACT 1996

1 The Police Act 1996 (c. 16) has effect subject to the following amendments.

General duty of Secretary of State

2 In section 36(2)(d) (general duty of Secretary of State) for "section 85" substitute "sections 84 and 85".

Regulations for police forces

3 (1) Section 50 (regulations for police forces) is amended as follows.

(2) For subsection (3) substitute—

"(3) Without prejudice to the powers conferred by this section, regulations under this section shall—

(a) establish, or

(b) make provision for the establishment of,

procedures for the taking of disciplinary proceedings in respect of the conduct, efficiency and effectiveness of members of police forces, including procedures for cases in which such persons may be dealt with by dismissal."

(3) In subsection (4) omit ", subject to subsection (3)(b),".

Regulations for special constables

4 (1) Section 51 (regulations for special constables) is amended as follows.
  (2) In subsection (2)(ba) (conduct of special constables) after "conduct" insert ", efficiency and effectiveness".
  (3) After subsection (2) insert—
    "(2A) Without prejudice to the powers conferred by this section, regulations under this section shall—
      (a) establish, or
      (b) make provision for the establishment of,
      procedures for the taking of disciplinary proceedings in respect of the conduct, efficiency and effectiveness of special constables, including procedures for cases in which such persons may be dealt with by dismissal."

Police Federations

5 In section 59(3) (representation only by another member of a police force except in certain circumstances) for "provided by" substitute "provided in regulations made in accordance with".

Police Advisory Board

6 (1) Section 63(3) (supply of draft regulations to the Police Advisory Board) is amended as follows.
  (2) In paragraph (a), for "regulations under section 50 or 52" substitute "regulations or rules under section 50, 52, 84 or 85".
  (3) After "a draft of the regulations" insert "or rules".

Representation at disciplinary and other proceedings

7 For section 84 substitute—
  "84 Representation etc. at disciplinary and other proceedings
  (1) The Secretary of State shall by regulations make provision for or in connection with—
    (a) enabling the officer concerned or a relevant authority to be represented in proceedings conducted under regulations made in pursuance of section 50(3) or section 51(2A);
    (b) enabling the panel conducting such proceedings to receive advice from a relevant lawyer or another person falling within any prescribed description of persons.
  (2) Regulations under this section may in particular make provision—
    (a) specifying the circumstances in which the officer concerned or a relevant authority is entitled to be legally represented (by a relevant lawyer);
    (b) specifying the circumstances in which the officer concerned or a relevant authority is entitled to be represented by a person (other than a relevant lawyer) who falls within any prescribed description of persons;
    (c) for securing that—
      (i) a relevant authority may be legally represented, and
      (ii) the panel conducting the proceedings may receive advice from a relevant lawyer,
      whether or not the officer concerned is legally represented.
  (3) Without prejudice to the powers conferred by this section, regulations under this section shall, in relation to cases where the officer concerned is entitled to legal or other representation, make provision—
    (a) for securing that the officer is notified of his right to such representation;
    (b) specifying when the officer is to be so notified;

(c) for securing that proceedings at which the officer may be dismissed are not to take place unless the officer has been notified of his right to such representation.

(4) In this section—

"the officer concerned", in relation to proceedings within subsection (1)(a), means the member of a police force or special constable to whom the proceedings relate;

"the panel", in relation to proceedings within subsection (1)(a), means the panel of persons, or the person, prescribed for the purpose of conducting the proceedings;

"prescribed" means prescribed by regulations under this section;

"relevant authority" means—

(a) where the officer concerned is a member of a police force (other than a senior officer), or a special constable, the chief officer of police of the police force of which the officer is a member, or for which the officer is appointed as a special constable;

(b) where the officer concerned is a senior officer, the police authority for the police force of which the officer is a member;

"relevant lawyer" means a person who, for the purposes of the Legal Services Act 2007, is an authorised person in relation to an activity which constitutes the exercise of a right of audience (within the meaning of that Act);

"senior officer" means a member of a police force holding a rank above that of chief superintendent.

(5) But in prescribed circumstances "relevant authority" also includes the Independent Police Complaints Commission.

(6) Regulations under this section may make different provision for different cases and circumstances.

(7) A statutory instrument containing regulations under this section shall be subject to annulment in pursuance of a resolution of either House of Parliament.

(8) Subsection (7) does not apply to a statutory instrument containing (whether alone or with other provision) any regulations under this section coming into force at a time that is the earliest time at which any regulations under this section are to come into force since the commencement of paragraph 7 of Schedule 22 to the Criminal Justice and Immigration Act 2008.

(9) A statutory instrument within subsection (8) may not be made unless a draft of it has been laid before and approved by a resolution of each House of Parliament."

Appeals against dismissal etc.

8 (1) Section 85 (appeals against dismissal etc.) is amended as follows.

(2) For subsections (1) and (2) substitute—

"(1) The Secretary of State shall by rules make provision specifying the cases in which a member of a police force or a special constable may appeal to a police appeals tribunal.

(2) A police appeals tribunal may, on the determination of an appeal under this section, make an order dealing with the appellant in any way in which he could have been dealt with by the person who made the decision appealed against."

(3) For subsection (4) substitute—

"(4) Rules made under this section may, in particular, make provision—

(a) for enabling a police appeals tribunal, in such circumstances as are specified in the rules, to determine a case without a hearing;

(b) for the appellant or the respondent to be entitled, in a case where there is a hearing, to be represented—

(i) by a relevant lawyer within the meaning of section 84, or

(ii) by a person who falls within any description of persons prescribed by the rules;

(c) for enabling a police appeals tribunal to require any person to attend a hearing to give evidence or to produce documents,

and rules made in pursuance of paragraph (c) may apply subsections (2) and (3) of section 250 of the Local Government Act 1972 with such modifications as may be set out in the rules.

(4A) Rules under this section may make different provision for different cases and circumstances."

(4) For subsection (5) substitute—

"(5) A statutory instrument containing rules under this section shall be subject to annulment in pursuance of a resolution of either House of Parliament.

(5A) Subsection (5) does not apply to a statutory instrument containing (whether alone or with other provision) the first rules made under this section after the commencement of paragraph 8 of Schedule 22 to the Criminal Justice and Immigration Act 2008: such an instrument may not be made unless a draft of it has been laid before and approved by a resolution of each House of Parliament."

Guidance concerning disciplinary proceedings etc.

9 (1) Section 87 (guidance concerning disciplinary proceedings etc.) is amended as follows.

(2) For subsection (1) substitute—

"(1) The Secretary of State may issue relevant guidance to—

(a) police authorities,

(b) chief officers of police,

(c) other members of police forces,

(d) special constables, and

(e) persons employed by a police authority who are under the direction and control of the chief officer of police of the police force maintained by that authority.

(1ZA) "Relevant guidance" is guidance as to the discharge of functions under regulations under section 50 or 51 in relation to the matters mentioned in section 50(2)(e) or 51(2)(ba)."

(3) In subsection (1A), after "section 50" insert "or 51".

(4) In subsection (5), after "section 50" insert "or 51".

Police officers engaged on service outside their force

10 (1) Section 97 (police officers engaged on service outside their force) is amended as follows.

(2) In subsection (6)—

(a) in paragraph (b), omit "or is required to resign as an alternative to dismissal";

(b) in paragraph (c), omit "or is required to resign as an alternative to dismissal".

(3) In subsection (7), omit ", or required to resign as an alternative to dismissal,".

Police Appeals Tribunals

11 (1) Schedule 6 (appeals to police appeals tribunals) is amended as follows.

(2) In paragraph 1(1) (appeals by senior officers) for paragraphs (b) and (c) substitute—

"(b) one shall be Her Majesty's Chief Inspector of Constabulary appointed under section 54(1) or one of Her Majesty's Inspectors of Constabulary nominated by the Chief Inspector, and

(c) one shall be the permanent secretary to the Home Office or a Home Office director nominated by the permanent secretary."

(3) In paragraph 2 (appeals by other members of police forces) for subparagraph (1) substitute—

"(1) In the case of an appeal by a member of a police force (other than a senior officer) or a special constable, the police appeals tribunal shall consist of four members appointed by the relevant police authority, of whom—

(a) one shall be a person chosen from the list referred to in paragraph 1(1)(a),

(b) one shall be a senior officer,

(c) one shall be a member of the relevant police authority, and

(d) one shall be a retired member of a police force who, at the time of his retirement, was a member of an appropriate staff association."

(4) Omit paragraph 6 (hearings).

(5) In paragraph 7 (effect of orders) for sub-paragraph (1) substitute—

"(1) Where on the determination of an appeal the tribunal makes such an order as is mentioned in section 85(2), the order shall take effect—

(a) by way of substitution for the decision appealed against, and

(b) as from the date of that decision."

(6) In paragraph 10 (interpretation)—

(a) for sub-paragraph (b) substitute—

"(b) "the relevant police authority" means the police authority which maintains—

(i) the police force of which the appellant is a member, or

(ii) the police force for the area for which the appellant is appointed as a special constable,

as the case may be."

(b) for sub-paragraph (c) substitute—

"(c) "appropriate staff association" means—

(i) where the appellant was, immediately before the proceedings from which the appeal is brought, of the rank of chief superintendent or superintendent, the Police Superintendents' Association of England and Wales; and

(ii) in any other case, the Police Federation of England and Wales."

PART 2

AMENDMENTS OF MINISTRY OF DEFENCE POLICE ACT 1987

12 The Ministry of Defence Police Act 1987 (c. 4) has effect subject to the following amendments.

Defence Police Federation

13 In section 3(4) (representation of a member of the Ministry of Defence Police by the Federation) for "on an appeal to the Secretary of State or as provided by" substitute "as provided in regulations made under".

Regulations relating to disciplinary matters

14 (1) Section 3A (regulations relating to disciplinary matters) is amended as follows.

(2) For subsection (1) substitute—

"(1) The Secretary of State may make regulations with respect to—

(a) the conduct of members of the Ministry of Defence Police and the maintenance of discipline;

(b) the suspension from duty of members of the Ministry of Defence Police.

(1A) Without prejudice to the powers conferred by subsection (1), regulations under this section shall—

(a) establish, or

(b) make provision for the establishment of,

procedures for the taking of disciplinary proceedings in respect of the conduct of members of the Ministry of Defence Police, including procedures for cases in which such persons may be dealt with by dismissal."

(3) For subsection (2) substitute—

"(2) The regulations may provide for decisions which would otherwise fall to be taken by the Secretary of State or the chief constable of the Ministry of Defence Police to be taken instead by—

(a) a person appointed in accordance with the regulations; or

(b) the Ministry of Defence Police Committee."

Representation etc. at disciplinary proceedings

15 For section 4 substitute—

"**4 Representation etc. at disciplinary proceedings**

(1) The Secretary of State shall by regulations make provision for or in connection with—

(a) enabling the officer concerned or the relevant authority to be represented in proceedings conducted under regulations made in pursuance of section 3A;

(b) enabling the panel conducting such proceedings to receive advice from a relevant lawyer or another person falling within any prescribed description of persons.

(2) Regulations under this section may in particular make provision—

(a) specifying the circumstances in which the officer concerned or the relevant authority is entitled to be represented by a relevant lawyer;

(b) specifying the circumstances in which the officer concerned or the relevant authority is entitled to be represented by a person (other than a relevant lawyer) who falls within any prescribed description of persons;

(c) for securing that—

(i) the relevant authority may be legally represented, and

(ii) the panel conducting the proceedings may receive advice from a relevant lawyer, whether or not the officer concerned is legally represented.

(3) Without prejudice to the powers conferred by this section, regulations under this section shall, in relation to cases where the officer concerned is entitled to legal or other representation, make provision—

(a) for securing that the officer is notified of his right to such representation;

(b) specifying when the officer is to be so notified;

(c) for securing that proceedings at which the officer may be dismissed are not to take place unless the officer has been notified of his right to such representation.

(4) In this section—

"the officer concerned", in relation to proceedings within subsection (1)(a), means the member of the Ministry of Defence Police to whom the proceedings relate;

"the panel", in relation to proceedings within subsection (1)(a), means the panel of persons, or the person, prescribed for the purpose of conducting the proceedings;

"prescribed" means prescribed by regulations under this section;

"relevant authority" means—

(a) where the officer concerned is a member of the Ministry of Defence Police (other than a senior officer), the chief constable for the Ministry of Defence Police;

(b) where the officer concerned is a senior officer, the Ministry of Defence Police Committee;

"relevant lawyer" means—

    (a) in relation to England and Wales, a person who, for the purposes of the Legal Services Act 2007, is an authorised person in relation to an activity which constitutes the exercise of a right of audience (within the meaning of that Act), and

    (b) in relation to Scotland or Northern Ireland, counsel or a solicitor;

"senior officer" means a member of the Ministry of Defence Police holding a rank above that of chief superintendent.

(5) But in prescribed circumstances "relevant authority" also includes—

    (a) in relation to England and Wales, the Independent Police Complaints Commission;

    (b) in relation to Scotland, the Police Complaints Commissioner for Scotland;

    (c) in relation to Northern Ireland, the Police Ombudsman for Northern Ireland.

(6) A statutory instrument containing regulations under this section shall be subject to annulment in pursuance of a resolution of either House of Parliament.

(7) Subsection (6) does not apply to a statutory instrument containing (whether alone or with other provision) any regulations under this section coming into force at a time that is the earliest time at which any regulations under this section are to come into force since the commencement of paragraph 15 of Schedule 22 to the Criminal Justice and Immigration Act 2008.

(8) A statutory instrument within subsection (7) may not be made unless a draft of it has been laid before and approved by a resolution of each House of Parliament."

Appeals against dismissal etc.

16 For section 4A substitute—

"4A Appeals against dismissal etc.

(1) The Secretary of State shall by regulations—

    (a) make provision specifying the cases in which a member of the Ministry of Defence Police may appeal to a police appeals tribunal;

    (b) make provision equivalent, subject to such modifications as the Secretary of State thinks fit, to that made (or authorised to be made) in relation to police appeals tribunals by any provision of Schedule 6 to the Police Act 1996 (c. 16) or Schedule 3 to the Police (Scotland) Act 1967 (c. 77).

(2) A police appeals tribunal may, on the determination of an appeal under this section, make an order dealing with the appellant in any way in which he could have been dealt with by the person who made the decision appealed against.

(3) The Secretary of State may make regulations as to the procedure on appeals to police appeals tribunals under this section.

(4) Regulations under this section may, in particular, make provision—

    (a) for enabling a police appeals tribunal, in such circumstances as are specified in the regulations, to determine a case without a hearing;

    (b) for the appellant or the respondent to be entitled, in a case where there is a hearing, to be represented—

      (i) by a relevant lawyer, or

      (ii) by a person who falls within any description of persons prescribed by the regulations;

    (c) for enabling a police appeals tribunal to require any person to attend a hearing to give evidence or to produce documents,

and regulations made in pursuance of paragraph (c) may apply subsections (2) and (3) of section 250 of the Local Government Act 1972 with such modifications as may be set out in the regulations.

(5) Any statutory instrument containing regulations under this section shall be subject to annulment in pursuance of a resolution of either House of Parliament.

(6) Subsection (5) does not apply to a statutory instrument containing (whether alone or with other provision) the first regulations made under this section after the commencement of paragraph 16 of Schedule 22 to the Criminal Justice and Immigration Act 2008: such an instrument may not be made unless a draft of it has been laid before and approved by a resolution of each House of Parliament.

(7) In this section—

"police appeals tribunal" means a tribunal constituted in accordance with regulations under this section;

"relevant lawyer" has the same meaning as in section 4."

PART 3
AMENDMENTS OF RAILWAYS AND TRANSPORT SAFETY ACT 2003

17 The Railways and Transport Safety Act 2003 (c. 20) has effect subject to the following amendments.

Police regulations: general

18 (1) Section 36 (police regulations: general) is amended as follows.

(2) In subsection (1) (power to make regulations about constables) after "conditions" insert "of service".

(3) For subsection (2) substitute—

"(2) The Authority shall also make regulations similar to the provision made by and under—

(a) sections 84 and 85 of the Police Act 1996 (representation etc. at disciplinary and other proceedings, and appeal), and

(b) Schedule 6 to that Act (appeals to police appeals tribunals)."

Police regulations: special constables

19 After section 37(1) (power to make regulations about special constables) insert—

"(1A) The Authority shall also make regulations similar to the provision made by and under—

(a) sections 84 and 85 of the Police Act 1996 (representation etc. at disciplinary and other proceedings, and appeal), and

(b) Schedule 6 to that Act (appeals to police appeals tribunals)."

Police regulations by Secretary of State

20 For section 42(3) substitute—

"(3) If regulations under this section make provision for a matter specified in section 50(3) or section 51(2A) of the Police Act 1996 (disciplinary proceedings), they must also make provision similar to that made by and under—

(a) sections 84 and 85 of that Act (representation etc. at disciplinary and other proceedings, and appeal), and

(b) Schedule 6 to that Act (appeals to police appeals tribunals)."

Regulations: further appeal

21 Omit section 43 (regulations: further appeal).

SCHEDULE 23   Section 127
INVESTIGATION OF COMPLAINTS OF POLICE MISCONDUCT ETC.

1 The Police Reform Act 2002 (c. 30) has effect subject to the following amendments.
2 In section 23(2) (regulations) after paragraph (q) insert—
"(r) for enabling representations on behalf of a person to whose conduct an investigation relates to be made to the Commission by a person who is not that person's legal representative but is of a description specified in the regulations."
3 Schedule 3 (handling of complaints and conduct matters etc.) is amended as follows.
4 In paragraph 6(4) (handling of complaints by appropriate authority: use of local resolution procedures) in each of paragraphs (a)(ii) and (b)(ii), for the words from ", a requirement to resign" to the end substitute "or the giving of a final written warning."
5 After paragraph 19 insert—

"Special procedure where investigation relates to police officer or special constable

19A Paragraphs 19B to 19E apply to investigations of complaints or recordable conduct matters in cases where the person concerned (see paragraph 19B(11)) is a member of a police force or a special constable.

Assessment of seriousness of conduct under investigation

19B (1) If, during the course of an investigation of a complaint, it appears to the person investigating that there is an indication that a person to whose conduct the investigation relates may have—
(a) committed a criminal offence, or
(b) behaved in a manner which would justify the bringing of disciplinary proceedings,
the person investigating must certify the investigation as one subject to special requirements.
(2) If the person investigating a complaint certifies the investigation as one subject to special requirements, the person must, as soon as is reasonably practicable after doing so, make a severity assessment in relation to the conduct of the person concerned to which the investigation relates.
(3) The person investigating a recordable conduct matter must make a severity assessment in relation to the conduct to which the investigation relates—
(a) as soon as is reasonably practicable after his appointment or designation, or
(b) in the case of a matter recorded in accordance with paragraph 21A(5) or 24B(2), as soon as is reasonably practicable after it is so recorded.
(4) For the purposes of this paragraph a "severity assessment", in relation to conduct, means an assessment as to—
(a) whether the conduct, if proved, would amount to misconduct or gross misconduct, and
(b) if the conduct were to become the subject of disciplinary proceedings, the form which those proceedings would be likely to take.
(5) An assessment under this paragraph may only be made after consultation with the appropriate authority.
(6) On completing an assessment under this paragraph, the person investigating the complaint or matter must give a notification to the person concerned that complies with sub-paragraph (7).

(7) The notification must—
- (a) give the prescribed information about the results of the assessment;
- (b) give the prescribed information about the effect of paragraph 19C and of regulations under paragraph 19D;
- (c) set out the prescribed time limits for providing the person investigating the complaint or matter with relevant statements and relevant documents respectively for the purposes of paragraph 19C(2);
- (d) give such other information as may be prescribed.

(8) Sub-paragraph (6) does not apply for so long as the person investigating the complaint or matter considers that giving the notification might prejudice—
- (a) the investigation, or
- (b) any other investigation (including, in particular, a criminal investigation).

(9) Where the person investigating a complaint or matter has made a severity assessment and considers it appropriate to do so, the person may revise the assessment.

(10) On revising a severity assessment, the person investigating the complaint or matter must notify the prescribed information about the revised assessment to the person concerned.

(11) In this paragraph and paragraphs 19C to 19E—

"the person concerned"—
- (a) in relation to an investigation of a complaint, means the person in respect of whom it appears to the person investigating that there is the indication mentioned in paragraph 19B(1);
- (b) in relation to an investigation of a recordable conduct matter, means the person to whose conduct the investigation relates;

"relevant document"—
- (a) means a document relating to any complaint or matter under investigation, and
- (b) includes such a document containing suggestions as to lines of inquiry to be pursued or witnesses to be interviewed;

"relevant statement" means an oral or written statement relating to any complaint or matter under investigation.

Duty to consider submissions from person whose conduct is being investigated

19C (1) This paragraph applies to—
- (a) an investigation of a complaint that has been certified under paragraph 19B(1) as one subject to special requirements, or
- (b) an investigation of a recordable conduct matter.

(2) If before the expiry of the appropriate time limit notified in pursuance of paragraph 19B(7)(c)—
- (a) the person concerned provides the person investigating the complaint or matter with a relevant statement or a relevant document, or
- (b) any person of a prescribed description provides that person with a relevant document,

that person must consider the statement or document.

Interview of person whose conduct is being investigated

19D (1) The Secretary of State may by regulations make provision as to the procedure to be followed in connection with any interview of the person concerned which is held during the course of an investigation within paragraph 19C(1)(a) or (b) by the person investigating the complaint or matter.

(2) Regulations under this paragraph may, in particular, make provision—
- (a) for determining how the time at which an interview is to be held is to be agreed or decided,
- (b) about the information that must be provided to the person being interviewed,

(c) for enabling that person to be accompanied at the interview by a person of a prescribed description.

Duty to provide certain information to appropriate authority

19E (1) This paragraph applies during the course of an investigation within paragraph 19C(1)(a) or (b).

    (2) The person investigating the complaint or matter must supply the appropriate authority with such information in that person's possession as the authority may reasonably request for the purpose mentioned in sub-paragraph (3).

    (3) That purpose is determining, in accordance with regulations under section 50 or 51 of the 1996 Act, whether the person concerned should be, or should remain, suspended—

        (a) from office as constable, and

        (b) where that person is a member of a police force, from membership of that force."

6 (1) Paragraph 20A (accelerated procedure in special cases) is amended as follows.

    (2) In sub-paragraph (1) (application of paragraph) for "a person appointed or designated to investigate" substitute "the person investigating".

    (3) In sub-paragraph (6) (investigation to continue after submission of report) for "appointed or designated to investigate" substitute "investigating".

    (4) In sub-paragraph (7) (definition of special conditions)—

        (a) for paragraphs (a) and (b) substitute—

            "(a) there is sufficient evidence, in the form of written statements or other documents, to establish on the balance of probabilities that conduct to which the investigation relates constitutes gross misconduct;";

        (b) in paragraph (c), for "is the subject matter of the investigation" substitute "it is".

    (5) Omit sub-paragraph (8) (interpretation).

7 (1) Paragraph 20B (investigations managed or carried out by Commission: action by appropriate authority) is amended as follows.

    (2) For sub-paragraphs (3) and (4) (action to be taken where special conditions are satisfied) substitute—

        "(3) If the appropriate authority determines that the special conditions are satisfied then, unless it considers that the circumstances are such as to make it inappropriate to do so, it shall—

            (a) certify the case as a special case for the purposes of regulations under section 50(3) or 51(2A) of the 1996 Act; and

            (b) take such steps as are required by those regulations in relation to a case so certified."

    (3) Omit sub-paragraph (5) (appropriate authority to notify DPP if special conditions are satisfied).

8 In paragraph 20D(2) (action by Commission on receipt of memorandum) for "appointed under paragraph 18 or designated under paragraph 19" substitute "investigating the complaint or matter".

9 (1) Paragraph 20E (other investigations: action by appropriate authority) is amended as follows.

    (2) For sub-paragraphs (3) and (4) (action to be taken where special conditions are satisfied) substitute—

        "(3) If the appropriate authority determines that the special conditions are satisfied then, unless it considers that the circumstances are such as to make it inappropriate to do so, it shall—

            (a) certify the case as a special case for the purposes of regulations under section 50(3) or 51(2A) of the 1996 Act; and

(b) take such steps as are required by those regulations in relation to a case so certified."

(3) Omit sub-paragraph (5) (appropriate authority to notify DPP if special conditions are satisfied).

(4) In sub-paragraph (7) (appropriate authority to notify person investigating if special conditions are not satisfied) for "appointed under paragraph 16 or 17" substitute "investigating the complaint or matter".

10 Omit paragraph 20G (special cases: Director of Public Prosecutions) and the cross-heading immediately preceding it.

11 (1) Paragraph 21A (procedure where conduct matter is revealed in course of investigation of DSI matter) is amended as follows.

(2) In sub-paragraph (5) (DSI matter is to be recorded as conduct matter) omit the words from "(and the other provisions" to the end.

(3) After sub-paragraph (5) insert—

"(6) Where a DSI matter is recorded under paragraph 11 as a conduct matter by virtue of sub-paragraph (5)—

(a) the person investigating the DSI matter shall (subject to any determination made by the Commission under paragraph 15(5)) continue the investigation as if appointed or designated to investigate the conduct matter, and

(b) the other provisions of this Schedule shall apply in relation to that matter accordingly."

12 (1) Paragraph 22 (final reports on investigations) is amended as follows.

(2) In sub-paragraph (1) (cases where paragraph 22 applies)—

(a) after paragraph (a) insert "or";

(b) omit paragraph (c).

(3) In sub-paragraph (4) (meaning of appropriate authority in the case of a conduct matter which was formerly a DSI matter) for the words from "a DSI matter" to "or (4)" substitute "a matter that was formerly a DSI matter but has been recorded as a conduct matter in pursuance of paragraph 21A(5)".

(4) At the end insert—

"(7) The Secretary of State may by regulations make provision requiring a report on an investigation within paragraph 19C(1)(a) or (b)—

(a) to include such matters as are specified in the regulations;

(b) to be accompanied by such documents or other items as are so specified.

(8) A person who has submitted a report under this paragraph on an investigation within paragraph 19C(1)(a) or (b) must supply the appropriate authority with such copies of further documents or other items in that person's possession as the authority may request.

(9) The appropriate authority may only make a request under subparagraph (8) in respect of a copy of a document or other item if the authority—

(a) considers that the document or item is of relevance to the investigation, and

(b) requires a copy of the document or the item for either or both of the purposes mentioned in sub-paragraph (10).

(10) Those purposes are—

(a) complying with any obligation under regulations under section 50(3) or 51(2A) of the 1996 Act which the authority has in relation to any person to whose conduct the investigation related;

(b) ensuring that any such person receives a fair hearing at any disciplinary proceedings in respect of any such conduct of his."

13 (1) Paragraph 23 (action by Commission in response to investigation report) is amended as follows.

    (2) In sub-paragraph (2) (action to be taken on receipt of report)—

        (a) for paragraph (b) substitute—

            "(b) shall determine whether the conditions set out in sub-paragraphs (2A) and (2B) are satisfied in respect of the report;";

        (b) in paragraph (c), for "the report does so indicate" substitute "those conditions are so satisfied";

        (c) in paragraph (d), after "appropriate authority" insert "and the persons mentioned in sub-paragraph (5)".

    (3) After sub-paragraph (2) insert—

        "(2A) The first condition is that the report indicates that a criminal offence may have been committed by a person to whose conduct the investigation related.

        (2B) The second condition is that—

            (a) the circumstances are such that, in the opinion of the Commission, it is appropriate for the matters dealt with in the report to be considered by the Director of Public Prosecutions, or

            (b) any matters dealt with in the report fall within any prescribed category of matters."

    (4) In sub-paragraph (5) (persons to be notified) for "Those" substitute "The".

    (5) For sub-paragraphs (6) and (7) substitute—

        "(6) On receipt of the report, the Commission shall also notify the appropriate authority that it must—

            (a) in accordance with regulations under section 50 or 51 of the 1996 Act, determine—

                (i) whether any person to whose conduct the investigation related has a case to answer in respect of misconduct or gross misconduct or has no case to answer, and

                (ii) what action (if any) the authority is required to, or will in its discretion, take in respect of the matters dealt with in the report, and

            (b) determine what other action (if any) the authority will in its discretion take in respect of those matters."

        (7) On receipt of a notification under sub-paragraph (6) the appropriate authority shall make those determinations and submit a memorandum to the Commission which—

            (a) sets out the determinations the authority has made, and

            (b) if the appropriate authority has decided in relation to any person to whose conduct the investigation related that disciplinary proceedings should not be brought against that person, sets out its reasons for so deciding."

    (6) In sub-paragraph (8)(a) (action by Commission on receipt of memorandum) for "is proposing to take the action" substitute "has made the determinations under sub-paragraph (6)(a)".

14 (1) Paragraph 24 (action by the appropriate authority in response to investigation report) is amended as follows.

    (2) In sub-paragraph (2) (action to be taken on receipt of report)—

        (a) for paragraph (a) substitute—

            "(a) shall determine whether the conditions set out in sub-paragraphs (2A) and (2B) are satisfied in respect of the report;";

        (b) in paragraph (b), for "the report does so indicate" substitute "those conditions are so satisfied";

        (c) after paragraph (b) insert "and

            (c) shall notify the persons mentioned in subparagraph (5) of its determination under paragraph (a) and of any action taken by it under paragraph (b)."

    (3) After sub-paragraph (2) insert—

        "(2A) The first condition is that the report indicates that a criminal offence may have been committed by a person to whose conduct the investigation related.

(2B) The second condition is that—

    (a) the circumstances are such that, in the opinion of the appropriate authority, it is appropriate for the matters dealt with in the report to be considered by the Director of Public Prosecutions, or

    (b) any matters dealt with in the report fall within any prescribed category of matters."

(4) In sub-paragraph (5) (persons to be notified) for "Those" substitute "The".

(5) After sub-paragraph (5) insert—

"(5A) In the case of a report falling within sub-paragraph (1)(b) which relates to a recordable conduct matter, the appropriate authority shall also notify the Commission of its determination under subparagraph (2)(a).

(5B) On receipt of such a notification that the appropriate authority has determined that the conditions in sub-paragraphs (2A) and (2B) are not satisfied in respect of the report, the Commission—

    (a) shall make its own determination as to whether those conditions are so satisfied, and

    (b) if it determines that they are so satisfied, shall direct the appropriate authority to notify the Director of Public Prosecutions of the Commission's determination and to send the Director a copy of the report.

(5C) It shall be the duty of the appropriate authority to comply with any direction given to it under sub-paragraph (5B)."

(6) For sub-paragraph (6) substitute—

"(6) On receipt of the report or (as the case may be) copy, the appropriate authority shall also—

    (a) in accordance with regulations under section 50 or 51 of the 1996 Act, determine—

        (i) whether any person to whose conduct the investigation related has a case to answer in respect of misconduct or gross misconduct or has no case to answer, and

        (ii) what action (if any) the authority is required to, or will in its discretion, take in respect of the matters dealt with in the report, and

    (b) determine what other action (if any) the authority will in its discretion take in respect of those matters."

(7) In sub-paragraph (7) (appropriate authority to give notice on making a determination under sub-paragraph (6)) for "a determination" substitute "the determinations".

(8) In sub-paragraph (8) (contents of notification authority is required to give of its determination) for paragraphs (b) and (c) substitute—

"(b) the determinations the authority has made under subparagraph (6);".

15 In paragraph 24A(2) (final reports on investigations into other DSI matters: obligation to submit report) for the words from "A person appointed" to "paragraph 19" substitute "The person investigating".

16 (1) Paragraph 24B (action in response to a report on a DSI matter) is amended as follows.

(2) In sub-paragraph (2) (circumstances in which appropriate authority must record matter as a conduct matter) omit the words from "(and the other provisions" to the end.

(3) After sub-paragraph (2) insert—

"(3) Where a DSI matter is recorded under paragraph 11 as a conduct matter by virtue of sub-paragraph (2)—

    (a) the person investigating the DSI matter shall (subject to any determination made by the Commission under paragraph 15(5)) investigate the conduct matter as if appointed or designated to do so, and

    (b) the other provisions of this Schedule shall apply in relation to that matter accordingly."

17 (1) Paragraph 25 (appeals to Commission with respect to an investigation) is amended as follows.

    (2) In sub-paragraph (2) (rights of appeal)—

      (a) for paragraph (a)(ii) substitute—

        "(ii) about any determination of the appropriate authority relating to the taking (or not taking) of action in respect of any matters dealt with in the report on the investigation;";

      (b) for paragraph (c) substitute—

        "(ba) a right of appeal against any determination by the appropriate authority that a person to whose conduct the investigation related has a case to answer in respect of misconduct or gross misconduct or has no case to answer;

        (c) a right of appeal against any determination by the appropriate authority relating to the taking (or not taking) of action in respect of any matters dealt with in the report; and

        (d) a right of appeal against any determination by the appropriate authority under paragraph 24(2)(a) as a result of which it is not required to send the Director of Public Prosecutions a copy of the report;".

    (3) In sub-paragraph (3) (power of Commission to require appropriate authority to submit memorandum on an appeal)—

      (a) before paragraph (a) insert—

        "(za) sets out whether the appropriate authority has determined that a person to whose conduct the investigation related has a case to answer in respect of misconduct or gross misconduct or has no case to answer;";

      (b) for paragraphs (a) and (b) substitute—

        "(a) sets out what action (if any) the authority has determined that it is required to or will, in its discretion, take in respect of the matters dealt with in the report;";

      (c) in paragraph (c), for "any person whose conduct is the subject-matter of the report" substitute "a person to whose conduct the investigation related";

      (d) after paragraph (c) insert "and

        (d) if the appropriate authority made a determination under paragraph 24(2)(a) as a result of which it is not required to send the Director of Public Prosecutions a copy of the report, sets out the reasons for that determination;".

    (4) In sub-paragraph (5) (determinations to be made by Commission on an appeal)—

      (a) after "shall determine" insert "such of the following as it considers appropriate in the circumstances";

      (b) for paragraph (c) substitute—

        "(c) whether the appropriate authority—

          (i) has made such a determination as is mentioned in sub-paragraph (3)(za) that the Commission considers to be appropriate in respect of the matters dealt with in the report, and

          (ii) has determined that it is required to or will, in its discretion, take the action (if any) that the Commission considers to be so appropriate; and

        (d) whether the conditions set out in paragraph 24(2A) and (2B) are satisfied in respect of the report."

    (5) In sub-paragraph (9) (action to be taken by Commission when it determines appropriate authority is not taking appropriate action) for "is not proposing to take the action in consequence of" substitute "has not made a determination as to whether there is a case for a person to whose conduct the investigation related to answer that the Commission considers appropriate or has not determined that it is required to or will, in its discretion, take the action in respect of the matters dealt with in".

(6) After sub-paragraph (9) insert—

"(9A) If, on an appeal under this paragraph, the Commission determines that the conditions set out paragraph 24(2A) and (2B) are satisfied in respect of the report, it shall direct the appropriate authority—

(a) to notify the Director of Public Prosecutions of the Commission's determination, and

(b) to send the Director a copy of the report."

18 (1) Paragraph 27 (duties with respect to disciplinary proceedings) is amended as follows.

(2) In sub-paragraph (1) (application of paragraph) in each of paragraphs (a) and (b), for "proposing to" substitute "required to or will, in its discretion,".

(3) In sub-paragraph (3) (recommendations that may be made by Commission in certain circumstances)—

(a) before paragraph (a) insert—

"(za) that the person has a case to answer in respect of misconduct or gross misconduct or has no case to answer in relation to his conduct to which the investigation related;";

(b) for paragraph (a) substitute—

"(a) that disciplinary proceedings of the form specified in the recommendation are brought against that person in respect of his conduct to which the investigation related;";

(c) in paragraph (b), for "include such charges" substitute "deal with such aspects of that conduct".

19 After paragraph 28 insert—

"Minor definitions

29 In this Part of this Schedule—

"gross misconduct" means a breach of the Standards of Professional Behaviour that is so serious as to justify dismissal;

"misconduct" means a breach of the Standards of Professional Behaviour;

"the person investigating", in relation to a complaint, recordable conduct matter or DSI matter, means the person appointed or designated to investigate that complaint or matter;

"prescribed" means prescribed by regulations made by the Secretary of State;

"the Standards of Professional Behaviour" means the standards so described in, and established by, regulations made by the Secretary of State."

SCHEDULE 24   Section 140

SECTION 327A OF CRIMINAL JUSTICE ACT 2003: MEANING OF "CHILD SEX OFFENCE"

The following is the Schedule to be inserted as Schedule 34A to the Criminal Justice Act 2003 (c. 44)—

"SCHEDULE 34A

CHILD SEX OFFENCES FOR PURPOSES OF SECTION 327A

Offences under provisions repealed by Sexual Offences Act 2003

1 An offence under—

(a) section 5 or 6 of the Sexual Offences Act 1956 (intercourse with girl under 13 or 16), or

(b) section 28 of that Act (causing or encouraging the prostitution of, intercourse with or indecent assault on girl under 16).

2 An offence under any of—
   (a) section 1 of that Act (rape),
   (b) section 10 of that Act (incest by a man), and
   (c) sections 12 to 16 of that Act (buggery, indecency between men, indecent assault and assault with intent to commit buggery),
   where the victim or (as the case may be) the other party was under 18 at the time of the offence.

3 An offence under section 1 of the Indecency with Children Act 1960 (indecent conduct towards child under 14).

4 An offence under section 9 of the Theft Act 1968 of burglary with intent to commit rape where the intended offence was an offence against a person under 18.

5 An offence under section 54 of the Criminal Law Act 1977 (incitement of child under 16 to commit incest).

6 An offence under section 3 of the Sexual Offences (Amendment) Act 2000 (abuse of position of trust).

Other offences

7 An offence under any of—
   (a) sections 5 to 8 of the Sexual Offences Act 2003 (rape and other offences against children under 13),
   (b) sections 9 to 15 of that Act (child sex offences),
   (c) sections 16 to 19 of that Act (abuse of position of trust),
   (d) sections 25 and 26 of that Act (familial child sex offences), and
   (e) sections 47 to 50 of that Act (abuse of children through prostitution and pornography).

8 An offence under any of—
   (a) sections 1 to 4 of that Act (rape, assault and causing sexual activity without consent),
   (b) sections 30 to 41 of that Act (persons with a mental disorder impeding choice, inducements etc to persons with a mental disorder, and care workers for persons with a mental disorder), and
   (c) section 61 of that Act (administering a substance with intent),
   where the victim of the offence was under 18 at the time of the offence.

9 An offence under section 62 or 63 of that Act (committing an offence with intent to commit a sexual offence and trespass with intent to commit a sexual offence) where the intended offence was an offence against a person under 18.

10 An offence under section 66 or 67 of that Act (exposure and voyeurism) where the victim or intended victim of the offence was under 18 at the time of the offence.

11 An offence under—
   (a) section 1 of the Protection of Children Act 1978 (indecent photographs of children), or
   (b) section 160 of the Criminal Justice Act 1988 (possession of indecent photograph of child).

12 An offence under section 170 of the Customs and Excise Management Act 1979 (penalty for fraudulent evasion of duty etc) in relation to goods prohibited to be imported under section 42 of the Customs Consolidation Act 1876 (indecent or obscene articles) where the prohibited goods included any indecent photograph showing a person under 18.

13 An offence under section 63 of the Criminal Justice and Immigration Act 2008 (possession of extreme pornographic images) in relation to an image showing a person under 18.

General

14 A reference in this Schedule to an offence ("offence A") includes—
   (a) a reference to an attempt to commit offence A,
   (b) a reference to a conspiracy to commit offence A,

(c) a reference to incitement to commit offence A,

(d) a reference to an offence under Part 2 of the Serious Crime Act 2007 in relation to which offence A is the offence (or one of the offences) which the person intended or believed would be committed, and

(e) a reference to aiding and abetting, counselling or procuring the commission of offence A.

15 A reference in this Schedule to an offence ("offence A") includes—

(a) a reference to an offence under section 70 of the Army Act 1955, section 70 of the Air Force Act 1955 or section 42 of the Naval Discipline Act 1957 as respects which the corresponding civil offence (within the meaning given by the section in question) is offence A, and

(b) a reference to an offence under section 42 of the Armed Forces Act 2006 as respects which the corresponding offence under the law of England and Wales (within the meaning given by that section) is offence A;

and section 48 of that Act (attempts etc. outside England and Wales) applies for the purposes of paragraph (b) as if the reference in subsection (3)(b) to any of the following provisions of that Act were a reference to that paragraph."

SCHEDULE 25
AMENDMENTS TO ARMED FORCES LEGISLATION

Section 145

PART 1
COURTS-MARTIAL (APPEALS) ACT 1968

1 The Courts-Martial (Appeals) Act 1968 (c. 20) has effect subject to the following amendments.

Power to dismiss certain appeals following references by the CCRC

2 After section 25B insert—

"Appeals following references by the CCRC

25C Power to dismiss certain appeals following references by the CCRC

(1) This section applies where there is an appeal under this Part following a reference by the Criminal Cases Review Commission under section 12A(1)(a), (7) or (8) of the Criminal Appeal Act 1995.

(2) Notwithstanding anything in section 12, 21 or 25 of this Act, the Appeal Court may dismiss the appeal if—

(a) the only ground for allowing it would be that there has been a development in the law since the date of the conviction or finding that is the subject of the appeal, and

(b) the condition in subsection (3) is met.

(3) The condition in this subsection is that if—

(a) the reference had not been made, but

(b) the appellant had made (and had been entitled to make) an application for an extension of time within which to seek leave to appeal on the ground of the development in the law,

the Court would not think it appropriate to grant the application by exercising the power conferred by section 9(3)."

Interim hospital orders

3 Section 16(5) (effect of interim hospital order made by Appeal Court) is omitted.

4 Section 25B(3) (as substituted by the Armed Forces Act 2006) (effect of interim hospital order made by Appeal Court) is omitted.

5 Before section 36 (but after the cross-heading preceding it) insert—

"35A Effect of interim hospital orders

(1) This section applies where the Appeal Court—

(a) make an interim hospital order by virtue of any provision of this Part, or

(b) renew an interim hospital order so made.

(2) The Court Martial shall be treated for the purposes of section 38(7) of the Mental Health Act 1983 (absconding offenders) as the court that made the order."

6 In section 36 (powers of Court under Part 2 which are exercisable by single judge), in subsection (1) after paragraph (h) insert—

"(ha) to renew an interim hospital order made by them by virtue of any provision of this Part;".

Evidence

7 (1) Section 28 (evidence) is amended as follows.

(2) In subsection (1), at the beginning insert "For the purposes of an appeal or an application for leave to appeal,".

(3) In that subsection, for paragraph (b) substitute—

"(b) order any witness to attend for examination and be examined before the Court (whether or not he was called in the proceedings from which the appeal lies); and".

(4) After subsection (1) insert—

"(1A) The power conferred by subsection (1)(a) may be exercised so as to require the production of any document, exhibit or other thing mentioned in that subsection to—

(a) the Appeal Court;

(b) the appellant;

(c) the respondent."

(5) In subsection (4), at the beginning insert "For the purposes of an appeal or an application for leave to appeal,".

(6) After subsection (4) insert—

"(5) In this section, "respondent" includes a person who will be a respondent if leave to appeal is granted."

Appeals against procedural directions

8 In section 36C (appeals against procedural directions), subsections (1) and (2) are omitted.

Detention of accused pending appeal to Supreme Court

9 (1) Section 43 (as amended by the Armed Forces Act 2006) (detention of accused on appeal by Crown) is amended as follows.

(2) In subsection (1) for "may make an order under this section" substitute "shall make one of the orders specified in subsection (1A)".

(3) In subsection (1A)—

(a) for "An order under this section is" substitute "The orders specified in this subsection are",

(b) the word "or" at the end of paragraph (a) is omitted, and

(c) after paragraph (b) insert—

"(c) an order that the accused be released without bail."

(4) After subsection (1B) insert—

"(1C) The Appeal Court may make an order within subsection (1A)(c) only if they think that it is in the interests of justice that the accused should not be liable to be detained as a result of the decision of the Supreme Court on the appeal."

(5) In subsection (2) for "under this section" substitute "within subsection (1A)(a) or (b)".

(6) For subsection (5) substitute—

"(5) The accused shall not be liable to be detained again as a result of the decision of the Supreme Court on the appeal if—

(a) the Appeal Court have made an order within subsection (1A)(c), or

(b) the Appeal Court have made an order within subsection (1A)(a) or (b) but the order has ceased to have effect by virtue of subsection (2) or the accused has been released or discharged by virtue of subsection (3)."

PART 2
ARMED FORCES ACT 2006

10 The Armed Forces Act 2006 (c. 52) has effect subject to the following amendments.

Consecutive custodial sentences

11 In section 188(4) (consecutive custodial sentences), after "Part 12 of the 2003 Act" insert "or under Part 2 of the Criminal Justice Act 1991".

Dangerous offenders

12 In section 209 (offenders under 18 convicted of certain serious offences), in subsection (7) for "sections 221, 222 and 227" substitute "section 226(2) of the 2003 Act (as applied by section 221(2) of this Act) and section 227 of this Act".

13 (1) Section 219 (dangerous offenders aged 18 or over) is amended as follows.

(2) In subsection (1) for the words from "a person" to the end substitute "—

(a) a person aged 18 or over is convicted by the Court Martial of an offence under section 42 (criminal conduct),

(b) the corresponding offence under the law of England and Wales is a serious offence, and

(c) the court is of the required opinion (defined by section 223)."

(3) For subsections (2) and (3) substitute—

"(2) Section 225(2) to (4) of the 2003 Act apply in relation to the offender.

(3) In section 225(2) and (3A) of the 2003 Act (as applied by subsection (2)), references to "the offence" are to be read as references to the offence under section 42 of this Act."

(4) For the italic cross-heading before section 219 substitute "*Required or discretionary sentences for particular offences*".

14 (1) Section 220 (certain violent or sexual offences: offenders aged 18 or over) is amended as follows.

(2) In subsection (1) for the words from "a person" to the end substitute "—

(a) a person aged 18 or over is convicted by the Court Martial of an offence under section 42 (criminal conduct),

(b) the corresponding offence under the law of England and Wales is a specified offence,

(c) the court is of the required opinion (defined by section 223), and

      (d) where the corresponding offence under the law of England and Wales is a serious offence, the case is not one in which the court is required by section 225(2) of the 2003 Act (as applied by section 219(2) of this Act) to impose a sentence of imprisonment for life."

  (3) For subsection (2) substitute—

    "(2) Section 227(2) to (5) of the 2003 Act apply in relation to the offender."

  (4) In subsection (3)—

    (a) for "section 227" substitute "section 227(2) to (5)",

    (b) before paragraph (a) insert—

      "(za) the reference in section 227(2A) to "the offence" is to be read as a reference to the offence under section 42 of this Act;", and

    (c) in paragraph (a) for "subsection (2)(b)" substitute "subsection (2C)(b)".

  (5) After subsection (3) insert—

    "(3A) The power conferred by section 227(6) of the 2003 Act includes power to amend section 227(2B) as applied by this section."

15 (1) Section 221 (dangerous offenders aged under 18) is amended as follows.

  (2) In subsection (1) for the words from "a person" to the end substitute "—

    (a) a person aged under 18 is convicted by the Court Martial of an offence under section 42 (criminal conduct),

    (b) the corresponding offence under the law of England and Wales is a serious offence, and

    (c) the court is of the required opinion (defined by section 223)."

  (3) For subsection (2) substitute—

    "(2) Section 226(2) to (4) of the 2003 Act apply in relation to the offender."

  (4) In subsection (3)—

    (a) for the words from the beginning to "is" substitute "In section 226(2) of the 2003 Act (as applied subsection (2))", and

    (b) in paragraphs (a) and (b) the words "in section 226(2)" are omitted.

  (5) Subsection (4) is omitted.

16 (1) Section 222 (offenders aged under 18: certain violent or sexual offences) is amended as follows.

  (2) In subsection (1), in paragraph (d) for the words from "section 221" to the end substitute "section 226(2) of the 2003 Act (as applied by section 221(2) of this Act) to impose a sentence of detention for life."

  (3) For subsection (2) substitute—

    "(2) Section 228(2) to (5) of the 2003 Act apply in relation to the offender."

  (4) In subsection (3)—

    (a) for "section 228" substitute "section 228(2) to (5)", and

    (b) in paragraph (a) for "subsection (2)(b)" substitute "subsection (2B)(b)".

  (5) After subsection (3) insert—

    "(3A) The power conferred by section 228(7) of the 2003 Act includes power to amend section 228(2A) as applied by this section."

17 (1) Section 223 (the required opinion for the purposes of sections 219 to 222) is amended as follows.

  (2) In subsection (1) for "219(2), 220(2), 221(2)" substitute "219(1), 220(1), 221(1)".

  (3) In subsection (2) for "section 229(2) to (4)" substitute "section 229(2) and (2A)".

  (4) In subsection (3) the words "to (4)" are omitted.

18 (1) Section 228 (appeals where previous convictions set aside) is amended as follows.

  (2) For subsection (1) substitute—

    "(1) Subsection (3) applies where—

      (a) a sentence has been imposed on any person under section 225(3) or 227(2) of the 2003 Act (as applied by section 219(2) or 220(2) of this Act),

(b) the condition in section 225(3A) or (as the case may be) 227(2A) of the 2003 Act was met but the condition in section 225(3B) or (as the case may be) 227(2B) of that Act was not, and

(c) any previous conviction of his without which the condition in section 225(3A) or (as the case may be) 227(2A) would not have been met has been subsequently set aside on appeal."

19 In section 237 (purposes of sentencing), in subsection (3)(b)—
(a) for "to 222" substitute ", 221", and
(b) for "any of sections 225 to 228" substitute "section 225(2) or 226(2)".

20 In section 256 (pre-sentence reports), in subsection (1)(c) for the words from "section" to the end substitute "section 219(1), 220(1), 221(1) or 222(1) (sentences for dangerous offenders)."

21 In section 260 (discretionary custodial sentences: general restrictions), in subsection (1)(b) for the words from "as a result" to the end substitute "under section 225(2) or 226(2) of the 2003 Act (as applied by section 219(2) or 221(2) of this Act) or as a result of any of sections 225 to 227 of this Act."

22 In section 261 (length of discretionary custodial sentences: general provision)—
(a) in subsection (1) for "falling to be imposed as a result of section 219(2) or 221(2)" substitute "imposed under section 225 or 226 of the 2003 Act (as applied by section 219(2) or 221(2) of this Act)", and
(b) in subsection (3) for "required minimum sentences" substitute "sentences that may or must be imposed".

23 In section 273 (review of unduly lenient sentences by Court Martial Appeal Court), in subsection (6)(b) for "section 219, 220, 221, 222, 225, 226 or 227" substitute "section 225(2) or 226(2) of the 2003 Act (as applied by section 219(2) or 221(2) of this Act) or by section 225, 226 or 227 of this Act".

Restrictions on imposing community punishment

24 In section 253(2)(h) (duties in complying with section 252) for "section 151(2) of the 2003 Act as applied by section 270 of this Act" substitute "section 270B(4)".

25 In section 254(1) (savings for powers to mitigate sentence etc.) for "and 270" substitute ", 270 and 270B".

26 (1) Section 270 (community punishments: general restrictions etc.) is amended as follows.
(2) After subsection (6) insert—
"(6A) The fact that by virtue of any provision of this section—
(a) a community punishment may be awarded in respect of an offence, or
(b) particular restrictions on liberty may be imposed by a community punishment, does not require a court to award such a punishment or to impose those restrictions."
(3) Subsection (7) is omitted.
(4) In subsection (8)—
(a) the word "Accordingly" is omitted; and
(b) for "151(2) of the 2003 Act as applied by this section" substitute "270B(4)".

27 After section 270 insert—
"**270A Community punishment available only for offences punishable with imprisonment or for offenders previously fined**

The power to award a community punishment is only exercisable in respect of an offence if—
(a) a person who is guilty of such an offence is liable to imprisonment; or
(b) in any other case, section 270B(4) confers power to award such a punishment.

270B Community punishment for offender previously fined

(1) This section provides for the award of a community punishment by a court in respect of an offence ("the current offence") committed by a person to whom subsection (2) or (3) applies.

(2) This subsection applies to the offender if—

(a) a person guilty of the current offence is liable to imprisonment,

(b) the offender was aged 16 or over when he was convicted;

(c) on three or more previous occasions the offender has, on conviction by a court for an offence committed by him after attaining the age of 16, had passed on him a sentence consisting only of a fine; and

(d) despite the effect of section 238(1)(b), the court would not (apart from this section) regard the current offence, or the combination of the current offence and one or more offences associated with it, as being serious enough to warrant a community punishment.

(3) This subsection applies to the offender if—

(a) a person guilty of the current offence is not liable to imprisonment;

(b) the offender was aged 16 or over when he was convicted; and

(c) on three or more previous occasions the offender has, on conviction by a court for an offence committed by him after attaining the age of 16, had passed on him a sentence consisting only of a fine.

(4) The court may award a community punishment in respect of the current offence if it considers that, having regard to all the circumstances including the matters referred to in subsection (5), it would be in the interests of justice to award such a punishment.

(5) Those matters are—

(a) the nature of the offences to which the previous convictions mentioned in subsection (2)(c) or (3)(c) (as the case may be) relate and their relevance to the current offence; and

(b) the time that has elapsed since the offender's conviction of each of those offences

(6) In subsections (2)(c) and (3)(c) "conviction by a court" means—

(a) a conviction by a civilian court in any part of the United Kingdom for a service offence or for an offence punishable by the law of that part of the United Kingdom; or

(b) a conviction in service disciplinary proceedings.

(7) For the purposes of subsections (2)(c) and (3)(c) a compensation order or a service compensation order awarded in service disciplinary proceedings does not form part of an offender's sentence.

(8) It is immaterial for the purposes of subsections (2)(c) and (3)(c) whether on previous occasions a court has passed on the offender a sentence not consisting only of a fine.

(9) This section does not limit the extent to which a court may, in accordance with section 238(1)(b) and (2), treat any previous convictions of the offender as increasing the seriousness of an offence.

(10) In this section—

(a) "service disciplinary proceedings" means proceedings (whether or not before a court) in respect of a service offence; and

(b) any reference to a conviction or sentence, in the context of such proceedings, includes anything that under section 376(1) to (3) is to be treated as a conviction or sentence."

Review of sentence on reference by Attorney General

28 In section 273 (reviews of unduly lenient sentencing by Court Martial Appeal Court) for subsection (7) substitute—

"(7) Where a reference under subsection (1) relates to a case in which the Court Martial made an order specified in subsection (7A), the Court Martial Appeal Court may not, in deciding what sentence is appropriate for the case, make any allowance for the fact that the offender is being sentenced for a second time.

(7A) The orders specified in this subsection are—

    (a) an order under section 269(2) of the 2003 Act (determination of minimum term in relation to mandatory life sentence);

    (b) an order under section 82A(2) of the Sentencing Act (determination of minimum term in relation to discretionary life sentences and certain other sentences)."

Compensation for miscarriages of justice

29 (1) Section 276 (compensation for miscarriages of justice) is amended as follows.

  (2) In subsection (1) for "subsections (2) and (3)" substitute "subsections (2) to (3A)".

  (3) At the end of subsection (3) insert "before the end of the period of 2 years beginning with the date on which the conviction of the person concerned is reversed or he is pardoned.

    (3A) But the Secretary of State may direct that an application for compensation made after the end of that period is to be treated as if it had been made within that period if the Secretary of State considers that there are exceptional circumstances which justify doing so."

  (4) For subsection (6) substitute—

    "(6) Section 276A applies in relation to the assessment of the amount of the compensation."

  (5) After subsection (7) insert—

    "(7A) But in a case where—

        (a) a person's conviction for an offence is quashed on an appeal out of time, and

        (b) the person is to be subject to a retrial,

    the conviction is not to be treated for the purposes of subsection (1) as "reversed" unless and until the person is acquitted of all offences at the retrial or the prosecution indicates that it has decided not to proceed with the retrial."

30 After section 276 insert—

"276A Miscarriages of justice: amount of compensation

  (1) This section applies where an assessor is required to assess the amount of compensation payable to or in respect of a person under section 276 for a miscarriage of justice.

  (2) In assessing so much of any compensation payable under section 276 as is attributable to suffering, harm to reputation or similar damage, the assessor must have regard in particular to—

    (a) the seriousness of the offence of which the person was convicted and the severity of the punishment resulting from the conviction, and

    (b) the conduct of the investigation and prosecution of the offence.

  (3) The assessor may make from the total amount of compensation that the assessor would otherwise have assessed as payable under section 276 any deduction or deductions that the assessor considers appropriate by reason of either or both of the following—

    (a) any conduct of the person appearing to the assessor to have directly or indirectly caused, or contributed to, the conviction concerned; and

    (b) any other convictions of the person and any punishment resulting from them.

  (4) If, having had regard to any matters falling within subsection (3)(a) or (b), the assessor considers that there are exceptional circumstances which justify doing so, the assessor may determine that the amount of compensation payable under section 276 is to be a nominal amount only.

  (5) The total amount of compensation payable to or in respect of a person under section 276 for a particular miscarriage of justice must not exceed the overall compensation limit.

That limit is—
> (a) £1 million in a case to which section 276B applies, and
> (b) £500,000 in any other case.

(6) The total amount of compensation payable under section 276 for a person's loss of earnings or earnings capacity in respect of any one year must not exceed the earnings compensation limit.

> That limit is an amount equal to 1.5 times the median annual gross earnings according to the latest figures published by the Office of National Statistics at the time of the assessment.

(7) The Secretary of State may by order amend subsection (5) or (6) so as to alter any amount for the time being specified as the overall compensation limit or the earnings compensation limit.

276B Cases where person has been detained for at least 10 years

(1) For the purposes of section 276A(5) this section applies to any case where the person concerned ("P") has been in qualifying detention for a period (or total period) of at least 10 years by the time when—
> (a) the conviction is reversed, or
> (b) the pardon is given,

as mentioned in section 276(1).

(2) P was "in qualifying detention" at any time when P was detained in a prison, a hospital or at any other place, if P was so detained—
> (a) by virtue of a sentence passed in respect of the relevant offence,
> (b) under mental health legislation by reason of P's conviction of that offence (disregarding any conditions other than the fact of the conviction that had to be fulfilled in order for P to be so detained), or
> (c) as a result of P's having been ordered to be kept in service custody, or remanded for mental health purposes, in connection with the relevant offence or with any other offence the charge for which was founded on the same facts or evidence as that for the relevant offence.

(3) In calculating the period (or total period) during which P has been in qualifying detention as mentioned in subsection (1), no account is to be taken of any period of time during which P was both—
> (a) in qualifying detention, and
> (b) in excluded concurrent detention.

(4) P was "in excluded concurrent detention" at any time when P was detained in a prison, a hospital or at any other place, if P was so detained—
> (a) during the term of a sentence passed in respect of an offence other than the relevant offence,
> (b) under mental health legislation by reason of P's conviction of any such other offence (disregarding any conditions other than the fact of the conviction that had to be fulfilled in order for P to be so detained), or
> (c) as a result of P's having been ordered to be kept in service custody, or remanded for mental health purposes, in connection with an offence for which P was subsequently convicted other than—
>> (i) the relevant offence, or
>> (ii) any other offence the charge for which was founded on the same facts or evidence as that for the relevant offence.

(5) But P was not "in excluded concurrent detention" at any time by virtue of subsection (4)(a), (b) or (c) if P's conviction of the other offence mentioned in that provision was quashed on appeal, or a pardon was given in respect of it.

(6) In this section—
"kept in service custody" means—
(a) kept in service custody under section 105(2) of the Armed Forces Act 2006, or
(b) kept in military, air-force or naval custody under section 75A(2) of the Army Act 1955 or of the Air Force Act 1955 or section 47G(2) of the Naval Discipline Act 1957 (as the case may be);
"mental health legislation" means—
(a) Part 3 of the Mental Health Act 1983, or
(b) the provisions of any earlier enactment corresponding to Part 3 of that Act;
"the relevant offence" means the offence in respect of which the conviction is quashed or the pardon is given (but see subsection (7));
"remanded for mental health purposes" means remanded or admitted to hospital under section 35, 36 or 38 of the Mental Health Act 1983 or under any corresponding provision of any earlier enactment;
"reversed" has the same meaning as in section 276 of this Act.
(7) If, as a result of the miscarriage of justice—
(a) two or more convictions are reversed, or
(b) a pardon is given in respect of two or more offences,
"the relevant offence" means any of the offences concerned."
31 In section 373 (orders, regulations etc.) in subsection (3)(a), after "113," insert "276A(7),".

Imposition of unpaid work requirement for breach of service community order or overseas service community order

32 In paragraph 14(b) of Schedule 5 (modifications of Schedule 8 to the Criminal Justice Act 2003 as it applies to overseas community orders), for "(3)" substitute "(3A)".

Suspended prison sentences: further conviction or breach of requirement

33 In paragraph 9(1)(b) of Schedule 7 (which provides for paragraph 9 of Schedule 12 to the Criminal Justice Act 2003, as it applies to an order under paragraph 8 of that Schedule made by a service court, to have effect with substituted sub-paragraphs (2) and (3))—
(a) in the substituted text of sub-paragraph (2), after "Part 12" insert "of this Act or under Part 2 of the Criminal Justice Act 1991"; and
(b) in the substituted text of sub-paragraph (3), after "287" insert "of the Armed Forces Act 2006".

PART 3
TRANSITIONAL PROVISIONS

Transitional provisions: compensation for miscarriage of justice

34 (1) Paragraph 29(3) has effect in relation to any application for compensation made in relation to—
(a) a conviction which is reversed, and
(b) a pardon which is given,
on or after the commencement date.
(2) Paragraphs 29(4) and 30 have effect in relation to—
(a) any application for compensation made on or after the commencement date, and
(b) any application for compensation made before that date in relation to which the question whether there is a right to compensation has not been determined before that date by the Secretary of State under section 276(4) of the 2006 Act.

(3) Paragraph 29(5) has effect in relation to any conviction quashed on an appeal out of time in respect of which an application for compensation has not been made before the commencement date.

(4) Paragraph 29(5) so has effect whether a conviction was quashed before, on or after the commencement date.

(5) In the case of—

    (a) a conviction which is reversed, or

    (b) a pardon which is given,

before the commencement date but in relation to which an application for compensation has not been made before that date, any such application must be made before the end of the period of 2 years beginning with that date.

(6) But the Secretary of State may direct that an application for compensation in relation to a case falling within sub-paragraph (5) which is made after the end of that period is to be treated as if it had been made before the end of that period if the Secretary of State considers that there are exceptional circumstances which justify doing so.

(7) In this paragraph—

"the 2006 Act" means the Armed Forces Act 2006 (c. 52);

"application for compensation" means an application for compensation made under section 276(3) of the 2006 Act;

"the commencement date" means the date on which paragraphs 29 and 30 come into force;

"reversed" has the same meaning as in section 276(1) of the 2006 Act (as amended by paragraph 29(5)).

SCHEDULE 26   Section 148
MINOR AND CONSEQUENTIAL AMENDMENTS

PART 1
FINE DEFAULTERS

Magistrates' Courts Act 1980 (c. 43)

1 In section 81(3) of the Magistrates' Courts Act 1980 (enforcement of fines imposed on young offenders) for paragraph (a) substitute—

    "(a) a youth default order under section 39 of the Criminal Justice and Immigration Act 2008; or".

Criminal Justice Act 2003 (c. 44)

2 (1) The Criminal Justice Act 2003 is amended as follows.

  (2) In section 221(2) (provision of attendance centres) after paragraph (b) insert—

    "(c) default orders under section 300 of this Act, or

    (d) youth default orders under section 39 of the Criminal Justice and Immigration Act 2008."

  (3) In section 300 (power to impose unpaid work requirement or curfew requirement on fine defaulter)—

    (a) in subsection (1)—

      (i) for "16" substitute "18", and

      (ii) omit paragraph (b), and

    (b) in subsection (2), omit from "or, as the case may be" to "young offender)".

(4) In Schedule 31 (modifications of community order provisions for purposes of default order) after paragraph 3 insert—

"Attendance centre requirement

3A In its application to a default order, section 214(2) (attendance centre requirement) is modified by the substitution for "not be less than 12 or more than 36" of "be—
  (a) not less than 12, and
  (b) in the case of an amount in default which is specified in the first column of the following Table, not more than the number of hours set out opposite that amount in the second column.

Amount	Number of hours
An amount not exceeding £200	18 hours
An amount exceeding £200 but not exceeding £500	21 hours
An amount exceeding £500 but not exceeding £1,000	24 hours
An amount exceeding £1,000 but not exceeding £2,500	30 hours
An amount exceeding £2,500	36 hours"."

(5) In paragraph 4(5)(a) of that Schedule (modifications of community order provisions for purposes of default order) omit ", (5)".
(6) In paragraph 5 of that Schedule, for "or 3" substitute ", 3 or 3A".

PART 2
OTHER AMENDMENTS

Prison Act 1952 (c. 52)

3 In section 43(1)(aa) of the Prison Act 1952 (provision by Secretary of State of young offender institutions), at the end insert "or other persons who may be lawfully detained there".

Criminal Justice Act 1961 (c. 39)

4 In section 38(3)(c) of the Criminal Justice Act 1961 (construction of references to imprisonment or detention in case of children and young persons) after "in accordance with" insert "a determination of the Secretary of State or of a person authorised by him, in accordance with arrangements made by the Secretary of State or in accordance with".

Children and Young Persons Act 1969 (c. 54)

5 (1) Section 23AA of the Children and Young Persons Act 1969 (electronic monitoring of remand conditions) is amended as follows.
  (2) In subsection (4)—
    (a) paragraph (a) is omitted; and
    (b) in paragraph (b), for "those arrangements" substitute "arrangements currently available in each local justice area which is a relevant area".
  (3) In subsection (8) for "Subsections (8) to (10) of section 3AA" substitute "Subsections (4) to (7) of section 3AC".

Criminal Appeal (Northern Ireland) Act 1980 (c. 47)

6 In section 13A(3) of the Criminal Appeal (Northern Ireland) Act 1980 (grounds for allowing appeal against finding of unfitness to be tried), in paragraph (a) for "the finding" substitute "a finding".

Wildlife and Countryside Act 1981 (c. 69)

7 In section 19XA(1) of the Wildlife and Countryside Act 1981 (constables' powers in connection with samples) for "by this section" substitute "by section 19".

Mental Health Act 1983 (c.20)

8 In section 37 of the Mental Health Act 1983 (powers of court to order hospital admission or guardianship), in subsection (1A)(c) for "any of sections 225 to 228" substitute "section 225(2) or 226(2)".

Repatriation of Prisoners Act 1984 (c. 47)

9 The Repatriation of Prisoners Act 1984 has effect subject to the following amendments.

10 Before section 1 insert—

> *"Transfer of prisoners to or from the United Kingdom".*

11 (1) Section 1 (issue of warrant for transfer) is amended as follows.

　(2) In subsections (2) and (3) for "warrant under this Act" substitute "warrant under this section".

　(3) In subsection (4)—

　　(a) for "warrant under this Act" (in both places) substitute "warrant under this section";

　　(b) in paragraph (b) omit the words "under this Act".

　(4) In subsection (5) (as it applies in cases in which the relevant Minister is the Scottish Ministers and in cases in which the relevant Minister is the Secretary of State) for "warrant under this Act" substitute "warrant under this section".

　(5) In subsection (6) after "warrant" (in the first place it appears) insert "under this section".

　(6) In subsection (7)(b) after "under" insert "any of".

　(7) In subsection (8)—

　　(a) after "similar to" insert "any of";

　　(b) after "respect to" insert "—

　　　(a) "; and

　　(c) at the end insert "; or

　　　(b) the transfer between different countries and territories (or different parts of a country or territory) of responsibility for the detention and release of persons who are required to be so detained in one of those countries or territories (or parts of a country or territory) but are present in the other country or territory (or part of a country or territory)."

12 (1) Section 2 (transfer out of the United Kingdom) is amended as follows.

　(2) In subsection (1) after "warrant" insert "under section 1".

　(3) In subsection (4)—

　　(a) in paragraph (a) for "warrant under this Act" substitute "warrant under section 1"; and

　　(b) in paragraph (b)(i) (as it continues to have effect in relation to prisoners sentenced for offences committed before 4th April 2005) after "33(1)(b)" insert ", (1A)".

　(4) In subsection (7) for "warrant under this Act" substitute "warrant under section 1".

13 (1) Section 3 (transfer into the United Kingdom) is amended as follows.

　(2) In subsection (1), after "a warrant" insert "under section 1".

(3) In subsections (2), (4) and (6), for "warrant under this Act" substitute "warrant under section 1".

(4) In subsection (7)—

    (a) at the beginning insert "Part 1 of"; and

    (b) for "warrant under this Act" substitute "warrant under section 1".

(5) Subsection (10) is omitted.

14 (1) Section 4 (temporary return) is amended as follows

   (2) In subsection (1)—

    (a) for "warrant under this Act" substitute "warrant under section 1";

    (b) in paragraph (a), after "Kingdom" (in the second place it appears) insert ", or from which responsibility for his detention and release has previously been transferred to the United Kingdom,";

    (c) in paragraph (b), after "transferred" insert ", or to which responsibility for his detention and release has previously been transferred,".

   (3) In subsection (2)—

    (a) for "a warrant under this Act" substitute "a warrant under section 1";

    (b) for "earlier warrant under this Act" substitute "earlier warrant under section 1 or section 4A".

   (4) In subsection (3)—

    (a) for "issued under this Act" substitute "issued under section 1";

    (b) after "an earlier warrant" insert "under section 1 or section 4A".

   (5) In subsection (4) for "warrant under this Act" substitute "warrant under section 1".

   (6) After subsection (5) insert—

    "(6) Any reference in subsection (5)(a) to the prisoner having previously been transferred into or from Scotland includes a reference to responsibility for his detention and release having previously been transferred to or from the Scottish Ministers (as the case may be).".

15 Before section 5 (operation of warrant and retaking prisoners) insert—

    "Supplementary and general provisions".

16 (1) Section 5 (operation of warrant and retaking prisoners) is amended as follows.

   (2) In subsection (1)—

    (a) for "under this Act" substitute "under section 1"; and

    (b) after "this section" insert "(apart from subsection (9))".

   (3) After subsection (8) insert—

    "(9) Where—

      (a) a warrant under section 4A has been issued, and

      (b) the relevant person is a person to whom subsection (3) of that section applies,

    subsections (2) to (8) above apply for the purposes of that warrant (but with the modifications contained in subsection (10)), except (without prejudice to section 4C(4) or any enactment contained otherwise than in this Act) in relation to any time when the relevant person is required to be detained in accordance with provisions contained in the warrant by virtue of section 4C(1)(b).

    (10) In their application for the purposes of a warrant under section 4A those subsections shall have effect as if—

      (a) any reference to the warrant under section 1 (however expressed) were a reference to the warrant under section 4A;

      (b) any reference to the prisoner were a reference to the relevant person;

      (c) in subsection (4)—

        (i) in paragraph (a) for "that person" there were substituted "the authorised person"; and

(ii) paragraph (b) were omitted; and

(d) in subsection (8)(a) for "transfer of a prisoner to or from Scotland" there were substituted "transfer of responsibility for the detention and release of the relevant person to the Scottish Ministers"."

17 (1) Section 6 (revocation etc. of warrants) is amended as follows.

(2) In subsection (1)—

(a) for "warrant under this Act" (in the first place they appear) substitute "warrant under section 1";

(b) in paragraph (b) for "this Act" substitute "that section".

(3) After subsection (1) insert—

"(1A) Subject to section 4A(8), if at any time it appears to the relevant Minister appropriate, in order that effect may be given to any such arrangements as are mentioned in section 4A(5)(a) for a warrant under section 4A to be revoked or varied, he may as the case may require—

(a) revoke that warrant; or

(b) revoke that warrant and issue a new warrant under section 4A containing provision superseding some or all of the provisions of the previous warrant."

(4) In subsections (2) and (3) after "subsection (1)(b)" insert "or (1A)(b)".

(5) In subsection (5)(a), for the words from "where" to the end substitute "in a case where—

(i) the warrant was issued under section 1 and provides for the transfer of the prisoner to or from Scotland; or

(ii) the warrant was issued under section 4A and provides for the transfer of responsibility for the detention and release of the relevant person to those Ministers;".

18 (1) Section 8 is amended as follows.

(2) In subsection (1) after the definition of "the prisoner" insert "; and
"the relevant person" has the meaning given by section 4A(5)(b)."

(3) In subsection (3)—

(a) in paragraph (a) after "section 1(1)(a)" insert "or 4A(5)(a)";

(b) in paragraph (b) for "such a party" substitute "a party to such international arrangements as are mentioned in section 1(1)(a)";

(c) after paragraph (b) (but before the "or" after that paragraph) insert—

"(ba) that the appropriate authority of a country or territory which is a party to such international arrangements as are mentioned in section 4A(5)(a) has agreed to the transfer of responsibility for the detention and release of a particular person in accordance with those arrangements,".

19 (1) The Schedule (operation of certain enactments in relation to the prisoner) is amended as follows.

(2) For the cross-heading before paragraph 1 substitute—

"PART 1
WARRANTS UNDER SECTION 1

Application of Part 1".

(3) In paragraph 1—

(a) at the beginning insert "This Part of";

(b) after "under" insert "section 1 of"; and

(c) after "; and in" insert "this Part of".

(4) In paragraph 2 (as it applies in England and Wales in relation to offences committed before 4 April 2005)—

    (a) in sub-paragraph (1A)(a) (which defines the enactments relating to release on licence) after "33(1)(b) insert ", (1A)"; and

    (b) after sub-paragraph (2) insert—

        "(2A) If the warrant specifies that the offence or any of the offences in relation to which a determinate sentence is to be served corresponds to murder or an offence specified in Schedule 15 to the Criminal Justice Act 2003 (specified violent or sexual offences), any reference (however expressed) in Part 2 of the Criminal Justice Act 1991 to a person sentenced for an offence specified in that Schedule is to be read as including a reference to the prisoner."

(5) In paragraph 2 (as it applies in England and Wales in relation to offences committed on or after 4 April 2005), after sub-paragraph (3) insert—

        "(3A) If the warrant specifies that the offence or any of the offences in relation to which a determinate sentence is to be served corresponds to murder or an offence specified in Schedule 15 to the Criminal Justice Act 2003 (specified violent or sexual offences), any reference (however expressed) in Chapter 6 of Part 12 of that Act to a person sentenced for an offence specified in that Schedule is to be read as including a reference to the prisoner."

(6) After paragraph 8 insert—

"PART 2
WARRANTS UNDER SECTION 4A TRANSFERRING RESPONSIBILITY TO THE RELEVANT MINISTER

9 This Part of this Schedule applies where a warrant is issued under section 4A providing for the transfer of responsibility for the detention and release of the relevant person to the relevant Minister (within the meaning of that section).

10 Paragraphs 2 to 8 above apply as they apply where a warrant is issued under section 1, but with the following modifications.

11 Any reference to "the relevant provisions" is to be read as a reference to the provisions contained in the warrant by virtue of section 4C(1)(b).

12 (1) Any reference to the prisoner is to be read as a reference to the relevant person.

    (2) Sub-paragraph (1) does not apply to the words "a short-term or long-term prisoner" in paragraph 2(3) (as it applies in Scotland to repatriated prisoners any of whose sentences were imposed on or after 1 October 1993).

13 In paragraph 2 (as it applies in Scotland to repatriated prisoners any of whose sentences were imposed on or after 1 October 1993) the reference to prisoners repatriated to Scotland is to be read as a reference to any relevant person—

    (a) in whose case the warrant under section 4A transfers responsibility for his detention and release from a country or territory outside the British Islands to the Scottish Ministers; and

    (b) whose sentence or any of whose sentences in that country or territory were imposed on or after 1 October 1993.

14 The reference in paragraph 7 to the time of the prisoner's transfer into the United Kingdom is to be read as a reference to the time at which the warrant under section 4A was issued."

Police and Criminal Evidence Act 1984 (c. 60)

20 (1) In section 37B of the Police and Criminal Evidence Act 1984 (consultation with the Director of Public Prosecutions) in subsection (9) (meaning of caution)—

  (a) after paragraph (a) (and before the word "and" immediately following it) insert—

      "(aa) a youth conditional caution within the meaning of Chapter 1 of Part 4 of the Crime and Disorder Act 1998"; and

  (b) in paragraph (b), for "of the Crime and Disorder Act 1998" substitute "of that Act".

  (2) In section 63B of that Act (testing for presence of Class A drugs) in subsection (7) (disclosure of information obtained from drug samples) in paragraph (aa) after "Criminal Justice Act 2003" insert "or a youth conditional caution under Chapter 1 of Part 4 of the Crime and Disorder Act 1998".

Criminal Justice Act 1987 (c. 38)

21 In section 1(17) of the Criminal Justice Act 1987 (application of Serious Fraud Office provisions to Northern Ireland), for "Attorney General for Northern Ireland" substitute "Advocate General for Northern Ireland".

Criminal Justice Act 1988 (c. 33)

22 The Criminal Justice Act 1988 has effect subject to the following amendments.

23 In section 36 (reviews of sentencing), in subsection (2)(b)(iii) for "any of sections 225 to 228" substitute "section 225(2) or 226(2)".

24 In section 160(1) (offence of possession of indecent photographs of children) for "Subject to subsection (1A)," substitute "Subject to section 160A,".

Criminal Justice (Evidence, Etc.) (Northern Ireland) Order 1988 (S.I. 1988/1847 (N.I. 17))

25 In article 15(5) of the Criminal Justice (Evidence, Etc.) (Northern Ireland) Order 1988 (possession of indecent photographs of children) after "Article 2(2)" insert ", (2A)".

Football Spectators Act 1989 (c. 37)

26 In paragraph 1(c), (k) and (q) of Schedule 1 to the Football Spectators Act 1989 (offences)—

  (a) for "Part III" substitute "Part 3 or 3A"; and

  (b) for "(racial hatred)" substitute "(hatred by reference to race etc)".

Criminal Justice (International Co-operation) Act 1990 (c. 5)

27 In section 6(7) of the Criminal Justice (International Co-operation) Act 1990 (transfer of overseas prisoner to give evidence or assist investigation in the United Kingdom), for the words from "having been" to the end of paragraph (b) substitute "—

  (b) having been transferred there, or responsibility for his detention and release having been transferred there, from the United Kingdom under the Repatriation of Prisoners Act 1984;

  (c) having been transferred there, or responsibility for his detention and release having been transferred there, under any similar provision or arrangement from any other country or territory,".

Broadcasting Act 1990 (c. 42)

28 (1) Section 167 of the Broadcasting Act 1990 (power to make copies of recordings) is amended as follows.

  (2) In subsection (4)(b), after "section 24" insert "or 29H".

  (3) In subsection (5)(b), after "section 22" insert "or 29F".

Criminal Justice Act 1991 (c. 53)

29 (1) The Criminal Justice Act 1991 is amended as follows.

(2) In section 43(5) (young offenders), for "under this Part" substitute "under any provision of this Part other than section 33(1A)".

(3) In section 44(6) (disapplication of certain provisions for prisoners serving extended sentences) for "section 46" substitute "section 46(2)".

(4) In section 46(3) (definition of persons liable to removal from the United Kingdom) after "for the purposes of this section" insert "and the following provisions of this Part".

(5) In section 46B(5) (re-entry into United Kingdom of offender removed early from prison), after "subsections (1)" insert ", (1A)".

(6) In paragraph 10(3)(d) of Schedule 3 (reciprocal enforcement of certain orders)—

(a) for "references in paragraph 3 to a day centre were references to" substitute "in paragraph 3 "day centre" meant", and

(b) at the end insert "or an attendance centre provided under section 221 of that Act".

(7) Sub-paragraph (6) extends to England and Wales and Northern Ireland only.

Prisoners and Criminal Proceedings (Scotland) Act 1993 (c. 9)

30 In section 10 of the Prisoners and Criminal Proceedings (Scotland) Act 1993 (life prisoners transferred to Scotland), after subsection (4) insert—

"(4A) The reference in subsection (4)(b) above to a person who has been transferred to Scotland in pursuance of a warrant under the Repatriation of Prisoners Act 1984 includes a reference to a person who is detained in Scotland in pursuance of a warrant issued by the Scottish Ministers under section 4A of that Act (warrant transferring responsibility for detention and release of offender).

(4B) Such a person is to be taken to have been transferred when the warrant under section 4A of that Act was issued in respect of that person."

Crime (Sentences) Act 1997 (c. 43)

31 The Crime (Sentences) Act 1997 has effect subject to the following amendments.

32 (1) Schedule 1 (transfer of prisoners within the British Islands) is amended as follows.

(2) In paragraph 8(2)(a) (as it continues to have effect in relation to prisoners serving sentences of imprisonment for offences committed before 4th April 2005), after "46" insert ", 50A".

(3) In paragraph 8(4)(a) (as it continues to have effect in relation to prisoners serving sentences of imprisonment for offences committed before 4th April 2005), after "46" insert ", 50A".

(4) Any reference in paragraph 8(2)(a) or (4)(a) to section 39 of the 1991 Act is to be read as a reference to section 254(1) of the Criminal Justice Act 2003 (c. 44) in relation to any prisoner to whom paragraph 19 of Schedule 2 to the Criminal Justice Act 2003 (Commencement No. 8 and Transitional and Saving Provisions) Order 2005 (S.I. 2005/950) applies.

(5) In paragraph 9(2)(a) (as it continues to have effect in relation to prisoners serving sentences of imprisonment for offences committed before 4th April 2005), after "46" insert ", 50A".

(6) In paragraph 9(4)(a) (as it continues to have effect in relation to prisoners serving sentences of imprisonment for offences committed before 4th April 2005), after "46" insert ", 50A".

(7) Any reference in paragraph 9(2)(a) or (4)(a) to section 39 of the 1991 Act is to be read as a reference to section 254(1) of the Criminal Justice Act 2003 in relation to any prisoner to whom paragraph 19 of Schedule 2 to the Criminal Justice Act 2003 (Commencement No. 8 and Transitional and Saving Provisions) Order 2005 applies.

33 (1) Schedule 2 (repatriation of prisoners to the British Islands) is amended as follows.

(2) In paragraph 2(2) (as it continues to have effect in relation to persons to whom it applied before 4th April 2005), in the definition of enactments relating to release on licence, after "33(1)(b)," insert ", (1A),".

(3) In paragraph 3(2) (as it continues to have effect in relation to persons to whom it applied before 4th April 2005), in the definition of enactments relating to release on licence, after "33(1)(b)," insert ", (1A),".

(4) In paragraph 5 (which modifies paragraph 2 of the Schedule to the Repatriation of Prisoners Act 1984 (c. 47) in its application to certain descriptions of prisoner), after sub-paragraph (1)(b) insert—

"(c) prisoners detained in Scotland in pursuance of warrants which—

(i) are issued by the Scottish Ministers under section 4A of the Repatriation of Prisoners Act 1984 (warrant transferring responsibility for detention and release); and

(ii) relate to sentences that were imposed before 1 October 1993."

Crime and Disorder Act 1998 (c. 37)

34 (1) Section 38(4) of the Crime and Disorder Act 1998 (which defines "youth justice services" for the purposes of sections 38 to 41) is amended as follows.

(2) After paragraph (a) insert—

"(aa) the provision of assistance to persons determining whether reprimands or warnings should be given under section 65 below;".

(3) After paragraph (b) insert—

"(ba) the provision of assistance to persons determining whether youth conditional cautions (within the meaning of Chapter 1 of Part 4) should be given and which conditions to attach to such cautions;

(bb) the supervision and rehabilitation of persons to whom such cautions are given;".

Youth Justice and Criminal Evidence Act 1999 (c. 23)

35 The Youth Justice and Criminal Evidence Act 1999 has effect subject to the following amendments.

36 (1) Section 35 (child complainants and other child witnesses) is amended as follows.

(2) In subsection (3) (offences to which section applies), in paragraph (a)—

(a) before sub-paragraph (v) insert—

"(iva) any of sections 33 to 36 of the Sexual Offences Act 1956,"; and

(b) in sub-paragraph (vi), at end insert "or any relevant superseded enactment".

(3) After that subsection insert—

"(3A) In subsection (3)(a)(vi) "relevant superseded enactment" means—

(a) any of sections 1 to 32 of the Sexual Offences Act 1956;

(b) the Indecency with Children Act 1960;

(c) the Sexual Offences Act 1967;

(d) section 54 of the Criminal Law Act 1977."

37 (1) Section 62 (meaning of "sexual offence" and other references to offences) is amended as follows.

(2) In subsection (1) at end insert "or any relevant superseded offence".

(3) After that subsection insert—

"(1A) In subsection (1) "relevant superseded offence" means—

(a) rape or burglary with intent to rape;

(b) an offence under any of sections 2 to 12 and 14 to 17 of the Sexual Offences Act 1956 (unlawful intercourse, indecent assault, forcible abduction etc.);

(c) an offence under section 128 of the Mental Health Act 1959 (unlawful intercourse with person receiving treatment for mental disorder by member of hospital staff etc.);

(d) an offence under section 1 of the Indecency with Children Act 1960 (indecent conduct towards child under 14);

(e) an offence under section 54 of the Criminal Law Act 1977 (incitement of child under 16 to commit incest)."

38 The amendments made by paragraphs 36 and 37 are deemed to have had effect as from 1 May 2004.

39 Where an order under section 61 of the Youth Justice and Criminal Evidence Act 1999 (c. 23) (application of Part 2 of Act to service courts) makes provision as regards the application of any provision of section 35 or 62 of that Act which is amended or inserted by paragraph 36 or 37, the order may have effect in relation to times before the making of the order.

Powers of Criminal Courts (Sentencing) Act 2000 (c. 6)

40 The Powers of Criminal Courts (Sentencing) Act 2000 has effect subject to the following amendments.

41 In section 12 (absolute and conditional discharge), in subsection (1) for "section 225, 226, 227 or 228" substitute "section 225(2) or 226(2)".

42 In section 24(5)(a) (first meeting: duration of contract), after "under paragraph" insert "9ZD,".

43 In section 28(a) (offender etc. referred back to court), for "Part I" substitute "Parts 1 and 1ZA".

44 In section 92 (detention under sections 90 and 91: place of detention etc.) omit subsection (3).

45 In section 116 (power to order return to prison where offence committed during original sentence)—

(a) in subsection (1)(b) for "under Part II of the Criminal Justice Act 1991 (early release of prisoners)" substitute "under any provision of Part 2 of the Criminal Justice Act 1991 (early release of prisoners) other than section 33(1A)", and

(b) in subsection (7), for "section 84 above" substitute "section 265 of the Criminal Justice Act 2003 (restriction on consecutive sentences for released prisoners)".

46 In section 130 (compensation orders), in subsection (2) for "section 225, 226, 227 or 228" substitute "section 225(2) or 226(2)".

47 In section 146 (driving disqualification for any offence), in subsection (2) for "section 225, 226, 227 or 228" substitute "section 225(2) or 226(2)".

48 In section 164 (further interpretative provisions), in subsection (3)(c) for "any of sections 225 to 228" substitute "section 225(2) or 226(2)".

49 (1) Schedule 1 (youth offender panels: further court proceedings) is amended as follows.

(2) In the heading for Part 1, at the end insert ": REVOCATION OF REFERRAL ORDER".

(3) In paragraphs 5(3), 9 and 14(2)(b), after "under paragraph" insert "9ZD,".

Criminal Justice and Court Services Act 2000 (c. 43)

50 In section 1 of the Criminal Justice and Court Services Act 2000 (purposes of the Chapter)—

(a) in subsection (1A)(a) for "authorised persons to be given assistance in" substitute "the giving of assistance to persons", and

(b) in subsection (4) for ""authorised person" and "conditional caution" have" substitute ""conditional caution" has".

Life Sentences (Northern Ireland) Order 2001 (S.I. 2001/2564) (N.I. 2)

51 In Article 10 of the Life Sentences (Northern Ireland) Order 2001 (life prisoners transferred to Northern Ireland), after paragraph (5) insert—

"(6) The reference in paragraph (4)(b) to a person transferred to Northern Ireland in pursuance of a warrant under the Repatriation of Prisoners Act 1984 includes a person who is detained in Northern Ireland in pursuance of a warrant under section 4A of that Act (warrant transferring responsibility for detention and release of offender)."

Crime (International Co-operation) Act 2003 (c. 32)

52 In section 48(2)(b) of the Crime (International Co-operation) Act 2003 (transfer of EU etc prisoner to assist UK investigation), for the words from "having been" to the end of paragraph (b) substitute "—
  (a) having been transferred there, or responsibility for his detention and release having been transferred there, from the United Kingdom under the Repatriation of Prisoners Act 1984;
  (b) having been transferred there, or responsibility for his detention and release having been transferred there, under any similar provision or arrangement from any other country or territory."

Sexual Offences Act 2003 (c. 42)

53 The Sexual Offences Act 2003 has effect subject to the following amendments.

54 (1) In section 83(6)(a) (notification requirements: initial notification) after "court" insert "or kept in service custody".
  (2) This paragraph extends to England and Wales and Northern Ireland only.

55 (1) In section 85(4)(a) (notification requirements: periodic notification) after "court" insert "or kept in service custody".
  (2) This paragraph extends to England and Wales and Northern Ireland only.

56 (1) Section 133 (interpretation) is amended as follows.
  (2) In subsection (1)—
    (a) in paragraph (a) of the definition of "cautioned", for "by a police officer" substitute "(or, in Northern Ireland, cautioned by a police officer)";
    (b) at the appropriate place insert—
    ""kept in service custody" means kept in service custody by virtue of an order under section 105(2) of the Armed Forces Act 2006 (but see also subsection (3));".
  (3) After subsection (2) insert—
    "(3) In relation to any time before the commencement of section 105(2) of the Armed Forces Act 2006, "kept in service custody" means being kept in military, air-force or naval custody by virtue of an order made under section 75A(2) of the Army Act 1955 or of the Air Force Act 1955 or section 47G(2) of the Naval Discipline Act 1957 (as the case may be)."
  (4) This paragraph extends to England and Wales and Northern Ireland only.

57 (1) In section 138 (orders and regulations), at the end insert—
    "(4) Orders or regulations made by the Secretary of State under this Act may—
      (a) make different provision for different purposes;
      (b) include supplementary, incidental, consequential, transitional, transitory or saving provisions."
  (2) The amendment made by sub-paragraph (1), and the repeals in Part 4 of Schedule 28 of sections 86(4) and 87(6) of the Sexual Offences Act 2003 (which are consequential on that amendment), extend to England and Wales and Northern Ireland only.

58 (1) Schedule 3 (sexual offences in respect of which offender becomes subject to notification requirements) is amended as follows.
  (2) After paragraph 35 insert—
    "35A An offence under section 63 of the Criminal Justice and Immigration Act 2008 (possession of extreme pornographic images) if the offender—
      (a) was 18 or over, and
      (b) is sentenced in respect of the offence to imprisonment for a term of at least 2 years."

(3) After paragraph 92 insert—

"92A An offence under section 63 of the Criminal Justice and Immigration Act 2008 (possession of extreme pornographic images) if the offender—
(a) was 18 or over, and
(b) is sentenced in respect of the offence to imprisonment for a term of at least 2 years."

(4) In paragraphs 93(1) and 93A(1) (service offences) for "35" substitute "35A".

(5) This paragraph extends to England and Wales and Northern Ireland only.

Criminal Justice Act 2003 (c. 44)

59 The Criminal Justice Act 2003 has effect subject to the following amendments.

60 (1) Section 23A (financial penalties) is amended as follows.

(2) In subsection (5), for paragraphs (b) and (c) substitute—

"(b) the person to whom the financial penalty is to be paid and how it may be paid."

(3) In subsection (6), for "to the specified officer" substitute "in accordance with the provision specified under subsection (5)(b)."

(4) After subsection (6) insert—

"(6A) Where a financial penalty is (in accordance with the provision specified under subsection (5)(b)) paid to a person other than a designated officer for a local justice area, the person to whom it is paid must give the payment to such an officer."

(5) Omit subsections (7) to (9).

61 After section 23A insert—

"23B Variation of conditions

A relevant prosecutor may, with the consent of the offender, vary the conditions attached to a conditional caution by—
(a) modifying or omitting any of the conditions;
(b) adding a condition."

62 In section 25 (codes of practice) in subsection (2) after paragraph (g) insert—

"(ga) the provision which may be made by a relevant prosecutor under section 23A(5)(b),".

63 In sections 88(3), 89(9) and 91(5) (days to be disregarded in calculating certain time periods relating to bail and custody under Part 10), before paragraph (a) insert—

"(za) Saturday,".

64 In section 142 (purposes of sentencing), in subsection (2)(c) for "any of sections 225 to 228" substitute "section 225(2) or 226(2)".

65 In section 150 (circumstances in which community sentence not available), in paragraph (d) for "any of sections 225 to 228" to the end substitute "section 225(2) or 226(2) of this Act (requirement to impose sentence of imprisonment for life or detention for life)".

66 In section 152 (general restrictions on imposing custodial sentences), in subsection (1)(b) for "any of sections 225 to 228" substitute "section 225(2) or 226(2)".

67 In section 153 (length of discretionary custodial sentences: general provision), in subsection (1), omit "falling to be".

68 In section 163 (general power of Crown Court to fine) for "any of sections 225 to 228" substitute "section 225(2) or 226(2)".

69 In section 224 (meaning of "specified offence" etc), in subsection (3) the definition of relevant offence is omitted.

70 Section 233 (offences under service law) is omitted.

71 In section 264 (consecutive terms), in subsection (6)(a)(i) after "means" insert "one-half of".

72 In section 305 (interpretation of Part 12), in subsection (4)—
    (a) for paragraphs (c) and (d) substitute—
        "(c) a sentence falls to be imposed under subsection (2) of section 225 if the court is obliged to pass a sentence of imprisonment for life under that subsection;
        (d) a sentence falls to be imposed under subsection (2) of section 226 if the court is obliged to pass a sentence of detention for life under that subsection;", and
    (b) paragraph (e) is omitted.

73 In section 273 (life prisoners transferred to England and Wales), after subsection (4) insert—
    "(5) The reference in subsection (2)(b) above to a person who has been transferred to England and Wales in pursuance of a warrant issued under the Repatriation of Prisoners Act 1984 includes a reference to a person who is detained in England and Wales in pursuance of a warrant under section 4A of that Act (warrant transferring responsibility for detention and release of offender)."

74 (1) Section 325 (arrangements for assessing etc risks posed by certain offenders) is amended as follows.
    (2) In subsection (8), for "section 326" substitute "sections 326 and 327A".
    (3) After that subsection insert—
        "(8A) Responsible authorities must have regard to any guidance issued under subsection (8) in discharging those functions."

75 In section 326(5)(a) (review of arrangements), for "and this section" substitute ", this section and section 327A".

76 In section 330(5)(a) (orders subject to the affirmative procedure) after "section 223," insert—
    "section 227(6),
    section 228(7)".

77 In Part 4 of Schedule 37, in the entry relating to the Magistrates' Courts Act 1980, in the second column, omit the words "In section 33(1), paragraph (b) and the word "and" immediately preceding it".

Criminal Justice Act 2003 (Commencement No. 8 and Transitional and Saving Provisions) Order 2005 (S.I. 2005/950)

78 In paragraph 14 of Schedule 2 to the Criminal Justice Act 2003 (Commencement No. 8 and Transitional and Saving Provisions) Order 2005 (saving from certain provisions of the Criminal Justice Act 2003 for sentences of imprisonment of less than 12 months), for "sections 244 to 268" substitute "sections 244 to 264 and 266 to 268".

Terrorism Act 2006 (c. 11)

79 (1) Schedule 1 to the Terrorism Act 2006 (Convention offences) is amended as follows.
    (2) In the cross-heading before paragraph 6 (offences involving nuclear material), after "*material*" add "*or nuclear facilities*".
    (3) In paragraph 6(1), after "section 1(1)" insert "(a) to (d)".
    (4) For paragraph 6(2) and (3) substitute—
        "(2) An offence mentioned in section 1(1)(a) or (b) of that Act where the act making the person guilty of the offence (whether done in the United Kingdom or elsewhere)—
            (a) is directed at a nuclear facility or interferes with the operation of such a facility, and
            (b) causes death, injury or damage resulting from the emission of ionising radiation or the release of radioactive material.
        (3) An offence under any of the following provisions of that Act—
            (a) section 1B (offences relating to damage to environment);

(b) section 1C (offences of importing or exporting etc. nuclear material: extended jurisdiction);

(c) section 2 (offences involving preparatory acts and threats).

(4) Expressions used in this paragraph and that Act have the same meanings in this paragraph as in that Act."

(5) After paragraph 6 insert—

"6A (1) Any of the following offences under the Customs and Excise Management Act 1979—

(a) an offence under section 50(2) or (3) (improper importation of goods) in connection with a prohibition or restriction relating to the importation of nuclear material;

(b) an offence under section 68(2) (exportation of prohibited or restricted goods) in connection with a prohibition or restriction relating to the exportation or shipment as stores of nuclear material;

(c) an offence under section 170(1) or (2) (fraudulent evasion of duty etc.) in connection with a prohibition or restriction relating to the importation, exportation or shipment as stores of nuclear material.

(2) In this paragraph "nuclear material" has the same meaning as in the Nuclear Material (Offences) Act 1983 (see section 6 of that Act)."

Natural Environment and Rural Communities Act 2006 (c. 16)

80 In paragraph 7 of Schedule 5 to the Natural Environment and Rural Communities Act 2006 (powers of wildlife inspectors extended to certain other Acts) after paragraph (d) insert—

"(da) section 19XB(1) and (4) (offences in connection with enforcement powers);".

Police and Justice Act 2006 (c. 48)

81 (1) The Police and Justice Act 2006 is amended as follows.

(2) In subsection (1) of section 49 (orders and regulations)—

(a) at the end of paragraph (a) insert "or";

(b) omit paragraph (c) and the "or" preceding it.

(3) In paragraph 30 of Schedule 1 (National Policing Improvement Agency: inspections) omit sub-paragraph (3).

Armed Forces Act 2006 (c. 52)

82 (1) The Armed Forces Act 2006 has effect subject to the following amendments.

(2) In paragraph 12(ah) of Schedule 2 (offences)—

(a) for "and 18 to 23" substitute ", 18 to 23 and 29B to 29G", and

(b) for "racial or religious hatred" substitute "hatred by reference to race etc".

(3) In paragraph 1(2) of Schedule 5 (service community orders: general)—

(a) for "12, 13, 15, 16(5), 17(5) and (6)" substitute "13, 16(5), 17(6)", and

(b) after "21" insert ", 25A".

(4) In paragraph 10(2)(b) of Schedule 5 (overseas community orders: general)—

(a) for "12, 13, 15, 16(5), 17(5) and (6)" substitute "13, 16(5), 17(6)", and

(b) for "and 23(1)(a)(ii)" substitute ", 23(1)(a)(ii) and 25A".

Offender Management Act 2007 (c. 21)

83 In section 1 of the Offender Management Act 2007 (meaning of "the probation purposes")—

(a) in subsection (1)(b) for "authorised persons to be given assistance in" substitute "the giving of assistance to persons", and

(b) in subsection (4) for ""authorised person" and "conditional caution" have" substitute ""conditional caution" has".

SCHEDULE 27   Section 148
TRANSITORY, TRANSITIONAL AND SAVING PROVISIONS

PART 1
YOUTH JUSTICE

Abolition of certain youth orders and related amendments

1 (1) Section 1, subsections (1) and (2) of section 6, the amendments in Part 1 of Schedule 4 and
the repeals and revocations in Part 1 of Schedule 28 do not have effect in relation to—
(a) any offence committed before they come into force, or
(b) any failure to comply with an order made in respect of an offence committed before
they come into force.
(2) So far as an amendment in Part 2 of Schedule 4 relates to any of the following orders, the
amendment has effect in relation to orders made before, as well as after, the amendment
comes into force—
(a) a referral order made under the Powers of Criminal Courts (Sentencing) Act 2000
(c. 6);
(b) a reparation order made under that Act;
(c) a community order made under section 177 of the Criminal Justice Act 2003
(c. 44).

Reparation orders

2 (1) Sub-paragraph (2) applies if the amendments of Schedule 8 to the Powers of Criminal
Courts (Sentencing) Act 2000 (action plan orders and reparation orders) made by paragraph
108(1) to (5) of Schedule 4 (reparation orders: court before which offender to appear or be
brought) come into force before the amendments of Schedule 8 to that Act made by
paragraph 62 of that Schedule.
(2) After paragraph 108(1) to (5) of Schedule 4 comes into force, and until paragraph 62 of
that Schedule comes into force, paragraph 3 of Schedule 8 to the Powers of Criminal
Courts (Sentencing) Act 2000 has effect as if—
(a) in sub-paragraph (5)(a) and (c), for "the appropriate court" there were substituted "a
youth court", and
(b) in sub-paragraph (6), for "appropriate" there were substituted "youth".
(3) Sub-paragraph (4) applies if the amendments of Schedule 8 to the Powers of Criminal
Courts (Sentencing) Act 2000 (action plan orders and reparation orders) made by paragraph
62 of Schedule 4 come into force before the amendments of Schedule 8 to that Act made
by paragraph 108(1) to (5) of that Schedule (reparation orders: court before which offender
to appear or be brought).
(4) After paragraph 62 of Schedule 4 comes into force, and until paragraph 108(1) to (5) of
that Schedule comes into force, paragraph 1 of Schedule 8 to the Powers of Criminal
Courts (Sentencing) Act 2000 has effect as if—
(a) for "an action plan order or" there were substituted "a", and
(b) the words "69(8) or, as the case may be," were omitted.

Making of youth rehabilitation orders: other existing orders

3 In paragraph 29(3)(c) of Schedule 1 (requirements not to conflict with other obligations), the
reference to a youth rehabilitation order is to be read as including a reference to any youth
community order within the meaning of section 147(2) of the Criminal Justice Act 2003
(c. 44) (as it has effect immediately before the commencement of paragraph 72 of Schedule 4
to this Act).

Instructions: other existing orders

4 In section 5(3)(c) (instructions not to conflict with other obligations), the reference to a youth rehabilitation order is to be read as including a reference to any youth community order within the meaning of section 147(2) of the Criminal Justice Act 2003 (as it has effect immediately before the commencement of paragraph 72 of Schedule 4 to this Act).

Fine default: section 35 of the Crime (Sentences) Act 1997

5 The amendments, repeals and revocations in section 6, Schedule 4 and Part 1 of Schedule 28 of provisions which are necessary to give effect to section 35 of the Crime (Sentences) Act 1997 (c. 43) (fine defaulters) do not have effect in relation to a sum ordered to be paid where—
   (a) the sum is treated as adjudged to be paid on conviction, and
   (b) the act or omission to which the sum relates occurred, or the order was made, before the commencement of those repeals and amendments.

Restrictions on imposing community sentences

6 In subsection (5) of section 148 of the Criminal Justice Act 2003 (restrictions on imposing community sentences), as inserted by section 10 of this Act, the reference to a youth rehabilitation order is to be read as including a reference to any youth community order within the meaning of section 147(2) of the Criminal Justice Act 2003 (as it has effect immediately before the commencement of paragraph 72 of Schedule 4 to this Act).

Attendance centre rules

7 The reference in paragraph 1(2)(a)(ii) of Schedule 2 to rules made under subsection (1)(d) or (e) of section 222 of the Criminal Justice Act 2003 includes a reference to rules made, or having effect as if made, before the coming into force of that section under section 62(3) of the Powers of Criminal Courts (Sentencing) Act 2000 (c. 6) (provision, regulation and management of attendance centres).

PART 2
SENTENCING

Release and recall of prisoners

8 Nothing in the amendments made by section 26 affects the operation of Part 2 of the Criminal Justice Act 1991 (c. 53) in relation to a long-term prisoner within the meaning of that Part who (for the purposes of that Part) has served one-half of his sentence before the commencement of that section.

9 Section 33(1A) of the Criminal Justice Act 1991 (c. 53) (which is inserted by section 26(2)) does not apply to a long-term prisoner serving a sentence (for one or more offences committed before 4th April 2005) by virtue of having been transferred to the United Kingdom in pursuance of a warrant under section 1 of the Repatriation of Prisoners Act 1984 (c. 47) if—
   (a) the warrant was issued before the commencement of section 26(2); and
   (b) the offence or one of the offences for which the prisoner is serving that sentence corresponds to murder or to any offence specified in Schedule 15 to the Criminal Justice Act 2003 (c. 44).

10 The amendments made by subsections (3) and (5) of section 28 do not apply in relation to any person who is released on licence under section 36(1) of the Criminal Justice Act 1991 before the commencement of section 28.

11 In section 255A and 255C of the Criminal Justice Act 2003 (which are inserted by section 29) "specified offence prisoner" is to be read as including a prisoner serving a determinate sentence by virtue of having been transferred to the United Kingdom in pursuance of a warrant under section 1 of the Repatriation of Prisoners Act 1984 if—

    (a) the warrant was issued before the commencement of section 29; and

    (b) the offence or one of the offences for which the prisoner is serving that sentence corresponds to murder or to any offence specified in Schedule 15 to the Criminal Justice Act 2003.

12 The amendment made by subsection (1) of section 32 applies in relation to any person who is recalled under section 254(1) of the Criminal Justice Act 2003 on or after the commencement of section 32 but it is immaterial when the person was released on licence under Part 2 of the Criminal Justice Act 1991.

Fine defaulters

13 (1) Section 39 and Schedule 7 do not apply—

    (a) in relation to a sum adjudged to be paid by a conviction if the offence was committed before the commencement of that section, or

    (b) where a sum ordered to be paid is treated as adjudged to be paid by a conviction, if the act or omission to which the sum relates occurred, or the order was made, before the commencement of that section.

    (2) Section 40 and paragraph 2(4) and (6) of Schedule 26 do not apply—

    (a) in relation to a sum adjudged to be paid by a conviction if the offence was committed before the commencement of that section, or

    (b) where a sum ordered to be paid is treated as adjudged to be paid by a conviction, if the act or omission to which the sum relates occurred, or the order was made, before the commencement of that section.

PART 3
APPEALS

Appeals against conviction etc.

14 The amendment made by section 42 applies in relation to an appeal under Part 1 of the Criminal Appeal Act 1968 (c. 19) if the reference by the Criminal Cases Review Commission is made on or after the date on which that section comes into force.

15 The amendment made by section 43 applies in relation to an appeal under Part 1 of the Criminal Appeal (Northern Ireland) Act 1980 (c. 47) if the reference by the Criminal Cases Review Commission is made on or after the date on which that section comes into force.

Prosecution appeals

16 (1) The amendment made by section 44 applies in relation to an appeal under Part 9 of the Criminal Justice Act 2003 (c. 44) if the proceedings on appeal begin on or after the date on which that section comes into force.

    (2) For the purposes of this paragraph, the proceedings on appeal begin—

    (a) if the prosecution appeals with leave of the Crown Court judge, on the date the application for leave is served on the Crown Court officer or, in the case of an oral application, on the date the application is made, or

    (b) if the prosecution appeals with leave of the Court of Appeal, on the date the application for leave is served on the Crown Court officer.

    (3) In this paragraph, references to service on the Crown Court officer are to be read in accordance with the Criminal Procedure Rules 2005 (S.I.2005/384).

17 (1) The amendment made by section 45 applies in relation to an appeal under Part IV of the Criminal Justice (Northern Ireland) Order 2004 (S.I. 2004/1500 (N.I.9)) if the proceedings on appeal begin on after the date on which that section comes into force.

(2) For the purposes of this paragraph, the proceedings on appeal begin—

(a) if the prosecution appeals with leave of the Crown Court judge, on the date the application for leave is made,

(b) if the prosecution appeals with leave of the Court of Appeal, on the date the application for leave is served on the proper officer, or

(c) if leave to appeal is not required, on the date the prosecution informs the Crown Court judge that it intends to appeal.

(3) In this paragraph, "the proper officer" has the same meaning as in the Criminal Appeal (Prosecution Appeals) Rules (Northern Ireland) 2005 (S.R (N.I.) 2005/159).

PART 4
OTHER CRIMINAL JUSTICE PROVISIONS

Alternatives to prosecution for offenders under 18

18 The amendments made by Schedule 9 do not apply in relation to offences committed before the commencement of section 48.

Protection for spent cautions under Rehabilitation of Offenders Act 1974

19 (1) Subject to the following provisions of this paragraph, the Rehabilitation of Offenders Act 1974 (c. 53) (as amended by Schedule 10 to this Act) applies to cautions given before the commencement date as it applies to cautions given on or after that date.

(2) A caution given before the commencement date shall be regarded as a spent caution at a time determined in accordance with sub-paragraphs (3) to (8).

(3) A caution other than a conditional caution (as defined in section 8A(2)(a) of the 1974 Act) shall be regarded as a spent caution on the commencement date.

(4) If the period of three months from the date on which a conditional caution was given ends on or before the commencement date, the caution shall be regarded as a spent caution on the commencement date unless subparagraph (7) applies.

(5) If the period of three months from the date on which a conditional caution was given ends after the commencement date, the caution shall be regarded as a spent caution at the end of that period of three months unless subparagraph (7) applies.

(6) Sub-paragraph (7) applies if—

(a) before the date on which the caution would be regarded as a spent caution in accordance with sub-paragraph (4) or (5) ("the relevant date"), the person concerned is convicted of the offence in respect of which the caution was given, and

(b) the rehabilitation period for the offence ends after the relevant date.

(7) The caution shall be regarded as a spent caution at the end of the rehabilitation period for the offence.

(8) If, on or after the date on which the caution becomes regarded as a spent caution in accordance with sub-paragraph (4) or (5), the person concerned is convicted of the offence in respect of which the caution was given—

(a) the caution shall be treated for the purposes of Schedule 2 to the 1974 Act as not having become spent in relation to any period before the end of the rehabilitation period for the offence, and

    (b) the caution shall be regarded as a spent caution at the end of that rehabilitation period.

(9) In this paragraph, "the commencement date" means the date on which section 49 comes into force.

20 In the application of subsection (7) of section 9A of the Rehabilitation of Offenders Act 1974 (as inserted by paragraph 4 of Schedule 10) to offences committed before the commencement of section 281(5) of the Criminal Justice Act 2003 (c. 44), the reference to 51 weeks is to be read as a reference to 6 months.

Extension of powers of non-legal staff

21 A designation made under section 7A of the Prosecution of Offences Act 1985 (c. 23) (powers of non-legal staff) which has effect immediately before the date on which section 55 comes into force continues to have effect on and after that date as if made under section 7A as amended by that section.

Compensation for miscarriages of justice

22 (1) Section 61(3) has effect in relation to any application for compensation made in relation to—

    (a) a conviction which is reversed, and

    (b) a pardon which is given,

on or after the commencement date.

(2) Section 61(4), (6) and (7) have effect in relation to—

    (a) any application for compensation made on or after the commencement date, and

    (b) any application for compensation made before that date in relation to which the question whether there is a right to compensation has not been determined before that date by the Secretary of State under section 133(3) of the 1988 Act.

(3) Section 61(5) has effect in relation to any conviction quashed on an appeal out of time in respect of which an application for compensation has not been made before the commencement date.

(4) Section 61(5) so has effect whether a conviction was quashed before, on or after the commencement date.

(5) In the case of—

    (a) a conviction which is reversed, or

    (b) a pardon which is given,

before the commencement date but in relation to which an application for compensation has not been made before that date, any such application must be made before the end of the period of 2 years beginning with that date.

(6) But the Secretary of State may direct that an application for compensation in relation to a case falling within sub-paragraph (5) which is made after the end of that period is to be treated as if it had been made before the end of that period if the Secretary of State considers that there are exceptional circumstances which justify doing so.

(7) In this paragraph—

"the 1988 Act" means the Criminal Justice Act 1988 (c. 33);

"application for compensation" means an application for compensation made under section 133(2) of the 1988 Act;

"the commencement date" means the date on which section 61 comes into force;

"reversed" has the same meaning as in section 133 of the 1988 Act (as amended by section 61(5)).

PART 5
CRIMINAL LAW

Penalties for possession of extreme pornographic images

23 In section 67(4)(a) the reference to 12 months is to be read as a reference to 6 months in relation to an offence committed before the commencement of section 154(1) of the Criminal Justice Act 2003 (c. 44).

Indecent photographs of children

24 (1) Section 69(3) applies in relation to things done as mentioned in—
        (a) section 1(1) of the Protection of Children Act 1978 (c. 37) (offences relating to indecent photographs of children), or
        (b) section 160(1) of the Criminal Justice Act 1988 (c. 33) (offence of possession of indecent photographs of children),
        after the commencement of section 69.
    (2) Section 70(3) applies in relation to things done as mentioned in—
        (a) Article 3(1) of the Protection of Children (Northern Ireland) Order 1978 (S.I. 1978/1047 (N.I. 17)) (offences relating to indecent photographs of children), or
        (b) Article 15(1) of the Criminal Justice (Evidence, Etc.) (Northern Ireland) Order 1988 (S.I. 1988/1847 (N.I. 17)) (offence of possession of indecent photographs of children),
        after the commencement of section 70.

Maximum penalty for publication etc. of obscene articles

25 Section 71 does not apply to offences committed before the commencement of that section.

Offences relating to nuclear material and nuclear facilities

26 The new section 2 inserted into the Nuclear Material (Offences) Act 1983 (c. 18) by paragraph 4 of Schedule 17 and the repeal in Part 5 of Schedule 28 of section 14 of the Terrorism Act 2006 (c. 11) do not apply in relation to anything done before the date on which Schedule 17 comes into force.

Reasonable force for purposes of self-defence etc.

27 (1) Section 76 applies whether the alleged offence took place before, or on or after, the date on which that section comes into force.
    (2) But that section does not apply in relation to—
        (a) any trial on indictment where the arraignment took place before that date, or
        (b) any summary trial which began before that date,
        or in relation to any proceedings in respect of any trial within paragraph (a) or (b).
    (3) Where the alleged offence is a service offence, that section similarly does not apply in relation to—
        (a) any proceedings before a court where the arraignment took place before that date, or
        (b) any summary proceedings which began before that date,
        or in relation to any proceedings in respect of any proceedings within paragraph (a) or (b).
    (4) For the purposes of sub-paragraph (3) summary proceedings are to be regarded as beginning when the hearing of the charge, or (as the case may be) the summary trial of the charge, begins.

(5) In this paragraph—

"service offence" means—

(a) any offence against any provision of Part 2 of the Army Act 1955 (3 & 4 Eliz. 2 c. 18), Part 2 of the Air Force Act 1955 (3 & 4 Eliz. 2 c. 19) or Part 1 of the Naval Discipline Act 1957 (c. 53); or

(b) any offence under Part 1 of the Armed Forces Act 2006 (c. 52);

"summary proceedings" means summary proceedings conducted by a commanding officer or appropriate superior authority.

Unlawfully obtaining etc. personal data: defences

28 The amendment made by section 78 does not apply in relation to an offence committed before the commencement of that section.

PART 6
INTERNATIONAL CO-OPERATION IN RELATION TO CRIMINAL JUSTICE MATTERS

Mutual recognition of financial penalties

29 (1) The amendments made by subsection (1) of section 80, and subsection (2) of that section, do not apply in relation to financial penalties (within the meaning of that section) imposed before that section comes into force.

(2) Section 82 does not apply in relation to financial penalties (within the meaning of that section) imposed before that section comes into force.

(3) Section 84 does not apply in relation to financial penalties (within the meaning of that section) imposed before that section comes into force.

(4) Section 87 does not apply in relation to financial penalties (within the meaning of that section) imposed before that section comes into force.

Repatriation of prisoners

30 The amendment made by section 93 does not apply to warrants under section 1 of the Repatriation of Prisoners Act 1984 issued before the commencement of that section.

PART 7
VIOLENT OFFENDER ORDERS

Penalties for offences

31 In section 113(7)(a) in its application in relation to England and Wales the reference to 12 months is to be read as a reference to 6 months in relation to an offence committed before the commencement of section 154(1) of the Criminal Justice Act 2003 (c. 44).

Service custody and detention

32 (1) In relation to any time before the commencement of section 105(2) of the Armed Forces Act 2006 (c. 52)—

(a) the definition of "kept in service custody" in section 117(1) of this Act does not apply; and

(b) any reference in Part 7 to being kept in service custody is to be read as a reference to being kept in military, air-force or naval custody by virtue of an order made under section 75A(2) of the Army Act 1955 (3 & 4 Eliz. 2 c. 18) or of the Air Force Act 1955 (3 & 4 Eliz. 2 c. 19) or section 47G(2) of the Naval Discipline Act 1957 (c. 53) (as the case may be).

(2) In relation to any time before the commencement of the definition of "service detention" in section 374 of the Armed Forces Act 2006—

(a) the definition of "service detention" in section 117(1) of this Act does not apply; and

(b) any reference in Part 7 to service detention is to be read as a reference to detention under section 71(1)(e) of the Army Act 1955 or of the Air Force Act 1955 or section 43(1)(e) of the Naval Discipline Act 1957.

PART 8
ANTI-SOCIAL BEHAVIOUR

Review of anti-social behaviour orders etc.

33 (1) The amendments made by section 123 do not apply in relation to an antisocial behaviour order, or a section 1B or 1C order, made more than 9 months before the day on which that section comes into force, unless the order has been varied by a further order made no more than 9 months before that day.

(2) In sub-paragraph (1) "section 1B or 1C order" means an order under section 1B or section 1C of the Crime and Disorder Act 1998 (c. 37).

Individual support orders

34 (1) The amendments made by section 124 do not apply in relation to an antisocial behaviour order, or a section 1B or 1C order, made more than 9 months before the day on which that section comes into force, unless the order has been varied by a further order made no more than 9 months before that day.

(2) In sub-paragraph (1) "section 1B or 1C order" means an order under section 1B or section 1C of the Crime and Disorder Act 1998 (c. 37).

PART 9
POLICE

Police misconduct and performance procedures

35 (1) This paragraph applies if paragraphs 7, 8(3), 15 and 16 of Schedule 22 come into force before the relevant provisions of the Legal Services Act 2007 (c. 29) come into force.

(2) Until the relevant provisions of the Legal Services Act 2007 come into force—

(a) section 84 of the Police Act 1996 (c. 16) (as substituted by paragraph 7 of that Schedule and as referred to in the subsection (4) of section 85 of that Act substituted by paragraph 8(3) of that Schedule) has effect as if, in subsection (4), for the definition of "relevant lawyer" there were substituted—
""relevant lawyer" means counsel or a solicitor;"; and

(b) section 4 of the Ministry of Defence Police Act 1987 (c. 4) (as substituted by paragraph 15 of that Schedule and as referred to in subsection (7) of the section 4A of that Act substituted by paragraph 16 of that Schedule) has effect as if, in subsection (4), for the definition of "relevant lawyer" there were substituted—
""relevant lawyer" means counsel or a solicitor;".

(3) In this paragraph "the relevant provisions of the Legal Services Act 2007" means the provisions of that Act which provide, for the purposes of that Act, for a person to be an authorised person in relation to an activity which constitutes the exercise of a right of audience (within the meaning of that Act).

PART 10
SPECIAL IMMIGRATION STATUS

Conditions on designated persons

36 In the application of section 133 to England and Wales in relation to an offence committed before the commencement of section 281(5) of the Criminal Justice Act 2003 (c. 44) (51 week maximum term of sentences) the reference in section 133(6)(b) to 51 weeks is to be read as a reference to six months.

PART 11
MISCELLANEOUS

Persistent sales of tobacco to persons under 18

37 The new sections 12A and 12B inserted into the Children and Young Persons Act 1933 (c. 12) by section 143 do not apply where any of the offences mentioned in those new sections were committed before the commencement of that section.

Sexual offences

38 The amendment made by sub-paragraph (1) of paragraph 57 of Schedule 26 is not to be read as affecting the validity of any supplementary, incidental, consequential, transitional, transitory or saving provisions included in orders or regulations made by the Secretary of State under the Sexual Offences Act 2003 (c. 42) before the commencement of that sub-paragraph.

SCHEDULE 28   Section 149
REPEALS AND REVOCATIONS

PART 1
YOUTH REHABILITATION ORDERS

Title	Extent of repeal or revocation
Children and Young Persons Act 1933 (c. 12)	In section 34(7), the words "section 163 of the Powers of Criminal Courts (Sentencing) Act 2000 or". In section 49— (a) in subsection (4A), paragraph (d) (but not the word "and" immediately following it); (b) in subsection (13)(c), sub-paragraph (i) together with the word "and" immediately following it.
Social Work (Scotland) Act 1968 (c. 49)	In section 94(1), in the definition of "supervision order", the words "the Powers of Criminal Courts (Sentencing) Act 2000 or".

Title	Extent of repeal or revocation
Children and Young Persons Act 1969 (c. 54)	Section 25. In section 70(1), the definition of "supervision order".
Northern Ireland (Modification of Enactments — No. 1) Order 1973 (S.I. 1973/2163)	In Schedule 1, the entry relating to section 25(2) of the Children and Young Persons Act 1969.
Transfer of Functions (Local Government, etc.) (Northern Ireland) Order 1973 (S.R. & O. 1973 No. 256)	In Schedule 2, the entry relating to section 25 of the Children and Young Persons Act 1969.
Bail Act 1976 (c. 63)	In section 4(3), the words "to be dealt with".
Magistrates' Courts Act 1980 (c. 43)	In Schedule 6A, the entries relating to Schedules 3, 5 and 7 to the Powers of Criminal Courts (Sentencing) Act 2000 (c. 6).
Contempt of Court Act 1981 (c. 49)	In section 14, the subsection (2A) inserted by the Criminal Justice Act 1982 (c. 48).
Criminal Justice Act 1982 (c. 48)	In Schedule 13— (a) in paragraph 7(2)(b), the words "(within the meaning of Part 12 of the Criminal Justice Act 2003)"; (b) in paragraph 7(3)(b), the words "within the meaning of Part 12 of the Criminal Justice Act 2003"; (c) in paragraph 9(3)(a), the words "under section 177 of the Criminal Justice Act 2003"; (d) in paragraph 9(4)(a), the words "(within the meaning of Part 12 of the Criminal Justice Act 2003)"; (e) in paragraph 9(5), the words "(within the meaning of the Part 12 of the Criminal Justice Act 2003)"; (f) in paragraph 9(6), the words "(within the meaning of Part 12 of the Criminal Justice Act 2003)". In Schedule 14, paragraph 60.
Mental Health Act 1983 (c. 20)	In section 37(8)(c), the words "a supervision order (within the meaning of that Act) or".
Health and Social Services and Social Security Adjudications Act 1983 (c. 41)	In Schedule 2, paragraphs 15(b) and 16.
Children Act 1989 (c. 41)	In section 21(2)(c), in sub-paragraph (i), the words "paragraph 7(5) of Schedule 7 to the Powers of Criminal Courts (Sentencing) Act 2000 or" and the word "or" at the end of that sub-paragraph. In section 105(6), in paragraph (b), the words from "or an" to the end of that paragraph. In Schedule 13, paragraph 35(3).
Criminal Justice Act 1991 (c. 53)	In paragraph 11 of Schedule 3— (a) in sub-paragraph (2)(a), the words "under section 177 of the Criminal Justice Act 2003"; (b) in sub-paragraph (4), the words "under section 177 of the Criminal Justice Act 2003". In Schedule 11, paragraph 3.
Children (Prescribed Orders – Northern Ireland, Guernsey and Isle of Man) Regulations 1991 (S.I. 1991/ 2032)	In regulation 8(1)— (a) sub-paragraph (a)(ii); (b) sub-paragraph (b)(i), (ii), (iv) and (v); (c) sub-paragraph (c)(ii) and (iii).
Prisoners (Return to Custody) Act 1995 (c. 16)	Section 2(2).

Title	Extent of repeal or revocation
Children (Northern Ireland Consequential Amendments) Order 1995 (S.I. 1995/ 756)	Article 7(2) and (3).
Crime and Disorder Act 1998 (c. 37)	In section 38(4)— (a) paragraph (g); (b) in paragraph (h), the words "or a supervision order". In Schedule 8, paragraph 13(1).

Powers of Criminal Courts (Sentencing) Act 2000 (c. 6)	Chapters 1, 2, 4 and 5 of Part 4.
	 In section 74(3)(a), the words "or with the requirements of any community order or any youth community order to which he may be subject".
	 In section 75, the words "action plan orders and" and "so far as relating to reparation orders".
	 In section 137(2)—
	 (a) paragraphs (a) to (c);
	 (b) in paragraph (d), the words "action plan order or".
	 In section 159, the words "paragraph 3(1), 10(6) or 18(1) of Schedule 3 to this Act,", "paragraph 1(1) of Schedule 5 to this Act," and "paragraph 7(2) of Schedule 7 to this Act, or".
	 In section 160—
	 (a) subsection (2);
	 (b) in subsection (3)(a), "40(2)(a)";
	 (c) subsection (5).
	 In section 163, the definitions of—
	 (a) "action plan order";
	 (b) "affected person";
	 (c) "attendance centre";
	 (d) "attendance centre order";
	 (e) "community sentence";
	 (f) "curfew order";
	 (g) "exclusion order";
	 (h) "supervision order";
	 (i) "supervisor";
	 (j) "youth community order";
	 and paragraphs (a), (aa) and (f) of the definition of "responsible officer".
	 Schedules 3 and 5 to 7.
	 In Schedule 8—
	 (a) in the heading, the words "action plan orders and";
	 (b) paragraph 1 and the heading preceding that paragraph;
	 (c) in the cross-heading before paragraph 2, the words "action plan order or";
	 (d) in paragraph 2—
	    (i) in sub-paragraph (2), in paragraph (a), sub-paragraphs (ii) and (iii) and in paragraphs (b) and (c) the words "action plan order or";
	    (ii) in sub-paragraphs (5) and (7), the words "action plan order or";
	    (iii) in sub-paragraph (8), the words "or action plan order" in both places;
	 (d) paragraphs 3 and 4;
	 (e) in the cross-heading before paragraph 5, the words "action plan order or";
	 (f) in paragraph 5(1)(a), the words "action plan order or";
	 (g) in paragraph 6(9)(a), (b) and (c), the words "action plan order or".
	 In Schedule 9, paragraphs 1, 2(2), (3)(a) and (4), 28(2), 33, 34(b), 39, 41, 42, 49, 80, 93(a), 126(b), 127, 129, 131 and 132.
	 In Schedule 10, paragraphs 4 to 6 and 12 to 15.
	 In Schedule 11, paragraphs 4(1)(a), (2) and (3) and 5.

Title	Extent of repeal or revocation
Care Standards Act 2000 (c. 14)	In Schedule 4, paragraph 28(3).
Criminal Justice and Court Services Act 2000 (c. 43)	Section 46. Section 52. Section 70(5). In Schedule 7— (a) in paragraph 4(2), in the entry relating to the Powers of Criminal Courts (Sentencing) Act 2000, the entries beginning "sections 63(1)(b)" and "in section 69"; (b) paragraphs 37(b), 69, 163, 164, 174, 175 and 192; (c) in paragraph 196, paragraphs (a), (b), (c) (i) and (iii) and (d); (d) in paragraph 197— (i) paragraph (a); (ii) paragraph (d); (iii) in paragraph (f), the definitions of "affected person" and "exclusion order"; (iv) paragraph (g)(i); (e) paragraphs 201, 202(2) and 204.
Anti-social Behaviour Act 2003 (c. 38)	Section 88. Schedule 2.
Criminal Justice Act 2003 (c. 44)	In section 147, subsections (1)(b) and (2). In section 148— (a) in subsection (2), the words "which consists of or includes a community order"; (b) subsection (3). In section 156(2), "or (3)(a)". In section 161— (a) in subsection (1), the words "aged 14 or over"; (b) subsection (7). In section 176, the definition of "youth community order". In section 197(1)(b), the words "the offender is aged 18 or over and". Section 199(4). Section 211(5). In section 221(2), paragraph (b) together with the word "or" immediately preceding it. Section 279. In section 330(5)(a), the entry relating to section 161(7). In Schedule 8, paragraphs 12, 15 and 17(5). Schedule 24. In Schedule 32, paragraphs 2(2), 8(2)(a), 14, 64(3)(a)(ii), 70(5)(a) and (7), 73, 89(2), 95 to 105, 106(2), 107, 122, 123(3), (5) and (8), 125, 127, 128, 129, 131(3) and 138.

PART 2

SENTENCING

Title	Extent of repeal or revocation
Criminal Justice Act 1991 (c. 53)	In section 45— (a) in subsection (3), subsection (2) of the substituted text, and (b) subsection (4). Section 46(1).

Title	Extent of repeal or revocation
	In section 46A—
	(a) in subsection (1), the words "Subject to subsection (2) below,";
	(b) subsection (2);
	(c) subsection (8).
	In section 50(2), the words from "but nothing" to the end.
Crime (Sentences) Act 1997 (c. 43)	In section 31(1), "(1) or (2)".
	In Schedule 5, in paragraph 7, the words "the corresponding subsection of".
Powers of Criminal Courts (Sentencing) Act 2000 (c. 6)	In section 17—
	(a) in subsection (1), paragraph (c) together with the word "and" immediately preceding it;
	(b) subsection (5).
	Section 92(3).
Criminal Justice Act 2003 (c. 44)	In section 142(2)(a), the words "at the time of conviction".
	In section 153(1), the words "falling to be".
	In section 224(3), the definition of "relevant offence".
	In section 227(1)(a), the words ", other than a serious offence,".
	In section 228—
	(a) in subsection (1)(b)(ii), the words from "or by section 226(3)" to the end, and
	(b) subsection (3)(a) and the word "and" immediately following it.
	In section 229—
	(a) in subsection (2) the words from the beginning to "18", and
	(b) subsections (3) and (4).
	Sections 233 and 234.
	In section 247—
	(a) in subsection (2), the word "and" (at the end of paragraph (a)) and paragraph (b), and
	(b) subsections (3), (4), (5) and (6).
	Section 254(3) to (5).
	In section 256—
	(a) in subsection (2), the words "or (b)";
	(b) subsections (3) and (5).
	In section 260—
	(a) subsections (3) and (3A);
	(b) in subsection (6), in paragraph (a), the words "or (3)(e)" and paragraph (b).
	In section 264A(3), the words from "and none" to the end.
	In section 300—
	(a) in subsection (1), paragraph (b) together with the word "or" immediately preceding it;
	(b) in subsection (2)—
	(a) the words from "or, as the case may be" to "young offender)";
	(b) the word "or" at the end of paragraph (a).
	Section 305(4)(e).
	Schedules 16 and 17.
	In Schedule 31, in paragraph 4(5)(a), ", (5)".
Referral Orders (Amendment of Referral Conditions) Regulations 2003 (S.I. 2003/1605)	Regulation 2(2) and (3).
Criminal Justice Act 2003 (Commencement No. 8 and Transitional and Saving Provisions) Order 2005 (S.I. 2005/950	Paragraph 30 of Schedule 2.

Title	Extent of repeal or revocation
Armed Forces Act 2006 (c. 52)	In section 221— (a) in subsection (3)(a) and (b) the words "in section 226(2)", and (b) subsection (4). In section 223(3), the words "to (4)". In section 270— (a) subsection (7), and (b) in subsection (8), the word "Accordingly". In Schedule 16, paragraphs 218 and 225.

PART 3

APPEALS

Title	Extent of repeal
Criminal Appeal Act 1968 (c. 19)	In section 4(2), the words "for the offence of which he remains convicted on that count". In section 6— (a) subsection (5); (b) in subsection (7), the definition of interim hospital order. Section 11(6). In section 14— (a) subsection (5); (b) in subsection (7), the definition of interim hospital order. Section 16B(3). In section 31, in the heading, the words "under Part 1". Section 31C(1) and (2).
Courts-Martial (Appeals) Act 1968 (c. 20)	Section 16(5). Section 25B(3). Section 36C(1) and (2). In section 43(1A), the word "or" at the end of paragraph (a).
Judicature (Northern Ireland) Act 1978 (c. 23)	In section 49— (a) in subsection (2), the words from "or, where subsection (3) applies" to the end; (b) subsection (3).
Criminal Appeal (Northern Ireland) Act 1980 (c. 47)	Section 10(6).
Mental Health Act 1983 (c. 20)	In Schedule 4, paragraph 23(d)(ii).
Criminal Justice Act 1988 (c. 33)	In section 36(9), the word "and" at the end of paragraph (ab).
Powers of Criminal Courts (Sentencing) Act 2000 (c. 6)	In section 155— (a) in subsection (1), the words from "or, where subsection (2) below applies" to the end; (b) subsections (2) and (3).
Criminal Justice Act 2003 (c. 44)	Section 272(1).

PART 4
OTHER CRIMINAL JUSTICE PROVISIONS

Title	Extent of repeal
Children and Young Persons Act 1969 (c. 54)	Section 23AA(4)(a).
Bail Act 1976 (c. 63)	Section 3AA(6) to (10) and (12).
Magistrates' Courts Act 1980 (c. 43)	Section 13(5). Section 24(1B).
Prosecution of Offences Act 1985 (c. 23)	Section 7A(6).
Criminal Justice (Terrorism and Conspiracy) Act 1998 (c. 40)	Section 8.
Access to Justice Act 1999 (c. 22)	Section 17A(5).
Powers of Criminal Courts (Sentencing) Act 2000 (c. 6)	In section 3— (a) in subsection (2), paragraph (b) and the word "or" immediately preceding it; (b) in subsection (5), in paragraph (b), the words "paragraph (b) and".
Sexual Offences Act 2003 (c. 42)	Section 86(4). Section 87(6).
Criminal Justice Act 2003 (c. 44)	Section 23A(7) to (9). In Schedule 3, paragraphs 13, 22 and 57(2). In Schedule 36, paragraph 50. In Part 4 of Schedule 37, in the entry relating to the Magistrates' Courts Act 1980, in the second column, the words "In section 33(1), paragraph (b) and the word "and" immediately preceding it".

PART 5
CRIMINAL LAW

Title	Extent of repeal
Criminal Libel Act 1819 (60 Geo. 3 & 1 Geo. 4 c. 8)	In section 1, the words "any blasphemous libel, or".
Law of Libel Amendment Act 1888 (c. 64)	In section 3, the words "blasphemous or". In section 4, the words "blasphemous or".
Nuclear Material (Offences) Act 1983 (c. 18)	Section 1(2). In section 6(1), the words "in this Act".
Public Order Act 1986 (c. 64)	Section 29B(3). In section 29H— (a) in subsection (1), the words "in England and Wales"; (b) subsection (2). In section 29I— (a) in subsection (2)(a), the words "in the case of an order made in proceedings in England and Wales,"; (b) subsections (2)(b) and (4). In section 29L(1) and (2), the words "in England and Wales".

Title	Extent of repeal
Sexual Offences Act 2003 (c. 42)	In Schedule 2, in paragraph 1(d), the words "in relation to a photograph or pseudophotograph showing a child under 16".
Terrorism Act 2006 (c. 11)	Section 14.

PART 6
INTERNATIONAL CO-OPERATION IN RELATION TO CRIMINAL JUSTICE MATTERS

Title	Extent of repeal
Commissioners for Revenue and Customs Act 2005 (c. 11)	In Schedule 2, paragraph 14.
Repatriation of Prisoners Act 1984 (c. 47)	In section 1(4)(b) the words "under this Act". Section 3(10). In section 8(1) the word "and" after the definition of "order".
Police and Justice Act 2006 (c. 48)	Section 44(4).

PART 7
ANTI-SOCIAL BEHAVIOUR

Title	Extent of repeal
Police and Justice Act 2006 (c. 48)	In Schedule 14, paragraph 55(5).

PART 8
POLICING

Title	Extent of repeal
Police Act 1996 (c. 16)	In section 50(4), the words ", subject to subsection (3)(b),". In section 54(2), the words "and the Central Police Training and Development Authority". In section 97— (a) in subsection (6), in each of paragraphs (b) and (c), the words "or is required to resign as an alternative to dismissal"; (b) in subsection (7), the words ", or required to resign as an alternative to dismissal,". In Schedule 6, paragraph 6.
Greater London Authority Act 1999 (c. 29)	In Schedule 27, paragraphs 95 and 107.

Title	Extent of repeal
Criminal Justice and Police Act 2001 (c. 16)	In section 125— (a) subsections (3) and (4); (b) in subsection (5), paragraph (b), together with the word "and" immediately preceding it.
Police Reform Act 2002 (c. 30)	In Schedule 3— (a) paragraphs 20A(8), 20B(5) and 20E(5); (b) paragraph 20G together with the cross heading immediately preceding it; (c) in paragraphs 21A(5) and 24B(2), the words from "(and the other provisions" to the end; (d) paragraph 22(1)(c) (together with the word "or" immediately preceding it); (e) in paragraph 25, the word "and" immediately after each of subparagraphs (2)(b), (3)(b) and (5)(b).
Railways and Transport Safety Act 2003 (c. 20)	Section 43.
Police and Justice Act 2006 (c. 48)	In section 49(1), paragraph (c) together with the word "or" immediately preceding it. In Schedule 1, paragraph 30(3). In Schedule 2, paragraph 19.
Legal Services Act 2007 (c. 29)	In Schedule 21, paragraphs 73 and 119.

The Criminal Justice and Immigration Act 2008 (Commencement No. 1 and Transitional Provisions) Order 2008

STATUTORY INSTRUMENTS
2008 NO. 1466 (C. 66)

PRISONS, ENGLAND AND WALES

Made   *7th June 2008*

The Secretary of State makes the following Order in exercise of the powers conferred by section 153(7) and (8)(b) of the Criminal Justice and Immigration Act 2008[1]:

Citation and interpretation

1.—(1) This Order may be cited as the Criminal Justice and Immigration Act 2008 (Commencement No.1 and Transitional Provisions) Order 2008.

(2) In this Order "the Act" means the Criminal Justice and Immigration Act 2008.

Commencement

2. Subject to articles 3 and 4, the day appointed for the coming into force of the following provisions of the Act is 9th June 2008—

(a) section 26 (release of certain long-term prisoners under Criminal Justice Act 1991) save insofar as subsection (2) inserts subsections (1C) and (1D) in section 33 of the Criminal Justice Act 1991[2];

(b) section 148(1) and (2) (consequential etc. amendments and transitional and saving provision) insofar as they relate to the provisions specified in paragraphs (c) and (d) of this article;

(c) the following paragraphs of Schedule 26 (minor and consequential amendments)—

(i) 9, 12(1) and (3)(b) and 19(1) and (4) (Repatriation of Prisoners Act 1984[3]);

(ii) 29(1), (2) and (5) (Criminal Justice Act 1991);

(iii) 31 and 33(1) to (3) (Crime (Sentences) Act 1997[4]); and

(iv) 40 and 45(a) (Powers of Criminal Courts (Sentencing) Act 2000[5]); and

(d) paragraphs 8 and 9 of Schedule 27 (transitory, transitional and saving provisions).

---

[1] 2008 c.4.

[2] 1991 c.53.

[3] 1984 c.47

[4] 1997 c.43.

[5] 2000 c.6.

Transitional provisions

3. The coming into force of section 26 of the Act is of no effect in relation to—
   (a) existing prisoners within the meaning of paragraph 8 of Schedule 12 to the Criminal Justice Act 1991;
   (b) long-term prisoners serving sentences of imprisonment for an offence under any of sections 11, 12, 15 to 18, 54 and 56 to 63 of the Terrorism Act 2000[6];
   (c) long-term prisoners serving sentences of imprisonment for an offence under any of sections 47, 50 and 113 of the Anti-terrorism, Crime and Security Act 2001[7];
   (d) long-term prisoners serving sentences of imprisonment for an offence under section 12 of the Sexual Offences Act 1956[8];
   (e) long-term prisoners serving sentences of imprisonment for an offence of aiding, abetting counselling, procuring or inciting the commission of an offence listed in any of paragraphs (b) to (d) of this article; and
   (f) long-term prisoners serving sentences of imprisonment for an offence of conspiring or attempting to commit an offence listed in any of paragraphs (b) to (d) of this article.
4. The coming into force of paragraph 19(4) of Schedule 26 to the Act is no effect in relation to long-term prisoners serving a sentence for one or more offences committed before 4th April 2005 by virtue of having been transferred to the United Kingdom pursuant to a warrant under section 1 of the Repatriation of Prisoners Act 1984 where the warrant was issued prior to the commencement of section 26 of the Act.

---

[6] 2000 c.11.

[7] 2001 c.24.

[8] 1956 c.69; section 12 was repealed by the Sexual Offences Act 2003 (c.42), sections 139 and 140, Schedule 6, paragraph 11(a) and Schedule 7.

EXPLANATORY NOTE
(This note is not part of the Order)

This Order brings into force section 26 and related provisions of the Criminal Justice and Immigration Act 2008 on 9th June 2008, subject to the transitional provisions in articles 3 and 4. Section 26 imposes a duty on the Secretary of State to release certain long-term prisoners (prisoners serving sentences of imprisonment of at least four years) subject to the release arrangements in the Criminal Justice Act 1991 ('the 1991 Act') at the half-way point of their sentence on licence until sentence expiry.

The transitional provision in article 3 provides that the duty to release prisoners at the half way point does not apply to prisoners who were serving their sentence at the time the 1991 Act was commenced and whose release arrangements are governed by paragraph 8 of Schedule 12 to the 1991 Act. Article 3 also provides that the duty to release does not apply to long-term prisoners who have committed certain offences under the Terrorism Act 2000, the Anti-terrorism, Crime and Security Act 2001 and the Sexual Offences Act 1956. Article 4 concerns the requirement in paragraph 19(4) of Schedule 26 to calculate the section 26 release date for a repatriated prisoner from the date on which the provisions of the warrant specified in paragraph 1 of the Schedule to the Repatriation of Prisoners Act 1984 take effect. By virtue of the transitional provision in article 4, that requirement will not apply to repatriated prisoners whose warrants were issued prior to 9th June 2008.

APPENDIX 3

The Criminal Justice and Immigration Act 2008 (Commencement No. 2 and Transitional and Saving Provisions) Order 2008

STATUTORY INSTRUMENTS
2008 NO. 1586 (C. 69)

CRIMINAL LAW, ENGLAND AND WALES
CRIMINAL LAW, NORTHERN IRELAND
CRIMINAL PROCEDURE, ENGLAND AND WALES
CRIMINAL PROCEDURE, NORTHERN IRELAND
LEGAL SERVICES COMMISSION, ENGLAND AND WALES
POLICE, ENGLAND AND WALES
PRISONS
REPATRIATION

Made   *17th June 2008*

The Lord Chancellor and Secretary of State makes this Order in exercise of the powers conferred by the Criminal Justice and Immigration Act 2008[1] on the Lord Chancellor by section 153(4), and the Secretary of State by section 153(7) and (8), of that Act.

Citation and interpretation

1.—(1) This Order may be cited as the Criminal Justice and Immigration Act 2008 (Commencement No. 2 and Transitional and Saving Provisions) Order 2008.

(2) In this Order—

"the 1968 Act" means the Criminal Appeal Act 1968[2];

"the 1980 Act" means the Criminal Appeal (Northern Ireland) Act 1980[3];

"the 2003 Act" means the Criminal Justice Act 2003[4];

"the 2008 Act" means the Criminal Justice and Immigration Act 2008.

Appointed dates

2.—(1) The date appointed for the coming into force of the provisions of the 2008 Act specified in Schedule 1, is 14 July 2008.

---

[1] 2008 c.4
[2] 1968 c.19
[3] 1980 c.47
[4] 2003 c.44

(2) The date appointed for the coming into force of paragraph 63 of Schedule 26 to, and section 148(1) of the 2008 Act so far as it relates to that paragraph, is 15 July 2008.

(3) Paragraph (1) is subject to Schedule 2 (Transitional and Saving Provisions).

SCHEDULE 1   Article 2(1)
PROVISIONS OF THE CRIMINAL JUSTICE AND IMMIGRATION
ACT 2008 COMING INTO FORCE ON 14 JULY 2008

1. Section 10 (Effect of restriction on imposing community sentences).
2. Section 11(1) (Restriction on power to make a community order).
3. Section 12 (Pre-sentence reports).
4. Section 13 (Sentences of imprisonment for public protection) and Schedule 5 (Offences specified for the purposes of sections 225(3A) and 227(2A) of the Criminal Justice Act 2003).
5. Section 14 (Sentences of detention for public protection).
6. Section 15 (Extended sentences for certain violent or sexual offences: persons 18 or over).
7. Section 16 (Extended sentences for certain violent or sexual offences: persons under 18).
8. Section 17 (The assessment of dangerousness).
9. Section 18 (Further amendments relating to sentences for public protection).
10. Section 20 (Consecutive terms of imprisonment).
11. Section 24 (Minimum conditions for early release under section 246(1) of the Criminal Justice Act 2003).
12. Section 25 (Release on licence under Criminal Justice Act 2003 of prisoners serving extended sentences).
13. Section 27 (Application of section 35(1) of the Criminal Justice Act 1991[5] to prisoners liable to removal from the UK).
14. Section 28 (Release of fine defaulters and contemnors under Criminal Justice Act 1991).
15. Section 29 (Release of prisoners after recall) save insofar as subsection (2) inserts subsections (9) and (10) of section 255A of the 2003 Act.
16. Section 30 (Further review and release of prisoners after recall).
17. Section 31 (Recall of life prisoners: abolition of requirement for recommendation by Parole Board).
18. Section 32 (Release of prisoners recalled following release under Criminal Justice Act 1991).
19. Section 38 (Imposition of unpaid work requirement for breach of community order).
20. Section 40 (Power to impose attendance centre requirement on fine defaulter).
21. Section 42 (Power to dismiss certain appeals following references by the CCRC: England and Wales).
22. Section 43 (Power to dismiss certain appeals following references by the CCRC: Northern Ireland).
23. Section 44 (Determination of prosecution appeals: England and Wales).
24. Section 45 (Determination of prosecution appeals: Northern Ireland).
25. Section 46(1) and (3) (Review of sentence on reference by Attorney General).
26. Section 47 (Further amendments relating to appeals in criminal cases) and Schedule 8 (Appeals in criminal cases).

---

[5] 1991 c.53

27. Section 52 (Bail for summary offences and certain other offences to be tried summarily) and Schedule 12 (Bail for summary offences and certain other offences to be tried summarily).

28. Section 54 (Trial or sentencing in absence of accused in magistrates' courts).

29. Section 55 (Extension of powers of non-legal staff).

30. Section 56 (Provisional grant of right to representation).

31. Section 57 (Disclosure of information to enable assessment of financial eligibility).

32. Section 58 (Pilot schemes).

33. Section 59 (SFO's pre-investigation powers in relation to bribery and corruption: foreign officers etc.).

34. Section 72 (Offences committed outside the United Kingdom).

35. Section 73 (Grooming and adoption) and Schedule 15 (Sexual offences: grooming and adoption) to the extent not already in force.

36. Section 76 (Reasonable force for purposes of self-defence etc.).

37. Section 93 (Delivery of prisoner to place abroad for purposes of transfer out of the United Kingdom).

38. Section 94 (Issue of warrant transferring responsibility for detention and release of an offender to or from the relevant Minister).

39. Section 95 (Powers to arrest and detain persons believed to fall within section 4A(3) of Repatriation of Prisoners Act 1984[6]).

40. Section 96 (Amendments relating to Scotland).

41. Section 97 (Power to transfer functions under Crime (International Co-operation) Act 2003[7] in relation to direct taxation).

42. Section 126(1) (Police misconduct and performance procedures) insofar as it relates to the provision specified in paragraph 47.

43. Section 140 (Disclosure of information about convictions etc. of child sex offenders to members of the public) and Schedule 24 (Section 327A of the Criminal Justice Act 2003: meaning of "child sex offence").

44. Section 141 (Sexual offences prevention orders: relevant sexual offences).

45. Section 142 (Notification requirements: prescribed information).

46. Sections 148(1) and (2) and 149 insofar as they relate to the provisions specified in paragraphs 48, 49 and 50 respectively.

47. In Schedule 22 (Police misconduct and performance procedures), paragraph 6 (Police Advisory Board).

48. In Schedule 26 (Minor and consequential amendments)—
  (a) paragraphs 2(1), (2), (4), (5) and (6), 59, 64, 65, 66, 67, 68, 69, 71, 72, 73, 74, 75 and 76 (2003 Act),
  (b) paragraph 3 (Prison Act 1952 (c.52)),
  (c) paragraph 4 (Criminal Justice Act 1961 (c.39)),
  (d) paragraph 6 (Criminal Appeal (Northern Ireland) Act 1980 (c.47)),
  (e) paragraph 7 (Wildlife and Countryside Act 1981 (c.69)),
  (f) paragraph 8 (Mental Health Act 1983 (c.20)),
  (g) paragraphs 10 to 19 (Repatriation of Prisoners Act 1984) to the extent not already in force,
  (h) paragraph 21 (Criminal Justice Act 1987 (c.38)),

---

[6] 1984 c.47
[7] 2003 c.32

452

(i) paragraphs 22 and 23 (Criminal Justice Act 1988 (c.33)),

(j) paragraph 26 (Football Spectators Act 1989 (c.37)),

(k) paragraph 27 (Criminal Justice (International Co-operation) Act 1990 (c.5)),

(l) paragraph 28 (Broadcasting Act 1990 (c.42)),

(m) paragraph 30 (Prisoners and Criminal Proceedings (Scotland) Act 1993 (c.9)),

(n) paragraph 32 and, to the extent not already in force, paragraph 33 (Crime (Sentences) Act 1997 (c.43)),

(o) paragraphs 41, 44, 45(b), 46, 47 and 48 (Powers of Criminal Courts (Sentencing) Act 2000 (c.6)),

(p) paragraph 51 (Life Sentences (Northern Ireland) Order 2001(S.I. 2001/2564(N.I.2))),

(q) paragraph 52 (Crime (International Co-operation) Act 2000 (c.32)),

(r) paragraphs 53, 56(1), (2)(a) and (4) and 57 (Sexual Offences Act 2003 (c.42)),

(s) paragraph 78 (Criminal Justice Act 2003 (Commencement No. 8 and Transitional and Saving Provisions) Order 2005 (S.I. 2005/950)),

(t) paragraph 80 (Natural Environment and Rural Communities Act 2006 (c.16)),

(u) paragraph 81 (Police and Justice Act 2006 (c.48)).

49. In Schedule 27 (Transitory, transitional and saving provisions), paragraphs 6, 10 to 12, 13(2), 14 to 17, 21, 27, 30 and 38.

50.—(1) The following entries in Schedule 28 (repeals).

(2) In Part 2 (Sentencing), the entries relating to the—

(a) Criminal Justice Act 1991 in sections 45, 46(1) and 50(2),

(b) Crime (Sentences) Act 1997 (c.43),

(c) 2003 Act, in sections 153(1), 224(3), 227(1)(a), 228, 229, 234, 247, 254(3) to (5), 256 and 305(4)(e), Schedules 16 and 17 and in paragraph 4(5)(a) of Schedule 31,

(d) Criminal Justice Act 2003 (Commencement No. 8 and Transitional and Saving Provisions) Order 2005 (S.I. 2005/950).

(3) In Part 3 (Appeals), the entries relating to the—

(a) 1968 Act,

(b) Judicature (Northern Ireland) Act 1978 (c.23),

(c) Criminal Appeal (Northern Ireland) Act 1980 (c.47),

(d) Mental Health Act 1983 (c.20),

(e) Criminal Justice Act 1988 (c.33),

(f) Powers of Criminal Courts (Sentencing) Act 2000 (c.6).

(4) In Part 4 (Other criminal justice provisions), the entries relating to the—

(a) Magistrates' Courts Act 1980 (c.43), section 13(5),

(b) Prosecution of Offences Act 1985 (c.23),

(c) Access to Justice Act 1999 (c.22),

(d) Sexual Offences Act 2003,

(e) 2003 Act, section 23A(7) to (9).

(5) In Part 5 (Criminal law), the entry relating to the Sexual Offences Act 2003.

(6) All the entries in Part 6 (International co-operation in relation to criminal justice matters).

(7) In Part 8 (Policing), the entries relating to the—

(a) Police Act 1996 (c.16) in section 54(2),

(b) Police and Justice Act 2006 (c.48) in section 49(1) and in Schedule 1.

SCHEDULE 2

TRANSITIONAL AND SAVING PROVISIONS

Article 2(3)

Restrictions on imposing community order

1. The coming into force of section 11(1) of the 2008 Act is of no effect in relation to any person who is sentenced to a community order within the meaning of section 177[1]of the 2003 Act before 14 July 2008.

Dangerous offenders

2. The coming into force of sections 13 to 18 and 25 of, Schedule 5 and paragraph 71 of Schedule 26 to, the 2008 Act (and the related entries in Schedule 28 (Repeals) to that Act) is of no effect in relation to any person sentenced under any of sections 225[2], 226[3], 227[4] or 228[5] of the 2003 Act before 14 July 2008.

Recall

3. The coming into force of sections 29 and 30 of the 2008 Act is of no effect in relation to any person who is recalled under section 254(1) of the 2003 Act before 14 July 2008.

Appeals in criminal cases

4.—(1) The amendments made by paragraph 6 of Schedule 8 to the 2008 Act (Powers of Court to substitute different sentence) and the related entry in Schedule 28 to that Act apply in relation to an appeal under Part 1 of the 1968 Act if the proceedings on appeal begin on or after 14 July 2008.

   (2) For the purposes of this paragraph, the proceedings on appeal begin—

      (a) if the Criminal Cases Review Commission refer the case to the Court of Appeal under Part 2 of the Criminal Appeal Act 1995[6], on the date the reference is made;

      (b) in any other case, on the date the notice of appeal or, as the case may be, notice of application for leave to appeal, is served on the Crown Court officer.

   (3) In this paragraph, the reference to service on the Crown Court officer is to be read in accordance with the Criminal Procedure Rules 2005[7].

5. The amendments made by paragraphs 7 to 9 of Schedule 8 to the 2008 Act (Interim hospital orders) and the related entries in Schedule 28 to that Act apply in relation to an interim hospital order made by the Court of Appeal under Part 1 of the 1968 Act on or after 14 July 2008.

6. The amendment made by paragraph 12 of Schedule 8 to the 2008 Act (Appeals against procedural directions) and the related entry in Schedule 28 to that Act apply in relation to a procedural direction given by a single judge under Part 1 of the 1968 Act on or after 14 July 2008 or, as the case may be, to a refusal by a single judge on or after that date to give such a procedural direction.

7. The amendments made by paragraph 13 of Schedule 8 to the 2008 Act (Detention of defendant pending appeal to Supreme Court) apply where an appeal lies to the Supreme

---

[1] Section 177 was commenced for certain purposes by S.I. 2005/950 as amended by S.I. 2007/391.
[2] Section 225 has been modified by S.I. 2005/643 and is amended by section 13 of the 2008 Act.
[3] Section 226 is amended by section 14 of the 2008 Act.
[4] Section 227 has been modified by S.I. 2005/643 and is amended by section 15 of the 2008 Act.
[5] Section 228 is amended by section 16 of the 2008 Act.
[6] 1995 c.35
[7] S.I. 2005/384; relevant amending instruments are S.I. 2007/699 and 2007/2317.

Court under Part 2 of the 1968 Act if the date of the decision of the Court of Appeal from which the appeal lies is on or after 14 July 2008.

8.—(1) The amendments made by paragraph 18 of Schedule 8 to the 2008 Act (Powers of court to substitute different sentence) apply in relation to an appeal under Part 1 of the 1980 Act if the proceedings on appeal begin on or after 14 July 2008.

(2) For the purposes of this paragraph, the proceedings on appeal begin—

(a) if the appellant appeals with leave of the Court of Appeal, on the date the application for leave is served on the proper officer,

(b) if leave to appeal is not required, on the date the notice of appeal is served on the proper officer,

(c) if the judge of the court of trial grants a certificate that the case is fit for appeal—

(i) on the date the application for the certificate is made to the court of trial or lodged with the proper officer, or

(ii) in a case where a certificate is granted without any application being made, on the date the certificate is granted, or

(d) if the Criminal Cases Review Commission refer the case to the Court of Appeal under Part 2 of the Criminal Appeal Act 1995, on the date the reference is made.

(3) In this paragraph, "proper officer" has the same meaning as in the Criminal Appeal (Northern Ireland) Rules 1968[8].

9. The amendments made by paragraphs 19 to 21 of Schedule 8 to the 2008 Act (Interim hospital orders) and the related entry in Schedule 28 to that Act apply in relation to an interim hospital order made by the Court of Appeal on or after 14 July 2008.

10. The amendments made by paragraph 24 of Schedule 8 to the 2008 Act (Detention of defendant pending appeal to Supreme Court) apply where an appeal lies to the Supreme Court under Part 2 of the 1980 Act if the date of the decision of the Court of Appeal from which the appeal lies is on or after 14 July 2008.

11. The amendments made by paragraph 26 of Schedule 8 to the 2008 Act (Detention of defendant pending appeal from High Court to Supreme Court) apply where an appeal lies to the Supreme Court under section 1 of the Administration of Justice Act 1960[9] if the date of the decision of the court below from which the appeal lies is on or after 14 July 2008.

12. The amendments made by paragraph 27 of Schedule 8 to the 2008 Act (Variation of sentences by Crown Court) and the related entries in Schedule 28 to that Act apply in relation to a sentence imposed, or other order made, by the Crown Court on or after 14 July 2008.

13. The amendments made by paragraph 28 of Schedule 8 to the 2008 Act (Variation of sentences by Crown Court) and the related entry in Schedule 28 to that Act apply in relation to a sentence imposed, or other order made, by the Crown Court on or after 14 July 2008.

14. References to the Supreme Court in paragraphs 7, 10 and 11 of this Schedule are to be read as references to the House of Lords until the coming into force of the following provisions of Schedule 9 to the Constitutional Reform Act 2005[10], namely—

(a) as regards paragraph 7, of paragraph 16(6) of that Schedule,

(b) as regards paragraph 10, of paragraph 33(6) of that Schedule, and

(c) as regards paragraph 11, of paragraph 13(5) of that Schedule.

---

[8] S.R. & O. (N.I.) 1968/218

[9] 1960 c.65. Section 1 was repealed as it applies to Northern Ireland by Schedule 7 to the Judicature (Northern Ireland) Act 1978. Section 1 was amended by Schedule 7 to the 1968 Act and by section 63(1) of the Access to Justice Act 1999.

Section 1 will be further amended and repealed in part by section 40(4) of, paragraph 13(1) and (2) of Schedule 9 to, and Schedule 18 to the Constitutional Reform Act 2005 (c.4), from a date to be appointed.

[10] 2005 c.4

EXPLANATORY NOTE
(This note is not part of the Order)

This Order brings into force the provisions of the Criminal Justice and Immigration Act 2008 (c.4) set out in Schedule 1 on 14 July 2008, and one other minor amendment on 15 July 2008. Commencement in the case of the provisions falling under article 2(1) and Schedule 1 is subject to the transitional and saving provisions contained in Schedule 2 to the Order.

NOTE AS TO EARLIER COMMENCEMENT ORDERS
(This note is not part of the Order)

Provision	Date of Commencement	S.I. No.
Section 26 (partially)	9 June 2008	2008/1466
Section 148(1) and (2) for certain purposes	9 June 2008	2008/1466
Schedule 26 (partially)	9 June 2008	2008/1466
Schedule 27 (partially)	9 June 2008	2008/1466

APPENDIX 4

The Criminal Justice and Immigration Act 2008 (Commencement No. 3 and Transitional Provisions) Order 2008

STATUTORY INSTRUMENTS
2008 NO. 2712 (C. 118)

CRIMINAL LAW, ENGLAND AND WALES
CRIMINAL LAW, NORTHERN IRELAND
CRIMINAL PROCEDURE, ENGLAND AND WALES
CRIMINAL PROCEDURE, NORTHERN IRELAND
MAGISTRATES' COURTS, ENGLAND AND WALES
POLICE, ENGLAND AND WALES
ANTI-SOCIAL BEHAVIOUR, ENGLAND AND WALES

Made   *13th October 2008*

The Lord Chancellor and Secretary of State, in exercise of the powers conferred on the Lord Chancellor by section 153(4), and on the Secretary of State by section 153(7) of the Criminal Justice and Immigration Act 2008[1], makes the following Order:

Citation and interpretation

1.—(1) This Order may be cited as the Criminal Justice and Immigration Act 2008 (Commencement No. 3 and Transitional Provisions) Order 2008.

(2) In this Order, "the 2008 Act" means the Criminal Justice and Immigration Act 2008.

Appointed Dates

2. Subject to articles 3 and 4, the date appointed for the coming into force of the provisions of the 2008 Act specified in the Schedule is 3rd November 2008.

Transitional and saving provisions

3. The coming into force of section 60 of the 2008 Act is of no effect—

(a) in relation to offences into which a criminal investigation within the meaning of section 1(4) of the Criminal Procedure and Investigations Act 1996[2], has begun, in England and Wales, before 4th April 2005 or, in Northern Ireland, before 15th July 2005: and

---

[1] 2008 c. 4.
[2] 1996 c. 25.

    (b) in relation to a case to which Part 1 of the Criminal Procedure and Investigations Act 1996 applies by virtue of section 1(1) or (2) of that Act before 3rd November 2008.

4.—(1) The Police Act 1996[3] and the Police Reform Act 2002[4] shall continue to apply in relation to specified matters as if the amendments in paragraphs 3, 4, 7 and 8 of Schedule 22 and in paragraphs 5, 12(4) and 19 of Schedule 23 to the 2008 Act had not been made.

    (2) In this article, "specified matters" means—

        (a) conduct by a police officer which may be or is being dealt with under the Police (Conduct) Regulations 2004[5];

        (b) conduct by a police officer which may be or is being dealt with under the Police (Complaints and Misconduct) Regulations 2004[6] as they are in force on the date this Order is made;

        (c) performance or attendance by a member of a police force which may be or is being dealt with under the Police (Efficiency) Regulations 1999[7]; or

        (d) anything which may be or is being dealt with under the Police Appeals Tribunals Rules 1999[8].

SCHEDULE

Article 2

PROVISIONS COMING INTO FORCE ON 3RD NOVEMBER 2008

1. Section 21(1) and (3) to (7) (Credit for period of remand on bail: terms of imprisonment and detention).
2. Section 22 (Credit for period of remand on bail: other cases).
3. Section 23 (Credit for period of remand on bail: transitional provisions).
4. Section 33(1), (3), (5) and (6) (Removal under Criminal Justice Act 1991).
5. Section 34(1), (3), (4)(a), (5), (6), (8) and (9) (Removal under Criminal Justice Act 2003), save insofar as subsection (6) provides that section 260(3A) of the Criminal Justice Act 2003 ceases to have effect.
6. Section 41 (Disclosure of information for enforcing fines).
7. Section 51 (Bail conditions: electronic monitoring).
8. Section 60 (Contents of an accused's defence statement).
9. Section 126(1) (Police misconduct and performance procedures) insofar as it relates to the provisions specified in paragraph 16.
10. Section 127 (Investigation of complaints of police misconduct etc.) insofar as it relates to the provisions specified in paragraph 17.
11. Section 129 (Inspection of police authorities).
12. Section 148(1) (Consequential etc. amendments and transitional and saving provision) insofar as it relates to the provisions specified in paragraph 18.
13. Section 149 (Repeals and revocations) insofar as it relates to the provisions specified in paragraph 19.
14. Schedule 6 (Credit for period of remand on bail: transitional provisions).
15. Schedule 11 (Electronic monitoring of persons released on bail subject to conditions).

---

[3] 1996 c. 16.
[4] 2002 c. 30.
[5] S.I. 2004/645, as amended by S.I. 2006/594.
[6] S.I. 2004/643, as amended by S.I. 2005/3311, 2005/3389, 2006/594 and 2006/1406.
[7] S.I. 1999/732, as amended by S.I. 2003/528 and S.I. 2003/2600.
[8] S.I. 1999/818, as amended by S.I. 2003/2597 and 2006/594.

16. In Part 1 of Schedule 22 (Police misconduct and performance procedures)—
    (a) paragraphs 1 and 2;
    (b) paragraphs 3, 4, and 7 for the purposes of making regulations; and
    (c) paragraph 8 for the purpose of making rules.
17. In Schedule 23 (Investigation of complaints of police misconduct etc.)—
    (a) paragraphs 1 to 3 and 12(1); and
    (b) paragraphs 5, 12(4) and 19 for the purpose of making regulations.
18. In Schedule 26 (Minor and consequential amendments)—
    (a) paragraph 5 (Children and Young Persons Act 1969 (c.54)),
    (b) paragraph 29(3), (4), (6) and (7) (Criminal Justice Act 1991 (c.53)),
19.—(1) The following entries in Schedule 28 (Repeals and revocations).
    (2) In Part 2 (Sentencing), the entries relating to the—
        (a) Criminal Justice Act 1991, section 46A; and
        (b) Criminal Justice Act 2003, section 260(3) and (6).
    (3) In Part 4 (Other criminal justice provisions), the entries relating to the—
        (a) Children and Young Persons Act 1969 (c.54), section 23AA(4)(a); and
        (b) Bail Act 1976 (c.63), section 3AA(6) to (10) and (12).

EXPLANATORY NOTE
(This note is not part of the Order)

This Order brings into force the provisions of the Criminal Justice and Immigration Act 2008 (c.4) set out in Schedule 1 on 3rd November 2008. Article 3 contains transitional and saving provisions in relation to the coming into force of section 60 of the Act. Article 4 contains saving provisions in relation to the amendments to the police misconduct and performance procedures and the investigation of complaints of police misconduct etc.

NOTE AS TO EARLIER COMMENCEMENT ORDERS
(This note is not part of the Order)

The following provisions of the Criminal Justice and Immigration Act 2008 have been brought into force by a commencement order made before the date of this Order.

Provision	Date of Commencement	S.I. No.
Section 10	14 July 2008	2008/1586
Section 11 (partially)	14 July 2008	2008/1586
Section 12	14 July 2008	2008/1586
Section 13	14 July 2008	2008/1586
Section 14	14 July 2008	2008/1586
Section 15	14 July 2008	2008/1586
Section 16	14 July 2008	2008/1586
Section 17	14 July 2008	2008/1586
Section 18	14 July 2008	2008/1586
Section 20	14 July 2008	2008/1586
Section 24	14 July 2008	2008/1586
Section 25	14 July 2008	2008/1586
Section 26 (partially)	9 June 2008	2008/1466
Section 27	14 July 2008	2008/1586
Section 28	14 July 2008	2008/1586
Section 29 (partially)	14 July 2008	2008/1586
Section 30	14 July 2008	2008/1586
Section 31	14 July 2008	2008/1586
Section 32	14 July 2008	2008/1586
Section 38	14 July 2008	2008/1586
Section 40	14 July 2008	2008/1586
Section 42	14 July 2008	2008/1586
Section 43	14 July 2008	2008/1586
Section 44	14 July 2008	2008/1586
Section 45	14 July 2008	2008/1586
Section 46 (partially)	14 July 2008	2008/1586
Section 47	14 July 2008	2008/1586
Section 52	14 July 2008	2008/1586
Section 54	14 July 2008	2008/1586
Section 55	14 July 2008	2008/1586
Section 56	14 July 2008	2008/1586
Section 57	14 July 2008	2008/1586
Section 58	14 July 2008	2008/1586
Section 59	14 July 2008	2008/1586
Section 72	14 July 2008	2008/1586
Section 73	14 July 2008	2008/1586
Section 76	14 July 2008	2008/1586
Section 93	14 July 2008	2008/1586
Section 94	14 July 2008	2008/1586
Section 95	14 July 2008	2008/1586
Section 96	14 July 2008	2008/1586
Section 97	14 July 2008	2008/1586
Section 126 (partially)	14 July 2008	2008/1586
Section 140	14 July 2008	2008/1586
Section 141	14 July 2008	2008/1586
Section 142	14 July 2008	2008/1586
Section 148 (partially)	9 June 2008	2008/1466
(partially)	14 July 2008	2008/1586
(partially)	15 July 2008	2008/1586
Section 149 (partially)	14 July 2008	2008/1586

Provision	Date of Commencement	S.I. No.
Schedule 5	14 July 2008	2008/1586
Schedule 8	14 July 2008	2008/1586
Schedule 12	14 July 2008	2008/1586
Schedule 15	14 July 2008	2008/1586
Schedule 22 (partially)	14 July 2008	2008/1586
Schedule 24	14 July 2008	2008/1586
Schedule 26 (partially)	9 June 2008	2008/1466
(partially)	14 July 2008	2008/1586
(partially)	15 July 2008	2008/1586
Schedule 27 (partially)	9 June 2008	2008/1586
(partially)	14 July 2008	2008/1586
Schedule 28 (partially)	14 July 2008	2008/1586

APPENDIX 5

The Criminal Justice and Immigration Act 2008 (Commencement No. 4 and Saving Provision) Order 2008

STATUTORY INSTRUMENTS
2008 NO. 2993 (C. 128)

CRIMINAL LAW, ENGLAND AND WALES
CRIMINAL LAW, NORTHERN IRELAND
ANTI-SOCIAL BEHAVIOUR, ENGLAND AND WALES
POLICE, ENGLAND AND WALES

Made   *15th October 2008*

The Secretary of State, in exercise of the powers conferred on the Secretary of State by section 153(7) of the Criminal Justice and Immigration Act 2008[1], makes the following Order:

Citation and interpretation

1.—(1) This Order may be cited as the Criminal Justice and Immigration Act 2008 (Commencement No. 4 and Saving Provision) Order 2008.

(2) In this Order, "the 2008 Act" means the Criminal Justice and Immigration Act 2008.

Appointed dates

2.—(1) Subject to article 3, the date appointed for the coming into force of the following provisions of the 2008 Act is 1st December 2008—

(a) section 61 (Compensation for miscarriages of justice);

(b) section 118 (Closure orders: premises associated with persistent disorder or nuisance);

(c) section 126(1) and (3) (Police misconduct and performance procedures) insofar as it relates to the entries specified in sub-paragraph (h);

(d) section 127 (Investigation of complaints of police misconduct etc.) insofar as it relates to the provisions specified in sub-paragraph (i);

(e) section 148(2) (Consequential etc. amendments and transitional and saving provisions) insofar as it relates to the provisions in sub-paragraph (j);

(f) section 149 (Repeals and revocations) insofar as it relates to the entries in sub-paragraph (k);

(g) Schedule 20 (Closure orders: premises associated with persistent disorder or nuisance);

---

[1] 2008 c. 4.

(h) in Schedule 22 (Police misconduct and performance procedures)—
  (i) paragraphs 3, 4, 7 and 8 to the extent not already in force; and
  (ii) paragraphs 5, 9, 11 and 17 to 21;
(i) in Schedule 23 (Investigation of complaints of police misconduct etc.)—
  (i) paragraphs 4, 6 to 11 and 13 to 18; and
  (ii) paragraphs 5, 12 and 19 to the extent not already in force;
(j) paragraphs 22 and 35(1), (2)(a) and (3) of Schedule 27 (Transitory, transitional and saving provisions); and
(k) in Schedule 28 (Repeals and revocations), the entries related to—
  (i) section 50(4) of, and paragraph 6 of Schedule 6 to, the Police Act 1996[2];
  (ii) Schedule 3 to the Police Reform Act 2002[3]; and
  (iii) paragraph 119 of Schedule 21 to the Legal Services Act 2007[4].

(2) The date appointed for the coming into force of the following provisions of the 2008 Act is 26th January 2009—
  (a) section 63 (Possession of extreme pornographic images);
  (b) section 64 (Exclusion of classified films etc.);
  (c) section 65 (Defences: general);
  (d) section 66 (Defence: participation in consensual acts);
  (e) section 67 (Penalties etc. for possession of extreme pornographic images);
  (f) section 68 (Special rules relating to providers of information society services);
  (g) section 71 (Maximum penalty for publication etc. of obscene articles);
  (h) section 148(1) and (2) (Consequential etc. amendments and transitional and saving provision) insofar as it relates to the provisions specified in paragraphs (j) and (k);
  (i) Schedule 14 (Special rules relating to providers of information society services);
  (j) paragraph 58 of Schedule 26 (Minor and consequential amendments); and
  (k) paragraphs 23 and 25 of Schedule 27 (Transitory, transitional and saving provision).

Saving provision

3.—(1) The Police Act 1996 and the Police Reform Act 2002 shall continue to apply in relation to specified matters as if the amendments in paragraphs 3 to 5, 7 to 9 and 11 of Schedule 22 and in paragraphs 4 to 10, 12 to 15 and 17 to 19 of Schedule 23 to the 2008 Act had not been made.

(2) In this article—
  (a) "specified matter" means—
    (i) conduct which may be or is being dealt with under the Police (Conduct) Regulations 2004[5];
    (ii) conduct which may be or is being dealt with under the Police (Complaints and Misconduct) Regulations 2004[6] as they are in force on the date this Order is made and which has come to the attention of the Independent Police Complaints Commission and the appropriate authority before 1st December 2008;
    (iii) performance or attendance which may be or is being dealt with under the Police (Efficiency) Regulations 1999[7]; or
    (iv) anything which may be or is being dealt with under the Police Appeals Tribunals Rules 1999[8];

---

[2] 1996 c. 16.
[3] 2002 c. 30.
[4] 2007 c. 29.
[5] S.I. 2004/645, as amended by S.I. 2006/594.
[6] S.I. 2004/643, as amended by S.I.s 2005/3311, 2005/3389, 2006/594 and 2006/1406.
[7] S.I. 1999/732, as amended by S.I.s 2003/528 and 2003/2600.
[8] S.I. 1999/818, as amended by S.I.s 2003/2597 and 2006/594.

    (b) "appropriate authority" has the same meaning as in the Police (Complaints and Misconduct) Regulations 2004.

EXPLANATORY NOTE

(This note is not part of the Order)

This Order brings into force the provisions of the Criminal Justice and Immigration Act 2008 (c.4) set out at article 2(1) and (2) on 1st December 2008 and 26th January 2009 respectively. Article 3 contains saving provisions in relation to the amendments to the police misconduct and performance procedures and the investigation of complaints of police misconduct etc.

NOTE AS TO EARLIER COMMENCEMENT ORDERS

(This note is not part of the Order)

The following provisions of the Criminal Justice and Immigration Act 2008 have been brought into force by a commencement order made before the date of this Order.

Provision	Date of Commencement	S.I. No.
Section 10	14 July 2008	2008/1586
Section 11 (partially)	14 July 2008	2008/1586
Section 12	14 July 2008	2008/1586
Section 13	14 July 2008	2008/1586
Section 14	14 July 2008	2008/1586
Section 15	14 July 2008	2008/1586
Section 16	14 July 2008	2008/1586
Section 17	14 July 2008	2008/1586
Section 18	14 July 2008	2008/1586
Section 20	14 July 2008	2008/1586
Section 21 (partially)	3 November 2008	2008/2712
Section 22	3 November 2008	2008/2712
Section 23	3 November 2008	2008/2712
Section 24	14 July 2008	2008/1586
Section 25	14 July 2008	2008/1586
Section 26 (partially)	9 June 2008	2008/1466
Section 27	14 July 2008	2008/1586
Section 28	14 July 2008	2008/1586
Section 29 (partially)	14 July 2008	2008/1586
Section 30	14 July 2008	2008/1586
Section 31	14 July 2008	2008/1586
Section 32	14 July 2008	2008/1586
Section 33 (partially)	3 November 2008	2008/2712
Section 34 (partially)	3 November 2008	2008/2712
Section 38	14 July 2008	2008/1586
Section 40	14 July 2008	2008/1586
Section 41	3 November 2008	2008/2712
Section 42	14 July 2008	2008/1586
Section 43	14 July 2008	2008/1586
Section 44	14 July 2008	2008/1586
Section 45	14 July 2008	2008/1586
Section 46 (partially)	14 July 2008	2008/1586
Section 47	14 July 2008	2008/1586
Section 51	3 November 2008	2008/2712
Section 52	14 July 2008	2008/1586
Section 54	14 July 2008	2008/1586
Section 55	14 July 2008	2008/1586
Section 56	14 July 2008	2008/1586
Section 57	14 July 2008	2008/1586
Section 58	14 July 2008	2008/1586
Section 59	14 July 2008	2008/1586
Section 60	3 November 2008	2008/2712
Section 72	14 July 2008	2008/1586
Section 73	14 July 2008	2008/1586
Section 76	14 July 2008	2008/1586
Section 93	14 July 2008	2008/1586
Section 94	14 July 2008	2008/1586
Section 95	14 July 2008	2008/1586
Section 96	14 July 2008	2008/1586
Section 97	14 July 2008	2008/1586

Provision	Date of Commencement	S.I. No.
Section 126 (partially)	14 July 2008	2008/1586
(partially)	3 November 2008	2008/2712
Section 127 (partially)	3 November 2008	2008/2712
Section 129	3 November 2008	2008/2712
Section 140	14 July 2008	2008/1586
Section 141	14 July 2008	2008/1586
Section 142	14 July 2008	2008/1586
Section 148 (partially)	9 June 2008	2008/1466
(partially)	14 July 2008	2008/1586
(partially)	15 July 2008	2008/1586
(partially)	3 November 2008	2008/2712
Section 149 (partially)	14 July 2008	2008/1586
(partially)	3 November 2008	2008/2712
Schedule 5	14 July 2008	2008/1586
Schedule 6	3 November 2008	2008/2712
Schedule 8	14 July 2008	2008/1586
Schedule 11	3 November 2008	2008/2712
Schedule 12	14 July 2008	2008/1586
Schedule 15	14 July 2008	2008/1586
Schedule 22 (partially)	14 July 2008	2008/1586
(partially)	3 November 2008	2008/2712
Schedule 23 (partially)	3 November 2008	2008/2712
Schedule 24	14 July 2008	2008/1586
Schedule 26 (partially)	9 June 2008	2008/1466
(partially)	14 July 2008	2008/1586
(partially)	15 July 2008	2008/1586
(partially)	3 November 2008	2008/2712
Schedule 27 (partially)	9 June 2008	2008/1586
(partially)	14 July 2008	2008/1586
Schedule 28 (partially)	14 July 2008	2008/1586
(partially)	3 November 2008	2008/2712

Index

References are to Paragraph Numbers